THE SPOILS OF WAR

THE SPOILS OF WAR

World War II and Its Aftermath:

The Loss, Reappearance,

and Recovery of Cultural Property

Edited by Elizabeth Simpson

Harry N. Abrams, Inc., Publishers

in association with The Bard Graduate Center
for Studies in the Decorative Arts

Editor: Ellyn Childs Allison

Editorial Assistant: Amy L. Vinchesi

Designer: Maria Learmonth Miller

Assistant Designer: Jennifer A. Davenport

For transcription of Cyrillic references, the Library of Congress system of transliteration is used throughout, except when an alternate form appears in a documentary title or text, or, in the case of proper nouns, when a commonly accepted variant spelling exists.

Library of Congress Cataloging-in-Publication Data

The spoils of war: World War II and its aftermath: the loss, reappearance, and recovery of cultural property / edited by Elizabeth Simpson.
      p.   cm.
Papers of a symposium sponsored by the Bard Graduate Center for Studies in the Decorative Arts, Jan. 1995, in New York.
Includes texts and excerpts of related treaties, conventions, and other official documents in the appendices.
   Includes bibliographical references and index.
   ISBN 0–8109–4469–3
   1. World War, 1939–1945—Destruction and pillage. 2. Cultural property, Protection of (International law) I. Simpson, Elizabeth, 1947–
D801.D6S67   1997
940.53'1—dc20   96–33258

CONTENTS

FOREWORD

Susan Weber Soros
Director, The Bard Graduate Center
for Studies in the Decorative Arts

The symposium "The Spoils of War—World War II and Its Aftermath: The Loss, Reappearance, and Recovery of Cultural Property" was a historic event that we at the Bard Graduate Center are proud to have hosted. The project is consistent with our aims as an academic institution dedicated to the dissemination of knowledge in the field of the decorative arts as seen in their historical and cultural context. As a new institution, with an international scope, we felt it appropriate to present a symposium that would reach out to the world cultural community on a pertinent and timely issue. I would like to recognize here the efforts of Bard Graduate Center faculty member Elizabeth Simpson, who organized the symposium and edited these proceedings.

The subject under discussion, cultural property displaced as a result of World War II, is one of the most important unresolved issues we face today. I first became interested in the topic during the 1980s when traveling through Central and Eastern Europe with my husband, George Soros, founder of the Open Society Fund. In my capacity at that time as Director of the Open Society Fund, I had the opportunity to meet with museum officials and cultural leaders, many of whom were concerned with artworks that were destroyed or lost during the war. With the media reports on the secret Russian repositories in the early 1990s, the entire world was made aware of the problem of displaced artworks. The time seemed opportune for a public symposium on the subject.

It is a particularly fitting topic for the Bard Graduate Center, because the losses of decorative arts in the war were staggering. The agencies and armies that fought for control of Europe did not limit their massive displacements to paintings and sculpture but swept all before them. Hitler's so-called Möbel-Aktion, or Furniture Project, removed over one million cubic meters of household objects from France alone.

At the end of the war, enormous numbers of objects were returned to the countries from which they had been taken. But today, half a century later, the fate of many thousands more remains unknown or undecided, the cause of considerable controversy. The Bard Graduate Center hopes that the information presented in this volume will help elucidate the issues relating to this controversy and that our common desire to preserve these displaced world treasures will help us all to resolve the problem of their disposition in an equitable fashion. As an independent academic institution, the Bard Graduate Center wishes to state that we are impartial and unbiased concerning the issues under discussion.

Our only regret is that the symposium could not address all the issues involved or include representatives from all the countries affected. We are, however, grateful to all those who did attend and to the international media, which reported the event so effectively. It is our hope that the Bard Graduate Center has contributed to the furtherance of the dialogue on restitution now in progress and that the path toward a solution will have been facilitated. We greatly appreciate the support of Harry N. Abrams, Inc., which shares our belief that this volume will be of universal and lasting significance.

ACKNOWLEDGMENTS

Elizabeth Simpson

Chairman, Symposium Organizing Committee
Editor, *The Spoils of War*

Tremendous effort has gone into the preparation of this volume of the proceedings of the Bard Graduate Center symposium "The Spoils of War"—as was the case with the organization and presentation of the symposium itself. I am privileged to have worked with some of the most accomplished specialists in their respective fields, and I am happy to be able to express my appreciation here. I wish to thank the members of the Editorial Board—Constance Lowenthal, Lynn Nicholas, Jonathan Petropoulos, and Stephen Urice—all of whom are contributors to this volume. Constance Lowenthal and Lynn Nicholas also served on the Organizing Committee for the symposium, along with Susan Weber Soros, Director of the Bard Graduate Center; Oscar White Muscarella; and Edward Wierzbowski. Osanna Urbay was Organizing Coordinator for both the publication and the symposium, managing the myriad details of these complex projects with cheerfulness and skill. Research and editorial assistants Jay Ottaway, Janis Mandrus, Heather Jane McCormick, Amy Coes, Kelly Moody, Jeanne-Marie Musto, and Svetlana Chervonnaya were responsible for the organization of various individual aspects of the projects. Assistance with legal citations and other legal matters was provided by Robin Villanueva, Melissa Pedone, Wendy Bond, Lucille Roussin, C. Michele McHugh, and Stefano Weinberger. It is in large part due to these people—to their creativity, commitment, and hard work—that the undertaking has been a success.

The symposium speakers and official guest participants are of course responsible for the international acclaim that the symposium received. Many traveled long distances and made sacrifices in order to attend. The presentations were all extremely interesting and well executed, and the speakers were conscientious in addressing the issues on which they had been asked to speak. The exceptional degree of preparation, high level of excellence in the presentations and discussions, and outstanding mutual cooperation of the participants produced a powerful effect. Although most of the topics were controversial, attitudes of the participants were positive and conciliatory, which contributed toward a greater appreciation of the difficulties faced by the various parties now involved in negotiations. The efforts of the participants are gratefully acknowledged here.

Many of the speakers and guest participants came as representatives of governmental agencies, academic institutions, research institutes, and other organizations. We received a great deal of help from a number of these agencies and organizations and would like to thank in particular the United States Department of State; the Office of the National Archives, Washington, D.C.; the Consulate General of the Federal Republic of Germany, New York; the Auswärtiges Amt (Foreign Office) of the Federal Republic of Germany, Bonn; the Embassy of the Republic of Belarus, Washington, D.C.; the Ministry of Culture of the Russian Federation; the Ministry of Culture of the Turkish Republic; the Art Recovery Project, Rijksdienst Beeldende Kunst, the Netherlands; the Forschungs-stelle Osteuropa an der Universität Bremen (Research Institute for Eastern Europe, University of Bremen); the Koordinierungsstelle der Länder für die Rückführung von Kulturgütern (Coordination Office of the Federal States for the Return of Cultural Property), Bremen; Kultura; the Museum für Vor- und Frühgeschichte, Berlin; and the International Foundation for Art Research, New York. We are grateful to Vitaut Kipel, Chairman of the Belarusan Institute of Arts and Sciences in the United States. In addition, we would like to thank Milton Esterow, Sylvia Hochfield, and the staff of ARTnews magazine for the many courtesies extended to us. The law firms of Herrick, Feinstein, L.L.P., New York, and Andrews & Kurth, L.L.P., Washington, D.C., have also been a great help.

As the symposium was international in its scope, with speakers coming from many countries, we provided simultaneous interpretation in English, German, Russian, and French. We were fortunate to have been able to engage some of the finest interpreters in the field: Daniel Rishik (organizer), Julia Erickson, Erika Konuk, Brigitta Richman, Andrew Tarutz, and Lynn Visson. Their work was greatly appreciated by all who attended the symposium, as evidenced by the cheers they received from the audience at the end of the conference. Round Hill-IVC, Inc., provided the booths and electronic equipment for the simultaneous interpretation; we would like to thank James Craft and his staff for their kindness and their help.

Similarly, for the publication of the symposium proceedings, translation of many of the papers submitted by the speakers and guest participants was required, along with research involving the knowledge of many languages. This work was carried out by advanced specialists, to whom we owe a deep debt of gratitude: Lynn Visson, Katrin A. Velder, Svetlana Chervonnaya, Peter Dreyer, and Aga Dreyer. The importance of their contribution to the volume is greater than I can adequately express.

The symposium was held at the Florence Gould Hall at the French Institute/Alliance Française in New York, which was a wonderful site for the conference. The staff of the Alliance Française were courteous, helpful, and efficient, and special thanks are due to Meredith Palin, Client Relations Manager, and Angelique d'Addario, House Manager for Performance Facilities. Security was provided by the Bard Graduate Center, and especially helpful in this and other related matters were Doru Padure, Facilities Manager; Richard Domanic, former Facilities Manager; Orlando Diaz; Terence Lyons; Jorge SanPablo; and Chandler Small. Additional security was provided by Sentinel Security Systems; we appreciated the willingness of the Alliance Française to accommodate our needs in this respect.

The symposium brochure was designed with the help of Stan Lichens and the Bard College Publications Office. Photographs that appear in this volume were obtained through a number of sources, with special help from Konstantin Akinsha, Klaus Goldmann, Jeanette Greenfield, Marlene Hiller, Sylvia Hochfield, William Honan, Manfred Korfmann, Wojciech Kowalski, Josefine Leistra, Constance Lowenthal, and Lynn Nicholas, and from Meredith Brosnan of the Sovfoto/Eastfoto agency, which allowed us the use of their outstanding archive. Many of the authors sent fine-quality reproductions or original

documents, and helped us obtain permission to publish their illustrations, for which we would like to express our appreciation. Photographs for the volume were reproduced by Jocelyn Miller, Bruce White, and Marcial Laviña, Photographer for the Bard Graduate Center Slide Library.

Other members (and former members) of the faculty and staff of the Bard Graduate Center contributed their efforts, especially Miao Chen, James Finch, Isabelle Frank, Rochelle Gurstein, Michele Majer, Karen Marshon, Missy McHugh, Melody Roberts, Elizabeth Smith, Leslie Tait, and Stefanie Walker. Others who worked with us include Karen Bysiewicz, Jennie Choi, Anna Eschapasse, Emma Guest, Elizabeth Kerr, Andrea Lowenthal, Vanessa MacDonna, Jennifer Olshin, and Suzanna Turman. We are grateful to all these people for their help.

I would particularly like to thank the staff of Harry N. Abrams, Inc., for their guidance in the preparation of this volume. We have very much appreciated the support of Paul Gottlieb, President, Publisher, and Chief Executive Officer, and Elizabeth Robbins, Vice President for Public Relations, Advertising, and Promotion, both of whom expressed an interest in publishing this work before the symposium had yet taken place. Sincere thanks are also due to Margaret Chace, Managing Editor, for her support throughout the project; Amy Vinchesi, Editorial Assistant, for her help with many details; Maria Miller, who designed the book; and most especially Ellyn Allison, who skillfully negotiated the difficult job of copyediting the manuscript and all that this entailed.

Funding for the symposium and publication of the proceedings was contributed by the following donors: for the symposium, the Samuel H. Kress Foundation, the Deutscher Akademischer Austausch Dienst, the Trust for Mutual Understanding, the Open Society Fund, Inc., and James H. Ottaway, Jr.; for the publication, the Samuel H. Kress Foundation, the Deutscher Akademischer Austausch Dienst, James H. Ottaway, Jr., the Malcolm H. Wiener Foundation, Inc., and Mrs. James J. Rorimer. We are very grateful for these contributions; without the generous support of these organizations and individuals, our work could not have been accomplished. In addition, we would like to thank Finnair for a grant-in-kind to cover the airfare of a number of the speakers; these and other travel arrangements were ably handled by Amilda Agudo of Journeycorp Travel Management. I would like to express my gratitude to the staff of the Development Office of the Bard Graduate Center for their help with these grants, especially Linda Hartley, Director of Development, and Andrea Morgan, past Director of Development; I am also grateful to Susan Gillespie, Vice President for Development and Public Affairs of Bard College, for her efforts on our behalf.

Finally, I would like to thank Susan Weber Soros, Director of The Bard Graduate Center for Studies in the Decorative Arts, who initiated the "Spoils of War" symposium project and provided continuous support throughout, and Leon Botstein, President of Bard College, for his belief in the programs and purpose of the Bard Graduate Center.

INTRODUCTION

Elizabeth Simpson

This volume records the events of the international symposium presented by The Bard Graduate Center for Studies in the Decorative Arts in New York in January 1995, marking the fiftieth anniversary of the end of the Second World War. The symposium dealt with the art and other cultural property that was willfully looted, damaged, or destroyed in vast quantities by Nazi armed forces and confiscation agencies during the war—and the consequences that ensued. One notable consequence was the removal at the end of the war of objects from German territory to countries of the former USSR, where they disappeared into private collections or were hidden in state repositories, many to be rediscovered nearly fifty years later by Soviet art historians.

Worldwide interest in these issues was generated by the announcements in 1991 of the whereabouts of many of these confiscated objects—first made public in articles written by Konstantin Akinsha, Grigorii Kozlov, and Alexei Rastorgouev, all contributors to this volume. This gave rise to the idea of a symposium, which was conceived by Susan Soros, Director of the Bard Graduate Center, in 1993, and which I began to organize soon thereafter. Interest in the subject increased with the publication in 1994 of Lynn H. Nicholas's prizewinning book, *The Rape of Europa: The Fate of Europe's Art Treasures in the Third Reich and the Second World War.* The unification of Germany in 1990, the dissolution of the Soviet Union in 1991, the institution of a series of goodwill agreements between Germany and countries of the former Soviet Union (1990–94), and the opening of official negotiations on restitution all contributed toward an atmosphere of international cooperation. It was this spirit of cooperation that made the symposium possible.

We encountered some initial difficulties in our efforts to organize the program. The topics to be addressed were highly controversial and had never before been the subject of public discussion. Indeed, many of the people we wished to invite had only recently felt free to speak openly without fear of recrimination. There developed a concern over parity in terms of the level of speakers' official positions, the number of participants allotted to particular delegations, and the amount of time that each was allowed to speak. Many of these difficulties were eased considerably by the diplomatic talents and hard work of the members of the symposium organizing committee, which included Constance Lowenthal, Oscar White Muscarella, Lynn Nicholas, Susan Weber Soros, and Edward Wierzbowski, who was especially helpful with Russian contacts. Negotiations were to continue up until the opening of the symposium, by which time—miraculously, it seemed—the program was finally in place. We were fortunate to be able to include as speakers or guest participants most of the world's leading authorities involved with the repatriation of cultural property destroyed or displaced as a result of World War II. It is due to the outstanding contributions of these participants that the undertaking was a success.

The nature of this success was manifold. Not only was this the first public meeting on the subject ever held, but it was also the first time that so many of those involved had been together in one place—in a less formal and more congenial setting than that of the courtroom or negotiating table. In fact, it was the first time that many had met. It was our wish that, by encouraging the spirit of goodwill and cooperation that had developed in the years preceding the conference, we might contribute to the efforts of the participants in the years to follow, as they worked toward solutions to the difficult problems associated with restitution and return.

The three-day conference began with an introduction to what has long been considered the right of the victor to "the spoils of war"—the taking of booty in armed conflict—and an overview of the unprecedented displacement of cultural property that occurred during World War II (Part 1). There followed a series of detailed assessments, given by official representatives from Poland, the Netherlands, Belgium, France, Russia, Ukraine, Belarus, Austria, Hungary, and Germany, of the cultural property destroyed, damaged, or missing in these countries as a result of the war (Part 2). Losses of Jewish ceremonial art and private property, which figured prominently in many of the talks, were also discussed in a separate presentation. As is obvious, any attempt to recoup wartime losses must depend upon an accurate account of property missing, although the difficulties involved in preparing such an account have not generally been appreciated. Losses from institutions can often be ascertained from prewar inventories, although many of these inventories have themselves disappeared. Losses by individuals can be especially difficult to track, as few families maintained lists of their possessions—nor would such property be easy to reclaim even if it could be identified. Official efforts to record and evaluate wartime losses are now under way in most of the affected countries, with the aim of eventual restitution and recovery.

The second day of the symposium was devoted in part to legal issues relating to the appropriation of cultural property during and immediately following the Second World War. These are generally little understood but underlie all negotiations relating to restitution (Part 3). The session began with a discussion of the laws and conventions relating to the protection of cultural property that were in force at the start of World War II, notably the 1907 Hague Convention, which forbade the seizure or destruction of cultural property in time of war and provided for compensation in case of violation. The agreements in force failed to prevent the widespread destruction and appropriation of cultural property by Nazi Germany, however, which were carried out without regard for international law, by authority of the Führer through the laws and directives issued under the government of the Third Reich.

The end of the war saw attempts by the Allies to create a program for postwar restitution, although no such program was put into effect due to lack of agreement on the details of the proposed provisions. Russian officials at the symposium suggested that the decisions of the Allied Control Council regarding restitution provided justification for the removal of property from the Soviet Zone of occupied Germany to the USSR, although a review of the relevant laws and directives passed by the Allied Control Council found no provisions to support this interpretation. The official Russian point of view, expressed by a number of symposium participants, differentiates between Nazi confiscations of cultural property, seen as illegal, and the "transfer" of property from the Soviet Zone at the end of the war, seen as legal and fully justified as compensation for the tremendous loss of life and property that resulted from the German invasion of the Soviet Union.

The remainder of the second day was devoted to discussions of repatriations effected after the end of the war (Part 4). With appreciation and great excitement, the audience welcomed the panel of former United States Army and Navy officers who had served in the Monuments, Fine Arts, and Archives section (MFA&A) of the Office of Military Government, United States, and in the Art Looting Investigation Unit, Office of Strategic Services. At the end of the war, Craig Hugh Smyth, S. Lane Faison, Jr., Walter I. Farmer, and Edith A. Standen served as directors of the Central Collecting Points at Munich and Wiesbaden for the collection and return of cultural property looted by the Nazis and recovered from German repositories. James S. Plaut was director of the Art Looting Investigation Unit, of which S. Lane Faison was also a member, and Bernard Taper served as art-intelligence officer for the United States Zone of Occupation (MFA&A). The panelists received a standing ovation at the end of the session, in recognition of their accomplishments and those of their colleagues. It is with regret that I note the death of James Plaut in January 1996 at the age of eighty-three.

Repatriations carried out during the Cold War period by the USSR and through the efforts of the United States Department of State were discussed in the next session of the symposium. This was followed by a case study on the now-famous Quedlinburg church treasures, precious medieval objects that were removed from a cave in Germany at the end of the war by an American soldier, Joe Tom Meador. A number of these objects passed to Meador's heirs after his death, and some were put up for sale, precipitating an investigation that resulted in the objects' return to Quedlinburg, and setting important precedent affecting wartime loot now in private hands in the United States and elsewhere.

Most of the third and final day of the symposium was dedicated to discussions of the art and other cultural property that was removed from German repositories in the Soviet Zone of Occupation and shipped to the USSR (Part 5). These shipments comprised state archives, library and museum holdings, and famous European art collections obtained by the Nazis through confiscation or forced sale—such as the Franz Koenigs collection of old master drawings from Rotterdam and paintings from the Hungarian Hatvany and Herzog collections —as well as the property of German citizens and state institutions, including ancient art from the Museum für Vor- und Frühgeschichte in Berlin, prints and drawings from the Bremen Kunsthalle and Dresden Kupferstich-Kabinett, and paintings from the Krebs, Koehler, Siemens, and Gerstenberg collections. Some of these objects have reappeared and are now known to be in private possession in the countries of the former Soviet Union and in museums and other state institutions there, including the State Hermitage Museum in St. Petersburg and the Pushkin State Museum of Fine Arts in Moscow, where a number of important collections have been featured in recent exhibitions. The ownership of this property is now hotly contested, and several talks were devoted to the legal issues bearing on its status.

Perhaps the most famous group of objects removed from Germany at the end of the war and now held in Russia comprises the so-called Treasure of Priam and other precious objects excavated by Heinrich Schliemann at the site of Troy. The Trojan treasures, missing from Berlin since 1945, were listed in the Russian documents found by Grigorii Kozlov in 1987 that first revealed the existence of the secret repositories. A case study on the "Treasure of Priam" was presented at the symposium. This included accounts of the objects' discovery by Schliemann, their transfer to Berlin, their subsequent disappearance at the end of the war, and their care, storage, and plans for exhibition at the Pushkin Museum in Moscow. The exhibition was opened in April 1996. The case of the Trojan treasures is especially complex, because many of the objects were removed illegally by Schliemann from Turkey. At least three countries now claim ownership of the objects: official statements submitted by Turkey, Germany, and Russia were read, indicating the basis for these nations' claims. Finally, the present director of the Troy excavations, Manfred Korfmann, spoke on the value of the objects to the scientific community and the need that they be made accessible for scholarly research.

The final session of the conference, entitled "Current Issues and Cooperative Efforts," featured presentations by three noted experts in the field of restitution (Part 6). Wolfgang Eichwede, through his position as Director of the Research Institute for Eastern Europe in Bremen, has headed the German project to help the countries of the former Soviet Union catalogue their wartime losses. Ekaterina Genieva, Director General of the Rudomino State Library for Foreign Literature in Moscow, has organized joint German-Russian conferences and exhibitions at her library, published inventories of German books held in the library's collection, and officiated successfully over returns. The last speaker, Lyndel V. Prott, Chief of the International Standards Section of the Cultural Heritage Division of UNESCO, proposed a series of principles for the resolution of claims relating to World War II losses. The speakers expressed their hopes—and frustrations—regarding their attempts to find constructive means by which the seemingly insurmountable difficulties threatening the process of repatriation and restitution might be overcome.

The publication of the symposium proceedings was made possible in large part by the hard work and good judgment of the editorial team, with special acknowledgment due to the members of the editorial board: Constance Lowenthal, Lynn Nicholas, Jonathan Petropoulos, and Stephen K. Urice. The published papers are written versions, in English, of the speakers' symposium presentations. Authors were given the opportunity to make changes and additions, and many added citations, which are included at the back of the volume. The papers are published as submitted, with little editorial intervention. Although the members of the editorial board have made every effort to correct inadvertent errors, it was not possible to corroborate every claim or figure—nor did we consider this approach to be desirable. We have chosen to let the participants speak for themselves, and their papers reflect their individual concerns, opinions, and interpretations. The papers are presented here in the same order in which they were heard; the order was determined by our wish to take a historical approach that would result in a lasting document. To my knowledge, no such comprehensive treatment of the subject has ever been attempted. It is our hope that the text will provide a general understanding of major issues as well as a detailed view of specific problems and controversies and that it will be useful to scholars, students, and laymen alike in the years to come.

Over a three-day period, we were able to accommodate a total of forty-eight speakers. In order that a greater number of experts could contribute to the dialogue, many more people were invited as official guest participants. These included governmental representatives of nations that suffered wartime losses—those on the program and those that we were not able to include—and scholars, lawyers, and other professionals who were directly involved in the issues under consideration. Along with the speakers, the official guests were given priority in the discussions that followed the spoken presentations. These exchanges were lively and often provocative; we regret that we are unable to document them in print. The guest participants were invited to contribute to this volume, and we are pleased that the papers of six official guests appear here (Part 7). Although unable to contribute, the Italian Ministero per i Beni Culturali e Ambientali and the German Koordinierungsstelle der Länder für die Rückführung von Kulturgütern have sent us their recent publications, whose titles are included in the bibliography. The final paper by a guest participant is a report on the displaced European archives that are now held in Russia, where millions of files await repatriation to their countries of origin.

Many of the published papers make reference to legal documents, and in order that these references may be fully appreciated, a series of seventeen legal appendices has been included at the back of the book. The documents are cited in their entirety or in part; as a group, they contain the relevant provisions of all major international treaties, laws, conventions, protocols, and official statements relating to wartime plunder, restitution, and repatriation. These key legal documents are often cited in writings on wartime losses, but rarely are they reproduced. It is our hope that this series of appendices may be of lasting value as a scholarly resource.

The final legal appendix is the UNIDROIT Convention on Stolen or Illegally Exported Cultural Objects, adopted at a diplomatic conference in Rome in June 1995. As of August 1996, the convention had been signed by twenty-two nations; it will come into force six months after the date of deposit of the fifth official notification of ratification. The parties to the convention recognize "the fundamental importance of the protection of cultural heritage and of cultural exchanges for promoting understanding between peoples, and the dissemination of culture for the well-being of humanity and the progress of civilization" and pronounce themselves "determined to contribute effectively to the fight against illicit trade in cultural objects by taking the important step of establishing common, minimal legal rules for the restitution and return of cultural objects between Contracting States, with the objective of improving the preservation and protection of the cultural heritage in the interest of all."

The essence of the convention is contained in Chapter 2, Article 3: "The possessor of a cultural object which has been stolen shall return it." Cultural objects are defined as those which "on religious or secular grounds, are of importance for archaeology, prehistory, history, literature, art or science," and include such objects as natural specimens, property of historical, archaeological, or ethnological interest, elements of historic monuments, and property of artistic interest, including paintings, drawings, prints, statuary, rare books and manuscripts, stamps, archives (including sound, photographic and cinematographic archives), furniture, and musical instruments.

While it may seem self-evident that the aims of the participants in the UNIDROIT conference were wholly laudable, the document produced an outcry within the international arts community after it was drafted. It was published by *The Art Newspaper* (no. 51, September 1995), along with a number of related articles. One of these consisted of excerpts from a statement submitted by a group of prominent American museums, auction houses, and associations of art dealers:

> UNIDROIT would inhibit the ability of U.S. museums to acquire and/or exhibit a vast array of objects, and would paralyze the public market for anything which could fall within the law's overly broad definition of cultural property. UNIDROIT is not limited to antiquities, and would encourage foreign governments to erect extremely broad and irresponsible export barriers in order to hoard and control works of art and culture of all types and from all ages. UNIDROIT would thus encourage illicit black market transactions in place of the currently lawful art trade.

These comments themselves are controversial, as they seem to suggest that forces within the "lawful art trade" would desire access to objects classified as illegally exported or stolen— those objects that the UNIDROIT convention was designed specifically to protect—with World War II contraband figuring prominently among them.

The interests of the international art market can thus be interpreted, in certain instances, to be contrary to the interests of the world community at large. The age-old battle continues over the illegal transfer of cultural property, in times of war and of peace, between those from whom property has been stolen and those who would profit from its theft. The basic issues are simple, but the details are often complex, and in the case of World War II losses, some of these complexities are evident. The Nazi confiscations and forced sales (as we now term these acquisitions) have been universally condemned as illegal transactions, although one doubts whether this judgment would have prevailed had the war's outcome been different. To the victor go the spoils: treaties drawn up at the conclusion of armed conflict implicitly favor the victor in terms of the redistribution of most kinds of property, especially monetary reserves and land (with its attendant natural resources and taxable citizens). The status of victor has traditionally implied the right to enemy property, which is exercised even where prohibited by international convention.

The "transfer" of property from the Soviet Zone of occupied Germany to the USSR was carried out as the prerogative of one of the victors, still seen by many in the former Soviet republics and elsewhere as justified recompense for the terrible losses the Soviet Union suffered. These "transfers" are termed "thefts" by others, executed in clear violation of the provisions of the 1907 Hague Convention. The legality of the removals continues to be debated, with negotiations currently at a standstill and no mutually acceptable solution in sight.

German officials continue their attempts to retrieve their cultural property. In September 1995, Germany awarded Walter Farmer the Commander's Cross of the Federal Order of Merit for his efforts to prevent the shipment of 202 paintings from German collections to America in 1945. German Foreign Minister Klaus Kinkel made use of the occasion to urge the Russians to follow Mr. Farmer's good example and acknowledge Germany's right to the artworks removed from Germany to the Soviet Union. In Russia, opinion is divided, with strong pressure from the conservatives and communists to nationalize the trophy art (see Grimsted, below, pages 244–45 and 250). In a March 1995 *Pravda* article criticizing the Bard Graduate Center symposium, the Russian participants who attended the conference were named and condemned variously as "incompetent," "blasphemous," and "anti-Russian." To their credit, all of the participants except one agreed to the publication of their presentations in this volume. While this book was in press, Irina Antonova, Director of the Pushkin State Museum of Fine Arts in Moscow, informed the publisher that she would not in fact allow us to print her contribution, underscoring the difficulties associated with the administration of the trophy collections and the seriousness with which the issue is regarded within the Russian political establishment. Therefore, I have prepared a report on Ms. Antonova's symposium presentation, which appears here, as she did not wish to contribute to the publication as an author. The optimism that prevailed in the first half of this decade has yet to be realized in the second.

As this high-profile contest over collections of artistic masterpieces plays out in the media and reverberates throughout the art world, one might well keep in mind the millions of ordinary people who suffered the effects of the war in Europe,

not to mention the disastrous consequences of the war in
the Pacific. In the tragedy of the Holocaust, entire communities
were wiped out, their members deported and murdered, and
their property confiscated—including religious objects, family
photographs, valuable heirlooms, or unassuming items of great
personal significance. Some of these objects were saved or
recovered, many now "heirless," with remnants preserved in
museums, such as the United States Holocaust Memorial
Museum in Washington, D.C. One might wonder whether the
loss of property should be considered important at all, when
confronted with human suffering on this vast scale. The
answer can be found in the papers presented in this volume.
To quote Lyndel Prott,

> It is understandable that the view is sometimes expressed
> that "things" are not as important as human beings... and
> that consideration of the fate of objects should always be
> secondary to that of the alleviation of human suffering.
> Yet we at UNESCO are constantly confronted by the pleas
> of people who are physically suffering to help them save
> their cultural heritage, for their suffering is greatly increased
> by the destruction of what is dear to them. Their cultural
> heritage represents their history, their community, and their
> own identity. Preservation is sought, not for the sake of
> the objects, but for the sake of the people for whom they
> have a meaningful life.

Let us hope that the impulse to preserve will prevail.

Colorplate 1.
Raphael (1483–1520). *Portrait of a Young Man.* **Oil on panel,**
75 x 59 cm (29½ x 23¼″). Formerly in the collection of The Czartoryski
Museum in Cracow. Lost during World War II (1940)

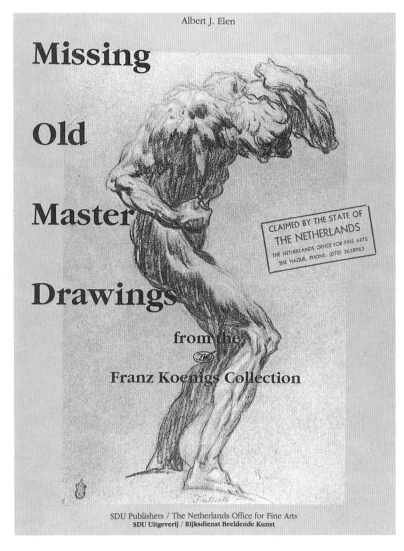

Colorplate 2.
Cover of the catalogue of drawings missing from the Franz Koenigs Collection (A. J. Elen, *Missing Old Master Drawings from the Franz Koenigs Collection, Claimed by the State of the Netherlands, 1989*). Depicted is a study of 1540–50 by Jacopo Tintoretto after a bronze statuette of Atlas (cat. no. 390). This drawing is now in the Pushkin State Museum of Fine Arts, Moscow (*Five Centuries of European Drawings: The Former Collection of Franz Koenigs*, cat. no 125).

Colorplate 3.
Andrea Mantegna (1431–1506), or after Andrea Mantegna. Studies of Saint John the Baptist and four other saints. Pen and ink on paper, 171 x 403 mm (6¾ x 15¾″). (A. J. Elen, *Missing Old Master Drawings from the Franz Koenigs Collection*, cat. no. 344.) Now in the Pushkin State Museum of Fine Arts, Moscow (*Five Centuries of European Drawings: The Former Collection of Franz Koenigs*, cat. no. 89)

Colorplate 4.
Medieval Cross of Saint Euphrosyne, the most important national relic of Belarus. Made in 1161 by the Polotsk jeweler Lazar Bogsha. Wood, enamel, precious metals, and stones. Lost in 1941

Colorplate 5.
Dressed Torah scroll from the synagogue at Danzig (now Gdańsk), part of the collection of ceremonial objects sold in 1939 to help finance the emigration of members of the Jewish community. Mantle: Prussia, first half of the eighteenth century; satin and velvet embroidered with silk and metallic thread. Pair of finials: Berlin, August Ferdinand Gentzmer, 1788–1802; cast, embossed and engraved silver, parcel-gilt. Pointer: Danzig, Johann Christian Franck (?), 1766–1812; cast and engraved silver. The Jewish Museum, New York

Colorplate 6.
Two beakers of the Burial Society of Worms, hidden during the war by a member of the Worms Jewish community. Left: Nuremberg, Johann Conrad Weiss, inscription date 1711/12; silver, 24.8 x 12.5 cm (9⅞ x 5″). Right: Worms (?), c. 1732; silver, 24.8 x 13 cm (9⅞ x 5⅛″). The Jewish Museum, New York

Colorplate 7 (above).
Reproductions of objects from the gold treasure of Eberswalde, ninth century B.C. The originals, formerly in the Staatliche Museen zu Berlin, Museum für Vor- und Frühgeschichte, were taken by the Soviet army from the Zoo flak tower in Berlin, May 1945. In 1994, it was officially revealed that the Eberswalde treasure was in the Pushkin State Museum of Fine Arts, Moscow.

Colorplate 8 (left).
Albrecht Dürer. *Quarry*. c. 1495. Watercolor, 29.2 x 22.4 cm (11½ x 8⅞″). Formerly in the collection of the Bremen Kunsthalle, and missing since 1945. Its whereabouts were made public in 1991 by Viktor Baldin. Currently in the State Hermitage Museum, St. Petersburg

Colorplate 9 (opposite).
Jeweled cover (c. 1225–30) of the Samuhel Gospels, a manuscript of the second quarter of the ninth century from the Quedlinburg church treasury. The Samuhel Gospels were removed from Germany at the end of the war by American soldier Joe Tom Meador. In 1990, a representative of Meador's heirs sold the manuscript to the German Kulturstiftung der Länder for almost $3 million, and the Gospels were returned to Quedlinburg.

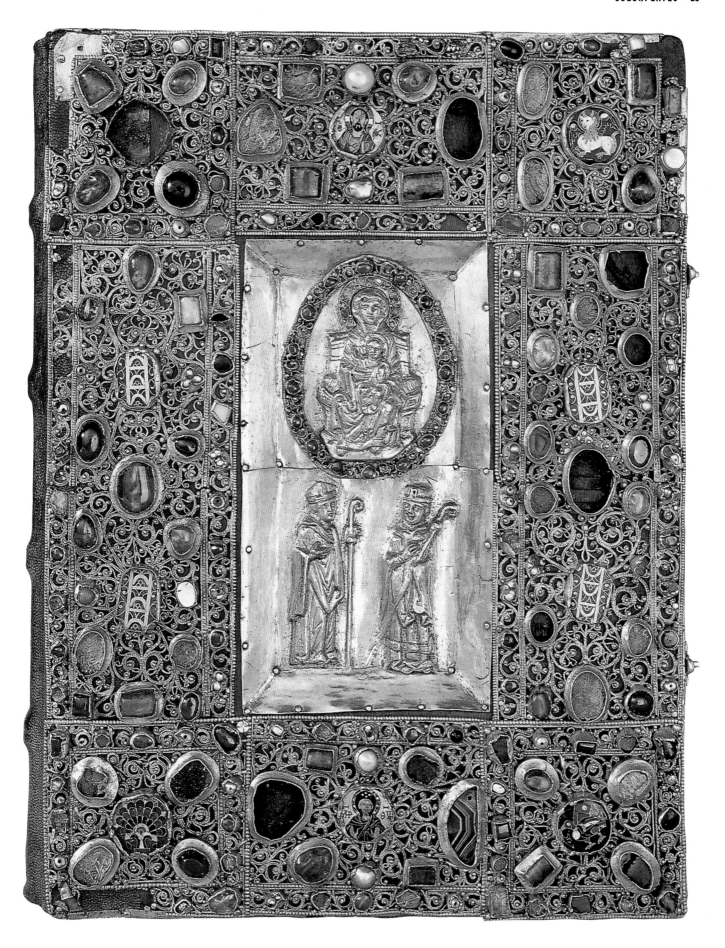

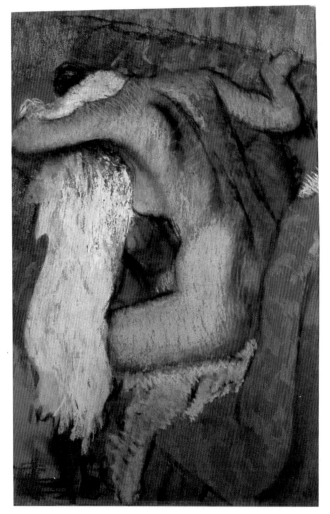

Colorplate 10.
The so-called Reliquary Casket of Henry I. This example of Quedlinburg gold-smiths' work (1230–40) incorporates eleventh-century German walrus-ivory panels depicting seated Apostles and tenth-century North Italian elephant-ivory panels. One of the Quedlinburg objects removed from Germany at the end of the war by Joe Tom Meador, the casket was returned to Quedlinburg church as part of the settlement of a lawsuit in Texas against Meador's heirs.

Colorplate 11.
Edgar Degas (?). *Femme s'essuyant* (Woman Drying Herself). c. 1888–92 or later. Pastel, 73 x 48 cm (28¾ x 18⅞″). Formerly in the Hatvany collection, Budapest. Transferred to the Russian city of Gorky (now Nizhnii Novgorod), and now in the Grabar Restoration Center, Moscow

Colorplate 12.
El Greco (or school of El Greco). *St. James Major as Pilgrim*. Late sixteenth century–seventeenth century. Oil on canvas, 92 x 47 cm (36¼ x 18½″). Formerly in the Herzog collection, Budapest. Transferred to the Russian city of Gorky (now Nizhnii Novgorod) in 1945, and now in the Grabar Restoration Center, Moscow

Colorplate 13 (opposite above).
Plan of the architectural remains on the citadel of Troy, with the fortifications and buildings of Troy II shown in yellow. Troia Excavations, 1994

Colorplate 14 (opposite below).
Remains of the fortifications of Troy II, showing the ramp near which Treasures A, B, E, F, J, and M were reported to have been found. Troia Excavations, 1995

Colorplate 15.
The Enemy Listens In, German propaganda poster from World War II

Colorplate 16.
German and Russian specialists examine the Trojan gold at the Pushkin State Museum of Fine Arts, Moscow, October 25, 1994. Seated from left: Mikhail Treister, Vladimir Tolstikov, Klaus Goldmann (with magnifying glass), Hermann Born, Wilfried Menghin, and Irina Antonova

Colorplate 17.
Gold ear ornaments from Treasure C, Troy. Archaeological Museum, Istanbul

Colorplate 18.
"Cypriote" loop-headed pin made of electrum, from the floor of Megaron IIA, Troy (Troy IIg)

Colorplate 19.
Three gold bars with incisions, from Treasure F, Troy. Third millennium B.C. Length: (left) 9.85 cm, (center) 10.4 cm, (right) 9.7 cm; weight: (left) 10.48g, (center) 10.39g, (right) 9.87g. From the Schliemann excavations. Formerly in the Museum für Vor- und Frühgeschichte, Berlin. Now in the Pushkin State Museum of Fine Arts, Moscow

Colorplate 20 (opposite).
Four ceremonial hammer-axes from Treasure L, Troy. Third millennium B.C. Top: nephritoid (?), length 25.9 cm; second from top: jadeite (?), length 28.2 cm; third from top: nephritoid (?) with gilding, length 31.1 cm; bottom: blue lazurite (lapis lazuli) with gilding, preserved length 27.8 cm. From the Schliemann excavations. Formerly in the Museum für Vor- und Frühgeschichte, Berlin. Now in the Pushkin State Museum of Fine Arts, Moscow

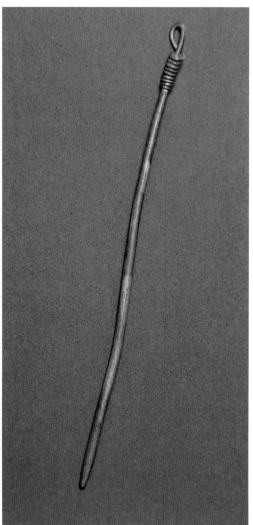

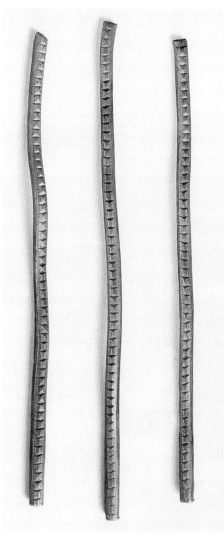

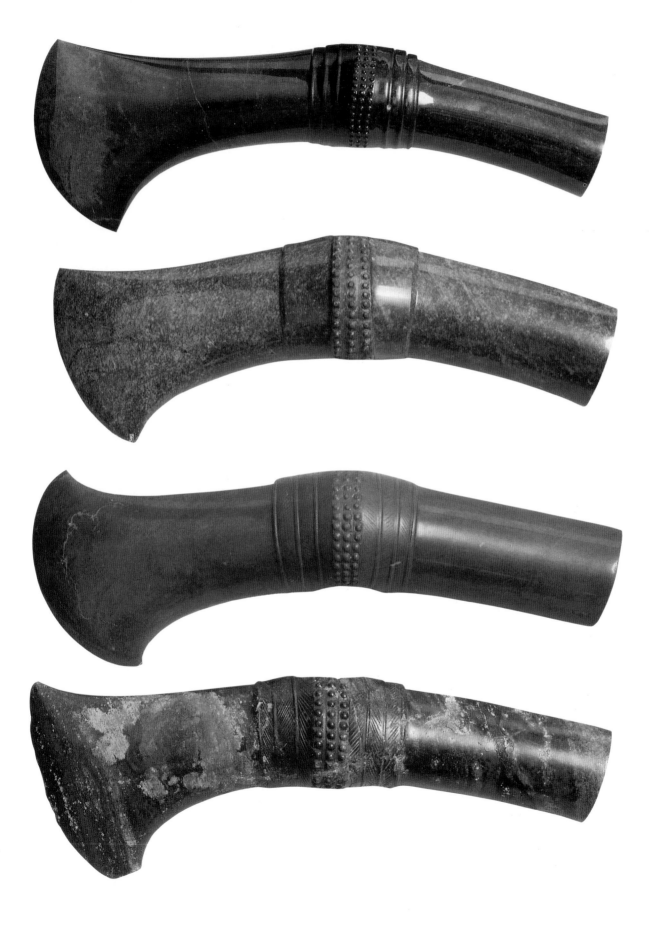

Colorplate 21 (opposite).
Objects from Treasures A and B, Troy. Third millennium
B.C., as illustrated in the Moscow exhibition catalogue
The Gold of Troy (1996). From the Schliemann
excavations. Formerly in the Museum für Vor- und
Frühgeschichte, Berlin. Now in the Pushkin State
Museum of Fine Arts, Moscow

Colorplate 22.
Bible. *Biblia: das ist: die gantze Heilige Schrifft ...*,
Volume 2. Wittenberg, Germany, 1541. Formerly in the
collection of J. H. von Hanstein. Now in the Rudomino
State Library for Foreign Literature, Moscow

Colorplate 23.
Owner's stamp and illustration of Saint Peter in G. B.
Cavalieri, *Omnium Romanorum pontificum icones ...*
(Portraits of all the Roman Pontiffs), [Rome] 1595.
Formerly in the Königliche Bibliothek, Dresden. Now in
the Rudomino State Library for Foreign Literature, Moscow

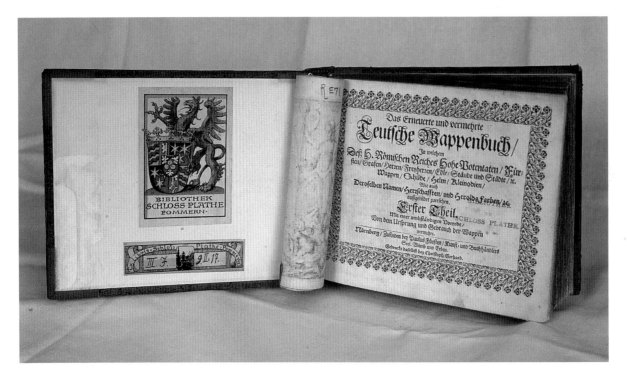

Colorplate 24. Owner's bookplate and title page in *Das erneuerte und vermehrte Teutsche Wappenbuch* ... (Coats of Arms of German Royalty, Nobility, etc.), Nuremberg, seventeenth century. Formerly in Schloss Plathe (Pommern). Now in the Rudomino State Library for Foreign Literature, Moscow

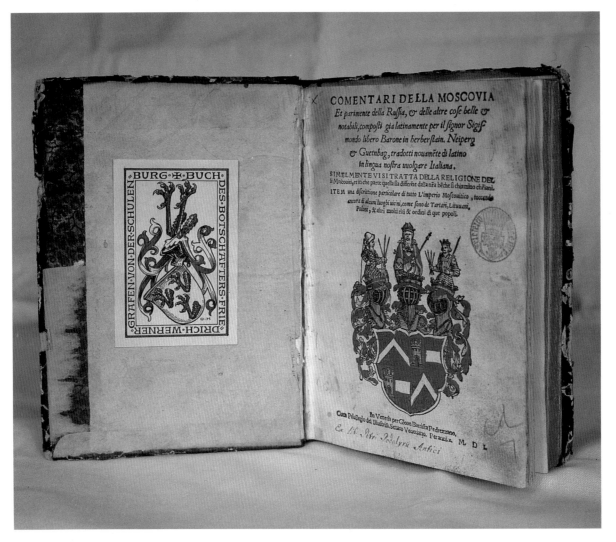

Colorplate 25. Owner's bookplate and title page in S. Herberstein, *Comentari della Moscovia* ... (Commentaries on Moscovia and the Provinces of Russia), Venice, 1550. Formerly in the collection of F. W. Graf von der Schulenburg. Now in the Rudomino State Library for Foreign Literature, Moscow

PART I

AN

OVERVIEW

"THE SPOILS OF WAR"

Jeanette Greenfield

In opening the Bard Graduate Center symposium, I began thinking more closely about the expression "spoils of war," which is one we all rather take for granted. It is an old term: "spoil," meaning not ruined things but valuable goods. It actually comes from the Latin *spolium,* originally meaning the hide stripped from an animal, and later the arms or armor stripped from an enemy—hence, booty, prey, or spoil. In time, anything stripped or taken from a country after its defeat in war came to be known as "spoils." That use of the word is recorded as early as 1300, and the English poet and translator John Dryden used the expression "spoils of war"[1] in 1697.[2] Of course, even though the expression itself appears to have entered the language only a few centuries ago, the act of plundering in time of war is ancient, timeless, and pandemic. The Bard symposium was focused on the events of the Second World War; but it is important to view those events in historical context. The history of the world is in part the history of wars, and so it is easy to cite endless examples of "spoils of war."

In the first millennium B.C., the ancient annals of Assyria record the enormous plunder of the Assyrian warrior-king Sargon II. In particular, a tablet from Assur which is now in the Musée du Louvre records his expedition to and sack of the Urartian city of Musasir in 714 B.C. There is a colorful and detailed inventory of everything he carried off, along with his explanation as to what prompted his actions: the king of that city, Urzana, "revolted against me, halted the return march of my expedition, [he failed to come bringing] his ample gifts, nor did he kiss my feet. He withheld his tribute, tax and gifts, and not once did he send his messenger to greet me. In the fury of my heart I made all of my chariots, many horses, all of my camp, take the road to Assyria."[3]

The Babylonians under King Nebuchadnezzar sacked Solomon's Temple in Jerusalem in 586 B.C. The Old Testament records that "What was of gold the captain of the guard took away as gold, and what was of silver, as silver" (Jeremiah 52:19).[4]

The Romans celebrated their military conquests with triumphal processions and displays of plunder. In A.D. 70, during the reign of Vespasian, the emperor's son Titus sacked Herod's Temple in Jerusalem. The Arch of Titus, commemorating this event, was erected posthumously in his honor about A.D. 81 in the center of Rome. Reliefs on the arch illustrate the triumphal procession with explicit representations, including a depiction of the Menorah, one of the most important of the spoils (fig. 1).[5] As described by the Jewish historian Flavius Josephus in *The Jewish War* (7.5.132 ff.):

> The most interesting of all were the spoils seized from the temple of Jerusalem: a gold table weighing many talents, and a lampstand, also made of gold. . . . there was a central shaft fastened to the base; then spandrels extended from this in an arrangement which rather resembled the shape of a trident, and on the end of each of these spandrels a lamp was forged. There were seven of these. . . . The law of the Jews was borne along after these as the last of the spoils.[6]

As art historian Richard Brilliant notes, Roman triumphal art is specific. It is therefore considered likely that the Menorah

1. Relief from the Arch of Titus, Rome, c. A.D. 81, depicting spoils from the Roman sack of the Temple in Jerusalem

illustrated on the Arch of Titus is a representation of the original taken from Herod's Temple. The sculptor presumably would have seen it among the spoils from Jerusalem that were stored in the Temple of Jupiter Optimus Capitolinus in Rome. The Hellenistic style of the metalwork and the depictions on the base panels have been seen as an indication that the Menorah shown on the Arch of Titus is indeed a faithful copy. It was a symbol of the Roman victory in Judaea that would have been understood by all who saw it.[7]

The Viking raid in 793 on the monastery on the Holy Island of Lindisfarne off the northeast coast of Britain is cited as the start of the Viking Age, which lasted nearly 300 years.[8] The Norsemen, who came by sea, sent fear throughout Europe, and their name became synonymous with pillage. Their "smash-and-grab" raids gave rise to the myth that prayers were said in every church in Europe asking for deliverance "from the fury of the Northmen."[9] They ranged far and wide in their distinctive vessels, even arriving at the Thames, where Olaf Haraldsson (later king of Norway) pulled down London Bridge in 1009, an event that gave rise to the children's song "London Bridge Is Falling Down."[10]

In 1096, the beginning of the first of the Crusades to the Holy Land set in motion another long march of murder and pillage. The Seljuk Turkish threat to the Christians in Byzantium led Pope Urban II to summon from across Europe a Christian army to liberate Jerusalem for the Church of God. Participation in the crusade was supposed to be an act of devotion in lieu of all penance, not to be undertaken for the gain of honor or money. However, in all the European territories the crusaders passed through, such as the Rhineland, Bavaria, Bohemia, and Hungary, the gold of Jews murdered on the way helped to finance the campaign.[11] The crusaders laid siege

to Jerusalem, which was captured in 1099. They slaughtered Muslims and Jews alike and the city was looted. From the Western Christians came the notion of "sacred theft" to justify the removal of holy relics.[12] One of the crusaders' motives was to subordinate the Eastern Church to the Western; the crusading period culminated with the Fourth Crusade of 1202–4 and the sack of Constantinople in 1204: gold, silver, satins, furs, and, in particular, relics were plundered.[13]

The most famous spoils—the four bronze horses from the Hippodrome—were used to decorate the facade of the Church of San Marco in Venice. These objects have come to symbolize the migration of treasures in war. Although their exact provenance is uncertain, they are considered to be either ancient Greek or Roman works.

As recognizable pieces, the horses of San Marco can be traced through the history of European wars and plunder. These same horses were taken from Venice in 1797 and later paraded by Napoleon Bonaparte in his triumphal procession on the Champ-de-Mars in Paris in 1798. Napoleon, the Corsican-born lieutenant who would rule as emperor of France between 1804 and 1815, led a campaign of conquest and "collecting" across the whole of Europe from 1796 until the end of his reign. His treasures filled the Musée Central des Arts (renamed the Musée Napoléon in 1803), later to become the Musée du Louvre. His campaign in Egypt is generally regarded as the beginning of Egyptology in France and of the "Egyptomania" that ensued. The Egyptian plunder brought to France influenced architecture and the decorative arts in the nineteenth century, and its influence can still be seen today. Napoleon's booty was studied by a special team of scholars and scientists led by Baron Dominique-Vivant Denon, who was later to become Director General of the Musée Napoléon.

Only after the military defeats of 1814 and the battle of Waterloo in 1815, and with the outcome of the Congress of Vienna, were many of the plundered masterpieces returned. Another instantly recognizable piece, the ancient *Laocoön* group, which had been removed from the Vatican and placed in the Musée Napoléon, was one of the returned treasures. The horses of San Marco continued their journey, returning to Venice, only to be taken down again from the church for safekeeping during the Second World War.[14]

At the turn of the sixteenth century, Spain had pointed her ships toward the New World. In 1519, the town of Panama was established as a base from which Spain was to expand its vast empire. The conquest of the Incas in Peru was led by Francisco Pizarro; the greed of the Spanish conquistadors for gold resulted in the devastation of Inca culture. In 1532, Pizarro ambushed the Inca king Atahualpa and took him hostage. The Spaniards gathered emeralds and countless plates, jugs, and other objects of gold and silver. Atahualpa offered the famous ransom of a room full of gold to save his life. The room would be seventeen feet wide and twenty-two feet long, to be filled halfway up with golden jars, pots, tiles, and other types of objects. The room would then be filled twice over with silver, to be added to the ransom of gold. The six metric tons of gold and the silver that made up Atahualpa's ransom would today be worth many millions of dollars. The ransom was paid, and the gold and silver were melted down. However, instead of releasing the king as promised, Pizarro ordered that he be garroted. The Spanish continued to pursue the "spoils" of their South American conquests with the utmost cruelty.[15]

Another seafaring nation that turned its eyes away from Europe in its conquests and treasure-hunting was England. In the early sixteenth century, Europeans began to establish bases on the coast of West Africa, which because of its supplies of gold came to be called the Gold Coast.[16] In 1867 the British clashed with the Ashanti ruler, King Kofi Karikari, and the Ashanti wars ensued. In 1874 a punitive expedition led by Sir Garnet Wolseley entered the city of Kumasi, the tribal capital of the Ashanti kingdom (now Ghana). The city was reported to have seemingly limitless amounts of gold—as Ashanti society was founded on gold. The king escaped from Kumasi, but the palace was ransacked of bags of gold dust, swords, plates, carved stools mounted in silver, and many other treasures; and the royal regalia ended up in the Museum of Mankind in London.[17]

Great Britain was a formidable presence in Nigeria throughout the nineteenth century, gaining control of the entire country by 1906 and ruling until 1960. In 1897, more than two thousand bronzes were taken by a British expedition in a punitive action against the king of Benin, the Oba. This was for failing to meet trading impositions and then murdering the acting consul of the British trading post and most of his party. The expedition, led by Admiral Rawson, found evidence of human sacrifice, which led to the description of Benin city as the "City of Blood." But the other sight that greeted Admiral Rawson was that of a vast collection of bronze plaques, portrait heads, and statues, as well as carved ivory figures of animals.[18] Most of the exquisite bronzes were removed to the British Museum, but many were also dispersed throughout the world. As a result, the Nigerian national collection is smaller than some foreign-held collections, such as those in Berlin or London.[19]

In China, two great "collecting" rivals, England and France, came to compete over the "spoils of war." By 1858, British and French forces had occupied Canton, and trading concessions were forced on the emperor. The Treaty of Peace, Friendship, and Commerce was signed by Queen Victoria and the emperor of China on June 26, 1858. However, problems arose with the exchange of the ratifications of the peace treaty, resulting in the capture and murder of English and French hostages by the Chinese. As retribution, and in order to destroy the emperor's prestige, the eighth earl of Elgin (son of the Lord Elgin who took the Parthenon marbles from Greece) ordered the destruction of the emperor's Summer Palace in Peking.[20] This is a most instructive episode in the saga of "spoils of war" because of the varying accounts it produced. The splendid palace was burned to the ground and many of its treasures are resurfacing today, more than one hundred years later, including exceptional porcelain. According to reports in the *Illustrated London News* in 1861,

> The loss inflicted cannot be estimated by any money valuation. Treasures of gold and silver, works of the highest Chinese art, which no sums could purchase, the accumulation of ages, the most valuable secret records of the empire, the sacred genealogical tablets of the dynasty, are all gone, and can never be replaced. The solid, indestructible stone, here and there a marble arch or gateway, and massive bronzes too ponderous to be removed, will alone remain to tell to a future generation where the beautiful palace once stood, and to bear undying record of the righteous retribution enacted by the allied armies of the foreigners.[21]

2. Looty, the Pekingese dog found by an officer of the British army during the looting of the Imperial Palace of Yuen-Ming-Yuen (the Summer Palace) near Peking, as depicted in the *Illustrated London News*, June 15, 1861

The attitude of the English to the plunder is best reflected in the name given to the little Pekingese dog found in the Summer Palace by Captain Dunne of the Ninety-ninth Regiment and presented to Queen Victoria. "At the loot of the Imperial Palace of Yuen-Ming-Yuen (the Summer Palace) near Pekin [sic], on the 8th of October last, a diminutive dog was found. . . . No other dog like it was found in the palace, and it is supposed to have belonged to the Empress or to one of the ladies of the Imperial family. By what name it was known to its small-footed mistress will in all probability remain a mystery. It has, however, appropriately enough, been renamed Looty" (fig. 2).[22]

Elsewhere there was speculation about how much the French had looted. The article "French Spoils from China" appeared in the same journal:

In all probability the real value of the booty taken by the allied armies during the late Chinese War will never be fully estimated. A figure something like two millions sterling has been mentioned as the market price of the mass of treasures dispersed after the capture of the Emperor of China's Summer Palace, the majority of which have been carried off by the troops of the "barbarians," and disposed of according to the desires or caprices of the individual victors. A certain quantity of the booty has been purchased by the Celestials [Royals] themselves at Shanghai, Hong-Kong, and elsewhere; other portions have found their way to India, carried thither by our troops; and a large remittance of curious objects has also been made to the capitals of each of the victorious belligerents, where they may be destined to fall into the possession of hands profane. It must be a galling souvenir to the Chinese Emperor when he remembers the fate of his beautiful Summer Palace and of the accumulated ancient treasures assembled in his charming residence. To what indignities may not some of the most sacred relics become exposed, passing from hand to hand of unappreciating amateurs! As to one portion, however, his Celestial Majesty may be tranquil. Promoted from the palatial abode of Hien-fou to that of Napoleon III., they have merely changed their address without compromising their dignity; for the thirty cases of valuable objects sent home as a present to the Emperor of France by the French expeditionary army were escorted with all due attention and honour from their recent habitat to that of the Tuileries, where they will be lodged, till such time as a permanent retreat can be found for their reception within the walls of the glorious Louvre. We had the satisfaction of visiting the collection last month, when it was opened for public inspection, and found it sufficiently interesting to warrant a pictorial record in the pages of the ILLUSTRATED LONDON NEWS. Our artist has selected some of the principal objects for the composition of his Illustration.[23]

There also appeared in the same journal an account of the plunder of the emperor's palace:

In the first accounts which were received of the taking by the French of the Chinese Emperor's Summer Palace it was stated that the French soldiers had looted it. The French General gives, however, an entirely different version of the matter. In his report to the French Government General de Montauban says:—

"I was anxious that our allies should be present at this first visit to the palace, which I suspected must contain great riches. After passing through several apartments of indescribable splendour, I had sentinels placed everywhere, and I selected two artillery officers to see that no one entered the palace, and that everything should remain as it was until the arrival of General Grant, who was sent for immediately by Brigadier Fattle. The English officers having arrived, we consulted what we had better do with all these riches, and we appointed three commissioners of each nation with instructions to set apart the objects of greatest value as curiosities, so that an equal division might be made. It would have been impossible to think of carrying away the whole of the property, our means of transport being very limited.

"Soon after a further search led to the discovery of a sum of about 800,000 francs in small ingots of gold and silver. The same commission also proceeded to make an equal division between the two armies, which gave about 80 francs to each of our soldiers. The division among the men was made by a commission, which was composed of all the chiefs of corps and of the different branches of the service, and was presided over by General Jamin. The commission, having deliberated in the name of the army, declared that the latter desired, as a souvenir, to make a present to the Emperor, the Empress, and the Prince Imperial of the whole of the curious articles carried off from the palace.

"The army was unanimous in approving of this offering to the chief of the State, who will consider it as a mark of gratitude of his soldiers for having been sent on the most distant expedition that was ever undertaken.

"At the moment of the division between the two armies I insisted, in the name of the Emperor, that Lord Elgin should make the first choice for the Queen of England.

"Lord Elgin selected a baton of command of the Emperor of China, in green jade of great value, and mounted with gold. A second baton similar in every respect having been found, Lord Elgin in his turn resolved that it should be reserved for the Emperor of the French. There was, therefore, perfect equality in this first choice.

"It would be impossible for me to describe to you, Monsieur le Maréchal, the magnificence of the numerous buildings which succeed each other over an extent of four leagues, and which composes what is called the Summer Palace of the Emperor, being a succession of pagodas, all containing gods in gold, silver, and bronze, of gigantic dimensions. One deity in bronze, Buddha, is about seventy feet high; gardens, lakes, and objects of curiosity heaped up for centuries past in the midst of buildings of white marble, roofed with dazzling varnished tiles of all colours; add to that the view over a delightful country, and your Excellency will have but a very feeble idea of what we have seen.

"In each of the pagodas there exist, not objects, but whole storerooms of objects of every kind. To mention to you only one fact: there are such quantities of the finest silk goods, that we have wrapped up in pieces of silk all the articles which I send to his Majesty."[24]

After all this, Elgin imposed a further convention upon China, signed on October 24, 1860, which also required the Emperor to pay enormous indemnities as further compensation—the sum of eight million taels.[25]

This sample chronicle of plunder as background to World War II shows that the events of the years 1939–45 were not really an aberration but merely a continuation. In the past, objects were taken on any pretext—"indemnity," "ransom," "punitive expedition," "sacred and religious crusade." Monstrous greed and barbarism were the common denominators. Nazi plunder was only exceptional in its scale, its ruthlessness, its planning, and even its recording. The nature of the materials taken differed, however, in that the Nazis certainly effected the greatest transport of paintings ever undertaken. In May 1945, soldiers of the United States Third Army discovered a huge cache of looted artworks deposited by the Germans in the salt mine at Alt Aussee, Austria, including thousands of paintings, among them the eight panels of the Ghent Altarpiece. This was to be a part of the long story about lost and returned paintings.[26] It has become clear in postwar times from such cases as that of the Quedlinburg treasures, removed to the United States by an American soldier, that plunder is not always one-sided. Moreover, revelations in recent years regarding works now in Russia from such famous art collections as the Krebs and the Koenigs collections and that of the Bremen Kunsthalle open up the unprecedented specter of two powerful nations engaging in successive plunder.

This unique situation also gives rise to fresh arguments about the status of "war booty." I use this term as opposed to "spoils of war," because war booty has separate legal connotations. International law has recognized the seizure of some war material and war booty in pursuit of the conduct of war. But it has limited the right of confiscation, especially from private citizens. According to the regulations annexed to the 1907 Hague Convention,* state-owned movable property found on the battlefield may be appropriated as "war booty."[27] This is quite different from the treasures we have been discussing. Looting and spoliation are precluded by the Hague Convention. Germany had destroyed over half a million museum objects and caused huge losses in untraceable items. The Soviet Union subsequently removed art from Germany through the work of its Trophy Commission, which was most active in 1945 and 1946. These two nations therefore have mutual claims to be reconciled. In the postwar era, there has been a strong impetus toward the idea of cultural restitution, although it should be said that the greater part of war spoils has probably never been returned. There is some precedent for the application of gold booty as reparations, but that is to be distinguished from art collections by its nature as currency. There is also a recent precedent set by the return from Israel to Egypt of archaeological objects from the Sinai, indicating that sometimes the victor may be prepared to make a voluntary surrender of "cultural" materials.[28] This brings me back to the meaning of "spoils of war." Although "spoils" suggests treasure, "spoil" has quite a different implication. It refers to the carcass of the animal left to rot. Nazi crimes against art began with censorship, confiscation, and deliberate destruction—and ultimately led to murder.[29] This last was the "spoil" of war, and it is against this almost unimaginable human loss that we should temper arguments over the "spoils of war."

---

* Editor's note: See Appendix 3; see also Kaye, below, page 102.

WORLD WAR II AND

THE DISPLACEMENT OF ART

AND

CULTURAL PROPERTY

Lynn H. Nicholas

The transfer of works of art from vanquished to victor is as old as warfare itself. The fact that it occurred in World War II is, therefore, not surprising. But the displacement of art in this war was unprecedented in a number of ways. Never before had objects been moved about on such a scale: not hundreds or thousands, but millions of objects of every description. Unprecedented, too, were the ideological, legal, and political arguments put forth to justify the removals. And, for the first time in history, the armies of most of the belligerents had highly trained art specialists in their ranks, whose duty it was to secure and preserve movable works of art, and whose professionalism, no matter what their ideology, saved most of the treasures of Europe for us.

The displacement of works of art began in Germany itself long before the actual outbreak of war. From the first day Hitler held office, he set about realizing his dream of a pure Germanic Empire. "Pure" and "Germanic" were the operative words, and art would not be exempt. The world must be purged of unsuitable works of art and the artists responsible for them. Hitler had no doubts about what was unacceptable: he disapproved of anything "unfinished" or abstract, such as the works of Vasily Kandinsky or Franz Marc—never mind that the latter had died fighting for Germany in World War I. But style was not the only criterion. Camille Pissarro was unacceptable because he was Jewish, George Grosz and Käthe Kollwitz because they were leftist and antiwar. It took even the Führer's closest colleagues quite a while to understand just what he did want. Goebbels, for example, had decorated his dining room with watercolors by Emil Nolde, a Nazi sympathizer, but when Hitler came to Goebbels's house, the Führer was not pleased, and Goebbels was forced to remove the pictures.

Pressure was put on the German art establishment as soon as Hitler came to power in 1933 and gradually increased. When, by 1937, the museums had not gotten rid of what they should, and indeed were actively resisting doing so, Hitler sent into the galleries committees of Nazi artists and theorists, who decided as they walked through what had to go. Sometimes agonizing decisions had to be made: one picture by Lovis Corinth, *Inntal Landscape* from Berlin's Nationalgalerie, was spared, but only after much discussion, when it was decided that the landscape features were sufficiently representational to outweigh the "degenerate" sky. Eventually, over sixteen thousand works were removed from public collections. To make sure everyone got the message, a selection was exhibited in the infamous "Degenerate Art" shows in Munich and other cities.

Although the Nazis found these "degenerate" works unacceptable for home consumption, they were not unaware of their market value. Göring was the first to grasp the commercial possibilities, and it was his agent who took Van Gogh's famed *Portrait of Dr. Gachet,* purged from a museum in Frankfurt, to Holland and sold it. The painting eventually came to New York, where it was sold in 1990 to a Japanese collector for $82.5 million—making it the world's most expensive picture. Later a special, secret marketing agency was set up where the best purged items could be obtained for

3. Empty frames at the Musée du Louvre, Paris, 1940

foreign currency—often for a few dollars or Swiss francs. For example, Ernst Ludwig Kirchner's *Street Scene,* now at the Museum of Modern Art in New York, was sold for $160. To increase sales, this agency put on a full-fledged auction in Lucerne in 1939. Joseph Pulitzer, there on his honeymoon, acquired Henri Matisse's *Bathers with a Turtle,* and a Belgian consortium bought ten major works by such artists as James Ensor, Picasso, and Marc Chagall. Dealers in many countries took full advantage of this deaccessioning by the Nazi authorities, and the rejects ended up in collections worldwide—in total, a tremendous loss to Germany.

As the restrictions imposed by the 1935 Nuremberg laws gradually became more drastic, private collections also began to leave Germany. Some collectors had seen the coming disaster early: Robert von Hirsch in 1933 persuaded the Nazi authorities to allow his incomparable collection, loaded with "Germanic" national treasures, to go with him to Switzerland by bribing Göring with Lucas Cranach's *Judgment of Paris.* The painting was retrieved by the Allies after the war from a mine at Heilbronn and returned to Hirsch. Others, like Justin Thannhauser, shipped collections first to France or Holland, and from there to the United States, where they still remain.

Though disturbed by these goings-on, art professionals in the rest of Europe were more concerned with the protection of their great collections from the physical dangers of war. The first measures taken were based on the experience of World War I. Everyone expected a static war centered on the fortifications of the new Maginot Line. But the events of the Spanish Civil War, with the bombing of Madrid and the terrifying last-minute rescue of the treasures of the Prado from their hiding place in a besieged rock quarry near Barcelona, made curators aware that they must now either put their collections in bombproof shelters in the cities or remove them to remote country refuges.

When in 1939 war did break out, evacuation of artworks began in earnest all over Europe. Polish curators shipped 160 magnificent tapestries from the Wawel Palace in Cracow by barge down the Vistula and then on to Rome (where the Vatican refused to take them in), to London, and finally to

Canada. There they not only spent the war but, trapped by Cold War politics, remained until 1960. Pictures everywhere were removed from their frames and packed in specially prepared cases (fig. 3). Statues were taken down or barricaded behind bizarre structures of brick and sandbags. Venetian collections left the city in trucks precariously balanced on barges. In Amsterdam, Rembrandt's *The Night Watch* was rolled up and evacuated. Scenery trucks had to be requisitioned from the Comédie Française to take away from the Louvre Théodore Géricault's enormous *Raft of the Medusa,* which was too delicate to roll. And, in a moment fraught with symbolism, the *Nike of Samothrace* was carefully lowered down the grand staircase of the museum. Most of the French treasures were first taken to the château of Chambord and from there redistributed to similar edifices around Le Mans and along the Loire. But the Maginot Line proved ineffective against the German advance so that the *Mona Lisa* and three thousand other important pictures had to be moved southward once again before the oncoming armies, this time in the midst of battle and streams of refugees. As the war went on, and the Germans took over Vichy France, the Louvre holdings would be moved three more times. The Soviet Union did not begin such operations until Hitler invaded in 1941. Only about half the collections of the State Hermitage Museum could be packed and evacuated to Sverdlovsk, in Siberia, before Leningrad (St. Petersburg) was besieged; the rest, mostly stored in cellars, stayed behind. Collections from all over the Soviet Union joined the Hermitage treasures in Siberia, but much could not be moved and would be exposed to the dangers of war.

Once in control of most of the continent of Europe, Hitler envisioned nothing less than the complete purification and rearrangement of its artworks in accordance with Nazi laws and theories. These operations were planned just as meticulously as the military ones and were carefully coordinated with them. There were four major, well-funded bureaucracies that concerned themselves exclusively with art matters, and they

4. Chaplain Samuel Blinder sorts Torah scrolls at the Offenbach Collecting Point, Germany, July 1945.

5. Polish monuments officer Karol Estreicher holding Leonardo da Vinci's *Portrait of a Lady with an Ermine* upon its return to Poland in May 1945

were backed by the full force of Nazi police and military organizations. Hitler's personal agency, the Sonderauftrag Linz, was established to build up a collection for a vast museum he intended to build in his hometown of Linz in Austria. He was inspired by the great Italian museums he had visited with Mussolini. The Führer monitored operations of the Linz organization daily, even during battles, through his assistant Martin Bormann. The agency received over 90 million Reichsmarks in its five years of existence, during which time Hitler collected some eight thousand paintings and "rights" to tens of thousands more. Göring, who amassed thousands of pictures and other objects, spent far more time on art matters. The Ahnenerbe (Ancestral Heritage) group operated by the SS specialized in archaeology. Alfred Rosenberg, ideological guru of the Nazi Party, established the Einsatzstab Reichsleiter Rosenberg, known as the ERR, which at first limited itself to collecting Jewish books, archives, and religious objects for a planned anti-Semitic think tank, but later expanded its activities to include works of art. By war's end these groups, and a number of lesser ones, would have accumulated literally tons of paintings, furniture, books, and every other form of art. The richest sources were collections confiscated from the state museums and citizens of the Slavic nations and from Jews everywhere. But the Nazis also bought huge quantities on the art market, which experienced a boom unequaled until the 1980s.

The Nazi art agencies had completely different policies for Eastern and Western Europe. In the East, Slavic cultures and their artifacts were to be eliminated completely and only "Germanic" items would be preserved. One example was the magnificent Veit Stoss altarpiece in the Church of Our Lady in Cracow. It qualified as Germanic because the artist had been born in Nuremberg. The fact that the altarpiece had been commissioned specifically for the church was ignored, and it was shipped off to the Reich. Other things, not Germanic, were simply considered too good for the inferior Slavs: Hans Frank, the Nazi governor of the semi-autonomous General-

gouvernement of Poland, ordered the chief of his art operations, Kajetan Mühlmann, to appropriate Leonardo da Vinci's *Portrait of a Lady with an Ermine* from the princely Czartoryski collection (fig. 5). When he fled before the Red Army in 1945, Frank took it with him to Bavaria.

These policies were continued with vigor in the USSR where, for example, the Tchaikovsky Museum in Klin and its contents, being all Slavic, did not qualify for preservation—it was ransacked and turned into a motorcycle-repair garage. But the panels of the Amber Room (see fig. 25), originally made in Prussia, were carefully removed from the walls of the Catherine Palace near Leningrad and put on exhibition in Königsberg (Kaliningrad). Many thousands more objects, books, and archives were taken to Nazi research institutes specializing in Eastern Studies. And this activity, competitively carried on by the SS and the ERR, would continue even as the German armies retreated for the last time.

In Austria and the conquered West, things were quite different. There was no need for Hitler to take away the national collections of these countries, for to him they had become provinces of the Thousand Year Reich. Indeed, a special art-protection agency, the Kunstschutz, was established within most German occupation governments to guard the stored masterpieces. To its credit, this group courageously, but unsuccessfully, tried to prevent Nazi looting. The chief of the Kunstschutz in France, Franz Count von Wolff-Metternich, was dismissed when he defied Göring.

In fact, the Führer did plan to rearrange Western Europe's patrimony and eventually take certain things back to the Fatherland: first and foremost, anything removed from Germany as a result of the hated Versailles Treaty, such as panels from the Dirk Bouts *Last Supper* from Louvain and the Ghent Altarpiece by Hubert and Jan van Eyck. Both of these works were taken back to Germany in 1942. Hitler also ordered a secret list made of everything else that had left Germany since 1500—whether due to war (especially the Napoleonic Wars), dynastic arrangements, or the art trade: the Holy Roman Regalia from Vienna, for example. He intended to collect most of the items on the list when the war ended and the Western nations were firmly in his power. There were only five copies of this top-secret three-hundred-page list, known as the Kümmel Report—one of which is in the library of the Metropolitan Museum of Art in New York.

The boom in the art market started as a natural response to the money lavished upon it both by the Nazis, using funds milked from the economies of the occupied countries, and by war profiteers seeking a safe investment for their cash. Vendors of all stripes besieged the Nazi agencies with offers to sell the family heirlooms, from the top-of-the-line Vermeer *Allegory of the Art of Painting,* sold in Vienna by a member of the Czernin family, to pure junk. Hitler's chief curator, Hans Posse, a top art historian who was also director of the Dresden Staatliche Gemäldegalerie, sometimes applying pressure, sometimes not, acquired such prizes as the Mannheimer collection and a part of the Koenigs drawings collection from Rotterdam. Representatives of German and Austrian auction houses and museums scoured the shops. Dealers trying to profit from the vast sums being spent by the Nazis resorted to the most byzantine international maneuvers to sustain their trade. Greed was rampant. Relatives betrayed one another for political or financial favors. Works of art were traded for tracts of conquered land in eastern Europe. And as the vise of the occupation tightened, survival became the motive for many a sale. A Jewish collector, scholar, or dealer, or an Aryan one with a Jewish wife, who could satisfy the Nazi craving for art, could make his freedom and that of his family part of the deal. The distinguished scholar Max J. Friedländer is a case in point. Friedländer had fled to Holland in the 1930s. After the arrival of the Germans, he was twice rescued from concentration camps by Göring's personal curator, Walter Andreas Hofer, who made him an "Honorary Aryan" and in exchange for his freedom required him to give expertises for the Reichsmarschall's collection. Friedländer must have particularly enjoyed authenticating the obviously fake Vermeer *Christ with the Woman Taken in Adultery,* by the famous forger Han van Meegeren, which Göring valued above all else in his collection (see fig. 69).

Massive though this trade was, it paled beside the confiscations, which were regulated and justified by an extraordinary array of laws and directives based on Nazi racial and political theory. In the Western occupied nations the emphasis was on Jewish collections. But not all such collections were automatically taken, for some lip service was paid to the local governments. The Nazis felt a peculiar need to give legal reasons for their looting and, as the tons of documents they left behind show, they went to the most elaborate lengths to do so. Confiscation of private collections was selective and limited to things "abandoned," that is, left in normally safe museums, houses, safe-deposit boxes, or commercial storage by those who had fled, especially German Jews who had managed to get their collections out of Germany. In France, the Vichy government, greedy for some of the spoils, played straight into Hitler's hands by declaring that French Jews who had left the country were no longer citizens. When, to Vichy's surprise, the Germans began to take the possessions of these families, the French protested that the confiscations violated the Hague Convention (1907), which prohibits the removal of the private property of the citizens of an occupied country. The Nazi response to that was that the objects in question no longer belonged to French citizens and that the convention, therefore, did not apply.

By 1942, not only works of art but the entire contents of abandoned dwellings were included in what could be "legally" looted. This amounted to plenty: over seventy thousand dwellings were cleared out in Paris alone. Those deported to concentration camps were considered to have fled, and their possessions too could be "legally" confiscated. Appeals were accepted: if a threatened person, by producing elaborate documentation, could prove he was Aryan he received a "certificat de non-appartenance à la race juive" and was allowed to keep his belongings.

Headquarters for confiscation operations in France was the Jeu de Paume, the lovely little Paris museum whose contents have now gone to the Musée d'Orsay. All looted works were taken there to be classified, photographed, and arranged in special exhibitions for the Nazi leaders, who could then take their pick. Göring visited some twenty times and eventually took more than six hundred items. Hitler, who had first choice, never came himself, but was sent albums with photographs of what was available from the magnificent collections of the Rothschilds, M. David David-Weill, all the major Jewish dealers such as Paul Rosenberg and Bernheim-Jeune, and many others. "Degenerate" works swept up in these operations, which could not be displayed in Germany, were quarantined in a special room (see fig. 51) and used as barter for old masters or sold off to dealers. It is estimated that more than twenty-two thousand items were shipped to the Reich from the Jeu de Paume alone.

As the tide of war turned, the restraint shown vis-à-vis state-owned objects in the West faltered badly: Himmler tried to take the Bayeux Tapestry from France but was thwarted by the fall of Paris. His colleagues in Belgium, in the interlude provided by the Battle of the Bulge, did better, making off by sea with Michelangelo's beautiful *Bruges Madonna.* Far bolder was the removal, ostensibly for protection, of about half the treasures of the Florentine museums—the Uffizi, the Palazzo Pitti, and others—to a remote castle on the Austrian border in the Alto Adige. The priceless works had been hidden in villas all around the city and were literally trapped between the warring armies; German art-protection officers darted in and out of the front lines to retrieve them. These objects, which later became bargaining chips in the negotiations for the surrender of Italy, were recovered by the Allies in 1945 and returned to Florence.

In Germany, as the bombing of its cities increased and as the Allied armies closed in from east and west, all the confiscated and purchased art, plus the great German museum holdings, was moved into hundreds of bunkers, castles, churches, salt mines, and even cow sheds (fig. 6). Most famous of these refuges was the salt mine at Alt Aussee, near Salzburg, where the cream of Hitler's collection was taken. But there were many others just as important both in Silesia and to the west of Berlin. Among the latter was Merkers, which held not only thousands of paintings from the Berlin museums, but also much of the gold reserve of the Reich. At the final surrender of Germany, all these hiding places awaited the attention of the Allied armies.

The fact that art-specialist officers were included in the armies of the Western Allies at all was something of a miracle. The British and American commands had, at first, not thought them necessary, and it was only by very persistent lobbying that members of the American museum establishment managed to convince President Roosevelt and the army that their presence in the field was essential. A small number of officers, known as "monuments officers," was eventually appointed, usually one with each army group. The Monuments,

6. German repository in a church at Ellingen, Bavaria, May 1945

7. Generals Bradley, Patton, and Eisenhower examining works of art stored by the Nazis in a mine at Merkers, Germany, April 1945

8. Allied monuments officers in Munich, 1945. Left to right: Marcelle Minet, France; Craig Hugh Smyth, United States; Hubert de Bry, France (back); Alphonse Vorenkamp, the Netherlands; Doda Conrad, United States; Raymond Lemaire, Belgium; Charles Parkhurst, United States; Pierre-Louis Duchartre, France

Fine Arts, and Archives section, as this group came to be called, performed extraordinary feats of salvage and preservation in Italy, France, and the Low Countries. But even after all they had experienced, the conditions they found in Germany were shocking to them. Once across the frontiers of the Reich, they found themselves in a surreal landscape of "skeleton cities" with no government and peopled by groups of homeless citizens, freed prisoners, displaced persons, and demobilized soldiers, who all wandered about burning priceless furniture to keep warm and who could pick up whatever they wanted in the unguarded refuges. Hidden somewhere in this chaos were the treasures of Germany and the Nazi acquisitions. Daily, the monuments men found thousands of irreplaceable things in danger of destruction. British officers discovered hundreds of uncrated pictures from Berlin's Nationalgalerie in a mine at Grasleben (fig. 9). Göring's collection was found scattered all over Berchtesgaden, where he had taken it on his special trains. Monuments men were greeted there by the Reichsmarschall's curator, Walter Andreas Hofer, who gave them a tour of the collections. The Rothschild jewels turned up at Neuschwanstein, and the Holy Roman Regalia (fig. 10) were found walled up in Nuremberg, which boasted elaborate underground bunkers filled with loot. Soviet art-specialist officers, attached to their Trophy Organization, found hundreds of similar caches: among them Schloss Weesenstein outside Dresden, which had been the last headquarters of Hitler's Linz organization; caves and mines containing the Dresden collections themselves; the refuges in Silesia; and of course the repositories for the tremendous holdings in and around Berlin, including the famous Friedrichshain and Zoo flak towers. There was a certain amount of competition to secure these objects: Anglo-American forces were ordered to take all such finds with them from the areas they relinquished to the Soviet army. Likewise, the Soviets removed everything they possibly could from those parts of Berlin that would later be controlled by the Western powers.

The primary duty of the British and American monuments men was to secure and sort out the vast quantities of art they were finding. This was a major undertaking, and the army command was, with some effort, persuaded to set up a number of Collecting Points, whose holdings would soon rival those of the greatest museums in the world. In two short weeks monuments officer Craig Hugh Smyth prepared Hitler's old administrative buildings in Munich—which were in terrible condition—to receive the thousands of tons of art being evacuated from Alt Aussee and other repositories in Austria and southern Germany. Another Collecting Point was set up by Walter Farmer in the Landesmuseum at Wiesbaden. The United States Office of Strategic Services (OSS), precursor of the Central Intelligence Agency, sent a special team, called the Art Looting Investigation Unit, to interrogate Nazi art officials and to analyze their records so that determination of ownership could begin. By the time the Collecting Points closed down in 1951 they had processed several million "items": art in truly industrial quantities.

9. In the Grasleben
mine, Germany,
1945, British officers
found hundreds of
uncrated pictures
from Berlin's
Nationalgalerie.

10. In Vienna, Ameri-
can officers inspect
returned Holy
Roman Regalia, Janu-
ary 1946. Left to
right: Colonel T. S.
Paul, and MFA&A offi-
cers Andrew Ritchie,
Perry Cott, and
Ernest De Wald

11. Recovered sculp-
ture in the Munich
Central Collecting
Point, July 1945

There now arose the question of what was to be done
with the huge amounts of art from so many different sources,
acquired in so many different ways, and belonging to so many
different nations. The Allies, despite years of discussion in
endless international committees, had never formulated a
definite policy on restitution. Agreement foundered on two
issues: restitution in kind and the use of works of art as assets
of reparation. But of course in 1945 there was no unified
policy on any aspect of the occupation of Germany, nor would
there ever be. Although discussions continued at many levels,
each Allied government essentially ran the zone under its
control as it pleased. The American military governor, General
Lucius Clay, wanted, above all, to be rid of responsibility for
the tons of art, removed from the various nations of Europe,
that were accumulating in the Collecting Points. It became,
therefore, U.S. and British policy to return a work to the
nation from which it had been taken, whether by purchase or
confiscation, and an international team was assembled to
claim items for their countries. The objects were shipped back
by the hundreds to East and West. Recuperation commissions
in the recipient nations were then left with the often nasty task
of deciding if sales had been forced or not, and just who would
keep the objects. The impeccable German records often were
useful in solving such problems, and many who had hoped to
hide their sales to the Nazis, keep the money, and then reclaim
their pictures were foiled by the evidence in these archives.
In such cases the disputed objects usually reverted to the
state. Most difficult was the problem of the so-called heirless
property of all categories, principally confiscated from Jews.
The American authorities in Germany eventually transferred
responsibility for the disposition of these things to the Jewish
Restitution Successor Organization, which distributed them to
Jewish communities worldwide.

The state collections of Germany were a different problem.
Given the condition of the German museums and the uncertain
state of Western relations with the USSR in 1945, General
Clay believed that temporary removal of the most precious
objects in the German collections to the United States would
be advisable. A number of officials in the Treasury and State
Departments felt that these works should be retained in
America indefinitely and be regarded as reparations. General
Clay vehemently rejected this idea and was strongly supported
by President Truman. In late 1945, about two hundred of the
most fragile pictures, most from Berlin's Kaiser-Friedrich-
Museum, were sent to Washington, D.C., and stored in the
vaults of the National Gallery of Art. Despite repeated
assurances by President Truman that they would be returned
to Germany someday, this act caused a near mutiny on the part
of the monuments officers, who felt that "safeguarding" the
pictures—a favorite Hitlerian euphemism—was unacceptable.
And in the United States there was such considerable outcry
by groups of museum professionals and the press that no
further works were brought to America. After being exhibited
to record-breaking crowds around the country, the paintings
were returned to West Germany in 1949.

12. One of many storerooms full of paintings at the Munich Central Collecting Point, 1945

Soviet policy was quite different. Almost all the objects collected by the Soviet Trophy Organization, regardless of ownership, were sent back to the USSR and stored in a number of cultural institutions. Thousands of items were later returned to Poland, East Germany, Hungary, and other East European countries. But many others, among which are works confiscated and purchased by the Nazis, and museum collections from West Germany, such as the famous Trojan gold, still remain in Russia and other nations formerly behind the Iron Curtain.

Of course, not everything was recovered by the official art specialists. Thousands of objects were stolen by civilians and military personnel and have been dispersed around the world. Many of these cases were pursued for years by agencies of the nations concerned, and sporadically things have been found and returned. Pollaiuolo's tiny painted panel *Hercules and the Hydra,* missing from the Uffizi, turned up in the hands of ex-German soldiers in California. Albrecht Dürer's delicate *Iris* from Bremen was discovered in an East German farmhouse. And priceless treasures of the church at Quedlinburg were recovered in 1990 from a small Texas town, where they had been kept for nearly fifty years by a GI who had stolen them from their hiding place in 1945 and simply mailed them home.

The fate of many thousands of objects still remains completely unknown. Among the most famous are the Raphael *Portrait of a Young Man* from the Czartoryski collection in Poland (see colorplate 1), Giovanni Bellini's *Madonna and Child* from Berlin, and of course the famous panels of the Amber Room from the Catherine Palace near St. Petersburg. Let us hope that they have not been destroyed, and that the recently revived interest in tracing the losses of World War II will soon bring them back into the light of day, which is where every work of art belongs.

PART 2

LOSSES DURING

AND AS A CONSEQUENCE OF

WORLD WAR II

INTRODUCTION

Lynn H. Nicholas

Before we can search for lost objects, we must know what they are and determine the exact circumstances of their displacement. We must discover if they were confiscated by governments, stolen by individuals, sold willingly or under duress, bartered for food, or simply hidden, forgotten, and randomly moved from place to place. Only when these problems have been solved can the processes of restitution and compensation be undertaken, and then only on a case-by-case basis, in which, inevitably, present-day political considerations and the emotional legacy of World War II will be major factors.

Determining what is missing is not a simple task. Many museum records have been destroyed or scattered, and private individuals often have inadequate documentation—or none at all. Wartime dealers and collaborators usually preferred to forget certain transactions altogether, and the heirs of thieves do not like to attract attention. Lists compiled by governments just after the war, never complete, were not kept up-to-date, or were destroyed as the years passed and interest waned.

With the end of the Cold War and the opening up of Eastern Europe, it has become apparent that large numbers of works of art previously thought to be lost are, in fact, stored in repositories in countries of the former Soviet Union. Conversely, reestablishment of communications with these nations has enabled Western officials to identify displaced objects that appear in their own jurisdictions. The continuing compilation and exchange of accurate information is vital to the discovery and survival of the thousands of works of every description that are still unaccounted for, and to this end, new commissions dedicated to the recovery of lost works have been set up in most of the European nations that participated in World War II. The constitution and funding levels of these commissions are extremely varied. Some work under the aegis of the countries' foreign ministries, others under ministries of culture or of finance. Nearly all must call on their scholarly communities for inventories and identification of the thousands of missing objects, which range from petrified dinosaur bones to illuminated manuscripts. The long-stored files and inventories of the recuperation commissions of the immediate postwar period have been exhumed, and the revived agencies, often spurred on by private individuals, are attempting to update their lists of missing objects so that concrete claims can be made.

The papers that follow are not simply dry catalogues: the losses discussed here are just as much psychological and emotional as material. Behind the enumerations of paintings, archives, and religious objects move the specters of lost families, lives, and cities; of destroyed memories and traditions which cannot be replaced; of patriotic passions and the terrible suffering of war. These discussions of cultural losses vividly illustrate the complex issues that enmesh the spoils of war.

The contributors to this part of the volume spoke during the first day of the New York symposium: they represent the nations most severely affected today by the loss of movable works of art resulting from the Second World War. There was, for example, no speaker from Italy, as its losses were principally to the physical fabric of the country, and items that were confiscated or illegally moved have, for the most part, been returned. Italy and other nations were represented at the symposium by a number of guest participants, several of whom have chosen to contribute essays to this book (see Part 7, below). The order of speakers on cultural losses was determined largely by the course of the war, moving from Poland, the first to be invaded by the German Wehrmacht, through Western Europe, on to the former USSR, and then to nations allied and annexed to the Reich, such as Austria and Hungary, as they in turn were taken by the Allies, and finally to Germany itself. Where possible, representatives were chosen from among officials of the present governments of these countries or from members of government-sponsored groups working on the assessment and recovery of wartime losses. The devastating effect of the war on Jewish cultural heritage was considered in a category by itself.

The symposium was conceived not as a strictly scholarly meeting, but as an informative one, in which the situation in each nation could be presented and discussed. And indeed, some of the most exciting moments of the conference occurred when national representatives, many of whom had never before met, were able to state their often passionate positions face-to-face. Two very separate problems of restitution emerged, and they were the same that bedeviled negotiators in 1815, 1919, and 1945: what should be returned to innocent victims, be they private individuals, museums, or governments, and what can be kept as spoils of war by nations that had their patrimony severely depleted by the defeated aggressor? To solve these problems the speakers suggested, among other things, the establishment of an international commission of adjudication, greater exchange of data, and stricter regulation of the illegal art trade.

But far more important in this session was the emergence of something quite different: the unequivocal commitment of the cultural officials of every nation to a just settlement. As the day progressed, it was the works of art themselves that seemed to dominate, overshadowing "national" requisites and promoting a common desire to find a way to release the long-hidden objects from arbitrary political bondage and restore them to public view, wherever that might be. The obstacles in the path of this seemingly simple idea would become clear in later sessions.

POLAND:

THE WAR LOSSES,

CULTURAL HERITAGE,

AND

CULTURAL LEGITIMACY

Jan P. Pruszyński

THEORETICAL PREMISES

Half a century after the last global armed conflict, we may talk more openly about the redress of certain grievances in respect to cultural losses, a subject that is very important not only for the past, but for our future. We cannot limit our activity to tort claims, nor to finding guilty and responsible persons. More important is listing items that are keepsakes of our history and that therefore make up a part of the national heritage. We owe a great debt to the past, which was once the present of our predecessors; however—and I speak not only from the Polish perspective—saving memorabilia, noble artistic creations, and important monuments seems to be in vain. Although we try to appreciate them and to inventory, to describe, and to restore the material evidence of history, the next armed conflict deprives us of them.

In order to begin to understand the concept of cultural heritage and the reasons why states insist on the restitution of cultural property that has been removed from their territory, one must first attempt to define these terms. When does an object form part of a nation's cultural heritage? In almost all legal regulations concerning the protection of cultural heritage, we find such property defined as that which is of historical, artistic, cultural, or scientific value to the nation and its people. Another kind of value should be added to this list—*patriotic,* that is, property that adds to a people's sense of identity[1] and continuity with generations past, as well as national community. A culture accumulates not only customs, habits, language, and beliefs, but certain objects. Not every one of them is created and formed within the nation. In each nation's cultural heritage we may find goods manufactured by migrants during a temporary sojourn abroad and examples of fine art and crafts bought in the past in culturally rich lands whose artists were renowned for their skill. Still other items may have been found, for example, during scientific excavations in lands having at that time no national identity or statehood, and here the possibility exists that the lands of origin will claim their rights in the future. Can we say that war trophies may be considered a part of the heritage of a conqueror? Museums are filled with souvenirs of courage in battle, sometimes seized in a conquered country. But an idealistic effort to make war more "civilized" brought the matter of protection of national cultural resources under international scrutiny during the nineteenth century, and the results were clearly stated in international agreements.[2] After the terrible experience of the Great War of 1914–18, the European states again affirmed that their cultural treasures could not be openly plundered.[3]* Another problem arises with changes in frontiers and the compulsory migrations of inhabitants, who leave behind a part of their inheritance. This very sensitive question must be solved *ex aequo et bono* (equally and fairly).

---

* Editor's note: As expressed in the provisions of the Treaty of Versailles (see Appendix 4; see also Kaye, below, pages 102–3).

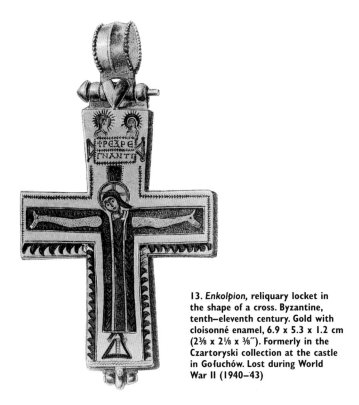

13. *Enkolpion,* reliquary locket in the shape of a cross. Byzantine, tenth–eleventh century. Gold with cloisonné enamel, 6.9 x 5.3 x 1.2 cm (2⅜ x 2⅛ x ⅜″). Formerly in the Czartoryski collection at the castle in Gołuchów. Lost during World War II (1940–43)

What is cultural heritage? We may answer: *everything,* depending on the level of cultural consciousness of a nation and the extent of its knowledge of the past and its personal links with its heritage, for "heritage" means documents of the past. And the value of these documents can change. Some of those things that we appreciate might not have been as important to our ancestors—and may not be considered as valuable by future generations.

How can one prove that an object belongs to one's heritage? To solve this problem is to get down to the crux of the matter! The quest for documentation of proprietary rights, and search for this documentation in archives, is of secondary significance. By formal legal process we may prove our rights to a certain material object but not to its cultural implications. Only some spoils of war are valuable items that are invento-ried, well known, and stored in public museums and cultural institutions, and, for the most part, many have been sold, bought, and owned by bona-fide possessors. The concept and theory, and hence the practice, of restitution change with time. Immediately after a war it may be seen as a form of redress of grievances: namely, the return of retrieved goods, or reparation in kind, which involves replacing objects wantonly destroyed by the enemy with similar objects, as a form of remuneration. Later, the issue becomes more sensitive. Due process must take into consideration a benefit of doubt and time limitations, must weigh the goodwill of the possessor, and so forth. And it is not true that the identification of an object leads automat-ically to its restitution. We should not desist, however, from efforts to recover a nation's cultural heritage, but rather seize whenever possible a favorable political moment or a rising interest that may result in the resolution of such problems.

It is most important that a nation should be understood to have the right to the material witnesses of its history and cultural heritage—documents, art objects, and monuments. We may term this right "cultural legitimacy." On this basis, a nation should be able to reclaim all cultural property that has been lawlessly expropriated, especially when carried out without provision for defense against the seizure, and this should be allowed without any time limitations. Future inter-national regulations regarding this right must be the subject of discussions by specialists in the field: art historians, historians, and lawyers.

POLISH LOSSES

A detailed list of losses incurred as a consequence of World War II is not easily compiled. It is difficult to explain in brief terms the situation in Poland during and after the war under the two occupation forces of the Nazi and Soviet regimes, especially with regard to the suffering caused by the martial regulations imposed,[4] the restrictions on personal freedom, and the loss of human rights. The main aim of both our neighbors, partners in the German-Soviet Treaty of Non-Aggression of 1939, was clearly stated in the long-denied "secret protocol" to the treaty, dated August 23, 1939. Much favored by Stalin, the protocol enabled Hitler's aggression to proceed without risk of war on two fronts: "Whether the existence of an independent Polish state is in the interest of both parties can be determined depending on future political events; in any case, both governments will approach this problem in a spirit of mutual friendship."[5]

"Be merciless! Do not spare Poland!" Hitler ordered his troops, police, and administration.[6] "Our main task is to settle in the Eastern territory [Poland] an exclusively German pop-ulation," exclaimed Nazi Generalgouverneur Hans Frank.[7]

Stalin's directives were almost the same, calling for the cleansing of the territories of Western Ukraine and Western Belarus of any Polish vestiges.[8] This meant the extermination

14. Attic red-figure kantharos, attributed to the Sotades Painter. c. 470–450 B.C. Height 8.5 cm (3³⁄₁₆″). Formerly in the Czartoryski collection at the castle in Gołuchów. One of 253 Greek vases removed from Poland during World War II, this example was not among the 56 returned in 1956 by the USSR.

15. *Madonna.* c. 1390–1410. Limestone, height 43 cm (16⅞″). Formerly in the collection of the Municipal Museum in Toruń. Lost during World War II (1944)

December 1939 and March 1940, over forty-three historical churches, seventy-four palaces, ninety-six manors, one hundred libraries, fifteen museums, and many art galleries were plundered, and the booty, carefully packed, was sent to Germany. It is significant that the stolen art objects were described as "safeguarded,"[15] and over five hundred of them, including the famous main altar of the Church of Our Lady in Cracow, and paintings, sculptures, and manuscripts, were exhibited in Berlin one year later.[16] Damage to historical architecture in Warsaw reached 92 percent, in Danzig (Gdańsk) 82 percent, in Poznań 52 percent, in Lublin 18 percent, and in Cracow 4 percent, with the total overall damage to the Polish architectural heritage calculated at 43 percent. These figures do not account for destruction to interiors and objects that were pillaged during the occupation. Even after the Warsaw Uprising of 1944, special German commando squads searched for precious objects in historical buildings before setting them on fire.[17]

No formal evaluation has been made of losses in former Polish territory in the east,[18] but only the ruined walls of most residences and churches bear witness to the former cultural existence of the Polish people there. The fate of museums was the same. In Warsaw, the collections of the Royal Castle, the Royal Palace in Wilanów, and the picturesque Palace-on-Water in Lazienki Park were removed almost completely; the losses of the National Museum in Warsaw—objects of gold and silver, coins, paintings, antiquities, and furniture—are estimated at 50 percent to 90 percent, partly because the Wehrmacht used the buildings of the museum as barracks. Among the identified and most precious lost objects we are still looking for are more than eighteen thousand items, such as *Saint Anne* carved by Veit Stoss during his years in Cracow, the famous sixteenth-century Reliquary of Wieluń, *Madonna with Child and Angels* by Bartolommeo dei Landi, *Adoration on Good Friday* by Jozef Chelmoński, once in the Poznań Museum, *Diana and Callisto* of the school of Rubens, *Madonna and Child with Angels* painted by Lorenzo di Credi (fig. 16), and, perhaps the most famous of all, *Portrait of a Young Man* by Raphael (colorplate 1), as well as manuscripts, engravings, and drawings. The most bitter loss is irreparable: libraries and archives plundered and burned for no military reason. The Krasinski Library in Warsaw was a notorious case: in underground magazines the rarest and most precious books and manuscripts had been stored on five floors. To set a fire there was not easy, but the brave German *Brandkommando* managed to do it![19] Many spoils left Poland under successive occupations, the partitions of 1772–95, and the annexation of its territories for over 120 years by Russia, Prussia, and Austria. We have lost almost all our royal regalia.[20] The aggressors solemnly assented not to use even the name of Poland. But these injuries are nothing by comparison with the devastation that took place in World War II during the occupation, the struggle between the German and Soviet armies in 1944–45, and the invaders' exercise of their supposed *ius spolii* (right to booty).

or deportation of all important members of Polish society: military officers and policemen, landowners and civil servants, scholars and persons actively engaged in political, religious, and welfare work, all of whom were blamed for their prewar activity—described as "anti-Soviet"—in favor of their state. All their property was nationalized and then most of it was laid waste, so that even if an owner or his heir, who might by chance survive, should return and prove his rights, no trace of his home would remain.

The Nazi expropriations, ordered by the German administration,[9] were more organized. After the first "big action"[10] came the activity of specialized and highly skillful "groups of action"[11] and of the Special Commissioner for the Protection of Monuments and Art Objects in the Generalgouvernement,[12] resulting in the pillaging of churches and residences, museums, and private collections—some very rich[13]—and the systematic search for all valuable and culturally important objects that were classified either as "Germanic" or as "harmful and anti-German."[14] For example, during the three months between

16. Lorenzo di Credi (1459–1537). *Madonna and Child with Angels.* Tempera on panel, diameter 85 cm (33½″). Formerly in the collection of the Poznań Museum. Lost during World War II (1943)

TOWARD RESTITUTION

Shall we deny the argument of S. Romilly that the rebirth of the state should be linked to material restitution and moral indemnity?[21] An eminent Polish scholar, active in the process of restitution after World War I, stated that the decrees of the enemies' administration, which are disadvantageous and discriminatory, are not binding because of their lawlessness.[22] The proposals made at that time to create an international court of arbitration for cultural restitution are interesting. Even during the Nazi occupation, Polish scholars, museologists, and conservators tried to inventory and record the destination points of German confiscations of fine-art objects from the Polish museums. Thanks to their initiative, in which they risked their lives and their freedom, the first restitutions made immediately after the war were possible—but that does not mean easy! From written records and the memories of the first envoys to Germany in 1945–49, we may conclude that the terrible reality of the occupation in Poland was not fully comprehended or investigated by an administration of Allies who demanded documents (stolen by Germans) to substantiate claims. Some very important objects were found, nevertheless, and returned to Poland between 1945 and 1949.[23] Instructions on how and where to find missing art objects had been given to members of the Department of Restitution in the Polish Ministry of Culture and Art; in some cases it was possible, owing to the activity of the same Polish

scholars during the Nazi occupation, to understand which objects had been plundered and even their destinations. Between 1945 and 1948, detailed questionnaires were prepared and sent to conservators, church administrations, and private persons, resulting in about thirty thousand files on missing objects.

Then, for almost forty years, the problem was abandoned for political reasons, with the sovereignty of Poland limited by the Soviet military and political presence in Eastern Europe. Some objects were handed over on the occasion of official visits of "friendship" between leaders of parties or heads of state. After the creation of the German Democratic Republic in 1949, there was no longer any practical possibility of searching for missing works presumably stored in their territory. On the other hand, many objects once stolen by the Nazis were later "found" in the Soviet Union, having been taken as war booty—for example, almost twelve thousand paintings returned from the Soviet Union to Poland in 1956! At present, the situation is no less complicated, due to problems involving statutes of limitation, formal negotiation, and the high costs and complexity of judicial procedures.

The example of the *Woman Washing,* a famous painting by Gabriel Metsu from the collection of the last king of Poland, is significant. Confiscated by the Germans, it appears in the catalogue of the Berlin exhibition of "safeguarded" art from the Generalgouvernement,[24] and hence is undoubtedly the property of Poland. Lost for many years, it was found at an auction house and returned to my country in 1994, not as a result of due process, but owing to the generosity of one of my compatriots abroad, who arranged for its purchase and return to his motherland. It has become clear that it is not enough to find a missing object, to recognize that object as important to a nation's cultural heritage, or even to establish legal right to property. Fifty years after the end of World War II, we are essentially no nearer our goal: the return of cultural property lost as a consequence of the war. This is not due to lack of knowledge about the status and location of this property or even due to lack of funds to pursue legal action; it is to a great extent due to the lack of will on the part of certain governments to redress damage inflicted in the past.

I wish to advance the suggestion that a comprehensive system of general rules be established, requiring that cultural property known to have been plundered from the nations of Europe as a result of the war be prohibited from the international art trade. Bilateral agreements to enable the search for this property, the documentation of losses, and the eventual retrieval of cultural goods should be encouraged. This is our cultural legitimacy! This series of papers—and the meeting of internationally known scholars that gave rise to this publication—shows, in one sense, how far we are from a solution to the problem. Nonetheless, we can do our best to let a spirit of optimism prevail, an optimism tempered by an understanding of the reality of the situation, in order to try to convince the governments involved to decide in favor of the rights of nations to their cultural patrimony.

A SHORT HISTORY

OF ART LOSS

AND

ART RECOVERY

IN THE

NETHERLANDS

Josefine Leistra

During the First and Second World Wars, the Netherlands remained neutral, but just before four o'clock on the morning of May 10, 1940, German soldiers crossed the border. No declaration of war had been issued. Four days later, after heavy bombing of Rotterdam, the Dutch capitulated. The royal family and the cabinet went into exile in London. A German nonmilitary, civil administration was set up in the Netherlands, under the authority of the Reichskommissar for the Occupied Netherlands, Arthur Seyss-Inquart. His headquarters were in the Ministry of Foreign Affairs building in the center of The Hague—incidentally, the building that now houses the Rijksdienst Beeldende Kunst (Netherlands Office for Fine Arts), the office responsible for art recovery since 1988.

The war ended for the Netherlands on May 5, 1945. During the five years of occupation, 210,000 people had died, including 198,000 civilians, 16,000 alone in the famine during the winter of 1944–45. At war's end, industrial goods, raw materials, means of transportation, cattle, practically the whole Rhine fleet, more than half of all railway equipment, including carriages, rails, and signposts, had been taken to Germany. Hitler himself had ordered the destruction of the harbors of Rotterdam and Amsterdam, and the airport was destroyed as well. In Paris in 1945, the Dutch government presented a memorandum containing the claims of the Netherlands to reparations from Germany. The amount claimed was 25.7 billion guilders in damages, of which 3.64 billion were the result of confiscation and looting.[1]

The bombs dropped on Rotterdam in May 1940 and the fires they caused miraculously did not affect the Boymans Museum, but 13 percent of the city's population became homeless and much art was lost from private houses, including the entire studio of the painter and sculptor Hendrik Chabot (1894–1949). Most of the old city center of Middelburg was destroyed, including the city's collection of antiquities, the city archives, and nineteen paintings the city museum had on loan from the Mauritshuis museum in The Hague. The Arnhem Open Air Museum was badly damaged and its important collection of traditional national costumes, which had been a gift from the Dutch people to Queen Wilhelmina on the occasion of her coronation in 1898, was lost. Also destroyed were some forty paintings, luckily not the most important ones, from the Amsterdam Rijksmuseum, which were on loan to cities that were damaged by bombs or fires.[2]

In July 1942, Seyss-Inquart ordered the delivery of all metal objects and church bells for use by the arms industry. By 1944, 4,400 of the 6,500 church bells collected in the Netherlands had been transported to Germany. In December 1941, Hitler approved the M-Aktion (Möbel-Aktion, or Furniture Project), acting on a proposal by Alfred Rosenberg. This operation was carried out in 1943 and 1944. Its purpose was to obtain household goods and furniture for bombed-out families in Germany. The goods were taken from the homes of Jewish families in France, Belgium, and the Netherlands: in the Netherlands, 29,000 homes were plundered. After the failed Allied landing in Arnhem in September 1944, all inhabitants of the city were ordered to leave. The Wehrmacht then systematically emptied the houses—all property was confiscated as punishment for aiding the Allied troops.[3]

These are a few of the losses that occurred in the Netherlands as a direct result of warfare. Most losses, of course, were caused by specific Nazi art policy. Unlike what happened in Poland, for example, there was no wholesale confiscation (or "safeguarding," as it was called) of valuable works of art in the Netherlands. Since the purpose was simply to integrate the country into the German Reich, there was no need to transport the national collections to Germany—they were already there, so to speak. So as a matter of policy the public collections were left in peace, with a few exceptions. In the end, Goebbels did order Dutch public collections transported to Germany, but military developments prevented this from happening.

The largest Dutch private collection, the royal collection, survived the war more or less intact, although Reichskommissar Seyss-Inquart published a statement on September 10, 1941, declaring all possessions of living members of the Dutch royal family forfeit. A Dutch commission managed to prevent the Nazis from transporting most of these to Germany by means of protracted negotiations. Among the losses were pieces of furniture, carriages, and a collection of paintings of hunting scenes. Some important material from the royal archives also went to Germany.[4]

In the Netherlands there were few private collections of international importance, but the population as a whole possessed relatively many works of art. In June 1940, the Netherlands government-in-exile had already issued a royal decree prohibiting all transactions with the enemy involving property. Later, transactions concluded between April 1, 1941, and May 5, 1945, by a payment of Reichsmarks by a non-resident to the Dutch Central Bank and subsequent payment in guilders by the Central Bank to the Dutch vendor were rendered void. This was done because in April 1941 the currency border between the Netherlands and Germany was abolished and the Dutch prewar claim of 400 million Reichsmarks, which was still outstanding, was simply canceled. The Netherlands Central Bank was now forced to exchange Reichsmarks for Dutch guilders and received in return a claim on Germany for the amount exchanged, so there was no real backing for this occupation money. There was also no restriction on the number of Reichsmarks to be exchanged. Since the currency borders still existed in Denmark, Belgium, and France, this put extra pressure on the Dutch market, where there was no control at all.[5]

Various German individuals and institutions took advantage of this situation. The first to do so was Kajetan Mühlmann. On May 15, 1940, one day after the Dutch capitulation, he was in The Hague, having been called there by Seyss-Inquart. His agency, the Dienststelle Mühlmann, bought art, which was sold to German buyers, with some going to the auction houses Lange in Berlin and Weinmüller in Munich, and to the Dorotheum in Vienna. One of the collections taken by

Mühlmann was that of Dutch collector Frits Lugt, who had left the Netherlands for Switzerland in 1939 and who lived in Oberlin, in the United States, from 1940 to 1945. He had many of his most valuable drawings sent over in sixty sealed letters. What was left in the Netherlands was put in the care of an assistant who, in the fall of 1940, reported that Lugt had ordered him to hide the collection. For this, all Lugt's possessions were confiscated by Mühlmann on the grounds of the owner's anti-German attitude. The collection, consisting of prints, drawings, and paintings, was taken to Alt Aussee near Salzburg. Some things stayed behind: furniture was discovered after the war in the offices of the Dutch Nazi Anton Mussert. Part of the collection was left intact when it was found out that the assistant had fabricated his report in the hope of getting a job. Some of the prints and drawings were saved in this way and were put under Dutch care in 1944.[6]

The painting collection of the Jewish doctor Alphonse Jaffé, who lived in London, had been placed partly in the care of the museum in Leiden, where it was confiscated and sent to Munich by Mühlmann.[7]

At the end of 1940, Mühlmann had tried to buy the Mannheimer collection, but he had to step aside when, at the beginning of February 1941, Seyss-Inquart received orders from Hitler to have the collection bought. It consisted mainly of French decorative art and belonged to the German-Jewish banker Fritz Mannheimer, who had become a Dutch citizen in 1936. A part of his collection was in the Netherlands, the rest in France. In 1939 Mannheimer died in France, leaving behind large debts caused by his passion for collecting. His estate was declared bankrupt. Hitler wanted the collection for his museum in Linz and gave orders that only Hans Posse's Referat Sonderfragen (Desk for Special Questions) could acquire the collection. Posse, appointed director of the Staatliche Gemäldegalerie in Dresden in 1913, had been charged by Hitler in June 1939 with "collecting" outstanding works of art in occupied territories for Hitler's planned but never realized Führermuseum of masterpieces in Linz.

The Mannheimer collection was eventually bought for Linz from the administrators of the Mannheimer estate under threat of confiscation by Seyss-Inquart, who could have declared it enemy property. The matter took years to settle, but in 1943 Seyss-Inquart paid the administrators 5.5 million guilders, which had been put at his disposal by the German office in the occupied Netherlands that managed confiscated enemy and Jewish property.[8]

Posse had arrived in the Netherlands on June 26, 1940, almost two months after the invasion. He established an office in The Hague. Two days after his arrival, he started negotiations for the purchase of the famous collection of old master drawings collected by Franz Koenigs, who had been born in Germany but lived in the Netherlands after 1922 and who had become a Dutch national. In 1933, forced by the depression, Koenigs used his collection as collateral for a substantial loan, stipulating that the drawings would be deposited in the Boymans Museum in Rotterdam instead of in a bank vault.

17. Rembrandt van Rijn. *Recumbent Lion*. c.1648–50. Pen and brown ink with brown wash, heightened with white, 143 x 210 mm (5½ x 8¼″). (A. J. Elen, *Missing Old Master Drawings from the Franz Koenigs Collection*, cat. no. 501.) Now in the Pushkin State Museum of Fine Arts, Moscow (*Five Centuries of European Drawings: The Former Collection of Franz Koenigs*, cat. no. 282)

Shortly before the invasion, Koenigs' Jewish bank asked that the drawings be either bought or packed for transport to the United States. The Rotterdam collector and harbor industrialist D. G. van Beuningen came to the rescue and bought the approximately 2,600 drawings. On June 28, 1940, about three months after his acquisition, Van Beuningen received a visit from Posse. A fifth of the collection, 527 drawings, was sold to Posse for Hitler's Linz museum for 1.4 million guilders. At the end of May 1941, after protracted negotiations, the drawings had arrived in Dresden.[9] The other approximately 2,100 drawings were donated by Van Beuningen to the Museum Boymans Foundation. To this day they have never left Rotterdam, except for exhibitions, and are still known as *the* Koenigs collection.

In October 1940, Posse had orders from Hitler to acquire the collection of Italian paintings, sculpture, and furniture belonging to Otto Lanz, who had died in 1935. The collection was known to the public because it had been exhibited at the Rijksmuseum in August 1940—it was the first collection of Italian art in the Netherlands. Although Göring also tried to buy it, Posse and Hitler won. The collection was sent to Germany in the summer of 1941 and from there to Austria.[10]

In May 1940, Reichsmarschall Göring bought the stock of the Jewish art dealer Jacques Goudstikker from the estate administrators after Goudstikker had died on board ship on his way to England, on May 14, 1940. Göring had the large collection, for which he paid 2 million guilders, taken to Berlin in a special train. He kept the best works for himself, sold a few to Hitler and the rest to his representative in the Netherlands, the banker Alois Miedl, who bought the art firm and its name in September 1940.[11]

The Einsatzstab Reichsleiter Rosenberg (ERR), established by Alfred Rosenberg in 1939, was represented in the Netherlands by an Amsterdam branch office. In 1940, the ERR confiscated all property belonging to the Freemasons, among which was the famous Biblioteca Klossiana. This library had been bought by Prince Hendrik (1876–1934), husband of Queen Wilhelmina, and had been presented by him to the order of Freemasons. It contained important incunabula and books on the occult, which were not available anywhere else in the Netherlands. Other parts of the library and the order's archive were of importance as well.

The library of the International Institute for Social History in Amsterdam was closed, and the ERR took over the building for its offices. In July 1940, the institute's very important collection of newspapers and the library of approximately 160,000 volumes were confiscated. German arguments over their final destination kept the materials in Amsterdam until the winter of 1944, when they were transported to Germany in eleven ships. The International Archive of the Women's Movement, established in Amsterdam in 1935, lost its whole collection after the institute was closed by the Sicherheitspolizei (Security Police) in June 1940. In August 1942, 499 crates containing books and archives taken from, among others, Jewish antiquarian book dealers and theosophic societies were transported to Berlin.

The important collection of Jewish books and manuscripts of the Biblioteca Rosenthaliana at the university library in Amsterdam, property of the Amsterdam municipality since 1880, was packed in 153 crates in June 1944 and sent to Germany to be placed in the Institut zur Erforschung der Judenfrage in Hungen, near Frankfurt. Very important as well were the 20,000-volume library and the archive of the seminary of the Portuguese-Jewish community in Amsterdam, which were also confiscated.[12]

18. Antoine Watteau (1684–1721). *Figure of a Child Blowing Bubbles*. Black and red chalk, 173 x 197 mm (6¾ x 7¾″). (A. J. Elen, *Missing Old Master Drawings from the Franz Koenigs Collection*, cat. no. 461.) Now in the Pushkin State Museum of Fine Arts, Moscow (*Five Centuries of European Drawings: The Former Collection of Franz Koenigs*, cat. no. 206)

Beginning in May 1942, Jewish people were ordered to deliver all works of art, jewelry and other valuables to Lippmann, Rosenthal and Co., an old, established bank, now a German organization with a stolen name. This firm had control over seized Jewish property and was accountable only to the German General Commissariat for Finance and Economic Affairs. Some of the Jewish depositories at the Lippmann, Rosenthal Bank were liquidated by the ERR, and some of these objects went to Linz. Typical is the fate of one very large collection of paintings from Haarlem that was confiscated in 1942 and brought to Lippmann, Rosenthal and Co., after which most of it was sold through the Lempertz auction house in Cologne. Only part of the collection was recovered after the war.

The collection of the Jewish Historical Museum in Amsterdam was confiscated as well. The museum had been established by a foundation in 1932. Eight years later, the building (the Waag, or Weighhouse) was closed and the collections turned over for safekeeping to the Municipal Museum. In February 1943 the museum director was informed that the Jewish Museum no longer existed and that the collections had to be delivered to the ERR. An attempt was made to delay transport and to declare the collection city property in order to save it, but this was unsuccessful, and at the end of April it had to be handed over to the ERR.[13]

These are a few examples of the works of art that left the Netherlands during the war. Only a rough estimate of the losses can be made. On the basis of prewar prices, the more than twenty thousand registered art losses were estimated in 1947 to represent a value of 150 million guilders. By a decree of July 1945 of the Dutch Military Authority, which represented the Dutch government after the German capitulation, every citizen was obliged to give information about artworks sold voluntarily or under duress to representatives of the German occupying forces, stolen or confiscated by the Germans, or otherwise lost during the war. This information was collected by the Stichting Nederlands Kunstbezit (SNK: Foundation for Netherlandish Art Property) and recorded on special forms. Thousands of these forms were used by the Allies at the Collecting Points in Germany, of which, for the Netherlands, the Collecting Points at Munich and Offenbach were the most important.[14]

The Biblioteca Rosenthaliana, for example, was found in a brick kiln near Hungen and returned to the Netherlands in the spring of 1946 via the Archival Depot in Offenbach. The library of the International Institute for Social History was found on the Weser River on board the ship that had carried it from Amsterdam. This library, too, was returned via Offenbach. In large part, the libraries of the Freemasons and of the Portuguese-Jewish community in Amsterdam were recovered as well. In 1946, much of the collection of the Amsterdam Jewish Historical Museum was identified among the objects in the Offenbach Collecting Point. It was returned before the end of the 1940s, but because of the losses outstanding, the museum could not reopen until 1955. In the British Zone

of occupied Germany, very few works of art from the Netherlands were found, but in 1945–46, three hundred church bells were returned from this zone. In the salt mines of Alt Aussee in Austria, the entire Lanz collection was found, as well as a large part of the Lugt collection (many Lugt paintings and 120 drawings remain lost). The Mannheimer collection returned from Hohenfurth in Bohemia.[15]

To give some idea of the restitutions effected, I will cite a few numbers: on October 8, 1945, a United States Army airplane brought the first twenty-six paintings from the Munich Collecting Point back to the Netherlands. Eleven days later, a second shipment left from Munich in trucks provided by the Netherlands. One year after the art-restitution program got under way, the Netherlands had received twenty-four shipments, consisting of 4,700 cultural objects, exclusive of archives. From the Archival Depot at Offenbach, about 5,000 crates in all were sent to the Netherlands.[16]

With these restitutions from the Collecting Points concluded, Dutch art-recovery work effectively ended in the 1950s, although the task was never officially terminated. The Dutch Ministry of Economic Affairs estimated in 1947 that approximately 80 percent of artworks of museum quality had been recovered. Of the large number of objects of lesser monetary value, not more than 25 percent were recovered. For paintings alone, there are *today* more than six thousand SNK forms describing lost works still outstanding.[17]

But it was not in the category of paintings that the most important loss was sustained. Not found after the war were the 527 drawings from the Koenigs collection. At the end of 1945, it was rumored they had been taken to the Soviet Union, but all efforts to locate them had failed. In 1987, the German Democratic Republic returned thirty-three missing drawings from the Koenigs collection to the Netherlands and this, together with the changing political climate in Eastern Europe, led to the reopening of the case.

In the Netherlands, as in other countries, recovery directly after the war was undertaken by the Ministry of Finance, since not only art but also liquid assets, machines, and means of transportation were involved. When only art recovery remained, the task was transferred by Royal Decree 233 of April 20, 1988, to the Ministry of Welfare, Health, and Culture, now the Ministry of Education, Culture, and Sciences. The execution of the task was given to the Netherlands Office for Fine Arts, which is part of the Ministry of Culture. The office is responsible only for the recovery of art; the recovery of books and archives is the responsibility of the State Archives. An explanatory note to Royal Decree 233 specifically mentions the Koenigs drawings; however, cases other than that of the Koenigs drawings in Russia have been handled as well, and as much information and assistance as possible is given to private owners searching for art missing since the war. But the first case taken on by the Netherlands Office for Fine Arts was the Koenigs collection case.

Work started in 1989 with the publication and international distribution of an illustrated catalogue by Albert J. Elen, *Missing*

Old Master Drawings from the Franz Koenigs Collection, Claimed by the State of the Netherlands (colorplates 2 and 3, and figs. 17 and 18). For several years, efforts were made to find the exact location of the drawings. In October 1992, the Russian minister of culture, Evgenii Sidorov, announced in an interview that the Koenigs collection had been found. This was the first time the presence of the drawings in Russia was acknowledged. One year later, the joint Russian-Dutch Koenigs Group, established in April 1993, was allowed to make an inventory of each of the 307 drawings present in the print room of the Pushkin State Museum of Fine Arts, Moscow. Naturally, it was a joy to see the drawings and a relief to find them in very good condition. A protocol of this first activity of the working group was signed, stating among other provisions that the 307 drawings in the Pushkin Museum would be exhibited and that the search for the still missing drawings would be intensified.

In November 1993, the working group met again, this time in The Hague, to discuss the Dutch claim on the drawings in Moscow. In the resulting report, the Russian members of the group concluded that the Dutch claim was founded. But the State Commission for Restitution of the Russian Federation has not discussed this report yet, and political circumstances have prevented any progress since then.

However, the exhibition of the drawings in the Pushkin Museum, which was agreed upon in the working-group meeting, did take place in October 1995. The exhibition and catalogue were entitled *Five Centuries of European Drawings: The Former Collection of Franz Koenigs*.[18] Obviously, there is *still* a Koenigs collection, formed by the approximately 2,100 old master drawings in Rotterdam, to which the drawings in Moscow also belong. To make this clear, a small counterpart exhibition was organized by the Netherlands government in the Rudomino State Library for Foreign Literature in Moscow. It presented drawings that were selected for their high quality and their art-historical relationship to the drawings in the Pushkin Museum. For example, the library showed the Rotterdam counterparts to Rembrandt's *Lion* and Giandomenico Tiepolo's *Burchiello* in the Pushkin Museum, as well as Lorenzo di Credi's *Angel,* belonging to his *Virgin* shown in the Pushkin Museum. Both Lorenzo di Credi drawings were once mounted in one passe-partout.[19]

In 1995, Alexei Rastorgouev and a Western collector each returned a Koenigs drawing, which brings the total of still missing drawings to 182, all by German artists. Today, the search for these drawings and negotiations for the return of the Koenigs drawings in Moscow continue.[20]

THE SPOILS OF WAR

REMOVED

FROM BELGIUM

DURING WORLD WAR II

Jacques Lust

In May 1940, Belgium, like its politically neutral neighbors, Holland and Luxembourg, was overrun and occupied by the German Wehrmacht. In June 1940 a German military occupation government (Militärverwaltung) was installed in Brussels. Belgium was considered the "unmittelbares deutsches Vorland," the direct foreland of Germany. The Belgian head of state, King Leopold III, remained in his country during the Second World War, while the Belgian government moved into exile from the south of France to England. These political contrapositions would lead Belgium, after the war, to the brink of a civil war. In spite of Belgium's prewar neutrality, National Socialist Germany saw its military strategic importance and its economic possibilities as a modern industrialized European state. During the Second World War, Belgium was plundered of its gold reserves, its economic production, and its laborers, who were forcibly sent to Germany. There were also specific interests in the natural riches of the Belgian colony in the Congo. Subsequently, it became obvious that Belgium and its people had also been robbed of cultural goods.[1]

The German military occupation government in Belgium relied for cultural matters on academic specialists, such as F. Petri and W. Reese, and on a Kunst-, Archiv-, und Biblio-theksschutz, which oversaw the protection of Belgian monuments, historical buildings, collections of museums, archives, and libraries. Also of concern was the *Sicherstellung* (safekeeping) of cultural goods of former German provenance, especially those works removed from Germany as a result of the settlement of the Treaty of Versailles after World War I.[2]

The first lootings took place during the military conquest of Belgium, and were committed by soldiers who ransacked homes left unprotected as more than half a million Belgians fled toward France. Beginning in June 1940, members of the German Sicherheitspolizei-Sicherheitsdienst (SIPO-SD) were installed in Brussels. Besides their brutal police activities directed toward the adversaries of National Socialism, they began to collect and to plunder archives and documents for political reasons.

They worked closely with the Einsatzstab Reichsleiter Rosenberg (ERR), which obtained through a directive (*Führererlass*) of 1940 the order to confiscate the cultural goods of the adversaries of National Socialism, such as Jews, Freemasons, and socialists.[3] The first goal of the SIPO-SD in Belgium was to seize the archives and cultural goods of the Freemasons' lodges in Brussels, Antwerp, Liège, and Verviers. A second target was Jewish organizations, such as the Belgian Federation of Zionists and the Alliance Israélite. A third target centered around socialist organizations: the archives of the newspaper *Le Peuple* and the *Vooruit* were confiscated, the International Institute for Social History was searched, and the libraries of the Houses of the People in Brussels were closed down and some of their holdings sent to Germany. There was special interest in the library of E. Vandervelde, the socialist leader. On November 26, 1940, 107 crates left Belgium for ERR headquarters in Berlin. The ERR in Belgium targeted the cultural goods, libraries, and archives of Belgian politicians and university professors who had fled Belgium before the end of May 1940 for France, England, or the United States.[4]

The ERR in Belgium prepared reports on the confiscated archives and libraries. The first report concerned the documentation of the archives of the duc de Guise, comte de Paris, who was living in the Anjou mansion in Brussels. ERR interest lay mainly in his contacts with French royalists and the right-wing nationalistic group Action Française.[5] The second report concerned the documentation found at the Antwerp home of Professor N. Gunzberg, who had fled. He was head of the Juridical Department of the University of Ghent, a leading member of the Jewish community of Antwerp, and a well-known Freemason.[6] The ERR devoted special attention to the papers of those professors forced to leave the Université Libre de Bruxelles (Free University of Brussels), which the Nazis branded the bastion of Belgian Jewry, Freemasonry, and liberal-socialist thinking in Belgium. In the 1930s, a group of professors and students had publicly reacted against Nazism, in magazines such as Le Flambeau, Cahiers du Libre Examen, and Solidarité.[7] In 1941, the occupation government tried to nominate a number of professors who supported the New Order. Finally they closed the university down on November 25, 1941. But in the meantime, the homes of the professors who had departed, including J. and P. Errera, D. Van Buuren, H. Grégoire, J. de Sturler, and A. Pinkus, and the eminent ministers A. Wauters, P. Hymans, and V. de Lavaleye, were raided by the ERR and the SIPO-SD (fig. 19).

Libraries and archives seen as enemy and international were confiscated outright by the ERR, as indicated by the following three examples. The contents of the communist book-shop OBLA, Brussels, were sent to Racibórz, Poland.[8] The records of the International Federation for Housing and Town Planning were confiscated and brought to Germany.[9] A similar fate overtook the archives and library of the international Jesuit college at Enghien, which was called a "Zentrale der anti-Deutschland speziell anti-national-Sozialistischen Information" (center for anti-German and anti–National Socialist information).[10]

Meanwhile, the Archivschutz was active in looking through the Belgian ministerial archives: a special interest was maintained in the archives of the ministries of National Defense, of Colonies, of Foreign Affairs, and of Economic Affairs, which were partly transferred for "safekeeping" from the south of France or Brussels to Germany.

FORMER GERMAN PROPERTY AND THE TREATY OF VERSAILLES

During the First World War, Belgium, like France, had become a bloody battlefield. In the first months of 1914, real terror and destruction reigned in Belgium. Hundreds of civilians were shot as hostages, and villages were burned down. In a heavy bombardment, the Germans destroyed the library of Louvain, one of Europe's oldest university libraries.

In accordance with the provisions of the Treaty of Versailles, the Belgians were compensated for this destruction, gaining the territory of Eupen-Malmédy, the side panels of the Ghent Altarpiece by Hubert and Jan van Eyck (from the Kaiser-Friedrich-Museum in Berlin), and the side panels of the Last Supper of Dirk Bouts (two from the Kaiser-Friedrich-Museum in Berlin and two from the Alte Pinakothek in Munich), supplemented by the enactment of various economic measures (see Appendix 4). Germany had to provide, as stipulated under Article 247 of the treaty, books for a new university library in Louvain. The new building was paid for by the United States during the administration of Woodrow Wilson.[11]

So in 1940, National Socialist Germany sought to reverse the reparations exacted from them by the Treaty of Versailles: Eupen-Malmédy was annexed by the German Reich, and the Archivschutz collected all documents concerning this territory, even medieval ones, and transported them to the Reich.

The Belgian government had brought the Ghent Altarpiece to Pau, in the south of France, for safekeeping. In July 1942, Ernst Buchner of the Alte Pinakothek in Munich got the order to transport the complete painting to Neuschwanstein, normally an ERR depot. (Near the end of the war, the altarpiece was deposited in the salt mine of Alt Aussee, where it was discovered

19. Official form of the Reichsministerium für die besetzten Ostgebiete, Belgium, recording the liquidation of the household of Professor A. Pinkus, Université Libre de Bruxelles, who was deported to and survived Auschwitz

by American troops.) In August 1942, Buchner brought the side panels of Dirk Bouts's *Last Supper* from Louvain to Germany, with the knowledge of the German military government, the Belgian administration, and the Belgian archbishop. At the end of August 1944, a few days before the liberation of Belgium, the *Bruges Madonna* of Michelangelo and the paintings of the Church of Notre Dame at Bruges were confiscated and taken to Alt Aussee.[12]

The Louvain library had become, for prewar Germany, a symbol of cultural humiliation. During the hostilities of May 1940 it went up in flames for the second time in twenty-six years. (After World War II it was not restituted or paid for: only a few dozen unidentified old books from the Wiesbaden Collecting Point were given to the University of Louvain.)[13]

THE MÖBEL-AKTION IN BELGIUM

At the outbreak of the war, the Jewish community in Belgium numbered about sixty-five thousand people, of whom less than one-tenth were of Belgian nationality. The majority were refugees from Poland and Russia who had come to Belgium in the 1920s, and in the 1930s from Austria and Germany.[14] The Nazi decrees against the Jewish community in Belgium started in October 1940 with the prohibition of the ritual slaughter of animals (October 23, 1940) and with the order that Jewish firms must be registered (October 28, 1940). Jewish property, along with the property of the inhabitants of Great Britain and its territories, France and its colonies, Egypt, Sudan, Iraq, Monaco, and, by the second half of 1941, the United States and the Soviet Union was declared "Feindvermögen," enemy property. The military government set up in occupied Belgium, in complete accordance with Belgian trading laws, the Brüsseler Treuhandgesellschaft (Brussels Trustee Corporation), to control, to check, and to liquidate enemy property. (Dr. Brauer of the Nationalgalerie in Berlin was their specialist on artworks.) From May 31, 1941, Jews were excluded from every form of economic life in Belgium. On July 22, 1942, the first roundups of Jews began in Brussels and Antwerp. The first deportation convoy left Belgium for Auschwitz on August 4, 1942. Between August 1942 and July 1944, 25,257 Jews were deported from Belgium, of whom only 1,291 survived the war.[15]

Meanwhile, the plundering and liquidation had started. The Reichsministerium für die besetzten Ostgebiete (Reich Ministry for the Occupied Eastern Territories) got the order in 1942 to activate the Möbel-Aktion (M-Aktion) project to liquidate the contents of households of enemies of the Reich. All interesting cultural goods, such as paintings, sculptures, books, and tapestries, had to be given over to the ERR. A special implementation project in Belgium began with the shipment of lift vans filled with cultural goods confiscated in 1940 in the port of Antwerp, to Cologne in 1942. In this instance, the ERR selected paintings from the shipment after it had arrived in Germany. This enormous operation followed a dreary and identical pattern throughout Belgium, as well as in Holland and France: the SIPO-SD sealed each building to be

cleared, and transport firms brought the contents to centralized depots, where selections were made. The most valuable cultural goods were brought to Paris or directly to Germany. Less exceptional furniture was given to the German victims of Allied bombardments. In this manner, more than forty-five hundred houses were liquidated in Belgium alone in less than two years.[16]

The ERR also targeted important art collections, such as the Andriesse and Lyndhurst collections. H. Andriesse, an industrialist who had fled Belgium in 1939, left behind a collection that consisted mainly of tapestries and seventeenth-century paintings by Flemish and Dutch masters. After receiving tip-offs from his former chauffeur, the ERR finally located these artworks in the Musées Royaux des Beaux-Arts in Brussels. H. Müchow, leader of the ERR in Belgium, and Dr. Graf, the inspector of the Devisenschutzkommando (Currency Control Commando), verified the contents of the sealed crates in the museum. J. Capart, the world-famous Egyptologist and director of the museum, could not prevent their seizure, and in December 1941 the confiscated works were transferred as enemy property to the ERR depot in the Jeu de Paume in Paris (fig. 20).[17]

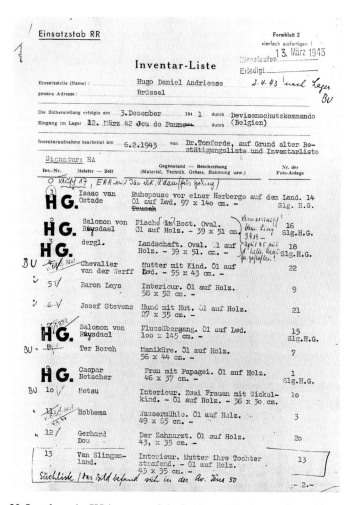

20. Page from the ERR inventory of the Andriesse collection, confiscated from Brussels in 1941

The E. Lyndhurst collection, mainly of eighteenth-century English paintings and drawings, was taken from the collector's Brussels home and out of the vaults of the National Bank. These works followed the same road to Paris, where some were seized by Göring's staff and transferred to the ERR depot in Nikolsburg (now Mikulov) in Czechoslovakia.[18]

THE ART MARKET IN BELGIUM

Some Belgian collectors and art dealers took the opportunity to sell their collections, some under pressure. Large sums were paid by Hans Posse and Erhard Göpel, who collected artworks for Hitler's Linz project, Walter Andreas Hofer for the Hermann Göring collection, Hans Herbst for the Dorotheum auction house in Vienna, and Kajetan Mühlmann's group in Holland. All of these German agencies were very active in the Belgian art market.

More than forty paintings out of the Van Gelder collection were sold to the Dorotheum, to the Linz collection, and to the Hermann Göring collection. The Van Gelder family owned a mansion near Brussels which housed an important collection, with one room dedicated to the work of Jacob Jordaens. Part of the collection was recovered after the war, but some of the paintings were last heard of in the Russian occupation zone in Germany.

Another important case is that of Emile Renders. Renders was a Brussels banker and connoisseur of the Flemish primitive masters. He sold his well-known collection of twenty paintings to Göring through Hofer and the Dutch art-dealer W. Paech. A part of his collection was used by Göring in a transaction with Alois Miedl, who had taken over Jacques Goudstikker's art business in Amsterdam. After the war the Belgian Office de Récupération Economique (ORE: Office of Economic Recovery) acquired ten paintings that had belonged to Renders from Germany, seven of which are today exhibited in Belgian museums in Bruges, Antwerp, Brussels, and Tournai. Although the ORE carried out extensive investigations, and although the American Monuments, Fine Arts, and Archives officers spent considerable time trying to locate these lost paintings, the rest of the collection was never found. Renders sued the Belgian state for ownership of the returned paintings in 1948. The following year, his demand was rejected, based on Article 2,279 of the Belgian Civil Law code, on the Declaration of London of January 5, 1943 (see Appendix 9), and on the resolutions of the Conference of Paris of January 15, 1946. An appeal was rejected on October 24, 1951.[19]

BELGIAN LOSSES AND RECUPERATION

In 1946, the first phase of the Belgian recovery and restitution effort began, with the newly created ORE, whose main task was the recovery of Belgian economic goods, such as trains, ships, and coal, and the settlement of German payments, in accordance with the resolutions of the Conference of Paris of 1946.

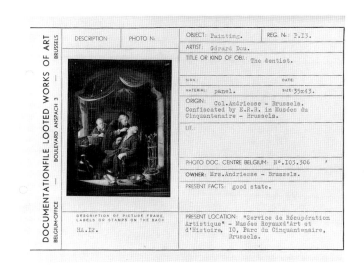

21. Inventory card prepared by the Belgian Office de Récupération Economique (ORE) after the war, documenting the recovered painting *The Dentist* by Gerard Dou (1613–75). The work had been confiscated from the Andriesse collection in 1941 by the ERR.

Within the ORE, a small unit was formed under the leadership of R. Lemaire, later professor at the University of Louvain. Supported by an administrative staff, scholars such as the renowned art historian and specialist on the Flemish Baroque, F. Baudouin, were sent to the American occupation zones in Germany and Austria. They were confronted with various difficult tasks: (1) to search in Germany and Austria for lost Belgian works of art, libraries, and archives, in close cooperation with the Allied forces and Collecting Points; (2) to form a center for the documentation of Belgian losses; (3) to contact private victims of looting; (4) to clear out the German depots left behind in Belgium; and (5) to maintain international contacts in case of disputes.

This first and crucial phase of ORE's work continued until 1952. The results were: the return of 492 artworks and 2,749 books from Germany and Austria, and hundreds of art objects and pieces of furniture found in Belgium and returned to their owners; the return of the archives of Eupen-Malmédy and other archives of private provenance; and the return from Hamburg, Germany, of some of the 4,568 church bells taken from Belgium.

The most notable returns of artworks were: the recovery of the Ghent Altarpiece for the Church of St. Bavo in Ghent and of the *Bruges Madonna* by Michelangelo (fig. 22) and ten paintings for the Church of Notre Dame in Bruges.

A second administrative phase started in 1956. A new search was undertaken by the Bundesamt für äussere Restitutionen (Federal Office for External Restitution) in Baden-Baden and the Belgian ORE. The Belgian government sent a list of 1,564 lost artworks, mainly paintings, sculptures, and tapestries, to the West German government. This search ended in 1964 without any tangible results.

A third phase began in 1993, due to the recent developments in Eastern Europe. The Office Belge de l'Economie et de l'Agriculture (OBEA), as successor of the ORE, resumed

22. Belgian soldiers loading Michelangelo's *Bruges Madonna* on a truck at the Munich Collecting Point in September 1945, in preparation for its return to Belgium

the Belgian state recovered only the telescope of the Royal Observatory from the Russian occupation zone in Germany and Austria.

In this "materialistic" account, one should surely not forget that Belgium counted tens of thousands of dead who were deported and killed during the war, and that National Socialism tried to erase, in five years, the culture, the history, and the memory of these victims.

the work officially stopped in 1967. A preliminary investigation convinced the OBEA that directly after World War II only some of the works of art that were lost were returned to their rightful owners.[20]

Still missing are 3,273 documented paintings, sculptures, tapestries, engravings, pieces of furniture, and drawings, although the official statistics represent a vast underestimate: first, losses were only documented in part, and second, these official figures are based on German documents and on the claims made after World War II. The losses of those who did not file claims were not taken into account. Third, the ORE mentioned only identifiable art objects in its claims. This is the main reason that 74 percent of the losses recorded are of paintings. Furniture made up only 5 percent of the recorded total, although in reality, these losses should be much higher than those of paintings. Fourteen percent of the recorded losses are the property of the Belgian state, of which one object in four belongs to the Musées Royaux des Beaux-Arts, Brussels. Tens of thousands of archives were not recovered after World War II and hundreds of thousands of books from private collections are missing (a large number were destroyed by the Germans during World War II). On the cultural level,

SPOLIATION AND RECOVERY

OF CULTURAL PROPERTY

IN FRANCE, 1940–94

Marie Hamon

SPOLIATION OF CULTURAL PROPERTY

Shortly before the declaration of war, the German government drafted a list of works of art that it wished to obtain based upon the principle of Germanic heritage. This inventory was completed in 1940 under the supervision of Otto Kümmel, director of the Staatliche Museen (State Museums), Berlin.

Confiscations began in France after the Germans entered the country, and they continued over more than four years, in spite of attempts made by various persons to curb them. Before being dispersed, most of the confiscated works of art passed through the Jeu de Paume, the small Paris museum the Germans had requisitioned, leading the French curators to believe that they would be able to carry out a separate inventory. Once installed on the premises, the Germans refused to keep their promises; however, they did not count on the tenacity of Rose Valland, the French curator who had been in charge of the collections of the Jeu de Paume for ten years. During the four years Valland spent with the Einsatzstab Reichsleiter Rosenberg (ERR), her activity was exclusively aimed at obtaining as much information as possible about the confiscations under way.[1] She went to the Jeu de Paume daily, except during a few periods of several days when the Germans told her to leave.

Rotating exhibits of the works of art seized by the ERR were continually being shown on the museum's walls in order to facilitate German appraisals and enable officials to choose what they wanted—Göring in particular, whose collections included over 1,375 works of art at the end of the war. These exhibits enabled Valland to take notes on the major works of art shown (artist, subject, owner) and to learn about confiscations in progress and shipments to Germany.

She was able to gather additional information from the daily events that took place in the Jeu de Paume, both from the activities of the German officials and from the museum attendants. She also managed secretly to consult the inventories drafted by the Germans, and she was able to make a number of partial copies that she gave to her supervisor, Jacques Jaujard, director of the Musées nationaux de France (National Museums of France).

National collections
In anticipation of the declaration of war, the National Museums had decided to safeguard their works of art. These were packed and transferred to various storage places, such as the châteaux of Sourches, La Pelice, Louvigny, Chambord, and Courtalain.

Some museums, such as the Musée de l'Armée, the army museum in Paris, could not be evacuated in time and were entirely emptied of their contents by the Germans.

The Schloss collection and other private collections
In this brief survey, we will only refer to a few collections and attempt to give a few figures.

The great art aficionado Adolphe Schloss had bequeathed to his wife a magnificent collection, made up, for the most part, of Dutch and Flemish paintings. This collection of 333 paintings was known worldwide for its scope, the selection of masters represented, and the quality of the works. The Schloss collection, in the opinion of the foremost experts (among others, the curators of the Musée du Louvre), was the last great collection of Dutch and Flemish art assembled in France in the nineteenth century. In it, works of the great primitive masters could be admired, such as the *Pietà* by Petrus Christus, a *Virgin* by Isenbrandt, and a *Venus* by Gossaert. Paintings by such seventeenth-century masters as Jan Brueghel, Brouwer, Van der Heyden, Van der Neer, Rembrandt, and Van Ruisdael were also represented. Other works had been chosen because of their quality and carried authentic signatures of minor masters, poorly represented in French collections, and for the most part very rare, such as Boursse, Brekelenkam, and Molenaer.

After the death of Lucie Schloss, the collection was bequeathed in co-ownership to her children, who sent it for safekeeping in 1939 to the château of Chambon, in Laguenne, about two kilometers from Tulle. This château belonged to the Banque Jordan, to which the collection had been entrusted at the start of the war. The German agencies started looking for it at the very beginning of their activities in France, having received orders to find it using all available means: police, informers, and so forth. Investigation by these agencies led them to discover the safe house of the Schloss heirs. Two of them were arrested; a third, who was not there, was not caught.

On April 10, 1943, the collection was discovered and transported to a German base in Tulle. In spite of protests by the Vichy government before the German general commanding the South Zone of France, the works were remitted to the French authorities, who stored them in the safes of the Bank of France in Limoges.

Finally, the paintings were shipped to Paris. The inventory of the collection was made between August 13 and August 23, 1943, on the premises of the Dreyfus Bank, which had been taken over by the Commissariat Général aux Questions Juives (General Commissariat for Jewish Questions). Several representatives of various administrations attended: the Delegation of the Police and Safety Services Headquarters of Paris; Jean-François Lefranc, expert administrator; Kornelius Postma, an expert on Flemish paintings; curators of the Louvre; bailiffs and civil servants from the Investigations and Verifications sections of the General Commissariat for Jewish Questions.[2]

The Louvre was able to preempt 49 out of 333 inventoried paintings, which it returned in 1945. The remaining 284 paintings were chosen by Germans. Of these, 262 were taken for Hitler's projected museum in Linz. As for the other 22 paintings, they were acquired by a mysterious character who went by the name of Buittenweg, a supposed Dutch art dealer, who in spite of police investigations was never subsequently identified. It seems that name had been fabricated to hide the identity of the purchaser, who wished to remain anonymous. These paintings had originally been chosen for Göring because of their value and interest. But Göring, whose influence was starting to decline in 1943, was afraid of upsetting Hitler by reserving part of the collection; furthermore, it seems that he did not want the scandal over the confiscation of the Schloss paintings to reflect on him. The 22 paintings selected for him had originally been appraised by the Germans, but when Göring withdrew, the allocation of his share to Buittenweg was facilitated by a new appraisal that allowed the paintings to be purchased at a lower price (which was never paid). After the war, five of these paintings were found in Germany. Two of the paintings were found in Hitler's collection in the salt mine at Alt Aussee.

A list of the missing works appeared in a catalogue of property confiscated during World War II, published in 1947 by the Bureau Central des Restitutions (Central Restitutions Office) of the French government.[3] The catalogue's purpose was to aid in the search for and identification of spoliated property. It was therefore not designed as a collector's catalogue. The photographic reproductions were sometimes very poor but were meant to aid—better than a description could—identification of the works of art. The catalogue was intended not only as a working instrument for experts in charge of recovering the art objects and other cultural property looted in France but also as a warning to potential buyers because it listed "the property acquired illegally which, therefore, could not be sold commercially without seriously involving their liability." This catalogue was widely distributed in Europe and the United States to experts and art dealers as well as to museums.

The Schloss family published a list of their collection, illustrated with photographs that were made by the Louvre prior to the removal of the paintings. Research carried out after the war showed that the 262 works meant for Hitler had been sent to Munich; there, some were stored at the Führerbau, from which they subsequently disappeared. A few were found in other areas of Germany. In total, out of 333 works, 171 were missing at the end of the war. More recently, some of the works have been found. In 1977, a painting by Jan van de Capelle, *Calm Sea,* was found in Germany and returned to the Schloss family. In 1990, the *Portrait of Adrianus Tegularius* by Frans Hals was recognized at the Biennale Internationale des Antiquaires in Paris and impounded. It is currently placed under official seal. During the past few years, various paintings from the Schloss collection have been identified in foreign museums. These are the *Fur-hatted Jew* by Rembrandt, the *Engraver in His Workshop* by Michael Sweerts, the *Rialto Bridge* and the *Piazza San Marco in Venice* by Francesco Guardi, and a *Still Life* by Dirck van Delen. Negotiations are under way to recover them.

Works from other major collections such as those of the Rosenbergs, Wildensteins, and Seligmanns were also confiscated. Some of these works were found after the war. The Rothschild collection, for example, taken from the château of Ferrières, was found in 1945 in salt mines in Austria, and easily identified through special markings on the works of art.

"Degenerate" art

In July 1943, around five hundred to six hundred works termed "degenerate" were taken from various collections, and a large number of them were burned in the Tuileries Garden in Paris. These were modern paintings (by, for example, Masson, Picabia, Léger, Braque, Picasso) considered unusable because of their Jewish inspiration and denounced by Hitler. Not all of them were destroyed, and a few were recovered after the war.

Computing the losses

It is very hard to compute the losses of cultural property in France during World War II. Ideally, all the files on the families whose property was looted should be examined, and the exact number of objects lost should be tallied. Because of time constraints, however, it has not been possible to carry out such a detailed investigation. The figures listed below were therefore computed approximately, using the catalogue of confiscated property published in 1947, with supplements published in 1948–49 and periodically updated until 1956.

It should be mentioned outright that for several reasons these figures must be considered inaccurate: (1) they are based only on official claims and not on actual losses; (2) some families whose property was stolen did not return, and thus no claims for restitution were made; (3) other families were not aware of the laws and did not file a restitution claim even though they had been robbed; (4) the numbers given in the catalogue are for both single objects and sets (bedroom or dining-room furniture, for example) and complete collections (jewelry or coins and medals), and in such collections, determinations of value are difficult to ascertain; (5) moreover, regarding looted books, there are statistics for books that have been recovered but not detailed accounts of the vast numbers that were lost. Based on the files of the Commission de Récupération Artistique (Artistic Recovery Commission), 2,290 families presented restitution claims.

Totals by Category

1. Paintings = 11,721
2. Sculptures = 2,236
3. Tapestries and rugs = 3,999
   - rugs[4] = 3,494
   - tapestries = 505
4. Furniture and miscellaneous decorative items[5] = 26,015
   - curios = 957 items and collections
   - bronzes, pewter, forged iron = 590 items and collections
   - ceramics and porcelains = 2,723 items and collections
   - crystal, glass, and stained-glass windows = 201 items and collections
   - lamps = 1,004 items and collections
   - furniture = 16,616 items and sets
   - gold-plated items and silverware = 3,346 items and collections
   - tall case clocks = 578
5. Archives and libraries[6] = 14,913
   - family archives and autographs = 389 collections
   - illustrations and illuminations = 461
   - incunabula = 355
   - libraries = 723 collections (taking into account only libraries for which the number of lost volumes is known, the number of volumes is 1,767,108)
   - newspapers and periodicals = 242 collections
   - rare books = 12,743 volumes
6. Various items = 1,652
   - weapons = 251 items and collections
   - enamels and gemstones = 412 items and collections
   - coins and medals = 49 collections (including several collections of over 500 coins belonging to a single museum and 1,000 belonging to a single family—in sum, around 7,500 items[7])
   - jewelry = 940 collections (around 28,000 pieces)
7. Music-related items = 1,765
   - musical scores = 267 scores and score sets
   - pianos = 1,338
   - violins = 129
   - other musical instruments = 31

Grand Total = 62,301 numbers (or more than 96,812 artworks, pieces of jewelry, and other objects, not including the itemized books, estimated at several million)

THE RECOVERY OF CULTURAL PROPERTY

Already in April 1941, Free France had denounced the actions of the occupiers and the governments now under their control, those actions being aimed at confiscating the property and denying the rights and interests of private individuals and legal entities. Also denounced were the methods used by the despoilers. In London, on January 5, 1943, the governments of the Allied nations made a solemn declaration warning neutral countries that they intended to do everything in their power to counter the expropriation methods used by enemy governments against the afflicted populations (see Appendix 9).[8] The following were signatory countries: South Africa, the United States, Australia, Belgium, Canada, China, the United Kingdom of Great Britain and Northern Ireland, Greece, India, Luxembourg, the Netherlands, New Zealand, Norway, Poland, the Czechoslovak Republic, the USSR, Yugoslavia, and the French National Committee. The latter accepted the solemn London Declaration and issued it as the ordinance of November 12, 1943.

In 1944, the staffs of French museums and storage places started to organize, feeling that the end of the war was near. Commissions were implemented in expectation of D-Day in order to develop future general and theoretical plans of action.

The first commission to salvage and protect cultural property had been established in Washington, D.C., on August 20, 1943, under the direction of Owen J. Roberts, a Supreme Court justice, bearing his name. In London, the MacMillan Committee preceded an inter-Allied organization established in 1944, under the direction of Paul Vaucher, to study the protection and recovery of artistic and cultural property. These commissions worked closely with the Supreme Headquarters, Allied Expeditionary Force (SHAEF). After several meetings, the Allies realized that information could only come from each country involved.

The French Artistic Recovery Commission was created under the instigation of Jacques Jaujard. At the first meeting, on September 19, 1944, the guidelines of what would become the future commission were set down. The commission's work was to gather all information on confiscated objects, as well as claim documents filed by injured families, in cooperation with the Office of Property and Private Interests under the authority of the Ministry of Foreign Affairs.

In the meantime, teams, headed by Rose Valland and others, traveled through Germany and Austria with the Allied forces looking for places where cultural property might be hidden.

Through the work of the Artistic Recovery Commission, as of June 5, 1950, 61,233 cultural works and art objects had been recovered by France: 58,477 were repatriated from Germany and Austria, 10 from Italy, 39 from Switzerland, 4 from Belgium, and 808 from Czechoslovakia; moreover, 1,895 were recovered in France itself because they had not been moved out early enough by the Germans. Nearly 500 private persons recovered around 45,441 cultural works and art objects, and the Musée de l'Armée, whose premises were emptied in 1940, recovered 1,444 military items.

The difference between what France recovered and the restitutions recorded is attributable to the fact that of the total, around 14,265 items fell into the following categories: (1) they were remitted to the State Property Department, (2) their owners were not identified before December 31, 1949, or never filed a claim for loss, or (3) the items were modern paintings or other miscellaneous items without artistic value or impossible to identify.

A minute portion (1,333), which had some artistic value, was entrusted to the supervision of the Direction des Musées de France, in expectation that their owners would be able to show proof of ownership. These works are still to be found today in a separate inventory list and will never become the property of the French state. They are part of a collection called "Musées nationaux Récupération" (National Museums' Recovered Art) and may be claimed at any time by their owners.

THE RESTITUTION OF CULTURAL PROPERTY BETWEEN 1964 AND 1994

Since 1956 was the deadline for filing claim documents, the official recovery procedure was terminated in 1964. Between 1964 and 1989, countries (Germany, Poland, and so forth) continued to proceed with hand-to-hand restitutions of objects and archives. Since the reunification of Germany in 1990, the potential for the recovery of cultural property located in the former German Democratic Republic has been recognized, and discussions took place in 1991 between France and the Federal Republic of Germany. These talks led to the establishment of a working group that is trying to gather as much information as possible on works of art and archives missing as a consequence of World War II.

The French Delegation to this task force is composed as follows:

1. Ministry of Foreign Affairs
   • Archives and Documentation Department: the director, head of the French Delegation; a permanent expert; an assistant
   • Department for the French Abroad: one or two representatives
   • Legal Affairs Department: a legal adviser

To these must be added experts, depending on the case involved:

2. Expert Group on Works of Art
   • French Museums: one or two representatives, depending on the case
   • Musée du Louvre: an expert
3. Expert Group on Archives
   • Ministry of Foreign Affairs: a national-heritage curator
   • National Archives (Archives de France): one or two experts, depending on the case
   • Defense archives: one or two experts, depending on the case

The Direction des Français à l'Etranger (Department for the French Abroad) of the Ministry of Foreign Affairs,[9] by its powers successor to the Office des Biens et Intérêts privés (Bureau of Property and Private Interests), has been responsible since the war for the restitution of confiscated property in cooperation with the Artistic Recovery Commission.

France has thus been able to recover twenty-eight works of art of French origin, eight of which were immediately returned to their owners. An exhibit of the remaining works was held at the Musée d'Orsay ("Oeuvres d'art restituées par l'Allemagne," October–December 1994), with the hope that among the visitors further owners could be found, to whom the Ministry of Foreign Affairs could return their property.

Contacts have now been established between France and a number of other countries in order to further the exchange of information on working methods and research techniques that will hopefully lead to the recovery and restitution of more works of art in the future.

RUSSIAN CULTURAL LOSSES

DURING WORLD WAR II

Mikhail Shvidkoi

I am glad to have had the opportunity to participate in the Bard Graduate Center symposium. This kind of scholarly discussion provides a better understanding of the past and, as Thomas Stearns Eliot wrote, the real future can be understood only based on the real past. I would not, however, wish this symposium to be regarded as a kind of circus-like or even knightly tournament organized by Russian and German participants for the entertainment of an American audience. As it is with love, so it is with our relations with Germany: a great many things are the concern only of the two parties involved, who have absolutely no need of advice from others, even if such advice is given with the best of intentions. The definition of the truth, however, knows no state borders. It should not be thought that the campaign to bring the truth to light began only within the last five or seven years. When I started dealing with this problem, primarily as a publisher, a producer of documentary films, and a journalist, it naturally seemed to me that either this had never been done or that it had been done badly.

In all fairness, it should be stressed that the first to begin the struggle for glasnost and for open information were the curators and the directors of major museums in Russia, including Irina Antonova, director of the Pushkin State Museum of Fine Arts, who participated in this symposium. They were state employees of a particular kind of state—a totalitarian state—and therefore their struggle was tinged with traces of bureaucracy, but this by no means implies that there was no struggle at all. Back in 1960, the director of the State Hermitage Museum, M. I. Artamonov, had requested that the closed archives and special repositories be opened up, but—as was subsequently the case when Irina Antonova appealed to the Ministry of Culture of the USSR—he was refused. We lived in a country in which not only individual museum holdings but also entire cities did not officially exist, and the museum directors are not to be blamed for this. In addition, the nature of the relations between the Soviet Union and the

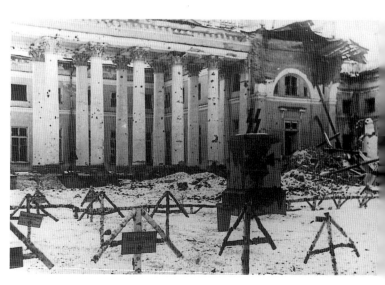

23. Cemetery for German SS soldiers on the grounds of the Alexander Palace, Pushkin (Tsarskoye Selo)

German Democratic Republic did not allow for any claims against one another.

Back in May 1957, Mikhailov, Topchiev, Zorin, and other members of the commission established by a decree of the Central Committee of the Communist Party of the Soviet Union (CPSU), "On cultural property of the GDR located for temporary preservation in the Soviet Union," reported to the Presidium of the Central Committee of the CPSU on work done to identify the losses inflicted by the fascist invaders on museums and cultural institutions of the USSR. In order not to cloud relations between the socialist countries, however, this was classified information for in-house use only. Since even our losses were classified information, it is clear how extremely difficult it was to clarify the real situation regarding German cultural property that was preserved in Russia. The atmosphere of secrecy hampered clarification of the fate of lost Soviet cultural property and of the real number of such losses. It hampered an understanding of what had returned to the USSR and what had been irretrievably lost. There is also an imperative need for Russian officials and researchers in the field of culture to get to the ultimate truth. In that sense, too,

25. The Amber Room in the Catherine Palace, Pushkin (Tsarskoye Selo), in an early-twentieth-century photograph. The amber panels were presented to Peter the Great by Frederick William I of Prussia in 1716 and later installed in the Catherine Palace by the Empress Elizabeth. The Germans took Pushkin in September 1941, dismantled the Amber Room, and reinstalled it in Königsberg Castle in 1942. It was recrated in 1945 and subsequently disappeared.

the Bard Graduate Center symposium should absolutely not be regarded as any attempt at summing up. It is only one of the first steps.

During the period of World War II, Nazi Germany deliberately removed cultural property and works of art from the occupied countries of Europe. This was, moreover, an operation conducted by the state. This was the goal of the creation in 1940 of the Einsatzstab Reichsleiter Rosenberg, which would later have divisions in the territory of the USSR in Minsk, Riga, Tallinn, and Kiev (Kyiv). The art objects removed by the ERR and by other Nazi organizations were carefully described and registered by those groups. Objects plundered by looters from the army were not included. The very best contents of Soviet museums were taken to Germany, and much of the rest, including museum documentation, was destroyed, since Hitler had declared that works of art on the Eastern Front were of no significance and should be destroyed. In the occupied territory of the USSR more than 427 museums were plundered (including 173 in Russia); 1,670 Russian Orthodox churches, 237 Catholic churches, 532 synagogues, and other buildings used for various religious purposes were destroyed or damaged. In particular, the unique palaces of the Leningrad (St. Petersburg) suburbs were totally plundered or burned down, including those at Pushkin (Tsarskoye Selo), Peterhof (Petrodvorets), Pavlovsk, Gatchina, and Oranienbaum (Lomonosov).

At Pushkin, the Catherine and Alexander palaces were totally plundered (fig. 26). Everything valuable was removed. The interiors were stripped: parquet floors, ceiling decorations, furniture, collections of paintings, tapestries, books from the palace libraries, Peter I's collection of 650 icons, and Catherine II's porcelain collection. Even the wooden and

24. The Monastery of New Jerusalem in Istra, near Moscow, built 1652–67. Destroyed by Germany during World War II

metal adornments on the doors were removed. The panels of the famous eighteenth-century Amber Room (fig. 25) were stolen. The ceiling decoration *The Feast of the Gods on Mount Olympus* was removed from the Hermitage pavilion, as was the seventeenth-century Gotthorp globe from the Admiralty pavilion.

At Pavlovsk, all the interior appointments of the palace were removed: the parquet floors, furniture, ceiling decorations, tapestries, door handles and adornments, collections of ancient coins, and books from the library of Peter I.

At Peterhof (see fig. 52), 34,000 precious objects from the Bolshoi, Marly, Monplaisir, and Cottage palaces were taken to Germany, including 4,950 pieces of eighteenth- and nineteenth-century Russian and Western European furniture; porcelain of the same period; statues, including the fountain sculptures of *Samson, Neva, Volkhov,* and *Neptune;** the contents of the picture gallery; and even the park gates.

In the fall of 1943, all valuable objects were removed from the Pushkin museum in Mikhailovskoye. The Pushkin house-museum was burned down, and the Sviatogorsk monastery destroyed. The Pskov-Pechersk monastery near Pskov lost all of its treasures. In Novgorod the sixteenth-century icons from the Cathedral of St. Sophia, the czars' and the metropolitans' thrones, and Boris Godunov's chandelier were sent to Germany, as well as icons from the Anton'ev monastery and also tiles from the refectory of the Vyazhishchsk monastery. The monument *The Millennium of Russia* was taken apart and prepared for removal to Germany, but this was prevented by the Red Army offensive.

Other victims of plundering and removal were the Rostov Museum of Fine Arts with 458 exhibits, the Don Cossack Museum in Novocherkassk with 471 exhibits, the Taganrog museum with 4,622 exhibits, the Krasnodar art museum with 784 exhibits, the Kalinin ethnographic museum with 6,000 exhibits, the Kalininskaia oblast' (Kalinin Oblast) picture gallery with 193 exhibits, the Kurskaia oblast' (Kursk Oblast) picture gallery with 84 exhibits, and the Novgorod state museum with 3,703 exhibits. According to incomplete data, in the seventy-three richest museums of the USSR 564,723 exhibits were destroyed or removed. The fifteen richest museums lost 269,515 exhibits.

I shall cite some data regarding the activity of German subdivisions in the removal of cultural property from the territory of Russia (based on documents of German origin):

- At Pskov, 1,026 church books were removed from the kremlin (fortress), including sixteenth- to eighteenth-century manuscripts and seventeenth-century printed books. Nearly 35,000 volumes were removed from the Pskov pedagogical institute, including 25,000 works of Russian scholars.

- At Novgorod, the library of the historical museum (fig. 27), which was "displaced," contained rare periodicals such as

26. A looted hall in the Catherine Palace, Pushkin (Tsarskoye Selo), strewn with the debris of Nazi occupation

Russkaia rech' of 1880 and *Bibliograf* of 1860. Books removed included editions of Voltaire of 1785 and of Jean Jacques Rousseau of 1796. All in all, 30,000 volumes were removed. Unique editions on archaeology, including 51 books on the history of ancient Russia, were removed from the Novgorod library for the German professor Engel. Publications on ethnography were removed for Professor Thiele.

- At Kursk, Russian eighteenth-century chronicles and a valuable edition by Mikhail Lomonosov (1785) of Dimitrii Kantemir's *Grammar* were removed from the library.

- At Smolensk, valuable autographs and manuscripts were removed: autographs of Peter I, Empress Anna, Peter II, Empress Elizabeth, Catherine II, Nicholas I, the Polish king Sigismund, and others; *The Life of Daniel Pereyaslavsky;* eighteenth-century chronicles; a sixteenth-century Gospel; *The History of Peter I;* and other manuscripts.

A few words about destroyed and ruined architectural sites. During the bombing of Novgorod, the belfry and frescoes of the Cathedral of St. Sophia were destroyed, and part of the

---

* Editor's note: The Neptune Fountain sculptures were returned to the USSR in 1947 (see Grimsted, below, page 246) and subsequently reinstalled on the grounds of the Petrodvorets (Peterhof) palace.

27. The State Museum of History in Novgorod was used as a barracks for German soldiers. Valuable books and other objects from the collection lie in the midst of empty bottles and rubbish.

28. This house in Voronezh, used by the Gestapo for a torture chamber, was demolished before the German retreat. February 1943.

arches collapsed. The walls and towers of the kremlin, the archbishop's palace, the Efim'evsk chapel, and the Hall of Facets collapsed. The Georgiev and Iur'ev cathedrals of the Nikolsky monastery and the thirteenth-century Church of Nikola on the Lipna were reduced to ruins, and the Church of Paraskeva was destroyed. The Church of the Dormition and a number of others with unique frescoes were destroyed as well.

In Gdov, a suburb of Pskov, the entire complex of ancient buildings within the fortress was blown up. These included the unique fifteenth-century Torshinsk church and the fifteenth-century church in the former Savvina hermitage, with its ancient iconostasis, which was shattered under the rubble. The ancient fortress walls of Ostrov were wiped from the face of the earth. Ancient residential houses were burned down, including the Pechenko house and the Catholic Priest's house. The world-famous Pogankin Chambers were blown up and the seventeenth-century Men'shikov Chambers destroyed. The only example of ancient wooden civic architecture in Pskov was burned down.

Since 1992, the State Commission on the Restitution of Cultural Property has been concentrating its efforts on the creation of a data bank to cover the whole range of problems involving the displacement of cultural property during or as a consequence of World War II: (1) the removal by Germany of cultural property from the territory of the USSR; (2) the return by Germany to the USSR of removed cultural property; (3) the removal of cultural property belonging to Germany and its allies to the USSR; (4) the return of cultural property by the USSR to Germany and other states of Eastern Europe.

This entire set of problems can be resolved only through careful work utilizing the federal and agency archives of Russia that relate to the activities of the main Trophy Organization of the Soviet army, the subdivisions of the Soviet Military Administration in Germany (SVAG; English acronym SMAG), and the agencies and scientific organizations of the USSR and Russian Republic (RSFSR: Russian Socialist Federated Soviet Republic), including the Committee on Arts Affairs of the USSR, the administration of cultural-educational institutions of the RSFSR, the Ministry of Finance and the State Bank of the USSR, the Academy of Sciences, and others.

There is a need for separate study of the activity of the German occupying authorities and the Wehrmacht, which handled the removal of cultural property from the USSR. The documents of the ERR discovered in the Ukrainian archives attest to a brilliantly planned system of removal and organization of cultural and art objects, involving skilled experts called upon to create collections for the libraries of the Hohe Schule in Germany, the museums of Bavaria and Nuremberg, and other German institutions from the contents of museums and libraries removed from the USSR. Entire railroad cars filled with cultural property from the palaces of the suburbs of Leningrad (St. Petersburg), Smolensk, Novgorod, Rostov, and Voronezh were sent off to Germany by the ERR. Working hand-in-hand in this field with the ERR was the staff of the Pleni-potentiary of the Eighth Army for the preservation of cultural

29. Empty frames hang in the looted dining room of Yasnaya Polyana, the estate of Leo Tolstoy in the region of Tula near Moscow, December 1941.

property, headed by Count Solms, who in the fall of 1941 also organized the dispatch to the Reich of five railroad cars with exhibits from the museums of Gatchina and Pushkin. (The Amber Room was among the valuable contents of this train.)

Members of the ERR were in constant contact with the other units of the Reich that dealt with the identification, deportation, and organization of plundered works of art. These included the departments and divisions of propaganda of the Wehrmacht, the Wehrmacht's economic inspection units, and the Sonderkommando Künsberg, which represented the interests of the Ministry of Foreign Affairs and the SS. In September 1941, threatened with having to leave Pyatigorsk, a subdivision of the Wehrmacht removed twenty-four large cases with art objects belonging to the Rostov museum from the Lermontov museum. In December 1941, the subdivision of economic inspection of the Wehrmacht, Economic Command IV of the Sixteenth Army Staff, delivered to Riga cultural property from the Novgorod kremlin and the monastery church in Tikhvin. On the Führer's order of March 1, 1942, and the order of the General Staff of the ground forces of September 30, 1942, the General Staff of the Wehrmacht assigned to various individuals the task of removing archives, libraries, and museum exhibitions from Pskov.

The above-mentioned Sonderkommando Künsberg was active in removing the czars' libraries from the suburbs of Leningrad and the contents of museums and libraries from Rostov and Taganrog. In addition to the ERR, Künsberg's "clients" were: the main Reich security agency, RSHA (Reichssicherheitshauptamt); the geographic service of the Ministry of Foreign Affairs; the state library; the Slavic Studies seminar; and the Hermann Göring economic library. The "Ingermanland" working group, which inspected the czarist palaces of Leningrad in November 1941 after the most valuable things had been removed by Solms and Künsberg, efficiently proposed that in the near future the remainder be removed, noting, moreover, that paintings and other works

of art had been plundered and that soldiers had taken as souvenirs more than a thousand icons from the belfry of the Alexander Palace.

During its inspection of the state of the Pavlovsk palace, the working group noted that the collection of engraved gems had been removed by the SS. Moreover, it was noted that Count Solms had removed from the Gatchina palace about four hundred portraits of German origin, and that "soldiers and officers had stolen various things." The group strongly recommended that the Neptune Fountain in Peterhof be sent immediately to Germany, since its proper location was seen as the city of party congresses of the Reich, Nuremberg, to which the fountain was delivered.

Plans are now being made for the publication of a catalogue of Russian losses based on existing and newly received archival documents and other museum materials. As is well known, the fascist ideological doctrine considered the Slavs a nation of slaves, and asserted that their culture and art were of no value whatever. Life, however, has refuted theory.

There is a certain desire to deal with the problem of losses only in terms of financial cost and value. In my view, this is wrong. The problem of the destruction or removal of artistic cultural property exists in a complex historical, political, and social-psychological context. A significant role is also played by national feelings, particularly in the fiftieth-anniversary year of the victory over fascism. But first and foremost we must know what we have lost—and whatever we find, we must return it as quickly as possible to cultural circulation for the benefit of humankind.

UKRAINE:

THE LOST CULTURAL

TREASURES

AND THE PROBLEM OF

THEIR RETURN

Alexander Fedoruk

In the sphere of culture, World War II, which was launched by an aggressive Germany, is still not over because stolen cultural treasures have not yet been returned to their legitimate owners. Taken by force from their legal owners and subjected to forced migration, they are still being held in various places as "prisoners of war." Those persons who pillaged cultural valuables "never had God in their hearts" and never believed in ideals. Those who stole valuable objects after the war did so in the guise of peacemakers acting under the flag of humanism. Their followers cynically attempted to totally destroy cultural treasures during the war and no less cynically tried to hide their plunder as far as possible from public view. Forcibly excluded from cultural life, these "prisoners of war" still await a better fate. We sincerely hope that the conference organized by the Bard Graduate Center will bring us at least one step closer to a successful solution, based on the legal norms governing the restitution to their countries of origin of the cultural treasures lost during World War II and its aftermath.

Despite dozens of conventions and resolutions, beginning with the Hague Conventions of 1899 and 1907 (see Appendix 3) and including the latest UNESCO documents designed to implement the program of the UNESCO "universal decade of culture" (1988–97), the problem of global losses of cultural property and of their identification and return to the states from which they were forcibly removed is still unresolved, relevant, and, to my mind, a deeply ethical issue. No analogies with Lord Elgin or the expeditions of Napoleon Bonaparte can ever justify the moral error of the supporters of the policy of "cultural prisons" and cultural property held as "prisoners of war."

At this stage of its formation as a nation and of the development of its political system, Ukraine has publicly declared that its national relics and cultural treasures, many of which were lost or have been found outside its territory, have experienced a tragic plight. The president and the government of Ukraine insist that the extent of the damages inflicted on its historic and cultural heritage be made public, that lists be compiled of the cultural property, monuments, and works of art that have been found in the territories of other states, and that there be a study of objective possibilities for their repatriation to Ukraine. This was the reason for the creation of the National Commission on the Restitution of Cultural Treasures to Ukraine.

As part of the former USSR, Ukraine was not able to exercise its sovereign right to the return of its cultural property, even though it was, in fact, subject to international law. Now, as a party to the Helsinki process, Ukraine has ratified international conventions that confirm the importance of cultural property and the primacy of law, including national legislation, regarding the return of cultural property to countries of origin and the return of national cultural property to a people.

It was not fortuitous that in September 1994 the Ukrainian town of Chernigov, which had been leveled to the ground by the Nazis, hosted an international conference under the aegis of UNESCO on the problems of the return of cultural property that had disappeared or been illegally removed during World War II. In his address to the participants of the conference, Leonid Kuchma, the president of Ukraine, stressed that the return of lost library property was an integral part of national cultural policy and of agreements on cultural cooperation, and should be considered in the context of international relations.

Ukraine also initiated the convening of an international roundtable designed to resolve problems regarding the return of lost library property that had been mistreated and banned, items that had become "prisoners of war." The participants, who represented the libraries of Eastern Europe, launched an appeal to the employees of libraries and scientific research institutions and to scientists, artists, and public figures to unite their efforts in developing long-term regional programs for the restitution of lost collections of books.

At the meeting of the roundtable, dramatic figures were cited. During the war, the holdings of the scientific library of Kyiv (Kiev) University and of the state historical, scientific-technical, and medical libraries were totally destroyed. From the central scientific library of the Academy of Sciences of Ukraine, the Germans removed more than three hundred twenty thousand copies of manuscripts, including many in Persian and Chinese, unique books and journals, and seventy-two thousand volumes from the V. Korolenko State Scientific Library. The collections of the Vinnitsa, Dnepropetrovs'k, Zaporizhya, Poltava, and Kyiv regional libraries were badly damaged.

There is evidence of the devastating scope of this pillaging. A legal document of August 26, 1943, states that the Germans took from library holdings 4,000 scientific books, 10,518 geographic maps, 2,500 works of German literature, 1,014 foreign journals, 2,508 technical journals, and all 50 geographic atlases. From Kyiv, the Germans took the holdings of the state historical library (3,000 volumes) and of the library of the Writers' Union, which were packed into seven cases. All the reference information material of the Kharkhiv scientific library, catalogued in 802 drawers and containing one million catalogue cards, was also found in Germany. The roundtable findings highlighted the need for thorough study of published archival documents concerning the policy of fascist Germany in the territory of occupied Ukraine (1941–44) and its tragic consequences for the development of Ukrainian culture.

In 1994 another special conference was held in Kyiv, dedicated to the problem of the migration of cultural property from Ukraine during World War II, as recorded in Einsatzstab Reichsleiter Rosenberg (ERR) archive documents in the central state archives of leading Ukrainian government and management bodies. During the war, the ERR was active throughout Ukraine, with the main group operating in Kyiv and a number of working groups active in other Ukrainian cities. Altogether, these groups included over 150 highly skilled experts whose main objective was to pillage and destroy Ukrainian cultural property. They prepared precise factual documents and submitted regular periodic reports. Today,

most of the contents of the ERR archives are in Germany (in the Federal Archive of Germany, in Koblenz), in Kyiv, in Moscow (in the center for the conservation of historical documents), and in the United States Holocaust Memorial Museum, in Washington, D.C.

The ERR and related materials in Kyiv can be found in four collections:

1. F.3676. Headquarters of the ERR for the Occupied Eastern regions, Berlin, Kyiv
2. F.3674. Headquarters of the ERR for the Occupied Western regions and the Netherlands (1940–43)
3. K.M. F-8. Collection of microfilmed documents from administrative organizations
4. F.3206. Reichskommissariat for Ukraine, Rivno

After attacking the USSR, Germany began systematically to destroy and pillage the cultural property of Ukraine. Germany became the aggressor, and the declaration of Field Marshal Walter von Reichenau that no historical or cultural property in the East was of any significance revealed the general policy of Nazism aimed at the destruction and pillaging of Ukraine's cultural property. Ukraine, Belarus, and Russia were precisely those countries of the East whose culture the Nazis intended to destroy.

This catastrophe, unprecedented in the history of humankind, had global consequences for the development of civilization on our planet. One of them was an awareness that the boundary separating existence from annihilation is precarious, and that the heritage of centuries of world culture can be easily lost. During the war, every sixth inhabitant of the territory of Ukraine perished. Over seven hundred cities and twenty-six thousand villages were completely destroyed, and 40 percent of the region's economic potential was lost. The war inflicted enormous losses on Ukrainian culture.

Contrary to all conventions in force at that time, cultural property became the victim not only of military operations but also of cynically planned action aimed at its destruction and theft. According to obviously incomplete data, nearly one thousand monuments of architecture were lost in ruined or damaged Ukrainian cities and villages, and 347 of these works were destroyed. The losses of the state archive holdings include forty-six million unique documents on Ukrainian history of the twelfth to the twentieth centuries. Over fifty-one million books disappeared from Ukrainian libraries, and new details about these losses keep coming to light. The German occupation army and its allies took a vast number of objects from the museums of Ukraine. New data published in 1987 shows that 151 museums were robbed and three hundred thousand exhibits were either destroyed or taken to the West. In the early 1990s, archival documents were published that made it clear that the losses of only twenty-one museums within the boundaries of present-day Ukraine account for 283,782 objects. Removed from the Museum of Russian Art in Kyiv and destroyed were 4,873 works. The art gallery in Kharkiv lost 1,348 canvases and sketches; 332 works of decorative art were sent to Germany, and the remainder were burned. Most recent data show that seventy thousand of the seventy-five thousand objects in the Kharkiv gallery on the eve of the war were removed. In 1943 the Nazis sent to Germany seventeen truckloads of objects exhibited in the Kharkiv historical museum and then set fire to the building. Considerable losses were also suffered by the museums of Dnepropetrovs'k, Donetsk, Lutsk, Odessa, Poltava, Rivno, Sumy, Kherson, Chernigov, Yalta, and other cities of Ukraine.

During the war, 5,113 manuscripts, 3,139 old printed books, and 2,346 engravings were taken from L'viv. The gallery of paintings lost 229 of its most famous works. The German occupation administration ordered the removal of 101 works from the picture gallery, including a Rembrandt self-portrait, and about three hundred paintings and decorative objects that were used to adorn the interiors of the officers' casino and administration buildings. In 1944 the German civil administration of the Galicia district sent 8,748 exhibits from the historical museum to Cracow and Visnicha. In 1946 a list was drawn up of museum works taken by the Germans. These included: an archaeological collection (over five thousand objects) from the excavations of Yaroslav Pasternak at the site of the ancient Ukrainian city of Plisetsko, 1,250 pieces from the collection of weapons, 154 decorative objects that adorned the city and guild administration offices, 121 gold articles, 67 paintings, 50 pieces of furniture, 90 plates and dishes, 180 books from the library holdings, and 54 museum exhibits. None of these and none of the Dürer drawings from the L'viv scientific library of the Academy of Sciences of Ukraine was ever returned to L'viv. Today these drawings are preserved in the Metropolitan Museum of Art, New York, the Art Institute of Chicago, the Barber Institute in Birmingham, England, and other museums.

That is only a small part of this tragic list. The Kyiv-Pechersk monastery lost the originals of the official charters of the Ukrainian hetmans, the archive of the Kyiv metropolitans, ancient manuscripts and acts of the fifteenth through the eighteenth centuries, coin collections, icons, collections of weapons, and portraits of the seventeenth and eighteenth centuries. Unique frescoes were taken from the Cathedral of St. Sophia, including the Zakharii composition; the *Virgin Mary and Archangel Gabriel* from the twelfth-century Cathedral of St. Michael; fragments of frescoes from the eleventh-century Tithes church; and valuable plates, dishes, and icons. In 1943 the Germans began removing works from the Kyiv Museum of Western and Oriental Art. Almost twenty-five thousand exhibits were lost, including paintings by Adrian van Ostade, Bernardo Strozzi, Hubert Robert, Jacob van Ruisdael, José Ribera, Jacob Jordaens, and Pieter Bruegel; bronze and terra-cotta articles; and marble and silver from ancient Egypt, Greece, and Rome. Only eight thousand of thirty-three thousand pages remained from the unique collection of engravings by Lucas Cranach and others.

Pictures, china, bronze, silver, ivory, and all of the scientific archives were taken from the museums of Odessa, and over two thousand icons were taken from the museums

and churches of the Odessa region. According to data of the Ministry of Education of Ukraine, the losses of the Odessa museum of history and archaeology in 1944 comprised more than one hundred thirty thousand objects. The invaders did not spare the museums of the Crimea. Nearly forty thousand exhibits were lost from the Simferopol regional history museum; nearly fifteen hundred were taken from the Kerch museum of history and archaeology; and over thirteen hundred works of art were removed from the palace museum in Alupka. Considerable losses were also sustained by the Yalta museum of regional history and the Kherson historical-cultural museum. Collections that were not totally lost or destroyed were not included in this count.

I emphasize that the magnitude of the losses suffered by Ukrainian museums, archives, and libraries resulted from the continuous, deliberate, and systematic pillaging and destruction of Ukrainian cultural property. The armies of Germany and its allies assigned special units to select and remove cultural property from the occupied territories. Among these units were the special German battalion commanded by von Künsberg of the ERR, the Romanian Service for the Confiscation and Collection of Trophies, and other units whose activity was condemned by world public opinion both during and after the

30. Ruins of the Kyiv-Pechersk monastery, destroyed during World War II

war. Though the tragic list of Ukrainian cultural property lost during World War II could be continued at length, and more time could be spent in analyzing the criminal activity of the invaders engaged in this destruction and pillaging, I shall not dwell further on these issues.

I wish to emphasize that the consequences of the immense cultural losses suffered by Ukraine during the Second World War have not yet been overcome. These terrible wounds on the body of Ukrainian culture are a perpetual reminder for us of past tragic events. The extent of these losses cannot be assessed in monetary terms. Every work of art or ancient object is historically and culturally unique and irreplaceable, and therefore no true compensation is possible. The rebirth and flourishing of Ukrainian culture urgently require the search for and restitution of cultural property lost or removed during World War II. Every small success and each individual step bring us closer to the reestablishment of historical legitimacy and to the end of this dramatic chapter in the history of humankind and the history of Ukraine, the chapter on the Second World War.

One of the most complicated problems is that of obtaining impartial and true information regarding the fate of Ukrainian cultural property lost during and after World War II. An initial approach to this problem revealed that under the totalitarian Soviet regime, instead of a detailed investigation of all aspects of this issue there were propaganda declarations filled with ideological clichés blessed by the political leaders of the former USSR. This applies both to losses of cultural property and to the reasons and circumstances surrounding their destruction or theft. It is paradoxical that not a single one of the efforts during and after the war to draw up an inventory of the wartime losses incurred by the archives, libraries, and museums of the former Soviet Union, including Ukrainian ones, was ever successful. In the best of cases, the assembled documents served merely to swell the holdings of archives, and as is well known, a good number of them disappeared. As a result, most cultural institutions that suffered during the war still do not have a full list of their lost property. This situation is of particular concern to the Ukrainian libraries, which in fact have only now begun compiling such lists. The situation is complicated by the fact that many archives, museums, and libraries no longer have their prewar catalogues and inventories or other wartime documents. Moreover, historical analysis of numerous older documents concerning the losses sustained by Ukrainian cultural establishments reveals that their information is quite incomplete and that further investigation and clarification are essential. And unfortunately, most of those people who were direct participants in those events and who could be of real assistance in reestablishing historical truth are no longer with us.

The policy of the Nazi leaders and their allies on Ukrainian territory also requires detailed scholarly research. We need to obtain a full picture of the theft of our cultural heritage, to study the ways in which these objects were removed and their routes of migration, and to determine their present-day location. Study of the materials of the special state commission and of the regional commissions are of great importance in determining the crimes of the fascist invaders and their allies, and the losses they caused to citizens, collective farmers, public organizations, and state establishments and institutions. It is equally important to study the documents of the Commission on the History of World War II and of the German war departments and the occupation administration involved in pillaging the cultural property of Ukraine, in particular of the ERR agency, as well as the materials of the Sonderkommando Künsberg and other organizations. The practical result of such research must be the most complete inventory possible of information concerning lost cultural property moved illegally beyond the borders of Ukraine during World War II. That will serve as the basis for a computer data bank that, using modern information technology, will be able effectively to obtain and process information on the lost works.

The complexity and scope of the tasks facing Ukraine in this area require scientific organization, identification of priorities, mobilization of available resources, and long-term planning. There is a need to coordinate the work of all the relevant departments, institutions, public organizations, and independent individuals on the basis of mutual understanding, solidarity, sincerity, and responsibility.

The problem of the identification and restitution of lost cultural property cannot be resolved by the will of one state acting alone. This issue requires broad cooperation with other states on the basis of goodwill and international legal norms. I would like to emphasize that Ukraine has ratified all international conventions governing the cooperation of members of the world community in this field, and has undertaken a commitment to adhere to the spirit and letter of these agreements. We expect a similar attitude from our partners. We consider that international cooperation on all levels can succeed on a bilateral basis, within the limits of regional programs, and on a global scale. In carrying out research and in organizing the return of cultural property lost during the Second World War, I would like to underline the particular need for close cooperation with the relevant organizations of the Russian Federation and the Republic of Belarus. Our relations with the Federal Republic of Germany are developing well and rapidly.

The latest scientific research has led us to analyze the conditions of the evacuation of cultural property from Ukraine to eastern areas of the USSR, and the activity of the Soviet military administration and the Allied administration in Germany entrusted with the restitution of the first objects discovered during the years immediately following the war. We still do not have information as to which Ukrainian cultural objects were found in the rear of the battlefields of the German-Soviet front or information regarding their specific location. Have they all been returned to us? We lack information on ways to bring about the return of our cultural property from Germany and other countries of Western and Eastern Europe since we do not have their inventories. Today we must deal with the problem of the cultural property removed from Ukraine to the eastern areas of the USSR that was never returned, as well as the problem of property taken from Ukraine by the fascists and their allies that was taken to the Soviet Union after the war and never returned to Ukraine.

Among the Soviet states, Ukraine, together with Belarus, suffered most from the pillaging of the German army and its allies, and Ukraine never received adequate compensation for these terrible losses. Initial experience with the identification and return of cultural property lost during the war has shown the urgent need for work on those aspects of international law that are relevant to this problem. In accordance with the protocol of intent to cooperate on the identification of lost cultural property and with the agreements concluded on the mutual exchange of some collections that had been removed during World War II, as a demonstration of goodwill and of practical action, Ukraine and Germany exchanged cultural property. In May 1993, Ukraine ceremonially handed over to the German people historic objects related to Goethe. In November 1993, the government of Germany received eight thousand fragments of ceramics and of glass vessels from the Kablovo archaeological site that had been found in Ukraine during World War I. In May 1994, a formal ceremony took place to mark the repatriation of valuable archaeological objects dating from the Neolithic period and the Bronze Age, which had been removed from the Kherson museum of history and archaeology in 1944 and kept in Germany for several decades after the war.

These actions had a positive effect on Ukrainian and German public opinion, and contributed to strengthening mutual confidence between the governments and peoples. Let us consider in the same context our cooperation with the Research Institute for Eastern Europe at the University of Bremen, regarding the fate of Ukrainian historic and cultural property lost during the war years. The possibility of creating a joint data bank for cultural property lost during the war and the free exchange of information on art objects are subjects currently on the agenda. I am sure that implementation of these projects would mark a real contribution toward the return of national cultural objects to their legitimate owners. I would like to note the positive nature of our dialogue with the authorities of Germany, Poland, Hungary, and other countries.

Some German cultural property, which was obtained either in the form of war reparations or simply as war trophies, has been kept in Ukraine. Until recently the presence of these objects was not publicly acknowledged, and it is now the task of the National Commission on the Restitution of Cultural Treasures to Ukraine to find them. We plan later to organize a special exhibition of cultural property taken from Germany. Together with our German colleagues, we are seeking ways to implement cultural policy in the field of restitution. We consider that direct contacts between archivists, librarians, museum workers, and scholars from various countries are particularly productive. There is a clear need to convene joint conferences, seminars, and roundtable meetings and to promote other activities designed to enhance international cooperation and a broad exchange of information. As is often the case, problems arise during the course of work that can only be resolved through joint efforts.

Today there is an urgent need for additional study of the international legal bases for the restitution of cultural property illegally moved from one country to another during and after World War II. It should also be noted that since the end of the 1940s there has been virtually no compliance with the provisions of the Hague Convention of 1907 and the Declaration of London issued by the Allied countries on January 5, 1943, which provided for the obligatory return of cultural property illegally removed during military operations or during the occupation (see Appendices 3 and 9). Moreover, such property has on occasion been openly exhibited in museums, archives, and other repositories or published in the mass media and scientific literature.

In our opinion, the United Nations Educational, Scientific and Cultural Organization (UNESCO) has a positive role to play here. We believe it would be useful to request the Director-General of UNESCO to organize or to assist in organizing an international conference under the aegis of UNESCO on the problems of the restitution of cultural property illegally removed from one country to another during and after World War II, and to take the initiative in convening a special session of the intergovernmental committee to contribute toward the return of cultural property to its country of origin or to provide for restitution if such property was acquired illegally. Such a session could consider both legal problems and means for the identification and restitution of national cultural property lost during the war. I am confident that the idea of holding such meetings would be supported by all those countries that experienced the terrible and destructive consequences of the Second World War. A step of great practical importance might be the creation under the aegis of the Soros Foundation of a single data bank on all (or at least the most outstanding) cultural property lost during the war. Such information could be shared by all participating countries.

THE TRAGIC FATE

OF BELARUSAN MUSEUM

AND LIBRARY COLLECTIONS

DURING THE

SECOND WORLD WAR

Adam Maldis

First of all, I would sincerely like to thank the Bard Graduate Center for the kind invitation to the symposium held in 1995 on the cultural and intellectual treasures lost during the Second World War. For Belarus, such participation was especially important because of the direct and indirect losses we incurred before, during, and after the war.

It is well known that during World War II Belarus lost one-fourth of its population, and recent research has raised this figure to one-third. Many cities of Belarus were destroyed, villages were burned, and architectural monuments were ruined. Nor did the war spare museums, libraries, and archives. According to available information, only the collections of the Grodno and Slonim historical museums were more or less untouched. Here we cannot agree with the conclusions of the Research Institute for Eastern Europe at the University of Bremen on the fate of works of art taken from the USSR during World War II, which state that during the war Belarus lost only 3 percent of its collections (while Ukraine lost 60 percent and Russia 35 percent).* The conclusion seems to be the opposite—that only 3 percent remained. The fact that our losses are little known in Europe and the world at large is a separate issue. Even in our own country only 3–5 percent of these losses have been studied.

The losses sustained during the first months of the war by the Mogilev historical museum were especially severe for the people of Belarus. The famous Saint Euphrosyne of Polotsk Cross, made in 1161 by the Polotsk jeweler Lazar Bogsha, disappeared from this museum (colorplate 4). It is known not so much for its gold- and silver-plating, enamel portraits of saints, and ornaments, precious stones, and pearls as for its inscriptions and the relics of the saints it contains. In June 1941 the cross disappeared and was never seen again.

Lazar Bogsha's masterpiece, however, was not the only extraordinarily valuable object in the Mogilev historical museum. Archival documents of 1945–46 show that prior to the war the museum also contained the gold and silver keys of Mogilev, two silver seals of the city, gold jewelry and tiles with pictures found during the excavations at Pompeii, the silver mace of King Sigismund III, tankards with portraits of Peter I and Alexei Mikhailovich, gold and silver crosses, pyxes, and censers. Museum documents refer to the Belynich (fifteenth century), Spas (1670), and Kazan' icons, the Iver icon of the Virgin, gem-studded icons of saints Nikolai, Peter, and Paul, and paintings by I. Aivazovsky, V. Borovikovsky, A. Watteau, I. Repin, and other masters. Such unique items as a flintlock pistol with gold Arabian hammered ornamentation, the throne made in 1780 for Empress Catherine II's visit to Mogilev, Napoleon's sleigh, gold and silver snuffboxes, porcelain figurines, and decorative fabrics are listed separately. Descriptions of the Mogilev holdings reveal that entire collections had been preserved: "coins . . . from the tenth to nineteenth centuries,

---

* Editor's note: See M. Hiller, below, page 83. The statement in question suggests that, according to Soviet estimates, 3 percent of the total losses sustained by the Soviet Union were objects from Belarusan institutions.

weighing up to six kilograms," "objects from burial mound excavations," "an ethnographic collection of Belarusan clothing from the seventeenth to nineteenth centuries," "cold arms and firearms from the tenth to fourteenth centuries" (280 items), "samples of wooden carvings by Belarus masters from the fourteenth to eighteenth centuries" (170 carvings), "a large paleontological collection," "an entomological and mineral collection," and many other items. Finally, the Mogilev museum also housed many unique and rare books and manuscripts: about twenty Gospels "with settings made by Belarusan masters of the sixteenth to eighteenth centuries," "175 Belarusan manuscripts and old printed books," and twenty-eight official documents of the kings and czars that were given to Mogilev.

The Cross of Saint Euphrosyne of Polotsk is also described among these treasures. Though it was appraised in 1944 at six million rubles, the cross is, in fact, of inestimable value to the people of Belarus. This is our most important national relic, which cannot possibly be replaced by the "Cross modeled after the Cross of Euphrosyne of Polotsk," which is now being made in Brest. Where did all these things disappear to during the summer of 1941? Some possibilities will be put forward in the second part of this paper.

The Minsk museums, in particular the art gallery of the Belorussian Soviet Socialist Republic (BSSR) and the historical museum of the BSSR, also suffered huge losses. According to postwar testimony found in the archives of the head of the Department of Arts of the BSSR government, of the writer F. Pestrak, and of E. Aladova, the director of the Art Gallery, approximately seventeen hundred masterpieces of Belarusan painting were taken from Minsk to Prussia. These included paintings by I. Aivazovsky, K. Brullow, V. Bialynitsky-Birula, M. Vrubel, F. Goretsky, S. Zarianko, A. Kuinji, I. Levitan, K. Makovsky, A. van Ostade, V. Polenov, I. Repin, F. Rushchits, V. Serov, I. Shishkin, and N. Iaroshenko. Also taken were thirty icons from the sixteenth and seventeenth centuries; letters of Belarusan artists; and about fifty sculptures of M. Antokolsky, P. Klodt, M. Kozlovsky, S. Konenkov, K. Rastrelli, F. Tolstoy, and others. The Art Gallery also had very rich collections of decorative and applied art. To cite E. Aladova: "a collection of Slutsk embroidered sashes, forty-eight items," "a huge collection of porcelain masterpieces from Russian, Chinese, and Western European factories," "art objects and dishes of Urech'e glass" (Urech'e is a small town in Belarus), "a huge collection of bronze and porcelain clocks from various eras," "a collection of masterpieces of bone carving by Russian and foreign artists," furniture ensembles, cupboards from Danzig (now Gdańsk), writing tables "made from various rare woods," "about a hundred carpets and tapestries," and many other things. During the first days of the war, almost all these treasures were packed into cases labeled "Königsberg." They never returned to Belarus. Only a very small part of the collections of the art gallery was handed over to the historical museum, which remained open during the occupation. After

the war, the stolen property removed from the art gallery was appraised at twelve million "gold rubles."

No less dramatic was the wartime fate of the Minsk historical museum (its director during the war was Mr. Anton Shukieloyts, who now lives in New York). Part of its treasures were plundered by marauders at the very beginning of the occupation, and nineteen ancient cannons were taken to Germany (including sixteen from the Radziwill Nesvizh collection, which had been transported to Minsk in 1940). The Germans then ordered that paintings, books, manuscripts, and Belarusan Jewish objects of decorative and applied art be sent to the Vienna Institute for Judaic Studies. Shukieloyts kept a detailed description of this part of the collection. It contained some twenty paintings, including I. Pen's *The Watchmaker*, a portrait of F. Skaryna by Y. Kruger, and other works. In June 1944 the Einsatzstab Reichsleiter Rosenberg (ERR) ordered the transfer of the entire collection of the Minsk historical museum to Höchstädt an der Donau (Bavaria). This operation was carried out under the supervision of Emma Haupt. After the liberation of Höchstädt by the Americans in 1945, a special Soviet commission arrived. Since there were no experts in this commission, however, all the objects were randomly shipped together. Belarusan masterpieces were mixed in with Ukrainian and Russian artworks. It was then, according to Shukieloyts, that the Minsk museum's valuable painting of the Mogilev school, *The Last Judgment*, disappeared.

The losses of the Baranovichi regional art museum, to which treasures from neighboring palaces and estates were brought in 1940, should also be noted. A document of September 19, 1944, shows that the Germans stole from this museum Rembrandt's *Portrait of an Old Man*, paintings by Jan Matejko, about sixty miniatures by Western European artists, icons, letters of Belarusan painters, church sculptures by Belarusan masters of the seventeenth and eighteenth centuries, about two hundred paintings by Soviet artists, a large seventeenth-century tapestry, a set of Louis XIV furniture, four Japanese vases, about one hundred sixty Western European statuettes, and "an art library in six languages." The fate of the Baranovichi treasures is unknown.

The records of the Belarusan commission that assisted the Extraordinary State Commission established to assess the losses of the USSR during World War II show that between 1941 and 1944 ten museums were destroyed in Belarus. The value of the lost artworks (11,641 items) was assessed at 163.4 million rubles. Those figures, however, are incomplete. M. Ianitskaya, an associate of the F. Skaryna National Center, has determined that the Belarusan commission did not take into account the losses of eight additional museums, including those in Bobruisk, Vitebsk, and Polotsk, and, strangely enough, the important historical museum in Mogilev which, according to the official version which was circulated for many years, had been plundered by the fascists.[1] Works of art preserved in the repositories of the state picture gallery of the BSSR were also not included in the commission's tally.

More than two hundred libraries of Belarus, especially the state (now the national) library, suffered irreparable damage during the occupation. An associate of the national library, T. Roshchina, calculated that 83 percent of the library's collection was plundered and destroyed. After the war some six hundred thousand volumes from this library were found in Germany, Poland, and Czechoslovakia, and were subsequently returned. About one million books, however, including rare and old printed volumes, have still not been located.[2]

During World War II, Belarusan collections were taken east as well as west. In 1939–40, expeditions from Moscow to Western Belarus (which had just merged with Eastern Belarus) removed valuable treasures from educational establishments and from private palaces and estates abandoned by their owners. Thirty thousand rare books and manuscripts from the Pinsk Catholic seminary[3] thus ended up in the central anti-religious museum in Moscow, and their fate is now unknown. An armchair made of deer horn was brought to Moscow from Nesvizh Castle as well as two ornamented chairs from the bishop's palace in Pinsk.[4] A delegation from the state historical museum in Moscow also took some paintings from the collections of the Mogilev and Minsk museums. In June–July 1941, exhibits from the Vitebsk and Gomel regional museums were brought (temporarily, of course) to Russia. The former ended up in Saratov and the latter went first to Uriupinsk and then to Stalingrad (now Volgograd). A list of valuable objects from the Gomel Museum, dated May 1946, has been preserved. It includes paintings, a marble sculpture by Leonardo da Vinci, three cast-iron and five bronze cannons, silver candlesticks, decorative boxes and cups, crosses, and medals. Postwar efforts to bring them back did not succeed.

The removal of cultural property from Belarus continued in the early postwar years, in particular in connection with the repatriation of the Polish population from the republic. Thus, a Novogrudok priest, Alexander Zenkevich, took with him a bound manuscript containing the birth records of the Polish poet Adam Mickiewicz (which are now in Częstochowa).[5] The paintings of the talented painter Lev Dobszynski, who lived in Losha (now the Grodno region), have also disappeared. Finally, the forced breakup of the collections of the Vilnius Belarusan Museum, which survived the occupation with almost no losses but could not withstand Stalinist totalitarianism during the first postwar year, was a huge loss to Belarusan culture.

It should also be noted that in the postwar years some Belarusan cultural property was returned from Germany to Russia: to Moscow, Novgorod, Leningrad (St. Petersburg), and other cities, but not to Belarus. This included two stone pagan idols, which had briefly adorned one of the parks in Berlin. Only a few works from the so-called Trophy Fund were subsequently returned to Minsk. One of the reasons for this was lack of access to the Trophy Fund archives.

With such huge losses of our national cultural property, it would have been logical to allocate considerable scholarly resources and state funds for their identification and return. But this has not been the case. In 1945–46, when the

Extraordinary Commission was functioning, only approximate estimates were made of the losses. In some cases the estimates were too low and in others they were excessively high. The question of restitution was, in fact, not put forward either then or later during the Cold War, and no efforts were made to provide a scholarly basis for such restitution. Today we must frankly and self-critically admit that during the long years of totalitarianism we were ashamed and even afraid to speak about our rights to the Belarusan cultural property that had been removed from Belarus (in particular, those objects that had ended up in Russia and Ukraine) as a result of military and other actions. Such patriotic aspirations were often labeled manifestations of nationalism, a failure to understand that everything in the USSR, including museum treasures, should belong to everyone—whereas in fact they belonged to no one. As a result, according to the calculations of M. Ianitskaya of the F. Skaryna National Center, losses of Belarus museums during the war were estimated at only 6 percent. Today we have concrete information about only 992 of the more than 11,000 objects listed in the documents of the Extraordinary Commission. The others are described only in a very summary manner.

For a long time in Belarus there was no state, or even public, body that dealt with issues of restitution. Investigation of losses remained the domain of a few isolated enthusiasts. It was only in 1989 that the Returns Commission, which I head, was created at the Belarus Cultural Foundation. I wish to emphasize that this is a public and not a state commission and receives no state funding. Nevertheless, in six years of work the Returns Commission has collected important factual material, prepared and published two books of documents and materials, and put forward several initiatives. As a result, the State Commission on Restitution was created at the Ministry of Culture in 1992, but since it is still dependent on private funding its effectiveness is limited. A research group financed by the Ministry of Culture was established at the F. Skaryna National Center. For over a year now, though, the State Commission on Restitution has ceased (or rather suspended) its activity, and the research group is no longer funded. It is true that individual studies are paid for by the State Commission on the Protection of the Historical and Cultural Heritage, headed by Dmitri Bubnovsky. In today's conditions of economic crisis, this commission alone deals with problems of restitution (the corresponding Belarus-Polish commission is working rather successfully). However, the financing of this commission is very limited. That is why I look with envy and even with a feeling of national inferiority at my Russian and Ukrainian colleagues, who represent high-level state bodies, while I only represent a public organization. Most important, their working conditions are much easier.

What should be done to keep Belarus from being a "white crow" in the area of restitution? I believe we must first of all establish an authoritative state body with a research group subordinate to it, whose primary task would be the identification of archival documents and prewar museum inventories and catalogues, which would give us the right to press for the return of lost cultural property. We have information that many of these inventories are in Moscow, but access to them is virtually closed to Belarusan researchers. Nor do we have the opportunity to work on the ERR holdings in the Federal Archive of Germany (Koblenz), which are of interest to us. However, we have not lost hope that this will be made possible. From known and as yet unknown inventories, we shall be able to create, albeit with some delay, a Belarus data bank closely linked to similar data banks in other countries. The first steps in this direction have already been taken. Thanks to the efforts of the art expert N. Vysotskaia, a partial list of the wartime losses of the Minsk art gallery (now the art museum) has been compiled. The data collected has been prepared for computerization (we hope for cooperation with private firms and foundations). Of course, here we also need professionals, including people who have been trained abroad.

We hope that as a result of further investigation, the fate of the treasures that disappeared from Mogilev, including the Cross of Euphrosyne of Polotsk, will finally come to light. For a while we thought that the cross was in the Pierpont Morgan Library, New York. In answer to an official inquiry, however, we received a reply in 1990 stating that this is not the case. Some reports then appeared in the Belarusan press based on personal recollections that the Mogilev treasures were evacuated in 1941 to a bank in Moscow, where Lavrentii Beriia himself gazed at them in amazement.[6] The "Moscow trail," however, does not exclude the "American trail." The cross and other valuable objects could have been used to pay for supplies or could have been sold abroad privately. Access to the relevant Moscow archive holdings would provide a clear, final answer.

While I am here in America, I should like to note that we are hoping for understanding and assistance from the United States on questions of restitution. A report appeared in the émigré press asserting that after the war the so-called Smolensk holdings ended up in the National Archives in Washington, D.C.,* together with the manuscripts of the Belarusan poet Vassily Koval. It would be very important to us to obtain xerographic copies or microfilms of these documents, as well as copies of the materials of the Polish folklorist and ethnographer Professor Józef Obrebski, which are now in the archives of the University of Massachusetts library. It would be important to study and publish them.

There is another important aspect to restitution. The return of cultural treasures can come about in various ways: through description, copying, publication, and exchange of exhibitions. While return in the literal and physical sense of the word is certainly preferable, the legal foundations and goodwill it requires do not always exist. Incidentally, we are counting on such goodwill in anticipating the return of the Khreptovich Library, which was temporarily removed to Kyiv

(Kiev); copies of F. Skaryna's publications, which are rare in Belarus but found abundantly in Moscow; and the Nesvizh portraits of the Radziwills, which the Belarus authorities illegally gave to B. Berut in 1950. Finally, we hope for a rebirth of the Vilnius Belarusan Museum in Lithuania. The people of Belarus, too, must show goodwill. Restitution is not a football match with only one set of goalposts. For example, we have demonstrated our goodwill by returning to Ukraine part of the library of Petlura and by giving back to Russia the Dutch trophy-book collection, which was later returned to the Netherlands.

Without disclosing all of our intentions, I would note that though we do have materials for exchange with Russia, France, and other countries, this requires the ratification and enactment of bilateral and multilateral agreements. It also requires that questions of restitution be taken into account in the signing of treaties among states and, finally, that an agreement be signed between all countries of the Commonwealth of Independent States and all European countries. Without going into detail, I shall note that Belarus has done considerable work on drawing up such an agreement. We believe that the return of national treasures, which in the past was the domain of a handful of enthusiasts, now under new conditions, conditions of a sovereign Belarus, will become a concern of the state, a part of state policy, and will serve the cause of our Belarusan national renaissance.

---

* Editor's note: According to Patricia Grimsted (see below, pages 246, 251), over five hundred files of the Communist Party Archives of Smolenskaia oblast' are still held in the National Archives in Washington, D.C.

THE DOCUMENTATION

OF WAR LOSSES

IN THE FORMER

SOVIET REPUBLICS

Marlene P. Hiller

The German troops who attacked the Soviet Union in the early hours of June 22, 1941, brought devastation to that land. The western parts of the USSR suffered huge losses in both human and economic terms. Damage was also inflicted on the Soviet cultural heritage on an unprecedented scale.

Loss of cultural treasures to this extent was new to modern European warfare. It is therefore all the more astonishing that it took so long for the academic community as well as the institutions concerned and the public to become interested in the matter. For almost four decades, dust was allowed to settle—often quite literally—on the archival documentation of these losses, as well as on at least some of the cultural objects under discussion. Memories of eyewitnesses have been allowed to fade. It is high time to recover whatever information can still be obtained. This is the task that we have tried to tackle since 1992 in close cooperation with Russian, Ukrainian, and American historians and art historians at the Research Institute for Eastern Europe attached to the University of Bremen.

I propose to put forward a set of five points that may help to outline the problems and possibly provoke further investigation into some of the lacunae that still exist with regard to our knowledge about who appropriated cultural treasures from Soviet museums, libraries, archives, and so forth, between 1941 and 1944; where these objects were taken and what happened during transport; who recovered them; and what happened to them in the period from 1945 to about 1950.

Since we are all too much inclined to reduce the problem to attractive paintings and icons, let me stress right at the beginning that the term "cultural treasures" embraces a wide variety of objects. Their origins and values differ widely, and they were coveted for many different reasons. They include:

- library collections (including up to one hundred thousand geographical maps), which were taken on ideological grounds, for academic research, as means for political, geographical, and economic information on Soviet cities and regions, or as collectors' items; the same can be said for archival material;
- museum artifacts: folk art, furniture, ceramics, coins, stamps, and so forth;
- scientific collections of such materials as medicinal plants, and natural-history exhibits, as, for example, lepidopterists' specimens;
- archaeological material from museums and university institutes and from the archaeological excavations that were undertaken through the war in the occupied territories;
- religious objects and ceremonial art of both Christian and Jewish communities;
- musical instruments, of which more than thirteen thousand were taken;
- architectural fragments and parts of monuments, such as the fountain from Peterhof, outside Leningrad (now St. Petersburg), or the bronze doors from the cathedral of Novgorod, which were claimed as masterpieces produced by German craftsmen.

And then there are, of course, the art treasures, about which we heard in the symposium that is documented here.

First point

In a general way, "loss" simply means that an object is no longer available in its former location, and perhaps also that its whereabouts are unknown. With regard to World War II, losses therefore resulted from: (1) destruction or major damage that occurred as a result of war, willful destruction by German forces, and sabotage actions of Soviet forces; (2) dislocation and eventual disappearance of these objects in the course of hasty evacuations in 1941; (3) organized shipments to Germany by various institutions, in particular by the Einsatzstab Reichs-leiter Rosenberg (ERR), by the Sonderkommando Künsberg of the Ministry of Foreign Affairs, and by Heinrich Himmler's Ahnenerbe. Not all of these objects were restored to their proper places by American or Soviet forces after the war; (4) failure to return objects to their proper places of origin once they were restituted: we know, for example, of archival material that has been in Kyiv (Kiev) since 1945–46 but is still listed as missing from Minsk; we also know of books in one St. Petersburg palace that are on the missing list of another, and so on; (5) private plunder by army or civilian personnel in the occupied territories of Eastern Europe during the last weeks of the war or during the restitution process.

Second point

Taking into account these different types of losses, we have no choice but to accept as final all those of the first category. The surfacing of objects of the last category, meanwhile, will be a matter of pure chance, although I am very happy indeed to be able to report some instances of private returns from German citizens to libraries and museums in the former Soviet republics. Efforts to locate missing cultural treasures must of necessity therefore concentrate *exclusively* on objects in the second, third, and fourth categories. This implies, however, that these efforts will have to take place in no small part within Russia, Ukraine, Belarus, and the Baltic republics themselves.

Third point

Pursuing this line of argument even further, we must differen-tiate between two types of documentation, each of which serves a different purpose and therefore requires its own method of assembling data: (a) the historical documentation of all wartime cultural losses in order to demonstrate the over-whelming extent of cultural losses during World War II; and (b) the precise and detailed documentation of those treasures that we can still hope to locate and consequently return.

Fourth point

A look at the archival material and other sources available for documentary purposes gives some grounds for optimism. German military and civilian documentation is, on the whole, fairly detailed, and much of it has survived the war. Some important documentation has surfaced only recently in Russian, Ukrainian, and Latvian *spetsfondy,* or special archives—that is, secret archival depots—and others are now being opened to the academic community in former East German archives.

With the help of these records we can in many cases recon-struct fairly adequate descriptions of local conditions (for example, to what extent buildings and collections were damaged and what evacuation measures were undertaken by Soviet institutions). We also learn a lot about the shipment of cultural objects to Germany.

In the beginning, only certain categories were transported to the Reich, mainly to Berlin. In particular, this was material confiscated for so-called research on problems related to the Nazi Weltanschauung, that is, for the most part Jewish, Bolshevik, and Freemasonic material, as well as works that could be used to prove early Germanic *grandeur* in the East. Most exhibits and collection pieces, however, were left on the spot—after all, the Germans meant to stay. When the receding Eastern Front, however, forced even the most dogmatic civil servants, party functionaries, and academics to accept the fact that the Eastern and Central European territories most definitely would not hold, increasingly hasty shipments of almost any-thing anybody considered valuable for whatever reason were organized. The objects were mostly stored in depots that could provide shelter against air raids and were consequently located in rural Bavaria, Austria, Saxony, Bohemia, and Silesia.

American officers attached to the MFA&A (Monuments, Fine Arts, and Archives section of the American military government) were literally overwhelmed by the millions of cultural objects with which they had to cope, scattered about western and southern Germany, Austria, and Bohemia in more than two thousand depots. Documentation on this is freely available, albeit of a patchy nature (especially with regard to the first weeks or months after the war ended). Personnel problems in American archives apart, this seems to be due to the sometimes unsystematic and surprising manner of filing World War II records. Nevertheless, these records allow us to draw a fairly accurate picture of most facets of United States involvement in the restitution policy in force after 1945.

Unfortunately, the same cannot be said for the documen-tation of Soviet policy. And this is of the utmost importance, since the Red Army in its forward thrust toward Berlin captured many German depots filled with plundered and evacuated cultural objects. So far, we are not in a position to document this; neither can we say much about what happened to these objects once they were returned to the Soviet Union. The records essential to an understanding of the situation— in particular, those of the six SVAG-*fondy,* special archives documenting the politics of the Soviet Military Administration in Germany (SMAG, or, in Russian, SVAG)—remain closed to academic researchers even today. In contrast, we can by now document the Soviet evacuation process in 1941 fairly well.

Fifth point

Documentation of losses necessarily involves dealing in numbers. Trying to evaluate the quantity of missing cultural objects is at best a tricky affair; in some cases it tends toward pure speculation. As an example of this, one might quote the 100–200 million objects that at the Nuremberg trials the

Soviet Union claimed to have lost. But even systematic efforts to assess the quantities involved quickly run into trouble.

As already mentioned, fairly detailed information on specific regions or cities can be ascertained from the German records; however, these records provide no basis for an overall quantitative analysis. To complement the picture, we must check the information gained from the German documents against that from Allied documentation on the depots found in 1945 and the restitution or other redistribution measures that followed (so far, as mentioned above, most of this documentation comes from United States sources, whereas Soviet records on this specific type of postwar politics unfortunately still remain inaccessible). We should then compare and cross-check this information with museum, library, and archival documentation from before 1941 as available in catalogues, inventories, and so forth, and with present-day inventories of the same institutions. This elaborate process is necessary not least because of the enormous problems caused by the fact that not all objects returned to the USSR in the 1940s were returned to their rightful owners. (To give another example: we are able to trace a valuable private collection from Riga—where it was seized by ERR officials—to Ratibor [Racibórz] in Silesia—where the Red Army took control in February 1945—to Vilnius and then, reportedly, to Minsk, with, for a very long time, none of the owners in Riga being the wiser regarding the fate of this collection.)

It is obvious even to the most uninformed observer that a thorough evaluation of the historical processes involves massive research, most of which has only just begun. Some data, however, is already available, and some gaps, outlined below, can be clearly identified.

United States documentation shows that 534,120 items were restituted to the Soviet Union from the American Zone of Occupation between 1945 and 1950. This included whatever was found in depots or Reich institutions, and also the more than twenty-four thousand objects turned over to the Americans by private German citizens in the spring of 1946, having been looted during the war.

About one million books that were still at the Offenbach Archival Depot in 1946 were never returned to the USSR because of a U.S. decision not to repatriate unclaimed Jewish property, property of the Baltic republics (whose annexation by the Soviet Union was not recognized), or that of exile groups and institutions like the Cossacks or the Russian Orthodox Church (see Kurtz, below, pages 115–16 and note 49). The same is true of a much smaller quantity (probably not more than ten thousand items) of ceremonial and other objects and of archival material.

While we can assume with some accuracy that up to three or four million books were shipped at various stages from the Soviet Union to the Reich, and while we also know that about two million of those fell back into Soviet hands in 1945 in Ratibor, we have no documentation on what happened to them afterward. (Since, for instance, the Lenin Library in Minsk got about six hundred thousand books back in 1946, we must assume that they were at least in part shipped back to the Soviet Union, but we cannot document the process.)

Soviet accounts of their losses go back to those established by the Extraordinary State Commission on the Registration and Investigation of the Crimes of the German-Fascist Occupiers. This commission counted 564,723 art treasures from seventy-three major museums as either destroyed or missing (283,782 of which were Ukrainian, 157,827 Russian, 14,750 Belarusan, 507 Latvian, and 1,016 Lithuanian); as far as we know, in only a few cases did these lists take into account that there had indeed been instances of restitution. Accounts of books missing range from 20 million to 200 million. As we heard at the Bard Graduate Center symposium, new efforts to evaluate losses are on the way. Obviously, we await the results with great interest.

Whatever the precise numbers of the losses, there can be no doubt that of all former Soviet republics the Ukraine suffered most: according to Soviet estimates, approximately 61 percent of all art treasures that were lost belonged to Ukrainian institutions—as against 35 percent from Russian, 3 percent from Belarusan, and 1 percent from Baltic ones. A quantitative analysis of the Property Cards from the files of the American Collecting Points, which redistributed looted objects, more or less bears this out. Nonetheless, we must take into account certain particulars. For instance, Belarusan libraries were plundered of 95 percent of their holdings, and so far we have no means of establishing how much was returned after the war.

In conclusion, I want to stress that we are still at the beginning with regard to the documentation of Eastern European cultural losses during World War II. While we are about to unravel quite successfully a lot of what actually happened (that is the perspective of a historian), precise documentation of individual losses has still only just started. Many of the problems involved in both these efforts have, however, no chance of being solved without close cooperation between researchers of all countries involved. Such cooperation is what the Bremen Research Institute for Eastern Europe stands for. We gladly welcome any proposition to join us in this effort.

JEWISH CEREMONIAL ART

AND

PRIVATE PROPERTY

Vivian B. Mann

One might assume, given the uniform aim of Nazi policy toward the Jews of Europe, that German policy in regard to Jewish holdings of art was also uniform.[1] In fact, this was not the case. The histories of three communities will illustrate the varying fates of Jewish communal holdings in lands ruled by the Nazis. The fate of private collections of art is another matter that will be considered later.

BOHEMIA AND MORAVIA

Before the Second World War, there were 153 Jewish communities of varying size in Bohemia and Moravia, lands that are now part of the Czech Republic. The first documentary mention of Jews in Bohemia dates to the tenth century;[2] during the sixteenth century the Jewish population of Prague doubled, making it one of the largest Jewish communities of the period. Over time, the Jewish community as a whole and its individual members played significant roles in the development of Bohemian and Moravian culture, and many of its members were at the forefront of the revival of Czech culture in the modern period.[3]

In 1906, Dr. Salomon Lieben (1881–1942), a historian in Prague, became concerned about the fate of ritual objects from synagogues destroyed during urban-renewal campaigns in the Jewish quarter of his city. With community support, he established a small Jewish museum and published a catalogue which included works such as the pewter Jewish Butchers' Guild Emblem of 1620 (fig. 31).[4] By the eve of World War II, there were approximately twenty-five hundred works of art and books in the Prague Jewish Museum, and other Jewish museums had been established—in Prešov, Mikulov (Nikolsburg), and Košice.

In 1942, Reinhard Heydrich, the Deputy Reich Protector of Bohemia and Moravia, established the Central Bureau for Dealing with the Jewish Question in Bohemia and Moravia. SS officer Karl Rahm was put in charge of the newly retitled Central Jewish Museum, and an order was issued to confiscate Jewish property in Bohemia and Moravia. As the Nazis depopulated the countryside of its Jewish inhabitants, the contents of Jewish homes and synagogues were sent to Prague. This is a point that bears emphasis. The confiscation of Jewish art holdings, as terrible as that may have been, was accompanied at every stage by the destruction of their owners. A people was systematically killed as its art was robbed. This terrible fact differentiates the Jewish experience from that of other peoples conquered by Germany.

31. Emblem of the Jewish Butchers' Guild, Prague. 1620 (restored 1841 and 1866). Pewter, cast and engraved, 113.5 x 35 cm (45 x 13¾"). Jewish Museum, Prague

32. Paintings in the storeroom of the Jewish Museum, Prague. 1942–45

As the Jews of Prague were sent to their death in the camps, the buildings of the community, including the synagogues, became warehouses: one building for household linens, another filled with Torah curtains and books, and another with synagogue and domestic silver. All of these objects were added to the holdings of the small, prewar Jewish Museum.

While lives were being snuffed out every day, eight Jewish curators and their helpers catalogued the tens of thousands of ceremonial objects coming into their storerooms, their dates of arrival coinciding with dates of deportation from Bohemian and Moravian cities and towns. The curators meticulously measured in millimeters, weighed silver in grams, described volutes and rococo ornaments, recorded provenances and silver marks.[5] In short, they did everything possible to record the information embodied in works of art concerning a culture and a people in the hour of their destruction.

The accounts of curatorial staff meetings during the war are equally remarkable.[6] The Nazis ordered exhibitions intended to show the perversity of Jewish life, which were to be viewed only by German personnel. Jewish curators spent hours devising the means by which the ethics and humanity of Judaism would be elucidated by the exhibits.[7] A section on the thirteenth-century Altneu Synagogue and its stylistic parallels in Bohemian Gothic architecture was a brave, if not pathetic, attempt to portray Jews as an integral part of Czech history.

The result of the Nazis' preservation of Jewish art is a collection whose numbers are staggering: twenty-five hundred Torah curtains, four thousand mantles or covers for the Torah, fifteen hundred binders to hold the Torah scrolls together, one thousand pairs of silver finials to decorate the staves of Torah scrolls, and so forth. Equally striking is what is missing from this collection. There are, for example, thirty-four pairs of candlesticks. This number is far too small to reflect a Jewish population of over three hundred thousand in Bohemia and Moravia before the war, since Jewish households inaugurate the Sabbath and festivals through the kindling of lights.

Or consider the paintings held by the Prague Jewish Museum (fig. 32), largely portraits of Jews and scenes of Jewish sites. Where are the other paintings, the other candlesticks, of the 153 prewar Jewish communities? Confiscated, no doubt, by individuals or German agencies who saw in generic objects and paintings of secular subjects something to add to their own possessions, or resources to be used to satisfy the Reich's need for cash, like the mound of gold wedding rings documented in wartime photographs.[8]

In a perverse way, German policy regarding Jewish communal and personal property in Bohemia and Moravia was constructive. An immense body of art was saved and, thanks to the curators who cared for this collection, a great deal of information regarding these works of art exists. Following the war, the museum was returned to a Jewish community that was enfeebled and decimated. Only fifteen thousand Czech Jews remained out of a population of over three hundred thousand. Unable to care for the museum, the community ceded it to the communist government in 1949. Only in 1994 did ownership of the collections revert again to a strengthened Jewish community.

DANZIG

The second case is that of the Jewish community of Danzig, today Gdańsk, Poland. For most of its history, Danzig's Jewish community was rather ordinary and relatively insignificant.[9] Then, in its final hour, an inspired leadership saw an opportunity for escape in the unusual political status of this Free City, and the Jewish community of Danzig became unique in the annals of European Jewry, the only Jewish community to voluntarily dissolve itself in an attempt to save, in their entirety, its people, its history, and its art.[10]

In many ways, the now lost Jewish community of Danzig was similar to other German Jewish communities. It had a relatively prosperous population that contributed to the political, social, and intellectual life of the city. The five synagogues existing in the early nineteenth century were unified into a single *Gemeinde,* or community, in 1883, finally complying with a Prussian law promulgated in 1847. Both the prominence of the community and its prosperity were symbolized by the building of the Great Synagogue of Danzig in 1887 (fig. 33). Originally, the architect had planned to place the building within a walled courtyard, but the mayor declared that the Jews of Danzig did not have to hide themselves, and the Great Synagogue was built fronting on a main thoroughfare.

An unusual aspect of Danzig Jewish life was the existence of a small museum in a room of the Great Synagogue. Established by the noted art connoisseur Lesser Gieldzinski in 1904, the Jewish Museum in Danzig was preceded only by the Jewish Museum of Vienna, organized in 1898.[11]

After World War I, Danzig's dual relationship with Germany and Poland led to its classification as a Free City under the supervision of the League of Nations.[12] As a result, there were no visa requirements in its port, and sixty thousand East Europeans journeyed through the city on their way to a safe

33. Interior of the Great Synagogue, Danzig (now Gdańsk). Built in 1887

refuge. In 1933, the rise of the Nazi party in Danzig resulted in increasing pressure on the Danzig Jewish community, whose members themselves began to emigrate. By November 1938, 4,500 Jews remained, out of an original population of 10,448. Of those still in the city, 3,000 had means enough to leave on their own.

On the night of December 17, 1938, two thousand members of the community met in the Great Synagogue. Spurred on by perceptive and eloquent leaders, they voted to sell all communal property to finance the emigration of remaining members of the community. With the cooperation of the Danzig city government, the community's archives were sent to Jerusalem; its real estate, including the Great Synagogue, was sold at a fraction of its value; and the synagogue building was dismantled brick by brick. The collection of ceremonial objects from the two active synagogues and the Gieldzinski museum were "sold," in return for funds to finance emigration, to the Joint Distribution Committee, an American-Jewish organization founded to aid refugees. On July 26, 1939, ten crates weighing over two tons arrived at the Jewish Theological Seminary in Manhattan accompanied by a letter stipulating that if, after fifteen years, there were no safe and free Jews in Danzig, the collection would remain in America for the education and inspiration of the world.[13] On September 1, 1939, the Germans invaded Poland, and Danzig became part of the Third Reich.

As a result of efforts by its farsighted leadership, the Danzig Jewish community saved nearly all of its members, with the exception of a few hundred elderly and infirm. The community also saved its tangible heritage, bequeathing to The Jewish Museum in New York the only single Jewish communal collection to survive the Second World War intact. The collection embodies a treasure of information about the history of Danzig silversmithing, patterns of patronage, and the taste of a Jewish community influenced by both the art of Germany and the art of Poland (colorplate 5).

WORMS

Had the first two case histories been typical, there would have been less reason to include the next topic in this essay on the spoils of war. Both of the histories cited document saved collections: one by dint of the Nazis' desire to establish a "Museum of the Extinct Jewish Race" in Prague, and one by dint of Jewish efforts to save a community's heritage. All the other Jewish communities of Europe suffered a different, harsher fate. Their treasures were looted by government agencies or by individuals and torn from their places of origin and use. Even those that survived the war could be traced to the synagogue, library, or school from which they were taken only in the rare instances when an inscription indicating origin or a careful caretaker's notes or photographs could be found.

The community and synagogue of Worms may be taken as an example of the common fate. During the eleventh century, the great teacher Rabbi Solomon son of Isaac (known as Rashi; 1040–1105) was head of the yeshiva, the advanced school of Jewish studies, housed in a building adjacent to the synagogue. Like many of his contemporaries, Rashi supported himself as a viticulturist, but it was not his achievements as a winegrower that assured the fame of the Worms Jewish community; rather it was Rashi's extensive commentaries on the Bible and the Talmud, which are still studied today. The synagogue was completed shortly before his birth, in 1034, and in the 1930s was the oldest surviving synagogue in Germany until Kristallnacht, the night of November 9–10, 1938, when it was totally destroyed.[14]

Before the war, the relatively small Worms community owned the following works of silver ceremonial art:[15]

1. a Renaissance goblet, dated 1609 (still extant);
2. a wine decanter, dated 1686 (lost);
3. a wine decanter belonging to the Burial Society, dated 1710;
4. two hexagonal beakers belonging to the Burial Society (colorplate 6). The first, dated 1711–12, was created by the Nuremberg silversmith Johann Conrad Weiss (active 1699–1751), and the second, dated by inscription to about 1732, appears to be a local Worms copy of the first. Not only are these beakers interesting examples of the silversmith's art, but their inscriptions record the history of the community through the names of members of the brotherhood charged with care of the sick, the dead, and the bereaved during the first half of the eighteenth century. Pride of place on the first beaker is given to the name of Samson Wertheimer (1658–1724), the Viennese Court Jew who was born in Worms and who donated the beaker to the Burial Society. These last items, the decanter and the two beakers of the Worms Burial Society, were saved through the individual initiative of a member of the community, who hid them throughout the war. They are today in The Jewish Museum, New York;[16]
5. a pair of beakers for use at weddings, made at Augsburg c. 1800 (lost);
6. a pitcher and basin for ritual hand washing, made at Augsburg c. 1700 (lost);
7. seven Torah shields, plaques placed over the staves of the scrolls, dated 1700–1856 (a single shield remains);
8. nine pairs of Torah finials from the seventeenth and

eighteenth centuries (a fragment of one seventeenth-century pair is extant);

9. five pointers for following the Torah reading, from the eighteenth and nineteenth centuries (two eighteenth-century examples remain).

Important works in other mediums included:

1. more than thirty Torah scrolls. The oldest of these was written by the great medieval sage Rabbi Meir of Rothenburg, who died in prison in 1293 for refusing to abjure his faith and was buried in Worms. Other early scrolls were dated 1643, 1650, and 1689. The extant portions of all but two of these, which remain in Worms, were sent to Jerusalem, along with an outstanding, illuminated Festival Prayer Book dated to the thirteenth century;

2. textiles, as follows: five silk and brocade Torah curtains, hangings before the Ark doors, existed before the war: one dated 1678, then the oldest extant in Germany; one dated 1698; another dated 1737, donated by Lob Segal Sinzheim, Court Jew in Vienna; and three unusual types—one for use on the New Moon, the beginning of Hebrew months, dated 1744; a curtain used at circumcisions; and a curtain hung on the occasion of weddings held in the synagogue. Only fragments of these elaborate textile compositions remained after Kristallnacht. The earliest curtains, from the Middle Ages, had been destroyed in a fire in 1615;

3. over six hundred Torah binders—the oldest collection extant before the war, the earliest example dated 1570—whose inscriptions were an invaluable demographic record of the community. (Today, thirteen remain in Worms; two are in Jerusalem);

4. a copper washing vessel from the forecourt of the synagogue, dating from the sixteenth century (lost);

5. the iron doors of the Ark, dated about 1350, among the oldest extant examples of Worms ironwork (one panel extant).

The example of Worms, a small but very prestigious community, should be multiplied by the thousands of European Jewish communities destroyed by the Nazis. After the war, works that could be assigned to a particular place returned to communities that survived. But most extant ceremonial art and the millions of books and archives robbed from Jewish institutions were "heirless": their owners killed; their institutions dissolved with the collapse of communities to maintain them.

Even before the war was over, the American Conference on Jewish Social Studies appointed a commission to explore ways of saving the cultural heritage of European Jewry. Under the leadership of Professor Salo Baron of Columbia University, the commission researched, as much as possible, works known to have belonged to Jewish institutions through published reports, interviews with displaced personnel, and press reports. The result was "The Tentative Lists of Jewish Cultural Treasures in Axis-Occupied Countries," published in 1946. The following year, the Jewish Cultural Reconstruction was formed to distribute archives, books, manuscripts, and ceremonial and fine arts that had originally belonged to Jews or their institutions and were now heirless property.[17] At one point, the JCR depot in Offenbach, Germany, held half a million books, as well as nearly eight thousand ceremonial objects and 1,024 Torah scrolls. These were distributed to institutions in Europe, South Africa, South America, Israel, and the United States by January 31, 1952. Distribution efforts in America were based in The Jewish Museum, New York.

PERSONAL HOLDINGS

Reports published even before the end of the war manifest an awareness of the breadth and depth of the Germans' looting of art treasures, especially those owned by Jews.[18] In Germany, shortly after Kristallnacht, museum officials were informed of the imminent confiscations of art belonging to Jews, which was to be stored in the Bavarian National Museum. The special attention paid to privately owned Jewish collections in conquered territories was acknowledged later by the pseudonymous writer George Mihan in his remarks on the situation in France published in 1944: "Jewish art collections came first. Under Rosenberg's personal supervision wagon loads of paintings, sculptures, tapestries and other objects of artistic value were stolen from Jewish houses and sent to Germany. It did not matter to the Nazis whether they were robbing Jews who were French citizens, foreigners . . . or people denationalised by . . . Vichy; the Germans broke into their homes and carried off whatever excited their cupidity."[19] The holdings of the many Jewish-owned art galleries in Paris were a special target; some gallery owners were able to hide portions of their stock or to send pieces abroad, which enabled them to start over after the war.

Occasionally, local authorities forestalled Nazi confiscation. The day after Kristallnacht, Maximilian von Goldschmidt-Rothschild sold his art collection to the city of Frankfurt for 2.3 million Reichsmarks. Yet, after the war, the city government of Frankfurt exchanged all of the illuminated Hebrew manuscripts in the municipal library for a parcel of downtown property, owned by a Jew, that the city had targeted for new roads, thus removing the manuscripts from the public domain to this day.

As a curator in a Jewish museum, I have heard many individual stories of works once owned, then irretrievably lost; of pieces whose ownership was documented before and during the war, so that afterward its rightful Jewish owner was able to claim the work from a German museum; of paintings lost for fifty years, whose owners never gave up hope and who eventually repossessed cherished works.

In 1985, a list of still unclaimed artistic property held by Austrian government agencies was published.[20] It included 655 paintings, 82 miniatures, 280 drawings including two by Michelangelo, 41 sculptures, fine furniture, tapestries, porcelain, ceramics, glass, arms, textiles, rugs, coins and medals, documents, theater literature, and so forth. The deadline for all individual claims was September 30, 1986, later extended.[21]

As we begin the fiftieth year since the end of World War II, the likelihood of successful claims by Jews or Jewish institutions grows dim. We are forced to recognize that the artistic patrimony of European Jewry will forever be represented by mere remnants of its past glory scattered in museums and private collections throughout the world.

AUSTRIA

Gerhard Sailer

Considering the fact that Austria was in the immediate combat area, the country suffered astonishingly few losses of movable cultural heritage during World War II, apart from the extensive damage to buildings and monuments.

The Austrian losses of cultural heritage during and after the Second World War have two causes, apart from the immediate effects of hostilities: (1) the so-called borrowing of art treasures from Austrian museums and monasteries for the furnishing of National Socialist administrative offices; (2) the transfer of art treasures for security reasons to monasteries, churches, castles, and palaces far from the major cities.

As regards the treasures removed by the Nazis, the following important works of art will serve as examples.

As early as 1938, Vienna's Kunsthistorisches Museum was obliged to "lend" tapestries to the Reich Chancellery in Berlin, to the Gauleitung (district administration) of Lower Silesia in Breslau, and to Karinhall (Hermann Göring's country estate in Brandenburg-Schorfheide). In the course of investigations as to the whereabouts of the tapestries in 1973–75, two of the Kunsthistorisches Museum's tapestries sent to Breslau in 1941 were found in the Warsaw National Museum in Poland. The People's Republic of Poland returned these two tapestries in 1983 with the comment that they had been "received from Russia." The question arises as to the present whereabouts of the third tapestry lent to Breslau: *Alexander in Battle and the Capture of Darius's Family* (Brussels, sixteenth century). The further question arises as to whether the three series of wall hangings lent to the Reich Chancellery in Berlin may have been taken to Russia and possibly have remained there until this day. We are concerned here with the following tapestries:[1]

The Life of Alexander the Great (Dutch, seventeenth century)

The series consists of eight pieces after paintings by Charles Le Brun, and cartoons made from the paintings for the Gobelins factory in Paris; without city or master mark:

1. *The Battle on the River Granicus*
   415 cm high x 810 cm wide
2. *The Battle at Arbela* (left portion)
   415 cm high x 319 cm wide
3. *Alexander Rages against King Darius's Chariot* (middle portion)
   415 cm high x 775 cm wide
4. *Alexander and Hephaestion in the Tent of Darius's Imprisoned Family*
   412 cm high x 573 cm wide
5. *Alexander Defeats King Porus* (left portion: fig. 34)
   415 cm high x 275 cm wide (the inventory gives the width incorrectly as 675 cm)
6. *King Porus Brought before Alexander* (middle portion: fig. 35)
   410 cm high x 520 cm wide
7. *Alexander Defeats King Porus* (right portion)
   415 cm high x 290 cm wide
8. *Alexander Enters Babylon in Triumph*
   415 cm high x 750 cm wide

34. *Alexander Defeats King Porus.* Seventeenth-century Dutch tapestry, one of a series of eight based on cartoons made for the Gobelins factory, Paris, after paintings by Charles Le Brun; without city or master mark. 415 x 275 cm (162⅜ x 108¼″). Removed from the Kunsthistorisches Museum, Vienna, as a "loan" to the Reich Chancellery in Berlin. Present whereabouts unknown

35. *King Porus Brought before Alexander.* Seventeenth-century Dutch tapestry, one of a series of eight based on cartoons made for the Gobelins factory, Paris, after paintings by Charles Le Brun; without city or master mark. 410 x 520 cm (161½ x 204¾″). Removed from the Kunsthistorisches Museum, Vienna, as a "loan" to the Reich Chancellery in Berlin. Present whereabouts unknown

Scenes from the Life of Decius Mus (Brussels, seventeenth century)

The series consists of five pieces with the city mark of Brussels, woven in the seventeenth century after cartoons by P. P. Rubens:

1. *Decius Mus Tells His Dream*
   374 cm high x 395 cm wide
2. *The Consecration of Decius Mus*
   374 cm high x 380 cm wide
3. *Decius Mus Takes Leave of the Lictors*
   374 cm high x 400 cm wide
4. *The Death of Decius Mus*
   370 cm high x 540 cm wide
5. *The Funeral*
   374 cm high x 567 cm wide

Scenes from the Life of Dido and Aeneas (Antwerp, seventeenth century)

The series consists of eight pieces woven in the seventeenth century by M. Wauters, after cartoons by Giovanni Francesco Romanelli:

1. *Venus and Aeneas*
   416 cm high x 375 cm wide; marked: M. W.
2. *Dido's Banquet*
   416 cm high x 643 cm wide; with an inscription on the bottom margin: LOF PRYS ENDE ER ZY VL—ALLE CONST BEMINDERS— M.W.
3. *Dido Sacrifices a Bull in the Temple of Juno*
   410 cm high x 498 cm wide; marked on the left of the picture: J.F. ROMANELLUS and, bottom right: M. WAVTERS
4. *Dido Shows Aeneas the Plan of the Palace under Construction*
   416 cm high x 568 cm wide; marked: M.W.
5. *Dido and Aeneas Flee before the Storm*
   414 cm high x 453 cm wide
6. *Mercury Urges Aeneas to Continue His Journey*
   420 cm high x 373 cm wide
7. *Aeneas Bids Farewell to Dido*
   415 cm high x 438 cm wide; marked: M. WAVTERS
8. *The Death of Dido*
   415 cm high x 511 cm wide

All three series were handed over to the Reich Chancellery against a borrower's receipt dated February 27, 1939. They disappeared at the end of the war.

In addition, the present whereabouts of two series of wall hangings lent to Karinhall in 1939,[2] the property of the Vienna Kunsthistorisches Museum, are still unknown, namely:

Hunting Scenes (Brussels, mid-seventeenth century)

These six tapestries were woven from sketches by Peter Paul Rubens. All the pieces bear the city mark and the signature of the weaver Daniel Eggermans.

1. *Diana and Her Retinue at the Hunt*
   365 cm high x 680 cm wide
2. *Bear Hunt*
   365 cm high x 700 cm wide
3. *The Death of Adonis* (fig. 36)
   365 cm high x 285 cm wide
4. *Hunting the Caledonian Boar*
   365 cm high x 640 cm wide

36. *The Death of Adonis.* Mid-seventeenth-century Flemish tapestry, one of a series woven from sketches by P. P. Rubens. Marked with the city mark of Brussels and the name of the weaver Daniel Eggermans. 365 x 685 cm (143¾ x 269⅝″). Removed from the Kunsthistorisches Museum, Vienna, as a "loan" to Karinhall, Göring's country estate near Berlin. Present whereabouts unknown

5. *Moors Hunt a Wild Bull*
   365 cm high x 933 cm wide
6. *Lion and Leopard Hunt*
   365 cm high x 644 cm wide

Hunting Scenes (Brussels, mid-eighteenth century)

The series consists of three pieces, all marked with the city mark of Brussels and the name of the weaver Frans van der Borght.

1. *Hunters with Hounds*
   407 cm high x 563 cm wide
2. *Two Hunters and Their Dogs Bring a Boar to Bay*
   407 cm high x 285 cm wide
3. *A Boar Throwing a Youth to the Ground* (*Adonis's Death*)
   407 cm high x 660 cm wide

In the case of the art collection of the Kunsthistorisches Museum, the works of art that had to be lent to the Reich Chancellery in Berlin were, above all, of high artistic and historical value—among them paintings by Angelica Kauffmann personally acquired by Emperor Joseph II. It would be beyond the scope of this paper to print here a list of the paintings that were taken, but the Kunsthistorisches Museum can make one available. It is also possible to obtain similar lists of the historical weapons taken from the Kunsthistorisches Museum, as well as of the losses of the Österreichisches Museum für Angewandte Kunst (Austrian Museum of Applied Arts), and of the Österreichische Galerie in the Belvedere in Vienna.

We know for certain that there are 560 Persian Pahlevi papyri and parchment scrolls in the State Hermitage Museum in St. Petersburg that had been sent by the Austrian National Library to the Egyptian Museum in Berlin in 1936 for restoration purposes. The director of the State Hermitage Museum, Dr. Mikhail Piotrovsky, has already expressed his willingness to return the collection,[3] which has been kept wrapped carefully in its original covers; it is the bureaucracy that has as yet to implement a successful restitution.

During the time that the St. Florian monastery in Upper Austria was administered by the National Socialist Gauleitung and the Reichsrundfunkanstalt (State Radio Institute), paintings (for example Bruegel's *The Burning of Rotterdam*),

copperplate etchings (for example, by Adam Scultori after Michelangelo), and tapestry table and chair covers all just "disappeared." Just after the war, valuable furniture that had been confiscated on the orders of the notorious National Socialist Gauleiter August Eigruber disappeared from the Upper Austrian monastery at Kremsmünster.

Much of the Austrian cultural heritage that had been hidden for reasons of safety throughout the war—in monasteries, churches, castles, and palaces (including the original furnishings of such buildings)—was lost immediately before and as a result of the end of hostilities because the Allied occupation forces, needing living quarters and office accommodation, ordered the re-storing of salvaged goods. This was often carried out hastily and without expert knowledge, so that cultural objects were stacked in unsuitable rooms and even out of doors. Constant re-storing led, for example, to the almost total loss of the art collection of the composer Richard Strauss. In some cases, stored museum pieces and the furnishings of castles taken for use in offices and soldiers' quarters were destroyed by unsuitable use. As a result of thoughtlessness and a "couldn't care less attitude" on the part of supervisory staff, looting was facilitated and soldiers, former prisoners of war, and the local population were easily able to "serve themselves"—and this they did.

Some wanton destruction also took place. A perfidious high point was reached on May 8, 1945, when, without any military necessity, a unit of the SS Division "Feldherrnhalle" blew up the castle at Immendorf in northeastern Lower Austria, completely destroying the building and its particularly valuable contents, which included an important private art collection, stored there since 1943, together with objects from Vienna's Österreichisches Museum für Angewandte Kunst and Österreichische Galerie (including works by Gustav Klimt).

Contrary to the situation in Germany, no officially sanctioned removal of cultural goods as war booty took place in Austria after the end of the Second World War. The reason for this obviously lies in the Moscow Declaration of October 30, 1943, in which the Allies declared Austria to have been a victim of aggression in 1938. Furthermore, the personal attitude and actions of individual officers of the Allied forces brought about the return of stored cultural goods to their original locations. This applied to the Western Allies (of whom I shall speak later) as well as the Soviet side, where, for example, considerable losses were avoided when Marshal Konev made ten lorries daily available for the return of museum property. In this connection, the name of a Russian cultural officer in Austria who later became world-famous should be mentioned: Boris Pasternak, the author of *Doctor Zhivago,* was stationed in the small town of Baden some twenty-five kilometers south of Vienna.

On the other hand, the removal, in the direction of Maribor, of about thirty cases of historic manuscripts and books from the university library in Graz by troops of the former Yugoslavia can be described as an exception, or better, as a violation of the Moscow Declaration. The university was recently offered the chance to buy back one of the eighty-five manuscripts that disappeared at that time. The furnishings of Grafenegg Castle in Lower Austria suffered a similar fate: Soviet soldiers removed works of art by the carload, leaving an empty palace. The large list of the lost items is available.[4]

One of my predecessors, Dr. Otto Demus, who was president of the Bundesdenkmalamt until 1964, stressed, in a letter dated April 2, 1948, that the Bundesdenkmalamt would endeavor to secure the return of all works of art that had been located in Austria in 1938. Above all, Professor Demus had in mind those cultural goods that were brought to the Munich Collecting Point by United States troops at the end of the war so that they could, in accordance with the London Declaration of January 5, 1943 (see Appendix 9), be returned to their rightful owners. Names such as Lieutenant Thomas Carr Howe (in civilian life director of a museum in San Francisco), Lieutenant George Stout (in time of peace the chief restorer at the Fogg Art Museum, Cambridge, Massachusetts), Captain Robert Posey, Major Malcolm Shaw, Lieutenant Colonel Ernest T. De Wald (in private life a professor at Princeton University), and Colonel Theodore S. Paul come to mind as being responsible for the prudent direct return of cultural property to the Austrian museums or their transfer to Munich from their places of storage at Alt Aussee, Bad Ischl, and Lauffen. Our archives make mention of Miss Eve Tucker, who diligently sought out Austrian art in the Munich Collecting Point; also Stephen Munsing and S. Lane Faison, Jr., who were sympathetic in their supervision. Thanks to the particularly correct behavior of the representatives of the United States Army, the top-grade works of art that had been stored for safety in the aforementioned places were recovered and returned to Austria.

In cases where the staff of the Munich Collecting Point was unable to determine the ownership of particular works of art that were obviously Austrian, the remaining articles were handed over by United States troops to the Austrian government. Already in a report dated December 20, 1948, Otto Demus put on record that he made the following statement at a meeting with Munsing, then head of the Munich Collecting Point: Austria would not retain any part of the restitution assets for itself and did not intend to take, for instance, any objects that might remain unidentified into state ownership as an enrichment of the public art collections.

Many works of art that have been brought to the Bundesdenkmalamt over the course of years and consist of the remaining assets of the Munich Collecting Point—that is, of objects found in the offices of the occupying forces after they had left, together with abandoned cultural goods—were returned, on the basis of several Austrian laws, to their owners or their heirs. It has taken over forty years to return some of these objects to their owners, especially when they were private persons. The reason for the long delay is to be found in the need for an especially correct procedure for the return of goods to their owners or heirs so that errors could be avoided. The majority of the valid claims made were examined and considered by independent judges rather than by the Austrian administrative authorities.

Lists of the objects collected in the Carthusian monastery of Mauerbach (near the western outskirts of Vienna) were made public in 1969 and 1986 in order to invite applicants and possible claims. From these lists it is clear that the artistic value of the remaining assets is not very high. Rumors that Austria is holding back valuable works of art are completely without foundation, particularly in light of the statement made by Professor Demus in 1948 from which I have quoted. The last court proceedings (in respect of twenty-seven claimants) will presumably be completed by 1996. The remaining assets whose owners are still unknown were given to the Austrian Jewish community on November 23, 1995, and will be auctioned for the benefit of needy persons who were persecuted by the National Socialist regime on grounds of race, creed, or political beliefs, as provided for by statute.*

I have already mentioned Miss Eve Tucker. She took a farsighted view in 1948 when she said: "The gigantic search for their lost heritage which the European nations have carried out during the past three years will probably continue for the next fifty years."[5] Miss Tucker's apparently pessimistic estimate of the time required for such an undertaking was exactly correct, as the Bard Graduate Center symposium has indicated.

---

* Editor's note: Approximately 8,500 Austrian Jewish-owned artworks confiscated by the Nazis during World War II were kept for nearly fifty years in government repositories. In 1984, *ARTnews* brought this matter to public attention with the first in a series of investigative articles on Jewish "heirless" property in Austria (A. Decker, "A Legacy of Shame," *ARTnews* 83, no. 10 [December 1984]: 54–76). Since that time, according to a recent report (S. Waxman, "Austria: Ending the Legacy of Shame," *ARTnews* 94, no. 7 [September 1995]: 122–25), 350 objects or groups of objects have been returned to survivors and their heirs. On 11 July 1995, the Austrian Parliament passed legislation allowing for the return of the remaining "heirless" property to the Austrian Federation of Jewish Communities (Bundesverband der Israelitischen Kultusgemeinden Österreichs). This property was sold at auction in Vienna on 29–30 October 1996, with 88 percent of the proceeds ($14.5 million) to go to the Austrian Federation of Jewish Communities and 12 percent to groups representing non-Jewish victims of Nazism in Austria.

THE RESTITUTION

OF WORKS OF ART

IN HUNGARY

István Fodor

During World War II and in the years that followed, Hungary suffered considerable losses of works of art. Monuments and buildings of extraordinary value were destroyed in immense numbers or suffered substantially—for example, the Buda Castle was demolished and left in ruins. A huge number of portable works of art (pictures, sculptures, decorative objects, and works of the goldsmith's art) were taken out of the country by the opposing parties, and a considerable portion has still not been recovered.

Hungarian cultural losses increased greatly after the German troops invaded the country on March 19, 1944. Following this catastrophe, the Germans took collections, most of them belonging to Jews, and subsequently transported them to Germany. The outflow of works of art increased again after October 1944, when the Hungarian fascist government—supported by the Germans—gained power in the country. At that time, many state-owned and museum collections were shipped illegally to the West, including the artifacts of the Museum of Fine Arts in Budapest and the Holy Crown of Saint Stephen and the royal regalia.

After recapturing the territory of Hungary from the Germans (1944–45), the Soviet army also confiscated quantities of art. Their special forces gained possession of the valuable collections stored in bank vaults and secured at other places, and after accumulating them in Budapest transferred them to the Soviet Union.

Since 1945, the democratic government of Hungary has done everything in its power to recover the works of art removed from the country during the war. The recovery of artifacts from the territory of the former German Reich began before 1947, and a considerable number of artworks have been returned to Hungary, mostly objects found in the zone occupied by the Americans. However, many works of art were never returned, and some of these have appeared on the international art market. As is well known, after the war the Holy Crown of Saint Stephen and the royal regalia were not given back to Hungary but were held in the United States until 1978.

Immediately after the war, steps were taken to regain possession of the Hungarian works of art held by the Soviets. On August 3, 1945, Géza Teleki, minister of religious and educational affairs, addressed a letter to the Soviet Supervisory Committee, requesting return by the Red Army of the Hungarian cultural objects that they had seized. This letter received no response. By this time, it had become clear that a considerable number of the Hungarian works of art that had been taken out of Hungary by the Nazis had fallen into Soviet possession in the Soviet-occupied zone of Germany. But exactly what had happened to them was unknown—and the mystery has yet to be solved.

During the period following 1948, when the communists gained power in Hungary, no one raised the issue of Hungarian works of art in exile in the Soviet Union—for obvious political reasons. Although in the beginning of the 1970s the Soviet Union returned some paintings by Hungarian artists, this took place in absolute secrecy, without the knowledge of the public.

37. *Coronation Scene.* **Tapestry from a Brussels workshop, perhaps by Maître Philippe. Sixteenth century. Wool, 324 x 525 cm (127½ x 206¾″). The subject depicted is probably the coronation of a French king, seen in the company of ancient religious and historical monarchs. Formerly in the Hatvany collection, Budapest. Presently in Russia**

39. Jacopo Tintoretto. *Portrait of a Venetian Nobleman.* **c. 1563–65. Canvas, 117.5 x 95 cm (46¼ x 37⅜″). This is a portrait of a member of the Morosini family, probably Battista Morosini. Formerly in the Hatvany collection, Budapest. Presently in the Grabar Restoration Center, Moscow**

38. Wastepaper basket of Napoleon I, emperor of France. Early nineteenth century. Brown wood with bronze ornamentation and the monogram of Napoleon, 52 x 45 x 57 cm (20½ x 17¾ x 22½″). Formerly in the Monte-nuovo collection, Budapest. Presently in Russia

The issue was next raised some twenty years later, in 1990, when Russian art historians made revelations in the international press about works of art stolen during World War II and secretly stored in Russia. Their articles dealt in detail with well-known paintings that had belonged to Hungarian private collections: works by El Greco, Goya, Tintoretto (fig. 39), Corot (fig. 40), Degas, and Manet.

In Hungary, the public and the official authorities followed these announcements with keen interest. In 1991 the Hungarian government dispatched a protocol to the Russian government requesting the return of the paintings. In 1992 the Hungarian government set up an official commission whose task it was to make preparations for the return of works of art taken from Hungary and held in the territory of the former Soviet Union. This commission signed the first official agreement with the State Commission on the Restitution of

Cultural Property of the Russian Federation on November 11, 1992. According to the agreement, each of the parties agreed to cooperate in the search for, registration of, and preparation for the return of properties that came into the other's possession during World War II or subsequently. In addition to accomplishing these objectives, the parties agreed to set up a joint Hungarian-Russian working group to study the issues involved.

Also in 1992, it was decided that, insofar as possible, the Hungarian researchers would compile a list of cultural losses and damages Hungary suffered as a result of World War II, and with this list a computerized data bank was to be established. This list was also to be published as a book, both in English and in Hungarian.

The next Hungarian-Russian restitution agreement was concluded in Moscow on May 21, 1993. The minutes signed by the chairmen of the state committees dealing with restitution —the Russian and the Hungarian ministers of culture— confirmed the intentions set out in the earlier agreement and also the establishment of a joint working group and its operational procedures. At the Grabar Restoration Center in Moscow, the Hungarian minister of culture and his colleagues were shown the previously mentioned, world-famous pictures from Hungary. It became evident that the Red Army had seized these pictures in Germany and transported them first

40. Jean-Baptiste-Camille Corot. *Portrait of Mariette Gambey.* c. 1869–70. Oil on canvas, 80 x 59 cm (31½ x 23¼″). Signed by the artist. Seen here in the Hatvany house, Budapest. Presently in the Grabar Restoration Center, Moscow

A data base for the works of art lost during the relevant period has been created at the Hungarian National Gallery in Budapest. The number of items recorded is currently about forty thousand. For some of these, the whereabouts are known or can be assumed, while for others such information is not available. Prior to the establishment of the data base, a substantial amount of research was carried out in archives, where work is continuing to produce an ever-increasing number of relevant details. Moreover, an exhibition of photographs showing lost works of art was organized in the Museum of Applied Arts in Budapest. A book written in English describing in detail some nine thousand lost works of art and historic documents will be published in the near future. The Hungarian Committee for the Restitution of Cultural Property has formed several working groups consisting of experts in libraries, archives, and legal matters who are busy solving problems relating to their areas of specialization.

In February 1995, the Pushkin State Museum of Fine Arts in Moscow mounted an exhibition entitled "Twice Saved," which included art previously held in their "secret repositories" —among other works, the famous paintings of the Hatvany and Herzog collections. A number of pictures of "unknown origin" that were exhibited may also have belonged to former Hungarian collections. We hope that in the future our Russian partners will provide more help concerning those locations in Russia where Hungarian works of art are "safeguarded." In this connection, it would also be essential to arrange for previously secret Russian archives to become accessible for such research. For us it is more than evident that success is only achievable if both partners act in a spirit of goodwill.

to Gorky (Nizhnii Novgorod), after which, in 1957, they were sent to the Grabar Center. In the meantime, the Hungarian committee handed over to the Russian committee a list of lost works of art; the number of items in question has increased month by month, with more than forty thousand objects registered to date.

In a decree of May 19, 1993, the Hungarian government set up the Committee for the Restitution of Cultural Property, chaired by the minister of culture. Hungarian experts visited Gorky, where they succeeded in locating some valuable books originally in the possession of the Library of the Calvinist College at Sárospatak. Later, in discussions held in Hungary with the director of the local library, preparations were made for the return of these books. The first meeting of the joint Hungarian-Russian restitution working group was held in Budapest in May 1994.

It must be emphasized that in the restitution agreements concluded so far, both parties have negotiated on the basis of *mutual* restitution; thus, the Hungarian committee has undertaken the obligation to locate and to make preparations for the return of works of art formerly in Russia that are presently in Hungary. However, it is obvious that there is a considerable difference in scale between the Russian and the Hungarian demands for restitution, in both the number of the artifacts and their quality.

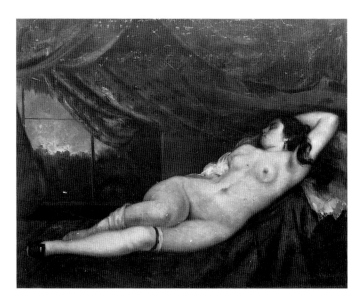

41. Gustave Courbet. *Nude in White Stockings.* 1862. Oil on canvas, 75 x 95 cm (29½ x 37⅜″). Signed by the artist. Formerly in the Hatvany collection, Budapest. Presently in Russia

THE LOSS OF

GERMAN ARTISTIC PROPERTY

AS A RESULT

OF

WORLD WAR II

Werner Schmidt

The calamity that Germany brought on Europe during the Second World War ultimately recoiled on the country itself. Whoever reports about the loss of German cultural property as a result of the war must be mindful of the Germans' historical guilt. I would like to emphasize this before commencing this presentation.

The heaviest loss suffered by Germany was the destruction of the historical centers of all its large cities, such as Dresden, which was razed to the ground by intensive bombing on February 13–14, 1945. Most of the architectural treasures in the old cities, from Cologne to Berlin and from Lübeck to Augsburg, were severely damaged or destroyed during air raids. The ground battles further devastated the cities. The resulting destruction of art treasures of all kinds can hardly be expressed in numbers.

Many works of art in museums were destroyed by the air raids. In the Wallraf-Richartz-Museum in Cologne and in the Historisches Museum in Frankfurt am Main, around four hundred paintings were burned during air attacks in 1942 and 1943. In the Neue Pinakothek in Munich, around forty thousand prints from the collection of graphic art fell victim to air strikes in 1944. The Staatliche Gemäldegalerie in Dresden was the one hardest hit by air warfare. On February 13 and 14, 1945, 199 paintings were lost, many of considerable importance and including such masterpieces as *The Stone Breakers* by Gustave Courbet, and paintings by Lucas Cranach the Elder, Dosso Dossi, Parmigianino, Domenico Fetti, Guercino, Guido Reni, Giovanni Lanfranco, Johann Heinrich Schönfeld, Luca Giordano, Pompeo Batoni, Julius Schnorr von Carolsfeld, Moritz von Schwind, Ferdinand von Rayski, Arnold Böcklin, Hans von Marées, and Ferdinand Hodler.

German museums suffered most losses in the confusion that prevailed once hostilities had ceased. On May 6, 1945, three days after the fighting had stopped, fire broke out in the Friedrichshain bunker in Berlin. It is estimated that 434 old master paintings and numerous other works from the Berlin collections were destroyed, among them masterpieces by Italian, Dutch, German, and French artists, such as the *Tondo* by Botticelli and *Saint Matthew and the Angel* by Caravaggio (fig. 42), as well as works by Giovanni Bellini, Petrus Christus, Fra Filippo Lippi, Luca Signorelli, Lucas Cranach, Carpaccio, Titian, Veronese, Tintoretto, Rubens, Van Dyck, Goya, Guido Reni, Francisco de Zurbarán, and Adolph Menzel.

A catalogue published in 1965 of paintings lost or missing from German museums comprises sixty-five hundred paintings, of which around five hundred were destroyed during air raids and around the same number in the confusion at war's end. Most of the works were plundered at that time and are still missing. Once hostilities had ceased, 97 paintings disappeared from the Weimar Museum, including *Landscape with Rainbow* by Caspar David Friedrich, which is still missing. Around 10,500 prints and 4,816 drawings were stolen from the Dresden Kupferstich-Kabinett (Prints and Drawings Collection) after the Red Army had assumed custody of the collection. There are many indications that the thousands of prints and drawings,

42. Caravaggio (1573–1610). *Saint Matthew and the Angel*. Oil on canvas, 223 x 183 cm (87⅞ x 72″). Formerly in the Staatliche Museen zu Berlin, Gemäldegalerie. Probably destroyed by fire in the Friedrichshain flak tower, Berlin, 1945

including numerous major works by Altdorfer, Cranach (fig. 43), Dürer, Van Dyck, Kollwitz, Menzel, and Rubens, were removed purposefully by individuals. During the last ten years, several of these works have turned up in the international "gray market," all of them originating in the territory of the Soviet Union. Of 513 paintings missing from the Dresden Gemäldegalerie, 59 have appeared to date.

After the war, the Soviet troops transported all cultural property of international renown that they could find within their occupation zone to the Soviet Union. All of these works disappeared into secret depots. In March 1955, the government of the USSR decided to return the paintings taken from the Gemäldegalerie, Dresden. Great effort was made at that time to convince the world that "the greatest paintings had been found in terrible condition in half-blocked shafts," as the Soviet minister of culture announced on May 1, 1955. This account was not in accordance with the facts.

Often cited as an example, the tunnel of the Rottwerndorfer quarry in the Erzgebirge, about twenty-five kilometers from Dresden, to which the most valuable paintings were evacuated, offered the best possible protection from air raids in 1943. Reports by the restorer Alfred Unger on air conditioning and regular controls, as well as a sketch made in January

1944 by Alfred Heese, a restorer at the Dresden Gemälde-galerie, show that careful measures were taken to create the necessary climatic conditions. When the air conditioning broke down on May 8, 1945, due to a power failure, the paintings could be taken from the tunnel as there was no longer any danger of a bombing raid. The most important and largest buildings to which Dresden's art treasures were evacuated from 1942 onward were in perfect condition when hostilities ceased: for example, Schloss Weesenstein, in which part of the contents of the Gemäldegalerie and the entire holdings of the Kupferstich-Kabinett were stored, and the Königstein fortress, in whose barracks the treasures of the Grünes Gewölbe (Green Vault) and the Armory were kept. The extensive castle buildings of Schloss Pillnitz suffered no damage either. It was therefore by no means necessary to remove the works of art from these places to the Soviet Union in order to conserve them. They could easily have been kept in the safety of the well-preserved buildings near Dresden.

In accordance with the government decision of January 7, 1957, the Soviet Union handed over to the German Democratic Republic (GDR) in 1958 and the following years the major part of the cultural property removed from museums in East Germany. From the Berlin museums, this included the collection of antiquities, among them the sculptural frieze from the Altar of Zeus at Pergamon, the entire coin collection, significant artifacts from the Egyptian Museum, the sculpture collection, and works from the Gemäldegalerie, the National-galerie, and the Kupferstichkabinett. Six truly regal collections were returned to Dresden: the Grünes Gewölbe, the Kupferstich-Kabinett, the coin collection, the porcelain collection, the armory collection, and the sculpture collection, as well as major works from museums in Dessau, Gotha, Leipzig, Potsdam, Schwerin, and Wörlitz. This represented a tremendous number of works of art of inestimable value.

43. Lucas Cranach the Elder. *Samson and the Lion*. c. 1509–10. Pen and ink with brown-gray wash, 15.1 x 20.5 cm (5¹⁵⁄₁₆ x 8″). Kupferstich-Kabinett, Dresden. After the Russian army took over on May 14, 1945, the drawing was removed from its mount and has been missing since that time.

44. Wu Yixian. *Rainstorm*. China, fifteenth century. Brush and ink, 174 x 53 cm (68½ x 20⅞″). Formerly in the Staatliche Museen zu Berlin, Museum für Ostasiatische Kunst. Now known to be in Russia

However, the Soviet Union continued to conceal the fact that works were still hidden in their special depots.

Detailed descriptions follow for several categories of German cultural property that is still held in the successor states to the Soviet Union, mostly in Russia. The first group comprises objects from the museums that were obviously excluded from the Soviet restitution after 1957 because they were situated in what was then West Berlin or in the Federal Republic of Germany, as property was only returned to the GDR. The Museum für Ostasiatische Kunst (Museum of East Asian Art) was on Prinz-Albrecht-Strasse in West Berlin. Until 1945 it housed one of the major collections of its kind. About 5,200 objects, 90 percent of its contents, were found in the Berlin Zoo flak tower in May 1945 and transported to the Soviet Union before the American occupation forces arrived on July 1, 1945. In addition to early Chinese bronze objects,

the Berlin collection includes important Chinese and Japanese paintings (fig. 44), as well as sculptures, pieces of lacquerwork, jade objects, and Noh costumes. These works are now kept in the State Hermitage Museum in St. Petersburg.

A second Berlin museum situated in former West Berlin is the Museum für Vor- und Frühgeschichte. From its contents, five treasure troves were removed in 1945. One of the treasure troves was the Eberswalde gold treasure dating from the ninth century B.C. (colorplate 7); another is the Schliemann treasure from Troy, which is now in the Pushkin State Museum of Fine Arts in Moscow and the State Hermitage Museum in St. Petersburg.

Around seventeen hundred drawings from the Bremen Kunsthalle, including numerous masterpieces by Corinth, Dürer (colorplate 8), Friedrich, Huber, Liebermann, Marées, Menzel, Corot, Daumier, Delacroix, Poussin, Toulouse-Lautrec, Watteau, Bernini, Carracci, Parmigianino, Pontormo, Tiepolo, Veronese, Van Dyck, Rembrandt, and Rubens, had been evacuated in 1943, together with fifty paintings and three thousand precious prints, to Schloss Karnzow in Brandenburg and were discovered there at the beginning of May 1945 by Soviet troops. An important part of this inventory has been turning up since 1989 in Russia in various institutions and private collections. In 1992, 138 drawings were exhibited in Moscow and St. Petersburg. At the time of the New York symposium, not a single drawing had been returned to Bremen.*

The second group I would like to mention are remainders, still kept in Russia, of collections supposedly returned in their entirety after 1955, for example, the small painting from the atelier of Lucas Cranach the Younger depicting Melanchthon on his deathbed, from the Staatliche Gemäldegalerie, Dresden. It is now in the State Hermitage Museum, which disclosed in 1993 to a group of German museum experts that it held certain individual works from these collections. It is not known, however, which objects are now kept in other Russian museums.

The academic documentation on the art treasures returned by the Soviets is also still missing from German museums. In 1945 and 1946, Soviet detachments confiscated inventories, academic indexes, photographic documentation, and reference libraries from German museums, along with works of art. They were not returned by the Soviet Union, nor were the vast inventories of German archives, which cannot be described in more detail here.

A large, important third category of cultural property only partially returned by the Soviet Union after 1955 comprises the libraries. In 1945 and 1946, Soviet detachments systematically confiscated the most valuable libraries they found. The missing books amount to 1.5 million volumes, including 220,000 from the State Saxon Library in Dresden, 206,000 from the Berlin State Library, 100,000 from the Bremen State

---

* Editor's note: Three Bremen drawings that appeared for sale in New York were returned to the Kunsthalle in March 1995, by order of a United States federal court judge. See Kline, below, page 157.

and University Library. Even more important than the number of volumes, however, is the value of individual books. For example, 1,500 books were removed from the sixteenth-century State Saxon Library in Dresden in 1946, together with 1,500 incunabula. The same selection process was used by the experts of the Soviet Trophy Commission in the case of the Leipzig university library, the Deutsche Bibliothek–Deutsche Bücherei (German Library), and the book museum of the Association of German Booksellers in Leipzig. Among these manuscripts, incunabula, and rarities were two Gutenberg Bibles.

An important public art collection in the territory of the GDR was excluded from the restitutions made by the Soviets: the armory of the Wartburg Castle near Eisenach. It comprises about eight hundred fifty items, including treasures such as the armor worn by Johann Friedrich II, duke of Saxony-Gotha, a work by Kunz Lochner in Nuremberg of about 1550. The entire armory of the Wartburg was removed on February 24, 1947. Perhaps it was not returned because it belongs to a foundation, such as the Bremen Kunsthalle, and is not state or municipal property.

This leads me to the fourth group, that of works from private art collections. During the war, the most important German private collections were evacuated to depots together with the contents of museums. Works belonging to museums and to individuals were thus transported to the Soviet Union together. When the museum contents were given back to the GDR, the private collections were systematically sorted out and remained in Soviet keeping. Naturally, the discrimination against private property was due to communist ideology. Affected were the main works of the Gerstenberg collection, including the painting *Place de la Concorde* by Edgar Degas, as well as the private collection of Bernhard Koehler with works by Cézanne, Courbet, El Greco, Van Gogh, Manet, and Seurat; the collection of Friedrich von Siemens, with paintings by Guardi, Delacroix, Menzel, and Toulouse-Lautrec; the collection of Else von Goldhammer, with 44 paintings by old masters such as Carpaccio, Lucas van Leyden, Rembrandt, Canaletto, Tiepolo, and Goya; as well as the Jantzen collection in Bremen with 107 bronze sculptures from the Middle Ages.

The Krebs collection, with about ninety Impressionist paintings, sculptures, and watercolors, including several paintings by Cézanne, Van Gogh, Renoir, Monet, Fantin-Latour, Signac, and Liebermann, was housed in the collector's country residence near Weimar and was removed by the Soviet army as late as 1949. Most of the collection is now in the State Hermitage Museum. The personal property of Wilhelm von Humboldt, of great cultural significance in relation to the castle in Berlin-Tegel built by Karl Friedrich Schinkel, where Humboldt resided, was confiscated in 1945. The Dresden collection of Victor von Klemperer was seized as Jewish property by the National Socialists in 1940. His collection of almost five hundred incunabula and early illustrated books from the fifteenth century was removed, together with the contents of the State Saxon Library.

The most precious and important private German collections still in Russia are the property of the House of Wettin. After the abdication of the last Saxon king, this royal family retained major works of art of all forms, including the famous font made by the Dresden gold- and silversmith Hans Kellerthaler, cast in 1617 (fig. 45). The Saxon court-silver chamber with riches from the eighteenth century also remained the private property of the House of Wettin. A large part of the Baroque silver plate from this collection was removed from Schloss Moritzburg near Dresden by the Soviet army in 1946. The whereabouts of these objects are a mystery to this very day. A large collection of approximately eighty thousand prints, the Kupferstich-Kabinett of the Saxon king Frederick Augustus II, remained the private property of the House of Wettin after his death in 1854. It is probable that the most valuable part of this collection, including a series of drawings in sepia by Caspar David Friedrich, was removed from Schloss Moritzburg by Soviet troops.

Missing works of art that reappear are welcomed and loved like the prodigal son. A. P. Ovsyanov, head of the Center for the Registration of Missing Cultural Property in Kaliningrad, in referring to our efforts to secure the return of preserved German cultural property, aptly described such works as "the last prisoners of the Second World War, which must be liberated."

45. Hans Kellerthaler. Baptismal Font of the House of Wettin. Dresden, cast 1617. Silver with gilding. Height 34 cm (13⅜″), diameter 77 cm (30⅜″). On loan to the Grünes Gewölbe (Green Vault) in the royal castle in Dresden, the font was transferred to the fortress of Königstein in 1940, and from there it was removed to the Soviet Union after May 9, 1945. Its current whereabouts are unknown.

PART 3

LAWS,
DIRECTIVES,
AND
CONVENTIONS

LAWS IN FORCE AT

THE DAWN OF WORLD WAR II:

INTERNATIONAL CONVENTIONS

AND NATIONAL LAWS

Lawrence M. Kaye

In August 1914, the magnificent library of the University of Louvain—an architectural masterpiece and repository of precious manuscripts and documents dating from the early Middle Ages to the modern era—was burned to the ground; and the cathedral of Reims, where for centuries the kings of France had been crowned, was severely damaged in a bombing raid. Both buildings had been specifically targeted because they were cultural and spiritual symbols of Belgium and France, the nations in which they were respectively situated. By destroying these cherished sites, Germany hoped to destroy the spirit of both nations, with which she was at war.

As heinous as these acts were on their own, they appear even more appalling when viewed in the context of the international laws in effect when they occurred. Only a few years before, Germany—as well as Belgium and France—had ratified the Hague Convention Respecting the Laws and Customs of War on Land, the first international treaty to codify the protection of cultural property during war.[1] The Hague Convention expressly forbade the destruction of, or willful damage to, historic monuments and buildings like those at Louvain and Reims (see Appendix 3).

Unfortunately, the failure of the Hague Convention to prevent the wanton destruction and plunder of cultural property during World War I foreshadowed the failure of international laws to prevent the despoiling of such property on a far larger scale during World War II.

This chapter presents a brief history of international and national efforts to protect cultural property up to the start of World War II. Although it is a history marked by failure, it reflects some successes as well—mainly in the ability of the victors to force the vanquished to return cultural property plundered during wartime.

INTRODUCTION: SOME BASIC LEGAL CONCEPTS

In order to comprehend fully the significance of the international agreements in place at the beginning of the Second World War, it is necessary to understand some basic legal concepts—especially the difference between international laws and national laws.[2] International law is the collection of rules that bind individual nations with respect to their relations with each other. National laws are simply the laws that individual nations have promulgated to govern what goes on within their own borders, mainly among their own citizens.

The concept that international laws *bind* individual nations raises a perhaps obvious but nonetheless critical difference between international laws and national laws: unlike individual nations, the world has no universal system for the compulsory enforcement of international laws similar to the courts, police forces, and other enforcement mechanisms of individual states. Therefore, agreements among nations—whether bilateral or multilateral, regional or universal in scope—depend in large part upon each nation's voluntarily abiding by the terms of those agreements, except, of course, in those instances when one nation forces another to abide by its will through warfare or other sanctions. Thus, when we speak of international agreements like the Hague Convention that purport to govern the future conduct of many nations, we must keep in mind that their success ultimately depends on the voluntary compliance of the signatory states.

Indeed, any attempt to pursue claims against a nation depends on that nation's agreement to have such claims adjudicated. Thus, while there is an international tribunal designed to resolve disputes among nations, namely, the International Court of Justice, its jurisdiction extends only to those nations that consent to appear before it.[3] Similarly, if one nation, or, for that matter, an individual or a company, wishes to initiate a lawsuit against another nation—for example, to recover artworks wrongfully confiscated during wartime—the suit may very well be dismissed on the grounds of sovereign immunity. Through sovereign immunity, a concept generally accepted by nations throughout the world, the sovereign or nation is immune from being sued anywhere, at least with respect to acts considered to be governmental, rather than commercial or private, in nature.[4] Nations, of course, may choose to limit their own immunity, and permit themselves to be sued, even in connection with their governmental functions. Indeed, that has been the trend in many nations for many years; but it is by no means universal. Sovereign immunity still poses a major obstacle to the recovery of cultural property taken during wartime.

Yet another potential obstacle to the recovery of cultural property taken during wartime is the statute of limitations. Statutes of limitations are laws—adopted by countries all over the world as well as by individual governmental entities within each nation—that prevent lawsuits from being brought after a certain time period has passed so as to avoid having the courts deal with so-called stale (old) claims. Some legal scholars contend that since the major international agreements adopted during and after World War II prohibiting the plunder of cultural property during wartime do not contain any such statutes of limitation, the implication is that there should be no time limit with respect to such claims.[5] But this is by no means clear; in any event, in private lawsuits brought to recover property looted during or shortly after World War II, the statute of limitations has played a major role in the success or failure of such claims.[6]

THE DEVELOPMENT OF INTERNATIONAL AND NATIONAL LAWS FOR THE PROTECTION OF CULTURAL PROPERTY BEFORE WORLD WAR II

Because the implementation of international agreements is so dependent upon each nation's voluntarily abiding by the terms of those agreements, one must appreciate what a significant achievement the Hague Convention was. For the first time, the international community codified in writing the notion that the cultural property of each nation is so important that it must be afforded special protection—especially in time of war.

The concept of special protection for cultural property, however, first emerged in Europe during the eighteenth century,

most notably in the writings of Emheric de Vattel, a leading legal scholar. Vattel's treatise *The Law of Nations* (1758) enunciated the basic principle: "For whatever cause a country is ravaged, we ought to spare those edifices which do honor to human society, and do not contribute to increase the enemy's strength—such as temples, tombs, public buildings, and all works of remarkable beauty. It is declaring one's self an enemy to mankind, thus wantonly to deprive them of these monuments of art."[7]

During the nineteenth century, as interest in art became more widespread—and as market prices for artworks reached unprecedented levels—recognition of the spiritual and material value of art contributed to the concept of national cultural heritage as the irreplaceable patrimony of a nation. Thus, the principle expressed by Vattel came to be accepted as part of international law, as expressed by the American jurist Henry Wheaton: "By the ancient law of nations, even what was called *res sacrae* were not exempted from capture and confiscation. . . . But by the modern usage of nations, which has now acquired the force of law, temples of religion, public edifices devoted to civil purposes only, monuments of art, and repositories of science, are exempted from the general operations of war."[8]

Condemnation of the looting of cultural property during war and the corresponding principle that plundered property should be returned to its country of origin were first addressed on an international scale by the 1815 Convention of Paris.[9] By that convention, the nations allied against Napoleon ordered the return of cultural property, either taken by France through force or acquired by it through treaty, to the countries of origin.[10] The allies' position was stated by the Duke of Wellington, who observed that the systematic looting by Napoleon of cultural property from the rest of Europe was "contrary to the principles of justice and the rules of modern war."[11]

The earliest known attempt to codify the principles of the protection of cultural property was the Lieber Code of 1863 (see Appendix 1). Written by Dr. Francis Lieber, a professor at Columbia College in New York, the Lieber Code was promulgated for use during the American Civil War—it was issued by President Lincoln for the Union army.[12] The Lieber Code provides for the protection during wartime of "property belonging to churches, to hospitals, or other establishments of an exclusively charitable character, to establishments of education, or foundations for the promotion of knowledge . . . museums of the fine arts, or of a scientific character."[13] The code provides further that "classical works of art, libraries, scientific collections, or precious instruments, such as astronomical telescopes . . . must be secured against all avoidable injury."[14] Although an invading nation may seize such cultural property, as long as that can be done without "injuring" it, the property must be held for safekeeping pending the resolution of the question of ultimate ownership, which would occur in the ensuing treaty of peace.[15]

The impact of the Lieber Code on international law was extraordinary. In 1874, the code served as the basis for the

Declaration of the Conference of Brussels, the first international attempt to codify the rules for the protection of cultural property (see Appendix 2).[16] Never ratified, the declaration would have prohibited wartime pillage of enemy property except for military reasons and specifically condemned the seizure or destruction of property belonging to art institutions, whether public or private.[17] In 1880, the Institute of International Law, a private but influential body, utilized the Lieber Code and the work of the Conference of Brussels six years earlier to prepare its own codification of rules for land warfare, known as the Oxford Manual.[18]

These efforts culminated at the dawn of the twentieth century in the adoption of the Hague Convention, an international agreement ratified by some forty nations, including France, Germany, Great Britain, Russia, and the United States. Despite international efforts between the world wars to adopt additional agreements to protect cultural property, in 1939 the Hague Convention was the only comprehensive multilateral international agreement in effect in Europe dealing with the protection of cultural property during wartime.

The Hague Convention is actually a series of agreements, adopted over several years at the turn of the twentieth century, that deal with the way belligerents are to conduct themselves during warfare. The key protections afforded to cultural property are set forth in Article 56 of the 1907 Hague Convention (see Appendix 3), which expressly forbids any "seizure of, destruction or wilful damage" to "institutions dedicated to religion, charity and education, [or] the arts and sciences," as well as "historic monuments, [and] works of art and science."[19] Other articles of the convention forbid any kind of "pillage," define particular categories of public property that may be requisitioned for strictly military uses, permit immovable public property to be used for military purposes as long as it is neither harmed nor destroyed, and prohibit any taking of private property.[20] It is fair to say that all of these provisions, taken together, afford protection from looting and destruction during wartime to virtually every kind of cultural property.[21] Lest there be any doubt, however, the preamble to the Convention declares that "in cases not included" in the rules adopted by the parties to the Convention, "the inhabitants and the belligerents remain under the protection and the rule of the principles of the law of nations, as they result from the usages established among civilized peoples, from the laws of humanity, and the dictates of the public conscience."[22]

The Convention also provides remedial measures in the event of violations of its rules. Article 3 states that "[a] belligerent party which violates the provisions of the said Regulations shall, if the case demands, be liable to pay compensation. It shall be responsible for all acts committed by persons forming part of its armed forces."[23] Article 56 specifies that violations of its provisions "should be made the subject of legal proceedings."[24] Although the Hague Convention did not expressly require the return of cultural property confiscated during wartime in violation of its provisions, nevertheless restitution of such property was a regular feature of treaties entered into after World War I.

At the beginning of World War II, the two-hundred-year evolution of a code of international rules to protect cultural property during wartime had borne fruit in the form of a widely ratified international agreement. Moreover, individual nations were also becoming increasingly interested in adopting their own sets of individual national laws to protect cultural property within their borders and prevent its unauthorized export to other nations. For example, Italian laws of 1902 and 1909—which can be traced back over four hundred years to a papal bull prohibiting the export by anyone of cultural property from the Papal States, and which are substantially the same as laws currently in effect in Italy—prohibited the sale or other transfer of cultural objects by public or private institutions and the export by anyone of any such objects; moreover, private sales of such objects by individuals could only be effected with the permission of the government, which had the right to preempt such sales by purchasing the objects itself.[25] A French law of 1913, still in effect today, placed similar limitations on certain objects that the government classified as protected property.[26] And in a law of 1918, the Soviet Union classified all cultural property as state property and prohibited any transfer or export thereof.[27]

These national laws were not designed to prevent the pillage of cultural property by invading armies during wartime. That obviously can only be the subject of international law. But these national laws are significant because they demonstrate how critically important the protection and preservation of each nation's cultural property and cultural heritage had become by the time of World War II.[28]

ENFORCEMENT OF THE HAGUE CONVENTION AFTER WORLD WAR I

Despite its comprehensive provisions for the protection of cultural property during wartime, the Hague Convention failed to prevent the wholesale pillage that was to occur during World War II. Indeed, the Convention also failed to prevent the pillage and destruction of cultural property during World War I. But after the First World War, relying on the principles articulated in the Convention, the victorious nations did effect the return of cultural property plundered during that war, as well as other remedies for violations of those principles. Since this experience foreshadowed the efforts at recovery of cultural property confiscated during World War II, it is worthwhile to review briefly some of the efforts after World War I to remedy violations of the Hague Convention.

Enforcement of the provisions of the Hague Convention was rigorously implemented in the Treaty of Versailles of 1919 (see Appendix 4). Remedies for the loss and theft of cultural property included not only the return of looted objects to their countries of origin and compensation for objects destroyed but a novel method of reparation—the replacement of lost objects with objects of comparable nature and value. Moreover, the treaty addressed not only claims arising from World War I but some claims involving Austria and Czechoslovakia dating as far back as the seventeenth century. Thus, no "statute of limitations" was recognized in this treaty.

Pursuant to the Treaty of Versailles, Germany was forced to return to France all "trophies, archives, historical souvenirs or works of art carried away from France by the German authorities in the course of the war of 1870–1871 and during [World War I]."[29] In addition, because of the total destruction of the Louvain library, the terms of the treaty required Germany "to furnish to the University of Louvain, within three months after a request made by it . . . manuscripts, incunabula, printed books, maps and objects of collection corresponding in number and value to those destroyed in the burning by Germany of the Library of Louvain."[30]

One extraordinary provision of the Treaty of Versailles pertained to the restitution of artworks to Belgium. Belgium demanded—and was granted—the return of works of art purchased by German museums in good faith on the open market, including the missing panels of the Ghent Altarpiece, painted by the Van Eyck brothers, which were returned to the Church of St. Bavo at Ghent from the Kaiser-Friedrich-Museum in Berlin,[31] and the panels of the triptych of the *Last Supper* by Dirk Bouts, two of which were in the Berlin museum and two in the Alte Pinakothek in Munich, all of which were returned to the Church of St. Peter in Louvain.[32]

World War I also resulted in the breakup of the Austro-Hungarian Empire, and both the Treaty of St. Germain of 1919 with Austria (see Appendix 5) and the Treaty of Trianon of 1920 with Hungary (see Appendix 6) included provisions obliging both of those nations to restore to the newly independent states of the Hapsburg monarchy cultural property taken before and during the war.[33] By the terms of the Treaty of Trianon, Hungary agreed to negotiate with the former states of the empire an "amicable arrangement" for the return of cultural objects "which ought to form part of the intellectual patrimony of the said States" (Article 177).[34]

The resolution of claims against Austria under the terms of the Treaty of St. Germain, however, was more complicated and more interesting. That treaty provided for a committee of three jurists to resolve claims to specific artistic, archaeological, scientific, and historic objects, put forward by Italy, Belgium, Poland, and Czechoslovakia (Article 195); it further provided that any objects of this nature that were not specifically included in such claims or otherwise referred to in the treaty could not be sold or otherwise transferred for twenty years (Article 196).[35] Items subject to arbitration by the designated committee included works by Michelangelo, Holbein, and Dürer, claimed by Czechoslovakia, and the Treasure of the Order of the Golden Fleece and the St. Ildefonso Triptych by Peter Paul Rubens, claimed by Belgium.[36] With respect to both the Czech and Belgian claims, the substantive issue was "whether movables purchased by a reigning Hapsburg sovereign out of revenues of which by law he had free disposal, became in law his absolute property, so that he was legally entitled to

remove his purchases out of the country whose revenues he had thus used, and so that further, on the dissolution of the Hapsburg monarchy, the modern states in which that country was incorporated or which had succeeded to its rights had no legal claim to recover the articles purchased."[37] In both cases, the committee concluded that Austria could keep all of the claimed objects.[38]

Poland fared much better in its claims for the return of cultural property. According to the terms of the Treaty of Riga of 1921 (see Appendix 7), by which the war between Poland, on the one hand, and Russia and Ukraine, on the other, ended and Poland attained independence, Poland was granted the return not merely of objects removed during World War I but also of all objects taken after the original partition of Poland in 1772.[39] Again, no statute of limitations was applied. The list of returned objects is staggering—the sword with which Polish kings had been crowned since the fifteenth century; 149 tapestries of wool, silk, and gold and silver threads dating from the sixteenth century and valued then at 115 million francs; 17 wagonloads containing 507 crates of artworks, including 600 paintings, 60 Gobelins tapestries, porcelains, armor, and furniture; and the collection of the Numismatic Society of the University of Warsaw.[40] The Treaty of Riga was unusual in that it provided that where the integrity of complete collections would be impaired by the return of only a part, other objects of the same artistic or scientific value could be substituted.[41]

ATTEMPTS BY THE LEAGUE OF NATIONS TO DRAFT CONVENTIONS FOR THE PROTECTION OF CULTURAL PROPERTY

In the early 1930s, the League of Nations focused its efforts on drafting conventions solely concerned with the protection of cultural property during periods of peace as well as war, as opposed to the approach of the Hague Convention, which included sections on cultural property within treaties dealing with broader issues of war in general. Although none of these draft conventions was adopted, a brief examination of their stated purpose and content affords an insight into attitudes prevalent at the beginning of World War II.

A draft Convention on the Repatriation of Objects of Artistic, Historical or Scientific Interest, Which Have Been Lost, Stolen, or Unlawfully Alienated or Exported was prepared by the International Museums Office and submitted to the League of Nations in 1933.[42] In the discussion of this draft convention, the league acknowledged the importance of national laws: "[A]t first sight, the formula of an international agreement may appear inadequate in a sphere where considerations with regard to home police organizations occupy the foremost position. Nevertheless, the examination of national laws reveals that there is absolute concordance between the preoccupations of a large number of countries."[43] Among the purposes of the proposed international agreement was "international collaboration in the protection of national artistic treasures" and "mutual assistance in the recovery of objects withdrawn from national collections."[44] The draft convention proposed two major rules: "[F]irst, with regard to objects illicitly exported by their owner, the obligation to repatriate them; secondly, with regard to objects illegally alienated, the cancellation of all transactions to which these objects may have given rise."[45] The draft convention provided for notification of any loss to the International Museums Office and in the event of disagreement, arbitration before, or other recourse to, the Permanent Court of International Justice for those nations that had accepted jurisdiction of the court.[46]

Significantly, when this draft convention was considered by the League of Nations, the problem of time limitations for the presentation of claims was discussed. It was noted in the discussion that "[M]ost of the legislative enactments relating to lost or stolen property prescribe that no claims shall be valid after a period of three years. Experience has shown, however, that it is very easy to conceal an object for a short period of time and then to dispose of it with impunity."[47]

The draft convention, which was criticized for a failure to distinguish between cultural property that was privately owned and that which was publicly owned, was not adopted.[48]

In 1936, a new draft convention, the International Convention for the Protection of National Artistic and Historical Treasures, was submitted to the League of Nations. This draft convention, which provided for the repatriation of objects of "remarkable paleo-ontological, archaeological, historic or artistic interest," as long as they had been officially documented before expatriation, was referred back to the Committee of the International Museums Office for further study, and, like the 1933 draft convention, was never approved.[49] In 1939, still another draft convention, the International Convention for the Protection of Historic Buildings and Works of Art in Time of War, was under discussion, but the outbreak of World War II ended this effort.[50]

POSTSCRIPT: THE ROLE OF PRIVATE LAWSUITS AND THE OBSTACLES POSED BY THE STATUTE OF LIMITATIONS

Although the Hague Convention failed to prevent the terrible pillage of cultural property during World War II, it is fair to say that the principles reflected by the Convention served as the basis for the repatriation of cultural property that occurred after the war. The process is a difficult one that is still ongoing today, as discussed in detail by many of the participants in the Bard Graduate Center symposium whose papers are published in this book.

Many recent efforts at repatriation have taken the form of private litigations, in which claimants, both sovereign and private, have sought, with varying success, to recover artworks stolen during the war, which have surfaced in places as far from the field of battle as New York and Texas. In these cases, however, the enemy with which the plaintiffs have to contend is the statute of limitations.

The statute of limitations almost always injects an enormous amount of expense and time into these cases. One of the best illustrations is the landmark American case of *Kunstsammlungen zu Weimar v. Elicofon*,[51] which involved the recovery of two magnificent Dürer paintings stolen during the war from a German museum. The courts spent no less than eight years addressing and determining issues relating to the statute of limitations.

The *Weimar* case involved two extraordinary fifteenth-century Dürer portraits from the collections of the Weimar Museum in eastern Germany. The paintings had been ripped from a triptych stored in the Schwarzburg Castle, where they had been moved for safekeeping during World War II. After occupation of the castle by American troops, the paintings were gone. They were discovered some twenty years after the war in the possession of a Brooklyn attorney, Edward I. Elicofon, who had purchased them in 1946 for $450 from an American serviceman who came to Elicofon's home, claiming that he had bought the paintings in Germany. Identification of the paintings was fortuitous—a friend of Elicofon's saw them in his house and remembered having seen them in a book on stolen artworks.[52]

Under the New York statute-of-limitations rule, a plaintiff has three years in which to initiate a lawsuit to recover stolen property in the possession of a good-faith purchaser. The period begins at demand and refusal, that is, from the time the plaintiff demands return of property from the possessor and the possessor refuses to comply. In *Weimar,* the limitations period commenced in 1966, when Elicofon, after allegedly learning of the paintings' true identity for the first time, held a press conference to announce his discovery and was immediately confronted with demands for their return by the Weimar Museum (at the time, an East German museum), the hereditary grand duchess of Saxony-Weimar-Eisenach, and West Germany, which claimed to be the sole representative of all of the German people pending unification. All of these demands were rejected.[53] Seeking to discredit New York's "demand and refusal" rule, Elicofon argued against its applicability to the case, and this was soundly rejected by the courts.

In addition, Elicofon argued that even if the demand and refusal rule applied, the Weimar Museum had a duty to make genuine and diligent efforts to look for the paintings and that it had not done so; its delay in making demand for the paintings, Elicofon argued, was therefore unreasonable and the lawsuit was not commenced in a timely fashion. The museum argued that such a "reasonable diligence" rule should not be engrafted upon the demand and refusal rule and that its only duty was to make demand once it learned of the location of the paintings, which it had done. The court, however, did not need to address this issue because it determined that the facts indisputably established that the museum had, in any event, made a diligent attempt to locate the paintings.[54] After extended litigation concerning all of these issues, the court awarded the paintings to the Weimar Museum.

However, plaintiffs have not been so fortunate in all of the cases of this nature brought in the United States. Indeed, only recently, one Mrs. DeWeerth, whose family lost a painting by Monet during the war in circumstances similar to those in which the Dürer paintings were lost, exhausted her attempt to get the United States Supreme Court to review a lower court's refusal to return the Monet to her, even after that court agreed that it had misconstrued the demand and refusal rule under New York law.[55]

It is therefore not surprising that plaintiffs sometimes decide to settle their claims, rather than risk the pitfalls of litigation, including those relating to the statute of limitations. And the potential for confusion and uncertainty is heightened by the fact that applicable statutes of limitations vary from nation to nation and, in some cases, from jurisdiction to jurisdiction within each nation. Few jurisdictions are as favorable to the plaintiff as New York.

Considering the importance accorded by the nations of the world to the preservation of each nation's cultural heritage, as reflected by the Hague Convention and other international agreements as well as by national laws, one may well ask why a nation or an individual from whom that property is wrongfully taken during wartime should lose the right to have the property returned because of the mere passage of time. As discussed above, this premise was implicitly rejected by the treaties concluded after World War I,[56] in apparent recognition of the principles favoring the repatriation of cultural property, long adhered to by the international community. It seems logical and appropriate that in recognition of these same principles, no statute of limitations should apply in any case seeking the return of cultural property looted during wartime, an issue I have addressed elsewhere.[57]

GERMAN LAWS AND

DIRECTIVES BEARING ON

THE APPROPRIATION

OF CULTURAL PROPERTY IN

THE THIRD REICH

Jonathan Petropoulos

It is my contention that an investigation of the Nazis' endeavor to appropriate cultural property is one of the best ways to understand the nature and structure of the regime. In this account of the laws and directives that comprised the looting program, the key features of Nazi rule become apparent. These include the following: (1) their programs grew more radical, beginning with modest and relatively nonviolent measures that steadily became more extensive and more malignant; (2) the policies stemmed from a combination of Hitler's personal orders and ministerial initiative, a complex interaction between the leader and his subordinates that scholars have explored for decades now without fully comprehending the implications; (3) many of the measures were first implemented outside of what the Germans called the *Altreich* (Old Reich: the nation's territory as of 1938)—specifically, in Austria, where the so-called Vienna model provided a crucial testing-ground for the Nazis' plundering operations; and (4) these laws and directives became inextricably linked with the Holocaust. The mass murder of Jews and others considered racially inferior was preceded by the expropriation of their property, with artworks standing out as a particularly important and visible component of that property.

To begin with point one concerning the gradual radicalization of the laws and directives that comprised the looting program, it should be noted that there was no organized appropriation prior to 1937. The book burnings of May 10, 1933, offer a possible exception, as members of the SA, flying high before the Blood Purge of June 1934, swept into libraries, universities, and institutes and carried off volumes that they thought fostered an "un-German spirit." But this event in the first days after the seizure of power was relatively spontaneous and quite exceptional. Not until the "degenerate art" campaign of 1937 was there an organized effort to secure cultural property.

The "degenerate art" campaign involved the removal of modernist artworks from state collections. Private property was not affected at that point in time—and, in fact, artists whose works were purged from museums, such as Emil Nolde, often requested the return of the works on the grounds that the art was private property on loan.[1] The purging—or, in Nazi parlance, the "cleansing"—of the state collections was carried out by a committee under the direction of the president of the Reichskammer der bildenden Künste (Reich Chamber for the Visual Arts), Adolf Ziegler. His cohorts included antimodernist activists, such as Wolfgang Willrich, various employees of the Propaganda Ministry, cultural bureaucrats from other ministries, and the director of the Folkwang Museum in Essen, Klaus Count von Baudissin. Previously, in April 1937, Willrich had been empowered by Goebbels to purge state collections, but museum directors proved uncooperative and refused to relinquish artworks.[2] Goebbels therefore brought President Ziegler into the picture (with a June 30 decree) and solicited an order from Hitler personally, dated July 14, 1937, that empowered the committee to attach works that featured abstraction or colors that did not conform to nature.[3] Ziegler's commission, armed with their Führer Decree, worked quickly and attached over five thousand works prior to the "Degenerate Art Exhibition," which opened in Munich on July 19, 1937.[4] The exhibition proved a propagandistic success from the very beginning, and eventually attracted over three million visitors as it traveled to various cities within the Reich. The apparently enthusiastic public reception induced other ministers to get involved, and on July 28 Göring, as minister president of Prussia, issued an order empowering Education Minister Bernhard Rust to pursue "degenerate" artworks within Prussia.[5] This order constituted a challenge to Goebbels and Ziegler, and Hitler was forced to intervene to resolve the dispute, which he did in an August 4, 1937, order affirming Goebbels's and Ziegler's jurisdiction over the program. Ziegler's committee continued their purges of the state collections into the autumn of 1937. It is significant that all the confiscations took place prior to May 31, 1938, when the law regarding "degenerate" art, drafted by Goebbels, was signed by Hitler.[6] This law is particularly interesting for two reasons. First, its tardiness shows that Hitler's directives from the previous year were sufficient to purge the state collections. Second, it is an example of the Nazis' utilization of an *ex post facto* law. They had little compunction about acting first and then later attending to the legality.

One finds a similar phenomenon in the next step in this radicalization process: the expropriation of artworks owned by Jews and communists in Austria after the Anschluss in March 1938. Himmler, Heydrich, and their SS and SD forces accompanied the Wehrmacht into Austria on March 13, and they immediately set off in search of declared enemies and their property. The most famous case was Louis Rothschild, arguably the wealthiest man in Austria, who was apprehended at the Aspern airport outside Vienna as he attempted to flee.[7] While he was imprisoned in the Gestapo headquarters at the Hotel Metropol, his palace on the Prinz-Eugen-Strasse was occupied and the contents, which included more than four thousand artworks, were secured on March 16 by the SS and

SD. Many other Jewish citizens in Austria (more specifically, in Vienna, where most lived) had their property attached in the period directly after the Anschluss. Yet the official directive for such actions did not come until April 26, with the Ordinance for the Registration of Jewish Property. This law required Jews to register all their possessions except household goods, and it included the provision that "objects would be secured in accordance with the dictates of the German economy."[8] Still, the most important collections belonging to Viennese Jews—those of the Rothschilds, the Bondys, the Lancoronskis, and others—were attached prior to the ordinance, in yet another instance where the deeds preceded the legal measures.

In June 1938, another crucial development took place in Austria as the concept of the *Führervorbehalt* (Prerogative of the Führer) was first articulated. By this point, large caches of art had been gathered in the Neue Hofburg in the heart of Vienna and at the Rothschilds' hunting lodge outside the city. By the end of the year, Himmler estimated that seventy million Reichsmarks worth of art were in these depots.[9] Of course, jurisdictional battles had broken out between various Nazi leaders. Hitler preempted his subordinates by borrowing a phrase from the Degenerate Art Law of May 31, 1938, which stated that "[Hitler] has authority over those objects which are given over to become property of the Reich."[10] This *Führervorbehalt* became the operative concept in future laws and directives, as it was applied first in Austria, then to the entire Reich, followed by Bohemia and Moravia, Poland, and finally all of the occupied territories.[11] Granted, this concept was not always respected by the subleaders, and they commandeered works for their own purposes. But it was an important directive in the history of the Nazis' plundering.

Within the *Altreich,* the legal measures providing for the expropriation of Jewish property came in the wake of the November 1938 Kristallnacht pogrom. The Nazis blamed the Jews themselves for inciting the riots and levied a tax, called a *Sühneleistung* (atonement tax), for the sum of one billion Reichsmarks. Previously, German and Austrian Jews had lost property as they emigrated, but the measures taken in the autumn of 1938 applied to those Jews who remained. In particular, the November 20 Ordinance for the Attachment of the Property of the People's and State's Enemies, and the December 3 Ordinance for the Employment of Jewish Property enabled government authorities to "Aryanize" Jewish businesses (including art dealerships) and seize Jews' property.[12] These various decrees were signed by Göring, as head of the Four-Year Plan, Minister of the Interior Wilhelm Frick, and Economics Minister Walther Funk. While they were often confusing and redundant—over four hundred anti-Jewish measures with economic import were signed during the Third Reich—they enabled the regime to pursue Jewish-owned artworks without legal restrictions.[13]

While 1937 brought the confiscation of state property, and 1938 saw the expropriation of private property within the Reich, the Nazis' policies became even more radical in 1939 as the military conquest of foreign lands entailed a new type of

46. Left to right: Arthur Seyss-Inquart, Kajetan Mühlmann, and Joseph Goebbels meet with Viennese Nazis after the Anschluss, March 1938.

plundering. Concomitant with the brutal attack on Poland in September of that year was the expropriation of cultural property belonging not only to Jews, but also to the state, to the Catholic Church, and to Polish aristocrats, among others. Two Nazi organizations undertook these operations. First on the scene were Himmler's SS and Heydrich's SD (these forces counting as one organization). They possessed orders from Hitler to attach property belonging to enemies of the Reich.[14] Himmler and Heydrich took steps to create special looting commandos, whose staffs included art historians and other scholars. The Sonderkommando Paulsen, led by a professor of Viking and early Germanic history, Peter Paulsen, was the best known of these commandos, partly because the unit located the Veit Stoss altarpiece from the Church of Our Lady in Cracow, which had been evacuated to Sandomierz on the Vistula River. While the SS and SD forces were the first to arrive in Poland, they were soon joined by a commando headed by the art historian Kajetan Mühlmann. Mühlmann, empowered by Göring on October 6, 1939, to confiscate artworks in conquered Poland, emerged as the central figure in the plundering of this area.[15] From Generalgouverneur of Poland Hans Frank, on November 15, and then on December 16, Mühlmann obtained two subsequent orders to confiscate property.[16] It is interesting that Göring, who was appointed Reichsmarschall on September 1, 1939, and who was by then Hitler's official successor, felt sufficiently powerful to issue such orders. Göring, as is well known, wore many hats, including heading the Haupttreuhandstelle Ost, an agency concerned with the economic exploitation of Poland. Mühlmann became one of the most prolific plunderers during the war—rivaled only by Alfred Rosenberg and his staff. Yet Mühlmann never received an official order from Hitler, even though he delivered volumes of photographs to the Führer documenting the prized works that he and his colleagues had

48. Hitler on his "art tour" of Paris in June 1940, accompanied by Albert Speer, Arno Breker (the leading sculptor in the Third Reich), and others

attached. Hitler did order Frank to undertake the liquidation of the "Polish upper crust" in a November 4, 1939, meeting; and he extended the *Führervorbehalt* to cover Poland.[17] But there were certain subleaders so powerful that they were able to issue orders that set loose plundering squads.

Himmler was another leader in this category. The Reichsführer SS not only drafted a December 16, 1939, decree (*Runderlass*) empowering the SS, the SD, and Mühlmann's commando to pursue "the confiscation of objects from Polish and Jewish possessions that are of cultural, artistic or historic value," but controlled an organization called the Ahnenerbe that attached artworks in the South Tyrol, the Baltic states, and Alsace-Lorraine.[18] The Ahnenerbe was purportedly a scholarly organization with the aim of providing scholarly evidence for the Nazis' Germanic ideology. But the Ahnenerbe was also a plundering agency.[19] Himmler exploited it for his own purposes. When Himmler was appointed the Reichskommissar for the Strengthening of Germandom in October 1939, a post in which he oversaw the resettlement of populations bordering on the Reich, he turned to the Ahnenerbe to arrange the transfer of cultural property.[20] Himmler then issued multiple directives to the Ahnenerbe's manager, Wolfram Sievers, that ordered the appropriation of cultural property in neighboring lands.

The plundering of France began after the cessation of fighting in the early summer of 1940.[21] Again, rival organizations emerged, and they all possessed orders from various leaders that supposedly empowered them to attach cultural property. The Foreign Office, headed by Joachim von Ribbentrop, became one of the first centers for the plundering bureaucracy in France. Ribbentrop possessed only verbal authorization from Hitler: on June 30, 1940, Hitler approved measures to expropriate Jewish-owned artworks.[22] Ribbentrop never secured a written commission to pursue artworks.

47. Generalgouverneur Hans Frank (left) and Kajetan Mühlmann in Cracow, 1940

Nonetheless, he was able to assemble a plundering squad headed by SS-Sturmbannführer Eberhard, Baron von Künsberg, who received a formal order via Ambassador Otto Abetz that was made known to the other occupation authorities on August 11, 1940.[23] Künsberg's commando faced considerable opposition, both from the French authorities and from the German Wehrmacht—more specifically, the Wehrmacht's art- and monuments-protection agency, called the Kunstschutz. Künsberg and his associates nonetheless attached a number of artworks and moved them to Paris, where they were stored in a building near the German Embassy on the rue de Lille.[24] At the end of the summer of 1940, it appeared that the Foreign Office would have the upper hand in this contest between competing groups, as Künsberg's group had secured some fifteen hundred paintings. The next most likely victor was Propaganda Minister Joseph Goebbels, who had launched a project called Rückforderung von Kulturgütern von Feind-staaten (Repatriation of Cultural Goods from Enemy States), which had the aim of recovering for the Germans all artworks of German origin or provenance taken by foreigners during the past four hundred years.[25] Hitler had authorized Goebbels to pursue this project in a Führer Decree of August 13, 1940, and Goebbels had enlisted the aid of museum experts, in-cluding Otto Kümmel, the director of the Staatliche Museen, Berlin (Berlin State Museums).[26] Lengthy lists were compiled that targeted Germanic artworks located abroad, and Goebbels made preparations to launch expert teams of his own. Hitler ultimately decided to wait until the peace negotiations with the French occurred before making claims on these Germanic works in their state collections; but, of course, such a con-ference never took place.[27]

As is well known, both Ribbentrop and Goebbels were outmaneuvered by Alfred Rosenberg, the Nazi ideologue who had been commissioned on January 29, 1940, to set up branch offices of the Hohe Schule, Nazi centers of higher learning. Rosenberg used these schools as the basis for his claims as a plunderer.[28] One of his objectives was to understand the

50. Alfred Rosenberg and Kurt von Behr of the ERR inspect looted objects in Paris, 1940.

enemies of National Socialism, and, to this end, he received permission from Hitler on July 5, 1940, to attach any archives or libraries that contained useful information about Jews, Slavs, communists, or Freemasons. Rosenberg, too, initially faced opposition from the Wehrmacht's Kunstschutz agency. His prospects looked dim at the end of the summer of 1940, when, in a stunning development, Hitler issued an order through the head of the armed forces, Wilhelm Keitel, dated September 17, 1940, that expanded the range of objects that Rosenberg's operatives could seize.[29] The Einsatzstab Reichsleiter Rosenberg (ERR), which was empowered to secure all "ownerless" (herrenlos) property, became dominant among the plundering agencies in France, eventually seizing over twenty-one thousand objects. Rival organizations, such as the Foreign Office, were required to hand over those works that they had attached (save for some modern works, which they sold or bartered on their own).[30] The competition in France remained fierce, inducing Rosenberg to seek an ally who could help protect his agency's prerogatives. Reichs-marschall Göring, who had attempted to pursue Jewish-owned artworks through his Devisenschutzkommando (Currency Control Commando), served this function; and he was quite successful in co-opting Rosenberg's agency through 1942. He issued a famous order on November 5, 1940, subject to the approval of Hitler, that determined how the seized artworks would be distributed. Hitler and his agents had first choice, followed by Göring, Rosenberg, and German museums.[31] Rosenberg later expanded the scope of his forces' activities to include furniture when Hitler approved his plans for the M-Aktion (Möbel-Aktion, or Furniture Project) on December 31, 1941.[32] Despite receiving a follow-up order from Hitler dated March 1, 1942, which authorized his pursuit of the property belonging to "Jews, Freemasons, and those opponents of National Socialism allied with them," Rosenberg ultimately lost much of his autonomy as Martin Bormann, the head of the Nazi Party Chancellery, proved successful in his efforts to dominate the ERR.[33]

49. Joseph Goebbels (right) consulting with Alfred Rosenberg (left), later head of the Einsatzstab Reichsleiter Rosenberg (ERR), and Nazi Party treasurer Franz Xaver Schwarz, 1934

51. Confiscated "degenerate" modern works in a separate room at ERR headquarters in the Jeu de Paume, Paris, 1942

Rosenberg also faced stiff competition in the Netherlands and Belgium in terms of attaching cultural property. Although small ERR staffs continued to operate in the Low Countries, they were overshadowed by Kajetan Mühlmann's operation, the Dienststelle Mühlmann, which fell within the bailiwick of Reichskommissar for the Occupied Netherlands Arthur Seyss-Inquart. The Dienststelle Mühlmann did not plunder to the same extent as the ERR in France; but Dutch Jews suffered terribly (with an extremely high mortality rate), and most of their property ended up in the hands of the Germans. Mühlmann's agency received much of this property, and processed it by selling it to the agents of the Nazi leaders.[34] Seyss-Inquart offered protection to Mühlmann, his longtime friend and fellow Austrian: he not only issued the necessary orders but provided sizable bank accounts to get the operation under way. In the summer of 1940, Seyss-Inquart also issued an ordinance that required Jews to take their valuables, including jewels and artworks, to Lippmann, Rosenthal and Co. Bank in Amsterdam. This "Aryanized" bank passed artworks on to Mühlmann's agency, which then sold them, giving first choice to Hitler, followed by Göring and the other Nazi leaders.[35] While Dutch Jews lost most of their artworks, Dutch and Belgian state collections remained largely unscathed, as the laws and directives in the West were decidedly moderate compared with those that prevailed in the East.

The ERR operated on the Eastern Front as well.[36] But here, where warfare was at its most brutal, they were but one of a number of agencies that confiscated cultural objects and sent them westward to the Reich. Ribbentrop had an agency that accompanied the advancing army groups: the Sonderkommando Ribbentrop was headed by Baron von Künsberg, who had been put out of business in France. Künsberg received his commission from Ribbentrop on August 5, 1941, and he arranged for three battalions to follow the army groups

into the Soviet Union.[37] The SS and SD also had plundering commandos in the region. All of these units were obliged to abide by the *Führervorbehalt,* but because Hitler had such a negative opinion of Slavic culture not a great deal was commandeered specifically for his collection. Depots in Berlin, including a massive building on the Hardenbergstrasse initially used by the Sonderkommando Ribbentrop, housed most of the plunder.[38] Much of the cultural property in the Soviet Union was destroyed in ideologically motivated acts of barbarism: Hitler's Führer Directive 33 stated that the German forces would be able to secure large areas only by "striking such terror into the population that it loses all will to resist."[39] At the International Military Tribunal at Nuremberg, the Soviet prosecutor General Rudenko stated that 427 of the 992 museums that fell into German hands were completely destroyed.[40] While not all the artworks in these museums perished, it is clear that the Nazis' policies became increasingly destructive over the course of time. This is what is meant by the radicalization of their policies.

In the latter half of the war, there were a number of directives issued concerning the disposition of the newly acquired art. For example, Hitler forbade the importation of modern art into the Reich, inducing the subleaders to participate in one-sided exchanges or "creative" initiatives such as sending the art to the Slovakian Protectorate.[41] There were also directives for safeguarding the looted art. But these measures lie beyond the scope of this paper, which is concerned with the process of attaching cultural property, and not so much with the subsequent arrangements.

To mention briefly the other important implications of these laws and directives concerning the seizure of cultural property, I would proceed to point two of my introduction, namely, that these measures tell us a great deal about the interaction between Hitler and his subordinates. Hitler was

52. The Great Palace at Petrodvorets (Peterhof), outside Leningrad (St. Petersburg), in ruins at the end of World War II

53. Heinrich Himmler (center) presents a painting to Hitler as a birthday gift, April 1939.

clearly the ultimate authority, as is suggested by the *Führervorbehalt*. But the subleaders possessed tremendous power—enough to commission their own plundering agencies, as in the case of Göring and the Sonderkommando Mühlmann in Poland and of Himmler and the Ahnenerbe. The Nazi regime was animated by this dynamic between "Führer absolutism," where Hitler's word was treated as law, and ministerial initiative, whereby the subleaders were expected to propose and implement new programs.[42] The laws and directives convey both the power of Hitler—who ultimately possessed more than five thousand paintings and numerous sculptures in his collection for the planned Führermuseum in Linz—as well as the decentralized nature of power in the Third Reich. The subleaders possessed a surprising degree of autonomy, as evidenced by their ability to circumvent the *Führervorbehalt* and amass sizable personal collections.[43]

Point three concerns the importance of the Vienna model. It is crucial to underscore that Austria served as a testing-ground for many of the Nazis' policies, both in the realm of plundering and, in a broader sense, with respect to the Holocaust. Just as Adolf Eichmann used his tenure in Vienna to refine his technique for dispossessing Jews of their property before emigration, the process of stealing artworks, first from Jews and communists, and then from the Catholic Church, was pioneered in Austria.[44] A number of monasteries and churches had their cultural property seized during the war—mostly by the SS and SD.[45] While the Austrian Nazis played leading roles in implementing these policies—the group includes Eichmann, Mühlmann, and Robert Scholz (a prominent art expert within the ERR), as well as a host of other functionaries—there is an element of truth in the claim that Austria was the first victim of Nazi aggression (though this formulation from the Moscow Declaration of 1943 is clearly very problematic).[46] A number of Viennese Jews possessed

remarkable collections, and it is not illogical that so many laws and directives were first tried out there.

Finally, as indicated in my fourth point, the connection between the looting measures and the Holocaust needs to be stressed. The expropriation of property was an important part of the Nazis' efforts to dehumanize the Jews. The theft of artworks was closely linked to their deportation to ghettos. In fact, one part of the plundering bureaucracy not yet mentioned, called the Vugesta, an acronym for Vermögens-umzugsgut der Gestapo (Property Transfer Authority of the Gestapo), was a Viennese office charged with processing all the property, including cultural goods, that surfaced when the local Jews were deported.[47] The Vugesta turned into a business, and leaders like Baldur von Schirach, the Reichs-statthalter (Reich governor) in Vienna, purchased works from this agency, as the owners were sent east to their horrible fate.

A number of scholars have noted that the persecution of the Jews often entailed not only racist motives but pecuniary ones. As historian Robert Koehl wrote, "While Heydrich and Eichmann seized the initiative in organizing the resettlement and killing of the Jews, they were continually abetted and even rivaled by other government and party agencies. Not the least of the motives involved in this initiative was the seizure of Jewish wealth."[48] Artworks, of course, comprised an important (not to mention easily transportable and inflation-resistant) component of this wealth. For the Nazis, artworks stood out as the most desirable objects available during the war.

The series of measures bearing on the appropriation of cultural property, then, involved a wide range of officials and agencies. Nearly all of the top Nazi leaders endeavored to participate in the looting programs due to a combination of racist, nationalist, and purely selfish motives. The result was a dizzying array of laws and directives. The import of these leaders' initiatives was not only a massive plundering operation, but a major step toward the dehumanization and murder of millions of people.

54. Hitler in the Berlin bunker under the Reich Chancellery, contemplating a model of the proposed Linz cultural complex, February 1945

THE END OF THE WAR

AND THE OCCUPATION OF

GERMANY, 1944–52.

LAWS AND CONVENTIONS

ENACTED TO COUNTER

GERMAN APPROPRIATIONS:

THE ALLIED CONTROL COUNCIL

Michael J. Kurtz

I would like to begin by stating that the views presented in this paper are mine alone, and do not necessarily represent the views of the United States government or of the National Archives and Records Administration.

This paper focuses on the Allied response to Nazi looting as expressed in the workings of the Allied Control Council in occupied Germany. Given the overall failure of the Allied Control Council to function as originally envisioned, most of our attention will be on the council's first year of existence, when the struggle to create an Allied restitution program was most intense. After that, the story becomes enmeshed in the zonal policies of the four occupying powers.

WARTIME BACKGROUND TO THE ALLIED CONTROL COUNCIL

To understand the workings of the Allied Control Council (ACC), we must begin with wartime Great Power diplomacy and the problem of rectifying the effects of Nazi looting. Only with this perspective can we understand the ACC's handling of restitution.

The first major Allied discussions concerning efforts to recover lost property began in 1942 in two main forums: a subcommittee of the exiled European governments planning for an eventual armistice, and periodic meetings of finance ministers, presided over by the British.[1] For the exiled governments, much of their planning revolved around restitution and reparations.[2]

Most of the discussion in early and mid-1942 took place among the exiled ministers of finance.[3] In the summer of 1942, they debated the text of a proposed declaration reserving the right to invalidate all transfers of property rights and interests in territory occupied by the Axis.[4] Because the United States had no representation in the finance ministers' group, the Americans had no influence on most of the negotiations that eventually led to the London Declaration of January 5, 1943, the Inter-Allied Declaration Against Acts of Dispossession Committed in Territories Under Enemy Occupation or Control (see Appendix 9).[5] The U.S. State Department belatedly requested that the American embassy in London send a representative to a crucial July 24 meeting on the proposed declaration.[6] But, typical of American reluctance to make any postwar political commitments, State Department instructions included only an expression of American sympathy and a request for a ten-day postponement until the American government formulated a policy on the declaration.

Several interesting points of contention arose during these negotiations, which illuminate the differences between the occupied states and the Big Three and the difficulties in implementing cultural restitution. First of all, the smaller nations, led by Belgium, wanted a statement of obligation binding all signatories to assist in the recovery of property.[7] The British led the opposition, arguing that the Belgian proposal turned the declaration into a treaty requiring a lengthy ratification process.[8] In reality, the British were reluctant to bind their hands with mandatory obligations to the smaller powers. The British, Americans, and Soviets wanted a free hand in all matters relating to the postwar settlement.

This reliance on general statements of principle, while at the same time maintaining operational flexibility, characterized the stance of the Big Three in other issues that arose. For example, at the urging of the United States a warning to neutral governments about trafficking in looted property was watered down to a warning to all persons in neutral countries.[9] Also, at American insistence the text was reworded from stating that the declaration related to the "Axis Powers and their associates" to "the governments with which the signatories are at war."[10] This allowed the Soviet Union, which was not at war with Japan, to sign the declaration. Getting the Soviets involved, though they expressed little interest in these negotiations, always remained a top American priority in wartime diplomacy.

The issuance of the declaration on January 5, 1943, began the next round of difficulties. While the text denounced all methods of dispossession, no mention of concretely implementing the declaration was included.[11] A pattern was set in regards to restitution: the pattern of laboriously developed agreements on principles, unaccompanied by specific procedures for implementation.

The Belgians, Dutch, and Norwegians wanted a subcommittee of experts to make recommendations on implementing the declaration in various countries. The British succeeded in restricting the subcommittee to a fact-finding role.[12]

Even this proved controversial. The subcommittee gathered data on existing legislation in Allied countries that invalidated forced transfers, Axis methods of disposition, and drafted a report documenting depredations.[13] The Polish government-in-exile submitted a report on events in eastern Poland, occupied by the Soviet Union.[14] At the furious insistence of the Soviets, this section was dropped from the final report. With little American input or interest, the British and Soviets successfully argued that all political disputes must be kept apart from the work of the technical committees.[15] Another pattern was set.

Concern in the United States about cultural preservation during the war and later restitution primarily came from the art and museum world.[16] However, by late summer 1943, the State Department did announce the establishment of an advisory panel to assist the government in formulating policies for the protection of fine arts and monuments during the war in Europe and for the return of any looted cultural items after the war.[17] Under the chairmanship of Supreme Court Justice Owen J. Roberts, the panel was generally referred to as the Roberts Commission. Members came from private organizations and federal agencies.[18] From its earliest deliberations, the Roberts Commission urged the British and Soviets to organize similar national commissions and began debating the definition of "works of art" and the scope of future restitution—topics that would bedevil Allied negotiations.

In the last two years of the conflict, postwar restitution, a goal generally accepted by all the Allies, became thoroughly embroiled in the diplomatic and political conflicts of the Great Powers. The smaller powers in a variety of forums, such as the Conference of Allied Ministers of Education and the Interallied Commission for the Study of the Armistice, urged the early establishment of an interallied body for cultural restitution. This proposed organization was to have extensive powers to control property in Germany, recover looted property stored in neutral countries, set up special restitution machinery for persecuted minorities, and settle claims.[19] This obviously would guarantee conflicts with neutral countries and with the Big Three, who did not favor any competing machinery apart from what they planned.

In the face of these pressures, the three major Allies had differing responses. The Soviets ignored the schemes and the organizations behind them.[20] The American and British governments were internally divided regarding the principles and machinery for cultural restitution.[21] From 1943 onward, the Big Three's discussions about the future of Europe continued on the working level in a forum known as the European Advisory Commission (EAC). This became more urgent in the post-D-Day environment.

On the larger issues involving postwar Germany, the Big Three could agree only on a brief surrender document restricted to military matters, zonal boundaries for the future zones of occupation, and a bare-bones structure for the future military government.[22] The approved governing structure included an Allied Control Council, composed of the commanders-in-chief from each zone, and a Coordinating Committee to implement ACC decisions. No agreement on principles for governing Germany was ever reached.[23]

In EAC discussions, which by early 1945 included the French, issues involving cultural restitution went nowhere. On the issue of an international body of experts to handle cultural restitution, the Americans officially had no position, the British favored it in a tepid fashion, the French agreed with reservations, and the Soviets blocked it. Concerning a restitution-in-kind replacement policy, vigorously pushed by the French, the other three Powers showed little interest. Nothing was accomplished regarding a final EAC policy on control of works of art and monuments, or in establishing a restitution commission.

Several important facts and problems emerge from this brief review of Allied wartime diplomacy, particularly as it concerned restitution. First of all, restitution policy was a vital concern to only one of the Big Four, France. The British and Americans had only a peripheral interest, and the Soviets had their own ideas on how to recoup their losses. Serious Allied disagreements on general postwar policy for Germany inhibited the development of a coherent approach to handling cultural objects. Cultural restitution became lost in the maze of other, greater conflicts. Finally, many issues revolving around cultural restitution were in themselves very complex. Issues such as the scope of the entire effort, restitution-in-kind, returning property to refugees, and the disposition of heirless property were difficult to resolve. The German collapse in May

1945 placed these problems squarely in the lap of the occupying powers.

THE ALLIED CONTROL COUNCIL AND CULTURAL RESTITUTION—THE FIRST YEAR

During the summer of 1945, restitution issues remained enmeshed with the broader and more volatile issue of reparations. These problems were thoroughly aired at a reparations conference held in Moscow in June, and at the Big Three's Potsdam Conference in July. Agreements were impossible to reach, and the issues involving property were deferred to a conference of foreign ministers set for the fall of 1945.

In this contentious environment, members of the Allied Control Council, and their deputies who functioned as a Coordinating Committee (CORC) for the council, began to wrestle with the issue of restitution after the foreign ministers in turn had failed to resolve the matter. The Soviet delegate to the CORC, General Sokolovsky, insisted that the Soviet Union could not agree to any restitution actions until an overall definition for the term "restitution" and the property covered by the term were settled.[24] That very point had eluded the EAC, the Potsdam Conference, and the foreign ministers.

Throughout October and November 1945, the CORC remained deadlocked on the definition and scope of restitution. The Soviet Union favored restricting restitution to only those items removed by force.[25] The other three powers insisted that the January 5, 1943, declaration included dispossession by any means.[26] In view of the deadlock, the Reparations, Deliveries and Restitution Directorate (DRDR), at the direction of the CORC, focused its efforts on reaching an agreement for the interim restitution of cultural works. The DRDR set up a Cultural Works Committee, which drew up a plan for restitution restricted to easily identifiable items of well-known ownership, which were taken during the occupation. In this scheme, all movable goods of religious, artistic, documentary, scholarly, or historic value, "the disappearance of which constitutes a loss to the cultural heritage of the country concerned," were included in the interim plan. The plan also provided for submitting descriptive lists of missing items and establishing panels of experts to review claims, with monthly reports to the DRDR required. The CORC approved the interim plan on December 12, 1945.[27] All this reflected what the Americans were already doing in their zone.[28]

The quadripartite interim cultural restitution plan awaited a final ACC decision on the definition and scope of a restitution program covering all categories of property. Finally, after months of debate in the CORC and the ACC, a final agreement on the definition of restitution was reached by the ACC on January 21, 1946.[29] The definition primarily reflected a proposal made by the American representative, General Lucius D. Clay.[30] Clay's proposal defined property liable to restitution as everything taken by force, with property obtained through other means eligible for return if consistent with reparations

agreements. This last point referred to industrial property. No Allied agreement, including this definition, ever specified that works of art or other cultural materials could be used for reparations purposes.

Also included in the definition of January 21 was a compromise agreement on the difficult issue of restitution-in-kind, that is, the replacement of a stolen, unrecoverable cultural item with a comparable German item. During the debate in the CORC, General Clay had supported the Soviet position on restricting restitution-in-kind to unique works of art, rather than a broad-based effort favored by the French. Clay categorically stated that he "would not commit the United States to replacement of objects of art item for item."[31] With the British supporting the Soviets and the Americans, the French reluctantly agreed to a provision which put the issue off a bit longer. The CORC revision, agreed to by the ACC, read: "As to goods of a unique character, restitution of which is impossible, a special instruction will fix the categories of goods which will be subject to replacement, and the conditions under which such goods could be replaced by equivalent objects."[32] The January 21 agreement did not authorize an immediate restitution-in-kind program. It merely provided for the preparation of a "special instruction" to define the parameters of such an effort.

The January 21 definition had several weaknesses. It did not indicate how the restitution and reparations efforts were to interact, included no precise delineation of the various methods of dispossession, and was silent on such issues as restitution to ex-enemy nations, restitution of property taken from German citizens, and the disposition of heirless property.[33] In effect, the ACC failed to resolve the difficult legal, political, and economic problems relating to property control. Most of the issues that the ACC sidestepped or ignored never were resolved at the quadripartite level, eventually forcing unilateral decisions by the zonal commanders.

Restitution procedures, issued on April 17, 1946, reflected the general Allied inability to operate programs on a quadripartite or unified basis.[34] The responsibility for implementing procedures, and thus controlling restitution, was placed on the zonal commanders. Their duties included searching for and locating looted property, the custody and preservation of this property, and providing assistance to Allied restitution missions. The procedures did not spell out the method of handling claims when they were received nor the parameters for the functioning of restitution missions. These were left to the discretion of the zonal commanders.[35] Clearly, there would be four restitution programs, not one.

Most of the restitution debates in the ACC, the CORC, and the DRDR focused on industrial property. But drawing up the "special instruction" for restitution-in-kind of unique works of art consumed a great deal of time in the CORC and the DRDR.

The debates between April and July 1946 foundered on several points: Soviet insistence that they could not account for cultural property removed from their zone of occupation; the French demand for a comprehensive object-for-object replacement effort; and the American position that such restitution should be a very rare occurrence. The Soviet position was consistent with its refusal to allow any investigation or accounting of activities carried out in its zone. This also reflected the general Soviet lack of cooperation in economic matters, and reports that the Soviets were using German cultural property for trophies of war and reparations.[36]

A final effort to prepare a detailed "special instruction" for restitution-in-kind collapsed when the Soviets objected to a proposed article that required: "In cases where the request for replacement is submitted by one of the Occupying Powers, the Allied Control Council will require the Commander of the Zone of that Occupying Power to submit a list of all similar or equivalent German-owned property removed from its Zone by the Occupying Power submitting the request and the basis on which such removals were made."[37]

Finally, on July 9, 1946, the CORC agreed to a brief American-drafted paper which listed five categories of items eligible for possible replacement.[38] These included: works of art by the masters of painting, engraving, and sculpture; important works of masters of applied art and outstanding examples of national art; historical relics; manuscripts and rare books; and objects of importance to the history of science. The paper clearly stated this instruction covered only items of great rarity, which the Allied Control Authority would consider on a case-by-case basis.[39]

During the discussion of the American proposal, General Harper, the United States delegate, explained that claims were to be submitted to the DRDR as the appropriate quadripartite forum.[40] Clearly, claims were not to be handled unilaterally in each zone of occupation, but were to be processed under the auspices of the Allied Control Authority. This point was reinforced again at the sixty-first meeting of the DRDR, on February 25, 1947.[41]

The French delegate argued once again for a more elaborate process for handling restitution-in-kind claims, with the American representative dissenting from the need for any procedure. The DRDR, representing the four occupying powers, agreed with the American position and stated that any zone commander could inform any government with a restitution claim that, "after having been notified by all four zones of the failure of all research pertaining to a restitution claim, the claimant nation, if it considers that the object falls into at least one of the categories established by CORC/M(46)34 Appendix 'A,' will be able to submit to the RD&R Directorate a claim for a replacement on an equivalent basis, so that any action taken on each claim may be based on the evidence presented and the merits of each case."[42]

This meant that no nation, including any of the four occupying powers, had the authority to obtain restitution-in-kind other than by submitting a claim on a case-by-case basis to the DRDR for study and approval. No claims were received by the DRDR for review or decision.

THE REALITY OF RESTITUTION AFTER THE FIRST YEAR

After this point, all efforts to implement restitution at the ACC level ended. American efforts to get a unified policy for restitution to ex-enemy nations were blocked by the Soviets, and the French would not agree to a proposal for setting a final date for filing restitution claims. The Soviets blocked American efforts to get quadripartite agreements on interzonal transfers of German cultural property and to recognize Jewish organizations as inheritors of heirless Jewish property.

Though agreements on interzonal transfers of German cultural property and the disposition of heirless Jewish property were ultimately reached among the three Western Allies, the Soviets refused cooperation. Despite repeated demands stated in the CORC and ACC and by the Western zonal commanders, the Soviets refused to let restitution missions enter their zone, provide an account of their restitution program, or report on their management of German cultural property.[43] Though ACC directives had abolished the Nazi Party and confiscated its property, as well as all items that glorified Nazi and German militarism, these issuances did not sanction the use of the German cultural heritage for reparations and restitution purposes.[44] These directives encompassed only the property of organizations or individuals directly linked to the Nazi regime.[45] Thus, these directives did not provide a legal basis for the wholesale removal by the Soviets of German cultural property.

The ACC impasse on restitution reflected the deep disagreements among the Allies over the political and economic future of Germany. Cultural restitution became enmeshed in the questions involving reparations and property in general. Above all, the fate of cultural restitution in the ACC reflected the rapid disintegration of relations between the Western Allies and the Soviet Union. Cultural restitution became one of the many flash points in the emerging Cold War struggle for the control of Europe.

CULTURAL RESTITUTION IN THE AMERICAN ZONE

Later chapters in this volume will explore in some detail operations in the American Zone of Occupation involving the return of looted cultural property (see below, Part 4: "Repatriations Following World War II: The Immediate Postwar Period, 1945–51"). But I believe it is appropriate to conclude this paper on the Allied Control Council by looking briefly at cultural restitution in the American Zone. After all, the failure of the ACC meant that cultural restitution was really a zonal phenomenon.

Early on, the American military, through the efforts of Monuments, Fine Arts, and Archives (MFA&A) officers, began working to uncover the sites where the Germans had hidden cultural property. Military Government Law No. 52 was enacted, prohibiting the sale or transfer of any work of art except as military government regulations permitted.[46] This was designed to prevent the dispersion of looted property. Eventually, the Americans located fourteen hundred repositories containing over fifteen million items of looted and German cultural property.[47]

These materials were brought together in Collecting Points for protection. Eventually, 3.45 million items were identified by foreign restitution missions and returned to the countries of origin.[48] During the years of greatest activity, between 1945 and 1949, the American military government returned German items to local control and initiated a far-ranging effort for the return of heirless Jewish property.

However, the growing Soviet control of Eastern Europe and the ensuing Cold War antagonisms led to American decisions in 1947 and 1948 to return looted property only to the owners and not to the countries of origin when the owners had fled the country for religious, racial, or ideological reasons.[49] This change in policy was a major deviation from restitution principles accepted from 1943 onward. This symbolized the final failure of Allied diplomacy in the arena of cultural restitution.

THE TRANSFER OF

THE CONTENTS OF GERMAN

REPOSITORIES INTO

THE CUSTODY OF THE USSR

Nikolai Nikandrov

Public opinion has been stirred by this subject, which for the last fifty years seemed to have been forgotten. There is now widespread interest in this topic and in the complex problems involved, which require general knowledge and experience in a field that is relatively new for Russia.

The establishment in 1992 of the Russian State Commission on the Restitution of Cultural Property provided an impetus to begin the systematization of archival materials concerning the displacement of museum and other cultural property during World War II. The State Commission on Restitution gives priority to identifying and searching for Russian losses, since during the last fifty years the authorities in the former USSR did not undertake any focused and systematic action in this area. Simultaneously, archival documents are being identified concerning the displacement of the cultural property of Germany to the territory of the former Soviet Union.

American and German researchers studying the problems and circumstances of the displacement of cultural and artistic property can make use of fundamental research studies and numerous publications in their work. Russia, however, is evidently one of the few states that does not have an exhaustive catalogue of its losses. We are obliged to start everything from scratch, by searching for and identifying archival sources that are not systematized and therefore have not been studied. Moreover, these sources are scattered throughout the archives of various Russian ministries, agencies, and institutions. I repeat: We are at the very beginning of this road. Our base of documents is still incomplete and because of its scattered and fragmented nature has not allowed for an exhaustive picture of the situation to date.

One of the major recipients of the loads of German cultural property removed to the USSR, and also the coordinator of their displacement, was the Committee on Arts Affairs of the USSR. Its archives present a clear picture of this process. During the period from 1945 to 1946, the committee received from German territory seventeen railroad trains consisting of three hundred fifty cars containing 12,644 items. So far no evidence has been found showing that the authorities and cultural institutions of the USSR were preparing special subunits (like the Einsatzstab Reichsleiter Rosenberg in Germany) designed to carry out large-scale removals of German cultural property.

The authorities of the USSR were seriously concerned both with identifying losses and with the possibilities for compensation for such losses. There was little to console them here, for on the territory liberated from the aggressor and in Germany, the repositories found by the few brigades of the Committee on Arts Affairs most frequently contained German and other foreign (non-Soviet) art objects. A large group of the documents in the committee's archives contains evidence of the discovery of cultural property in castles, secret repositories, and mines in the territory of Germany occupied by Soviet troops. I shall briefly deal with one such episode.

In February 1945, a brigade of the Committee on Arts Affairs was sent to the region of hostilities at the First Belarusan

Front to find depots of museum property that had been removed from the occupied part of the Soviet Union. Repositories containing such objects were discovered on the grounds of the Focke-Wulf airplane-engine factory in the village of Hochwald in the Imeritz region. Inspection of these repositories was carried out by the brigade with the approval of the Military Council of the Sixty-ninth Army, whose units were then participating in the assault along the Oder and were preparing to storm Berlin. The inspection revealed paintings, porcelain, furniture, religious objects, and coins, some of which had been plundered and damaged. The command of the Sixty-ninth Army and the Trophy Division of the First Belarusan Front decided to send the property that had been discovered to the Soviet Union. The items were taken from the repositories to a train six kilometers away. Six hundred nineteen cases were loaded onto the train, which was hidden in the forest to avoid its being bombed from the air.

The brigade was working in a region where hostilities were taking place, and because emergency measures were required to prevent plundering and misuse only the number of items was recorded (without verification of the contents of the cases). Cases filled with smaller items were packed inside larger cases, banded with iron, and covered with camouflage. The train arrived in Moscow, where expert registration of the art objects was carried out at the Pushkin State Museum of Fine Arts.

Other trains, which were put together at bases in Potsdam, Berlin, Leipzig, and other cities in Germany, were sent off by the administration responsible for these trophy objects with the participation of the Committee on Arts Affairs, which was given detailed descriptions of the contents. Each train was headed by the chief of transportation, to whom military guards were assigned, and who represented the Trophy subdivisions of the Soviet army. The formation, dispatch, and transfer of these trains to the Committee on Arts Affairs was carried out in accordance with the orders of the commander in chief of the Soviet Occupying Forces in Germany and of the Soviet Military Administration in Germany (SVAG; English acronym SMAG). The final comparison of the initial lists with the actual contents of the cases was done by the recipients of the shipments—the representatives of the Committee on Arts Affairs, of the Trophy subdivisions, and of the museums in which, on the committee's instructions, the exhibits were to be stored.

The SMAG command also gave its approval for the removal of museum objects that had been discovered. After such approval was received, the Plenipotentiary of the Committee on Arts Affairs gave instructions to provide each brigade with transportation and appropriate manpower to export these objects to the Soviet Union. As a rule, the reason for this was the lack of appropriate repositories which could have met museum standards and rules.

The most important of these objects were studied by major Soviet art experts, archaeologists, and scholars, who reported on the results of their investigations to the Central Committee of the VKPb (All-Union Russian Party of Bolsheviks).

Inspection of the Potsdam castles and palaces revealed that the most valuable canvases had been taken by the Germans to the region of Thuringia and to the Hohenzollern Palace in Rheinsberg, and that part was found in Lehnin and part in Potsdam. It was proposed that

- historical ensembles with monumental sculpture be preserved;
- the most valuable items in a number of repositories be removed;
- the work of German masters be removed only in exceptional cases and in extremely small quantities;
- examples of eighteenth-century furniture (not more than thirty) that had been evacuated to various points be removed and used to restore the interiors of eighteenth-century Leningrad (St. Petersburg) suburban palaces destroyed by the Nazis.

An inspection of Berlin's museum sites showed that the majority of the museum buildings had been nearly destroyed. It became clear that part of the museum property of Berlin had been evacuated by the Germans to western regions of Germany, and that part was in repositories in Potsdam. Among the emergency measures taken to preserve the enormously valuable objects hidden in the flak tower on the grounds of the Berlin Zoo was a proposal to send them to warehouses located in the city abattoir and in the Treskow palace, where packing of the objects could be organized.

Monuments of classical and Eastern sculpture and cases with works of art and art objects were discovered in the basement of the Mint. Since the basement had been flooded before Berlin was taken by the Soviet troops, these required thorough restoration. In November 1945, after receiving approval from the SMAG command for the removal of museum objects, the Plenipotentiary of the Committee on Arts Affairs appealed to the SMAG commander in chief, Marshal Zhukov, to provide seventy train cars for removal of property from the Berlin base, and twenty for removal of property from Leipzig.

There were plans to send the monumental friezes of the Pergamon altar, which had been discovered in the flak tower of the Berlin Zoo, by road transportation to Frankfurt an der Oder, from where they were to be sent to the Soviet Union in accordance with a decree of the Soviet government. In November 1945, the departure of one of the trains from Berlin was postponed because some of the art objects had been stored in the flooded basement; because of possible temperature fluctuations it was deemed extremely risky to send them off in winter.

Displaced cultural property discovered in German territory was removed and exported to the Soviet Union on the orders of the commander in chief of SMAG. It is absolutely clear and confirmed by documents that cultural property was displaced to the USSR in cases where there was a lack of clarity with respect to origin or in order to ensure its preservation and to provide more favorable conditions for a final decision regarding its fate. To avoid tiring the reader with additional facts, I shall consider only one of the basic aspects of this question. I have in mind the assessment of the legality or illegality of actions in removing cultural property both by Germany, which had unleashed World War II in Europe, and by the USSR, which had suffered as the result of the aggression.

According to the conclusion of specialists of the Institute of State and Law of the Russian Academy of Sciences, which was prepared on the instructions of the State Commission on Restitution, all cultural property displaced to the USSR on orders of the commander in chief of SMAG is in Russia on a legal basis insofar as the commander in chief of SMAG was acting on the basis of the laws of the Allied Control Council. Certain cases require further discussion and negotiations. It is absolutely clear that, in the last analysis, the fate of cultural property of German origin displaced to the territory of the USSR can be resolved through the international legal acts adopted as a result of the defeat of Germany and its allies. These are the peace treaties with Italy, Bulgaria, Hungary, and Romania, acts of the Allied Control Council, and the orders of the commanders in chief of the zones of occupation in Germany.

The Allied Control Council, which had supreme authority in occupied Germany as a whole, and the commander in chief of SMAG, who had supreme authority in the Soviet Zone of Occupation,* issued a number of laws concerning confiscation of the property of Nazi organizations (Control Council Laws No. 2 and No. 58; SMAG Civil Code Edict No. 80), of the Wehrmacht (Control Council Law No. 34), and of war criminals (Control Council Law No. 10), and others.†

In implementing the Potsdam Agreement on the denazification of Germany, the Allied Control Council, having abolished the National Socialist Party, all of its units, all organizations affiliated with it, and sixty-three other Nazi institutions, also decreed in one of its first laws (Law No. 2 of October 10, 1945) that all movable and immovable property, holdings, and archives belonging to them should be confiscated. Expanding the scope of Control Council Law No. 2, SMAG issued Order No. 126 of October 31, 1945, On the Confiscation of the Property of the National Socialist Party, Its Organs, and of Organizations Affiliated with It.

The process of denazification also affected the fate of libraries, whose holdings were reviewed in entirety in connection with the removal of literature that promulgated fascism and militarism in Germany. SMAG Order No. 39, On the Removal of Nazi and Militarist Literature, provided for the removal from private libraries, bookstores, and publishing houses of all books, pamphlets, albums, and other literature containing propaganda for fascism, racist theory, the seizure of foreign territory, and also any kind of literature aimed against the USSR and other Allied nations. These sanctions were also applicable to all military literature, textbooks, and manuals for military educational institutions and armies. One copy of all publications was sent to the Academy of Sciences of the USSR to be used for scholarly purposes. Such literature was not subject to return, but in order that it be available for study within the territory of Germany, another copy of these publications was given to the Deutsche Bibliothek–Deutsche Bücherei (German Library) of the city of Leipzig, which was the national bibliographic center for Germany (opened by SMAG Order No. 12 of September 8, 1945). At the present stage of study of archival materials, there has still been no analysis of the result of SMAG's activity in implementing this order. However, information in the documents that have been studied seems to indicate that this activity was considerable.

The displacement of cultural property resulting from decisions of military tribunals concerning its confiscation affected, for the most part, the private collections, libraries, and other property of convicted individuals. Allied Control Council Law No. 10 and Directive No. 38 established the legal basis for the Allied powers to bring certain categories of individuals before military tribunals. Law No. 10, Punishment of Individuals Guilty of War Crimes and Crimes Against Peace and Against Humanity, was passed in accord with the Moscow Declaration of October 30, 1943 (On the Responsibility of the Hitlerites for Brutalities Committed . . .), and with the London agreement of August 8, 1945 (On the Judicial Prosecution and Punishment of Major War Criminals of the European Countries of the Axis . . .). SMAG Order No. 126 established that the entire immovable and movable personal property of those sentenced by military tribunals to confiscation of property was to be handed over to the Soviet state. Allied Control Council Law No. 9 of November 30, 1945 (On the Confiscation of Property Belonging to I. G. Farbenindustrie and Control of It . . .), was the basis for the SMAG order published in March 1946 stating that property of the directors of Farbenindustrie, amounting to forty-six cases, was being given to the Committee for Cultural and Educational Institutions of the Russian Federation for purposes of restoring the museums of the USSR. These cases were found in the Wintershalle mine in Bernburg, Saxony-Anhalt. The wording "for purposes of restoration of museums of the USSR" was interpreted in this case as meaning "for purposes of compensation for losses."

In accordance with a SMAG order of March 1946, the Committee for Cultural and Educational Institutions received cultural property and objects, found in mines and repositories, from the following:

- The Zerbst Palace Museum
- The collection of negatives of the State Recording Library
- Staatliche Museen, Berlin (archaeological collections)
- Museum für Völkerkunde (Museum of Ethnography), Berlin
- The Oranienbaum Palace Museum
- Paintings and portraits from the Potsdam palaces
- Coins and medals, including valuables from the Meissen Hussar barracks

---

* Editor's note: Officially, the Allied Control Council was responsible for the overall governance of occupied Germany, while the zonal commanders had operational control; in fact, as there was no mechanism to enforce this hierarchy, in certain respects the zones of occupation might function autonomously.

† Editor's note: See Kurtz, note 44 (page 260), for references pertaining to Allied Control Council laws mentioned here.

SMAG Order No. 334, of November 29, 1946 (On the Sending to the Soviet Union of Property Belonging to the Belaieff Music-Publishing House in Leipzig), contained the phrase "as a means of compensating for losses caused by the war to the musical manuscript holdings of the USSR." On May 13, 1946, the Allied Control Council adopted Directive No. 30, Elimination of German Military and Nazi Monuments and Museums. On the basis of this directive, SMAG ordered that the cultural property of the Zeughaus (military-historical museum) of the city of Berlin and its libraries found in the Count Moltke mine (in the city of Schönebeck, Saxony-Anhalt), be handed over to museums of the USSR.

Directive No. 30 of the Allied Control Council ordered that by January 1, 1947, all military museums and exhibitions in German territory be eliminated and also that all Nazi monuments, posters, statues, and so forth be completely destroyed and eliminated. Possibilities for preservation were provided only for objects of extraordinary artistic value.

Among the property transferred to the USSR from Germany, there was also cultural property belonging to the Allies. During the period 1945–46 the Pushkin State Museum of Fine Arts transferred to the Polish government more than twenty-two thousand works of art.

At the end of the 1950s, the leadership of the Soviet Union undertook on its own initiative a large-scale return to the German people of cultural property that had been displaced to the USSR during the postwar period. According to existing information, some cultural property still remained in Russian repositories, including those objects whose origin was difficult to determine.

At the end of the 1950s, when a large-scale transfer to the German Democratic Republic (GDR) of a great number of cultural and art objects was being prepared, the Soviet authorities evidently heeded the view of eminent scholars, including outstanding museum specialists, regarding the usefulness or even the necessity of keeping some of the objects of German origin in the Soviet Union, along with those works whose origin was difficult to determine. The major motivation here was that these remaining objects could, at least to some extent, compensate for the Soviet Union's losses during the war. Moreover, it was assumed that since the GDR was not able to return anything, a great deal must have been located in the territory of the Federal Republic of Germany. At the present time, certain Russian museums have begun preparing these objects for display and in order to make them public. It goes without saying that the problems relating to this property are complex and serious.

Recent agreements between Russia and various European countries have included provisions for the return of lost or illegally displaced cultural property. These provisions now require careful preparation and a clarification of our position. In particular, in the previously mentioned conclusion of the Institute of State and Law of the Russian Academy of Sciences, there is a clause stating that cultural property of religious and private charitable organizations should be returned, even in those cases where displacement to the USSR of cultural property that belonged to these organizations was carried out on the basis of an order of the commander in chief of SMAG.

In the view of Russian legal experts, articles of the agreements between Russia and Germany of 1990 and 1992 concerning the process of the mutual return of cultural property (see Appendix 14 and Appendix 15) require additional legal interpretation to clarify the concepts of "unlawful transfer" and "lawful transfer" regarding cultural property of German origin displaced to the territory of the former Soviet Union. The Russian side intends to study most carefully the circumstances of the displacement of each collection, each collection of books, and each piece of cultural property, considering that irreplaceable cultural losses should be replaced by objects of the same type and of the same quality. The conflicts that have quite naturally existed up to now between the parties can be overcome only by reliable documentation of losses, which must be checked through the use of archival materials.

In resolving the question of the removal of cultural property, it is inadmissible to put Germany and Russia (USSR) on an equal footing. Convinced that the art of Slavic peoples did not represent anything of value, Hitler's army deliberately and skillfully devastated our land. Germany was the aggressor. It bears the responsibility for this international crime. The USSR is a state that was subject to aggression and therefore has the indisputable right to compensation for losses inflicted on it by the aggressor. Germany must take measures to identify all unreturned cultural property removed during the period of occupation of the territory of the former USSR and to return it to Russia. Russia should take measures to return to Germany that part of displaced cultural property which was removed unlawfully. The Department of Restitution of the Ministry of Culture of the Russian Federation is carrying on an intensive search in the archives, museums, and other Russian cultural institutions with the full understanding that its efforts are designed to promote a settlement of such complex and unique problems.

PART 4

REPATRIATIONS

FOLLOWING

WORLD WAR II

INTRODUCTION

Edith A. Standen

The Collecting Points in occupied Germany were run by the Monuments, Fine Arts, and Archives section (MFA&A) of the Office of Military Government, United States (OMGUS). One of their functions was to house, protect, and eventually restitute works of art that can only be described as loot, objects that had been taken from countries occupied by the German armies and transported back to Germany. But I am sure that I speak for all MFA&A officers when I say that this was not our chief concern. Even the name of the organization suggests this; you cannot restitute a monument. The greatest priority to us was the well-being of works of art of all kinds and of any ownership. In the Collecting Points were masterpieces of the greatest beauty, mostly from publicly owned German and Austrian collections, such as the museums of Berlin, Frankfurt, Munich, Vienna, and many more cities. Much restitution was made from the Collecting Points; the MFA&A officers obeyed army orders and carried out all their instructions effectively. But it is the existence on German museum walls of some of their proudest possessions that gives all of us the deepest satisfaction.

I say "we," as a former MFA&A officer, but the greatest honor must be paid to the officers of the conquering American army who went into Germany, Italy, or any other enemy or occupied country while the fighting was still going on, or immediately afterward. Two of these remarkable men, Craig Hugh Smyth and Walter Farmer, are contributors to this volume, but others, sadly, are no longer alive. James Rorimer, later director of the Metropolitan Museum of Art, New York, served with the Seventh Army, met the French heroine Rose Valland in Paris, and learned from her how to find the loot when he went with the combat troops into Germany. Frederick Hartt was with the invading army in Italy, caring for works of art all the way up the peninsula. Both these men wrote enthralling books about their experiences. Immediately after the war, John Skilton put a roof over the stupendous Tiepolo frescoes in the Würzburg Residenz; they would otherwise not have survived the winter of 1945–46. Walker Hancock, fortunately still with us, is writing his memoirs; he made a temporary Collecting Point at Marburg that rescued and preserved many treasures. These men, with others, deserve the gratitude of everyone who likes to look at works of art.

The Collecting Points, of course, were also repositories for the loot. The Nazis who stole and the organizations they controlled had to be investigated in order to identify and take their booty into custody. This work was done largely by the United States Office of Strategic Services (OSS); the first and fifth contributors to this section, James Plaut and S. Lane Faison, Jr., with Theodore Rousseau, a Metropolitan Museum curator, now dead, made up the small group who investigated

interest in preserving works of art than in their other, literally vital, activities. To set up a Collecting Point for art, looted or German-owned, was an almost superhuman task. Professor Smyth, in his symposium contribution published here, describes how the one at Munich was created and functioned, and Professor Faison, its final director, tells how, after several years of intense and valuable activity, it was brought to a close.

Munich was the site of the first Collecting Point; the second was at Wiesbaden, where conditions were much the same, though the city was less badly damaged. Walter Farmer did a similarly herculean job and has also earned the same measure of thanks from all lovers of art. Here I can add a personal note. When I took over the Wiesbaden Collecting Point from Walter Farmer in early 1946, I found an organization in perfect working order. The building was in good condition. It was heated. It was lighted. It was weatherproof and secure. The German staff had been well chosen and were hardworking and loyal. Photography and conservation work were being undertaken by competent professionals. The only new responsibilities that fell to me were the reception of representatives from countries that had been occupied and robbed and the actual shipment of restituted objects. Interesting and, I hope, satisfactory work, but I was a dwarf standing on the shoulders of giants, the men who have truly earned your applause.

55. Captain Edith Standen in the Central Collecting Point, Wiesbaden, 1946, holding looted antique weapons

the Nazi confiscation agencies and the criminals who headed them. Bernard Taper, also a contributor, carried on their work.

The second and third contributors to this section belong to the category I have described, the men who saved masterpieces. Craig Hugh Smyth's summary of his prestigious career does it scant justice; he has been the head of two of the most important educational establishments in the art-historical world and has published books that every student of Italian art knows well. But the book that must be mentioned here is his *Repatriation of Art from the Collecting Point in Munich after World War II: Background and Beginnings, with Reference Especially to the Netherlands*; it was the third Gerson Lecture at the University of Groningen, in the Netherlands, and was published in 1988. It is extremely informative and thorough, but does not do justice to the difficulties faced by its author. He was the creator as well as the "officer-in-charge" of the Munich Collecting Point, but what this entailed is not adequately recorded in his contribution here or his book. Munich was wrecked. The civilian economy scarcely existed; nothing from it was available to the occupying army; and the leaders of that army, like the military government in general, had less

INVESTIGATION OF THE

MAJOR NAZI

ART-CONFISCATION

AGENCIES

James S. Plaut

I was pleased and flattered to have been asked to participate in the Bard Graduate Center symposium, and I am happy to contribute to the proceedings; but I must warn you that at my age one's memory is quite unpredictable. The events under discussion occurred fifty long years ago. Some recollections still shine like beacons, but far too many have been lost in the mists of time. With this confession, I can now begin.

The Art Looting Investigation Unit of the Office of Strategic Services (OSS) was formed in 1944 in anticipation of the forthcoming occupation of Germany by the Allied forces. Instigated by President Roosevelt's special commission led by Supreme Court Justice Owen J. Roberts, the unit was established to provide an intelligence component to the Monuments, Fine Arts, and Archives (MFA&A) branch of the United States Army. Its mission was twofold: first, to provide information helpful in the art-restitution process, and second, to provide evidence for the prosecution of Nazi leaders at the Nuremberg trials.

The unit comprised six officers and supporting staff. Immediately following the German surrender, an interrogation center was established in Alt Aussee, Austria, in close proximity to the salt mine where the greatest concentration of Nazi plunder from Western Europe was concealed. From June 1945 until the spring of 1946, leading participants in Nazi art-looting operations were detained for varying periods of time and helped to clarify the nature of the looting process and identify the whereabouts of countless masterpieces. The results of our interrogations are incorporated in three major reports, dealing with the most comprehensive looting efforts—namely, the Göring collection;[1] the proposed Führermuseum at Linz, Austria[2] (Hitler's hometown); and the operations of the so-called Einsatzstab Reichsleiter Rosenberg (ERR) in France.[3]

In 1944, Justice Roberts met with General William Donovan, director of the Office of Strategic Services, with the hope that a special intelligence unit, the Art Looting Investigation Unit, could be formed and administered by the OSS. Donovan assented, and the new unit was placed under the control of the counterintelligence branch, largely because it was believed that certain Nazi agents would be using art-confiscation activities to conceal their true roles as espionage perpetrators. (In fact, this did not occur. Only one art dealer was found to be involved in espionage, and that at a low level of importance.) Our unit was given the code name, appropriately, of Project Orion, because we truly were the hunters. The late Francis Henry Taylor, then director of the Metropolitan Museum of Art in New York, was asked by the Roberts Commission to select as members of the new unit those professionals in the field of fine arts in whom he had personal confidence and who he thought would be most adaptable to the work to be done.

I had been serving in the Office of Naval Intelligence since 1942, and Taylor, a close friend and colleague, asked me to become director of the unit. The second officer selected was Theodore Rousseau, who had been on the staff of the National Gallery of Art in Washington, D.C., prior to the war and was serving as United States naval attaché in Spain and Portugal. Rousseau was named operations officer, but in fact

56. Officers of the Art Looting Investigation Unit (OSS) Theodore Rousseau (left) and James Plaut at their interrogation center, Alt Aussee, Austria

he and I shared full responsibility for the unit's activities. S. Lane Faison, Jr., professor of fine arts at Williams College, a speaker at the New York symposium and contributor to this section, was detached from his naval station to join the unit in 1945. Taylor secured detachment from the army of two other distinguished professionals—Charles Sawyer, director of the Addison Gallery of American Art in Andover and the Worcester Art Museum in Massachusetts, and John Phillips, curator of the Mabel Brady Garvan Collections and professor at Yale University. Sawyer served as the unit's liaison officer in Washington, and Phillips ran our London office. Somewhat later, Otto Wittman, who after the war became director of the Toledo Museum of Art, Toledo, Ohio, joined our unit. From this compilation, you will recognize that ours, at least in numbers, was a very small undertaking. However, the results of our activities far outstripped the scale of the operation.

At Alt Aussee, for the better part of a year during the summer of 1945 and the following winter, hundreds of Nazi officials and collaborators were detained for interrogation. Whereas our contacts with the MFA&A personnel were irregular, these colleagues frequently brought suspects and informants to us for interrogation. Like all such "roundup" activities, a relatively small number of detainees provided the most significant information. Fortunately, Alt Aussee lay in the very center of what became known as "the last redoubt," a relatively small geographical area chosen by the Nazis as a safe haven for themselves and their families as the Allied forces swept eastward. This resulted in a compact concentration of the Nazi elite and their followers such that we were able to find and detain many of the looting operators close at hand.

At the outset we decided that Rousseau, Faison, and I, the only field operators, would each report upon one of the most important looting programs. Rousseau chose the Göring collection and Faison the activities of the planners of the projected Führermuseum at Linz. I chose the official Nazi looting organization in France under the leadership of Minister Alfred Rosenberg (ERR). In addition to these three reports, we issued reports on the interrogation of leading conspirators.

Without the unwitting collaboration of the Nazis themselves, we could never have achieved positive results.

When the United States Seventh Army occupied Bavaria, the late Captain James Rorimer discovered in the fabled castle of Neuschwanstein a meticulously prepared inventory of all objects taken by the Nazis from public and private collections in Belgium, France, Italy, and the Netherlands. The information was exhaustive, with descriptions of provenance, condition, dimensions, and whereabouts of custody. This information was indispensable in determining locations of storage and identifying virtually every object in Nazi custody that was confiscated from these countries. Here I must remind you that our mandate was limited to the investigation of looting activities in Western Europe. In deference to our Russian allies and because of the huge depredations that took place in Eastern Europe, those areas were beyond the scope of our investigation.

In our intensive, often frustrating work at Alt Aussee we became lucky at times and benefited from the revelations of a few individuals who had been centrally involved in the looting process. Bruno Lohse, a Munich art dealer, had served as executive officer of the ERR in Paris. His knowledge was encyclopedic and, hoping to please his captors, he held nothing back. Equally responsive was Fräulein Gisela Limberger, Göring's secretary, who, while professing her own innocence, became a fountainhead of incriminating information.

Eventually, we turned Lohse over to the French authorities. He spent some time in a French prison and, when released, resumed his career as a Munich dealer. Limberger was released outright after interrogation. In his interrogations, Faison received similar windfalls. Because our "network" grew, we were led to Gustav Rochlitz, one of Göring's chief art procurers, who had taken refuge in a nearby village. Rousseau and I apprehended him and drove him to Paris, where he was detained by the French authorities. As the Nuremberg trials drew near, Rousseau interrogated Göring in prison and found him despondent, indifferent, and degradingly unheroic.

The Alt Aussee center was closed in 1946. Rousseau and I traveled to Switzerland in December 1945 and January 1946 to seek the cooperation of the Swiss government in the restitution of looted art that had found its way through many complex and devious channels into the hands of private collectors and art dealers—notably, Emil Bührle, the arms manufacturer, and Theodor Fischer, the well-known dealer and auctioneer. At first, citing the national tradition of nondisclosure, the Swiss authorities were uncooperative, but in time, bowing to international pressure, they helped to expedite the restitution process.

I retired from active duty in the summer of 1946. Before retiring, Rousseau went to Japan on a special mission. Faison remained for some time and returned to Germany in 1950 to become final director of the Munich Collecting Point. In closing, I wish particularly to thank and congratulate Lynn Nicholas. Her book, *The Rape of Europa*,[4] is an extraordinary achievement—a work of impeccable scholarship, written so enthrallingly that the reader is enveloped in a web of intrigue and depredation that only the Nazis could have concocted. And so it was.

THE ESTABLISHMENT

OF THE

MUNICH COLLECTING POINT

Craig Hugh Smyth

I should begin by saying that the University of Groningen in Holland invited me to give the university's Gerson Lecture in 1986 specifically on the subject of the Central Art Collecting Point in Munich and the start of repatriating art to looted countries. Groningen published this lecture as a book in 1988, with appendices containing relevant archival documents, including monthly reports.[1] Lynn Nicholas, in her book of 1994, has given an excellent summary of the same subject.[2] Therefore, I keep now to an abbreviated outline of events.

The need for Allied storage depots in Germany—later called Collecting Points—began to be foreseen well before the occupation of Germany. Prior to the invasion of Europe, at Eisenhower's headquarters in England, known as SHAEF, there was a policy branch of the Monuments, Fine Arts, and Archives section (MFA&A). The policy branch was headed by Major Mason Hammond, the first American monuments officer in the war, starting in Sicily. Hammond's branch considered what would be necessary in Germany to protect art and cultural materials from damage, theft, and loss—including looted art that had to be located and held for repatriation. The policy branch recommended what it called "warehousing." At the end of hostilities, the establishment of Collecting Points was officially requested by Major Bancel LaFarge, chief of MFA&A, United States Forces European Theater, architect in civilian life. On May 20, 1945, thirteen days after the German surrender, Eisenhower's headquarters (SHAEF), now at Versailles, issued an order to this effect, headed with the words, "By directive of the Supreme Commander."

MFA&A personnel had always been too few for the needs in the field. Toward the European war's end, the army and navy transferred to MFA&A a few more officers deemed qualified. Having been a member of the curatorial staff of the National Gallery of Art in Washington, D.C., before naval service, I was one of them. The navy on land and at sea is a notable teacher of organization and responsibility—in my case very fortunately, in view of my future MFA&A assignment. Along with another naval lieutenant, Thomas Carr Howe, Jr. (director in civilian life of the California Palace of the Legion of Honor), I was ordered to SHAEF at Versailles, was indoctrinated there for two weeks by the MFA&A chief, British Lieutenant Colonel Geoffrey Webb (a Cambridge University medievalist), then was sent for several days to London for further indoctrination by Sumner Crosby, representative of the Roberts Commission (a Yale medievalist), and also taken to meet Sir Leonard Woolley, Archaeological Advisor to the British War Office. Orders were then drawn sending Howe and me to MFA&A headquarters at Frankfurt. Briefed on arrival there by LaFarge and by Naval Lieutenant George Stout—of whom more later—Howe was assigned to evacuating repositories, and I was assigned to Munich, to set up a Collecting Point. My instructions were that a Collecting Point was to be ready for the first loads from Austrian repositories in no less than two weeks.

No one had considered yet exactly how a Collecting Point should be organized. Stout and LaFarge stressed that the Munich

57. The Führerbau, Munich, in June 1945, viewed from the Königsplatz, with one of the two temples to Nazi heroes (Ehrentempel), at right. Both structures have a covering of camouflage.

58. The Königsplatz, Munich, in June 1945. Left to right: the two Ehrentempel, the Verwaltungsbau (Nazi Party Central Administration Building), and the Staatliche Antikensammlung (State Museum of Antiquities). The Ehrentempel were leveled and removed soon after the photograph was taken.

Collecting Point must serve for immediate safe storage, but must also serve as a long-term repository and center for cataloguing loot. There was a day to consider, while I was driven in a jeep from Frankfurt to Munich on June 4. The jeep ride produced the numbering system used at Munich to identify and keep track of each object from the moment of arrival. Reaching the headquarters of the Military Government Detachment for Bavaria in Munich at 5:00 P.M., I was quickly billeted in a row house requisitioned for the detachment, and had a meeting with the three people necessary to see about getting a building, or buildings, for the Collecting Point: the Property Control Officer for Munich, the MFA&A officer for Bavaria, Lieutenant Daniel Kern, and the MFA&A officer for the Seventh Army, occupying Munich, Lieutenant James Rorimer—who before the war was curator of the Metropolitan Museum of Art's Cloisters and who, some years after the war, became the Metropolitan Museum's director. Rorimer had decided where the Collecting Point should be. He hurried me to the Königsplatz to see the building complex that had been Nazi Party Headquarters for all Germany. As viewed from the Königsplatz, on the left is the Führerbau (fig. 57), where the Munich Pact was signed in 1938—seen here with remnants of its camouflage —and on the right the Verwaltungsbau (fig. 58), the Nazi Party's Central Administration Building, housing the party's central files. (Between them are two structures that our forces removed, temples to Nazi heroes.) The buildings had suffered from bombing, but much less than the Alte Pinakothek and the Neue Pinakothek, two museums of comparable size. In the Nazi headquarters, Hitler had stored some of his art for the Führermuseum at Linz. The buildings had been sacked by the populace (fig. 59). Rorimer thought one building enough and preferred the Verwaltungsbau, then occupied by Seventh Army troops. He had already asked SHAEF to designate it for use as the Collecting Point, and SHAEF had done so.

As it turned out, our final decision was to have both buildings, plus the complex of other structures that went with

59. A room in the basement of the Verwaltungsbau, as found when the building was taken over for use as an art collecting point in June 1945

them. General Patton's Third Army was moving in to replace the Seventh Army. Its MFA&A officer, Captain Robert Posey, was an architect in civilian life, and familiar with some of the repositories. He was sure the space of both buildings was needed. In addition, one subsidiary structure—the heating plant—was absolutely necessary. Other structures belonging to the complex would be needed for a guard battalion and transport drivers.

But immediately there was a standoff with the Third Army. It wanted the buildings for General Patton's headquarters. Learning this, I was able to come to the buildings with a supporting Military Government officer in time to welcome the

Third Army staff officer sent to inspect them, and argue that the buildings were the only ones remaining, after the bombing of Munich, large enough to house and protect works of art for which the Third Army would now have the heavy responsibility. Captain Posey helped greatly from his office—as did his assistant, Lincoln Kirstein, the famed American essayist and patron of the arts, of all people, who was helpful from then on in every way. There was much delay. Approval for the Collecting Point occupancy did not come until three days before the first loads of art were to arrive from Austria.

In the diary that I was directed to keep, the entry for June 5, the day following my arrival in Munich, summarizes what needed to be done, and subsequent entries tell how and when things were accomplished.[3] With little likelihood of there being more than one or two army enlisted men assigned to the Collecting Point, almost everything would have to be accomplished with the help of German personnel. These must be found by using "white lists" of non-Nazis: first of all, trustworthy personnel to bring order in the buildings, to clean, and to inventory, and trained archivists to gather Nazi Party files, wherein was recorded the entire Nazi Party membership of Germany and beyond. Army Intelligence had done nothing about this. Summoned when we finally had the buildings, Intelligence left soon, leaving our archivists to finish—work probably indispensable when it came to the denazification of Germany.

An architect and construction workers were needed—to repair bomb damage and make the buildings waterproof, secure, and eventually heatable—plus a maintenance staff. Very fortunately, on the sixth day there arrived an architect from SHAEF via the Twelfth Army Group: Naval Lieutenant Hamilton Coulter, just transferred to MFA&A, to serve as second officer and supervise building repairs. He was a perfect choice. He took charge of repairing roofs, filling in windows, repairing spaces for art and offices (figs. 60 and 61), and repairing the electric, heating, and water systems. Later, we were able to take on one more officer from the Third Army to help him. We quickly had Third Army bomb squads search the whole complex for explosives. They did not find everything, and, very sad to say, one young worker was killed. A new search followed.

Professional handlers of art had to be found for moving and storing objects, clerical staff to keep records, and professional museum people to supervise, serve as curators, and help identify objects for repatriation—not to mention a conservator from the Alte Pinakothek for objects in need of emergency care.

Most important was security. A battery of military guards had to be got from the Third Army. These we supplemented with German police—a combination to ensure care—and finally with a protective fencing around the whole Collecting Point. The Third Army delayed in providing the fence. Our good luck was to be in naval uniform: we won army sympathy, and not being expected to know its procedures, could manage regularly to go to the top at the Third Army, not up the chain

60. The future space of the Munich Collecting Point's office of the registrar, before repairs

61. Office of the registrar for the Munich Collecting Point, following repairs

of command. Scrounging the city and countryside for construction materials we did with the help of two enlisted men.

By the end of two weeks, we had enough secure space and enough personnel ready for the first shipment from Alt Aussee—where George Stout was supervising the whole operation of packing and shipping. Funding came from the Bavarian state, with the government's paymaster part of the Collecting Point staff.[4] By the end of the summer, when the first repatriation of easily identifiable objects began, there were 107 civilian employees, including such curators and handlers as seen in figure 62, plus 114 temporary construction workers, plus the battery of army guards. The photographer had his studio, and space had been readied for emergency conservation (fig. 63). Besides loot from repositories in Austria, Czechoslovakia, and Bavaria, we housed the contents of both Pinakotheks, most of the Glyptothek collection, the Graphische Sammlung, and Münz-Sammlung, and the Theater Museum collection—as well as art from the Budapest National Museum, discovered in Bavaria. By now the Collecting Point also had a library, formed of books from two museums, and a document center, both for use in establishing the ownership of looted objects.

Now, three concluding observations. First, President Truman's policy for unilaterally repatriating looted objects from the United States Zone of Germany suddenly saddled the

Munich Collecting Point with *de facto* responsibility for repatriation. When accredited representatives of looted countries were invited to have offices in the Collecting Point and to document, with the help of staff, the ownership of objects, in order to prove they were from their countries, the officer-in-charge had to rule on whether the documentation was sufficient for an object to be released for repatriation—easy to do at the start, for the Ghent Altarpiece (fig. 64) or Michelangelo's *Bruges Madonna* (fig. 65). Other shipments were less spectacular. The difficult problems arose after my time. In April 1946, with the requisite service points, I received orders from the Commander of U.S. Naval Forces, Germany, relieving me of active duty.

Second, it was in the Munich Collecting Point that the Zentralinstitut für Kunstgeschichte was conceived—and from which it was born. At the outset, it occurred to me to change the names Verwaltungsbau and Führerbau to Gallery I and

62. Boxes being packed with small paintings for repatriation at the Munich Collecting Point

63. Emergency first-aid conservation studio at the Munich Collecting Point. Visible at left is Leonardo da Vinci's *Portrait of a Lady with an Ermine* from Cracow (see fig. 5); at right, on the shelf, is a portrait by Giorgione from Budapest; and on the table in the foreground is a painting by Bernardo Bellotto from Warsaw.

64. A case containing a panel of the Ghent Altarpiece is being loaded at the Munich Collecting Point on August 21, 1945, for return by air to Belgium. (Lieutenants Thomas C. Howe and Craig H. Smyth are at right.)

65. A gathering outside the Munich Collecting Point to observe the repatriation of Michelangelo's *Bruges Madonna* in 1945. Standing, left to right: Lieutenant Colonel Ernest De Wald, MFA&A officer, U.S. Forces Austria; Emile Langui, Belgian official; Captain Steven Kovalyak, U.S. Army; Lieutenant Craig H. Smyth; Dr. Andrew Ritchie, civilian adviser to MFA&A, U.S. Forces Austria; Commander George Boas, U.S. Naval Attaché, U.S. Embassy, Belgium; Major Bancel LaFarge, senior officer of MFA&A, Twelfth Army, U.S. Forces Europe

GEORGE STOUT
IIC Honorary Fellow 1966

66. George Stout, Department of Conservation, Fogg Art Museum, Harvard University. Cover photo, *Studies in Conservation,* **May 1966**

Gallery II as a peaceful sign. It seemed evident to us immediately that these buildings could well be the place for postwar study of art to begin in the bombed-out city. By autumn, there was talk among all concerned about an institute in the future. Plans then quickly matured.

Finally I want to take a larger view. The person ultimately responsible for there being an MFA&A at all, and hence the Collecting Point, was George Stout (fig. 66), Harvard conservator. This, I think, none of us ever knew, and he was not one who would ever say so. A letter from Paul Sachs in the United States National Archives names Stout as "the real father of the whole show" and designates the Roberts Commission, from which MFA&A stemmed, as his "brain child."[5] His purpose was to preserve—preserve above all—and secondly to repatriate the displaced.

In wars since then, has there been such an effort to preserve humankind's heritage? Is there the possibility that this can be encouraged henceforth in conflicts everywhere?

CUSTODY AND CONTROVERSY

AT THE WIESBADEN

COLLECTING POINT

Walter I. Farmer

The end of the war found me stationed near Frankfurt. I was a captain in the army and adjutant in a general-service engineering regiment. We had just completed three bridges over the Rhine and were now building prisoner-of-war stockades. In my capacity as adjutant I was often up at SHAEF (Supreme Headquarters, Allied Expeditionary Force) on regimental business. The regiment was on alert to return to the United States.[1]

In the spring of 1945, I had read stories in the *Stars and Stripes* about the discovery of great art caches in various mines all over Germany and Austria. God knows, I had seen enough destruction and wondered how anything could have survived.

One day at SHAEF I presented myself to the HQ of MFA&A.[2] Was it possible they could use me? After a long interview with Charles Kuhn and Bancel LaFarge, I detected they had quite an interest in my architectural and engineering background. As I was about to leave they said to me, "If your colonel will release you, we will take you." How wonderful![3] Three years with the Engineers were enough. The colonel would release me if I would put the regiment on a ship at Le Havre. That accomplished, I went back to Frankfurt and reported in. There I was told what I was to do.

I had two jobs: (1) I would be the MFA&A officer for the Regierungsbezirk Wiesbaden (Wiesbaden Administrative District), and (2) I was to put into usable condition the vast Landesmuseum in Wiesbaden. It had been selected to be the Central Collecting Point for German-owned works of art. I was given no guidelines or instructions. I was taken on a tour of the Reichsbank in Frankfurt, where I saw the masses of crated works of art that had been evacuated there from the salt mines southwest of Berlin in March 1945. It was the only safe and secured building in that part of Germany. The Reichsbank was also headquarters for the Financial Section of SHAEF. They needed all the space for their operations and were clamoring for the art to be removed to another location as soon as possible.

The Landesmuseum had been selected because it was repairable. Standing alone amid total devastation, it had not taken a direct hit. The block-square building had housed the Wiesbaden archaeological, natural history, and paintings collections. There was not a single window; the doors were blown off; part of the roof was gone—no water, no heat, no light—but it was salvageable. It had housed a Luftwaffe barrack, a machine shop, and city offices, and had been a refuge for displaced persons. When I arrived, it was a United States Army supply depot.[4]

Off I went to the Arbeitsamt (Labor Exchange) and arranged for a continuous supply of sappers (army engineers) and, of course, an interpreter. The high barbed-wire fence went up first to confine my space. And then out went all of the tenants—not without clashes, but *out.* Then over two thousand windows and the skylights went in; crews cleaned out the trash; doors were hung; a carpenter's shop was functioning; mechanics repaired the furnace; coal was ordered; the plumbing started to work; new slates were on the roof—and on and on and on.

All the while, in connection with my regional duties, I supervised the shoring up and reroofing of damaged castles and the boarding up of the Staatsarchiv (Office of Public Records).[5] I also investigated the art repositories that were being reported. I discovered that the works-on-paper collection of the Wallraf-Richartz-Museum, Cologne, was stored in a damp castle, surrounded by a moat. I brought it to the Collecting Point: this was the first collection to enter there.

Originally, I was the only MFA&A officer in Wiesbaden, and I had to hunt and find both personnel and materials. I received no aid from the city other than a positive answer to my constant demands for more and more workmen. Late in July, Sergeant Kenneth Lindsay joined us to assist with the administration. Finally, I hired the upper-level professionals. The photographic team came from Photo Marburg, conservators arrived, and the registrar and secretaries were appointed. The Arbeitsamt located an American-born architect, Otto Seeler, who knew the local building trades and could work well with my foremen.

All the changes were necessary because, unfortunately, the former staff had all been members of the Nazi Party and I was obliged to fire them. However, I was able to reinstate several elderly museum professionals who had taken early retirement rather than join the party. Dr. Kutsch and Dr. Bleibaum gave devoted service, as did the eminent young director of the Städelsches Kunstinstitut, Ernst Holzinger, who came over from Frankfurt and served as consulting curator (fig. 67).

Above all else, I was concerned about security and took every precaution against break-ins or theft. The museum was

67. Dr. Ernst Holzinger (right), director of the Städelsches Kunstin- stitut, Frankfurt am Main, and Captain Walter I. Farmer, director of the Wiesbaden Collecting Point, standing in front of a rack with paintings from the Kaiser-Friedrich- Museum, Berlin, 1945

surrounded by a ten-foot-high barbed-wire fence, which was lighted with headlights removed from abandoned trucks. I demanded that a tank company have guns positioned to cover every line of fire. GI's guarded the perimeter of the building; German police guarded the galleries now used as storerooms. A secret policeman guarded the Germans, and I guarded the guards. By the second week of August everything was ready.

A registration area had been set up near the entry point for the incoming shipments. Every museum collection evacu- ated from Berlin was assigned its own space. The paintings from the Nationalgalerie had never been crated, so I had racks ready for them. Captain James Rorimer arrived in the lead jeep, and for the next ten days trucks came bumper to bumper loaded from the Frankfurt Reichsbank. Tanks lined the road to guard them. Imagine the pressure, but imagine the joy when shouts went up: "The painted queen [*Nefertiti*] is here! The Guelph Treasure is here!" It was a perfect operation.

The convoys brought objects from sixteen major museums of Berlin, six thousand cases. After these were stored, other local museum collections were brought to us for storage (see "Collections Stored at the Wiesbaden Collecting Point," below). By the time I left, over twenty-eight thousand cases had been inventoried. Crates were checked and rechecked to verify their contents, and an inventory system was established to control them. Paintings that needed conservation were examined and given temporary treatments. At Captain Rorimer's suggestion, I created a treasure room carefully guarded and secure. Jim said that I had more gold and jewels in that room than any room since the time of Montezuma. It must be remembered that all were German-owned works of art excepting the looted church treasures from Poland and the Holy Crown of Saint Stephen and regalia from Hungary.[6]

Top-flight government officials from many countries, including the Vatican, as well as some U.S. top brass, came to visit the Collecting Point. Among them was Colonel Henry McBride from the National Gallery of Art in Washington, D.C., who came in early November. To my surprise he found fault with everything and praised nothing, leaving me to wonder why all the trained museum people who were members of MFA&A had vigorously applauded my efforts and endorsed my procedures.

Little did I realize that he was building up a story to sell to the folks back home. He wanted to convince himself that the Wiesbaden Collecting Point could not safeguard the most priceless German art treasures: he wanted them all shipped to the National Gallery in Washington. He had even brought a carefully thought-out list of the very best works from the Kaiser-Friedrich-Museum in Berlin.*

---

* Editor's note: The Wiesbaden staff was unaware at this time of the top- secret decision by President Truman and General Lucius Clay in July 1945 at the Potsdam Conference to remove temporarily to the United States a selection of German-owned artworks. Truman's initial decision was said to be motivated by reports of inadequate storage facilities. By the time McBride was sent to Germany in November to carry out this order, conditions had greatly improved, and the removal seemed unnecessary.

On November 6, 1945, I was dealt a tremendous blow. A soldier from the military government headquarters in Wiesbaden hand-delivered a copy of a telegram they had received ordering the removal to Washington of the most famous paintings we were safeguarding. Now I understood the purpose of McBride's visit. The text of that telegram was distributed at the New York symposium and is reproduced here:

From 7th US Army
To Office Mil Govt for Stadtkreis Wiesbaden
BT

Higher headquarters desiges [sic] that immediate preparations be made for prompt shipment to the UNITEK [U.S.] of a selection of at least two zero zero German works of art of greatest importance X Most of these are now in Art Collecting Point Wiesbaden X Selections will be made by personnel from Headquarters CMA US Forces CMA European theater who will assist in packing and shipment by motor transport to Bremen X

From CG Seventh Army to Director CMA Office of Military Government for Stadtkreis Wiesbaden CMA REF NO able three three zero two seven X

You will provide sufficient material and personnel X This headquarters is to be informed by telephone of progress and anticipated requirements X Operation to be completed by two zero November X Transportation and military security during transit will be provided by this headquarters X

My emotions overcame me, and I wept tears of rage and frustration. It seemed to me that everything that had been done to demonstrate the integrity of the United States government in the matter of its handling of German cultural properties would be discredited if this shipment took place. So great was my personal confidence in the value of our mission that I was prepared to face a court-martial by disobeying orders. After I calmed down, I called all the members of MFA&A in Europe to come to a meeting in my office on the following day. We had to protest this disastrous decision.

Thirty-two officers answered my appeal. Everyone there shared my sense of shame at our government's behavior, and it was a highly vocal meeting. By the end of the day, our collective expressions of defiance and passionate convictions had been codified into a document finally drafted by Everett Lesley that has become known as the Wiesbaden Manifesto, the only act of protest by officers against their orders in the Second World War.[7]

Having just ten days to prepare for the transport of the works, I asked for assistance from the MFA&A office in Höchst. Lamont Moore, a former National Gallery staff member, was selected to supervise the packing and escort the shipment. McBride's list had been given to us, but since we had never received the crate lists we'd begged for from Berlin, every crate had to be opened and its contents searched for the chosen pictures. Eventually 202 paintings were selected. When a painting on the list was found, it was photographed and its condition was examined and recorded by Moore. Emergency conservation treatments were given by our conservator. Crates

The Wiesbaden Manifesto

U.S. Forces, European Theater Germany
7 November 1945

1. We, the undersigned, Monuments, Fine Arts and Archives Specialist Officers of the Armed Forces of the United States, wish to make known our convictions regarding the transportation to the United States of works of art, the property of German institutions or Nationals, for purposes of protective custody.

2a. We are unanimously agreed that the transportation of these works of art, undertaken by the United States Army, upon direction from the highest national authority, establishes a precedent which is neither morally tenable nor trustworthy.

b. Since the beginning of United States participation in the war, it has been the declared policy of the Allied Forces, so far as military necessity would permit, to protect and preserve from deterioration consequent upon the processes of war, all monuments, documents or other objects of historic, artistic, cultural or archaeological value. The war is at an end, and no doctrine of "military necessity" can now be invoked for the further protection of the objects to be moved, for the reason that depots and personnel, both fully competent for their protection, have been inaugurated and are functioning.

c. The Allied Nations are at present preparing to prosecute individuals for the crime of sequestering, under pretext of "protective custody," the cultural treasures of German-occupied countries. A major part of the indictment follows upon the reasoning that, even though these individuals were acting under military orders, the dictates of a higher ethical law made it incumbent upon them to refuse to take part in, or countenance, the fulfillment of these orders. We, the undersigned, feel it is our duty to point out that, though as members of the Armed Forces we will carry out the orders we receive, we are thus put before any candid eyes as no less culpable than those whose prosecution we effect to sanction.

3. We wish to state that from our own knowledge, no historical grievance will rankle so long, or be the cause of so much justified bitterness, as the removal, for any reason, of a part of the heritage of any nation, even if that heritage may be interpreted as a prize of war. And though this removal may be done with every intention of altruism, we are none the less convinced that it is our duty, individually and collectively, to protest against it, and that though our obligations are to the nation to which we owe allegiance, there are yet further obligations to common justice, decency and the establishment of the power of right, not of expediency or might, among civilized nations.

were rebuilt and refitted, and the shipment left on a train bound for Le Havre and a ship that would cross the Atlantic in early December. It was the height of lunacy in our opinion. Surely these paintings were safer with us in Germany than on the high seas. What could higher authorities be thinking of?

Along with the paintings went word of our protest. First Janet Flanner, better known as "Genêt," published an article in the *New Yorker* that announced the impending arrival of the ship in December.[8] Next, in January, Lieutenant Charles Kuhn, who had just returned to Harvard to teach, published in the *College Art Journal* his report on the senseless transport of the 202 along with the text of our protest.[9]

Feelings against the removal of the German paintings were beginning to build in Washington and throughout the nation, thanks to the *College Art Journal* publication and efforts of other museums and academic leaders, who circulated a resolution calling for the immediate return of the paintings to Germany.[10] The national press had begun to cover the story, and the propaganda value of the shipment was now being publicly debated.

The paintings went into storage at the National Gallery in Washington while the State Department and the Truman administration deliberated the political consequences of their removal from Germany. But there were no more shipments of German art. Four years later, the paintings did return to Wiesbaden after a tremendously popular exhibition of them in Washington and the national tour of a reduced number to thirteen American cities.[11]

After the removal of the 202, it had seemed to me that we might redeem our honor by mounting a public exhibition at the Wiesbaden Landesmuseum drawn from the collections which we were guarding. What a pleasure it was to select from such an outstanding array of paintings, sculptures, and church objects to fill a few of our refurbished galleries and reassure the German people that their treasures were safely kept! Our exhibition of February 1946 inaugurated a series of shows that continued until all the visiting collections were returned.[12]

Shortly before I left my post to return to the United States, I had one other memorable opportunity to be of service. The Wiesbaden Collecting Point became the repository for the first shipments of synagogue treasures that had been looted in Poland, Russia, and elsewhere and warehoused in Germany by the Nazis. My colleague Jim Rorimer sought my advice on the renovation of factory buildings in nearby Offenbach for service as a Collecting Point. There, more than three million books and Torah scrolls would be sorted and identified before attempts could be made to return them to the ravaged communities of Jewish people who had once held them (see fig. 4). Entire libraries that had been seized would eventually go back home or to Israel, thanks mainly to Leslie Poste, Seymour Pomrenze, and Isaac Benkowitz.[13]

COLLECTIONS STORED AT THE WIESBADEN COLLECTING POINT

Artworks from the Berlin State Museums
Ägyptische Abteilung (163 cases): Egyptian antiquities
Antikenabteilung (89 cases): classical antiquities
Gemäldegalerie (1,188 paintings): paintings
Islamische Abteilung (49 cases): ceramics, sculpture, carpets
Kunstbibliothek (14 cases, 742 portfolios): books, prints
Kunstgewerbemuseum (45 cases): decorative arts from all periods
Kupferstichkabinett (2,300 portfolios): prints, drawings
Münzkabinett: coins of all periods
Museum für Deutsche Volkskunde (30 cases): folk art
Museum für Völkerkunde (92 cases): ethnological collection
Museum für Vor- und Frühgeschichte (6 cases): prehistoric art
Nationalgalerie (681 paintings): paintings
Ostasiatische Kunstabteilung (4 cases): ceramics, sculpture
Skulpturenabteilung (350 cases): sculpture
Zeughaus (121 cases): arms, armor, uniforms, flags

Other German Collections
Berlin, Schloss Charlottenburg (74 cases): tapestries, porcelain, Prussian regalia
Cologne, Wallraf-Richartz-Museum (80 cases): prints
Düsseldorf, Stadtmuseum (12 cases): coins
Frankfurt, Städelsches Kunstinstitut and other museums (20,000 cases): paintings, sculpture, drawings
Karlsruhe Museum (193 cases): paintings, prints
Kassel Museum (55 cases): sculpture, prints, drawings
Krefeld, Kaiser Wilhelm Museum (73 cases): paintings, sculpture
Lüneburg, Grasleben (13 cases): archaeological collection
Lüneburg, Grasleben (773 cases): church treasures
Mainz, Städtische Gemäldegalerie (207 cases): paintings, antiquities
Mannheim Museum (34 cases): textiles
Potsdam, Garnisonskirche (1 case): textiles
Potsdam, Schlösser und Gärten (353 cases): tapestries, paintings, furniture
Stuttgart, Staatsgalerie (1 case): paintings
Wiesbaden, Archaeological Museum (27 cases): sculpture, tapestries, artifacts
Wiesbaden, Staatsarchiv (1 case): archives
Worms, Stiftung Heylshof (10 cases): paintings

Displaced Treasures from Other Countries
Hungarian State Coronation Regalia (1 chest)
Polish Church Treasures

INVESTIGATING

ART LOOTING FOR

THE MFA&A

Bernard Taper

Starting in early summer of 1946, for two years I had the job of art-intelligence officer for the Monuments, Fine Arts, and Archives (MFA&A) section of the United States Military Government in Germany. My assignment was to search out and recover displaced, misplaced, or looted artworks. Some assignment, indeed! Tens of thousands of precious artworks, wrongfully obtained by the Nazi conquerors during the war, or wrongfully acquired after the war by the German populace through random looting or black-market transactions, were still missing—who knew where? And most of these to this day have never been found. The whole MFA&A section consisted of just a handful of people. They had all they could do to store, care for, catalogue, and restitute in orderly fashion the troves of art and archives that had been discovered in salt mines and hundreds of other repositories at the war's end, in 1945. For the continuing investigative function, which remained part of the MFA&A's mission as long as it existed, there were on the roster as full-time agents during my tenure just myself, as art-intelligence officer for the whole United States Zone of Occupation, and Edgar Breitenbach, in Bavaria. Obviously, what we could accomplish, compared with what needed to be done, was necessarily token. But as a moral symbol it was, I believe, important.

I'll try to give an idea of some of the things we did in those days. My story is not as heroic or as glamorous as those of the earlier Monuments people, whom I look on as legendary figures, truly chivalric in their courage, enterprise, and dedication to a cause. One such was my predecessor as art-intelligence officer, Lieutenant Walter Horn, a medieval-art scholar. Born in Germany, Horn was one of the rare individuals who chose exile after 1933, not because of fear of racial persecution—in appearance he was the absolute Aryan ideal—but because of his abhorrence of Nazi ideology. Returned to his homeland as a member of the victorious Allied forces, Horn was the one who, in August of 1945, brilliantly tracked down the missing crown and regalia of the Holy Roman Empire, which the Nazis had hidden away deep in a secret vault in Nuremberg to serve as a rallying symbol for a future Nazi resistance movement. What special satisfaction cracking this case and thwarting this last desperate Nazi fantasy must have given Horn!

As Horn's successor, I had my share of successes and achievements, but none as glorious as his. Of the numerous investigations I was involved in during those two years, the one that most preoccupied and tantalized me was the search for the Raphael painting from the Czartoryski collection at Cracow—the *Portrait of a Young Man*. There were nights when I dreamed of it. I knew the painting only from a small black-and-white photograph that had been given to me by Major Karol Estreicher, the art-restitution representative from Poland, but in my dreams it was always in sumptuous color (see colorplate 1). I worked closely on this search with Major Estreicher. Together we interrogated the infamous Kajetan Mühlmann, the former art adviser to Generalgouverneur Hans Frank. And I took care to keep Estreicher informed of my

68. Bernard Taper in 1946, around the time he joined the MFA&A

continuing solo efforts, of which the most important was a twelve-hour-long interrogation I conducted of Mühlmann's successor as art adviser to Frank, a man named Wilhelm Ernst von Palezieux, whom I was able to track down in the French Zone of Occupation.

Promising leads kept emerging in this quest, but over time all came to nothing. Exactly what happened to the Raphael is still unclear. Generalgouverneur Frank and his entourage made stops on their hasty flight from Cracow. Whether he brought the painting with him along with a small number of other art treasures of the highest merit, whether it got left behind at Schloss Muhrau, where he made one stop, or whether it was included in the final, smaller selection that accompanied him to Neuhaus, where he was captured—none of this can be determined with certitude. My own present hunch, developed after reading State Department accounts of subsequent investigations in the late 1950s, is that the Raphael is not something Frank would have left behind, and that he did bring it along to Neuhaus but quite possibly left it in another residence he owned there that the Americans who arrested him did not know about. But regarding what might have happened thereafter my crystal ball becomes clouded. The Raphael is possibly the most important painting lost in the war whose fate remains unknown.

In 1989 Thomas Hoving, former director of the Metropolitan Museum of Art, visited the Czartoryski Museum and wrote about it in the magazine *Connoisseur*. After his return from Cracow, he wrote to me, in reply to a query as to whether he had learned any new information about the Raphael. His sense, he said, was that the people at that museum had pretty much given up hope of ever seeing that painting again.

But his own intuition, Hoving added, though he knew not why, was that the painting still exists and will surface again one day. "If it ever turns up," he added, "we can be sure it will emerge sometime after 1995, when the final statute of limitations falls regarding the Nazis." A striking prediction—and it leaves me with a question that I hope a jurist will address—

namely, is there such a statute of limitations, did it in fact run out at the end of 1995, and what would be its implications for those who have suffered art losses?*

Let me return now to some of the other aspects of my art-intelligence job, less exalted than the search for the Raphael, but worthwhile nonetheless. One of my first tasks, after I took on the job in 1946, was to try to establish some system of priority for investigations and to arrange effective liaison with other investigative branches of the military and with the denazified local police forces. We got some good results from these arrangements, particularly in the Frankfurt area, where many art dealers were suspected of having engaged in shady transactions during the war. The Netherlands had filed 279 claims with us for artworks that had been expropriated from the Goudstikker collection. I arranged to provide lists to the Frankfurt dealers and required them to certify what works they had sold and to whom.

Then, under my guidance, German police officers were utilized to track these works down. This was the first time the German police had been used for such a task. It was deemed to be time for them to be given such responsibilities. I don't have a record of how many restitutable art objects were ultimately discovered in this way, but I believe it to have been a goodly number.

As most accounts have noted, the great troves of looted art that had been discovered in the salt mines and elsewhere were essentially official loot—collections assembled by Hitler and Göring and by the designated confiscation agencies. The Nazis' looting, in the West at any rate, had customarily been meticulously documented by their own functionaries. But there was another kind of art looting that Edgar Breitenbach and I found ourselves investigating in our time that was quite a different story. It was what might be called second-generation loot or loot twice removed—the result of random, often impulsive, whimsical or ignorant behavior—and almost always undocumented. Thus, it was not easy to track down. This was the kind of looting that took place when Munich fell and the mob broke into Hitler's Munich headquarters and made off with numerous paintings from the Adolphe Schloss collection —a fine collection of small, mostly Dutch and Flemish masters that had been confiscated by the Vichy Commissioner of Jewish Affairs from the Schloss family after the fall of France. Most of the Munich looters, you can be sure, had no idea what they had gone off with. Recovering what they had grabbed called for a somewhat different kind of detective work—cultivating informants, keeping an eye on the local black markets, and the like. In Bavaria, Breitenbach pursued these missing works patiently—like a wily fisherman—and from time to time made some good catches.

And this spontaneous, unorganized kind of looting was also what took place at the collapse of German resistance in southern Bavaria, when the peasants from the Berchtesgaden

---

* Editor's note: There is no such "final statute of limitations." See Kaye, above, pages 101, 104–5; Maurer, below, page 144; and Kline, below, page 158.

region swarmed over the abandoned train, loaded with Göring's possessions, that Göring had sent from Karinhall to escape the advancing Soviet army. Before the German troops had fled, the most important artworks had been transferred to a nearby air-raid shelter, but the shelter had not been large enough to hold everything.

The peasantry that came swarming had heard the train was loaded with schnapps, and the firstcomers got their fill thereof. Those who came later had to be satisfied with things like a school of Rogier van der Weyden painting, a thirteenth-century Limoges reliquary, four late Gothic wood statues, and other such baubles—whatever they could grab. It was a real mob scene. Three women laid hands on the same Aubusson carpet, and a heated struggle ensued until along came a local dignitary, who said to them, "Women, be civilized, divide it among you." So they did. Two of the women used their portions as bedspreads, but the third cut hers up to make window curtains. Edgar Breitenbach and I learned such details, and much more, in the course of a series of belated investigative forays we made in the fall of 1947. By the time we finished, we had gotten to know much of the populace quite intimately, and we had retrieved a fair number of interesting art items, along with a quantity of kitsch.

We had also, I've got to admit, had a good time. Breitenbach was not only an effective investigator but an entertaining companion on a mission of this sort. Born in Hamburg, he had studied under Erwin Panofsky at the University of Berlin before emigrating to the United States, where eventually he became chief of the prints and photographic division of the Library of Congress. A squat, middle-aged man, with a stubby pipe invariably smoldering in his mouth, he always seemed to be having the time of his life, even when trying to act solemn. During our Berchtesgaden investigations, he habitually dressed in Bavarian peasant garb, and not long after we had arrived there on our first visit, I heard that the German chief of police of Berchtesgaden had sent out a puzzled inquiry, wanting to know who this man was who was running around the country in lederhosen, speaking with a Hamburg accent through a pipe and claiming to be an American officer and a doctor of arts. Also with us on at least one of these Bavarian investigations, and most helpful, was Dr. Hans Roethel, later renowned for the great collection of early Kandinskys at his Munich gallery. No lederhosen for young Dr. Roethel but only fastidious sartorial elegance, such as would grace the most high-toned exhibition reception.

Those of us, like me, who came along after the War Department's Office of Strategic Services (OSS) had done its superb reports on art looting found them an invaluable basis for our own investigations. Throughout my tenure, we sought to enlarge and build on that foundation by continued questioning of the principal players—such art advisers as Hans Posse, Karl Haberstock, Walter Hofer, and Mühlmann—as well as such art dealers as Hans Wendland, and others. Sometimes one of them would complain, "I've already told all I know about that matter." Nevertheless, every once in a while some-thing new would emerge—some lapse, perhaps, in the selective amnesia that every one of them, even the most garrulous, suffered from when it suited him—and new leads would develop that we could act on or that would shed further light on the murky history in which they had been involved.

Of these interrogations, the most extensive and significant was one I conducted together with Otto Wittman, Jr., an OSS officer, of the art dealer Hans Wendland. A shadowy, rather slippery figure, Wendland was the key link in the complex of transactions by which important artworks confiscated from French Jewish collections by the Einsatzstab Reichsleiter Rosenberg (ERR) passed through the hands of Göring and then made their way by diplomatic pouch to Switzerland for sale by the Fischer Gallery of Lucerne. Wittman and I questioned Wendland for ten straight days at the Wannsee Interrogation Center in Berlin to establish a coherent, authoritative history of this unsavory episode in the history of art dealings, and of Wendland's role in it. The report we assembled provided the possible whereabouts of a number of important paintings that had been questionably acquired.[1] It also led to the extradition of Wendland to France. And it also provided, I understand, some of the documentation needed to persuade the Swiss government to change its policy in regard to the wartime art transactions that had occurred—a policy of traditional leniency favoring the dealers, while putting virtually impossible obstacles in the way of those who had been victimized and who in postwar years were seeking to recover what had been taken from them.

In addition to the continuing interrogations of the agents and dealers, I also thought it worthwhile to revisit the memories of some of the top Nazi culprits, those who hadn't been executed. At Spandau prison in 1948 I interrogated Albert Speer; Baldur von Schirach, the Governor of Vienna; and Walther Funk, the former Minister of Economics and head of the Reichsbank. Speer was cooperative and helpful, like the Speer we've come to know through his books. Von Schirach was truculent but, when pressed, informative. Funk at some length convinced me he knew nothing.

I never interrogated Hermann Göring, but my MFA&A colleague H. Stewart Leonard did. That interrogation took place at Nuremberg on August 30, 1946, six weeks before Göring committed suicide. In that interrogation, Leonard told me, Göring acted very much the Renaissance man, the connoisseur he prided himself on being, who could recall, in impressive detail, the minutiae of almost every one of his transactions. In the course of that session, Leonard had the satisfaction of breaking the news to Göring that the painting he valued most of the 1,300 in his collection, the one he had actually paid more for than for any other work—his supposed Vermeer, *Christ with the Woman Taken in Adultery* (fig. 69)—was a fake. Göring refused at first to believe it, citing that he had also been shown a companion painting (presumably the work known as *Christ in the House of Mary and Martha*) that had gone on the market about the same time, and which the Rijksmuseum in Amsterdam had purchased, though it was in quite bad shape. Furthermore, he recalled that he had received a telegram from Alois Miedl, the dealer who worked with Göring's adviser, Walter Hofer, urging him to decide quickly on this second religious "Vermeer" because the Rijksmuseum was interested in that one, too. Short of an unbroken provenance, what better endorsement of the work's authenticity could he have had than that? So he closed the deal. *"Furchtbar alt"* was the way the painting looked when he bought it, he remembered, and it was in such poor condition that a costly restoration job had been required, though it had cleaned up very nicely, he had to admit.

"You say," he asked plaintively, "it's not genuine?"

"No," replied Leonard, "it's not genuine." And he told Göring about the forger Han van Meegeren, who at that very moment was in a Dutch jail, painting yet another such religious "Vermeer" in order to clear himself of the charge of having sold a national treasure to the enemy. With that, Göring could argue no longer but had to accept reality. Shaking his head, Göring lamented about the swindles of dealers and the perils of the art trade, and about the betrayal of trust. At that moment, Leonard told me, Hermann Göring looked as if for the first time he had discovered there was evil in the world.

The account of this episode given here is pretty much as it was told to me by Leonard not long after the event, and I have been able to verify its substantial accuracy from a transcript of the interrogation at the National Archives in Washington, D.C.[2] I have related the story now, because it's one I have not seen in any of the Göring biographies and thus belongs in

69. Master forger Han van Meegeren's notorious fake Vermeer *Christ with the Woman Taken in Adultery*. During World War II, the painting was owned by Hermann Göring.

its small way to history. I wish that Leonard were alive to tell it himself, but he died in 1952 at the age of forty-one in St. Louis, Missouri, where he was assistant director of the Saint Louis Art Museum.

At the end of August 1948, after two years of this art sleuthing, I left Germany and returned to the United States. Things were changing rapidly. Two months before, currency reform had been instigated in the Western zones of occupation, and the famous West German "economic miracle" was getting going. Goods had begun to appear in the stores, and at last the rubble was being cleared off and the rebuilding of the German cities was under way. Our art section's task was not over. For some years to come, the process of safeguarding, inventorying, and restituting looted art to the formerly occupied countries would continue. But the main discoveries had already been made, and our finds hereafter would be occasional and, for the most part, of minor works. There were vast losses to be mourned, but not all that much we could any longer do about them.

For me, those years had been an extraordinary, complicated experience, painful much of the time as I wrestled with feelings that were an uneasy mix of righteousness and shame. The righteousness, obviously, was directed at all that the Germans had done; the shame was over what the Allies had done in return, which I was not convinced we needed to have done to win the war, particularly the blanket bombing of the cities. As I picked my way through a city's rubble, conscious that the bodies of children were still immured in those brick and concrete heaps, I sometimes thought how horrified the world had been just a decade before when German planes bombed Guernica, killing some eight hundred people, and I grieved over the callousness with which we accepted and justified our own thousandfold more devastating raids.

Nevertheless, I was proud of the work that our MFA&A agency had done, and remain proud. Our efforts to try to tidy up, in the world of art at any rate, some small part of the epic mess that had been made, seemed to me to have been meaningful behavior, not merely as equity but also as ritual and symbol. It had been gratifying to me that ours was an organization that was concerned with preserving Germany's art heritage as well as with restituting to other nations the things that Germany had pillaged from them. It was good, I thought, that amid all the sickening evidence of man's depravity and destructiveness I should have had the opportunity to help preserve some of the things mankind had done that one could not only bear to contemplate but even take joy in.

TRANSFER OF CUSTODY

TO THE GERMANS

S. Lane Faison, Jr.

My appointment by the United States Department of State as the final director of the Munich Central Collecting Point (CCP) came through Ardelia Hall, Chief of the Office of International Information and Cultural Affairs in Washington, D.C. It was probably due to my experience five years earlier, in 1945, as a member of the Art Looting Investigation Unit (ALIU) of the Office of Strategic Services (OSS). Three of us spent that summer quizzing Nazi art personnel. My particular task was to find out about Adolf Hitler's massive art collection, which he intended to become the crown jewel in a sort of Acropolis-on-the-Danube in the old Austrian city of Linz. As a great new cultural center, Linz was to replace Vienna, scene of Hitler's failures as a student of art and architecture. From my friend and commander-of-unit, James S. Plaut, you have just heard (see above, pages 124–25). Our attractive bivouac in these days was near the great Austrian salt mine at Alt Aussee.

In 1950 the State Department decided to end its participation in the work of the two United States Zone centers for repatriation of art found in U.S.-occupied Germany and Austria. These were set up at Wiesbaden and Munich. Appointed to wind up affairs at Wiesbaden was my friend the late Thomas C. Howe, director of the California Palace of the Legion of Honor, San Francisco, and in 1945 a leader of the transport team that moved thousands of works in ninety truckloads from the Alt Aussee mine to the Munich CCP. As my senior, Tom reported for both of us to HICOG (the United States High Commissioner in Germany) in Frankfurt. Please note that I did not report to OLCB (Office of the Land Commissioner of Bavaria) in Munich, but via Tom to HICOG Frankfurt.

Sailing together from New York, Tom and I reached our respective destinations in the early days of December 1950. You have already heard about the Wiesbaden CCP from its first two directors, Walter Farmer and Edith Standen; likewise

70. Officer S. Lane Faison, Jr., in 1943, before his transfer into the OSS (Art Looting Investigation Unit)

from Craig Smyth, the first director of CCP Munich (see pages 131–34, 122–23, and 126–30). In both areas, setting up a CCP was achieved despite incredible obstacles. Nevertheless, Allied policy to repatriate works of art to the occupied countries from which they had been moved forged steadily ahead. This policy was a noteworthy decision to avoid the traditional "finders-keepers" disposition of such art practiced by victors like Napoleon.

On my first visit to Wiesbaden, I met Theodore Heinrich, my predecessor at CCP Munich. He, Tom Howe, and I called on our chain-of-command representative in Frankfurt at HICOG . This was William Daniels, Chief of the Property Division in the Office of External Affairs. Daniels's reception of Tom and me was not excessively cordial; indeed, his main concern was with how soon we would go home.

Heinrich then drove me to Munich. During that beautiful ride on the Autobahn he filled me in on background history. After Craig Smyth's tour of duty, several directors had come and gone, among them H. Stewart Leonard, who lost a vigorous battle to oppose repatriation of certain works to Italy, and Stephen Munsing, who had moved across the Königsplatz to the former Führerbau to become director of Amerika Haus. Heinrich, who had succeeded Munsing, was also responsible for the Wiesbaden CCP.

The Munich CCP occupied the Verwaltungsbau, the former official Nazi Party building in Munich. In addition to the CCP, it now housed other offices. Their directors included Dr. Eberhard Hanfstaengl, administrator of all Bavarian art museums and castles, and Dr. Ludwig Heydenreich, a distinguished art historian who presided over the scholarly Zentralinstitut für Kunstgeschichte inaugurated by Craig Smyth in 1945. Heinrich introduced me to all these persons and of course to the personnel of the CCP, especially the hardworking Fräuleins Boehm and Haars. I also met briefly Dr. George N. Shuster, on leave from the presidency of Hunter College to serve as United States Land Commissioner of Bavaria.

For the most part, work at the Munich CCP continued on in its orderly routine. Lists were constantly reviewed and checked against claims and works in storage. New claimants were directed to make very specific descriptions of what they had lost, when, and how. Appointed representatives of the nations occupied by Germany (especially France, the Netherlands, and Belgium) assisted in the process. When a work had been identified as having come from such a nation *after the date of occupation,* it was returned to the *government* of that nation. To that source, the owner could then make a claim for restitution.

Occasionally, even at this late date, works were brought in for potential return. On August 1, 1951, for example, the resident U.S. Officer at Traunstein brought in a large canvas, rolled and damaged, that had just been confiscated in the area. A former German foot soldier had "picked it up" in the ruins of Monte Cassino. It was soon identified as one of the altarpieces of the great abbey church, an *Assumption of the Virgin* by Paolo de Matteis. Restitution to Italy was easily accom-

plished through the Italian consul in Munich. There was no such problem as H. Stewart Leonard had faced in 1947, when Italy demanded return of works taken from important collections and presented as gifts to Hitler and Göring by Mussolini. Question: was Italy "liberated" or was it an Axis partner? Leonard's vigorous fight against return was overruled.

As a considerable portion of the treasure now at CCP Munich had been brought there from the Alt Aussee salt mine, I had many reminders of our OSS/ALIU unit at Aussee in 1945. For example, Walter Andreas Hofer, Göring's chief curator, called to press his own claim for a fifteenth-century *Madonna*. The Göring collection was also in the CCP, brought there in 1945 by Tom Howe—not from Aussee but from Berchtesgaden, where the great Göring train from Karinhall/Berlin had ended up in a railway tunnel. I was favored with a visit from Frau Emmy Göring herself, with a claim of her own.[1]

These matters, interesting and generally pleasant enough, were subordinate to what I call the two leitmotifs of my nine months' tenure. The first, already alluded to, was the tug-of-war between HICOG (in the person of William Daniels) and Tom and me as CCP directors. Time—the end-of-August termination date—was on Daniels's side, with occasional support from OMGUS (Office of Military Government, United States) in Berlin. On our side there was the work to be completed, and strong support from Ardelia Hall in Washington. She could and did get cables sent on our behalf, ending with the authoritative signature, "Acheson."

The second leitmotif emerged around the middle of January 1951, in conversations with Ludwig Heydenreich of the Zentralinstitut für Kunstgeschichte. Through our common interest in art history we had developed a friendly approach to current problems. It was his offhand remark about sending back to Austria works still awaiting identification of wartime provenance that took my breath away. Back to Austria? This was something Ted Heinrich had not divulged to me, nor to Tom Howe.

The origin of this policy appeared to go back to about 1945, and it may have involved an alleged agreement between the Austrians and General Mark Clark of the United States Fifth Army. The irony of all this was that most of what had been brought from Aussee to Munich in 1945 had previously been sent there *from Munich* to save it from the great bombardments. Obviously, there was no proof that these works had been acquired in Austria. Even if they had been, there was the question of whether they should go back to a former Axis partner. Under a controversial Allied decision made in November 1943, however, Austria was to be considered "liberated" from Axis occupation. *Ergo,* repatriate. No matter whether that policy or the traditional argument of "finders-keepers" applied, the conclusion was inescapable. I had to carry out a shipment to Austria before the United States transfer of custody to the Germans. The address of the receiver was the Palace of the Archbishop of Salzburg.

As time went on, the impact of such an unwanted end to my Bavarian sojourn steadily grew, and it damaged many friendly associations. Eventually, of course, the secret was out. Packers from Munich Military Post Engineers arrived on August 17, but already a week beforehand a news reporter of the *Abendzeitung* had gone on the attack with a powerful Anglo-German pun. Remember that Hitler's collection was destined to go to Linz, and that a Linzer torte is a famous dessert. As the reporter's unlikely name was Christliebe, it was from such a hallowed source that I was charged with committing a Linzer torte! By August 22, wires were buzzing between the offices of the High Commissioner in Frankfurt and the Land Commissioner in Munich. The latter, Dr. George Shuster, got me on the phone in a rage and tore me apart. Two days later, in his office, he had cooled down, and he treated me graciously. We discovered a common bond in a love for German Baroque and Rococo architecture, and a shared belief that Dominikus Zimmermann's masterpiece was the pilgrimage church at Steinhausen, not the Wieskirche. Remarking that "this business has taken a bit of my shirttail," he wished me well. I suppose I should have kept him informed, but I had assumed that HICOG, to which I reported, was doing that.

The shipment that left was large in quantity, but notably dull in quality. As always the case, finer things are more easily identified. To this day, the Austrians have been plagued with lawsuits about these poor remnants.

THE ROLE OF THE

STATE DEPARTMENT

REGARDING NATIONAL AND

PRIVATE CLAIMS FOR

THE RESTITUTION OF STOLEN

CULTURAL PROPERTY

Ely Maurer

The symposium presentations documented in the preceding section were indeed a hard act to follow.[1] And I hope that some of the approval that was displayed will extend to the smaller operation of the restitution that I am about to describe. I refer to the role of the State Department in the postwar recovery of looted cultural property that mainly was looted in Europe and found its way to the United States. What was involved here in the United States was an operation of modest dimensions in comparison with the extensive restitution operation of the Collecting Points in Germany. But the operation here had the same objective as that of the Collecting Points and was important in depriving those who engaged in thievery and pillage of looted objects and in restituting such objects to their rightful owners.

Here, I might note that Ardelia Hall, who headed the State Department operation in the early years, was a Monuments, Fine Arts, and Archives adviser to the State Department. She had served as an MFA&A officer in Europe and continued in the department, working in close cooperation with her counterparts in Europe.

I might start by pointing out that the State Department adopted a position and a policy in favor of restitution for cases involving stolen cultural objects that had come to the United States. The department position in favor of restitution is based on three principles. The first principle involves morality: stolen property should be restored to its owner. The second is that it is good foreign policy and good foreign relations to make such restorations. The countries that see their masterpieces come to the United States are aggrieved and have made outcries to us and pressed us for our help. Any aid that we can give to them helps to assuage their concerns. The third principle is that such restitution action is in our own self-interest. Masterpieces that have been displaced to the United States are not only part of the patrimony of their particular country of origin, they are also the heritage of mankind, in which we all share and from which we all benefit.[2] In the case of the particular subject of this volume, involving art looted during war, an additional motive comes into play. In recovering cultural property of this kind, we are correcting a violation of international law. In these cases, pillage has occurred or there has been a failure to "respect" works of art in private hands or in the possession of state museums. Such actions are condemned by provisions that appear in the Hague Convention of 1907 (Convention Respecting the Laws and Customs of War on Land), Articles 46, 47, and 56 (see Appendix 3).

What has the State Department done to implement this policy, this position in favor of restitution? I wish to point out first that the State Department does not have the legal power to seize stolen cultural property and return it to a victimized country or individual. We are therefore forced to look to other forms of aid. For instance, we can use our good offices or try to conciliate or mediate disputes so as to recover stolen or looted property. In fact, there was a major episode of this nature involving the two Albrecht Dürer paintings stolen from the Weimar Museum during the war.* When the paintings surfaced in New York in the 1960s, the embassy of the Federal Republic of Germany (FRG) asked the State Department for assistance. Our undersecretary for political affairs, George C. McGhee, took it upon himself to invite Edward Elicofon, who was the possessor of the Dürer paintings; Wildenstein, who was his mentor, head of the Wildenstein Gallery; and the lawyer for Elicofon to have lunch with him at the State Department. He pointed out that Elicofon had bought these major artworks, worth millions, for a pittance of $450 from a GI who had come to his door; that there was a possible violation of the National Stolen Property Act (stolen property crossing international borders); and that the retention of the paintings in the United States was an embarrassment to our good foreign relations. McGhee asked Elicofon if he would not, in his role as a good citizen and in the interests of the United States, give up the paintings. The request of the undersecretary was unavailing, and Elicofon refused to turn over the paintings. We therefore urged the FRG to initiate a lawsuit, indicating that we would render as much help as we could. A lawsuit was brought, and ultimately Elicofon was defeated. In this case, the use of good offices was not successful, but on other occasions we have brought about recoveries, and we think this procedure oftentimes is a good way to start.

In addition to using our good offices, when an uninformed claimant comes to the State Department with a case, we try to explain what our law is and the favorable jurisprudence that has developed here for the recovery of looted and stolen cultural property. Here again, we may suggest that the best way for the claimant to proceed may be to initiate litigation; and several claimants, after consulting their lawyers, have followed this course.

To compensate for our lack of legal power, we can suggest the application of legal powers held by sister agencies in the U.S. government. I am referring here to the Justice Department, the Customs Service, the Defense Department, and the Internal Revenue Service. The Justice Department has in its purview the National Stolen Property Act, which makes it a crime for persons to transport, in international commerce or over state borders, objects worth $5,000 or more that are known to be stolen. The Customs Service administers customs provisions that permit seizure of property if smuggled in or improperly declared, and the return of the property to the true owner. The Defense Department can subject a member of the armed services suspected of theft to court-martial, impose fines and penalties, and recover items that have been looted. The Internal Revenue Service may charge a violation of the Income Tax Law or of the Estate Tax Law, where stolen cultural property is involved.

The above-mentioned method was used in the case of the Quedlinburg treasures; the Justice Department, the Customs Service, and the Internal Revenue Service were alerted to the possible application of their legal controls.[3] It will be recalled that the German government felt it had to ransom the Quedlinburg treasures, since it was fearful that if the objects remained on the market, they might be purchased by individuals and lost forever. I understand that legal remedies in the control of the Internal Revenue Service, the Department of Justice, and the Customs Service may still be effective in reducing the gains of the Meador-Cook family.†

When we encourage claimants to initiate a lawsuit, we also encourage them to make known to the court our expressed policy favoring restitution of cultural property so as to provide support for their case. Also, where our special expertise is involved, the State Department may intervene in litigation, as we have done, for instance, with respect to unrecognized regimes, the interpretations of international law, and the application of the law of successor states.

Finally, let me give you some idea of the range and volume of recovery activities in which the State Department has been engaged. During the period from 1944 to 1954, the dominant force in the State Department was Ardelia Hall, who, as we have said previously, was a Monuments, Fine Arts, and Archives adviser to the department. She was a persistent, zealous person, passionate in her attempts to recover stolen cultural property, and she succeeded greatly in that effort. When she arrived at the State Department, she republished a circular previously published by the Roberts Commission.[4] At this time there was a great influx of returning military personnel, and numerous stolen items were surfacing in the United States. She sent the circular to museums, university art faculties, and art dealers, advising them to be on the alert for cases of possible looted property and exhorting them to report such cases to the government. She then enlisted the help and cooperation of our governmental sister agencies in recovering stolen items. As a result of this circular and the cooperative efforts of our sister agencies, sixty-six cases came under her control. These sixty-six cases involved sixteen hundred items. Ardelia Hall wrote several articles on her activities;[5] the last article, published in 1954,[6] advised that of those sixty-six cases, fifty-one cases, involving about thirteen hundred items, had been successfully concluded by the end of September 1954. With respect to the fifteen other cases and the three hundred remaining items, she reported jubilantly that all were under active investigation. It was quite clear that she expected a successful outcome in these cases.

Ardelia Hall retired from the State Department in 1964. I was one of the lawyers who had served her in her work, and when she retired, her area of activity fell to me. I later acquired the same responsibility with respect to stolen cultural property not connected with war. During the period in which I have been involved, there has not been the great influx that

* Editor's note: See Kaye, above, pages 104–5.

† Editor's note: See the case study below, pages 148–58.

occurred earlier, in the 1950s. There has been a resurgence of cases recently, perhaps because some persons holding looted property believe that enough time has elapsed so that stolen items might safely be put on the market.[7] These persons may be disappointed, because the statute of limitations does not begin to elapse until the victimized country or individual learns the location of the looted object or the identity of the possessor.

During the period of my tenure, several interesting cases of wartime looting have come before the State Department. One is that of two small masterpieces by Pollaiuolo that had been in the Uffizi Gallery, *Hercules and the Hydra* and *Hercules and Antaeus*. The Italian government was very upset when these paintings were found to be missing. Several years later, they surfaced in California in the hands of a former German officer who had served in northern Italy. He had picked up these paintings there, gone home to Germany, and then emigrated to the United States. When the location of these paintings became known, Rodolfo Siviero, who headed an art-recovery section within the Italian foreign ministry, rushed to California. He talked with the German immigrant but was not able to persuade him to relinquish the two paintings. Siviero then traveled to Washington, D.C., where he and the Italian ambassador talked with the secretary of state and asked for help. The secretary agreed to help and called the attorney general, who sent a team of lawyers from the Justice Department and FBI agents to California to interrogate the possessor of the paintings. The team informed this individual of a violation of the National Stolen Property Act, for which he could be prosecuted and punished. They also found that the possessor had intended to become a United States citizen and informed him that his refusal to relinquish the paintings could jeopardize his citizenship application. The man then decided to give up the paintings, which were sent to Washington, D.C. A ceremony was held there, in which the paintings were turned over by the United States attorney general to Siviero in the presence of the chief justice of the United States Supreme Court and officers of the State Department.

Many engrossing stories such as this can be told. We have already mentioned the cases of the Dürer paintings and the Quedlinburg treasures. Also pertinent are the DeWeerth case,* the case of the eight postage stamps, the case of the Polish archives, the case of the medieval Vellum of Indulgences, and the case of the Tintoretto painting (*Holy Family with Saint Catherine*). All these have their fascinating details. Two cases that do not involve looted property are of interest and should be mentioned here.

One case involved the Holy Crown of Saint Stephen and the royal regalia of Hungary. These the United States took under protective custody, which led to criticism that we were behaving like Hitler and his agents; it was thought that we had intended to keep these treasures. In fact, Hungarian refugees wanted us to keep them out of the hands of the communist regime. We kept them in Fort Knox, and when an opportune time came, we returned them to Hungary, in 1978.

Another case involved art that Hitler and the German Propaganda Ministry had commissioned German artists to create. Six thousand pieces of "German war art" came to the United States. We considered that this art was legitimate war booty that could be kept by us under the laws of war, because the art had been used to promote the German war effort. Ultimately we returned as a matter of grace all but about three hundred items, which contained Nazi swastikas and other Nazi symbols, portraits of German war leaders, and so forth.

In addition to the recovery cases mentioned above, the State Department has played a leading role in preventing the enactment of legislation that would have hindered the recovery of stolen cultural property. To benefit a constituent, one United States senator tried to get a law passed that would have established a "law of repose," as he called it. The proposed law would have permitted a work of art, such as the *Mona Lisa*, to be stolen, put in a basement or vault for five years, and then become the irrevocable property of the possessor. We strongly opposed this legislation, and the interested agencies in the government rallied in opposition to it: it died in committee. In another case, legislation was promoted in New York that would have made the recovery of stolen property more difficult. The State Department took the lead in writing to Governor Mario Cuomo urging that the legislation be vetoed. Similar letters were sent by the Justice Department, the United States Information Agency, and the National Endowment for the Arts. Governor Cuomo vetoed the legislation.

This is the story that I can tell. As Lynn Nicholas has said in *The Rape of Europa*,[8] this is not the end of the story. Stolen art objects from Eastern Europe continue to appear; and it can be expected that items will reach the United States and that the State Department will continue to play its part in the recovery and restitution of these items.

---

* Editor's note: For the DeWeerth case, see Kaye, above, page 105.

INSTANCES OF

REPATRIATION BY

THE USSR

The following is a summary of the symposium presentation given by Irina Antonova on the returns made by the Soviet Union to the German Democratic Republic (GDR) during the Cold War period (see above, page 15).*

A document prepared by the Institute of State and Law of the Russian Academy of Sciences, "On the Legal Bases for a Solution to Questions Concerning Cultural Property Removed to the USSR as a Result of World War II," demonstrates, in the view of Ms. Antonova, the legality of the presence in the Soviet Union of the objects removed from Germany at the end of the war. Her only regret is that the document was not prepared earlier and was not backed expeditiously by law. The cultural property removed officially from Germany to the USSR in 1945–46 was housed in the vaults of museums, libraries, archives, and other state institutions, thereby ensuring both its preservation and the possibility of its being made available to scholars and the public. In the case of property removed unofficially, much of this ended up in the hands of private individuals; these removals included cases of "looting and plundering" as well as cases of "honest acquisitions."

Not wishing to discuss the actions of the Soviet leadership regarding the removals, Ms. Antonova nonetheless made reference to the difficulties that she and her colleagues had faced as a result of these actions: "We all were hostages to many erroneous decisions on which history has passed judgment." These included the decision to impose a "regime of secrecy" on the displaced objects in the state repositories. Beginning in the 1960s, members of the administrations of the museums in which many of these objects were held repeatedly "raised the question of the need to open up the closed collections." Those who did so included Directors Artamonov and Piotrovsky of the State Hermitage Museum in Leningrad (St. Petersburg), and, from the Pushkin State Museum of Fine Arts in Moscow, Deputy Director Vipper and Director Antonova herself. Those whom Ms. Antonova approached regarding this issue included Ministers of Culture Furtseva, Demichev, Zakharov, and Gubenko, and in the 1990s Mr. Yakovlev and Mr. Kozyrev.

The return of cultural property to Germany can be said to have begun in 1949, with the decision of the Soviet government to return the archives from the Hanseatic cities of Hamburg, Lübeck, and Bremen, in exchange for the archives of the Kaliningrad region and the city of Tallinn, which were at that time in the British Zone of Occupation. The transfers were begun in July 1952 and concluded at the end of the 1980s. In all, 74,998 archival units were handed over. Additional transfers of cultural property were effected, including nineteen such transfers between September 1958 and July 1960 alone. The final Protocol of the Transfer by the Government of the USSR to the Government of the GDR of Cultural Property Saved by the Soviet Army was signed in Berlin on July 29, 1960.

---

* Editor's note: This summary has been prepared by the editor from a transcription of Ms. Antonova's presentation (in translation) as documented in the official taped record of the symposium proceedings.

In accordance with the Protocol, 1,571,995 objects; 121 cases of books, sound archives, and musical scores; and more than 3 million archival files were returned. More recently, the collection of German books held in the Pulkovo Observatory was handed over in 1993.

The objects returned included "works of the highest merit": the collection of the Gotha library, which had been preserved in the Academy of Sciences of the USSR (29,818 units); German archival materials from the state archives of the USSR and Ministry of Foreign Affairs of the USSR (214,924 files); the treasures of the Grünes Gewölbe (Green Vault) in Dresden; 800,623 works of art that had been held in the State Hermitage Museum in Leningrad, including reliefs from the Pergamon altar, ancient Egyptian papyri, and European paintings; and from the Pushkin State Museum of Fine Arts, 354,271 works of art including drawings, paintings, coins, and antiquities.

Never before had any state that was a victim of aggression entailing such monstrous consequences, that in war had lost millions of its citizens, hundreds of thousands of artifacts of culture and art, thousands of unique secular and religious buildings, more than 400 museums and more than 700,000 exhibits, made such gifts to countries whose deeds had warranted judgment by an international court. We cannot fail to recall that our losses were not merely the inevitable consequence of the destruction caused by modern warfare. What took place was an operation deliberately planned to destroy the culture of a country.

One of the most notable returns was that of the paintings from the Dresden Gemäldegalerie, an act "unprecedented in world history." And for all of those who participated in the "epic story of the appearance of the Dresden collection" in the USSR, this was one of the most important and thrilling events of their lives.

No one ever again will see the treasures of the exhibits the way we saw them in those unforgettable years or experience that feeling of pride, happiness, and inspiration that flowed from our participation in the salvation of these great creations.

Beginning in 1939, the Dresden paintings were removed for safety to a number of repositories. In 1945, after the bombing of Dresden, the paintings were moved to quarries and mines in various parts of Saxony. In some of them, such as the limestone mine at Pockau-Lengefeld, the works were deeply buried, in this case to a depth of fifty-two meters. Moreover, explosives were stored in the mines. Temperature and humidity controls broke down, "and dampness and water dripping down the walls created a threat to the paintings' security." With the exception of Raphael's Sistine Madonna, which was found in a crate, paintings were found on the ground or leaning against one another and against the walls of the shafts. There was also the threat of looting. The search for the paintings of the Dresden Gemäldegalerie was carried out by the battalion of the Fifth Guards of the army of the First Ukrainian Front. The story of the paintings' discovery would later be called by

the Süddeutsche Zeitung "the most breathtaking detective story of the twentieth century."

The Dresden collection arrived at the Pushkin State Museum of Fine Arts in August of 1945, at the time when the museum's own collections had only just been reassembled. During the war, the museum building had been damaged, although by the time of the arrival of the Dresden paintings, the most essential repairs had been made. In 1946, the galleries would again be opened to the public. During this period, the work of the museum staff consisted mainly in the preparation of the museum's own collections for exhibition and the processing of "new acquisitions"; the latter activity would continue for a decade.

During these years the restoration workshop of the museum was reminiscent of a field hospital. Nearly all of the paintings arrived from Germany "bandaged up"—with warning stickers on those parts that had been damaged, applied by the restorer Stepan Churakov at the sites of their discovery. The most difficult and complicated work was carried out by the chief restorer of the museum, the wonderful artist Pavel Korin. It is he who saved from destruction Titian's masterpiece The Tribute Money and Francia's Crucifixion of Christ, Rubens's Bathsheba, and many other treasures of the collection. It was possible to start working on many panel paintings only after two or three years, once the thick wood had dried, as it was impossible to dry the wood of these paintings artificially. At the opening of the collection it was rightly noted that the works had been saved twice—first by the soldiers who recovered them after the war, and then by the restorers and museum associates who cared for them.

The paintings from the Dresden Gemäldegalerie were exhibited from May 2 through August 20, 1955. People travelled long distances to see the legendary treasures, sometimes standing in line for days in order to buy tickets. The demands on the museum staff were tremendous—with the work day extending from dawn until nearly midnight—and yet in the museum and in Moscow there reigned a joyous atmosphere. In all, 1,200,000 people attended the exhibition. On August 25, the closing ceremony took place, and the act was signed for the transfer of the first painting to the GDR: Dürer's Portrait of a Young Man. The remaining works were then documented, and exhaustive condition reports were prepared. In all, 1,240 paintings were transferred to Dresden, some of which came from Kiev. On June 3, 1956, the paintings were exhibited in Dresden; prior to that, they were displayed in Berlin.

I admit that it is hard for me—from many points of view—to discuss totally objectively the problems of displaced cultural property and the losses that occurred during the years of World War II. The war—and these are not just empty words—deeply affected the lives and the hearts of the people of my generation. For me, a specialist in Italian art, the Sistine Madonna will never be solely a masterpiece by Raphael. That image is forever fused in my consciousness and in my memory with the heroic salvation of my country and my people from destruction, fused with the heroic deed of a mother who sacrificed the life of her son. Of course, the emotional side of my impressions does not prevent me from clearly understanding that today the dialogue must be continued. We have now marked the fiftieth anniversary of the end of the Second World War. But the war has not truly ended, as long as we have not settled the unresolved issues in the area of cultural property. I think that we need to recall the concept of conscience, a concept that Hitler referred to—unfortunately—as a chimera. In 1945, in New York, the great German writer Thomas Mann gave a lecture entitled "Germany and the Germans." In that speech he expressed the following profound thought: "In the last analysis, the misfortune that befell Germany is only a reflection of the human tragedy in general. All of us need mercy."

INTRODUCTION

Constance Lowenthal

As we turn to the well-known case of the discovery and return of the Quedlinburg treasures, our attention focuses not only on the past but also on the present. The story is rich and colorful—involving an American soldier, precious medieval reliquaries and manuscripts, some citizens in a small town in Texas, and the highest levels of the international art market. The objects in question formed part of the treasury of the church of Quedlinburg (fig. 71) for approximately a thousand years and were gifts to the church from Ottonian emperors and members of their families. They were mentioned in the tenth century and inventoried in the thirteenth; among medievalists, they are famous. The treasury remained largely intact, even through the upheavals of Lutheran reformation, until the Second World War.

The contributors to this section are three thoughtful men who became involved with the treasures' discovery and return. Their papers narrate their own experiences and expound their views of the case today in the light of subsequent events. The Quedlinburg case is not only colorful but significant. This is not a case of official return, nation to nation. This case posed different problems that required different solutions. The Quedlinburg treasures were not sitting in Fort Knox under the control of the United States government like Hungary's Crown of Saint Stephen. Their fate did not rest on a United States government decision. The objects were in private hands, in possession of the heirs of Joe Tom Meador, the American soldier who sent them to Texas in 1945 and who died in 1980. The return of the objects to the church followed after the story played out in the press, sometimes known as the court of public opinion, and after the case entered the United States court system. After the initial return for a fee of one of the works, the Samuhel Gospels (colorplate 9),[1] a settlement arranging the return of the other objects held by Meador's heirs to the church of Quedlinburg was reached out of court.

These contributors provide an appreciation of the issues that bear upon a case in which war booty was found in America in private hands. Laws and expectations in the United States are quite different from those in other countries. What kind of payments, if any, should be made to effect recovery of one's possessions? What kind are necessary? What legal action can be taken? At what expense? With how much confidence can its outcome be predicted? What are the rights of the original owner? And what are the rights of the possessor? Can a thief or his heirs be considered legitimate owners and therefore have the right to sell? What is in the public interest?

71. Church of St. Servatius, Quedlinburg, Germany, seen from the southwest. Some of the most valuable items from the Quedlinburg treasury were removed for safety during World War II. Although the cache was guarded by the occupying United States Army, objects were taken by an American soldier, who shipped them home to Texas.

After the first financial transaction, in which the German Kulturstiftung der Länder (Cultural Foundation of the States) agreed to pay a finder's fee of nearly $3 million to the heirs of Joe Tom Meador, there was an outcry and an uproar. My voice was one of many that protested the arrangement, as I commented to the press and wrote about it in the *Wall Street Journal*.[2] I was an observer, but our contributors were players in the drama.

The precious objects recovered in Texas* included several reliquaries and objects of liturgical use, among them the Reliquary Casket of Henry I (colorplate 10).[3] Henry I, known as the Fowler, was the early-tenth-century ruler of Saxony, and the father of Otto I. The longest side of the box measures twenty-nine centimeters, approximately eleven inches, and its panels are carved from walrus and elephant ivory. Strips of gilt silver and gilt copper repoussé and openwork are placed around the edges and are inset with glass and semiprecious stones. Another outstanding object is an ecclesiastical comb,[4] also connected to Henry I, made of elephant ivory and carved in the eighth century; it is of Umay-

yad origin, and is embellished with a German-made jeweled mounting of tenth-century date. Such ceremonial combs were used in the consecration ceremonies for bishops; they symbolize the combing-out of evil that a new bishop is expected to accomplish.

Five other reliquaries were in the group,[5] one a crystal flask in the shape of two birds, carved back-to-back.[6] Its origins are in tenth-century Fatimid Egypt, but the gilt silver mounts are fourteenth-century German. Two monstrance reliquaries in the form of towers (thirteenth century) were among the loveliest objects in the collection; these were made of rock crystal (so the relics inside could be visible), gilt silver, garnets, and blue and green glass.[7] Some of the Quedlinburg reliquaries are believed to contain dried blood of Christ or a hair from the head of the Virgin Mary. An unusual piece is a fifteenth-century capsule in the form of a heart; it is believed to contain wax from an Easter vigil candle burned at the Lateran basilica in Rome and blessed by the pope.[8]

Two luxury manuscripts were recovered from the Meador heirs. The Evangelistary of 1513 was bound with a gilt-silver cover, decorated with precious stones.[9] The Samuhel Gospels (colorplate 9), a Carolingian manuscript of the ninth century, was written in gold letters and bound with an even more lavish, jewel-encrusted cover. It was this work that was transferred in 1990 to the Kulturstiftung der Länder for some $3 million, variously characterized as a finder's fee or a sale price. This was a separate transaction that preceded the lawsuit.†

A bank vault in Whitewright, Texas (population: 1,760), was the unlikely place where these objects turned up.

---

* Editor's note: A total of ten objects was recovered. Nine of these (excluding the Samuhel Gospels) were exhibited in the Dallas Museum of Art in 1991, after which they were returned to Germany (Anne Bromberg et al., *The Quedlinburg Treasury*, exhib. cat., February 16–April 14, 1991 [Dallas Museum of Art, 1991]). Two Quedlinburg objects known to have been in the possession of Joe Meador, a crucifix and a rock-crystal reliquary, were never found (see Kline, below, page 157 and figs. 72 and 73). Of the works listed as missing on a United States Army inventory prepared in Munich, December 17, 1947, the following were never recovered: "all relics out of an embroidered case" (inventory no. 4), "reliquary in form of a plate, silver partly gilded, about 1250" (no. 5), "memorial coin of Emperor Wilhelm II" (no. 10), "reliquary in form of a plate with intarsia" (no. 11), "painted box, contents: sealed documents concerning relics" (no. 12), "all coins from a glass case" (no. 13), "two gold and silver crucifixes" (no. 14), and "several old embroideries" (no. 15). Of these, the missing crucifix known to have been in the possession of Meador (see fig. 72) is surely one of the crucifixes originally inventoried as no. 14; the missing rock-crystal reliquary (see fig. 73) may be the reliquary inventoried as no. 5, although if this identification is correct, the description as listed in the inventory is not accurate.

† Editor's note: In 1992, an out-of-court settlement was reached in which the Meador heirs agreed to relinquish their claims to the remaining objects, in exchange for a total of $2.75 million, most of which they had already received in a series of payments made by the German government for the purchase of the Samuhel Gospels. See Kline, below, pages 156–58.

SEARCH FOR THE TREASURES

Willi Korte

The St. Servatius Church of Quedlinburg, a small town in the Harz Mountain region of eastern Germany, has had a treasure from its beginning, but the treasure has not always included the same objects, and it has not always been in the church or belonged to it.

There has been a church treasure since the tenth century, and since 1170 there has been a treasure chamber called the "Zither" in the church. Throughout the Middle Ages the treasure grew. After the Reformation, beginning in the second half of the sixteenth century, it started to shrink again. Due to greed and to need—to pay for repairs to the church building, for example—more and more pieces were sold, and others disappeared. However, the most significant objects stayed together or eventually found their way back to Quedlinburg. In 1803 the church and its treasures became the property of the Kingdom of Prussia. Following the Napoleonic Wars, Jerome Bonaparte, brother of Napoleon and king of Westphalia, took the treasure to the city of Kassel and kept it there for two years. After the Kingdom of Westphalia collapsed in 1813, the treasure was taken to the Prussian city of Halberstadt, only a few miles from Quedlinburg, where it remained until it was returned to St. Servatius in 1821.

The darkest days of the church and its treasure began on July 2, 1936, when Heinrich Himmler and the SS celebrated the thousandth anniversary of the death of King Henry I, called the Fowler, the first German king and founder of Quedlinburg; King Henry's widow, Queen Mathilde, established the convent church there. Himmler saw Henry I as one of the Germanic guiding stars in whose footsteps the Nazis should follow. From then on, the SS celebrated the anniversary in Quedlinburg every July 2. It was their plan—and construction began immediately—to turn the church into a national holy shrine of the SS. In December 1937, Himmler obtained the key to the treasure chamber, and on Easter 1938, the last religious service was held in the church. On September 1, 1939, the day Nazi Germany invaded Poland, the SS packed up the treasure and removed it to the vault of the local savings-and-loan association. In October 1943, out of fear of air raids, the SS took the treasure to the Altenburg cave, not far from the church. From that cave, American Lieutenant Joe T. Meador removed many of the most valuable pieces in April 1945.

Joe Meador used the military postal service to send his souvenirs home to Whitewright, Texas, in the summer of 1945. Upon the arrival of some of the items, his mother expressed her concern in a letter to Meador about the spirits of the Middle Ages inhabiting her house. After keeping the treasure in his mother's home and the family hardware store, Meador finally created his own shrine in the late 1960s, renting an apartment in Dallas, where he led a flamboyant weekend life, impressing his friends who thought of him as a man of wealth and culture. But the spirits of the Middle Ages caught up with him after all: he died rather miserably from cancer in 1980.

The greed that had plagued the history of the treasure for centuries also guided Meador's brother and sister, who were his heirs. Two years after their brother's death, they began to appraise and sell parts of the treasure, and in the course of doing so dealt with some of the world's leading art and rare-book dealers, who mostly did not question the provenance of the goods. At least, we know that none of them alerted the authorities. But when I first began to work on this case, of course none of these details was known.

In October 1988, Sam Fogg, a London dealer, offered the Samuhel Gospels, part of the long-lost Quedlinburg treasures, for $9 million to the Foundation for Prussian Cultural Heritage (Stiftung Preussischer Kulturbesitz) in Berlin. In the beginning of 1989, I was in Washington, D.C., working for the foundation at the National Archives, researching traces of lost treasures from the Berlin museums. Through a few phone calls and a handful of documents, I learned about Quedlinburg, its lost treasure, and the Gospels that were being offered for sale. Unfortunately, nothing was definite, just a few historical references and vague hints that prominent New York dealers might be or had been involved; yet those few clues were to change my life during the next two years.

A problem arose when officials at the foundation told me that even though they hoped I could find "something," the Quedlinburg case would not be part of my official assignment—after all, Quedlinburg was in hostile East Germany. Working on the case in an unofficial capacity and without a budget, I couldn't do much more than study old United States Army and military-government records in the National Archives and make phone calls to New York. But phone calls to whom? I could hardly call New York art and manuscript dealers, state my name, inquire about a stolen gospel book and other treasures from Quedlinburg, and expect to get any results.

The first help came from a New York law professor who shared my interest in missing and stolen works of art and who agreed to inquire on his own. The professor confirmed what I had heard, that a New York manuscript dealer, Roland Folter of H. P. Kraus, had been asked to appraise the Samuhel Gospels. I now needed to put more weight behind my efforts. The suggestion from Berlin to have an article published in the *New York Times* led me to the idea that I might get the *Times* actively involved. It was *Times* correspondent Bill Honan who in the end, despite the few documents and sketchy information available, was persuaded to join in this story. In particular, his efforts with Folter paved the way for me to negotiate later with this expert myself—and do so on much more solid ground.

By now, it was the fall of 1989, and I realized that my recent research in the National Archives had produced some useful information; but in order to completely reconstruct the events surrounding the Quedlinburg treasures, and in particular to learn the names of those in all the American army units in Quedlinburg during April–May 1945, I would need to research the United States Army records in Washington, D.C., and St. Louis. Also, I would need to approach the dealers in New York myself—in an official capacity.

November 9, 1989: the Berlin Wall opened, and with this event came new hope for the Quedlinburg case. At the end of November, I met with various cultural officials in Berlin and

pleaded my case: now that the border was open, one might talk to the church officials in Quedlinburg, get their authorization, and finance the treasure hunt. The authorization finally came—shortly before we went to court in Dallas in June 1990. But by then, the *New York Times* had published the name of the thief and his heirs, and I had already located the church's treasures in Texas.

In the meantime, however, by mid-January 1990 I was back in Washington, without any additional support from Germany—West or East—but getting more and more determined to pursue the Quedlinburg case anyway. By February, I was working exclusively on the mystery of the missing treasures; I had found more encouraging documents in the archives, and one of the New York dealers declared a willingness to talk to a German "official." Since I had no clear mandate to work on the case, I realized that I needed to talk to a good lawyer. Bill Honan suggested Tom Kline, from Andrews & Kurth in Washington, D.C., which happens to be a Texas law firm. Kline had successfully litigated the Cyprus (Kanakaria) mosaics case.

In early March 1990, I received information from New York that some years before, Roland Folter had been asked to appraise not only the Samuhel Gospels but also a second medieval manuscript. Using prewar photographs of the covers of the two books missing from Quedlinburg, I could verify that the second manuscript on the market was the Evangelistary of 1513, also stolen from the Altenburg cave. This discovery led me to believe that all the lost objects might still be in one place. My hopes grew that I could find the source of the two books and the rest of the loot—which were obviously offered by someone in the United States—especially since, after countless hours in the archives, I began to understand which American military outfits were in Quedlinburg and when. At the same time, my fears grew as well, as I realized that "they" might find out about my efforts. It took many more calls and several visits with reluctant New York manuscript dealers and experts before I could decipher their cryptic information, but at the end of that month I knew that a bank in rural Texas had something to do with the efforts to sell the manuscripts.

Before I could board a plane to Texas, my unofficial project was officially put on hold. Both the Stiftung Preussischer Kulturbesitz in Berlin and the federal government in Bonn informed me that there was a serious offer from Switzerland for the return of the Samuhel Gospels for a reasonable finder's fee; this opportunity should not be endangered. The view in Germany was that paying for their return was the only way to get the objects back. I wanted to go after the source of this offer—but then I did not want to have a second disappearance of the magnificent Carolingian manuscript on my conscience.

By the end of April, I learned that the Gospels were safe and that therefore I could go back to work. Soon thereafter I learned the names of the town—Whitewright—and bank in Texas, and in early May, I finally made that flight to Dallas. Whitewright has only one bank—across from the Meador hardware store—but I still did not know whether the thief or the sellers had also come from that town. I had long lists with names of officers and soldiers who should have been in Quedlinburg at the end of World War II, but during my first visit to Texas, I could not make a clear match. However, I decided to introduce myself to the president of the bank to show him the *New York Times* article on the return of the Samuhel Gospels, express my determination to find the other missing pieces, and judge his response. Of course, he had nothing to say, but two days later I had my first meeting with his lawyers in Dallas. Now, Tom Kline became a necessity. From that day on, I spent most of my time in law offices, negotiating, drafting papers, trying to reach agreements. We did obtain permission to view and photograph what were supposed to be "other pieces" from the Quedlinburg treasure. The permission was rescinded, and the next day Bill Honan had a story in the *New York Times* that said that the Evangelistary—one of the "other pieces" we were supposed to see in Dallas—had just been offered for sale in Switzerland. A lawsuit was filed in federal court two days later, and a temporary restraining order was granted.

Before the lawyer in me took over from the historian, Bill and I had dinner in Washington after my first trip to Texas. I told him I could not continue my investigation, now that I was negotiating. Over fish and white wine we discussed some ideas about what to do next in Texas in order to get to the bottom of this case. A few weeks later, the story made the front page of the *New York Times* . . .

JOURNALIST ON THE CHASE

William H. Honan

I sometimes think of Joe Tom Meador, the United States Army officer who stole the Quedlinburg treasures, as being rather like the man who killed the world's last dodo bird. When the man was arrested, he told the judge: "Your Honor, I did *not* kill the dodo bird. I saw it fly into a plate-glass window and break its neck. Only *after* I realized it was dead did I cook it and eat it."

The judge believed the man's story and acquitted him, but just before he left the courtroom the judge said, "Tell me, sir, for the record, what did the world's last dodo bird taste like?" The man replied, "Oh, Your Honor, it's hard to say, but somewhere between a white rhinoceros and a bald eagle."

Joe Tom Meador was like that man in the perhaps apocryphal story because he, too, fooled the world while he greedily savored for himself alone a treasure that belonged, in a sense, to all humankind. But, unlike the man who killed and ate the last dodo bird, the truth finally caught up with Meador.

Willi Korte, Tom Kline, and I helped bring that about, but we were not alone. Klaus Goldmann, the German museum curator who is also a contributor to this volume, discovered the United States Army documents buried in an archive in Munich (see editor's note, above, page 149) that provided essential background for our prosecution of this case. And it was my *New York Times* colleague Karl Meyer, also a symposium participant, who put the documents from Goldmann into my hands and encouraged me to pursue the matter. Constance Lowenthal of the International Foundation for Art Research was also helpful throughout.

It was both Klaus's and Karl's idea that Willi and I might work in cooperation, sharing leads and information as we went along. And that we did. For my part, in 1990 I began by interviewing Roland Folter, the New York City rare-book and manuscript dealer, as it had been rumored that Dr. Folter had been asked to appraise the two great medieval manuscripts that were among the missing treasures of Quedlinburg.

Dr. Folter acknowledged that he had been shown slides of the Quedlinburg manuscripts some years before and then had lost touch with the would-be seller. After a little encouragement, he also revealed that his contact had been a banker who lived in Texas. I immediately called Willi and told him of Dr. Folter's revelations and added that, since Dr. Folter had been born in Germany, Willi might be able to get even more out of him than I had if he interviewed him in his native German. Willi agreed to come to New York, where he met Roland Folter, about which you have just heard (see above, page 151). Shortly afterward, the government of West Germany announced it had paid a finder's fee of $3 million to acquire one of the long-lost Quedlinburg treasures—the Samuhel Gospels, a sumptuously illustrated, gold, silver, and jewel-encrusted manuscript from the ninth century.

Part of the acquisition deal, I was told when I explored the matter, was that the Germans were bound to secrecy and would not reveal the identity of the seller. After some pestering, however, I finally got a West German official to reveal that the seller was an American lawyer who lived in Texas but that the actual owner's name had been concealed from him.

As you can see, all signs were pointing to Texas and, on the strength of a tip from Dr. Folter, Willi journeyed to White-wright, a small farm town in Texas. While he was not able to extract a confession from anyone, or locate the treasures, Willi came back East thoroughly Westernized and declaring that he had come close enough to the treasures to hit them with a horseshoe if he had known in which direction to pitch. I was not so sure. It later turned out, however, that Willi's instinct was absolutely correct.

Meanwhile, I was preoccupied with another approach to the case. I figured that the Texas lawyer who sold the Samuhel Gospels to the West German government did not hit a home run his first time at bat. I assumed he must have attempted to get the treasures appraised or sold at least once or twice before finally pulling off the multimillion-dollar sale.

I guessed that his first feelers would have been aimed at rare-book and manuscript dealers, or perhaps art or estate appraisers in Texas. So my job would be to call such dealers asking if they recalled ever having been invited to appraise or buy medieval manuscripts of my description. I drew blanks for about two or three weeks. But one fine day in May 1990, I called a certain Thomas Taylor, who owned and operated a bookstore in Austin. When I told Taylor what I was looking for, there was a long pause, and then he said a little mysteriously, "Hold on. I want to take your call in my back office."

I had to wait two minutes, but it seemed like two hours! When he picked up the phone again, Taylor said, "I have not seen the manuscripts myself, but I know someone who has." When I asked who that "someone" was, he said: "I'm sorry, but I cannot give you the man's name. He spoke to me in strict con-fidence, and I would lose a friend if I gave his name in this connection to a reporter." I tried every journalistic wile I could think of to get Taylor to reveal his friend's name, but he was resolute. Maybe I should have said: "Just between you and me, whisper it." Instead, I said, "How about this? I'll send you a letter addressed 'to whom it may concern' expressing my interest in hearing from the gentleman who saw the medieval manuscripts. When you get the letter," I said to Taylor, "you can forward it to the gentleman. If he cares to reply to me, fine. On the other hand, if he decides not to and tears up my letter, you have done your job of protecting his identity." Some-what grudgingly, Taylor agreed. I mailed my letter and waited.

I soon fantasized that my letter had become lost in a pile of incoming orders for books about stolen art. About eight or ten days later, however, my phone rang and I heard the voice of an elderly man with a very slight Southwestern accent. The man said he had received my letter and decided to respond because—what do you know?—he was a regular reader of the *New York Times* and knew my byline. He said his name was Dechard Turner and that he had been director of the Human-ities Research Center at the University of Texas at Austin. He said that several years ago a man by the name of Meador had shown him slides of two medieval manuscripts which, Meador told him, he had inherited from his brother, who had found them "in the gutter" in Germany at the war's end.

Turner said, "When I looked at the slides, I thought I might faint! These were the most valuable manuscripts ever to have entered the state of Texas." Turner also said he had told Meador that the manuscripts were doubtless stolen and should be returned, but Meador evidently didn't like hearing that, and so he disappeared and Turner never heard from him again. Turner also recalled that some years before, a Dallas antiques dealer had told him a story about having been asked to appraise a couple of medieval manuscripts under very suspicious circumstances.

Turner said that after he had been visited by Meador, he intended to ask this Dallas antiques dealer if the same people could have been involved in the two cases, but he never got around to it. He suggested that I might wish to pursue the matter, and told me the Dallas dealer's name was John Carroll Collins. Within minutes, I had Collins on the phone, and he turned out to be a reporter's dream. He had a great memory and, better yet, he had kept a detailed diary.

He told me that nearly a decade before this, a group of men and women, led by a certain Dr. Cook, had asked him to appraise a couple of absolutely extraordinary medieval manuscripts. His suspicions were aroused, he said, because they would not allow him to photograph or measure the manuscripts, and when he told them the objects were probably stolen, they laughed it off. Collins's recollections about the manuscripts suggested that they were indeed the same ones that had been shown to Turner several years later. What clinched the matter was that Collins told me the date 1513 was inscribed on the cover of one of the manuscripts.

I immediately dug into the old United States Army documents supplied to me by Klaus Goldmann through Karl Meyer and saw that one of the Quedlinburg manuscripts was, in fact, inscribed with the date 1513. With this, I had the last names of two people—Meador and Cook—who had repeatedly attempted to have the Quedlinburg manuscripts appraised in Texas throughout the 1980s.

I puzzled over this and at one point called Willi. I would not give him the names. I still darkly suspected that Willi was working for the West German equivalent of the C.I.A., but I told him I had implicated two people and said that one had a common and one an uncommon name. Together, we speculated about various possible relationships between these two people, but I thought that the best way for me to pursue these leads was to go to Texas. Willi had made a stab at it. Now it was my turn.

Time is too short to describe *that* adventure in detail, but basically what I did was devise a hypothetical profile of the Quedlinburg thief. I assumed—simply because I had to begin somewhere—that Meador had told Turner the truth when he said he had inherited the manuscripts from his late brother. In essence, I traveled to Texas looking for a dead Meador connected with Cook. I started the search in Dallas and then continued it by driving from county to county in a great circle around the city. I visited courthouses, newspaper offices, undertakers' parlors, and libraries, always casting and retrieving a net that I hoped would prove the right mesh to catch the dead man for whom I was looking. Apart from the morticians, who turned out to have much better files than the county clerks in that part of the country, a particularly useful source of information turned out to be the genealogy sections of libraries that keep on file local newspaper obituaries.

It was, in fact, at one such library in Sherman, Texas, about eleven miles south of the Oklahoma border, and just a few miles from the birthplace of Dwight Eisenhower, that I found the obituary of a man named Joe Tom Meador, who was said to be survived by his brother, Jack Meador, and his sister, Jane Meador Cook. There, at last, was the explanation for the Cook-Meador connection. Both Joe Tom Meador's brother and his sister had attempted to have the manuscripts appraised—Jane Meador Cook and her husband, Dr. Cook, through the antiques dealer John Carroll Collins, and Jack Meador through the library director Dechard Turner.

I can remember looking up at the ceiling of that library and muttering, to the annoyance of a lady wearing cowboy boots seated across from me, "You son of a bitch. I got you." That evening, I called Willi, who had become a good friend and resourceful collaborator over the previous months. I told him that I had found the thief, but added: "Just to be sure I have the right guy, I want to ask you a question. His obituary states that he served with the Eighty-seventh Battalion during the Second World War. Is *that* one of the units that you found had been stationed at Quedlinburg in April 1945, when the treasures disappeared?" Willi did not need to check his files. His files were in his head. Without a pause, he said: "Yeah, but you don't have the name quite right. One of the four units stationed there was called the Eighty-seventh *Armored Field Artillery* Battalion."

I spent the next several days gathering material from people who remembered Joe Tom Meador, and within a week I was back in New York City shepherding a three-thousand-word story onto the front page of the *Times*.[1]

It was still a long way from returning the treasures to Germany, but it was a beginning.

LEGAL ISSUES RELATING TO

THE RECOVERY OF

THE QUEDLINBURG

TREASURES

Thomas R. Kline

When I was first approached about the Quedlinburg treasures in early 1990, the story of their disappearance had the quality of a myth: by apocryphal accounts, the "Quedlinburg box" had vanished from storage in the closing days of the war. Willi Korte came to me—because of my experience with the recovery of the Kanakaria mosaics for Cyprus[1]—with historical records showing that the Altenburg cave near the German city of Quedlinburg had been under guard by United States forces at the time of the disappearance of the famous box. Dr. Korte signed me up to assist his efforts, but my role was that of an attorney and not a treasure hunter. I left that work to Dr. Korte and to Bill Honan of the *New York Times.* My job was to ensure that nothing was done in the hunt that would jeopardize the making of a lawful claim to the treasures.

After the German Kulturstiftung der Länder (Cultural Foundation of the States) reached agreement to purchase the Samuhel Gospels (see Lowenthal, above, pages 148–49 and colorplate 9) in May 1990,[2] Dr. Korte continued his work and found the remaining missing Quedlinburg treasures—at least the vast majority of them[3]—and Bill Honan identified the Meador heirs who possessed them.[4] On behalf of the Quedlinburg church, Dr. Korte and I made claim on the bank that held the treasures and attempted to reach a quick settlement that would resolve all issues before the astonishing levels of publicity overwhelmed our efforts. The family, however, reneged on an agreement to let us photograph the objects and place them in safekeeping pending further discussions. Instead, they insisted on moving the objects to Switzerland before there could be further talks.

The church then had no choice but to litigate to prevent the Quedlinburg treasures from disappearing. Dr. Korte and I believed the church lacked sufficient information to make a criminal complaint, and we could not wait for government wheels to grind. Settlement negotiations broke down late on a Friday night in June 1990, and we filed suit at 9:00 A.M. the following Monday morning.[5] By 1:30 P.M. or so, the court entered a temporary restraining order preventing the movement of the treasures and allowing us to inventory them.[6] Under applicable law, obtaining the order required a showing of imminent harm—in this case the likely disappearance of movable property—and some likelihood of success on the merits, that is, that the church had a strong claim of ownership. These presentations were made by sworn affidavit from Dr. Korte, attaching documents showing the church's original ownership of the treasures. Thereafter, we obtained an order setting the terms for photographing the objects, and proceeded to document them. (We also defeated an effort by the family to have a protective order, or "gag rule," applied to the litigation and thereby protected the public's right to be informed about proceedings in the case.)[7] In the course of photographing the objects, we learned that the family had moved some of them early in the morning on the day we filed suit, before the temporary restraining order was in place.[8] We then obtained an order from the court allowing expedited discovery of the history of the movement of the objects, so that we could satisfy ourselves that the family had produced all the objects from Quedlinburg they still possessed.[9]

We took the testimony of a number of members of the family and were able to establish that two of the missing treasures that had been held by the late Joe Meador, the original thief, were no longer in the possession of the family (figs. 72 and 73; see editor's note, above, page 149). During the course of these events, the family changed counsel and, through their new lawyers, offered to settle the case. In Germany, a team was assembled to handle decision making in the case, with representatives of the church of Quedlinburg, the Interior Ministry, and the Cultural Foundation of the States. I assumed representation of the foundation in the United States in its dispute with the Meador heirs and made claim on them for return of the funds already paid under the initial agreement for the purchase of the Samuhel Gospels.[10] At this point, the active litigation ceased and the case proceeded on a path to settlement.

As has already been mentioned, before the lawsuit was filed, when the Meador heirs were negotiating anonymously through numerous intermediaries, the Cultural Foundation of the States agreed to pay $3 million for the Samuhel Gospels alone. Our record of litigation successes put the Quedlinburg church in a position of strength, which enabled it to obtain a settlement for the return of all the Quedlinburg treasures still in the possession of the Meador heirs for less money than the family had originally agreed to for the sale of the Samuhel Gospels.[11]

The *Quedlinburg* case is just one of a number of instances in which victims of cultural-property theft have brought claims and pursued them to settlement on favorable terms or to success in United States courts. These cases have concerned stolen art and cultural property from Poland,[12] Cyprus,[13] Turkey,[14] Greece,[15] and other countries as well.[16] Most of these cases concerned disappearances and thefts that occurred long ago. I have handled one of these recent cases on behalf of the Bremen Kunsthalle, an institution with considerable wartime losses, as Dr. Werner Schmidt has indicated above (see page 97).[17]

This case concerned three drawings stolen from the Bremen Kunsthalle at the end of World War II. An individual offered them to a number of art dealers in New York City, one of whom reported him to Dr. Constance Lowenthal of the International Foundation for Art Research. The FBI seized the drawings and, ultimately, the United States government commenced a civil lawsuit to determine ownership of the drawings. Dr. Korte and I collaborated on this case together. I am pleased to report that under order from a federal judge in New York City these three drawings were returned to the Bremen Kunsthalle in March 1995.[18] Three more prisoners of war have now gone home. Our litigation victory in the *Bremen Kunsthalle* case, the settlement of the *Quedlinburg* case from a position of strength, and other recent successes provide important lessons that theft victims must learn.

While there have been some voluntary returns of stolen property based on individual acts of goodwill, and law-enforcement efforts have been responsible for some recoveries,

civil lawsuits remain the last refuge of the victim of theft. Because of this, I would like to discuss the reasons for the recent successes and review the lessons of these cases for theft victims who must litigate questions of ownership in United States courts. First and foremost, I must stress that under United States law, a thief cannot pass title to a stolen object. Almost without exception, the United States does not allow a transfer of stolen property to a good-faith acquirer to create title. Nevertheless, three significant issues will affect legal claims for the recovery of stolen art and cultural property in U.S. courts: initial ownership, theft, and the passage of time.

Initial ownership can be established in cultural-property cases the same way it would be done in any other type of litigation, that is, both by documentation of ownership and through the testimony of living witnesses. Frequently, initial ownership is proven by showing that the objects before the court are genuine and are, indeed, the same ones described

72. Reliquary cross. Northwestern Germany, second half of the twelfth century. Cast bronze with champlevé enamel on gilded copper backing, 7 x 5.5 cm (2¾ x 2¼″) Stolen from the Quedlinburg church treasure in 1945. Present whereabouts unknown

73. Reliquary. Carved rock crystal: Fatimid, tenth century. Inscribed and gilded silver band: Lower Saxony (Quedlinburg), 1230–50. Underplate of silver mount: fifteenth century. 7 x 5.5 cm (2¾ x 2⅛″). Stolen from the Quedlinburg church treasure in 1945. Present whereabouts unknown

or depicted in historical literature. In the *Quedlinburg* case, scholars had documented the church's treasures before they disappeared. With this documentation in hand, and with the testimony of living scholars, it would have been relatively easy to prove that the Quedlinburg church was the original owner of its treasures. Because of the need to prove initial ownership, I always advise museum and cultural officials and individual collectors of the importance of documenting their collections. With regard to historical losses, it is most important to gather and preserve the existing documentation (and also witness recollection) so that these records will be available in the future.

With regard to proof of theft, it is generally easy to establish theft in cases brought to recover art and cultural property looted during wartime. Typically, the circumstances of the disappearance of the objects indicate that they were not voluntarily given away, sold, or abandoned but were definitely taken without the consent of the owner. The Quedlinburg treasures, for example, had been placed in a cave for protection from the ravages of warfare and were under guard by United States forces at the time of their disappearance. Since an individual soldier may not lawfully seize artwork or other personal property during wartime,[19] Joe Meador's appropriation of the treasures was—beyond question—a theft. We were able to make the same point forcefully in the Bremen Kunsthalle's recent case, since the historical documentation allowed us to show that the drawings in question had been placed in storage for safekeeping but were never returned. Again, a party seeking to recover stolen property in a United States court must prove the specific circumstances of the theft; therefore, it is imperative to preserve existing documentation and eyewitness accounts.

The passage of time creates some of the most difficult issues in cases brought to recover stolen art and cultural property in the United States, and this was the primary legal issue in the Quedlinburg treasures litigation. In Texas, as in most states, the statute of limitations for recovering stolen property is quite short, especially by comparison with European statutes of limitations. Every U.S. state has a statute of limitations that is intended to cut off stale claims. Typically, the statutory period for bringing such a claim is only two to six years. In the *Quedlinburg* case, the Meador family—the brother and sister of the thief—admitted that the two-year Texas statute of limitations had not begun to run during the time the treasures were in the hands of their brother. They did claim, however, that the property became theirs two years after his death, whether or not the church knew of the thief's identity or the whereabouts of its property prior to his death.

There are a number of important principles applied by United States courts that mitigate the effect of these short statutes of limitations. In Texas, as would be the case under the law of most states, the church could have avoided the effect of the statute-of-limitations defense by proving that it had been diligent in pursuing the recovery of its property. Under this theory, generally referred to as the "discovery rule" or the "due diligence rule," the cause of action to recover the property does not accrue—and the statute of limitations does not begin to run—as long as the theft victim diligently searches for its property.[20] The discovery rule was the basis for success in the case I handled for the Greek-Orthodox Church of Cyprus, which recovered mosaics that had been missing for twelve years, even though the court applied the Indiana six-year statute of limitations.[21] In each of these cases, the most critical issue with regard to the statute of limitations is the diligence of the theft victim in reporting its losses and conducting a search for its lost artwork. "Due diligence" efforts can include investigating the circumstances of the loss, reporting the loss to law-enforcement agencies and to recognized registries, and alerting art experts and the art world generally. If the victim has been diligent in trying to recover its losses, the statute of limitations will not begin to run. Once the theft victim has obtained information suggesting the identity and location of the thief, it must act promptly to make its claim and, if necessary, to bring suit.

New York law differs from that of most other states in this country and merits special mention because so many wartime and other losses appear on the art market in New York. Under New York law, the statute of limitations does not begin to run until the victim makes a demand for the return of the object and the demand is refused.[22] In New York, a claim can be brought many decades after the theft without being barred by the statute of limitations, as long as the theft victim acted promptly to sue after the demand is rejected by the possessor. This approach does not mean, however, that New York law allows a theft victim to be lax in searching for its property, or to delay unreasonably in making the demand. The theft victim must still be diligent, because the possessor has available the defense of "laches." The defense of "laches" is based on unreasonable delay by the victim in bringing the claim, which causes prejudice to the possessor, such as a change in position, during the period of delay.

Ultimately, the *Quedlinburg* case was settled out of court, and the various legal issues involved were never presented to the court or ruled upon. However, any claim for return of property made in United States courts would be analyzed along the lines I have discussed. I would like to add one comment, in response to Bernard Taper's question (see above, page 136), that I am not aware of any special fifty-year statute of limitations in the United States for claims relating to Nazi seizures.

I am, of course, very pleased that after the Quedlinburg treasures were found we were able to place them under the protection of the United States courts and to negotiate an acceptable settlement for the church. I am also pleased by our recent court victory for the Bremen Kunsthalle. I look forward to future successes, which will only be possible if theft losses are documented, and if the theft victims are diligent in making their losses known to the art world and pursuing their recovery.

PART 5

REAPPEARANCE

AND

RECOVERY

INTRODUCTION

Constance Lowenthal

The papers presented in this section would have been inconceivable as recently as six years ago. The political events of the intervening years—Mikhail Gorbachev's glasnost, the reunification of Germany, and the subsequent dissolution of the Soviet Union and the Warsaw Pact—have transformed Europe and radically changed the lives of millions of individuals in hundreds of regions and cities. While economic and political transformations dominate the news of Eastern Europe, this chapter focuses on the huge numbers of works of art that were moved eastward at the end of the Second World War. This subject has hardly been neglected, but much is added in the papers that follow, which take up the subject of works now known to be in Russia, both in government repositories and in private hands. These papers address important historical issues, such as the circumstances of the removal of these works, the reasons the art was sent to the former USSR, and the change in Soviet policy that made the open secret of the art's presence in the Soviet Union into a deep, dark secret, revealed only recently at great risk to those who first made it public.

Long believed lost and feared to have been destroyed, much art displaced after the war has surfaced in the former Soviet Union in recent years. Among the most important of these works of art are Edgar Degas's *Place de la Concorde* and the Schliemann gold, now acknowledged to be, respectively, in the State Hermitage Museum, St. Petersburg, and the Pushkin State Museum of Fine Arts, Moscow. The Schliemann gold, the so-called Treasure of Priam, is the subject of the next section. The Degas canvas was much missed at the major Degas exhibition at the Metropolitan Museum of Art, New York, the Grand Palais, Paris, and the National Gallery of Canada, Ottawa, in 1988. A recent series of dramatic, unofficial articles and official announcements has raised the hopes of elated owners and cheered the scholars who crave access, for the first time in two generations.

Our knowledge of the existence of Soviet repositories of art displaced in the Second World War owes much to recent political events as well as to some of the individuals whose papers follow. In the last few years, important stories have appeared in *ARTnews* and other publications, reporting the existence in the former Soviet Union of art missing since the war. There was Viktor Baldin's announcement in 1989 that he had and would return many old master drawings from the collection of the Bremen Kunsthalle. After a few sightings on the international art market, the government of the Netherlands was able to "find" over three hundred Koenigs collection drawings in Russia.* The State Hermitage Museum in St. Petersburg opened "Hidden Treasures Revealed," an exhibition of Impressionist and modern pictures from German private collections in the spring of 1995, with a full catalogue,[1] and the Pushkin State Museum of Fine Arts in Moscow opened an exhibition called "Twice Saved," without a catalogue, in February 1995. Pictures that had been locked away in secret were shown publicly for the first time in fifty years.

Utilizing such new information, this subject was discussed at the Bard Graduate Center symposium in a public international forum—the first such gathering to take place. The first three papers in this section treat the displaced art itself—how it was discovered, where it is, what it is, what its fate may be, and the condition it is in. The last three papers focus on legal considerations, seen very differently by representatives of two of the countries involved: Germany and Russia.

It is particularly fascinating, and I hope auspicious, that many of the contributors are too young to have been combatants in the war; in fact, many were not even born at the time. The issue of the discovery of the missing art (and, I must add, the contents of libraries and archives) and the determination of its fate are proving compelling for a generation that has matured in the postwar era. Perhaps this is a favorable sign. If the question of alliances, of victors and vanquished, can be diffused by the relative youth of many of the negotiators, this may help make it possible to find a solution. If loss of life, destruction of cities, and memories of other great suffering can be distanced by a new generation, perhaps these national wounds will not be the sole determining factors in the ultimate disposition of the cultural property displaced as a result. It is hoped that other considerations—the growth of a healthy European region reaching far to the east, goodwill, international law, and mutual respect—will also play their roles.

---

* Editor's note: In 1945, Viktor Baldin, then a Russian officer, removed 362 drawings and 2 paintings belonging to the Bremen Kunsthalle from Schloss Karnzow in the Soviet-occupied zone of Germany. In 1947, he presented the works to the A. V. Shchusev State Research Museum of Architecture in Moscow and subsequently tried repeatedly to have the works returned to the Bremen Kunsthalle, but without success (see S. Salzmann, *Dokumentation der durch Auslagerung im 2. Weltkrieg vermissten Kunstwerke der Kunsthalle Bremen* [1991]; K. Akinsha and G. Kozlov, *Beautiful Loot* [1995], 243–46). The Koenigs collection of paintings and drawings was sold to D. G. van Beuningen in 1940, to be given to the Boymans Museum in Rotterdam. Later that year, Hans Posse arranged to purchase 527 drawings from Van Beuningen for the Führer's museum in Linz. These were stored in the Dresden Kupferstich-Kabinett from May 1941 and were subsequently removed for safety with other works from the Dresden collection, eventually to be sent to Schloss Weesenstein, where they were discovered by Soviet forces in May 1945. By 1996, 38 of these works had been returned to the Netherlands, and 307 have been acknowledged to be in the Pushkin State Museum of Fine Arts, Moscow (A. J. Elen, *Missing Old Master Drawings from the Franz Koenigs Collection, Claimed by the State of the Netherlands* [1989], 5, 9–25, and Addenda; C. Dittrich, *Vermisste Zeichnungen des Kupferstich-Kabinettes Dresden* [1987]; and see also Leistra, pages 54–57, and Koenigs, pages 237–40, in this volume).

THE DISCOVERY OF THE

SECRET REPOSITORIES

Konstantin Akinsha and

Grigorii Kozlov

In 1991, after we published our first article in *ARTnews* magazine[1] about the secret repositories of cultural property removed from Germany by the Soviets at the end of World War II, we never imagined that almost four years later the problem of trophy art would still exist and that most of the art in the repositories would still be there. We thought, in our naiveté, that as soon as the problem was brought to the attention of the world everyone would agree that the art in the special repositories had to be brought to light and returned to the countries of origin.

The first publications concerned with the so-called special repositories and private trophies began to appear in the Soviet and the Russian émigré press in 1990 and 1991. Some, like Professor Alexei Rastorgouev's plan to resolve the problem, were prepared primarily for Soviet officials, not the press.[2] The first information about the location of the Koenigs collection drawings from the Boymans–van Beuningen Museum in Rotterdam and the drawings from the Bremen Kunsthalle was published in both the Soviet and the international press in 1990.[3] There was interest in this news throughout the world. But Soviet officials didn't respond at all.

In our first article, we named many of the trophy masterpieces hidden in the Soviet Union, but we didn't publish any of our documentary evidence or even name the locations of the secret repositories—the State Hermitage Museum in St. Petersburg, the Pushkin State Museum of Fine Arts and the State Historical Museum in Moscow, and the Beer Tower in the Trinity–Saint Sergius Monastery in Sergeyev Posad (then still called Zagorsk; fig. 74). Our hope was that officials would have the will to resolve the problem.

This hope faded very soon. In the course of the next year and a half, Soviet officials refused even to admit the existence of the special repositories. In September 1991 we published in *ARTnews* an article that included photographs of the documents proving that the Trojan gold found by Heinrich Schliemann, many Post-Impressionist masterpieces from German private collections, and the Koenigs collection had been transported to the Soviet Union after World War II.[4] We

74. The Trinity–Saint Sergius Monastery in Sergeyev Posad (Zagorsk). The Beer Tower (right), restored in the 1950s by Viktor Baldin to hold trophy artworks, is one of the largest secret repositories in Russia.

named the main special repositories. In October 1991, the last minister of culture of the USSR, Nikolai Gubenko, organized a press conference to inform journalists that Mikhail Gorbachev had signed a decree establishing a government commission to deal with the trophy-art problem. Mr. Gubenko finally admitted the existence of the special repositories but at the same time refused to name or describe any trophy artworks hidden in them.[5] And the state commission had a very short life: a few months later it collapsed, together with the Soviet Union.

Mr. Gubenko had one very reasonable conception. He repeated many times that the problem of trophy art could be resolved only through the cooperation of all Soviet republics whose property was damaged or lost during the war. As a result of the fall of the Soviet Empire, the lion's share of trophy masterpieces was appropriated by the Russian Federation. Ukraine and Belarus, which were more severely damaged during the war than Russia, lost the opportunity to influence the fate of the trophy art hidden in Moscow and St. Petersburg.

In 1992 President Boris Yeltsin signed a decree establishing a State Commission on the Restitution of Cultural Property. It was headed by Evgenii Sidorov, the minister of culture of the Russian Federation. But the commission members continued to state that they had no information about the fate of the Trojan gold, although such information was published by us in both ARTnews and the German magazine Antike Welt.[6] We published the documents that traced the gold from the moment of its discovery in the Zoo flak tower in Berlin to the moment of its delivery and registration in the Pushkin State Museum of Fine Arts. All of these documents were available in the archives in Moscow and could have been consulted by anyone.

Mr. Sidorov did officially inform the Dutch government that works from the Koenigs collection were in Russia. He organized a secret show of these works for the Dutch ambassador in Moscow, taking the drawings from the Pushkin Museum and transporting them to the Central Museum of the October Revolution for the exhibition. But the ambassador was made to promise that he would not reveal where he had seen them or where they had been stored. Nevertheless, the story was leaked to the Russian press.[7]

Mr. Sidorov has been candid about the role of the press in revealing the story of the hidden trophy artworks. In November 1993, he told the newspaper Segodnia, "At first the journalists began to work. There are art historians who had access to the special repositories. When somebody stated that we didn't have all these trophy artworks, an article appeared, and everything became public."[8]

But we would like to emphasize that it wasn't necessary to have access to special repositories or to classified materials. At a time when Mr. Sidorov was asking President Yeltsin to declassify documents about the special repositories, the documents were in open access in the central Moscow archives. They were sometimes difficult to locate, but they were there, and they were the main source for our research. Today the secret repositories are secret no longer. But many interesting facts about their creation are still largely unknown.

The origin of the repositories goes back to August 1943, when Igor Grabar, the well-known Russian art historian, addressed a letter to Nikolai Shvernik, a very powerful official. Shvernik was the head of a committee with a long name: the Extraordinary State Commission on the Registration and Investigation of the Crimes of the German-Fascist Occupiers and Their Accomplices and the Damage Done by Them to the Citizens, Collective Farms, Public Organizations, and Institutions of the USSR.[9]

Grabar proposed that Soviet museums damaged by the Nazis should receive compensation after the war equivalent to their losses, in the form of artworks from enemy collections. Shvernik supported the idea. The Extraordinary State Commission gave an order to compile a list of objects in German museums that were exceptionally valuable. By the end of 1943, dozens of experts in different disciplines were composing lists that covered not only the visual arts but libraries and archives and scientific collections of all kinds. The work was controlled and organized by the Bureau of Experts, headed by Grabar.[10]

Grabar was thinking about more than Germany. In a letter to Shvernik, Grabar wrote, "I think it's a timely measure to establish now a special division of the Extraordinary State Commission to make up lists of objects in the museum collections of Germany, Austria, Italy, Hungary, Romania, and Finland that could be named as eventual equivalents." These lists were compiled, and they were remarkably detailed. They included not only short descriptions of the desired objects and their locations, but even the specific rooms or galleries in which they could be found.[11]

It's interesting that the Trojan gold treasure was mentioned in the lists twice. One scholar explained that it had to be brought to the USSR after the war because it had "extreme value for research on the history of South Russia and the ethnic origins of the Slavic population."[12]

If Grabar's original idea could be described as "restitution in kind," very soon the character of the activity of the Bureau of Experts deviated from this basic purpose. The bureau had no knowledge about the losses of Soviet museums because a large part of Soviet territory was still under Nazi occupation. The experts who had to find equivalents for the losses simply began to compose lists of the masterpieces in enemy collections that they thought should be brought to the USSR after the war. The word "equivalent" became no more than a euphemism.

During the bureau's meetings, some of the experts began to discuss what to do with all these trophy artworks. During one session, Grabar made a surprising proposal. He said, "It seems that there could be a museum in Moscow without equal in the world."[13] Boris Iofan, the well-known Soviet architect who was a member of the bureau, echoed this idea. He said, "There are excellent Greek architectural remains in German museums; at least there are Oriental architectural remains that are so closely related to our cultural tradition, or paintings, which it would be possible to take as equivalents. A superb museum of fine arts could be established in Moscow."[14]

75. Design for the Palace of Soviets in Moscow, a skyscraper supporting a statue of Lenin. The complex, never built, was to have included a museum of world art filled with works taken as compensation for Soviet art looted or destroyed by Germany.

76. Artworks from Germany are removed from a truck at the Pushkin State Museum of Fine Arts, Moscow, in summer 1945. Irina Antonova (lower left), present director of the museum, assists.

The idea of creating a supermuseum in Moscow after the war seems to have become very popular in official cultural circles. A representative of the Research Institute of Museology in Moscow, speaking at a meeting organized by the institute to discuss the problem of selecting equivalents, proposed that in addition to compensation for its losses, the Soviet Union should exact what he called a "penalty." This "penalty" had to include cultural valuables. He sketched for his colleagues an ambitious plan to create not one but two immense museums in Moscow after the end of the war: a museum of world history and a museum of the history of science and technology. The exhibits for these future institutions should be received as a "penalty" from enemy countries.[15]

In March 1944 Sergei Merkurov, the director of the Pushkin Museum, made a proposal to Mikhail Khrapchenko, head of the Committee of the Council of People's Commissars. Merkurov, too, had an ambitious plan. He wanted to establish a museum of world art in Moscow after the war. Khrapchenko also became enthusiastic about this idea, and together they drew up a detailed letter to Viacheslav Molotov, at that time the deputy head of the council, second only to Stalin. The letter stated that the capital of the world's first proletarian state had no real museum of world art, whereas "the capitals of the most important states have such museums."

Merkurov and Khrapchenko thought that the Museum of Modern Western Art and the Museum of Oriental Cultures could be united with the Pushkin State Museum of Fine Arts, which would be the heart of the future institution. "The museums of the Axis countries," Khrapchenko and Merkurov wrote, "are full of wonderful masterpieces that must be given to the Soviet Union as compensation. All valuables received from the Axis countries must be concentrated in one place and can play the role of a perfect memorial dedicated to the glory of Russian arms."[16]

This glorious memorial would be the Museum of World Art in Moscow. The collection, swelled by trophy-art master-pieces, would require a much bigger building than the Pushkin Museum. Merkurov thought about the Palace of Soviets, which was to be built only fifty meters from the Pushkin Museum (fig. 75). His plan was to incorporate the museum and its additions into the complex of the proposed Palace of Soviets. As part of the most impressive manifestation of communist grandeur, it would be a suitable home for the Museum of World Art.

A decree of the State Committee of Defense was attached to the letter to Molotov. It asserted the necessity for the museum and gave it the exclusive right to receive artworks from Axis countries sent as compensation to the USSR.[17]

The idea of the supermuseum wasn't forgotten after the victory in 1945. What had been forgotten was the basic idea of collecting "equivalents" for Soviet losses. In a decree of the State Committee of Defense dated June 26, 1945, and signed by Stalin, the purpose of removing the Dresden Staatliche Gemäldegalerie collection was expressed very clearly: "Give the order to the Committee on Arts Affairs of the Council of People's Commissars of the USSR (Comrade Khrapchenko) to remove to the repositories of the committee in Moscow the most valuable artworks . . . from the trophy storages in Dresden for the enriching of state museums."[18]

On August 22, 1945, Khrapchenko reported to Molotov that the masterpieces of the Dresden museums had arrived in Moscow. He wrote: "The Committee on Arts Affairs of the Council of People's Commissars has decided to include the newly arrived valuables in the collection of the Pushkin State Museum of Fine Arts. In combination with the permanent collections of the Pushkin Museum, it could help to create in Moscow a rich Museum of World Art, comparable in quality to such art museums as the Louvre in Paris, the British Museum in London, and the State Hermitage in Leningrad."[19]

But the idea of a supermuseum wasn't realized. The Pushkin Museum did mix trophy artworks with its permanent

77. By the end of 1945, every available space in the Pushkin Museum was used to store trophy artworks.

collection and prepared an exhibition. Invitations were issued to the opening of the combined exhibition. But it never opened because of political events. The beginning of the Cold War made this plan impossible.[20]

In summary, two ideas should be emphasized. First, the creation of the special repositories involved a massive campaign of looting art collections in occupied territories—and not only in the Axis countries. Poland, which was a victim of aggression by both Nazi Germany and the USSR in the Second World War, was heavily looted, too. Second, the removal of more than 2.5 million objects was part of Stalinistic foreign policy.

During the course of the war, only two nations organized well-planned stripping of museums and cultural institutions in the countries occupied by their military forces. These nations were Hitler's Germany and Stalin's USSR. The similarity between Hitler's project to build a Führermuseum in Linz (see fig. 54) and Stalin's idea to build a Museum of World Art in Moscow is striking, but not so exceptional. It is one more point of comparison between the two most monstrous totalitarian regimes of the twentieth century.

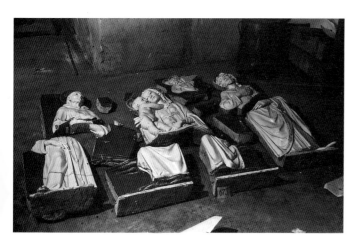

78. Artworks stored by the Germans in the Friedrichshain flak tower in Berlin were destroyed or badly damaged by fire. Making things worse, many of these objects, such as this relief by Andrea della Robbia, were then transported to the Soviet Union in unheated trucks and trains. The final destination of the Della Robbia relief was the State Hermitage Museum in Leningrad (St. Petersburg).

DISPLACED ART

IN PRIVATE HANDS

Alexei Rastorgouev

The subject of my paper differs somewhat from the topics dealt with by the other participants in the Bard Graduate Center conference, although in terms of the disastrous consequences of war, actions of individuals are often no less destructive than processes sanctioned by the state. But there is one distinction that makes this aspect of the problem more difficult to study. During the first two days of the symposium, we tried with a greater—and often lesser—degree of accuracy to define the nature of the displacement of cultural valuables sanctioned by states before, during, and after World War II. No matter how these removals took place, and whether or not from today's point of view there is justification for them, they are nevertheless described in an enormous number of documents that have been preserved and can therefore today be a subject for scholarly work.

The history of the displacement of art during the last few decades, and a simple analysis of the antiques market, however, shows us that the war also led to the large-scale movement of many works of art, including some of unique quality, into private hands. All of this has taken place more or less in silence. Only a few archival materials help us to understand what was hidden in private hands after the war, and the work of researchers on this subject—unfortunately, I am speaking from my own experience—is more reminiscent of investigations of a private detective than of normal scholarly work. Nevertheless, there is a need to collect this information carefully and cautiously, as has been demonstrated, for example, by the story of the Quedlinburg treasures (see above, pages 148–58) or of the so-called Baldin group of the Bremen Kunsthalle drawings collection (see the editor's note, page 161). In these two cases, cultural property of the highest quality wound up in the possession of private parties. Unfortunately, this is a tiny fragment of what remains to be discovered.

In considering specific works of art that came into private collections in Russia as a result of the war, we see an amazing variety of outcomes, events, and stories. The removal of art from the territory of Germany and other countries through which the Soviet army had marched involved an enormous number of people. Various trophy commissions of the army, the ministries, the Academy of Sciences, the state repositories, and the union and republic organizations all acted independently, often going through the same museum or bank repositories several times. This was done by individuals, almost all of whom were imitating what the government was doing right before their eyes. As one elderly lady said to me after the appearance of my first articles on trophy art in Russia, "My father was the administrator of the Sanssouci palace in Potsdam. He was a very well educated man with a doctorate in history, and we have four paintings he asked never be shown to anyone." Unfortunately, she faithfully continues to honor his wish, and does not even know what kind of paintings these are since they are packed into a tight roll. Her sister in Kaliningrad, however, has several drawings by an artist whose name she did mention: these are Canalettos, bearing several German stamps.

The trophy collections of less well educated but high-ranking officials were less professionally chosen but incomparably bigger. Each Soviet officer when leaving Germany had the right to bring to Russia a certain quantity of baggage, and for generals, these quantities could amount to whole railroad cars. This was the norm for the pyramid-like hierarchy of the Stalinist system. The documents that have been preserved serve to confirm this general rule, which was applicable even to Marshal Zhukov himself, who was forced to justify his removal of an excessive number of valuables for his own use, having violated the unwritten export norm. In the possession of such families, one can see entire rooms and sometimes entire houses that are of German origin. If these are, for example, from Göring's hunting lodge or the study of General Field Marshal Keitel, the art—stolen by the Germans from all over Europe well before Russian involvement—is of the highest quality. Strangely enough, such collections sometimes have documentation that confirms the legality—according to Soviet laws of the time—of their removal to Russia. I have even seen objects from the Schlossmuseum in Gotha which, according to the original documents, were bought in a secondhand store in the Soviet-occupied zone of Germany in 1948. This does not contradict what is known regarding the mores of that time.

But the most important works of art from German collections that wound up in private hands in Russia are not those of the members of the Trophy Organization or generals, but belong to some of the most capable and talented—I don't know how to put it—thieves? collectors? saviors of German cultural property? In this case, these words are synonymous, as is shown by the history of the drawings of the Bremen Kunsthalle collection (see Schmidt, above, page 97).

Divided up into several parts by junior officers who had stumbled on the cases from the Bremen Kunsthalle in Schloss Karnzow, in Brandenburg, this collection experienced all the characteristic vicissitudes of such trophy art in Russia. These included the forced relinquishment of part of it by private individuals to the A. V. Shchusev State Research Museum of Architecture in Moscow; free movement about the market and acquisition of other items by various museums within the country; division among the various states of the former USSR; theft from one museum (I have in mind the Baku part of the collection); the presentation of some works to the German embassy in Russia; mention at the trial concerning criminal activity of the Communist Party of the Soviet Union (CPSU); the illegal removal from the country and the secret sale of some of the works back to Bremen and others to Western collections; and, finally, a preliminary agreement on the return to Germany. Almost everything possible had happened to these works, but their story has not yet ended. In the last analysis, thanks to the relatively high level of cultural sophistication of those people who divided up this collection in Schloss Karnzow, this is not the worst such story, because the best things in the collection survived.

All of us, regardless of whether we were allies or adversaries during the last war, are concerned with these questions: what

disappeared into the private collections of the former Soviet Union? What is still preserved there? What will happen to these things in the future? I shall here select just one example—but a very telling one—to give a more or less full answer. This concerns the fate of the Kupferstich-Kabinett (Prints and Drawings Collection) in Dresden.

As a result of the war, the Dresden Kupferstich-Kabinett lost no fewer than 4,816 drawings and 10,384 prints (I am using the figures for the number of works still missing, cited in Werner Schmidt's preface in C. Dittrich, *Vermisste Zeichnungen des Kupferstich-Kabinettes Dresden.*[1] From the end of 1942, the overwhelming majority of the Dresden drawings and prints were hidden in the castles of Wurschen and Weesenstein. In February–March 1945, the works of art in the Wurschen castle were moved first to Dresden and then to Schloss Weesenstein, where they were discovered by Soviet special forces on May 12, 1945. That date marks the beginning of a new chapter in the history of the Dresden collection. At the end of May 1945, the holdings of the Schloss Weesenstein were moved to the well-known Schloss Pillnitz, which contained the major repository of trophy art in Saxony. At the end of May 1946, when the Soviet military left Pillnitz, 2,617 drawings and 21,019 other works of graphic art remained there—primarily reproductions or works of German nineteenth- and twentieth-century painters, that is, only those the Soviet trophy commissions had not thought good enough to remove.

In 1958, an enormous number of works of art from East Germany's collections were returned from the Soviet Union. As far as I know, all of these East German works of art, and in particular those from the Dresden collections, were subject to mandatory return. Regardless of how we now view this action—and I think that it was just as poorly conceived as the removal of this cultural property to Russia—it led to the return to Dresden of much of what had been preserved in state collections in Russia. A lot, but not all.

Among the exceptions, which are both public knowledge and known to me privately, I shall indicate only the holdings of incunabula and rare books from the Dresden print collection, materials that still today are available for general use at the museum of books of the former Lenin—now the Russian State—Library in Moscow. All these books bear the stamp of the Dresden Kupferstich-Kabinett, and consequently were not accidentally forgotten in Russian collections, but rather are cultural property that was deliberately not returned.

Unfortunately, I do not have specific documentation proving that in the museums there are things from Dresden that were deliberately kept for the Soviet Union, although the testimony of museum employees allows us to say this with reasonable confidence, at least insofar as that collection whose history we are considering, the Dresden print collection, is concerned. One thing is important for our subject: a significant part of the Dresden drawings and prints that were not returned (4,816 drawings and 10,384 prints) are now in private collections. Thus, according to the catalogue of lost Dresden drawings, Russian private collections may contain: six drawings by Dürer, sixteen drawings by Cranach, twenty-six drawings by Menzel, twenty-nine drawings by Rubens, twenty-seven drawings by Rembrandt, and so forth. I will not repeat the entire list. It is likely that many of them are still in Russia. I would like to cite below a few drawings that definitely are.*

The title page of the catalogue of Dresden losses reproduces the Adolph Menzel drawing of 1880 *The Staircase of the Wallpavillon in the Zwinger Complex, Dresden*[2] (fig. 79). Another no less exciting example is a drawing that does not belong to the Dresden collection but was among those acquired by Hans Posse for the Führermuseum in Linz and was preserved in Dresden, later to share the fate of the Dresden collection. This is the drawing ascribed to Albrecht Altdorfer (fig. 80) from the well-known Dutch collection of Franz Koenigs, *The Judgment of Paris*.[3] The third example, which is not listed in the catalogue of losses from the Dresden collection, is the fifteenth-century drawing from the circle of Israhel van Meckenem *Saint Luke Drawing the Virgin* (fig. 81). By means of these examples, I would like briefly to indicate the fate of trophy art in Russian private collections.

The Menzel drawing, which, as I see it, is one of the most significant losses from the Dresden collection, raises a question for us: how, in fact, did works that according to the documents should have all been transferred to Russian state collections wind up in private hands? This question can be answered only by living witnesses, who are hardly likely to be persuaded to talk. Hundreds of Dresden drawings that never reached either museums or the windows of antiques stores are circulating among Russian collectors. It is easy to recognize them by two of the most common types of museum stamps, which can be found in the catalogue of losses from the Dresden collection, or by the blue paper of the albums in which the drawings from the Gottfried Wagner Collection were glued.[4] It seems that there was never a full catalogue of this last group of drawings and that the works by no means always received museum stamps. Therefore, only the blue paper of their albums and the annotations on the backs can help to determine their Dresden origin. There are hundreds of such drawings. They must have been stolen from Schloss Weesenstein or Schloss Pillnitz in 1945–46, as they were not registered in any of the museums that were receiving trophy art. The drawing of the Van Meckenem circle, which has lost its blue backing, seems to belong to this group.

On the back of Menzel's masterpiece, there are traces of a stamp, which has been cleaned off, and the work is signed only with initials. We may therefore conclude that it was forgotten for many years and shared the fate of the mass of German drawings from the Dresden collection that today still fill Russian collections. Such names as Carl Vogel von Vogelstein, Carl Schumacher, Johann Wilhelm Schirmer, Ludwig

79. Adolph Menzel. *The Staircase of the Wallpavillon in the Zwinger Complex, Dresden.* 1880. Drawing in black chalk and graphite, 32.3 x 24.1 cm (12¾ x 9½"). Signed "A.M." and dated "80." Formerly in the Kupferstich-Kabinett, Dresden (C. Dittrich, *Vermisste Zeichnungen des Kupferstich-Kabinettes Dresden*, cat. no. 773). Now in Russia

80. Albrecht Altdorfer. *The Judgment of Paris.* 1509. Brush drawing in white on red prepared paper, 22.6 x 17 cm (8¾ x 6¾"). Formerly in the Koenigs collection (A. J. Elen, *Missing Old Master Drawings from the Franz Koenigs Collection*, cat. no. 82). Removed to Russia at the end of the war. Returned to the Boymans–van Beuningen Museum, Rotterdam, in April 1995

Richter—and if not the name at least the monogram of Adolph Menzel—do not say much to a Russian collector. Only the stamp of the Dresden collection makes such a work desirable. Once the stamp is gone, even such a wonderful German nineteenth-century drawing as Menzel's can lose its attribution, vanish, and finally perish altogether.

Fortunately, this drawing, along with several others, was identified as a work by Menzel, and here begins the second part of the story. Once the works were identified, they very quickly disappeared from view, and there are grounds for believing that at least some of them were taken out of the country, since today this is very easy to do. Although there is

---

* Editor's note: The three examples cited were in Russia at the time of the Bard Graduate Center symposium. Subsequently, in April 1995, the Albrecht Altdorfer drawing from the Koenigs collection (illustrated here as figure 80) was presented to the Boymans–van Beuningen Museum, Rotterdam, by the author (see below, page 170).

81. Circle of Israhel van Meckenem. *Saint Luke Drawing the Virgin.* Fifteenth century. 20.6 x 14.1 cm (8 x 5½"). Formerly in the Kupferstich-Kabinett, Dresden. Now in Russia

no assurance of this, we can hope that some day they will return to Dresden. During the last few years, several Dresden drawings have appeared at European auctions, and not all of these sales have been challenged.

Quite different are the circumstances of the drawing from Van Meckenem's circle. It is not listed in the Dresden catalogue of losses but bears the museum stamp, and it is more than likely that it comes from the old part of the collection, specifically from the albums of the Gottfried Wagner Collection. In the collection where the work is presently held, it was until very recently considered a nineteenth-century forgery, and only the stamp, which had not been recognized initially by the owner, finally drew attention to it. Since the Dresden collection had never been split, and since not a single drawing from it had ever been sold, the presence of the stamp clearly shows it was stolen. Unfortunately, the Dresden drawings do not always bear the museum's stamp, and the judgment of an incompetent collector can forever remove many valuable works of art from the field of vision of professionals.

Finally, a drawing from the Koenigs collection opens up one of the most tragic and puzzling stories in the annals of trophy art (see Leistra, above, pages 54–57; editor's note, page 161; and Koenigs, below, pages 237–40). It is now known that most of the drawings missing from the Koenigs collection are preserved in the collection of the Pushkin State Museum of Fine Arts in Moscow. Acquired under duress by Hans Posse for the Führermuseum in Linz, they are now claimed by the Netherlands, in accordance with the tenets of international law and wartime documents signed by the Allies of the anti-Hitlerite coalition. But more than one hundred drawings have disappeared from the collection and have still not been found.

As with the Dresden works, these were stolen by private individuals. Five of them were in the collection of the art

historian and professor A. A. Sidorov who, judging by notes on the back of some of them, got them from various collectors in Russia. Yet another was submitted to the British Museum for appraisal by the well-known employee of the KGB Victor Louis, who could have been working for his agency or simply in his own interest. After the drawing was taken into custody in 1988 and returned to the Netherlands, Louis denied that such an occurrence had ever taken place.

Eleven more Koenigs drawings were acquired by the Pushkin State Museum of Fine Arts from a private individual, the widow of an artist named Nechaev, who confidently puts forward a highly unlikely version of their origin. Nechaev allegedly brought them from Berlin in the 1940s. This would indicate that the drawings were stolen from Schloss Weesenstein or from Dresden and were displaced from the territory of the Soviet-occupied zone right after the war.

At the end of the 1980s, another Koenigs drawing was offered for sale in New York and subsequently returned to the Netherlands; most probably, it had left Russia fairly recently. I have now discovered two more Koenigs drawings in private hands. They lay unrecognized for more than thirty years in a folder of reproductions in the private library of a man who did not collect art and who is now dead. I have drawn your attention to one of them, Altdorfer's *The Judgment of Paris,* number 82 in the catalogue of lost Koenigs drawings (fig. 80). The other is a portrait by Hans Brosamer, number 132 in the catalogue. Unfortunately, the location of these two drawings gives no clue to the whereabouts of the others. Nevertheless, perhaps some of the lost works are in museums and not in private hands.

These are my examples. In conclusion, I would like to reflect on the implications. I have seen in private collections in Moscow and St. Petersburg—I don't know of collections of importance in Kyiv (Kiev) or Kharkiv, and my experience is limited to those cases in which owners have consulted me—paintings from the Dresden Gemäldegalerie, books from the Gotha library, and paintings and drawings from the Bremen Kunsthalle and from Aachen, Leipzig, Magdeburg, and other collections, including private collections from a variety of countries, including Belgium. From this experience I can conclude one thing: in addition to private removal of trophy art to Russia, there was a colossal amount of theft within the trophy commissions themselves. This is natural, since the state ideology of acquisition easily motivated private initiative. I think that today 70 percent of the Western European art on the market in Russia—painting, graphics, and applied arts—is trophy art. The works have been in Russia, are there, and will remain. This is not a declaration but an unfortunate reality. The ignorance of the parties involved is the greatest source of danger for these works in private hands. Our art market is populated with many who are poorly educated and criminal, and whose dealings are hidden both from the Russian public and from Western authorities. By losing a stamp or a signature, a work is deprived of its history and in some sense ceases to exist—it is taken from the world, and its spiritual death only briefly precedes its actual physical demise. In all three of my examples the works were on the brink of perishing because they had lost their context. That is what is frightening, not the displacement from one owner to another.

Of course, by landing in one of the Russian museums that willingly purchase trophy works, these things can regain their history. Though such purchase is hardly legal by European standards, it is justified in our country to which, unfortunately, these norms do not apply. These works can recover their context only if they are not hidden away in these museums. Today it is impossible to guarantee this, and therefore no one knows how much longer displaced art will continue to wander in the circles of silence. Harsh measures are senseless and dangerous. One cannot declare these works state property, since the state itself still has somehow to justify its right to own those things from German collections and collections of the countries of the Hitlerite coalition that are said to have been taken as compensation for Russia's national artistic losses during World War II. The confiscation of property was too common a tradition in the former USSR to be continued in the new Russia. It is not advisable to attempt to return trophy art to Germany by decree, because laws enacted for the forcible transfer of property may result in the consignment of these works to secrecy again for many more years. We must seek solutions by removing the works from hiding one by one, and simply by becoming aware of their existence. Therefore, in concluding my paper I wish to express my deep gratitude to those collectors who have allowed me to photograph objects in their collections, though none of them wishes his name to be mentioned. Nevertheless, this openness represents a step forward—and a hope for the future.

In conclusion, I shall add the most recent news concerning the history of the two drawings that I recognized as belonging to the Koenigs collection, which are mentioned in this paper. One of them I bought from the last owner and in April 1995 gave without remuneration to the kingdom of the Netherlands. The other was then bought by the Russian Stolichny Bank with the intention of returning it to the Netherlands. Thus, the two small examples cited here confirm my assertion: the most important thing that can be done for those works now in private hands as a result of the war involves research and their eventual publication. Returned to the light of day, in one way or another they will determine their own future—in the two cases mentioned above, a promising one.

THE HISTORY OF

THE SOVIET REPOSITORIES

AND THEIR CONTENTS

Valery Koulichov

From the vantage point of historical distance it is, of course, easy to judge a people and their past. The Russian people are shedding the vestiges of their totalitarian past, characterized not just by a lack of glasnost but by total disregard of law. This process is painful and not as quick as we would like it to be. The road to democracy is far from smooth and there are still roadblocks to overcome before we can be called a democratic society.

Returning to the last months of World War II, I would like to emphasize the special importance given to equivalence in dealing with the problem of reparations for art losses. By the time the Allied Control Council was established, a special procedure for determining art equivalence and its practical application had been developed. The said procedure was to be adopted by the Allied Control Council, but for a number of various reasons—one of them being the fact that the Soviet Union did not fully agree with the proposed concept—it was not adopted.

Is there anything wrong with the idea of compensation for immeasurable cultural losses suffered by a nation in the wake of its occupation by an adversary army? Should that nation and its people be stigmatized for their desire to be compensated somehow for these losses? One should also take into account the dominant feelings and atmosphere of the first postwar months. As an example, we can refer to the serious consideration given by the Allied Control Council to the proposal of Poland to strip Germany of the right to have any museums. If that proposal had been adopted, Germany would have no museums at all. Then Poland came forward with detailed claims against Germany demanding equivalence for its cultural losses and even appealed to the United States government asking it to donate some objects from Munich collections. The United States was in principle against this idea of compensation and refused the request. However, it should be noted that this kind of political thinking was typical of the immediate postwar period.

With the start of the Cold War, the general political climate and the relationship between the Allies in particular underwent changes. By the end of the 1940s, former war allies were no longer political allies.

As to the Russian secret repositories—or "secret foundations," as they were named upon the arrival of the first displaced cultural property in the former Soviet Union—I would like to dispel the impression that from the outset these special foundations were secret basements of some kind, with arched ceilings and silent guards who did not allow access. Mrs. Antonova, who at that time was a young art historian, can very well confirm how the artworks arrived in the Soviet Union and the manner in which they were received. I have gone through many archival documents that deal with the procedures involved in receiving this cultural property in our country. There are numerous documents concerning the review of the inventory, the opening of the crates, and the comparison of the lists with the contents of the crates, and I can say with full confidence that there was no hint of secrecy in these documents. Only later on did they become secret. The documents themselves demonstrate the great care with which the museum curators received this valuable freight.

As to the physical condition in which these objects arrived, I will cite just one group of figures given by the department then called the People's Commissariat of Finance (that is, the future Ministry of Finance of the Soviet Union) for one of the deliveries of these trophies from occupied Germany to the Pushkin State Museum of Fine Arts that went through that ministry. In this delivery, there were 572 crates containing paintings and other objects from German museums. Out of the total of 572 crates, 304 were sent to the state restoration workshop, which later became known as the Grabar Restoration Center. Of these, only 40 crates were later returned to the Pushkin State Museum. The procedure for accepting and receiving this cultural property was very far from a clear-cut attempt at hiding stolen things. For those objects brought to the Pushkin Museum, many museum officials were in fact involved: the museum director; the curators, including the chief curator and the curator of the "special repositories"; and the heads of the various museum departments—paintings, drawings, and so forth. All of them took part in receiving these objects for the purpose of their preservation. I have studied more than a hundred of these documents, and they all attest to the fact that many people were involved in receiving the art trophies.

It is worth recalling here that at first some of the best things that arrived at the Pushkin Museum were collected and gathered together in two rooms. Of course, access to them was limited. Repairs as yet unfinished, the war-damaged museum wasn't yet fully open, but at first one needed only the permission of the museum director, Sergei Merkurov, in order to be able to have a look at these things. Then with political changes in the country as a whole, the regime tightened considerably.

By late 1948 and early 1949, with the emergence of the German Democratic Republic (GDR), the situation had changed. By then, it was already clear that we would have to be friends with this new German Republic, and there were all kinds of political considerations that would have a role to play. Then the regime tightened further, and by the end of that period, only Marshal Voroshilov, who was responsible for culture, could give permission to show the collection. I personally have looked through a lot of archival materials, with the exception of some CPSU Central Committee documents that are still inaccessible. I have not found a single document that states any order—even an instruction—to seal these repositories. The situation was rather difficult because of the political climate in the country in that period. Most important decisions were made where the real power was— that is, at the Central Committee level. There was a special department responsible for culture, and it was here that the most important decisions were made. The decisions were then swiftly, precisely, and unswervingly carried out by all subordinates in the organization.

The archival materials clearly show that museums themselves did not initiate the closing of these repositories to public access. Of course, considering the irretrievable cultural losses suffered by the nation, one might imagine how the museums could consider the art trophies delivered from defeated Germany as a kind of compensation for the losses and suffering caused by the war. Can we blame that generation embittered by the brutalities of a devastating war for accepting the war trophies as restitution in kind? But notwithstanding these feelings, museums had nothing to do with initiating the closing of the repositories. Political considerations were the only reasons for hiding these valuable cultural treasures from the public view. So the regime of secrecy had begun by the early 1950s.

At that point, there was an intensive correspondence between the Soviet government and the government of the GDR. This correspondence was not only at the intergovernmental level but also at the interparty level and at other institutional levels, including that of the Academies of Sciences of the two countries. The two sides were working to agree on a list of objects that would be returned to East Germany. At that time, the regime was not so strict and so secretive. It would be wrong to assume that the many people in the museums involved in preparing paintings, drawings, and other cultural objects did not know what they were doing or were not aware of the origins of these objects. Until 1956, an atmosphere of relative secrecy prevailed.

After this came a period that can be termed transitional. Apparently at that point the Soviet party leadership began to give consideration to the future fate of all these treasures— to whether they should open up the repositories or even give the artworks back. One can assess their decisions in different ways, but however they are judged, these decisions resulted in what has now become a fact of history. At that time, a number of proposals and plans were discussed. I cannot say that I have discovered documents demonstrating that there was any specific decision-making mechanism, but one can assume the existence of two approaches under consideration for the resolution of the problem. One was to open the repositories, bringing the art they held out into the public view. At the time, this seemed quite feasible, considering the massive returns to the German Democratic Republic of 80 percent of the art displaced from Germany. The second approach was to keep the repositories secret, for use in future bargaining with the West for the return of displaced Soviet property. The second approach eventually prevailed. Subsequently, in the late 1950s and 1960s, a real period of secrecy began—a period of total and absurd secrecy. Our museum directors and curators experienced this regime of secrecy only too well. The director of the Pushkin State Museum, Irina Antonova, has sincerely admitted that until recently she did not know that a sizable and interesting part of Heinrich Schliemann's finds from Troy, the bronzes and ceramics, were in fact in the State Hermitage Museum in St. Petersburg. Despite the fact that the director of the Hermitage, Dr. Piotrovsky, knew about the Schliemann finds in his collection, such information was not shared, even among colleagues at the highest level.

The regime of secrecy was such that even the curators of individual departments within a single museum would not have discussed art objects in their custody: a curator of paintings would not have shared information with a curator of prints and drawings. That was the kind of secrecy that reigned in the Soviet museums. One can logically ask why nobody had spoken out against it, why everybody had so blindly obeyed the instructions. Now, after that reality has become history, it is very easy to be bold and brave and blame these people. But the old system was omnipotent: we were all part of that system, and the system oppressed us all. It oppressed both its supporters and its opponents. The subject of special museum repositories remained taboo during the Khrushchev era, all through Leonid Brezhnev's years, and long after Mikhail Gorbachev came to power.

I cannot recount all of the numerous attempts by museum officials to convince Soviet authorities of the necessity to open up the special repositories. One of the last attempts was made by the Pushkin State Museum Director, Mrs. Antonova, on August 16, 1991. Only three days remained before the tanks were moved into Moscow. In less than five months, the Soviet Union would collapse. Gorbachev was still relaxing at his Phoros dacha. Nevertheless, the answer was still a firm no— the time had not yet come.

Of course, one would be justified in asking why now, after such a long time has elapsed and such profound changes have taken place in Russia, is the country so slow in opening up its special repositories? It is extremely difficult for me to answer this question, because time acts for us now in a different way. As with many other problems, Russian political leaders and Russian society as a whole are deeply divided concerning this issue. There are different points of view even within the Russian State Commission on the Restitution of Cultural Property. The most important problem facing us now as a nation is our need to determine national aims and agree on a concept of nationhood—a concept that would create a framework for resolving these questions without detriment to our national pride, in the interest of both our own national culture and that of the world, and with due consideration for the claims of our partners in the negotiating process. But one question still looms large: how can we explain to the ordinary Russian man in the street why, in the case of the Quedlinburg treasures, Germany raised the necessary funds to buy the works back from an American owner—when Russians for some reason are only blamed or pressured to return art treasures as a "gesture of goodwill"? And not only that, but give them back with apologies for having retained these things for so long. And that is what is expected from us. It is extremely hard to explain this to the Russian man in the street, especially to middle-aged and elderly Russians with their bitter and emotional reaction to the events of World War II and their effects on the nation. It is now difficult to predict what kind of legal framework our parliament—the State Duma—will finally

adopt, but before solving this problem internationally we Russians must develop our own ideas of what we must do.

As for the closed repositories, they are closed no longer. The process of bringing their contents out into the public view has started and will accelerate (see colorplates 11 and 12). But this will not happen overnight. For what we are dealing with is not only cultural property but also the subject of international claims. That is why we must study the contents of our repositories carefully. This is an enormous job, considering the number of objects there are and the complexities surrounding these objects. It would be naive to believe certain journalists' allegations that the Russians are so ignorant that they have no understanding of what they are really holding. The real problem lies in the necessity of carrying out a careful and thorough study of the objects. Of course, we should have started this work long ago. This delay is our fault and our misfortune. We deeply regret that scholars had their first opportunity to examine the objects from the Schliemann gold collection only last year (see colorplate 16). But this is only part of the problem. The second part is that it is hard for us to accomplish everything all at once. Of course we want to bring out the best pieces into the public view. To my mind, the return of these long-considered-lost art treasures to the world is a much more urgent task than resolving the difficulties surrounding their ownership and settling the various and often conflicting claims. The most important objective is the return of these works of art to humanity.

Returning to the question of why this process did not start earlier, I would like to explain the way in which the whole process of decision making was affected by so-called nomenclature thinking, one of the most amazing features of the Soviet political system. How did this mechanism work?

The initial decision to establish the institution of special repositories could only be repealed by the same agency that had adopted it. If such a decision were made by the Presidium of the Central Committee of the Communist Party of the Soviet Union it could be repealed only by decision of the same body. But to effect such a change was extremely difficult. One might submit many motions to the parties in power with no result. Even if this issue were finally to be presented for the Presidium's consideration and—most improbably—the decision to change a policy were finally made, in order for the decision to be confirmed by the CPSU Central Committee, it had to be written according to certain standards: it should be presented in a document of no more than three pages, double-spaced, and written so simply that even a nonspecialist could understand it. In view of this bureaucratic procedure, the presentation of such a complex issue in this abbreviated format was a nearly insurmountable task.

Among the archives I looked through before coming to New York was a very interesting document relating to a small Thuringian town near the Hochwald mine. Near the end of the war, the Germans deposited in the mine hundreds of crates containing objects from Berlin collections. Not far from that place, there was a camp for displaced persons. With the approach of the Red Army, the inhabitants, most of whom were Russian and Ukrainian youths brought to Germany by force from occupied territories, dispersed and hid themselves in the mine. There they discovered the depository containing the crates. Since it was cold, they started breaking pieces of wood from the crates to make a fire. Inside the crates they found theater costumes. The people quickly put on the costumes for warmth. Looking for more things, they opened up the remaining crates one after another. Driven by bitterness, hatred, and a desire for vengeance, they were looking for more loot. And suddenly in one of the opened boxes they saw a beautiful *Madonna and Child.* And the beauty of the painting made them step back and pause in admiration. For the moment, the old feelings of hatred and vengeance had disappeared. These ordinary Russian and Ukrainian people stared at the divine image, and the sight of it somehow reconciled them to their situation and the reality around them. The people carefully gathered the works they had found and put them back into the crates.

Around that time, a military unit of the Soviet army arrived, and the people took the soldiers into the mine and showed them the crates. And the cultural treasures began their journey to the east . . .*

At this international forum we have heard polemics, arguments, and different points of view. But I would like to set all political and legal considerations aside for the moment and, in a way, ask that we follow the example of those Russian and Ukrainian people, who set their bitterness aside in admiration of the eternal beauty of art. Let us reflect together in silent admiration of these great works of art, which were hidden from humankind for half a century. It will not be long before these treasures are finally returned to public view. Let us consider them together in the hope that our admiration will help us find a civilized way of resolving the terribly complex and confused issues involving art displaced during and after the war.

---

*   Editor's note: For a different account of the circumstances of the rifling of the contents of the Ransbach mine in Thuringia, see L. Nicholas, *The Rape of Europa* (1994), 332–35; and K. Akinsha and G. Kozlov, *Beautiful Loot* (1995), 139–40.

LEGAL ISSUES BEARING ON

THE RESTITUTION OF

GERMAN CULTURAL

PROPERTY IN RUSSIA

Wilfried Fiedler

THE LEGAL BASIS FOR THE GERMAN REQUEST FOR RESTITUTION

In spite of the grave war and postwar events, the legal basis for the German request for restitution cannot be found in measures or standards pertaining to war or its aftermath. It rather is based on treaty regulations made after the opening up of Eastern Europe in 1989. This fundamental political change was sealed with a number of treaties.

The Good-Neighborliness Treaty

In particular, the new departure was manifested in the Treaty between the Federal Republic of Germany and the Union of Soviet Socialist Republics on Good-Neighborliness, Partnership and Cooperation (see Appendix 14) and in the Treaty on the Development of Comprehensive Cooperation in the Field of Trade, Industry, Science and Technology, both of which were signed on November 9, 1990.[1] The conclusion of these bilateral instruments was tied up with a number of historic multilateral decisions terminating the East-West confrontation, as, for example, by the adoption of the Charter of Paris for a New Europe in November 1990.[2]

Article 16 of the 1990 German-Soviet Good-Neighborliness Treaty reads:

> The Federal Republic of Germany and the Union of Soviet Socialist Republics will advocate the preservation of cultural treasures of the other side in their territory. They agree that lost or unlawfully transferred art treasures which are located in their territory will be returned to their owners or their successors.

This provision of the treaty was confirmed by Article 15 of the German-Russian Cultural Agreement of 1992 (see Appendix 15).[3]

Negotiations since 1993

Since February 1993, there have been negotiations between Germany and Russia to organize the restitution of cultural property. In this context a dispute arose about the interpretation of the second clause of Article 16 of the Good-Neighborliness Treaty, which is the central clause in favor of restitution. During the negotiations, both sides defined the purpose of the negotiations. In March 1994 both sides agreed "that the subject of the work of the Joint Commission will be those items of cultural property which were taken from their respective countries during or as a consequence of the Second World War."[4]

Another important advance was also achieved in March 1994, when both sides granted free access for experts to works of art that were hidden for more than forty years:

> Both sides . . . will grant these experts free access to such cultural property at the places where it is located in order that they may together identify it and prepare reports, and will ensure that they have favorable working conditions.[5]

HISTORICAL FACTS AND STARTING POINTS

The lawyer who is concerned with the question of the German cultural heritage in Russia must deal with a great number of historical facts, which can neither be denied nor concealed. Among those are all measures taken by the powers involved in the war during and after military operations. These facts are the historical starting points for the legal conflict that exists today, fifty years after the end of World War II, not only between Germany and Russia but also between many other states.

The Nazi raids and destruction of property

In the first place, the facts are dominated by the Nazi raids. The Nazi officials seized numerous works of art in each of the occupied territories and brought them to Germany. Particularly the activities of the Einsatzstab Reichsleiter Rosenberg (ERR: Task Force Rosenberg) and the SS organization Ahnenerbe (Ancestral Heritage) were notorious for their looting of works of art.[6]

Additionally, in many states cultural property of great value was destroyed during hostilities. Especially in the Soviet Union this destruction was considerable. The lack of respect and the disregard for the cultural identity of foreign peoples become obvious when we look at the conduct of the special units involved. The present negotiations between Russia and Germany are characterized by the fact that there has never been any uncertainty about German actions in Eastern Europe during World War II. The German side always deeply regretted the unfortunate events and has indicated this repeatedly to the Soviet Union. It is my understanding that it is a basic characteristic of the talks that no one has ever tried to play down this issue—for only one who is fully aware of all the historical facts can come to the right conclusion, which is necessary to ensure that peoples may live together peacefully in the future.

The restitution of Soviet cultural property

It is fortunate that at the end of the war the Allied Armed Forces arranged for the collection and restitution of the works of art that had been brought to Germany. In that way, the works of art that had been held in about a thousand German depots and collected in four central Collecting Points were returned to their countries of origin.[7] This is the reason for the well-known restitution of many hundreds of thousands of works of art to the Soviet Union. Due to these returns, there is no longer a considerable number of Russian works of art in Germany. Therefore, the proposed restitution of the works of art that were brought from Germany to Russia cannot be compensated by the restitution of equivalent works of art of Russian origin. This was always called a regrettable "asymmetry" by the Russian participants. The "asymmetry," however, is due to the restitution accomplished by the Allies after World War II.

The fact of the restitution of the Soviet works of art is itself satisfactory in almost every way. The works of art plundered in Soviet territory were returned after the war to the Soviet Union in many trainloads and carloads. Uncertainties remain, however, because we do not know if and how many of these works of art were returned to their place of origin. Let me clarify that statement: we do not know, for example, whether Ukrainian cultural property returned after the war has been stored in other parts of the Soviet Union. Much the same can be said of the returned cultural property of Belarus. It is, in these examples, the negotiators for Ukraine and Belarus, on the one hand, and Russia, on the other, who must address those uncertainties.

THE REMOVAL OF GERMAN CULTURAL PROPERTY TO THE SOVIET UNION AFTER 1945

If we return to the political situation in postwar Germany, we realize that at the very moment when the works of art plundered by German special units were being returned to the Soviet Union, in the Soviet-occupied zone of Germany, the search for works of art, libraries, and archives was continued on an entirely different basis. This resulted in the transfer by the Soviet Union of more than 2.5 million works of art from Germany to the cities of the USSR. Today, a great number of these works are still kept in storage, partly in secret depots, partly in the cellars of some famous Russian museums. Many of these works of art were restituted to the former German Democratic Republic in the 1950s and 1960s.[8] But even today there are hundreds of thousands of pieces of German cultural property hidden in Russia. During the last conference between Russia and Germany, in June 1994, Germany named about two hundred thousand works of art, two million books, and three kilometers of archives to be restituted to museums, libraries, archives, and collections in Germany.[9]

The number of works of art removed from Germany by the Soviet Union is not a fabrication of the Germans; it can be gathered from Soviet documents that were inaccessible for a long time—and especially from the official statements of the Central Committee of the Communist Party of the Soviet Union (CPSU).[10] These records indicate the incredible extent of the removal of cultural property from Germany. At the same time, the outstanding importance of this cultural property for the cultural identity of the German people becomes obvious. From the very beginning, the Soviet communists realized that the plundered works of art were irreplaceable parts of the cultural achievement of the German people. It was the Central Committee of the Communist Party of the Soviet Union itself that mentioned the great importance of the valuables for the history of the national culture in Germany.[11] So it is no surprise to discover that the German cultural treasures stored in the former Soviet Union are tantamount to a walk through the entire history of Germany. The valuable inventories of the museums of Berlin, including the gold treasure of Eberswalde, two Gutenberg Bibles, the valuable books of the Gotha collection, the collection of the Bremen Kunsthalle, and the estate of Wilhelm von Humboldt—to mention just a few examples —were taken to the Soviet Union. The famous "Treasure of Priam"[12] is only one part of the German art treasures that are stored in Russia.

It is not necessary to describe the circumstances of the removal once again.[13] I want to mention, however, that German cultural property was not only removed by regular divisions of the Red Army but also by the so-called trophy commissions, which acted at the express order of Joseph Stalin and organized the removal according to carefully elaborated plans.[14] Stalin expressly ordered the art raids. With regard to the removal of German and other cultural property, his spirit stands behind all actions of the trophy commissions at the end of the war and in the postwar era. In addition, the numerous private plunderings by Soviet soldiers must be mentioned. Today, their booty is increasingly a part of the illegal art trade.[15]

THE SOVIET ATTITUDE TOWARD THE TRANSFER OF GERMAN CULTURAL PROPERTY

It is an extremely interesting fact that the Soviet trophy commissions did not carry off German cultural property during the war. The removal only took place after the end of military operations, when German cultural property was no longer in danger as a result of hostilities. When Soviet documents say that the German cultural property was brought to Moscow for reasons of saving, safeguarding, and storing, this does not accord with the facts. However, these statements have bearing on an important legal issue: not even Stalin and the CPSU insisted that the works of art removed from Germany became Soviet property. The removal did not take place expressly to acquire ownership. Recently, it has been maintained that the looted objects are now Russian property; however, this is not based on legal or historical facts.

THE INTERPRETATION OF THE TREATIES

The interpretation of the treaties signed since 1990 causes significant difficulties for the participating nations. According to the exact terms of the above-mentioned Article 16 of the German-Soviet Good-Neighborliness Treaty, "lost" cultural property will be returned.

Lost cultural property
But what is the meaning of the word "lost"? The removal of German cultural property is characterized by the fact that the removed objects were hidden for more than forty years. Only after the opening up of Eastern Europe in 1989 did the dimensions of the removal—except for that part that had already been returned to East Germany (the GDR)—become obvious. Up to that moment the existence of German cultural property in Soviet repositories had been denied. In the context of the contractual provisions regulating the return of items, the status of an object can only be determined based on the extent of knowledge of the country that is seeking its missing property. Consequently, those items of cultural property whose whereabouts were unknown to the rightful owner at the time the treaty was concluded have to be classified as lost. If any government agencies of one of the contracting parties had knowledge of the whereabouts of cultural property that was inaccessible to the other side, this does not alter the fact that the property must be considered lost within the meaning of the treaties.

The Vienna Convention on the Law of Treaties
It is obvious that an international treaty must be interpreted according to the international law in effect at the time when it was signed. Both the Soviet and the Russian parties to the treaty, on the one hand, and the German party to the treaty, on the other, understood that the effective international law was applicable and that this included, among other things, the Vienna Convention on the Law of Treaties, which is dominated by the rule *pacta sunt servanda*.[16] The treaties signed with the Soviet Union and Russia since 1990 clearly stressed that the unfortunate and tragic past of the states and peoples involved had to come to an end and that partnership and cooperation would be the basis for future relations between the contracting parties.[17] This was the purpose of the treaties, on which was based the extensive economic, financial, and political collaboration that ensued, and there is no indication that the restitution of cultural property should be treated differently from other important subjects.

"Unlawfully transferred" cultural property
The interpretation of this phrase has important implications for the negotiations now in progress. Article 16 of the Good-Neighborliness Treaty applies not only to the lost cultural property but also to that which was "unlawfully transferred." Neither by the directions of the Allied Control Council nor on any other legal basis was the Soviet Union allowed to remove cultural property from Germany, no matter how it has tried to justify it,[18] for the Hague Convention of 1907 (see Appendix 3) as part of the customary international law was also binding for every state during and after World War II. According to those provisions, "works of art and science" and "institutions dedicated to . . . the arts and sciences" on occupied territory are protected against confiscation irrespective of whether they are private or public property.[19] There does not exist any "right of the victor" detached from international law and permitting any kind of confiscation and taking of booty, nor did any such right exist in 1945. Germany never and in no way accepted as legal the removal of cultural property to the Soviet Union. Article 56 of the Hague Convention prohibits any unilateral seizure of cultural property. This provision concluded a legal battle that had lasted almost the entire nineteenth century, after the looting by Napoleon's army.[20]

INTERNATIONAL LAW IN EFFECT DURING AND AFTER WORLD WAR II

Looking at the incredible destruction and the many victims of World War II, we might conclude that the Hague Convention was not considered applicable in this case. But all one needs to do is to look at the statements made at the Nuremberg trials regarding the scope of the Hague Convention.

The Nuremberg trials

The Nazi war criminals were accused of "pillage and destruction" of works of art, including both private and public property. The charge was expressly based on Article 56 of the Hague Convention.[21] This regulation was also one of the reasons for the sentences meted out.

The judgment of the Nuremberg trials stated:

> . . . that it was supported by evidence that the territories occupied by Germany had been exploited in the most merciless way and that actually a systematic plundering of public and private property had taken place.[22]

The humanitarian functions of the Hague Convention

The Hague Convention stresses in its preamble that it had not been possible to provide for all circumstances that might arise in practice. However, any ambiguities or omissions addressed by the Allies had to be considered within the framework provided by the convention itself for future events. In these cases the inhabitants and the belligerents of the countries involved

> remain under the protection and the rule of the principles of the law of nations, as they result from the usages established among civilized peoples, from the laws of humanity, and the dictates of the public conscience.[23]

We must ask why cultural property is protected by the effective international law and especially by the UNESCO conventions since 1954 in such a particular way. It was already obvious in the Hague Convention: the regulations for the protection of international cultural property had a humanitarian character from the very beginning. The main function is not to protect the institutions of the state but the particular intellectual achievements of the "inhabitants," and this means the intellectual identity of individuals and peoples.

The removal of cultural property—additional humiliation of peoples and minorities

So it can be explained why the removal of cultural property for reasons of compensation and reparations is illegal under effective international law. To humiliate a neighboring people further and to destroy its cultural identity by systematically and totally removing its cultural property comes close to the behavior of a dictator such as, for example, Adolf Hitler. This is not the behavior of a progressive government based on peace and committed to the increasing importance of human rights despite all setbacks.[24]

The abuse of the idea of compensation

Fortunately, the United States realized after 1945 that Hitler's crimes could not be compensated by a questionable confiscation of German works of art.[25] So there are good reasons why the idea of compensation is not part of Articles 16 and 15 of the treaties of 1990 and 1992, respectively, even if supporting measures for the future are not excluded. The effective international law does not allow a unilateral compensation for war losses by a "free choice" out of the captured war "trophies." Otherwise, just that part of the German people that had to bear the greatest hardship during the Nazi period would have had to suffer again. The collections of Jewish owners were not spared by the Soviet trophy commissions, nor did they spare the collections taken from Holland and France. Religious objects were not spared either, as is demonstrated, for example, by the looting of the medieval windows of the Marienkirche in Frankfurt an der Oder, a church of the fourteenth century.

The Russian tradition of protecting cultural property and the influence of the communist regime under Joseph Stalin

The particular importance assigned to the international protection of cultural property in Article 56 of the Hague Convention is a result of the great effort of Russia and especially of the legal adviser of the Russian Foreign Ministry Frédéric de Martens. The Hague Convention of 1907 was his achievement.[26] The German request for restitution comes much closer to what he had in mind than any effort to justify the orders of Joseph Stalin. By ordering the removal of German cultural property, Stalin ignored the older Russian tradition in an almost brutal way.

THE GERMAN-RUSSIAN

NEGOTIATIONS

OVER

THE CONTENTS OF

THE RUSSIAN REPOSITORIES

Armin Hiller

On November 9, 1990, Germany and the Soviet Union concluded a Good-Neighborliness Treaty (see Appendix 14) with which, along with other bilateral treaties and multilateral decisions on ending the East-West conflict, a comprehensive political architecture was created whose objective was, and still is, to transform earlier confrontation and demarcation into a reliable partnership and to build a future in which the two countries, despite the dark chapters in their past, can develop forward-looking bilateral relations that fit smoothly into a merging, democratic Europe. It was therefore no coincidence, but rather the political logic of this new beginning, that an obligation on the mutual return of cultural property removed from their countries in time or as a consequence of war was included in the treaty. The agreement to return such property was reaffirmed in the German-Russian Cultural Agreement of 1992 (see Appendix 15).

These agreements on returning cultural property by no means establish new law. They merely codify international law in bilateral treaties. Against this background, Germany and Russia took up negotiations on returning cultural property in 1993 and agreed on a format for the implementation of the obligations they assumed in the so-called Dresden Protocol. To this end, they established a Joint Commission with German and Russian co-chairmen and set up joint groups of experts on museums, libraries, archives, and law accordingly.

In Dresden and at the subsequent meetings of the Joint Commission in Moscow and Bonn, more detailed protocol arrangements were agreed upon regarding the implementation of the provisions on the return of cultural property, for example, access to all the sites where cultural property is held, exchange of confiscation, transportation, and missing-property lists, and determination of individual cases that should be given priority.

However, in the Joint Commission, the Russian side displayed a growing tendency to mark time, which prevented further progress from being made and even called into question protocol arrangements that had already been agreed upon. Although Chancellor Helmut Kohl and President Boris Yeltsin brought forward on May 12, 1994, the date for the next meeting of the Joint Commission in order to make it possible for tangible results to be achieved sooner, this did not influence Russia's negotiating positions. This led to irritation and doubt in Germany as to the will and readiness of the Russian side to honor the obligations assumed in the Good-Neighborliness Treaty and the Cultural Agreement.

The Russian negotiating commissions used the legal interpretation of the treaty text as a means of blocking progress and made the term "unlawfully transferred" a particular hurdle. With a logic that is difficult to follow, the Russian side argues that the cultural property stolen by the German occupiers in the USSR was "unlawfully transferred"—an assertion that the German side has at no point in time disputed—while the cultural property taken from Germany by their own military and occupation authorities on a large scale was transferred to the Soviet Union "lawfully."

Some of the cultural property taken from Germany was returned by the USSR to the German Democratic Republic (GDR) in the 1950s. Some of it disappeared for half a century in secret depots. With regard to earlier operations to return cultural property, it must be said that the Soviet Union carefully sought to avoid appearing to have acted contrary to international law in the transfer protocols to the GDR. At no point in the relevant decisions and documents of the Soviet leadership is there any mention of booty, in the sense of Soviet property, or of reparations. They order the return of such property without conditions or compensation.

One is certainly not entertaining any illusions as to the Soviet dictatorship's relationship to justice if one points out that it locked the cultural property that it wanted to keep in secret depots and decreed this to be a state secret because it feared the legal and moral stigma of stealing such property. The question is, however, how today's Russia, which has declared its commitment to democratic reforms in its domestic policy and to international law and the validity of treaties in external affairs, intends to deal with the burden of the past. The question is whether it wants to adhere to and defend bilaterally and internationally a position that the Soviet government and the Central Committee of the Soviet Communist Party (CPSU) did not want to become public.

It is not necessary to enter into a complex discussion of international law and the application of the Good-Neighborliness Treaty and its provisions on returning cultural property (a detailed position paper of the German government, distributed at the Bard Graduate Center symposium, is appended here, pages 181–85) to realize that an understanding of international law and contractual fidelity are of vital importance in dealing with bilateral questions of return. When the Soviet Union took cultural property from Germany during and after the Second World War, the Hague Convention of 1907 (see Appendix 3) had long been established international law. According to those provisions, "works of art and science" and "institutions dedicated to . . . the arts and sciences" in occupied territory are protected against confiscation irrespective of whether they are private or public property. This fundamental concept of protection applied, and still applies, to the victors and the vanquished alike. It expresses the consensus and desire of the international community to prevent the cultural identity of peoples from being impaired, even in wartime. This was established law in 1941, as it was in 1945. The same concept must apply today because otherwise the way would be open again for the theft and plundering of cultural property in our troubled time fraught with military conflict. Events in the former Yugoslavia and elsewhere should serve as a reminder and warning.

By this point at the latest, it becomes obvious that the international community cannot stand on the sidelines in matters regarding cultural property removed during or as a consequence of war. It is directly affected as this relates to central issues of international protection of cultural property. Experts on international law rightly point out that both negotiating partners have a great responsibility, which exceeds the bilateral realm, to guarantee the established minimum standards under international law and not to establish conditions that can be invoked to jeopardize the protection of cultural property in wartime.

A leading Russian politician from the cultural sphere recently asserted that his government insisted on a legal solution while Germany was striving for a political solution, thus ignoring the law and fostering political voluntarism. This is obviously due to a misunderstanding. Germany bases its claims against Russia on treaties and international law. However, deviation from the principle of *pacta sunt servanda* would be unacceptable. And so would attempts to subordinate international law to national law.

Germany and Russia came to precise agreements in the Good-Neighborliness Treaty, which can be regarded as the basis for their relations with one another and with the international community. Article 1 (paragraph 6) reads: "They guarantee the precedence of the universal rules of international law in their domestic and international relations and confirm their resolve to honour their contractual obligations." In order to legally justify the removal, owing to war, of cultural property a peculiar Russian expert opinion refers to Stalin's orders, to decrees of the Soviet military authorities in 1945, and to alleged but unproven decisions of the Allied Control Council or similar sources. It will surprise no one that this meets with incomprehension and disapproval in Germany and other Western countries.

These and similar interpretations can and will not be Russia's last word on the return of cultural property. A country that is resolved to undergo democratic reforms and play an active role in constructing the European House will carefully weigh its interests. It will respect established international law, honor existing treaties, and decide to act in keeping with Russian cultural traditions. This is no easy task during the current difficult phase of transition in which reformers and their ideas have to grapple daily with the spirit of the past. However, Russia owes it to itself and its European neighbors to face up to this demand.

The negotiations with Russia on the return of cultural property are at a difficult stage. Even individual cases that have already been negotiated have come to a halt. For instance, the Russian State Commission on the Restitution of Cultural Property recommended that the rest of the Gotha library and the so-called Baldin collection* be returned to Germany. At the same time, the commission stated that it did not know which authority in Russia could implement its recommendations and actually order the return. This is, in the context of negotiations between governments, a rather unusual state of affairs.

---

* Editor's note: On Viktor Baldin and the Bremen Kunsthalle collection, see the editor's note, page 161.

The situation is similar with regard to the so-called 101 prints. These are mainly prints by the old masters from the Bremen Kunsthalle collection, which were transferred to Russia during the war and presented to the German embassy in Moscow by a private individual some time ago. In this case, too, the Russian commission recommended their return but insisted that they be examined beforehand by experts from both countries in order to establish their authenticity and provenance. This examination has taken place. The Russian authorities nevertheless continue to refuse to issue an export license for these works of art. Russia has announced, however, that an act or a presidential decree is being prepared in order to remove any legal uncertainties. This is intended to create the national framework for the return of the property and ensure that the government has scope for action in this sphere.[1]

To sum up:

For Germany, it is a matter of regaining part of its cultural heritage. This is a national task of great importance to the German government. Existing treaties and established international law form the basis for finding a solution.

From a political point of view, a mutually agreed-upon solution to the problem of returning cultural property is in keeping with the new quality of German-Russian bilateral relations. Chancellor Kohl and President Yeltsin jointly declared this on November 21, 1991.

Russia must decide whether to continue treating German cultural property as a hostage of war or whether to make it a harbinger of peace within the framework of radically changed relations between our two countries. This concerns Russia's political self-perception and raises the question as to how Russia intends to integrate itself into the European community based on shared values, a community for which international law, contractual fidelity, and respect for the cultural identity of other countries are indispensable.

The international community must ensure that the protection of cultural property under international law and its peace-enhancing potential are not impaired. This is no less important now than it was in the past.

The German government will constructively pursue the negotiations with Russia. Time, patience, and political sensitivity are required on both sides. Germany does not expect the impossible from Russia, but it does expect it to honor the spirit and letter of the Good-Neighborliness Treaty and to attune the domestic legislation it has announced to international law.

AGREEMENTS BETWEEN GERMANY AND RUSSIA ON THE RETURN OF CULTURAL PROPERTY TRANSFERRED FROM THEIR COUNTRIES IN TIME OR AS A CONSEQUENCE OF WAR: THE LEGAL SITUATION FROM THE GERMAN POINT OF VIEW

I

"Germany and Russia have become partners. That partnership is characterized by openness and trust. Even in matters on which our views and interests may differ we seek sensible solutions together in a spirit of friendship."

1. This is an extract from a speech which the Federal Chancellor [Helmut Kohl] made in Bonn in May of this year [1994] during the visit of President [Boris] Yeltsin. It illustrates the new quality of German-Russian relations and is a suitable motto for resolving the difficult problem of returning cultural property.

2. The actual implementation of agreements on the return of cultural property is proving increasingly difficult. In discussions among experts it has become clear that one of the main reasons lies in the widely different standpoints regarding the legal significance of those agreements. It would therefore seem appropriate to examine once more all the facts that make up the current legal situation.

II

3. The legal analysis of the situation has to be seen in the political context. Since the political dimension of the agreements on the return of cultural property is obvious, this paper will first draw attention to the overriding, common political aims which led to and found their legal expression in the agreements.

4. This concerns primarily the common intention of the two countries in 1990. In that year, which brought the ending of the Cold War and the division of Europe, Germany and the Soviet Union decided to dispel the shadows of the past once and for all and enter into a new era of cooperation based on partnership. It was a fundamental political change sealed with a number of treaties. The new departure was particularly manifest in the Treaty on Good-Neighborliness, Partnership and Cooperation (the Good-Neighborliness Treaty) and in the Treaty on the Development of Comprehensive Cooperation in the Field of Trade, Industry, Science and Technology, both of which were signed on November 9, 1990. The conclusion of these bilateral instruments was tied up with a number of historic multilateral decisions terminating the East-West confrontation, ranging from the Two-plus-four Treaty between the former occupying powers and the two German states (September 12) to the adoption of the Charter of Paris for a New Europe at the CSCE (Conference on Security and Cooperation in Europe) summit on November 21, 1990.

5. One hardly need mention that Russia adopted these foreign-policy decisions and international agreements of the Soviet Union. From the beginning the Russian Federation left

no doubt that it wanted to be regarded as the state in international law in continuation of the Soviet Union.

6. Politically, the 1990 treaties were and continue to be a whole in that they manifest a new identity of political intent, envisage a program of comprehensive cooperation, and seek to establish a new relationship of broad-based partnership. The common architecture of the treaties was and remains crucial for the stability of that partnership. Although the underlying mutual interest is not necessarily expressed in specific articles, it is inherent in the treaties as a whole. The common force of the treaties can only fully come to bear if the interpretation of their individual provisions, too, serves the overriding common objectives. In this way the purpose of the treaties will be fulfilled and the partnership deepened. The overriding mutual interest in developing that partnership is the essence of the treaties. It must not be overshadowed by particularism, which is oriented to specific commitments rather than the overall purpose, and is thus open to misinterpretation.

III

7. Article 16 of the 1990 German-Soviet Good-Neighborliness Treaty reads: "The Federal Republic of Germany and the Union of Soviet Socialist Republics will advocate the preservation of cultural treasures of the other side in their territory. They agree that lost or unlawfully transferred art treasures which are located in their territory will be returned to their owners or their successors." The agreement to return such property was reaffirmed by Germany and Russia in Article 15 of the German-Russian Cultural Agreement of 1992: "The Contracting Parties agree that lost or unlawfully transferred cultural property which is located in their sovereign territory will be returned to its owners or their successors." In the negotiations so far on the implementation of this agreement considerable differences have arisen as to the interpretation and meaning of these provisions. The key elements therefore call for closer examination.

Art Treasures/Cultural Property: What Is Meant?

8. At their first meeting in Moscow on March 23–24, 1994, the German-Russian Commission defined these terms as follows: "The two sides agree that . . . the subject of the work of the Joint Commission are those items of cultural property which were taken from their respective countries during or as a consequence of the Second World War" (paragraph 5 of the Moscow Protocol of March 24, 1994). That covers the abstract part of the subject. But what does it mean in practice?

9. As regards the theft of art treasures by Nazi Germany in the Soviet Union and the whereabouts of the booty, the legal situation is quite clear. So too are the facts to a large extent. From the summer of 1943 various Nazi agencies, but especially Einsatzstab Reichsleiter Rosenberg and Ahnenerbe, an SS organization, saw to the large-scale removal of cultural property to Germany. This theft was not only a breach of international law but also a direct attack on the cultural identity of the peoples of the Soviet Union, as indeed it was intended to be according to the Nazi ideology underlying the war of conquest against the Soviet Union.

10. The bulk of this stolen Soviet property, together with art treasures taken from other occupied territories, was stored in depots in southern Germany. When American troops entered the country they found more than one thousand such depots, which were placed under the authority of the Monuments, Fine Arts, and Archives of the military administration. In the winter of 1945–46 the depots were closed and their contents sent to four central Collecting Points (Munich, Wiesbaden, Marburg, and Offenbach), where they were inventoried. With the assistance of representatives of the territories occupied by Germany during the war, transport was organized for the return of cultural property to its countries of origin. The Soviet Union, too, was represented. Between 1945 and 1948 thirteen large consignments of such goods were taken back to the Soviet Union. They comprised several hundred thousand objects, including, for instance, more than 1,100 icons from Pskov and Novgorod.

11. The scientific processing of all available data relating to these activities has not yet been completed. However, experts reached the conclusion long ago that the great majority of the works of art taken from the Soviet Union to Germany were returned in the early postwar years, that is, to the extent that their destruction or loss during the war had not made them irretrievable. Nonetheless, the German authorities are trying to trace objects still remaining in Germany in order that they may be returned.

12. Of course, the German side has only limited knowledge of the removal of German cultural property to the Soviet Union during the war and its whereabouts there. Although large numbers of objects were returned to the former GDR, the German government must assume that there are still about two hundred thousand museum objects, some two million books and a good three kilometers of archive material from Germany stored in Russia. This property includes such unique testimonies to German culture and history as eighty objects from the early German gold treasures found at Eberswalde, two Gutenberg Bibles, and outstanding collections of paintings. These are therefore part of the cultural heritage, part of Germany's and her people's cultural identity.

Much the same applies to those objects of ancient civilizations which had a permanent place in German museums and had considerable influence on the nation's cultural life. In many instances the process of cultural integration began with the discoveries made by German archaeologists. One particularly outstanding example is the "Treasure of Priam," which belongs to the Berlin Museums and is still being kept in the Pushkin Museum, Moscow.

What Is Meant by "Lost or Unlawfully Transferred Cultural Property"?

13. So far German and Russian experts have not been able to find a common answer to this question. If an international treaty leaves such room for interpretation, an attempt must be made to find the answer with the help of the rules of interpretation embodied in the 1969 Vienna Convention on the Law of Treaties. The general rule for interpretation is contained in Article 31: "A treaty shall be interpreted in good faith in accordance with the ordinary meaning to be given to the terms of the treaty in their context and in the light of its object and purpose."

14. If in our interpretation we start from the "ordinary meaning" of the words, then it would seem that one word in the Good-Neighborliness Treaty and the Cultural Agreement is clear beyond any doubt: the tiny word "or." By choosing to write "lost 'or' unlawfully transferred cultural property," the contracting parties obviously wanted to show that two different categories of cultural property are meant—lost property on the one hand and unlawfully transferred property on the other—and that for each of these categories viewed separately there exists an obligation to return the property.

15. The word "lost," too, has a clear meaning in general parlance. It is used to describe things the whereabouts of which are unknown. Whose knowledge that they are lost matters? In the context of the contractual provisions governing the return of such items, it can only be that of the country that lost them. Consequently, those items of cultural property had to be classified as lost, the whereabouts of which were unknown to the rightful owner at the time the treaty was concluded. If any government agencies had knowledge which was inaccessible to the other side, that does not alter the fact that the property was lost within the meaning of treaties. It is significant that up to 1989 the Soviet Union had denied that any German cultural property was still in its possession.

16. "Lost" cultural property can of course only be the subject of further consideration if it turns up again. Accordingly, the two sides agree on the necessity of exchanging relevant information. Thus paragraph 3 of the protocol of the first meeting of the German-Russian Commission held in Moscow on March 23–24, 1994, reads: "Both sides deem closer and more open cooperation indispensable between their respectively appointed experts for the purpose of jointly elaborating proposals for identifying and listing items of cultural property for possible return to their owners. To this end both sides will grant these experts free access to such cultural property at the places where it is located in order that they may together identify it and prepare expertises and will ensure that they have favourable working conditions."

17. Where, however, lost cultural property turns up again, its legal status needs no further clarification, for in the agreements quoted above the two sides unequivocally declared that "lost . . . cultural property . . . will be returned to its owners." The mutual obligation to return lost cultural property has thus been clearly established.

18. Under the Good-Neighborliness Treaty and the Cultural Agreement the two sides are likewise obliged to return unlawfully transferred cultural property. As regards this category of property it appears today to be particularly difficult to proceed on the basis of the original joint intention of the contracting parties. Sometimes it is as if these words are only being used in order to reopen the wounds of a painful past. But precisely this is what the authors of the Good-Neighborliness Treaty wanted to avoid, as the second sentence of the preamble makes particularly clear: "Desiring to set the final seal on the past and, through understanding and reconciliation, render a major contribution towards ending the division of Europe. . . ."

19. Thus the contracting parties wanted a forward-looking final settlement. They realized that in the matter of cultural property removed during the war the views of the two sides differed considerably on account of the past. Whereas the illegality of the theft of cultural property from the Soviet Union during the Second World War has never been disputed by the Federal Republic of Germany, the legal positions of the two sides differed sharply regarding the cultural property taken from Germany to the Soviet Union in 1945 and subsequently. However, in choosing the words "unlawfully transferred," it cannot have been the intention of the contracting parties to refer merely to unresolved controversies concerning the past since it was their declared intention to set the seal on the past.

20. The apparent contradiction proves meaningless if one applies the above-quoted rule contained in Article 31 of the Vienna Convention on the Law of Treaties, which says that not only the object and purpose of the treaty but also the context of other provisions of that treaty must be taken into account in order to arrive at the correct interpretation. Fundamental significance attaches to Article 1, sixth paragraph, of the Good-Neighborliness Treaty in this context: "They [the contracting parties] guarantee the precedence of the universal rules of international law in their domestic and international relations and confirm their resolve to honour their contractual obligations."

21. According to the general rules of international law, whose precedence has thus been bindingly reaffirmed, cultural property is specially protected against confiscation and removal from the country in times of war. Also significant is the reference in Article 15 of the Good-Neighborliness Treaty to the exceptionally large degree of mutual cultural affinity and respect through a long period in the history of both sides: ". . . conscious of the mutual enrichment of the cultures of their peoples over the centuries and of their unmistakable contribution to Europe's common cultural heritage. . . ."

22. The intention of the contracting parties at the time the treaty was concluded emerges clearly against this background.

They wanted to express their respect for each other's cultural heritage as protected by international law and to free themselves from the burdens of the past and recommence their cooperation with a clean slate. Thus the words "unlawfully transferred" have to be seen in the context of the mutual intention in 1990 to avoid argument over the events of 1945 and thereafter. In 1990 and 1992 the Soviet Union/Russia and Germany confirmed that they respect each other's cultural identity without reservation, that therefore the continuing unilateral relocation of cultural property is in their present mutual opinion unlawful, and that hence cultural property which has been unilaterally relocated must today be regarded as unlawfully transferred property and returned to its owners.

23. Only this interpretation reveals the logic in the equal-ranking juxtaposition of the two categories of property lost or unlawfully transferred. Otherwise it would be difficult to understand why lost property should be returned directly and unilaterally removed property only after further historical consideration of the legality of its removal. The parties wanted to agree on the return of both categories of unilaterally removed property.

24. This interpretation of the agreements is based on the principles of systematic and teleological interpretation prescribed by international law and is future-oriented. Even if one did not wish to adhere to those principles and insisted on regarding the agreements in isolation in relation to the past, that would not alter the outcome: authoritative for an assessment of the situation under international law relating exclusively to the time the property was removed is the Hague Convention of 1907 respecting the laws and customs of war on land, especially its Article 46, second paragraph, and Article 56. According to those provisions "works of art and science" and "institutions dedicated to . . . the arts and sciences" on occupied territory are protected against confiscation irrespective of whether they are private or public property. There does not exist any "right of the victor" detached from international law and permitting any kind of confiscation and taking of booty, nor did any such right exist in 1945.

25. However, an assessment based on the past could lead to the result that the unilateral removal of cultural property in order, say, to ensure its safekeeping could be justifiable for a time. The attitude of the Soviet Union seemed to suggest that this was its understanding of the legal situation. The Soviet Union apparently never regarded itself as the owner of the German cultural property in question since it kept most of the items in secret storage on its territory for over forty years. In those cases in which it admitted to holding the property, that is to say, when German art treasures were returned to the GDR, it spoke of "temporary custody." Were Russia to claim ownership of unilaterally removed German cultural property today, that from a legal point of view would be a case of *venire contra factum proprium* (to go against one's own action), that is to

say, difficult to reconcile with the principle of protection of good faith as established in international law.

IV

26. The previous section covered the international-law aspects of immediate importance for the interpretation and application of the provisions of the Good-Neighborliness Treaty and the Cultural Agreement quoted in paragraph 7. The political discussion on the return of cultural property has also included legal arguments that have no basis in the relevant contractual provisions. In order to present a complete picture, those arguments, too, are outlined below.

27. One of them is "restitution in kind." The Russian experts on the Joint Commission argued thus: "If it proves impossible to return cultural property removed from the territory of the Soviet Union during the Second World War it should be replaced with objects of the same kind and quality, including items which after the termination of hostilities were taken from Germany to the Soviet Union."

28. This is an understandable political position considering the sorrowful events of the Second World War, and there are historical precedents in treaty law (Treaty of Versailles, individual peace treaties after the Second World War), but as a legal opinion it is not borne out by general international law. Above all, it is a position which was neither set out during the negotiations nor in any way mentioned in the treaty provisions.

29. Reference is therefore also made in this connection to the *pacta sunt servanda* principle, perhaps the most important tenet of international law. Coming back to the political aspect, it is again emphasized that the fundamental mutual interest underlying the 1990 accords is inherent in their totality and not necessarily in specific provisions. It is generally known that Germany has made and is still making exceptional contributions to the fulfillment of these agreements. There is no need, however, to go into *quid pro quo* detail here.

30. Another argument which has no contractual basis in the agreements relates to the joint letter from the two German Foreign Ministers to the Foreign Ministers of the Four Powers on the occasion of the signing of the Two-plus-four Treaty in Moscow on September 12, 1990. That letter contains, *inter alia*, the following passage from the Joint Declaration by the two German governments on June 15, 1990: "The expropriations effected on the basis of occupation law or authority (between 1945 and 1949) are irreversible. The Governments of the Soviet Union and the German Democratic Republic do not see any means of revising the measures taken then. The Government of the Federal Republic of Germany takes note of this in the light of the historical development." It has been variously deduced from this that Germany no longer insists on the return of cultural property. The Russian government did not make the same deduction because it knew that neither the joint letter from the two German Foreign Ministers nor

the Joint Declaration by the two German governments of June 15, 1990, had anything at all to do with the question of cultural property. In fact the letter dealt with the matter of land reform in the territory of the former GDR.

31. Nonetheless, the background to that letter is interesting in this context as well to the extent that one can infer from it the degree of importance which the Soviet Union attached to measures introduced "on the basis of occupation authority" in 1990. The fundamental Soviet objective in this connection is reflected, for instance, in the following passage from a paper on fundamental principles for a final international settlement with respect to Germany which was presented at a two-plus-four meeting of Foreign Ministers in Berlin: "The united Germany will recognize the legitimacy of the measures taken and orders issued by the Four Powers together or in each of their former occupation zones with regard to denazification, demilitarization and democratization. The legality of these decisions, including questions of land and property, will not be subject to a review by German courts or other German authorities."

32. This Soviet negotiating position led to the aforementioned letter from the two German Foreign Ministers expressing their recognition of the irreversibility of the land reforms carried out in the Soviet-occupied zone. The quotation makes absolutely clear what the Soviet Union had in mind with regard to recognition of measures taken "on the basis of occupation authority," i.e., measures with regard to "denazification, demilitarization and democratization." But the question of recognizing the transfer of German cultural property to the Soviet Union "on the basis of occupation authority" was never a subject of the 1990 negotiations. To this extent, too, any attempt to establish Russian ownership of German cultural property "on the basis of occupation authority" would today be a *venire contra factum proprium*.

33. Furthermore, although the German government knows of the existence of Allied Control Council documents relating to the restitution of cultural property of the victorious powers which had been removed to Germany, it has no knowledge of any documents which contain an authorization to remove German cultural property. If such agreements did exist (Russia has so far not presented any such document) they would not be compatible with international law as applicable then and now. Moreover, they would to Germany be *res inter alios acta* because third parties cannot make decisions affecting the legal positions of the party concerned protected by international law without the involvement of that party. It is also clear from the way these matters were dealt with by the occupying powers at the time that there can hardly have existed Control Council agreements providing for the removal of German cultural property since the actions of the Four Powers on the basis of occupation sovereignty did not manifest any legal intention to acquire permanent owner-

ship of German cultural property. As explained above (paragraph 25), the attitude of the Soviet Union over many years also suggested that its sole intention was to take temporary possession of the removed German cultural property.

V

34. The German government will continue its efforts to settle the present legal controversy through diplomatic channels. Its aim, as Foreign Minister Klaus Kinkel has said on various occasions, is to reach an amicable settlement of the matter of the return of cultural property, which is also important for the development of bilateral relations, in the spirit and according to the letter of the Good-Neighborliness Treaty.

35. However, the current legal positions on the proper interpretation of the agreements on the return of cultural property (Article 16 [2] of the 1990 German-Soviet Good-Neighborliness Treaty and Article 15 of the German-Russian Cultural Agreement of 1992) are far apart. In order to settle the matter in a spirit of partnership, therefore, it may also be appropriate to put these legal issues before the International Court of Justice or an arbitration tribunal. Germany would be willing to do so.

LEGAL ASPECTS OF

THE RUSSIAN POSITION

IN REGARD TO

THE RETURN OF

CULTURAL PROPERTY

Mark Boguslavsky

In the search for ways to settle reciprocal Russian-German claims for the return of cultural property, the legal bases are two similarly worded articles from treaties concluded in the 1990s between Russia and Germany.* These are the second paragraph of Article 16 of the Treaty on Good-Neighborliness, Partnership and Cooperation between the Union of Soviet Socialist Republics and the Federal Republic of Germany of November 9, 1990 (see Appendix 14) and Article 15 of the Agreement between the Government of the Russian Federation and the Government of the Federal Republic of Germany on Cultural Cooperation of December 16, 1992 (see Appendix 15).

Negotiations on the reciprocal return of cultural property between Russia and Germany began in February 1993, nearly fifty years after the end of World War II. On February 9–10, 1993, a meeting was held in Dresden at which the parties stated their basic views on the objectives and goals of the negotiations. "It was emphasized that questions of the return of cultural property involve complex political, historical-cultural, economic, legal, and moral aspects of Russian-German relations and require a responsible and careful approach" (paragraph 5, Protocol of the Dresden meeting of February 10, 1993).

At the Dresden meeting, a decision was taken to create a joint Russian-German commission on the reciprocal return of cultural property. One of the tasks of this commission was to "determine the conditions for such return" (paragraph 6, Protocol of February 10, 1993). Joint expert groups, including a group on legal questions, were also established. The first meeting of the joint commission took place in Moscow in March 1994, and the second was held in Bonn in June of that year. Two meetings of the group on legal questions were also held. These meetings revealed a difference in interpretation of the provisions of the international treaties concluded between Russia and Germany on questions of the reciprocal return of cultural property.

The goal of this chapter is not only to provide the reader with information concerning the basic legal questions that emerged in the course of the official Russian-German negotiations on the reciprocal return of cultural property displaced during and after World War II, but also to present the author's comments on these problems. The basis for these comments is an analysis of international legal documents, archival materials, and the published works of both Soviet (Russian) and foreign authors.

It is well known that during World War II Hitler's Germany engaged in a massive seizure of cultural property. Following Hitler's special instructions, a number of subdivisions were established that deliberately and intentionally removed objects of historical and artistic value from the occupied territories to Germany. This criminal activity of the Nazi

---

* Editor's note: For a description of cultural losses suffered by the USSR during World War II, see Shvidkoi, above, pages 67–71; on the transfer of the contents of the German repositories to the USSR, see Nikandrov, above, pages 117–20.

state was submitted for consideration at the postwar Nuremberg trials. Hermann Göring, Joachim von Ribbentrop, Hans Frank, Alfred Rosenberg, and others were accused of the theft of cultural property.[1]

While all of the countries of Europe occupied by the Nazis suffered from the looting,[2] particularly heavy losses were inflicted on the cultural heritage of the former Soviet Union (Belarus, Ukraine, and Russia), Poland, and Yugoslavia. During the war the Nazi invaders flagrantly violated international legal norms and above all the Hague Convention of 1907 on the laws and customs of war (see Appendix 3). From the point of view of modern international law, the Nazi seizures of cultural property could not be—and never were—considered as lawful legal actions.

Even while the war was going on, the Allies thought it necessary to warn the invaders concerning the inadmissibility of massive plundering of cultural property. On January 5, 1943, the Declaration of London was published (see Appendix 9), and in it the Allies stated that they recognized as invalid any transfer or transaction on the part of the Axis powers involving plundered property.[3]

The legal basis given in Soviet publications for the restitution of cultural property removed by the Nazis from the territory they had occupied during the war was the principle of the material responsibility of a state that had perpetrated violations of international law or acts of aggression that were most serious international crimes. "Of course," wrote L. N. Galenskaia, "when the occupying power seizes the cultural property of another state, in so doing it damages it. However, damage in this case is not solely material: there is a loss of the cultural property of a people, and such actions are considered as international crimes."[4]

The Soviet doctrine of international law considers restitution to be one of the forms of material responsibility of a state. Responsibility concerning restitution entails the elimination or reduction by the state that has committed the damage it has caused the other state by restoration to its former condition (restitutio in integrum), inter alia through the return of property it has plundered and unlawfully removed from the territory of the other state occupied by its troops. Such restitution is distinguished from another type of material responsibility, namely reparations, which are understood as meaning compensation by the state that is to blame in cash or in kind (for example, supplies of equipment), for the damage it has caused the other state as a result of its illegal actions.[5]

After the end of World War I, the rule regarding the return of cultural property seized during armed conflicts was enshrined in the treaties of the Versailles system. The Versailles treaty with Germany of 1919 (see Appendix 4) set forth the obligation of Germany to return all seized objects of value that could be identified on the territory of Germany or its allies (Article 238). The demand for the return of works of art, historical monuments, archives, and so forth that were removed both during and prior to the period of World War I follows from the texts of the Versailles Treaty, the Trianon treaty with

Hungary of 1920 (see Appendix 6), and the St. Germain treaty with Austria of 1919 (see Appendix 5). For example, the Versailles Treaty required the return of objects of value removed during the period of the Franco-Prussian War, 1870–71 (Article 245).

After the end of World War II, obligations regarding restitution were included in the texts of the peace treaties of 1947 with Italy, Hungary, and Bulgaria, and obligations regarding the Soviet Union were included in the texts of the treaty with Finland, the peace treaty with Japan of 1951, and the state treaty with Austria of 1955.[6]

On the basis of an analysis of international legal practice, Professor L. N. Galenskaia concludes that "at the present time there are both customary and treaty norms of international law, which bind all states to return cultural property removed from occupied territories during the period of hostilities. This obligation is equally applicable to the occupying authorities, and to third states on whose territories such objects of value were found."[7]

The provisions of international law regarding the return of cultural property to the countries from which they were removed during hostilities as a result of the occupation of a country by a foreign power are contained in the Hague Convention and Protocol of 1954 (see Appendix 10). According to Article 3, Part I, of the 1954 Protocol, each party is obligated to return cultural property located on its territory "to the competent authorities of the territory previously occupied" if such cultural property was removed during the war.

The Protocol to the Hague Convention of 1954 also provides for other cases of the return of cultural property, namely, of that which during the war was temporarily taken to another location for purposes of preservation. A special article (5) of the Protocol of 1954 states that such cultural property must be returned to that state in which it was formerly located. A classic example in international practice is the case of the Polish tapestries from Wawel Palace, Cracow. They were sent to Canada before the outbreak of the war, and for a long period of time Poland tried to gain their return. The tapestries were finally given back to Poland, and the Hungarian Crown of Saint Stephen was returned by the United States in a similar fashion.

The provisions cited above and, first and foremost, the provision regarding responsibility for the actions of Nazi Germany are, as I see it, significant for an understanding of the official position of the Russian side at the negotiations which took place in 1993–94. Basic problems emerged during the negotiations concerning the interpretation of the concept of "unlawfully transferred cultural property." The criterion of illegality became the first legal question on which the interpretation of the parties did not coincide. In the view of the Russian side, from a legal point of view there was a need for different approaches in defining this concept as applied to cultural property removed during the war by Germany from the territory of the former Soviet Union, and as applied to cultural property removed from Germany by the Soviet Union.

In the view of the Russian party, "unlawfully transferred cultural property" includes all cultural property removed from the territory of the Soviet Union during World War II. Such property is subject to return regardless of any subsequent transactions as a result of which the owners of such property acquired them. This leads to the conclusion that as a result of the principle of responsibility Germany has a strict obligation to engage in restitution of all cultural property removed during the war from the territory of the Soviet Union.

Cultural property removed from the territory of Germany to the former Soviet Union is in a different situation. The legality or illegality of such removal of property to Russia after the war can be determined on the basis of those legal norms which were in force at the time of removal, that is, in 1945–46. The displacement of cultural property from Germany to the territory of the Soviet Union is defined in the documents of the Allied Control Council and by the normative acts adopted on the basis of those documents. A special regime must be applied to cultural property removed during the process of denazification and demilitarization of the German state. Cultural property displaced from Germany to the territory of the Soviet Union in accordance with the documents of the Allied Control Council and the Soviet military administration in Germany is considered as legally removed cultural property.[8] Claims concerning the return of cultural property can be considered following artistic appraisal and legal qualification in accordance with the rules of international law and of universal legal practice.

The second question, which was raised in different forms during the negotiations, was the question of so-called substitution (restitution in kind). From the Russian point of view, the list of cultural losses incurred by the Soviet Union during the war can and must include lost objects of value. If restitution is impossible, these objects are subject to replacement by objects of the same kind, and, insofar as possible of the same value, from among that cultural property taken from Germany to the Soviet Union following the end of hostilities.

To understand this provision, which was put forward during the negotiations by the Russian side, I believe there is a need to refer to precedents in international treaty practice. On the basis of the principle of substitution, the Treaty of Versailles (Article 247) had already stated that to replace the destroyed books, manuscripts, and incunabula of Belgium's Louvain library, Germany was obligated to return an appropriate quantity of cultural property of the same kind and value, as well as the Ghent Altarpiece, which had been taken from the Church of St. Bavo in Ghent, and the side panels of the Dirk Bouts triptych of the *Last Supper* to Louvain.

The principle of substitution is the basis for the provisions of the peace treaties of 1947 (Article 75, paragraph 9, of the peace treaty with Italy; Article 24, paragraph 3, of the peace treaty with Hungary; Article 22, paragraph 3, of the peace treaty with Bulgaria). Thus, paragraph 9 of Article 75 of the peace treaty with Italy reads as follows:

If in individual cases it is impossible for Italy to provide restitution of objects of artistic, historical or archaeological value which are part of the cultural property of the Allied nation from the territory of which these objects were removed by the Italian armies, Italy undertakes to give to the relevant Allied nation objects of the same kind and approximately equal in value to the objects removed, insofar as such objects can be obtained in Italy.

Of course, Germany is not a party to these treaties, and due to various circumstances that are beyond the scope of the present paper, a peace treaty was not concluded with the Soviet Union. But the inclusion of the relevant provisions in these and other international agreements attests to existing international practice concerning these issues and therefore to the existence of international legal custom. It should also be noted that in the process of drawing up the peace treaties of 1947 this principle was cited by the representatives of various states that had suffered from fascist aggression, in particular by the representative of Greece.[9]

During the recent negotiations, the German party referred to the fact that after the end of World War II the principle of substitution had virtually not been applied. This assertion requires more detailed consideration. Indeed, as was correctly pointed out by Professor W. Kowalski of Poland in his work specifically devoted to problems of restitution, the normative materials prepared by the Allied powers had initially contained a provision concerning substitution. The definition of restitution adopted by the Allied Control Council on January 21, 1946, thus contained this concept. On February 25, 1947, the Allied Control Council issued instructions concerning the implementation of substitution. The quadripartite procedure for restitution approved by the coordinating committee on April 17, 1946, stated that "property of a unique nature, for which restitution is impossible . . . can be replaced by equivalent objects." Because of the differences in the positions taken by the representatives of the Allies on this question, the Allied Control Council authorities did not further rule on it, but this does not imply rejection of the force of the principle.[10]

This principle however, was not in fact implemented because of a change in the directive of the commander in chief of the United States forces in Germany, who referred to the need to comply with the principle of the unity of cultural property in Germany. The existence of different opinions between the Allies on this question, however, as is noted above, cannot invalidate this principle, which had become an international legal custom.*

As for compliance with the principle of the unity of a collection, that question must be resolved by specific negotiations. The need for conducting, in each individual case, not only artistic appraisal but also legal qualification stems from the understanding referred to above concerning the legality of the removal of cultural property from Germany to the USSR.

The result of such qualification can be, first of all, the determination of the legality or illegality of removal; second, the determination of the category of property to which one or another object of cultural property removed to the USSR belongs, and specifically whether it belongs to the category of German property or to the category of so-called Allied property, which is understood as the property of states that fell victim to Nazi aggression and of the former allies of the USSR during World War II (France, Belgium, the Netherlands, and others); third, to identify whether this cultural property was private property, *inter alia* that of individuals who had suffered or perished in the Nazi camps and prisons; and fourth, to determine whether this cultural property was the property of religious or charitable organizations and communities.

Different points of view were expressed in Russia and in Germany concerning the problem of the existence or determination of the right of ownership to cultural property displaced to the USSR after the war.

The first point of view stated that all cultural property removed from Germany must be considered as belonging to the German people or, in other words, that the German state or German citizens and legal residents continued to retain the right of ownership concerning such property.

The second point of view stated that all cultural property located at the present time in the territory of Russia, which had been removed from Germany or in any case legally removed from Germany, must be considered as an integral part of the national cultural heritage of Russia.

For a number of reasons, and above all as a consequence of the regime of secrecy, the issue of the right of ownership of cultural property as of the present (January 1995) remains an open question.

An answer to this extremely complex question involves historical and legal considerations. After the end of the war, the supreme organs of power and of administration of the Soviet Union did not adopt any kind of normative act establishing or proclaiming the USSR's right of ownership of this property. Objects of value from museums were not included in the single list of state museum holdings that then existed in the USSR. Nor were the archives that had been removed included in the list of archive holdings. All of these objects of value were placed in separate special repositories for purposes of preservation. Regarding the archive holdings, back in 1945 a special meeting of the People's Commissariat for Internal Affairs (NKVD), which at that time was responsible for all the archives, declared that the archives brought to the USSR from Germany were in the USSR for temporary preservation, and that their fate and legal status were to be decided on at a later date.

The decision regarding the fate of the paintings from the Dresden Staatliche Gemäldegalerie was highly significant in terms of museum objects. This question was considered by what was then the highest ruling body in the USSR, the Presidium of the Central Committee of the Communist Party of the Soviet Union (CPSU). In a note of March 3, 1955, to the Presidium of the Central Committee of the CPSU, the then Minister of Foreign Affairs of the USSR, V. M. Molotov, the closest associate of Joseph Stalin, raised the question of the disposition of the contents of the Dresden Gemäldegalerie. This document noted that there was virtually no access to the collection of paintings from this gallery and further stated:

> The present situation regarding the paintings of the Dresden Gallery is abnormal. Two solutions to this question can be proposed: either to declare that the paintings of the Dresden Picture Gallery as trophy property belong to the Soviet people and provide broad access to them for the public, or to return them to the German people as its national property. In the present situation the second decision seems more correct. The handing over of the paintings of the Dresden Gallery will promote a further strengthening of friendly relations between the Soviet and German peoples and at the same time will promote a strengthening of the political positions of the German Democratic Republic.[11]

As a result of this note, the second option was exercised, based, of course, primarily on the political and more specifically on the foreign-policy interests of the Soviet Union at that time. As I see it, however, the legal aspect of that solution to the problem cannot be ignored.

On the basis of the decision, negotiations were held from January 3 to January 8, 1957, between the governments of the USSR and the German Democratic Republic (GDR). In a joint statement, "the parties declared their readiness to consider questions linked to the return on a reciprocal basis of cultural property (works of art, archival materials, etc.), in order to conclude the settlement initiated by the Soviet Government of similar issues which arose during the war."

On September 8, 1958, the Protocol was signed on the transfer to the GDR of German cultural property that had temporarily been located in the USSR for purposes of preservation. A number of protocols were then signed, and ultimately the Final Protocol (July 29, 1960). In all of these documents, cultural property was defined as "located (or having been located) for temporary preservation in the USSR." Of course, these decisions of the Soviet leadership and the international documents (the agreements between the USSR and the GDR) can now be criticized, but it is hard to deny that they defined the legal status of the cultural property that was under discussion. That property was held by, but not owned by, the Soviet state. Such was its position as set forth in the international legal documents.

From a civic-legal point of view, the question of the right of ownership to such property could not arise either for the Soviet state or for Soviet legal professionals because in the legislation of the USSR, as distinguished from that of other countries, there was no institution of ownership by prescription (acquisition of title by virtue of time held). This was first introduced into Russia in the law on property of the Russian Federation of 1990. At the present time the Civil Code of 1995 (part I, page 234) is in force, providing for a statute on acquisition of title by virtue of time held, but only regarding publicly accessible holdings, which up to the present time could not be applied to cultural property displaced to the USSR and which until 1994 was located in a closed and secret repository.

As for private collections and possible claims of owners and their successors (including heirs), the following should be borne in mind:

1. The right of private property is recognized in Russia by the Constitution of 1993 and by Russian legislation in effect (page 213, part I of the Civil Code, which entered into force on January 1, 1995);
2. For claims for recovery of private property from a possessor *mala fide,* proof is required of the existence of the right of ownership and the lack of legal grounds for recognition of the right of ownership of the present holders of the property in Russia;
3. In the case of a decision by a court in the United States, in the Federal Republic of Germany, or in the majority of other states of the world concerning the return of property, *inter alia* of cultural property from the USSR, such a decision cannot be executed in Russia because these states have not concluded an international agreement with Russia on the execution of judgments. (Agreements with the United States, Germany, and a few other countries are solely in the form of an exchange of notes regarding the implementation of judicial assistance.)

In the discussions held, primarily at meetings of the legal group of the joint commission, the parties did not succeed in reaching an adequate decision concerning the question of compensation of expenditures and labor costs borne by the Soviet Union (Russia) for the conservation and restoration of the cultural property located at present in the Russian repositories. The Russian side asserted the principle of the necessity for full compensation for such types of expenditures. This was not fully recognized by the German side.

Another important legal question is that of the statute of limitations. In the view of the Russian side, the statute of limitations should not be applied to demands of one state on another state concerning the return of cultural property. In those cases when action for return of cultural property is brought in the courts of a state (for example, in the United States, Germany, or Russia), the applicable dates of the statute of limitations are those established by the legislation of the relevant state (in the United States by the legislation of the individual states). In Russia, such dates are established by civil legislation.

In conclusion, it should be noted that the present article has focused on those differences of opinion of a legal nature that arose during the execution of the agreements between Russia and Germany. An approach shared by all states, based on the recognition of special regulations governing cultural property during periods of armed conflict, would help to overcome these differences.

It is noteworthy that such an approach was demonstrated back in 1935 in the United States with the adoption of the so-called Roerich Pact (see Appendix 8). On April 15, 1935, in Washington, D.C., in the presence of President Franklin D. Roosevelt, the U.S. and twenty countries of Latin America signed the Treaty on the Protection of Artistic and Scientific Institutions and Historic Monuments. This was one of the first international legal documents based on the recognition of this principle. In a radio address on the signing of the treaty, Roosevelt said: "In proposing this pact for signing by all countries of the world, we hope that its universal recognition will become an essential principle for the preservation of modern civilization. This treaty is of greater significance than the text of the actual document."[12] In 1947, after World War II had inflicted incalculable disasters on all of mankind and on the cultural heritage of many countries, N. Roerich wrote in his diary: "So it is. The events which have shaken the entire world during the last few years have only served to reaffirm the truth of the late president's words. He understood that the meaning of the Pact lies in the public protection of culture."[13]

SCHLIEMANN'S "TREASURES"

FROM THE

SECOND CITY OF TROY

Elizabeth Simpson

Troy, the Homeric Troia or Ilios, was believed by the ancient Greeks to have been a historical city in Asia Minor, and the Trojan War, immortalized in the *Iliad* and the *Odyssey,* was considered to have actually occurred. The Homeric epics, probably composed in the eighth century B.C., are the oldest surviving records of the conflict. The war itself, however, took place in an earlier, more glorious age. This heroic era is now known to scholars as the Late Bronze Age, the period of greatest power and prosperity of the Mycenaean Greek kingdoms; Troy, besieged by the followers of Agamemnon after the abduction of Helen by the Trojan prince Paris, may have fallen some time in the thirteenth century B.C.[1] The scale of the undertaking and the tragedy of the war's consequences would profoundly affect the generations that followed. The Greek historian Thucydides, writing in the fifth century B.C., understood that the Trojan expedition was, for its time, the greatest that had ever taken place.[2]

Those who sought to achieve their own conquests were drawn to the famous city. In 480 B.C., before crossing the Hellespont, the Persian king Xerxes sacrificed a thousand oxen at the traditional site of Troy;[3] and Alexander the Great, who slept with the *Iliad* under his pillow,[4] first cast his spear into the soil of Asia there.[5] But by the time that Julius Caesar visited Troy, the Homeric city could no longer be recognized, although its general location was still known, marked by later constructions.[6] Throughout succeeding periods, the fame of the ancient city remained undiminished, and many pilgrims journeyed to the area to search for the ruins. It was not until the nineteenth century, however, that the Homeric city was identified with the mound of Hisarlık, located in northwest Anatolia near the entrance to the ancient Hellespont (the Dardanelles).[7]

Hisarlık was first investigated in 1863 by Frank Calvert, a British expatriate diplomat who owned a portion of the site.[8] In 1868, Calvert met the wealthy German merchant Heinrich Schliemann (fig. 82),[9] whom he impressed with his belief that the mound of Hisarlık covered the ruins of the ancient city. Wishing to enlist Schliemann's help with the investigation of the mound, Calvert made his lands available to Schliemann for excavation,[10] in return for which he asked that half of the objects found on his property be given to him.[11] Schliemann began a trial excavation at the site in 1870, digging in the western area of the mound (which was not Calvert's land), although without the proper governmental *firman* (permit). Because of this impropriety, he was forced to stop his work and was not allowed to begin again until the following year. Schliemann was to engage in other illegal acts in his efforts to circumvent the Turkish authorities, the ultimate, perhaps, being his removal of "Priam's Treasure" from the site in 1873.[12]

82. Photograph taken in 1880 of the archaeologist Heinrich Schliemann, discoverer of the "Treasure of Priam"

As with those who had preceded him, Schliemann was drawn to Troy through the influence of the Homeric epics;[13] he was the first, however, to attempt to unearth the ancient city in a major program of excavation, which he carried out intermittently between 1870 and 1890, the year of his death.[14] His energy, persistence—and his ample supply of the necessary funds—allowed him to excavate not only the city of Troy but also those of its Greek adversaries—Mycenae,[15] Tiryns,[16] and Orchomenos.[17] At Troy, Schliemann's determination was such that he inadvertently dug down through what little remained of the Late Bronze Age levels, revealing a city of a much earlier period—which, however, he took to be the city of Priam, king of Troy at the time of the Trojan War.

Subsequent archaeological excavations at the site—by Wilhelm Dörpfeld in 1893 and 1894;[18] Carl Blegen of the University of Cincinnati between 1932 and 1938;[19] and Manfred Korfmann of the University of Tübingen[20] beginning in 1988 and currently under way—have revealed in detail the stratified remains of nine major building phases, dating from about 3000 B.C. through the fourth century A.D. The sixth (Troy VI) was most probably that of the Trojan War.[21]

Troy VI was preceded by five other major phases, the richest of these being Troy II, which dated to the second half of the third millennium B.C. The "Burned City" of Troy II, with its fortified citadel (colorplate 13), was the city that Schliemann initially identified—wrongly—with the city of Priam. The walls of the Troy II citadel were marked by monumental gateways, one of which was reached by a paved, stone ramp (colorplate 14). It was near this ramp in 1873 that Schliemann

found the "Treasure of Priam" (figs. 83 and 84),[22] now also known as Treasure A, one of many "treasures" that would be recovered from the site (see Easton, below, pages 194–99).*

Schliemann allegedly "cut out the Treasure with a large knife," at great peril to his safety, gave the objects to his wife, Sophia, to pack into her shawl[23] (which could never have occurred, as Sophia was in Athens at the time),[24] and proceeded to crate the most valuable pieces and ship them out of the country in secret. Thus began the well-known series of thefts and removals of these famous finds,[25] which have since come to symbolize the problems associated with the plunder of cultural property—both the plunder of cultural sites and plunder as wartime booty. It is for this reason that we have chosen to present the "Treasure of Priam" as our final case study, as the

* Treasure A, called the "Treasure of Priam" by Schliemann, is still often referred to in this way, although the finds are a millennium older than the supposed date of the Trojan War. The combined treasures have been called collectively the "Treasure of Priam," complicating the issue even further; the "Schliemann gold," even though many materials other than gold are represented in the collection; the "Troy gold"; and other variations.

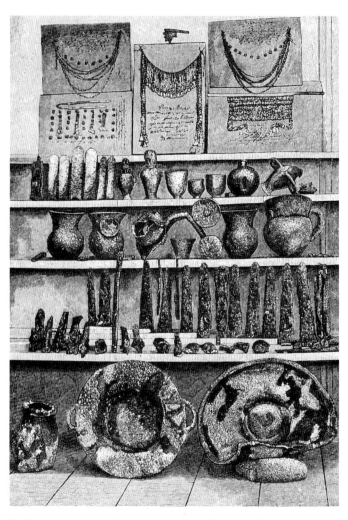

83. "General view of the Treasure," the so-called Treasure of Priam (Treasure A), as published by Heinrich Schliemann in *Ilios* (1880). What Schliemann called the "key of the treasure chest" (top, center) is actually a chisel with a lump of corrosion attached.

84. Heinrich Schliemann's wife, Sophia, wearing gold jewelry from Treasure A

world watches while the most recent episode of this drama plays out—with the Trojan treasures now in Moscow (see Goldmann, below, pages 200–203).[26] The ownership of the treasures is hotly contested, and the claimant nations Russia, Germany, and Turkey state their cases here (see Urice, below, pages 204–6).

One of the greatest losses caused by the removal of the treasures to secret repositories at the end of the Second World War was the loss to science (see Korfmann, below, pages 207–11): for almost fifty years, these important objects were totally inaccessible to scholars. Indeed, the Trojan treasures were thought to have been destroyed, and that they are again available for study is cause for celebration. Russian archaeologists and conservators have begun to collaborate with their foreign colleagues in the study of the objects, and, in April 1996, the larger part of the Trojan treasures was placed on display in a major exhibition in the Pushkin State Museum of Fine Arts, Moscow (see Tolstikov, below, pages 212–13). The State Hermitage Museum, St. Petersburg, plans to exhibit a second group of Trojan finds in 1997. Old images of the artifacts, evocative as they may be (fig. 84), are no substitute for modern photographic reproductions, which have now been made widely available through the distribution of the fine catalogue of the Moscow exhibition (colorplates 19–21). It is our hope that this example of cooperation may serve to encourage those who hold other items of wartime plunder to release those works to the world community.

THE EXCAVATION OF

THE TROJAN TREASURES,

AND THEIR HISTORY

UP TO THE DEATH

OF SCHLIEMANN IN 1890

Donald Fyfe Easton

During his excavations at Troy, Heinrich Schliemann found twenty-one groups of metal objects, which he referred to as "treasures."[1] These groups together consist of over thirteen hundred items, some of which are themselves clusters of corroded bronzes, groups of gold beads, or pairs of earrings. If we count every single object, including every individual bead, the treasures contain well over ten thousand pieces. Some include objects of nonmetallic materials: faience, carnelian, and other semiprecious stones. The treasures are conventionally distinguished by the letters A to H and J to S. This nomenclature derives from the 1902 Berlin catalogue by Hubert Schmidt, but three of his nineteen groups (H, R, and S) need subdivision,[2] and not all of his attributions are correct. His catalogue, of course, lists only what was in Berlin and does not pretend to be a full account of the treasures as originally found.

Where were the treasures found, and what did they contain?
By modern standards, Schliemann's documentation is poor, so there is always some uncertainty. But it seems that the treasures come from several different periods. The earliest is probably Treasure R2, a gold ring and some gold beads.[3] This lay in a sloping stratum of destruction-debris outside the citadel wall of Late Troy I (fig. 85), a phase for which I have proposed a date of circa 2650 B.C. (Current views as to all these dates differ by up to four hundred years, and there are new discussions in the light of recent carbon-14 results.)[4] Lying at a slope in the same deposit was a human skeleton. Possibly the ring, beads, and skeleton all came from an earlier burial churned up when Troy I was leveled off after its destruction.

The stately architecture of Middle Troy II[5] included an enormous central building: Megaron IIA. From in and around this come four treasures: G, N, R1, and Q (fig. 86).[6] These are small collections of jewelry: gold, electrum, silver, and bronze. Whether these groups were found *in situ* in their original place of deposition or all lay in a destruction-deposit is unclear.

The American excavations of the 1930s produced evidence indicating that Middle Troy II was destroyed by fire,[7] a deduction confirmed by the new excavations under Professor Manfred Korfmann.[8] For this event I have suggested a date of circa 2350 B.C. Pits dug into the destruction-debris suggest that in many places the inhabitants tried to dig out their lost valuables. Perhaps they succeeded, for Late Troy II,[9] despite its meaner architecture and pottery, has yielded more metalwork than any other period. However, this was also a period when, as we know from crucibles, tuyeres, slag, ingots, and the many stone molds,[10] the inhabitants were themselves active metalworkers.

The final phase of Late Troy II, which (I have argued) may have ended about 2150 B.C., produced several groups of metalwork finds that seem to have been *in situ* when excavated (fig. 87). On the west side of the citadel, over the then-buried circuit wall of Middle Troy II and in among some buildings whose plans were never recorded, Treasure A (Priam's Treasure, so called) was deposited during Late Troy II in a stone cist or box set in the ground.[11]

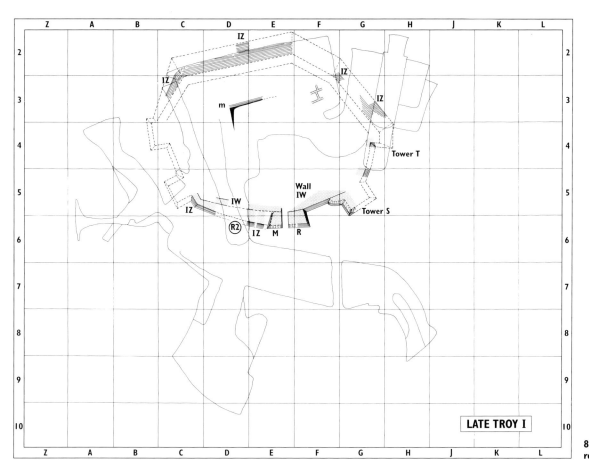

85. Find-spot of Treasure R2, recovered from Late Troy I

86. Find-spots of Treasures G, N, Q, and R1, probably recovered from Middle Troy II

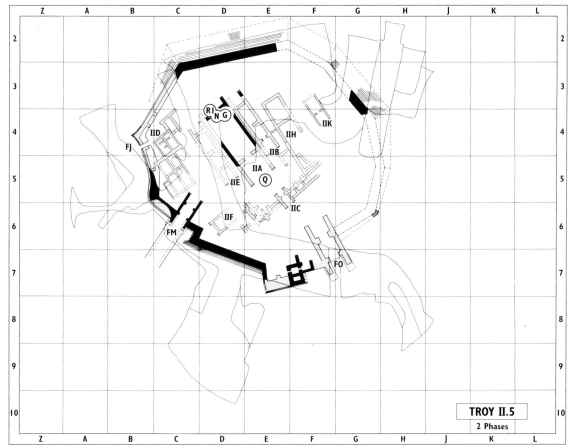

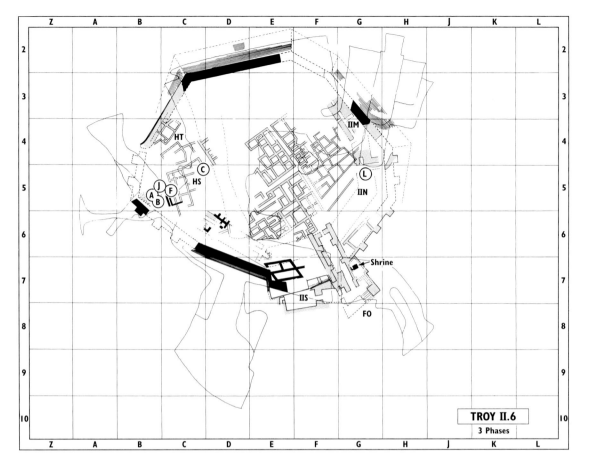

87. Find-spots of Treasures A, B, C, F, J, and L, probably *in situ* when recovered from Late Troy II

Treasure A was large and tightly packed. It contained nineteen vessels: three of gold, twelve of silver, one of electrum, and three of bronze. There were also six silver ingots, eight bronze spearheads, thirteen bronze daggers, fourteen bronze flat axes, three bronze chisels, one saw, one knife, and three other blades. In one of the silver jars was a hoard of gold jewelry including six bracelets, four torques, two headdresses, one headband, four basket earrings, fifty-six shell earrings, and 8,700 beads. In all, 183 objects plus, perhaps, one gigantic necklace using all the beads.[12]

Immediately beside it was Treasure B;[13] and thirteen meters further north, in the same stratigraphic position, was Treasure J: a collection mostly of gold jewelry.[14]

What were these collections? Despite the stone cist, I do not think that Treasure A was a burial. In a burial, the objects would usually be spread out on and around the corpse. It is more likely that the stone box functioned as a safe, and that the collection represents someone's wealth. Treasures B and J may have been buried in the same relative position for the same reason.

Treasure L had a similar position.[15] It was found buried below floor level, seemingly by means of a niche in a massive mudbrick wall. But this was a lapidary's hoard. There were four ceremonial stone axes—a damaged one of blue stone (possibly lapis lazuli), plus three green ones in mint condition (see colorplate 20). Perhaps the craftsman was making three

new axes from an older and damaged prototype.[16] There were also six rock-crystal pommels, forty-seven rock-crystal lenses, a clump of small gold tacks and other objects, and a piece of iron. Some beads of carnelian and amber are included in Schmidt's Berlin catalogue, but may not belong.[17]

Treasure F, says Schliemann, was found *on* the wall of House HS.[18] It included one bronze vessel, six bronze weapons and tools, a broken pot containing a quantity of gold jewelry, and, in the bronze jar, two gold bracelets and three gold ingots. The gold jewelry was "more or less embedded" in a white powder.

One wonders about this white powder. In two other cases (Treasures D and E), it was again found in jars containing gold jewelry.[19] Could they have been cremations? The idea is tempting, but I am not convinced. These groups are not otherwise distinctive,[20] and it sounds, rather, as though Treasure F had been deliberately set into a niche in the wall—a practice noticed in the new excavations.[21] It makes better sense as a hoard. The white powder may derive from wrapping material.

We know the approximate find-spot of Treasure C[22] but not its precise position because it was discovered and stolen by workmen in March 1873.[23] It may or may not have been found *in situ*.

Then we have a scatter of treasures, which, though dating to Late Troy II, seem to have been found in secondary positions in the destruction-deposit (fig. 88). Here I include Treasure M (an unilluminating object of faience);[24] Treasures

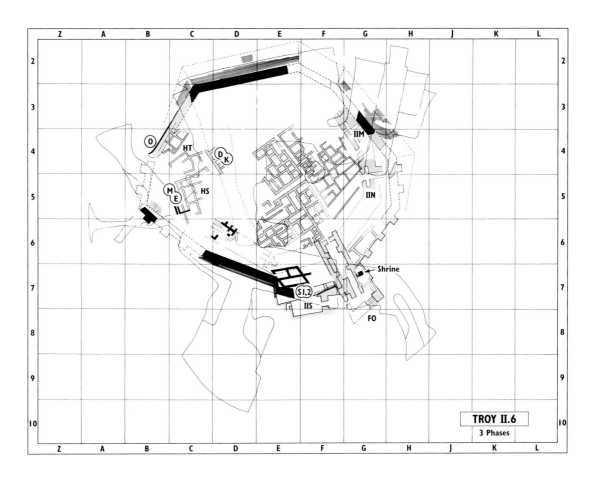

88. Find-spots of Treasures D, E, K, M, O, S1, and S2, probably in disturbed contexts when recovered from Late Troy II

D and K (gold jewelry in a fallen jar, and some loose bronzes—all from the same room);[25] Treasure E (more gold jewelry found in two fallen jars, with three bronze tools nearby);[26] and Treasure O (two gold pins in a deposit outside the circuit wall).[27] Typologically, one of these pins would fit better in Troy III but is not necessarily out of place in Late Troy II.[28] Lastly, there are Treasures S1 and S2: a dagger and fragments of two bronze kettles found in the same locality as fragments of two skeletons.[29] These may represent earlier burials disturbed at the end of Troy II by leveling.

The remaining Troy treasures consist only of some Early Bronze Age jewelry rescued from the wheelbarrow (Ha), and so of uncertain provenance; and three gold discs and six bronzes from Troy VI or VII (Treasures Hb, P) (fig. 89).[30] These are of Late Bronze Age date but of uncertain association.

What did Schliemann do with his treasures, and to what extent were his actions legal?

The subsequent movements of Schliemann's treasures and the legality of his actions vary considerably according to the year of excavation. And we must consider questions relating both to ownership and to export. I must emphasize that, on the legal side, all that follows is provisional and is largely based on Schliemann's own statements. A fully accurate picture requires study of the Ottoman archives and of the history of Turkish antiquities laws. It also requires the opinion of a properly

competent lawyer, which I am not. But it does seem that, during these years, we can observe the Turkish government acting increasingly strongly to retain its own antiquities, and changing the legal basis on which Schliemann was allowed to operate. We do not see Schliemann moving in quite the same direction. First, ownership.

From the excavations of 1872–73, we can disregard the stolen Treasure C. This was largely recovered by the Turkish police and was placed in the Imperial Museum in Constantinople (now the Archaeological Museum, Istanbul),[31] where it still remains.[32] We are concerned with Treasures N, P, R1, and R2 (from 1872) and A ("Priam's Treasure"), B, S1, and S2 (from 1873).

Schliemann's permit obliged him to share his finds with the state, which owned the western part of the site.[33] (The eastern part was owned by a British resident, Frank Calvert.)[34] But we know that in the case of Treasure A Schliemann avoided any division by smuggling the objects out of Turkey to his home in Athens.[35] The same may well apply to the other treasures excavated in 1872–73, because it is clear that very little went to Constantinople.

In 1874 the Turkish government sued Schliemann in the Greek courts for the return of half of his entire Troy collection, including these treasures.[36] The text of the final settlement is not preserved in Athens (though it may be in Istanbul). According to Schliemann, Turkey relinquished all rights to the collec-

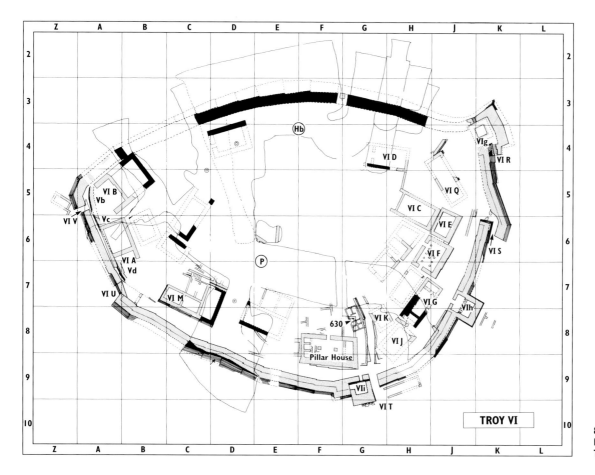

89. Find-spots of Treasures Hb and P, recovered from Troy VI or Troy VII

tion in exchange for an indemnity of £2,000.[37] If this is correct (and Schliemann is not always a reliable witness), then it all became Schliemann's property. It was this collection that went, via a three-year exhibition in London, to Berlin in 1881 as an outright gift to the German people.[38]

His new permit in 1878–79 again required division of the finds.[39] This affected Treasures D, E, F, G, M, and O (from 1878) and Ha, Hb, and J (from 1879). We know little of what went on. Divisions must have been made, because the Istanbul Archaeological Museum still has parts of Treasures D, F, J, and O.[40] Originally they had more, but there was a theft at some date before November 1881.[41] This may account for some of the more than 330 items that could not be located in 1902 and that are still missing.[42] The collection may also have been diminished by Schliemann himself, who bought back much of his collection in 1885.[43] So we cannot now assess how fairly the divisions were carried out. But in these years, at any rate, we see Schliemann acting in an apparently legal manner.

Some items from the 1878–79 treasures—parts of Treasure F, at least—had already been displayed in London[44] and went to Berlin in 1881, along with the earlier material. Parts of Treasures D and G, along with two earrings retained from Treasure A, went after Schliemann's death to the National Museum in Athens.[45] Most of the rest he bequeathed to the

Berlin Staatliche Museen (State Museums), where they went after his death, in 1890,[46] if not at some earlier date.[47]

The excavations of 1882 produced Treasures K and Q. Under the then law, two-thirds of the Trojan finds belonged to Turkey,[48] and Schliemann received a new permit.[49] A legitimate division did take place at the Dardanelles in July 1882, apparently a rather disorganized affair, from which twenty-two crates of objects went to Berlin.[50] But we also hear of a *secret* dispatch of twenty-one baskets made to Athens with the help of the Italian consul.[51] This was undoubtedly intended to circumvent the division. The dispatch certainly included Treasure Q,[52] and very possibly Treasure K. To these objects Schliemann did not have a good title. Selected items from both treasures went to Berlin in 1882,[53] and the rest followed later.

The excavations of 1890, again conducted under a new permit,[54] revealed Treasure L, the lapidary's hoard. This treasure is unique in having been found on the eastern half of the site and thus possibly on Frank Calvert's land.[55] Under a law introduced in 1884, there was now to be no division at all, and all finds were to go to the state.[56] Once again, Schliemann used the Italian consul to smuggle the treasure away to Athens,[57] where he kept it hidden lest disclosure provoke a new court case.[58] It is difficult to imagine that he had any good title to the objects. After his death in 1890 they went to Berlin.[59]

Now, questions of export. For export from Turkey, a ministerial decree of April 1872 apparently prohibited Schliemann from exporting *any* of his finds, even his own share.[60] But this decree seems to have become a dead letter. It was not invoked in the Greek court case,[61] and there is no indication that it affected matters in later seasons.

Export from Greece seems to have caused Schliemann more worries. It was forbidden to export Greek antiquities; so, in practice, export of the Trojan antiquities depended on having a customs declaration documenting their original import. It looks as though Schliemann was in the habit of being fraudulent in these declarations;[62] and he expected that Berlin would use the resulting documents after his death.[63] But though this performance with customs documents may all have been a practical necessity, I am not sure that it was a legal one. Greek official advice at one stage, indeed, was that it was not.[64] Some objects slipped through easily in any case. Parts of Treasures K and Q went in Schliemann's personal luggage when he traveled to Marienbad in August 1882.[65]

Conclusion

Thus, by the year after Schliemann's death, the story had begun as it was to continue—with a mess. There were (1) Troy treasures in Constantinople that had been recovered from thieves or claimed by the Imperial Museum in the divisions of 1878–79. There were (2) treasures in Athens that derived almost entirely from Schliemann's share of the same divisions of 1878–79. There was (3) the majority of the treasures in Berlin: the bulk of these derived from the material whose ownership Schliemann had apparently obtained by agreement with the Turks in 1875, together with some of the treasures shared out in 1878–79; but the collection in Berlin also included objects that had evaded a division in 1882 or that had been illegally taken out of Turkey in 1890. And (4) over 330 items had gone missing, at least some of them in a theft from the Imperial Museum at Constantinople.

The legal standing of these groups probably varied. But before that can be properly judged, we need more information from the Turkish archives and from Turkish legal history. What *did* the antiquities laws and decrees really require? What really *were* the terms of Schliemann's permits? And what really *was* agreed between Turkey and Schliemann at the conclusion of the court case in 1875?

THE TROJAN TREASURES

IN BERLIN.

THE DISAPPEARANCE

AND SEARCH FOR

THE OBJECTS

AFTER WORLD WAR II

Klaus Goldmann

In its April 1991 issue, *ARTnews* revealed the existence of secret art repositories in the former Soviet Union in an article written by Konstantin Akinsha and Grigorii Kozlov.[1] One such secret repository was found to contain Heinrich Schliemann's Trojan treasures, sought since the end of World War II by its owner, the Berlin Museum für Vor- und Frühgeschichte (Museum for Pre- and Early History), part of the former Prussian State Museums. Having been informed by friends in the United States of the forthcoming publication, the author of this chapter asked his Berlin friends Professor A. Jähne and G. Wermusch, who are both fluent in the Russian language, to fly to Moscow at the end of March 1991 to interview both authors of the above-mentioned article. With this visit to Moscow, the final chapter of a forty-year search had begun. This happened in a period when the reunification of Germany had just begun, and even the directors of the various former Prussian State Museums in East and West Berlin had no knowledge of the holdings of one another: the East Berlin museums were not allowed to share information with West Berlin museums regarding the art objects that the Soviets had returned to the former German Democratic Republic (GDR) in 1955, 1958–59, and later.

The history of Schliemann's Trojan collection in Berlin is summarized here. After the Trojan antiquities were acquired by Berlin's Museum für Vor- und Frühgeschichte in 1881[2] as "a gift to the German people, forever to be shown in the German capital," many photographs were taken of the objects. However, nearly all of the museum's photodocumentation was destroyed in February 1945, as the museum's repository at Lebus an der Oder was situated for many weeks on the German-Russian front.

Just days before the outbreak of World War II on September 1, 1939, the museum transferred all its treasures for safekeeping to the ground floor of the building. The fact that this was done so early indicates the close connections existing between all levels of government agencies and officials of the Prussian State Museums during that period.[3] On the ground floor of the Gropius Building, which served as the home, since 1921, of the Berlin Museum für Vor- und Frühgeschichte, all precious metal objects and pieces considered to be irreplaceable were hastily packed into three crates. Each crate had a full inventory list packed inside and was sealed. All three crates remained sealed throughout the war.[4]

On January 23, 1941, these crates along with most of the museum's other "irreplaceable" treasures were brought to the deep vault of the Prussian State Bank, as the museum's shallow ground floor provided poor security. Losses and damages by air raids were the greatest fear. This same year, construction of several anti-aircraft artillery towers (flak towers) was begun. The towers were large bunkers constructed of steel and concrete, which were used as air-raid shelters as well. The towers' walls could withstand every means of warfare available at that time—and they did. Two of these bunkers were planned from the very beginning to be used as repositories for Berlin's cultural treasures. Even an optimal

90. Aerial photograph of Berlin in 1945, showing the Zoo flak tower, with its four turrets, at center

Abschrift.

Der Reichsminister und Chef

der Reichskanzlei   Rk.1126 A.   Berlin W 8,den 6.März 1945.

Betrifft Kunst- und Kulturgüter der Preuss.Staatsverwaltung.

Auf das Schreiben vom 16.Februar 1945.

_____

.... Der Führer hat angeordnet, dass diese Sicherung nunmehr schleunigst vorgenommen werden soll.

Ich darf Sie bitten, die Sicherung der Kunstschätze u.s.w. in diesen Sinne schnellstens zu bewerkstelligen. Die nunmehr vorliegende bestimmte Anordnung des Führers verpflichtet alle für die Mitwirkung in Frage kommenden Dienststellen, die Angelegenheit mit allen zu Gebote stehenden Mitteln zum schleunigen Abschluss zu bringen. Sollten sich dabei wider Erwarten unüberwindbare Schwierigkeiten ergeben, so bitte ich um Verständigung, damit ich in geeigneter Weise eingreifen kann. Ueber Fortgang und Abschluss der Angelegenheit bitte ich, mich auf dem Laufenden zu halten.

....   gez.Dr. L a m m e r s

An den Reichsminister
für Wissenschaft, Erziehung
und Volksbildung,
Herrn R u s t .

                                         Beglaubigt

                                         Verwaltungsobersekretär.

91. "Führer Decree" of March 6, 1945, ordering evacuation to the west of the Prussian State Museums' holdings

air-conditioning system was installed. In September 1941, the Museum für Vor- und Frühgeschichte was assigned two rooms, with a total space of forty-eight square meters, at the Flakturm Zoo (Zoo flak tower). The Flakturm Zoo is here illustrated (fig. 90) as photographed by British air reconnaissance on March 23, 1945, with the anti-aircraft artillery clearly visible on the tower top.

Security was extremely tight. Not only military installations and operations but industrial and other economic data were classified as "top secret" (colorplate 15), including all matters relating to the safekeeping of German or foreign-owned art. Any breach of security could lead to imprisonment or even death.

Until the end of January 1945, the Berlin museum collections suffered only minor losses from the continual air raids. Many of the museum buildings were damaged, but none of the repositories in and around Berlin had been harmed.

On February 1, 1945, Dr. Karl Hermann and Robert Hiecke, two high-ranking officials of the Ministry of Science and Education who were responsible for the Prussian State Museums, held a meeting with all department directors of the State Museums. The officials ordered the immediate evacuation of all museum collections remaining in flak-tower bunkers and elsewhere in Berlin to an area west of the Elbe River. This area was chosen because it had been designated as part of the United States and British occupied zones in case of Germany's "unconditional surrender." Most of the department directors opposed this order. Everybody in Germany was aware of the constant danger from Allied air attacks on the highways, the railway network, and the waterways. Evacuation would imperil the most valuable objects of the Berlin collections. In view of this protest, the director general of the Prussian State Museums asked Hitler himself to make the decision, which was rendered on March 6, 1945.

A "Führer Decree" (fig. 91), the Third Reich's top executive order, advised the Prussian State Museums to start evacuation immediately, beginning with the highest ranked holdings. Official help was to be given in the event of any obstacles. From this moment on, the Berlin directors were required to obey unconditionally and they did, but with one notable exception, which will be discussed later. The bulk of the museum's most prized objects left the Berlin repositories between March 6 and April 7, 1945, headed for several salt mines, and were later surrendered to the United States Army. Most of this art was subsequently handed over by the United States combat forces into the custody of the Finance Division of the Supreme Headquarters, Allied Expeditionary Force (SHAEF), U.S. Group Control Council (Main). By order of the highest authority in Washington to General Dwight D. Eisenhower on April 10, 1945, all currency and artworks found in Germany were to be moved to a place of safekeeping in the proposed United States Zone. This order was classified not only "top secret" but "eyes only," which meant in this case that only four individuals should be informed: Supreme Commander (General Eisenhower), Chief of Staff (Lieutenant

General Walter B. Smith), General McSherry, and Mr. Murphy (Political Adviser) (fig. 92).

On April 4, 1945, the United States Third Army (Patton's army) took the Merkers mine, where they found not only the wealth of the Reichsbank—more than two hundred fifty tons of gold—but also a tremendous number of artworks from the Prussian State Museums' collections, including several crates from Berlin's Museum für Vor- und Frühgeschichte.

To turn now to another most important repository, the salt mine at Grasleben was taken by the United States Ninth Army on April 12, 1945. This repository held several thousand crates, which also contained parts of the Prussian State Museums' collections. They included large parts of the ethnographic holdings, archives, and museum collections from other parts of Germany, as well as Polish treasures. Some days before the mine was occupied by Allied forces, two convoys of trucks with trailers arrived at Grasleben. Their payload was the crated artworks of the Prussian State Museums that had previously been sheltered in the flak towers—treasures of the highest value. Included were some fifty crates belonging to the Museum für Vor- und Frühgeschichte, the true owner of the Schliemann collection!

Until the end of May 1945, the Grasleben mine was completely "off limits," even for high-ranking United States Army officers. It had a special code name: "Conquer." Only Lamont Moore and Sheldon Keck, both Monuments, Fine Arts, and Archives (MFA&A) officers, were ordered to visit Grasleben early in May to remove some materials to the Reichsbank building in Frankfurt am Main, which was then the United States central repository for confiscated currency and artworks. They escorted a convoy of special holdings belonging to the Prussian State Museums Sculpture Gallery and the former Kaiser-Friedrich-Museum in Poznań, as well as Polish church treasures. All this was taken from what later became part of the British Zone and which, by former agreement between the Allies, should have remained in that zone. In September 1945, the British found important holdings of the Berlin Nationalgalerie in the mine (see fig. 9). In April 1987, Lamont Moore told the author in a telephone interview that he surely had not seen these paintings there; if he had, he would have secured them. Had he been in another part of this mysterious mine, or had the paintings been at another place outside the mine at that time? These are the kinds of difficult questions that I faced in my effort to track the missing crates of Berlin's Museum für Vor- und Frühgeschichte.

For decades, the search for the Schliemann treasures has been an excruciating task. No detailed evacuation lists of the museum's holdings could be found after the war—although they had existed! The Zoo flak tower was handed over to the Red Army on May 1, 1945. No looting of this repository by German or Russian soldiers was ever reported. Professor W. Unverzagt, the late director of Berlin's Museum für Vor- und Frühgeschichte, claimed he had handed over the three crates containing the Schliemann collection to a high-ranking Russian commission. But why had he done so? This was against

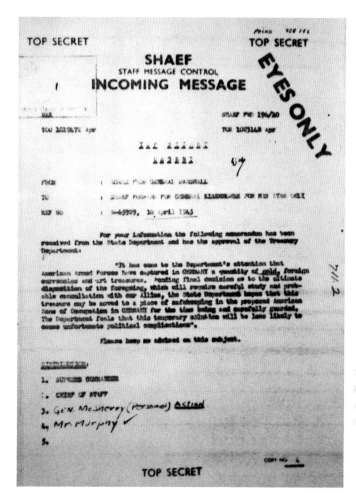

92. Memorandum of April 10, 1945, forwarding a proposal from the U.S. State Department to General Dwight D. Eisenhower to evacuate the holdings of German repositories to the proposed American Zone of Occupation

Hitler's strict order, violation of which brought risk of death. What parts of the museum's collection had been removed to the Grasleben salt mine in April 1945? He insisted it had been some fifty crates, but in the return of property from Grasleben to West Berlin in 1956 (via British Collecting Point Celle), only thirty of these crates were accounted for! Where are the contents of the missing twenty crates today?

Parts of the Berlin museums' holdings, captured by United States troops at Merkers and Grasleben, had been brought to the Reichsbank at Frankfurt am Main. As late as June 22, 1945, this material (or a part of it?) was released to the custody of the MFA&A Reparations, Deliveries and Restitutions Division by Captain Dunn of the United States Group's Finance Division. There is evidence of important inconsistencies between the lists of what had been confiscated at Merkers in April 1945 and of what was transferred to the MFA&A on June 22, 1945. Could the Schliemann treasures have disappeared between the two dates?

There is also, of course, a high-level political aspect to the story of the disappearance of the Schliemann collection in 1945. At the Potsdam Conference of July–August 1945,

Joseph Stalin submitted a document to President Harry Truman and Prime Minister Clement Attlee in which he demanded the return of all property that he believed should be classified as Russian war booty. The list covered most shipments to the west by United States troops before Russian accession of its assigned occupation zone. Among other objects, the treasures of Merkers were mentioned, together with crates of the records of the Königsberg Canal Board (Office of East Prussian Waterways) that were stored with the Berlin museums' crates and which U.S. troops had confiscated in the Merkers mine. German documents prove that all these had been removed from the mine on April 17, 1945, but even Truman was told by his advisers that no one knew anything about the existence of these materials (fig. 93). Could the Schliemann treasures have been in this group of crates that had disappeared?

Early in 1991, there was an offer to sell some tiny gold tassels of apparent Trojan origin to the Staatliche Museen, Berlin. The holder of the tassels, who remains anonymous to this very day, told the intermediary that he had bought these golden tassels on the Berlin black market in autumn 1945. Could this prove the story that the Berlin museum's holdings were looted from the flak tower? Subsequently the museum acquired the tassels. They were clearly ancient, possibly of Trojan origin, but definitely not part of the former holdings of the Schliemann collection in the Museum für Vor- und Frühgeschichte.

In April 1991, *ARTnews* published the above-mentioned article on secret art repositories in the former Soviet Union. Subsequent contacts with Konstantin Akinsha and Grigorii Kozlov and later findings of World War II documents on this topic revealed that the Trojan treasures really had gone to Russia in June 1945. They were inventoried by the staff of the Pushkin State Museum of Fine Arts, Moscow, in July 1945,

using the original lists of the Berlin museum, which had been crated with the collection in 1939. The Pushkin's inventories are cosigned by Irina Antonova, then a young member of the Pushkin staff, but not a member of the Soviet Trophy Organization, as has been frequently but wrongly asserted. The last available documents date from 1958.

During that year some 1.5 million works of art that had been confiscated from the Soviet-occupied zone of Germany were returned to East Berlin, capital of the German Democratic Republic (GDR). The Soviet government and the government of the GDR said all (!) of the confiscated art had been returned to the GDR with this operation. At this time the Museum für Vor- und Frühgeschichte had no counterpart in East Berlin; hence the holdings returned from the USSR remained without an official home between 1958 and 1963. In the same period the GDR Secret Police (Stasi) arranged an operation with the code name "Light." Archives and artworks believed to be heirless (formerly owned by Jewish or German noble families but as yet unclaimed) should be brought to "light" to be sold on the international art market by a "special plan which was to be coordinated with the Ministry of Finance." Was it not conceivable that some of the treasures could have been marketed for "hard currency" so badly needed by the GDR government?

All these conjectures were open for discussion up until October 24, 1994. On that day, at 3:05 P.M. Moscow time, members of the staff of Berlin's Museum für Vor- und Frühgeschichte were permitted for the first time to inspect all the Schliemann treasures (colorplate 16), but these represented only about 20 percent of the contents that had been packed in the three crates in 1939. There is every hope in Berlin that in time the rest of the contents of the three crates, of such great value for the study of early European history, will be shown soon and returned to its original home.

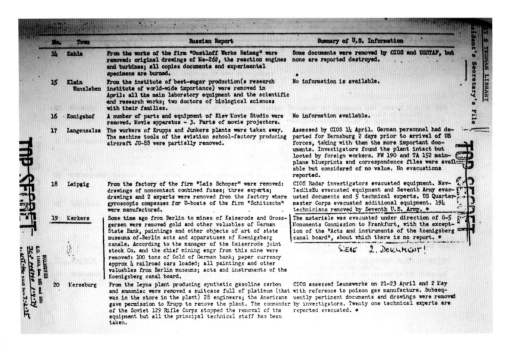

93. Document from the file of President Harry Truman's secretary relating to the transfer of valuables and documents by the United States Army, including records of the Königsberg Canal Board

CLAIMS TO OWNERSHIP

OF THE TROJAN TREASURES

Stephen K. Urice

Competing claims to ownership of cultural property present some of the most difficult, intractable issues in international law. In recent years, a large body of law—multilateral and bilateral treaties,[1] national and local laws, and court opinions—has addressed the interrelated issues of stolen or illegally exported cultural property. Thus, by now, the *legal* principles concerning cultural property either stolen or removed from the borders of a nation contrary to that country's export laws are fairly well understood by a reasonable number of legislators, lawyers, archaeologists, museum curators, dealers, collectors, and others directly affected by the issues. Popular interest in these matters is widespread and, at least in the United States, recent cases have attracted substantial media attention.[2]

The symposium documented here is evidence of an increasing interest in a subset of these cases, those involving cultural property displaced during time of war. Although several such matters have reached American courts (including three celebrated New York cases),[3] the discussions that took place at the symposium make clear that a great deal of thinking not merely about the legal but also about the ethical, political, and moral issues implicated by these cases lies ahead. I wish to express my appreciation to the organizers for providing the forum in which these issues could be discussed in a spirit of mutual respect.

The organizers asked me to summarize the claims of three nations for the treasures removed by Heinrich Schliemann from the site of Troy. I was not asked to present my own work or independent thinking on the topic; rather, the organizers requested that I serve as a neutral, objective observer, summarizing position papers that representatives of Turkey, Germany, and the Russian Federation prepared and submitted. This paper, then, is not intended to weigh the relative strengths or weaknesses of a nation's position. Nor is it intended to serve as an adjudication of the merits of competing claims. Instead, the purpose of this paper is to heighten awareness of the complex claims that each of these nations believes it has over the treasures, thereby engendering a better understanding of the situation from multiple points of view.[4]

I shall first discuss Turkey's position, for Turkey is where Schliemann excavated the objects; then Germany's, where Schliemann placed them; and finally the Russian Federation's, for that is where most of the treasures are located today.[5] The relative balance of legal or nonlegal arguments in any one nation's position results from the materials submitted to me and not from my editorial efforts.

TURKEY

The Turkish position—set out in a two-page statement dated January 12, 1995—focuses on archaeological, scientific, and historical concerns rather than on legal arguments. According to Turkey, those concerns dictate a *reunification* of all of the antiquities removed by Schliemann, which are now in the possession of some forty different collections throughout the

world, and a *return* of those antiquities to the site from which they were excavated. Turkey asserts that current archaeological activity at the site will benefit from the presence of the returned objects. Moreover, historical understanding of the antiquities and of the site will be promoted if the objects are in close proximity to the ongoing archaeological fieldwork.

Turkey notes the difference between nineteenth-century archaeological practice, which emphasized the individual object, and current practice, which takes a broader view in its efforts to reconstruct all aspects of an ancient civilization. That shift in practice and the interest in promoting historical and scientific values provide substantive reasons for the reunification and return of the Schliemann antiquities, including the Trojan treasures.

GERMANY

The German position was outlined in an eleven-page document dated September 1994 entitled "Agreements between Germany and Russia on the Return of Cultural Property Transferred from Their Countries in Time or as a Consequence of War: The Legal Situation from the German Point of View" (see pages 181–85) and in a two-page statement entitled " 'Priam's Treasure'—the German View," which I received on January 4, 1995. Germany's materials address possible claims not only of the Russian Federation but also of Turkey.

The German position asserts that Heinrich Schliemann made a gift of the treasures to the German people in 1880–81 and that Germany publicly displayed the objects, never concealing their presence in Berlin, from 1881 until 1939, when they were "moved to safe premises in Berlin to protect [them] from the effects of the war." Germany states that in June 1945, the Soviet occupying power removed the treasures from Berlin to Moscow, where they are now in the Pushkin State Museum of Fine Arts.* Germany takes the position that the collection remains German property under international law and cites several multilateral and bilateral agreements, specifically:

1. relevant articles of the Convention Respecting the Laws and Customs of War on Land (the Hague Convention of 1907, see Appendix 3);
2. the 1990 Treaty on Good-Neighborliness, Partnership and Cooperation—a bilateral agreement between Germany and the Soviet Union (see Appendix 14). Article 16 of that treaty provides in relevant part that "[The parties] agree that lost or unlawfully transferred art treasures which are located in their territory will be returned to their owners or their successors;"
3. the German-Russian Agreement on Cultural Cooperation of 1992 (see Appendix 15). Article 15 of that agreement states in pertinent part that "The contracting parties agree that lost or unlawfully transferred cultural property which is located in their sovereign territory will be returned to its owners or their successors."

---

* Editor's note: It has also been acknowledged that certain items from the Troy treasures are in the State Hermitage Museum, St. Petersburg.

The German position asserts that the treasures are cultural property within the meaning of the two bilateral agreements; that the collection is lost or, alternatively, is unlawfully transferred cultural property; and that accordingly the objects must be returned. The German position makes it clear that there are differences in interpretation and application of the treaty language to the case at hand. Germany's materials state that Germany would be willing to put the legal issues before the International Court of Justice or an arbitration tribunal.

Germany asserts that Turkey could not substantiate a legal claim based on removal of the objects in violation of Turkish law. Further, Germany holds the position that by Turkey's actions in settling a court case in Athens in 1874–75—in which Schliemann paid the Turkish government 50,000 francs, in exchange for which Turkey renounced all claims to the exported finds—Turkey is now foreclosed to assert legal title to the treasures. Germany asserts further that Turkey's subsequent actions in granting additional permits to Schliemann after that case was settled indicates Turkey's tacit understanding that its claims against Schliemann and the treasures were settled. Finally, Germany notes that Turkey never asserted a claim to the treasures when Schliemann took the objects to Berlin in the nineteenth century or at any other time in the intervening years when they were in Germany, suggesting that a Turkish claim would be time-barred by applicable statutes of limitations.

RUSSIAN FEDERATION

The Russian Federation's position is set forth in a two-page letter dated January 11, 1995, which outlines the Russian position without setting forth specific legal claims. In that letter, it is emphasized that the case of the Trojan treasures "is just one element in the total complex of Russian and German mutual claims to cultural treasures moved during the [Second World War] and in its aftermath from the territories of both countries." The Russian position notes that the Trojan treasures and other properties are currently the subject of negotiations between Germany and the Russian Federation and that it is the mutual desire of the parties that the "content, direction, and argumentation of these negotiations remain confidential."

The Russian Federation puts particular emphasis on seeing the treasures in the broad context of all cultural property moved as a result of the war. Thus, the Russian position holds that the legal context must reflect the current bilateral discussions between Russia and Germany and the ongoing efforts of domestic Russian legal developments.

As to the nonlegal aspects, the Russian Federation indicates that there is widespread popular opinion in Russia that all of the relocated cultural treasures currently in that country—including the Trojan treasures—belong to Russia as the victors in World War II. As the statement puts it, "This belief is rooted in the emotional perception of the past war, which brought innumerable sufferings to millions of people." On the other hand, the Russian position accepts that the resolution of the situation should "benefit the world culture as a whole." In this regard, even while the negotiations are proceeding and despite the controversies, the Pushkin State Museum of Fine Arts is actively working to prepare a public exhibition of the Trojan collection it now holds (see Tolstikov, below, pages 212–13).*

I want to thank again the representatives from Turkey, Germany, and the Russian Federation for having supplied me with materials with which to summarize their perspectives on this case. Before I close, allow me this brief personal observation.

The Preamble to the Convention for the Protection of Cultural Property in the Event of Armed Conflict (the Hague Convention of 1954: see Appendix 10), to which Turkey, Germany, and Russia are all parties,[6] states that "cultural property belonging to any people whatsoever" is "the cultural heritage of all mankind." As we see from the differing views of Turkey, Germany, and the Russian Federation, and as we see in the ongoing disputes over other displaced cultural treasures, giving meaning to this broad, international perspective of cultural property is a difficult task, fraught with legal, ethical, moral, and political considerations. Although attorneys tend to view these controversies from exclusively legal perspectives, it is important for the rest of us (and even for attorneys) to be aware of and sensitive to the nonlegal issues. Of course, a reasoned legal analysis is essential. However, in view of the realities of international law—in which insurmountable issues of jurisdiction and enforcement are often present—it is naive to think that the law alone can effect satisfactory resolutions, giving each party a sense that justice has prevailed (see Kaye, above, pages 100–105). Thus, as a practical reality and, perhaps, even as an ideal, we must also consider the ethical and political considerations affecting competing claims for cultural properties. As one acute observer recently put it, "The law is not designed to make us honorable, only bearable."[7] While a world without the rule of law is unthinkable, legal codes alone cannot assure that the cultural property of any one nation will remain truly the cultural property of us all.

---

*   Editor's note: The exhibition opened on April 16, 1996.

THE VALUE OF THE FINDS

TO THE

SCIENTIFIC COMMUNITY

Manfred Korfmann

This contribution and, especially, many of the remarks relating to the "treasures" excavated by Heinrich Schliemann at Troia (Troy) are based mainly on (1) the results of the modern excavations at Troia; (2) the publications of the Troia treasures, especially those of Schliemann, Götze, and Schmidt;[1] and (3) close inspection of the objects by the author, which was made possible by kind invitation of the directors of the Pushkin State Museum of Fine Arts in Moscow (October 1994) and the State Hermitage Museum in St. Petersburg (November 1994).[2] Such "inspection" produces many impressions and hypotheses. But one statement must be made at the outset as a result of these visits: the ugly imputation that the scholar Heinrich Schliemann may have falsified the "Treasure of Priam," or put it together from different sources, or even bought portions of it, is as completely nonsensical as the suspicion that Schliemann hired a modern jeweler to produce the treasures.

THE DATING OF SCHLIEMANN'S "CITY OF PRIAM" (THE BURNED CITY, OR TROIA II)

Schliemann's dating of the treasures of Troia was off by something like 1,200 years: there was no connection whatsoever with Homer's Troia, the Trojan War, or Priam.[3] The residential remains of Troia II—and the treasures—are clearly much older than supposed by many. The last phase of the Burned City seems to end, according to our dating supported by archaeological arguments, sometime in the twenty-fifth or in the very beginning of the twenty-fourth century B.C. that is, in the middle of the Early Bronze Age of the eastern Mediterranean (fig. 94).

THE POTENTIAL OF THE TROIA II FINDS FOR CULTURAL AND SCIENTIFIC STUDIES

The entire citadel with its palaces and fortifications—including bastions—was strongly status-oriented and suggestive of a residential complex that most probably also had a cultic function (see colorplate 13). The Troia II citadel complex gives evidence of the rise of a highly advanced civilization at the very border between Asia and Europe. But cultural progress can also be detected in other types of finds from the site, for example, the ample use of bronze (an alloy of copper and tin) and the quickly rotating potter's wheel, found here at Troia for the first time in the Aegean cultural sphere.[4] The use of bronze led to military strength. The use of the potter's wheel most probably played a role in the organization of society within the settlement and undoubtedly had an impact on trade and trade objects—and, of course, created a completely new sense of appropriate pottery shapes.

The very existence of the treasures shows in itself the high level of culture of the Troia II civilization. One must acknowledge, and one should also admire, the technological and technical skill of the metalworkers and especially the goldsmiths of the time—about 4,500 years

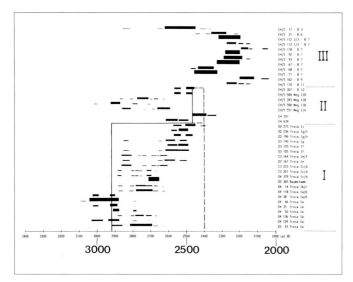

94. Calibrated carbon-14 dates for samples from Troy I–III. The horizontal bars indicate the probable dates (in years B.C.) of the samples listed at the right, from bottom to top.

INTERPRETATION OF THE FUNCTION OF THE TREASURES

The treasures from Troia are today in different places—but they must be studied as one scientific unit. One should not just consider the finds from the treasures housed in Moscow and—as we now know—in St. Petersburg. To my knowledge, at present objects from the Troia treasures are in at least six other museums in four different countries. In any scientific investigation, all these objects must be treated together—along with all the other finds from Troia, and of course together with the monuments of Troia itself. Therefore, in the following discussion I do not differentiate, for example, between finds from Çanakkale or Istanbul in Turkey or those from Moscow or St. Petersburg in Russia.

On the basis of past and present excavation results, we can presume that there is no single interpretation suitable for all the treasure finds. It is possible that the collection includes items from cultic inventories, funerary gifts, and actual treasure hoards. First, the splendid houses of Troia II should be considered (see colorplate 13). These were certainly used as residences and were evidence of high status, signifying power, wealth, and prominence in the religious hierarchy. With regard to the treasure finds, the objects mainly bring to mind cultic equipment, objects of adornment for cult figurines, or—as Machteld Mellink suggested during our visit in November 1994 to St. Petersburg—"temple treasures" in general. This hypothesis is supported by the extraordinary size of some objects, especially the bronze objects, which precludes "normal" everyday usage. The end of a handle of a bronze pan[13]—now in St. Petersburg—and the pan itself[14]—now in Moscow[15]—are of enormous size.

ago. There are some special items and aspects of the treasures worth mentioning.

Iron appeared at Troia long before it came into general use. Among the different metal types and their alloys present in the Troia II finds, the iron found in Treasure L is of extreme interest.[5] According to Ernst Pernicka, it is quite safe to assume that the iron found in that treasure is not meteoric, indicating a high level of competence in the extraction and working of metals.[6] It is significant that iron, meteoric as well as smelted, also appears at this early date at Alaca Höyük in northern Anatolia as well as in Mesopotamia and Egypt.[7] Its appearance with gold or generally "in contexts that indicate some special, precious, or ritual status for the iron within them"[8] gives evidence of the importance of iron in the third millennium B.C. It was not until more than 1,500 years later that iron became a common commodity and as such came to dominate the ancient world.

Among the many other remarkable items of the treasures, an extraordinarily large double magnifying lens of rock crystal is of particular importance (fig. 95, at top).[9] There is no doubt that the use of such a lens, and possibly also the many smaller ones in the collection,[10] was intentional even in the third millennium B.C., and it is likely that lenses like this were used for extremely delicate goldsmith's work or for carving seals. Thus, this piece may be the oldest magnifying lens in existence.[11]

Also noteworthy among the finds are gold, rodlike ingots, which are marked with notches (see colorplate 19).[12] The nearly identical weights of the five Moscow rods (about 10 grams) and their regular subdivisions raise the question of whether they conform to one of the weight systems known from Mesopotamia, Syria, or Egypt. Further study of these rods may provide important, detailed information about the weights-and-measures systems used at Troia and in international trade during the third millennium B.C.

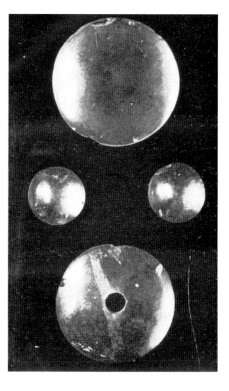

95. Rock-crystal lenses, probably from Treasure L, Troia

Also thought to have served a cultic function are the four stone axes from Treasure L (see colorplate 20).[16] They are of excellent craftsmanship and were obviously made in imitation of metal axes—but were surely much more precious than those, even those of gold. Doubtless they are scepters, symbols of power and dignity, made of archaic materials, perhaps to stress the antiquity of the tradition and its value as such.

The extremely thin gold sheet used in ear ornaments (colorplate 17, and see fig. 84) and diadems suggest that much of this jewelry may have been made especially for funerary purposes. Some of the objects, although not all of them, show signs of burning. This is normally explained by the catastrophic destruction of the settlement of Troia II by fire. Apart from this, the results of recent excavation allow the possibility of cremation burials. In 1993, for the first time, Early Bronze Age cremation burials were identified at Troia, although belonging to a later period, that of Troia V (or IV?).[17] Some of the treasures might therefore be attributable to tombs of special persons cremated and buried within the citadel. In order to clarify such a hypothesis, samples of soil in which the objects were found should be analyzed; this will be possible, because some of the finds bear traces of this soil still attached. This is true of objects in Istanbul, Moscow, and St. Petersburg. In addition, metal analyses of these objects should be carried out on a larger scale—an international project including all kinds of analyses should be considered for the immediate future.

Finally, it seems certain that there is some actual hidden treasure among the objects in the Troia treasures. This can be deduced from the circumstances of the finds. Some pieces bear signs of considerable use or, in some cases, are even broken and no longer usable (fig. 96). This indicates that it was their pure value in gold that was most important. In other cases, pieces were bent in such a way that they could have been fitted into containers, such as pottery vessels. To sum up: no single interpretation alone can be used to explain the existence of the many treasures from Troia II.

TRADE AND THE TROIA TREASURES

Comparable find-complexes of roughly the same period are known from Maikop,[18] north of the Black Sea at the foot of the Caucasus Mountains; from Alaca Höyük,[19] Horoztepe,[20] and Eskiyapar[21] in northern Turkey, to the south of the Black Sea; from the settlement of Poliochni[22] on the island of Lemnos, just west of Troia in the north Aegean; and even in far-distant Ur,[23] in Iraq. Regarding specific kinds of items, forms of objects, and even materials, a relation between all these sites can be posited. Here again, further metal analyses of the Troia objects would be of great importance, especially analysis for lead isotopes. This kind of research should help to determine the origin of the raw materials used, the extent of long-distance trade in metals and other products, and evidence for migrant metalworkers in the third millennium B.C.

Of great significance is the hypothesis that central Asia played an important part—if not the leading role—in providing

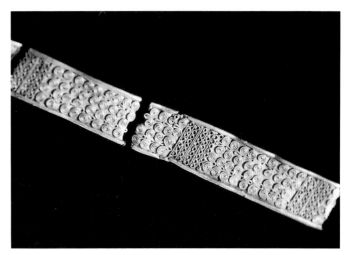

96. Gold bracelet fragments from Treasure F, Troia. Archaeological Museum, Istanbul

tin for all these sites.[24] There are few known sources of tin within Eurasia. But tin was a valuable commodity, as it is a necessary component of bronze, an alloy of roughly one part tin and nine parts copper. Whoever controlled the metal-trade routes and related commerce at the beginning of the Bronze Age was also obviously in a good position to manufacture metal objects—for example, bronze weapons—thereby ensuring their commercial and military advantage. The Trojans would have been well situated, geographically, to control and hold this market in the metals trade, especially as Troia is directly en route between Asia and the Aegean; and indeed, Troia II is one of the earliest known sites in the world where bronze appears—and, if bronze was manufactured at Troia, one of the earliest where tin was used.

Indeed, there is evidence that some of the raw materials represented among the objects in the treasures came to Troia through extensive trade over long distances. A look at the finds in Moscow at the end of October 1994 made it clear that one of the four large stone axes from Treasure L (found by Schliemann only in 1890, the last year of his life) was cut from the dark blue stone lapis lazuli (see colorplate 20, at bottom). Until then, the material from which the ax was made had not been identified with certainty.[25] The lapis lazuli of the Old World is supposed to have come only from northern Afghanistan, and it is only found there in the neighborhood of tin deposits. This supports my hypothesis that north Anatolia, Troia, and the Aegean obtained not only lapis lazuli from Afghanistan, but also very likely the important metal tin. The existence of a trade route over the Turkmenian steppe and across the Black Sea is a clear possibility.[26]

Some amber beads—which cannot be assigned to the treasures with certainty[27]—may give evidence for trade contacts with the somewhat nearer region of the Baltic Sea. In addition, beads of red carnelian are represented in the treasures.[28] Possibilities for the origin of this carnelian are not only India or Georgia, but—as I have learned at the New York symposium from my colleague Dr. Vladimir Tolstikov—the Crimean

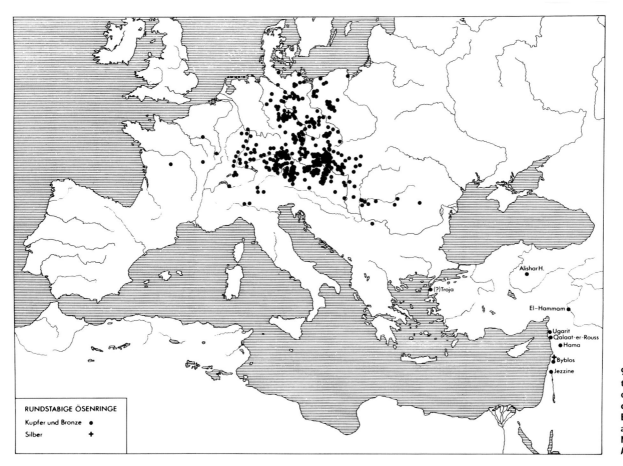

RUNDSTABIGE ÖSENRINGE

Kupfer und Bronze ●

Silber ✛

97. Map showing the distribution of torques (neck circlets) in central Europe, Anatolia, and the eastern Mediterranean. After Gerloff

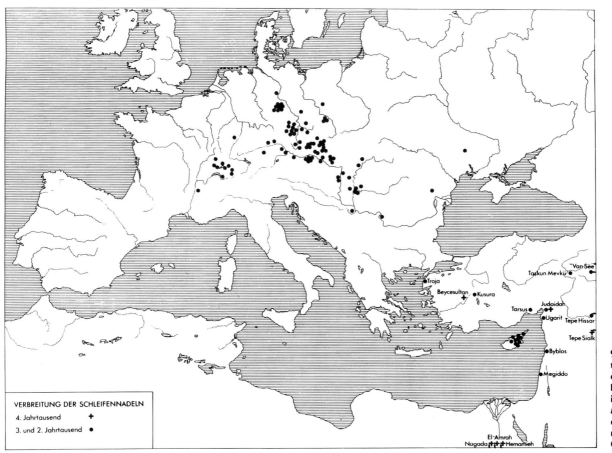

VERBREITUNG DER SCHLEIFENNADELN

4. Jahrtausend ✛

3. und 2. Jahrtausend ●

98. Map showing the distribution of "Cypriote" loop-headed pins in central Europe, Anatolia, and the eastern Mediterranean. After Gerloff

peninsula situated to the north of the Black Sea. Treasure finds of this kind indicate that due to Troia's key geographic position, its upper class contributed to—and played an important role in—"world trade," not only during the Mycenaean period but also a thousand years before that time.

THE TROIA TREASURES AND THEIR IMPORTANCE FOR DATING IN THE BRONZE AGE

Not long ago, the beginning of the European Bronze Age was dated somewhere in the eighteenth or the seventeenth century B.C. Recently, evidence from Troia has supported the theories of those who suggested a much earlier date for the beginning of the Bronze Age in Europe. I was surprised that the objects from the treasures in Moscow included quite a number of neck circlets of a special kind, so-called torques. Schliemann had called these objects bracelets,[29] but in fact they are not bracelets. The torques had been bent in order that they could be fit into pots or boxes. Their original form can be reconstructed based on a similar example from the hoard from Eskiyapar in northern Anatolia.[30] The Eskiyapar torque is gold, as are most of the Troia pieces. Thus, Troia constitutes an important link between many other sites where such early neck circlets are known, for example, Ugarit (Ras Shamra) in Syria, or, in distant central Europe, sites of the Alsace region (fig. 97). In Troia, this fashion is now well datable and, as we can see, very old.

Similarly, a precious-metal find from the new excavations at Troia recently contributed to the discussion of the chronology of European prehistory: the object is an ornamental pin made of electrum with a very characteristic top in the shape of a loop (colorplate 18). Here, too, the question of the beginning of the European Early Bronze Age is raised, because this type of pin marks the start of this period in central Europe and has a wide distribution (fig. 98).[31] The pin was found on the floor of the biggest palace or cult building of Troia II,[32] and, according to the radiocarbon analysis of the surrounding area, it must be dated to about 2450 B.C. or somewhat later. Thus, the conventional dating of the beginning of the Early Bronze Age in Europe can be pushed back by more than half a millennium. There are other arguments as well (deriving from carbon-14 and dendrochronological analysis) that lead to the same conclusion: the Bronze Age of southeastern and central Europe starts about 2300 B.C. Finds like the pin and the torques from Troia argue for the consideration—or conclusion—that the impetus for the European Bronze Age came from the southeast, beginning in or passing through Anatolia.

FINAL REMARKS

I wish to conclude with a reference to the very familiar photographs of the famous Treasure A, parts of which are now housed in Berlin, Moscow, and St. Petersburg.[33] With regard to the Moscow and St. Petersburg exhibition plans, it is to be anticipated that the great expectations created by Schliemann himself, then afterward inflated by the mass media, will only bring disappointment when the objects are exposed to unbiased inspection. In my opinion, this will be felt by most people outside the field of archaeology. From the time of the discovery of the objects up to the present, too many mistaken and falsified claims have been associated with the Schliemann finds. Whoever has seen the fabulous archaeological treasures of pharaonic Egypt, Mesopotamia or Mycenae, Latin and South America, or even crown jewels of today will be forced to admit that the Troia treasures are only modestly impressive. For several years, parts of the Troia treasures have been on view in the Istanbul Archaeological Museum; to my knowledge, their exhibition has caused no great general excitement. The reputation of the Schliemann treasures nowadays obviously rests more on emotional, political, and juridical issues.

But for the scientific world, one point is clear: the treasures—all of them—are of extreme importance, especially in the context of the other finds from Troia. Scientists should now work together on an international scale. All who have studied the Troia treasures would agree that the previous publications are completely insufficient, and this is why so many questions about the material persist! For example, many of the objects have been neither drawn nor photographed. Cooperation in the evaluation, analysis, and publication of the finds is absolutely necessary. At the same time, the legal aspects of the problem should be clarified with mutual respect for the various positions. However, my conviction is that scientific interests and political and juridical ones should be kept strictly separate. Troia and its former inhabitants and their cultural legacy should be given their due priority and respect.

SOME ASPECTS OF THE PREPARATION OF THE CATALOGUE FOR THE EXHIBITION "THE TREASURE OF TROY: HEINRICH SCHLIEMANN'S EXCAVATIONS" AT THE PUSHKIN STATE MUSEUM OF FINE ARTS, MOSCOW

Vladimir Tolstikov

In January 1993, after an official decision was made by the minister of culture of the Russian Federation regarding the exhibition at the Pushkin State Museum of Fine Arts of the Heinrich Schliemann collection from the Troy excavations, I received this collection and was entrusted with its preservation and processing. Processing the collection took over three months, as the task required scrupulous care in studying the state of preservation of these unique objects, verifying and clarifying existing documentation, and compiling new documentation. This work was hampered by the total lack of photographic documentation in the museum for this collection: during the entire period of their preservation in Moscow not a single one of the objects had ever been photographed, and the old photographs, published by Schliemann in the *Atlas* of 1874, as well as the drawings of several objects in the well-known Schmidt catalogue, were not up to modern standards.[1]

Thus, the most important and urgent task facing us was to photograph the Schliemann collection. In May and June 1994, I photographed all of the two hundred sixty inventoried items in the collection. Moreover, each piece was photographed from two or three angles, and detail photographs and shots of individual elements were also taken of the most important objects (colorplates 19 and 20).

At the same time, the staff of my department and my colleagues Dr. Liudmila Akimova and Dr. Mikhail Treister began compiling catalogue cards for each object. These scholars were working on the preparation of the catalogue for the exhibition "The Treasure of Troy: Heinrich Schliemann's Excavations," scheduled to open in April 1996.* The objects are arranged in the catalogue and will be displayed at the exhibition in groups of "treasures," in accordance with the system introduced by Schliemann himself and used in the Schmidt catalogue (colorplate 21). During the process of work on the exhibition catalogue, our group took measurements and weights of the objects, which, incidentally, have already revealed a great number of significant differences from the data cited in the Schmidt catalogue. At the same time, I should like to emphasize that the director of the museum, Mrs. Irina Antonova, the chief curator Tatiana Potapova, and our group decided not to conduct any kind of research or analyses that could cause even minimal damage to the surfaces of the objects of this unique collection. Such indispensable special scientific studies should be conducted using modern methods and equipment and require special consideration.

It should be noted that beginning in the 1920s, the Pushkin State Museum has maintained a continuous tradition of archae-

---

* Editor's note: *The Treasure of Troy: Heinrich Schliemann's Excavations,* catalogue of the exhibition held at the Pushkin State Museum of Fine Arts, Moscow, April 16, 1996–April 15, 1997 (Moscow: Ministry of Culture of the Russian Federation and the Pushkin State Museum of Fine Arts; Milan: Leonardo Arte, 1996). The catalogue has also been published under the title *The Gold of Troy: Searching for Homer's Fabled City* (New York: Ministry of Culture of the Russian Federation and the Pushkin State Museum of Fine Arts in association with Harry N. Abrams, Inc., 1996).

ological excavation of the major settlements and necropolises of antiquity in the Crimea and on the Taman Peninsula in the territory of the ancient Cimmerian Bosphorus (Kerch Strait). The museum staff thus includes experienced specialists not only in the field of classical art but also in the areas of ancient metallurgy and archaeology. We were therefore equipped to carry out the complex, professional work required for the preparation of a new catalogue of the Schliemann collection.

From the outset, Mrs. Antonova, my colleagues, and I all agreed that at the preparatory stage of work on the catalogue there was a need to organize viewings of the collection for outstanding Russian and foreign scholars and specialists in the fields of Trojan archaeology and the archaeology of Asia Minor and Greece in the Bronze Age. Despite the fact that the organization of the visits of foreign colleagues required a great deal of time and effort on the part of the museum staff, from October through December 1994 these visits successfully took place. At the invitation of the Ministry of Culture and of the museum, the following specialists were able to inspect the Schliemann collection:

- Dr. Wilfried Menghin, Dr. Klaus Goldmann, Dr. Burkhardt Goeres, and Hermann Born from Germany
- Dr. Manfred Korfmann from Germany
- Dr. Engin Özgen, Dr. Ufuk Esin, and Dr. Mehmet Özdoğan from Turkey
- Dr. Machteld Mellink from the United States
- Dr. Donald Easton from the United Kingdom

We are also expecting the arrival of colleagues from Greece, Dr. Katie Demakopoulou and Dr. George Korres, and I should like to take advantage of this opportunity to express to them our sincere gratitude for the assistance rendered us during our recent visit to Greece as part of the program of preparing the catalogue.

In addition, thanks to Professor Korfmann, director of the current excavations at Troy, our group was invited to visit Tübingen to see the exhibit prepared there by Professor Korfmann on materials recovered from recent excavations at Troy, as well as literature on the site and other scholarly materials.

Our foreign colleagues were given an opportunity to acquaint themselves in detail with all two hundred sixty items of gold, silver, bronze, and stone in the Schliemann collection. An exchange of views and information took place in a friendly working atmosphere, and possibilities for scientific cooperation in the future were discussed. Our German colleagues from the Museum für Vor- und Frühgeschichte, Berlin, noted that all of the objects are in a good state of preservation. During the meetings, our group received important information for the catalogue on the results of the most recent archaeological excavations at Troy and in Anatolia and on new discoveries that can augment our understanding of the Trojan antiquities in the Schliemann collection.

At the time of the New York symposium, research on the objects was being concluded and corrections were being made to the text of the catalogue entries. At the same time, the introductory section was being written, along with several scholarly articles intended for the catalogue. This progress was reported in my symposium presentation.

PART 6

CURRENT ISSUES

AND COOPERATIVE

EFFORTS

INTRODUCTION

Milton Esterow

When I first heard about the plans for the conference that this publication documents, I had some reservations as to whether it would be worthwhile. By the end of the final session, I no longer had any. Although there were moments during the three days when it sounded as if we were still in the middle of the Cold War, I believe the conference was a great success. I congratulate Susan Soros, Dr. Elizabeth Simpson, and the staff of The Bard Graduate Center for Studies in the Decorative Arts. As far as I know, there has never been such a gathering anywhere in the world. It was long overdue.

The success of the conference is proof that the restitution issue is at the forefront of concern for many people and that we can come together to cooperate toward a solution. What we have learned is that the issue is much more complicated than we imagined. As Dr. Eichwede asked in the concluding session, "Are we going to use this opportunity or lose this opportunity?" And as Dr. Genieva said in discussing the return to Germany of books from the Rudomino State Library for Foreign Literature in Moscow, "We didn't become enemies. We became friends."

The subject of the spoils of war has interested me since 1964, when I wrote about it while I was a reporter for the *New York Times*. At *ARTnews*, we published Andrew Decker's articles about Austria's inept handling of art stolen from Jews by the Nazis. And in 1991 we published the series of articles that revealed for the first time the existence of the secret repositories in the former Soviet Union. The articles were written, as many of you here know, by Konstantin Akinsha and Grigorii Kozlov, who took part in the New York conference and who are contributors to this volume. They are responsible for one of the most important pieces of journalism in many years. Their articles in *ARTnews* received two of the most distinguished awards in American journalism. What they did was very brave, and I salute them again here today.

One excellent model of restitution was the recent return to Egypt of objects excavated in Sinai by Israeli archaeologists between 1969 and 1981. A political agreement between the two countries resulted in the recovery by the Egyptians of thousands of valuable objects dating back more than five thousand years. The delay has been beneficial to both sides. Not only will the finds be returned in first-rate condition, but the objects will be accompanied by scholarly documentation. Eventually, a new museum will be built for the objects in El 'Arîsh, near the Israeli border. As the writer Meir Ronnen, Jerusalem correspondent for *ARTnews,* has pointed out, "This amicable and civilized arrangement is without precedent in the annals of political agreements."[1] The Egyptian-Israeli accord sets a new standard.

Throughout the conference, we heard not infrequently such words as *multilateral* and *bilateral, morality* and *ethics, international law* and *protocols.* But I think we should also keep in mind something else. It has been said many times but it's worth repeating: great works of art are not merely objects to be collected in museums, arranged, looked after, and exhibited. They are our inheritance from the masters, and their history is part of the history of mankind. It is with pleasure that I introduce the papers in this section, which address current issues and cooperative efforts relating to the recovery of this inheritance.

MODELS OF RESTITUTION

(GERMANY, RUSSIA,

UKRAINE)

Wolfgang Eichwede

ILLUSIONS

Only a few years ago, I still had a dream: artworks thought to have disappeared or even to have been destroyed are being rediscovered; state vaults shrouded in darkness for decades are opening up; private collectors and former soldiers (or their descendants) who had obtained icons here and drawings there realize that they want to save, not steal. They inform the surprised public that they are planning to return the treasures to their places of origin, to the places they belong. Nations understand that reconciliation is a matter of deeds rather than words. Since Germany, for historical reasons, has less to return but wants to match the other side, and because she is aware of her guilt, having initiated the murderous activities more than fifty years ago, she is looking for a means to balance the disparity and convey her goodwill. Trophy art is becoming art again. In the words of a Russian author, Rembrandt and El Greco are being given to the world a second time. Conferences cease to be a forum for playing hide-and-seek and become a market for ideas on how restitution and gestures of gratitude can come together. Everyone is a winner. Even titles of ownership lose their divisive character within the dynamics of cooperation. Rather than demanding, people are building together. Art celebrates its peace.

REALITIES

Today we know that reality does not support such dreams. As far as the Russian-German negotiations are concerned, the window of opportunity that seemed to be opening up three years ago has long since shut. Silence is increasing from one discussion to the next, and already irritability is noticeable. Protocols no longer reflect a rapprochement, but rather gloss over increasing disagreement. How to prove the other side wrong seems to have become the guiding principle, rather than how to develop terms of exchange in cooperation with it. Hundreds of thousands of art treasures were lost during the war. Now we are close to losing our chance in peacetime to agree on what still can be saved. History shows that it is only in rare instances that the wounds of war can be healed. In this case, we have the opportunity, but we are losing it. The absurdity of the situation is obvious: the great powers were able to agree on the reorganization of the political geography of Europe and on German unity, but not on the handling of stolen altars.

ASYMMETRIES

Each side, Russian as well as German, believes that it is right. Claims based on signed treaties are pitted against demands arising from historical experience. Germany insists on observing international conventions; Russia points out that Germany was the aggressor and started the looting. Consequently, the administration in Moscow tries to bend the German-Russian Good-Neighborliness Treaty of 1990 (see Appendix 14), which provides for the return of cultural property, to fit its view of history (or even to withdraw *de facto* from the agreement). Meanwhile, the government in Bonn is taking pains to reduce to a minimum the material burdens resulting from historical guilt.

Next to the asymmetry of the arguments is set the asymmetry of possession. Being the loser of the war, Germany today holds almost no treasures from the former Soviet Union and possesses nothing (or very little) that it could return, although Hitler's armies had looted on a grand scale. In the late 1940s, the American occupying forces transferred much of what was found in the Western zones of Germany to the Soviet allies; these returns were acknowledged by the Soviet side via a signed receipt (but the Germans cannot honestly claim these actions as their own). Russia as a victorious power, on the other hand, has to this day at its disposal state repositories (which are still not completely open) containing property looted from Germany, officially confiscated right after the war. A considerable amount of this property was handed over to the German Democratic Republic (GDR) during the 1950s. But altogether there remains an asymmetry—the country that started the war demands restitution of its property without having anything to return itself. Or, to put it differently: the former victims are called upon to restitute property to the former aggressor without receiving anything in return. A one-way solution will not work. Legal principles derived from treaties collide with a historical sense of justice.

Lines of argument threaten to cancel each other out. As a result, each side may live with the feeling of being right in itself, but nobody will have been helped. Germany will not have been helped, since it will still miss its losses. Russia also will not have benefited, since it will have missed the chance for additional initiatives that could have brought at least partial compensation for its war damages. It is true that Russia has the German "trophies" to make up for its losses, but at the same time it knows that it is operating outside international norms. This is likely to dampen the joy that might be derived from the possession of these treasures. What is needed here is a "new thinking": gestures of reconciliation instead of a mutual standoff, a willingness to embark upon joint projects, instead of reviving the Cold War on the cultural front. Restitution of cultural property can only be effected if interests merge. Even those who wish to avoid the moral aspects of the problem will have to concede pragmatically that one must offer something to the other side in order to get something oneself. In the interaction between states, rigid adherence to principles without searching for fair compromises is a narrow-minded policy certainly bound to fail. And in the present disagreement, the positions of the two opposing sides are not necessarily mutually exclusive. It is true that they do follow different lines of reasoning and are meant to impose pressure; nonetheless, these positions would allow for a common ground if this were desired. Neither party in the negotiations needs to sacrifice its own stance, but each must be willing to accept the legitimacy of the other. Immediately, resolution would cease to be impossible and become possible. Diplomacy would succeed through creativity.

BLOCKADES

Looking back, it seems as though Russia could have been moved to a solution in 1992 if Germany, for its part, had been willing to make a convincing opening gesture. At the time, the Russian inclination toward a solution became apparent during many meetings with high-ranking representatives of the administration in Moscow. These officials felt the topic of confiscated (and locked-up) art to be—and I quote—"embarrassing" and wanted not only to tackle but to resolve the problem in such a way that both countries could build a foundation for their cultural dialogue. In the end, there was a lack of courage to take the big step. There certainly should have been a German offer at this point. Delay and the strengthening of legal positions, however, could not replace it. As early as 1993, the Russian position began to harden. Domestic policy opposition started to leave its mark on the sensitive issue, and nationalist voices became louder and louder. While movement had still been apparent before the end of the preceding year, now paralysis began to set in. Political agreements as well as diplomatic contacts were losing their viability. Germany was even said to have lost its right to demand restitution of its cultural property, in a statement prepared by Russian lawyers, because, they said, the allies of the German Reich had had to give up this right in their peace treaties of 1947. What was good for Hitler's allies, they said, was even more applicable to the main culprit.

This thesis implies that at present, one must act according to the conventions of 1947—indeed, that since there was no treaty with Germany at the time, one must simulate today the harsh clauses of 1947, as if there had been no German-Russian friendship treaty in 1990. If this logic prevails, history confers merciless damnation. Learning ceases to promote change. But there are other lines of argument from Moscow politicians which are presented with greater seriousness. So far, they indicate, there is no legal mechanism within Russia that could enable restitution to be carried out as a regulated procedure. Who has the right to make which decisions? they ask—which institutions must be included? which of the demands that have been brought forward must be taken into account? Effecting domestic procedures from international obligations, they say, takes time and care.

But the experience of the last few years shows that time does not work in favor of a solution. Are these objections voiced only as a delaying tactic? In the Russian Parliament (Duma), efforts have been made to render invalid international obligations and bilateral agreements via Russian laws. These efforts are a poor beginning for a new constitutional state. If, fifty years after the war, art from Germany that was once removed as a consequence of war is now pronounced "Russian state property," Russian politics would lose its rationality, pursuing a policy of nationalization of property while at the same time moving toward a free-market economy.

BUT STILL . . .

It is obvious that no reconciliation on displaced art is in sight at this point. While German diplomacy temporizes, the Russian side is tending toward a more negative position. Passivity is impending everywhere. Nevertheless, we must try to develop models of solutions that demonstrate that it is more advantageous to work toward cooperation than to remain locked in conflict. It is hardly possible to resist nationalistic tendencies by giving in to them, but only by proving them to be unproductive, through examples of openness and cooperation with the rest of the world. Meanwhile, we Germans must learn to understand that people from Ukraine and Russia can only view possible restitution to the Federal Republic through the prism of their own losses. Any successful strategy for a solution will have at its innermost core an appreciation of the other cultures. This appreciation will make it possible to modify expectations and to accept without resentment the fact that some of the displaced cultural property should be allowed to remain with the current possessor by mutual consent. The key word is "giving" in both directions.

GRATEFULNESS AND ADMONITION

We have been speaking of states, governments, and museums. But it is courageous individuals who have broken up empires of taboos with their sensational research and their sharp pens, reopening new worlds for art. They are barely a handful— Ekaterina Genieva, Konstantin Akinsha, Grigorii Kozlov, Alexei Rastorgouev, and Viktor Baldin—to name just five. They have thoroughly changed the cultural images of their countries with their impressive openness and their courage to confront history. The Bard Graduate Center conference would probably not have been possible without their efforts. Without these efforts, Germany could not ask for restitution. At the same time, they all advocate cooperative gestures and accompanying actions. This is an important point that the German side should not overlook. In the view of these individuals, settlements that are solely based on German demands will have no chance to succeed.

POSSIBLE EXCHANGES

The Amber Room

A concrete example: the fate of the Amber Room from the Catherine Palace at Pushkin, near St. Petersburg, is surrounded by legends. Hardly any other wartime loss has become so well known. According to all reports, it must be considered lost. So why cannot the chancellor of the new Germany build—for a second time—for the president of the new Russia what the Prussian king Frederick William I once—in 1716—gave to the Russian czar Peter the Great? Parts of the room have already been restored, and the projects could complement one another. A symbol of theft (in 1941) would once again become a symbol of friendship. In return, it might be agreed that Russia

would start restitution to Germany in grand style. Proceeding step by step, the effort would soon gain its own momentum. The palaces of the czars surrounding St. Petersburg or the churches of Pskov would offer further projects. In a workshop in Novgorod, more than 1.2 million fragments of frescoes from a destroyed church have been collected. There, over a period of thirty-five years, murals from the fourteenth century have been undergoing reconstruction, in the manner of an enormous puzzle. Means are severely limited, and the progress of the work suffers because of the extreme scarcity of materials. The visitor, overwhelmed with admiration, asks himself why efforts could not merge, why young people from Germany could not do internships here, why German companies and sponsors could not help out. No one in Germany denies the devastation suffered by the countries of the former Soviet Union through Hitler's invasion. Everyone understands the value of nurturing culture in times of dramatic change. Our societies' openness will grow when remembrance takes the form of dialogue.

Bremen

Bremen is progressing along that path, although it has not yet led to success. This example reveals the full dilemma of the present situation. A reminder: the Bremen Kunsthalle moved substantial numbers of its drawings, watercolors, and paintings to Brandenburg during the war. They were found there by Soviet soldiers and "privately" taken home as booty. Since they were not officially seized by the authorities, they are today classified as "illegally" removed property in Russia, too. In 1990, a Soviet veteran, Viktor Baldin, contacted the north German Hanseatic city and made the astonishing announcement that he had taken away more than three hundred fifty drawings in May 1945. Baldin said that his only wish now was to give them back to Bremen. Unfortunately though, he had given them over into Russian state custody and was powerless over their fate. Some one hundred other works with the Bremen stamp have since appeared in Russia. The negotiations concerning these works are complicated and are part of a different story. More than once, a positive conclusion was imminent, and there was no lack of dinner speeches and toasts in festive settings. In the spring of 1993, after visits by mayors and ministers, a "protocol of intent" was signed that was generally seen as a model breakthrough. The Russian side announced its willingness to give back the drawings and paintings, and in return Bremen promised the gift of valuable drawings, as well as committing support for the restoration of Novgorod on an impressive scale. Included also was the initiation of joint research projects for the clarification of Russian cultural losses incurred during World War II. German companies promised generous funding. Celebrated but not realized, the "Bremen Protocol" is still pending. Delays repeatedly followed signals of imminent restitution. Recently, those signals have been decreasing. Two years ago, Moscow had hoped to set a precedent (restitution for mutual benefit). Today, it seems as though Moscow feared setting a precedent. Because of confusion within the Russian power structure, strident talk and false pathos have gained unreasonable ground. Still, there are no convincing alternatives to the "philosophy" of a network of interests such as the "Bremen Protocol" formulates, unless one decides to define one's self-esteem through "trophies." However, Russia is too proud and too great for that.

Ukraine

A third approach leads us to Ukraine. Two-thirds of all cultural losses suffered by the former Soviet Union are losses of Ukraine. This fact is usually overlooked in the Russian-German controversy. The war extended over Ukraine's entire territory, and there is hardly a country that suffered to such an extent. Yet the Ukrainians are anxious to research their losses, not in a spirit of confrontation, but in one of cooperation with the Germans. The Museum of Western and Oriental Art in Kyiv (Kiev) recently presented a well-researched list of its missing works, including 475 important paintings. Despite intensive research carried out by scholars from Ukraine and the Bremen Research Institute for Eastern Europe, clues to the whereabouts of these works seem to have been lost in the destruction of the war and its aftermath. Considering the extent of these losses, this lack of information remains a mystery. At the same time, researchers are taking inventory of what German cultural goods are still in Ukraine. These goods, however, are not about to be declared Ukrainian state property. What is on the agenda is the question of how a balance can be struck between compensation for one's own losses and restitution to Germany.

Meanwhile, a diplomacy of concrete reciprocal gestures has been initiated. An engineer from Ukraine, for instance, recently contacted Bremen with the news that he wanted to return the famous self-portrait of Hans von Marées, the nineteenth-century German painter. He claimed that his father had taken the painting from its refuge in Brandenburg as a soldier and that the piece bears the stamp of the Bremen Kunsthalle. The cultural ministry in Kyiv officially agreed to the transfer to Bremen, with no strings attached. Today, the painting is hanging in its original spot in the museum. As a sign of gratitude, the young man was given a one-year scholarship in the Federal Republic of Germany. Almost concurrently, more than seven hundred valuable books on ancient history and prehistory, dating from the nineteenth and twentieth centuries, were returned to Kyiv. These books had been seized in 1943 by the Einsatzstab Reichsleiter Rosenberg (ERR) and were removed to the Reich. For decades, they were kept in the Pfahlbaumuseum on Lake Constance where Hans Reinerth, former director of the museum and one of the organizers of the Nazi plundering raids, had taken them. His successor at the museum, Günther Schöbel, had only recently been able to identify the holdings, which were still packed in their original boxes. Without hesitation, he decided to send them directly back to their owners in Kyiv as quickly and as unbureaucratically as possible. The operation, including its financing, was carried out as a private initiative. Just a few

weeks earlier, the director of the German Goethe Institute in Kyiv, Ute Countess Baudissin, had returned to the Historical Archive of the Ukraine a certificate of Peter the Great including the seal of the czar and his signature from 1700. The document had been stolen in Kyiv during the war by German units. It had reached the countess through an American soldier who asked that it be returned to the legal owner.

In this way, a network of citizens' initiatives has developed, and this could set an example for state authorities. The Ukrainian government has demonstrated its openness. It should not be difficult for Bonn to reciprocate with constructive steps of its own. The situation is favorable to progress.

INFORMATION AND ACCESS

The accounts of individual cases require a few concluding remarks. Acceptance of the provisions of the Hague Convention of 1907 (see Appendix 3) is paramount, but it is also true that titles of ownership alone cannot solve the problem of displaced art. The historical context precludes a one-sided solution. Policy based solely on legal provisions will inevitably lead to a dead end. Since the Russians may pass laws that will limit their own sphere of action, it would be advisable for the German side to indicate ways out of the impasse.

In a number of joint statements, the two parties have promised each other unlimited information. It is simply absurd that several Russian archives, which could supply information on their own wartime losses, are inaccessible to Western researchers to this day. This policy of continued secrecy leaves unanswered a myriad of questions. We do not know, for example, what Soviet cultural goods previously plundered by Hitler's divisions the Red Army was able to recover during its advance. In addition, we do not know the location of hundreds of thousands of books and artworks from Russia and Ukraine which were restituted by the Americans to the USSR soon after 1945. In this respect, it is not only the Germans who are awaiting the opening of the archives.

Some progress has been made toward access to the Russian repositories. In this regard, however, the "great step forward" to normalcy is required. An open world cannot tolerate sequestered art. Obstructions and excuses only testify to a guilty conscience. The first spectacular exhibitions at least have indicated the scope of the treasures that have been kept from the public so unnecessarily and for so long.

MODELS ONCE AGAIN

Pilot projects and symbolic gestures have already been mentioned. The modalities of restitution can vary within a wide spectrum. Cultural foundations involving Germany and Ukraine, which could absorb the topic of restitution within a broader framework, would be desirable from this perspective for their value in diluting the issue of restitution as a whole. The aim would be to intensify relations to a point where restitution loses its sting, and no longer implies a loss of prestige. At the moment, of course, pragmatic approaches that are quickly realizable will be needed.

Among conceivable gestures that might be made are loans or gifts of objects from collections, which would be allowed to return "home" as part of the agreement. Gifts from the rest of the holdings in the galleries or institutions involved would, of course, also be possible.

A completely different avenue might lie in answering restitution with support for contemporary culture. This could be done, for example, by building a Museum of Modern Art in Kyiv. The collection of twentieth-century art in Ukraine is riddled with gaps, due to the tragic history of the country. There are numbers of artists and museum professionals in Germany who would be excited to help fill these gaps, making it possible to exchange newer works for long-lost art.

Finally, the cultural infrastructure of our eastern neighbors remains an area in permanent need of help. Again, restoration projects on various scales could be undertaken. Or perhaps technical projects or the construction of exhibition space might take precedence. These are only suggestions intended to open the door to further proposals.

The "Bremen Protocol" of 1993 recorded the intention to exhibit the drawings of the Kunsthalle on their return to Bremen, with the participation of the State Hermitage Museum. Further projects for mutual benefit were planned. In 1995, French Impressionist paintings from private German collections were placed on view in St. Petersburg. Might it not be possible to initiate joint exhibitions in Germany as well and thus start the procedure of restitution? This could be done in such a way that each participant would be bound by agreements that are acceptable to all.

The establishment of a foundation as the institutional base for German efforts has been suggested repeatedly. Such a foundation could secure a high measure of independence and help keep political concerns at bay. Most important, however, would be the implementation of concrete measures that are as object-oriented as possible. The institutions whose collections are at stake should be part of the process, since they are the most knowledgeable about the subject. The Russian-German Library Commission on Restitution has done exemplary work already. It is the politicians' task now to open up the decision-making process. Again, the pioneering efforts of the Pfahlbaumuseum need to be recognized as an example. Peoples, not just ministry officials, must come together. International organizations such as UNESCO can play a part as mediator in this matter, but the addition of further options should not lead to more diversionary tactics or obstructionist policies. In that they can provide a forum for the definition of common interests and the initiation of models for solution, however, such organizations are always welcome. It is not time to resign, but time to send a signal.

GERMAN BOOK COLLECTIONS

IN RUSSIAN LIBRARIES

Ekaterina Genieva

I am very pleased that the organizers of this extremely timely conference have found it possible to include a discussion of the displaced books and library collections that became spoils of war (see colorplates 22–25). Together with artworks and archives, on both sides, enormous quantities of books were displaced and were lost forever.

For some twenty years now, I have been working in the Rudomino State Library for Foreign Literature in Moscow. This largest repository of foreign books in the territory of the former Soviet Union, now the Russian Federation, was founded over seventy years ago, in 1922, by Margarita Rudomino, a figure well known in both Russia and Germany. For the seventy years of the Soviet regime, the Library for Foreign Literature was the only existing source of information on Western culture.

In 1945, Rudomino was serving in Germany, holding the rank of lieutenant colonel. She had been sent there by the Soviet government as an associate of the staff of the Plenipotentiary State Special Defense Committee. This organization was responsible for the removal and repatriation of property from Germany in accordance with the Teheran, Yalta, and Potsdam conferences. The removal of books, so-called trophy literature, was headed by Rudomino, the director of the Library for Foreign Literature.

The expropriation of books from Germany to the Soviet Union was justified by the widespread devastation of hundreds of Soviet libraries and the loss of millions of books. The books were removed openly, for the Germans, understanding the responsibility they bore for the acts that had been perpetrated on the territory of the Soviet Union, did not block this process. I am not attempting here to speak of the guilt of Germany, for that guilt is obvious. I shall merely note that this guilt cannot be compensated by any kind of material equivalents.

I should like to focus on the fate of the displaced book collections as they began their journey toward their new place of residence and also on their fate in their new foreign environment. Margarita Rudomino quite reasonably attempted to select for shipment to the Soviet Union those books that could, without detriment to the national dignity and heritage of the German people, fill some of the gaps caused by Russian losses. Her understanding of the utter senselessness of trying to take everything at once differed sharply from the attitude of the administrators of other Soviet trophy-literature divisions. They often took to the Soviet Union everything at hand, even contemporary popular magazines.

The Deutsche Bibliothek–Deutsche Bücherei (German Library) in Leipzig was a subject of particular interest, and the question arose of sending its books to the Soviet Union. Arguing that the Leipzig library was part of the national cultural legacy Germany would need for its cultural rebirth, however, Rudomino was able to prove to the Moscow leadership that this was undesirable. On her initiative, two million books from that library were evacuated to Thuringia, assembled in the summer of 1945, and returned to the Leipzig library, which reopened in November 1945. Rudomino was also able to convince the Soviet commander in chief, Marshal Zhukov, not to confiscate the contents of the Sächsische Landesbibliothek (State Saxon Library) in Dresden. Zhukov's order, however, was delayed, and the books were sent in error to the Soviet Union. They were returned, in part, in 1957.

However, it was not contrary to her will and her conscience that Margarita Rudomino was involved in sending to the Soviet Union the greatest cultural legacy of the German people, the Deutsches Buch- und Schriftmuseum der Deutschen Bücherei (the German Museum of Books and Manuscripts). The archives of the Library for Foreign Literature for the 1940s through the 1950s include charts showing the presence of incunabula from German libraries and indicate the number of copies in these collections. In the files for 1945, there is an interesting and rather lengthy document entitled "List of certain German libraries whose holdings it is useful to make available to the USSR regardless of repatriation payments in books by Germany to the Soviet Union."

In Germany a very competent and effective Soviet library commission had information concerning the most valuable German collections. Forty percent of the twenty thousand state, municipal, and private libraries in Germany were in the Soviet Zone of Occupation. Works from some of those libraries were plundered by the local population, and others were stolen by Soviet soldiers before the books were placed in protective custody and sent off to the Soviet Union. In the archives of my library there is a document signed by Rudomino stating that altogether about eleven million books were removed to the Soviet Union. Five million were sent to Moscow and Leningrad, two million to Minsk, three million to Kyiv (Kiev), and for one million a destination was not specified.

These books vary greatly in quality. Some were extremely valuable editions, but there were also ordinary German publications published in many copies. The fate of these books after their arrival in the Soviet Union also varied considerably. Many were used to round out the holdings of various libraries in the country, were included in their catalogues, and turned out to be extremely useful to Soviet readers. But hundreds of thousands—I hope no more than that—never reached readers. Dispersed throughout repositories of the Moscow and Leningrad libraries, they wound up in basements. Quite a number of cases of books taken to the Soviet Union were never even opened. It is clear from contemporary archives that, although Soviet leaders at the level of Molotov, Mikoyan, and Beriia made the final decisions concerning the removal and displacement of these books to the Soviet Union, for forty-five years it was not considered acceptable, and simply was not permitted, to talk about these treasures. The war had ended, but its prisoners continued to exist and were often detained in thoroughly inappropriate conditions.

It is a historical irony that in 1992 the Rudomino State Library for Foreign Literature, with its rare-book holdings including so many German trophy books, was the initiator of the first German-Russian roundtable on the issue of book restitution.* I was gratified to see at the Bard Graduate Center

symposium several participants in that truly historic event, which included representatives of German and Russian ministries and German and Russian librarians, jurists, politicians, scholars, and other experts. The publication of the catalogue of German sixteenth-century books in the rare-book collection of the Library for Foreign Literature, which was prepared jointly with German colleagues, was timed to correspond with the beginning of the roundtable. In the catalogue, for the first time since the transfer of these books to Moscow, the owners' stamps and bookplates were described (colorplates 23–25). This was the first step toward openness regarding library information on trophy books, clearly demonstrating the desire to make available as quickly as possible to all interested persons and institutions exhaustive information concerning the books, their original historical affiliation, state of preservation, and present location. I am very pleased to say that this catalogue, which is the result of the first fruitful postwar cooperation between German and Russian specialists, is still relevant today. I think that after the work by the Library for Foreign Literature, with support from the Ministry of Culture of the Russian Federation, on the restitution and return of books to the university library of Amsterdam, we can hope that in the very near future yet another such return will take place.†

While we were preparing for the roundtable, I heard quite a few skeptical comments asserting that "provincial" Russia, which had endured such losses, would not participate in the roundtable as a sign of protest, that the major national libraries of Russia, the Russian State Library (the former Lenin Library) in Moscow or the Russian National Library in St. Petersburg, which had received the most valuable German trophy books, would refuse to discuss the problem, that there was no point in thinking that Russian libraries would ever in the foreseeable future open up their repositories to international experts, and that it was total madness even to think it would be possible to talk about library restitution.

The first day of the roundtable was very difficult. Since emotions held sway, the speakers listened but did not hear each other. Some hotheaded Germans talked about a schedule of German trains to take the German trophy books back home.

---

* Editor's note: For documentation of the German-Russian roundtable discussed here, see Klaus-Dieter Lehmann and Ingo Kolasa, eds., *Restitution von Bibliotheksgut: Runder Tisch deutscher und russischer Bibliothekare in Moskau am 11. und 12. Dezember 1992, Zeitschrift für Bibliothekswesen und Bibliographie,* Sonderheft 56 (Frankfurt am Main: Vittorio Klostermann, 1993).

† Editor's note: In 1992, under the direction of Ekaterina Genieva, a selection of 608 books that had been confiscated by the ERR from the Netherlands and later removed to the Soviet Union (1946) was exhibited both at the Rudomino State Library for Foreign Literature in Moscow (June) and at the university library in Amsterdam (September). Two editions of the catalogue were printed, both of which listed the books' original owners, which included the city library of Amsterdam, trade unions and public organizations, scientific and theosophic movements, literary and historical societies, clubs, and private persons. In the second edition of the catalogue, prepared for the exhibition in Amsterdam, the names and addresses of approximately ninety owners were given. Following the Amsterdam exhibition, the books were returned to the Netherlands.

The Russians heatedly accused the Germans of destroying the libraries of Smolensk, Voronezh, and Kharkiv. Yet it should be stressed that this was the first professional meeting that included the people who held these book collections, and one at which each of the parties involved was looking for revelations. In fact, in only a few days the Russian archives began opening up their collections. It was hard for the participants to accept the fact that the most outstanding specialists of the countries involved had been engaged in this problem of trophy art. It was difficult to listen to our colleagues from the Bremen Research Institute tell of their search for Russian losses. It was hard to accept the atmosphere of secrecy that had surrounded the transfer of trophy books to the USSR. And it was quite impossible to accept the fact that in forty-five years the Russian side had not regularized the situation regarding its losses.

The second day of the roundtable was completely different. Emotions abated, and a businesslike discussion began on the legal aspects of the issue, which were still extremely unclear, on proposed pilot projects of the Russian and German libraries, and on imposing a moratorium on the work of book dealers, primarily foreign ones, who were besieging library directors with their trade in stolen books. A decision was made that German and Russian colleagues would work jointly to seek lost cultural property and to exchange their results. To this end, the establishment of a Russian-German Library Commission on Restitution was proposed; this commission has continued to work successfully up to this day.

There was also discussion of German compensation for Russian losses. There was talk of Russian libraries' returning part of their trophy holdings and the need to discuss what would be returned. The German side indicated that it would make available to the Russians copies of publications, subscriptions to German periodicals, equipment, and support for visits to Germany by Russian professionals. All this was by no means an easy process. Quite a few efforts were required to include in one of the resolutions of the Library Commission on Restitution a provision concerning unimpeded and unlimited free access to the repositories. It was in fact due to that particular provision that the Gutenberg Bible was discovered in a special top-secret repository of the Lenin Library.

Once again we should recall Margarita Rudomino. The Gutenberg Bible from the collection of the Deutsches Buch- und Schriftmuseum was hidden in the basement of the ancient family castle of Baron Raunstein. Right after the departure from the region of the American troops, the Raunsteins themselves reported the book's location to the Soviet military command. Why did they do that? Their behavior was not unusual but, as further events showed, it had dramatic consequences. Believing in the strength of long-standing German-Russian cultural relations, they hoped that at some point in the future this great book would once again return to Germany. All that is known of the family's fate is that they disappeared at the end of the 1940s. Perhaps their secret is preserved in some yet unopened Russian archives.

Thus, the Raunsteins' Gutenberg Bible was brought to the USSR. Those who took this treasure to the USSR included the son of Margarita Rudomino, a twenty-year-old lieutenant also serving in Germany. Though it recently came to light that the bible was subsequently given to the Lenin Library, its fate in the USSR was shrouded in secrecy. Even the Lenin Library's curators and possibly its administration did not know that the book was secreted in its depths. Years passed, and in 1970, Rudomino's post as director of the Library for Foreign Literature was taken over by the daughter of Prime Minister Kosygin. Tortured by the knowledge of the Gutenberg Bible, Rudomino on several occasions tried to speak about it to the Soviet leadership but got the answer that has now been reported so often: Wait—the time has not yet come. Before her death, she shared this secret with me. Why did it bother her so much? Though she herself had taken books from Germany for Soviet libraries, as a professional librarian Rudomino understood that involuntarily she had become a party to a crime. For half a century, some of the greatest treasures of world culture, preserved in inappropriate conditions, had not been accessible to readers. In other words, the books were slowly and spiritually dying.

I, too, tried to share the secret of the Gutenberg Bible with various staff members and specialists, and got the same answer: Wait—the time has not yet come. A very highly qualified expert once said to me: "You are mistaken. The Gutenberg Bible is in Moscow State University." I thought that since so much time had passed the treasure might have been moved yet once again. But Margarita Rudomino was right. When, through the joint efforts of the Russian-German Library Commission on Restitution, the top-secret room in the Lenin Library was opened, the German and Russian librarians saw that Gutenberg Bible, which, because of ill will, lack of culture, and cowardice, had been slowly and spiritually perishing in that prison.

I think that it is not so much the legal aspects of this Soviet detective story, and not so much even the question of physical conservation of the books that are important, but rather the moral aspects of the greater issue. Is it not madness to hide this book from readers? The fate of the Gutenberg Bible, for example, clearly differs from that of the famous Elgin Marbles in the British Museum. The latter were immediately made accessible to viewers, while the Gutenberg Bible will only be accessible at some time in the future.

In an era of glasnost, what will be the fate of the German trophy books? Various solutions are possible. We could recognize the *de facto* present state of affairs and keep the holdings where they are now. How could this be justified? The consequences of the war are irreversible. In that case, particularly in an era of new technology, and in conditions of a united Europe and wider global community, certain contacts could, in fact, be simplified. It would also be possible to consider the return and transfer of valuable objects in cases where ties have been reestablished and when such objects can fill existing gaps.

We might give thought to a compromise involving the restoration of old ties and the creation of new ones. For example, duplicates of publications could be made available through microfilm, microfiche, or electronic means. Such solutions have become possible not only because of the changes in the attitude of German and Russian librarians during the last few years, but also because questions of book restitution are considerably simpler than questions of the restitution of objects of art. Even such an extraordinary book as the Gutenberg Bible exists in more than one copy. Given the unique character of books, the members of the Russian-German Library Commission on Restitution have appealed to the governments of their countries to separate questions of book restitution from all other restitution issues. Such an approach could guarantee the logical conclusion of some of the proposed projects in the foreseeable future.

One of these is the need to return the half of the Gotha library (Forschungs- und Landesbibliothek Gotha) that has remained in Russia. A dispersed collection loses its coherence. Either the rest of the Gotha collection should be sent to Russia, an impossible step, or, as the Russian-German Library Commission on Restitution is insisting, the books should be returned to Germany. It is also possible that through the use of such an approach, the effort to return 13,500 books to Germany, prepared through the first pilot project between the Library for Foreign Literature and the State Library in Berlin, will also finally be completed. According to competent specialists, the 13,500 books are not needed by a single library in Russia but are needed in Germany.

Here I agree with Dr. Eichwede (see above, pages 216–20). Although I, too, would very much like to see various legal conclusions and norms drawn up in the near future, I do not truly believe they would help us resolve this confused, painful, and agonizing problem, one we ourselves sometimes exaggerate. Claims to property by the German side, by the Germans who were the aggressors, are outweighed by that country's guilt. It is not, therefore, relevant to speak about ownership rights since such claims lose any validity when the scale of guilt is taken into account. But claims to ownership on the Russian side, and demands for compensation for damages, also do not hold up if we take into account the wrong done in terms of noncompliance with international law regarding the protection of cultural property, the present state of affairs, and the present state of a significant number of the trophy holdings in Russia.

This issue can also be viewed from the other side. If one looks at history not only from the perspective of guilt and atonement, one sees that the people involved, in the past and the present, are different. Nevertheless, the same problem has remained, and there is still that ominous Russian question, "What is to be done?" I am not ready to say here what should be done to resolve this. I can, however, say what should not be done. We should not continue to wage war through peaceful means. We should not place too many hopes on the omnipotence of the law. We should not imagine that highly complex problems can be resolved through financial transactions. We must attempt together to prevent excessively hotheaded politicians from using this complex situation for purposes that are by no means always positive.

The emotions that overwhelmed all of us during the three days of the roundtable only hinder a practical and professional solution to the problem and, more importantly, have an adverse impact on public opinion. Even though the commission has been working so successfully, and is insisting on the return of the portion of the Gotha collection now in Russia, not a single German book within the jurisdiction of the Russian-German Library Commission has yet been returned to Germany. On the other hand, Germany, regardless of whether it received physical compensation, agreed in 1992 alone to give three million deutsche marks to Russian libraries to help meet their needs in supplementing their holdings. Believe me—a specialist—that modern German books and magazines are significantly more important to us today than the German books written in Gothic script that we have in the Tomsk and Ryazan libraries. I think we can find an enormous number of ways to use our own hands and our own reason to create models of restitution. If our talk of a united Europe is not merely rhetoric but a real attempt to create this unity, we need to give careful thought to each individual collection of books removed to Russia, Belarus, and Ukraine, and to think about what would be reasonable in terms of restitution. I will not lose hope that we shall achieve a solution to this problem within our lifetimes. In conclusion, I should like to say what it is I find so particularly exciting. The problem of book restitution, which could have made us all enemies, has made us friends. That is the guarantee of what I am talking about— that we will succeed in building a mutual society in which there will rule not hatred but tolerance and compassion. And then we will truly be able to say that we have created a shared European community.

PRINCIPLES FOR THE RESOLUTION OF DISPUTES CONCERNING CULTURAL HERITAGE DISPLACED DURING THE SECOND WORLD WAR

Lyndel V. Prott

INTRODUCTION

It was difficult to speak at the end of such a rich conference and do justice to the exchanges that had taken place. It is understandable that the view is sometimes expressed that "things" are not as important as human beings—who could ever forget the picture of the box of abandoned wedding rings and all that it represented in terms of human tragedy[1]—and that consideration of the fate of objects should always be secondary to that of the alleviation of human suffering. Yet we at UNESCO are constantly confronted by the pleas of people who are physically suffering to help them save their cultural heritage, for their suffering is greatly increased by the destruction of what is dear to them. Their cultural heritage represents their history, their community, and their own identity. Preservation is sought, not for the sake of the objects, but for the sake of the people for whom they have a meaningful life.

UNESCO (United Nations Educational, Scientific and Cultural Organization), founded in 1945, is the specialized agency for the protection of cultural property, a mission given to it by its constitution. It is not surprising, therefore, that one of its very first standard-setting activities concerning the tangible cultural heritage should be an effort to prevent for the future the kind of horrendous destruction and looting of the cultural heritage that had taken place all over Europe during the Second World War. It was thus soon engaged in the negotiations that resulted in the adoption of the UNESCO Convention for the Protection of Cultural Property in the Event of Armed Conflict (the Hague Convention) of 1954 and its Protocol (see Appendix 10).

The suspicion with which certain politicians in the Eastern bloc then regarded international organizations had not spared UNESCO. The removal and destruction of so much of the cultural heritage in the territory of the Soviet Union was fresh in memory and unforgiven in that country. It was the preparatory work on the Hague Convention of 1954, designed finally to outlaw such looting and destruction, that brought the USSR actively into the work of UNESCO. But the Hague Convention did not, of course, have any retroactive effect.

THE EXISTING LAW

Other papers in this volume show how the law on the international return of cultural heritage taken during conflict has developed. To set this law in a broader context, it should be noted that the effort to protect the cultural heritage from the vicissitudes of conflict is part of the wider development over the last three centuries, and most intensively over the last hundred years, toward more humane international behavior during wartime.

Before the Second World War, there were a number of treaties that dealt with specific instances of looting. These included the Treaty of Westphalia of 1648, the post-Napoleonic settlements, and the Treaty of Versailles of 1919 (see Appendix 4). Apart from that, there were also many strong ethical statements, going back to classical times in Europe, deploring wartime looting. Unfortunately, very little had developed in the way of undoing the harm once the conflict was over, other than including a clause in a bilateral or multi-lateral peace settlement. There are many well-known cases in which the "spoils of war" taken in European conflicts are still held by the victors. One of particular interest is the case of Sweden, which acquired much important cultural property from many countries during the wars of Gustavus Adolphus during the seventeenth century.

WORLD WAR II AND POSTWAR LEGAL DEVELOPMENTS

The Declaration of London of 1943 (see Appendix 9) marked a new departure in many ways. First, it was announcing the rules *prospectively,* rather than waiting for a peace treaty that could simply dictate them by virtue of the victors' dominance. Second, it was specifically addressed also to neutral states and third parties, including those in neutral states, to warn them against suspect transactions. Third, it made clear that looted objects were to be returned, even where they were in the hands of third parties whose title would normally have been protected by local law as to "bona-fide" (good-faith) acquirers.

The Declaration of London was adopted by legislation so extensively in Western European states that it became something of a common law in the postwar period (although, in some cases, not for very long). The high-minded enthusiasm of 1943 did not always last: the law that had undoubtedly developed by 1945 was only partially applied to the events that had taken place during the preceding six years. Thus, instead of a general settlement for all the systematic and episodic loot-ing that occurred, leaving only the odd, concealed case to be dealt with five decades later, there are still very large numbers of displaced cultural objects far from their prewar locations. It must be said, of course, that many postwar governments were in most difficult economic circumstances and distracted by major problems of reconstruction.

PROBLEMS ATTACHED TO THE EXISTING LEGAL RULES

Many of the issues that bedevil the application of law today would most probably have been solved if a general resolution of issues, delayed by the political context between 1948 and 1989, had taken place. For example, the need to resolve the issue as to time limitation of claims would have occurred much more frequently in different jurisdictions as case after case had to be dealt with. A body of precedents in many countries, or of statements in bilateral agreements, would have shown by weight of experience how the international com-munity had decided to settle these issues.

The issue of time limitation is one of the most interesting and difficult if one seeks to resolve it solely in terms of existing law. It can certainly be argued that the Declaration of London, where no limitation of claims was mentioned, was not intended to be subject to one. This was certainly the view of Ardelia Hall, one of its early commentators, who wrote that the recovery program

> . . . provides for an appropriate continuation of the cultural restitution programs. For the first time in history, restitution may be expected to continue for as long as works of art known to have been plundered during a war continue to be rediscovered.[2]

On the other hand, the declaration is not an international agreement and, because it affected private law matters (such as title to property), it had to be implemented by national legislation. Should this legislation have set limits? The Swiss legislation implementing the declaration was adopted on December 10, 1945, and was repealed on December 23, 1947. The Swiss special tribunal's interpretation of that legislation had held the Swiss federal government liable to pay compen-sation to persons in Switzerland who were required to return cultural objects to the original owners where they would normally have been held by Swiss law to have acquired them "bona fide."[3] No doubt, the Swiss government wanted to restrict its potential liability as far as possible. It is not clear that any of the Allied and Associated Powers that put pressure on the neutrals to adopt the rules of the Declaration of London ever protested about this repeal, although it must have been realized that other objects might surface in Switzerland later.

Whatever decisions might have resulted from claims through the national courts under legislation adopted in accordance with the Declaration of London, it is clear that such decisions, though they might have produced useful precedents for private claims, would not have decided the issue for claims between states. The International Court of Justice has discussed problems in interstate claims of "laches" (undue delay on the part of a claimant state) and "estoppel" (condoning of the conduct of the defendant state by the claimant state), but neither of these defenses could strictly be relevant here, as the states making claims now have been generally unaware of the exact location of the objects that they are now claiming. These defenses might be argued against the claims of certain countries that are now claiming back cultural objects that had been centralized in the capital museums of a former federation and whose locations had therefore been known; but if these claimant states were unable to pursue their claims legally before, these defenses may still not succeed.

Finally, it has to be said that the Declaration of London, though a clear statement of principles, was expressed to relate solely to objects taken by the powers with whom the Allied and Associated Powers were at war—it says nothing about objects taken by members of their own forces, although I would argue that there is a clear moral implication that such behavior would not be condoned by them, and this is certainly the view that has been taken by the United States.

PROPOSALS FOR THE RESOLUTION OF REMAINING CLAIMS

The failure to implement a general program of returns, and the secrecy surrounding the location of many important cultural objects, which is dissipating only now, explains why, fifty years after the end of the Second World War, many legal principles have still to be decided on. There is, however, as one will have seen, no lack of legal materials on which to draw. I therefore think it quite possible to propose principles that would constitute an appropriate basis for the settlement of outstanding claims.

I phrase these as proposals, not because they are not well grounded in existing legal principle, but for the following reasons: first, because I do not believe we can ignore the social, cultural, and economic developments of those intervening years, which, for transfers on the scale now being discussed, are obviously important; and, second, because of the general political delicacy of the subject in almost every jurisdiction, although it is much more delicate in some than in others.

The sources of these proposed principles are the Declaration of London of 1943, and the Protocol to the UNESCO Convention for the Protection of Cultural Property in the Event of Armed Conflict (the Hague Convention) of 1954, which in effect legislated the principles of the Declaration of London for future conflicts. I will also make reference to the UNESCO Convention on the Means of Prohibiting and Preventing the Illicit Import, Export and Transfer of Ownership of Cultural Property of 1970 (see Appendix 11) and the UNIDROIT Convention on Stolen or Illegally Exported Cultural Objects (see Appendix 17), which was adopted by a diplomatic conference in Rome on June 24, 1995. The UNIDROIT Convention has limited the rights of a purchaser of a stolen cultural object where he or she would normally be protected by the "bona-fide" rule. This is a recent confirmation of the principle in the Declaration of London that misappropriated objects must be returned.

Finally, there are principles that have been recommended by the International Council of Museums (ICOM) for the resolution of disputes about movables. These principles were proposed in 1978 in connection with the debate on the return of materials taken during colonial times,[4] and some seem to me to have relevance for the present debate, for example, that every state has a right to a representative collection of its own cultural heritage.

Why should states that are not parties to these instruments pay any attention to them? Or for that matter, to instruments to which they are party, but which are not retroactive? As far as the Declaration of London is concerned, it was accepted by all the major powers of 1943 except those of the Axis. It was applied in the zones of occupation of Germany after the Second World War, and its principles were adopted by legislation in the neutral European countries, Sweden, Switzerland, and Portugal. The Federal Republic of Germany adopted these principles in its own legislation when it became independent once again. Principles drawn from the declaration were also included in the peace treaty between the Allies and Italy. Its principles have, therefore, very substantial acceptance.

While the UNESCO Convention for the Protection of Cultural Property in the Event of Armed Conflict (the Hague Convention) of 1954 controls protection of cultural property from damage and destruction in armed conflict, the removal of such property from occupied territory and its return are dealt with in the Protocol. The Protocol to the Hague Convention has been adopted by seventy-five states:[5] a number of states that are not party to the Protocol, such as Australia, Canada, the United Kingdom, and the United States, had accepted similar principles in the Declaration of London, and some states that were not party to the Declaration of London, such as Austria, Hungary, and Switzerland, are party to the Protocol.

The UNESCO Convention of 1970 is not primarily designed to deal with the protection of cultural heritage in wartime—that is the function of the Hague Convention of 1954 and its Protocol. However the 1970 Convention does provide (Article 11) that

> the export and transfer of ownership of cultural property under compulsion arising directly or indirectly from the occupation of a country by a foreign power shall be regarded as illicit.

There are eighty-five states party to this Convention,[6] a number of which were not party to the Declaration of London nor are party to the Hague Protocol. Both the 1970 UNESCO Convention and the UNIDROIT Convention, the final text of which has recently been adopted,[7] are good indications of developments in the general law of protection for the cultural heritage. Both indicate an increased concern for the recovery of displaced cultural heritage. These developments since the Second World War indicate an acceptance of principles for the recovery of cultural objects displaced in peacetime, which apply even more strongly to cultural heritage displaced in times of conflict, for which the rules were developed much earlier.

Finally, much that was stated in the appeal of the Director-General of UNESCO in 1978 is highly relevant to the present situation. This *Plea for the Return of an Irreplaceable Cultural Heritage to Those Who Created It* is attached as Appendix 12.

THE PRINCIPLES

Principle I
Cultural objects that have been taken from territory occupied during or immediately after hostilities in the Second World War by any belligerent will be returned to the country from which they have been taken (Declaration of London, Hague Protocol).

Principle 2

Where there have been successive displacements, the objects will be returned to the territory where they were located at the outbreak of hostilities in 1939.

The problem of successive looting has to be faced; for example, there are cases where cultural objects were taken by German soldiers or Nazi authorities from the Netherlands, Poland, or other countries under Nazi occupation and then taken from Germany by Soviet soldiers during their occupation of Germany. Although this principle has not so far been enunciated in any international instrument, it seems appropriate to regulate it in this manner so that claims for the same object can be dealt with once, rather than give rise to a series of claims.

The reason for limiting this principle to displacement after the outbreak of war should be evident: the commitment of states to the Declaration of London makes a clear starting point directed specifically to the events subsequent to the outbreak of war. Claims for the return of cultural objects displaced (by whatever means) before that date should be dealt with, after their return to the country that held them in 1939, between the government of that country and the claimant on the basis of other principles,[8] by bilateral negotiation. Should that fail, the claim could be brought to the UNESCO Intergovernmental Committee for Promoting the Return of Cultural Property to its Countries of Origin or its Restitution in Case of Illicit Appropriation. It does not seem appropriate that the general resolution of claims to objects displaced during the Second World War should be delayed or prevented by claims that have their origin in events remote from that time and that conflict. The UNIDROIT Convention has limited claims under that instrument to breach of export controls, which prevents complication of claims on that basis by intervention of claims of much older origin.

Principle 3

Principle 1 will apply whether transfers of the cultural objects concerned have taken the form of open looting or plunder, or of transactions apparently legal in form, even when they purport to have been voluntarily effected (Declaration of London).

Principle 4

Cultural property taken from an occupied territory shall never be detained as war reparations (Hague Protocol, Article 3).

It is clear that citizens, especially veterans' groups, of countries that suffered severe losses of cultural property during the Second World War may have an emotional attachment to the idea that their country is entitled to "spoils of war." However, this idea is now contrary to international humanitarian law, and it is important that this be understood and accepted. One method of dealing with this politically very delicate issue is to show such groups that important cultural objects of their own heritage will be returned in recompense for their relinquishing "spoils of war" that are not as significant for their national

heritage. For these reasons, such a principle must go in tandem with the next (Principle 5).

Principle 5

Where cultural objects displaced during or immediately after hostilities in the Second World War have passed into the hands of third parties, the state that is responsible for their removal from the country where they were located in 1939 shall reacquire them for return to the state from which they were taken, by repurchase, indemnity or other appropriate means (Hague Protocol, Article 4).

This principle is designed to cover the case of cultural objects that were sold on to and are held by third parties, some of whom may attract in certain countries protection as "bona-fide" acquirers. It cannot be sufficient for one country to demand the return of displaced goods from a country that holds them in state hands (for example, in state museums) while at the same time refusing responsibility for the return of cultural goods taken by it from that state on the ground that it no longer has the goods in question in its possession. Where an object is still in the territory of the state under whose occupation it was removed, that state is responsible for its return and may have to regain possession from private individuals, whether by purchase, expropriation, or other legal action, in order to be able to return it. If the object is in the territory of a third state, the state responsible will have to negotiate with the private holder, or with the third state itself if, for example, it is now in a state-owned collection of the third state.

Principle 6

No time limits can be set.

Although time limits are set for claims in private law in all legal systems, there is good reason to suggest that this should not be the case here. Sufficient cases are at hand to show that goods identifiably looted from another country are still appearing, and in view of the amount of material still missing, much of it will continue to appear for some time to come. There are precedents for this view. The peace settlements after the First World War dealt with the return of works of art that had been taken long before the events of that war—in some cases as early as the seventeenth century—reflecting practice at the 1815 Congress of Vienna that dealt with manuscripts taken from the library at Heidelberg in 1622.[9]

Principle 7

Cultural objects being repatriated are to be accompanied by the relevant scientific documentation where available.

It is evident that objects looted in war will, in many if not most cases, have become detached from their scholarly documentation. However, in some cases the documentation may also have been taken. It may be the case that an object has found

its way into an institution in another country where new scholarly documentation has been prepared. The importance of the sharing of scientific information has been asserted in a number of UNESCO and ICOM documents.[10]

Principle 8
Restitution by replacement is an available remedy where unique cultural objects have been destroyed.

Article 247 of the Treaty of Versailles required that Germany should provide the University of Louvain with manuscripts, incunabula, books, maps, and collectibles of the same number as and of similar type and value to those destroyed by Germany through the burning of the library of Louvain during the First World War. This principle should be further explored with regard to significant cultural materials that can be proven to have been taken away during occupation, but whose present location has not been discovered and which may, in fact, have been destroyed.

Restitution by replacement is not possible in all cases. However, it remains important that people who are asked to return to another nation cultural objects of primary interest to them should see a compensating benefit to their own culture. One possibility that has been suggested is the restoration of Novgorod cathedral as recompense by Germany for the destruction of Russian cultural property during the war. However, there are many other imaginative solutions that might be explored, such as the technological and financial support of existing museums; the granting of scholarships to artists and writers; the training of conservators, librarians, and curators; the establishment of cultural centers, art schools, and museums to replace those known to have been destroyed; and the support of existing craftwork and its further development. The important point is that the new flowering and accessibility of the damaged culture should be highly visible, in order to make clear to the population that the resolution of the issues remaining after the "cultural warfare" of the 1940s can produce equally significant benefits for both sides.

REQUIREMENTS FOR A SUCCESSFUL RETURN PROGRAM

Where there are many outstanding claims between countries, it is clear that there is good reason to try to establish some kind of general program of restitution that would regulate the problem as far as possible in accordance with mutually acceptable principles and, allowing for the odd object that will still surface, will regulate the bulk of the outstanding claims for once and for all. For such a program to be successful, however, there are several preliminary requirements.

Inventories
Before a successful settlement of claims can take place, there is an enormous job of identification and documentation to be undertaken. Lists of what was taken and the circumstances of its loss must be prepared. While in some countries that work has been largely done, in others it has not.

The demands for restitution will not be satisfactorily resolved by returns on the basis of inventories, where inventories of lost material are adequate in some countries but not in others. Because of the political delicacy of the issue in some countries, the authorities must show that there will be an even-handed settling of claims. That cannot be done if one country has a good inventory of lost material and has identified its current locations, and other countries with major losses have, for whatever reasons, not been able to document these losses.

This is clearly a job in which dedicated art historians can help, by drawing up inventories of losses and trying to locate the objects in question. Sophisticated means of searching can now be employed—for example, the use of computerized data based on the catalogues of auction houses—and some objects may be located by alert specialists working in museum storerooms or simply in the course of checking literature and exhibition catalogues if these specialists are aware of what they must look for. Even if a specific object under investigation cannot be located by these means, such lists are important, as they will enable other missing objects to be found when they appear on the market or are identified by their present holders. The publicity surrounding the recovery of the Quedlinburg treasures has, for example, encouraged other holders of important cultural property taken from Germany and now in the United States to return it.

Identifying categories of special importance
Certain cultural objects are of particular importance to the people of the country that has lost them, and it is evident that many of those displaced during the Second World War or its aftermath will fall into this particularly sensitive category. These would include

- objects that are indispensable to people in understanding their origin and culture,[11] such as objects of spiritual value; objects of special importance to the national history (such as crown jewels or other objects of particular national significance);
- elements of dismembered objects, stolen from sites, or pieces that were once part of a complex object.

These categories are derived from *A Plea for the Return of an Irreplaceable Cultural Heritage to Those Who Created It* (see Appendix 12). Repatriation of objects displaced during the Second World War will concern many thousands of objects over time. It is logical, therefore, that emphasis should be placed first on these categories, since their loss has been the most painful.

Publicity
Clearly the controversy surrounding the return of cultural heritage taken during the Second World War or its aftermath has attracted major publicity. This is important, as it reinforces the public conscience that cultural objects should not be dis-

placed during conflict and, if so displaced, should be returned. The general media discussion and publicity given to returns will also reassure people in all jurisdictions that their claims will be heard. It will encourage those with knowledge about objects taken or their present location to volunteer information for those making the inventories, and it may encourage spontaneous return on the part of others. Finally, it will shore up the changes in mentality that have occurred in the twentieth century to make it clear that the principles of the Declaration of London and Hague Protocol are now generally accepted as international law and that reconstituting of cultural heritages dispersed during conflict must be a normal part of peace settlements.

METHOD OF PROCEDURE

From all that precedes, it should be evident that I believe that, while drawing on the substantial body of existing legal principles, claimant states should not be unduly legalistic in their application. This is, after all, a cultural and an emotional issue as well as a legal and political one. Sensitive handling now may create the decisive step in the development of the law of return of the so-called spoils of war. Insensitive handling could set the development of precedent and of public ethics back many years. Views have been expressed at this conference, on all sides, that there is now a consensus to resolve this problem. With due attention to the sensitivity of the issues, they should be resolved by the use of principles that, even if they were not absolutely clear in 1945, are certainly now generally accepted.

For these reasons I believe the first step should be that states wishing to make claims must agree on certain basic principles. Perhaps only seven or eight, such as those suggested above, are needed. These could then be embodied in a bilateral agreement. This agreement should be made public, so that the people in both countries can see the very reasonable ethical and legal basis on which returns will be made. Each accord will also help other states in their efforts to settle a similar group of principles.

If bilateral agreement is not reached, it would be possible to seek an arbitrator to settle appropriate principles for such returns, or to ask an organization such as UNESCO to convene a meeting of experts to agree on such principles.

The process would then require a prioritization of claims, along the lines suggested above for the most significant categories of material. This may mean many months of careful work. Finally, for specific claims that the bilateral authorities find themselves unable to resolve, there could be recourse to the mediatory functions of the UNESCO Intergovernmental Committee for Promoting the Return of Cultural Property to its Countries of Origin or its Restitution in Case of Illicit Appropriation, whose statutes are able to encompass claims arising from the Second World War. A copy of these statutes is attached in Appendix 13.

CONCLUSION

The problem has remained unsolved for fifty years. If it is not resolved in the next few years, it will remain a constant source of friction, limiting the development of new political harmony. It is my firm belief that the emergence of this issue at the end of the twentieth century provides an unparalleled opportunity to reaffirm the law created in 1954 on the recovery of cultural heritage displaced as a result of conflict. This, in an age in which culture-based conflicts are showing increasing vitality, would be a significant gift from this millennium to the next.

PART 7

CONTRIBUTIONS
BY GUEST
PARTICIPANTS
IN THE
CONFERENCE

LOSSES OF

CULTURAL PROPERTY

FROM THE TERRITORY OF

THE CZECH REPUBLIC

DUE TO WORLD WAR II

Pavel Jirásek

The beginning of the expansion of the Third Reich into Czechoslovakia began with the Munich Pact of September 1938, when, due to France's and Britain's policy of appeasement, the country lost almost one-third of its historic lands and was, in fact, doomed to destruction. The events of March 15, 1939, when German military units occupied the territory of Bohemia and Moravia and the newly established protectorate became part of the Third Reich, and when Slovakia declared independence, were only a logical consequence of Munich. From today's vantage point, it can be said that it was Munich 1938 that most strongly influenced even the postwar Czechoslovak development, the victory of the left wing and the following forty years of the totalitarian regime.

The Czech territory was thus totally occupied by 1939. Due to the absence of military operations, the cultural monuments were not destroyed at that time—neither was there much pilfering of cultural objects, not even at the time of escalated Nazi terror after the assassination of the Deputy Reichsprotektor, Reinhard Heydrich, which cost the lives of tens of thousands of people. Apart from this, the Czech territories were not crossed by any military front before the end of World War II. That is why (with some exceptions) no outflow of cultural objects to Germany can be noted until 1945.

One of these exceptions is the Jezeří Castle, which was vacated and then adapted by Nazis as a special prison in which senior French military officers were interned. The contents of the Bouzov Castle, an important monument which since 1699 was in possession of the Order of Teutonic Knights, were partly destroyed, partly stolen after the expulsion of the owners and its occupation by the fascists.

Special mention should be made, of course, of the Jewish art and ceremonial objects that were assembled by the Nazis after 1942, with the aim of establishing a rare world attraction in Prague after the planned liquidation of the Jewish population—a museum of an extinct nation. The present Jewish museum, whose original collections, assembled before 1950, were handed over in 1994 to the Federation of Jewish Communities, has amassed objects from 153 Jewish religious communities in the territory of Bohemia and Moravia. Most of their original owners never returned from behind the gates of Dachau, Auschwitz, Majdanek or other concentration and death camps.

The situation changed drastically at the end of the war, when the military front crossed the Czech territory. The north of Moravia and of Silesia was most painfully affected. By the end of March 1945, during the liberation fights in the vicinity of the Silesian capital Opava, the beautiful building of the present Silesian Provincial Museum was destroyed by fire, and most of the collections of this oldest museum in the Czech lands were destroyed. A great part of those collections was, however, removed before the end of the war and placed in several castles of the region. The objects were not properly protected against destruction or theft. There is also a justified suspicion that the administration of the Third Reich managed to dispatch part of the collections via the still occupied

territory to Germany before the arrival of the Red Army. The number of lost objects is estimated at about five thousand. They include the works of important European artists, the oldest dating to the thirteenth century. In the archive of the museum is kept a list of those objects, in some cases accompanied by their photographs.

Among other painful losses of cultural heritage can be mentioned the castle in Mikulov and its contents. During World War II, collections from occupied France were brought to the castle. Also stored there was an important castle library as well as art and historical objects. The castle was occupied by German soldiers who, at the end of the war, stole many of its valuables. The greater part of the edifice, including the contents, was, however, burnt to ashes when the Germans poured gasoline over it and set fire to it on their retreat.

A rather unusual case concerns the fate of the so-called Pazaurek Collection. Dr. G. E. Pazaurek, born in Prague, was director of the Provincial Industrial Museum in Stuttgart beginning in 1905. In 1932, he bequeathed to the Prague Museum of Applied Arts his comprehensive glass collection, numbering 2,400 important pieces of glass dating from classical times through the nineteenth century. One of the reasons for this donation was Pazaurek's antipathy toward Nazi Germany, resulting in conflicts with pro-Hitlerite employees of the Stuttgart museum. In the year of the bequest, 2,034 pieces from this collection were transferred to Prague. Dr. Pazaurek kept the rest—366 pieces of glass—temporarily in his own possession for study purposes at his Altmanshof manor in Germany. After his death in 1935, however, the transport of the remainder of his collection to Prague was systematically prevented by the German authorities. In 1939, the collection was transferred to the Silesian Museum of Applied Arts in Wrocław (the then-German Breslau). During the investigation in 1948, the former director of the Wrocław museum testified that the collection, together with other exhibits, was hidden away from the advancing Red Army in a Lower Silesian monastery. Further postwar search was unsuccessful. After a resumed search by Polish authorities, 16 pieces of glass, mostly damaged, were found in 1962. In the same year, during the restitution proceedings, they were handed over to Czechoslovakia. At the same time, the Prague Museum of Applied Arts handed over to Poland a collection of approximately 3,000 medals, removed to our territory at the end of the war. The fate of the remaining 350 pieces of glass is still uncertain. It can be supposed that after 1945 they were dispersed, as indicated by the fact that in 1961 the Prague Museum of Applied Arts purchased one goblet from this collection in a Prague antiques shop.

Other evidence exists regarding the destruction of cultural property. The paintings by the most prominent Czech Baroque painter, Petr Brandl, were lost from the collections of the Lobkowitz family; lost also were some of the contents of the Valtice castle. These are typical examples of property that had survived German invaders but was destroyed after the liberation by the Red Army.

Other museums and castles affected by World War II are the Konopiště castle, the Sovinec castle, and the Museum of Czech Sokol, and certainly there would be many others if a more detailed search of archives were made.

It is necessary to state that the most tragic period for the movable cultural heritage in Czechoslovakia was to occur after the war, from 1946 through 1954, following the 1948 communist revolution. The losses of art objects and collections that occurred during this period are estimated to be four to five times higher than the war losses. At this time, the nationalized aristocratic and church estates were ransacked and pillaged. Alas, documentation of this heritage began only in 1954; because of the wide range of archival materials destroyed prior to that date through neglect or purposefully, it has been impossible to find necessary information on the missing works.

A new wave of ransacking began, paradoxically, after the raising of the Iron Curtain. Open frontiers and the growth of the antiquities market have caught the Czech Republic unprepared. Criminal activity in this sphere has increased by ten to fifteen times. Although the state has adopted some technical and legislative measures that have already resulted in a reduction of these criminal acts, it is estimated that over one hundred thousand works of art have been displaced illegally from Czech territory since 1989.* The central register of stolen monuments is computerized, including information and photographs.

Ninety-five percent of these records have been compiled since 1989. The police are gradually penetrating back into the more remote years, and before long the data base will hold information on identified stolen works from the period of World War II as well. Should losses from the period of the war be settled separately from the others, the Ministry of Culture of the Czech Republic is prepared to support this work and to participate in any prospective international cooperation.

---

* Editor's note: See Pavel Jirásek, "Institutions Form Network to Fight Art Theft," *ICOM News* 1, vol. 48 (1995), 8–9, for an account of the measures being taken to counteract the current threat to the cultural heritage of the Czech Republic.

THE RECOVERY OF CULTURAL

PROPERTY IN SLOVAKIA

Jana Bahurinská

The Bard Graduate Center conference was organized at the right place and at the right time. The timing of the conference could not have been more appropriate, as the symposium followed on the heels of the 1989 revolution in Eastern Europe against communism. Since the fall of communism there in 1989, Europe has been marked by a new political climate, which has facilitated the discussion and resolution of problems related to the reappearance and recovery of cultural property looted or otherwise removed in the past.

The proposals expressed by Lyndel V. Prott at the conference, together with the experience of German and Russian experts in the field and the legislative initiatives presented, have proved invaluable to the Slovak Ministry of Culture, which is in the process of setting up a commission on the restitution of cultural treasures. The delegation should compile an up-to-date, comprehensive list of missing works of art and objects, many of which are believed to be in Hungary, Germany, the Russian Federation, and the United States.

We Slovaks have attempted to recover our Slovak cultural heritage held by Hungary since the time of the Austro-Hungarian Empire. Regrettably, many of our works have yet to be returned. With regard to World War II, we have in our possession lists of missing works that were prepared by our museums and galleries, archives, and libraries just after 1945. Some of the listed works were recovered between 1945 and 1948. After 1948, the political situation in Slovakia (then part of Czechoslovakia) became highly unfavorable. During the early 1950s, many works of art, rare books, and religious artifacts were destroyed by the communist government. It is not known whether certain works were looted by the Nazis or the Red Army or destroyed by the communists. After 1956, when Hungary was experiencing political changes, several attempts were made to discuss the recovery of the Slovak cultural heritage held by Hungary and looted from Slovakia during World War II. All official dialogue was carried out in accordance with the "Štrba Agreement."* In the 1960s, there were some new but unsuccessful attempts on the part of Czechoslovakia to recover the works. After 1968–69 and the occupation of the country by the Soviet army, it became impossible to pursue this endeavor further. Many important documents, lists, and agreements were permanently locked in archives, making it virtually impossible for art historians and lawyers to study them and continue their work. Since 1989 new avenues of possibility have opened, facilitating the resolution of this problem. We know that we need to study and compare existing lists of artworks missing since World War II, and we must coordinate the claims process at the level of the Slovak Ministry of Culture.

Thanks to the symposium, we have gained much useful information regarding the process of recovering cultural heritage; I am sure that we shall use it successfully in Slovakia.

---

* Editor's note: The Štrba Agreement, signed in 1949 at Štrba Mountain Lake in High Tatra, included provisions relating to the exchange and recovery of cultural property looted from Slovakia after 1938.

WORLD WAR II CULTURAL LOSSES OF POLAND:

A HISTORICAL ISSUE OR

STILL A "HOT" POLITICAL

AND LEGAL TOPIC?

Wojciech Kowalski

It was wonderful to meet Bernard Taper at the New York conference, "The Spoils of War." He was an Art Intelligence Officer (MFA&A) in Germany, and from 1946 to 1948 tried to recover artworks looted from Poland (see above, pages 135–38). Most vigorously, as he relates, he sought the Czartoryski *Portrait of a Young Man* by Raphael, alas without success. Almost half a century later, serving as Commissioner of Polish Cultural Heritage Abroad for the government of Poland, I began to search for the portrait again, but as yet the only result is a color photograph of the painting (see colorplate 1). I presented this photograph to Mr. Taper during the conference, in response to his statement that he had only had use of a black-and-white reproduction.[1]

Mr. Taper told me also about a communication he had received from Thomas Hoving, the former director of the Metropolitan Museum of Art, after his visit to the Czartoryski Museum in Cracow. Hoving informed Taper that the museum people there had "all but given up hope on the Raphael," although he himself still suspected that the picture existed and would surface one day. This story reflects two important aspects of the difficulties Poland has had in trying to trace her war losses. Why did Bernard Taper have only a black-and-white photograph when looking for such an important work of art? Why have Polish museologists "all but given up hope" on the most valuable known cultural war loss of their country?

In answer to the first question, it is necessary to point out that art collections in Poland were only in very exceptional cases well inventoried and documented before 1939. The very small number of publications and catalogues produced resulted from a generally low level of knowledge about the historical importance of art in Poland in the nineteenth and early twentieth centuries. The aristocracy possessed many paintings and objets d'art, but, with few exceptions, there was no tradition of systematic collecting and consequently of the cataloguing of works of art in a thorough and scholarly manner. Artworks were mostly kept in residences and palaces in order to indicate the wealth and importance of the owner's family. Most of the cultural property removed to Russia during the course of political events in the nineteenth century could not be repatriated due to lack of documentation, although Poland had very good legal grounds for such restitution based on the Riga Treaty of 1921.[2]

However, lack of documentation was not the only cause of the catastrophe that the events of World War II wreaked in the field of Polish culture. Postwar restitution was incredibly difficult because of the unprecedented scale and severity of looting, both by the Nazis and by the Red Army. All that was of value was removed both officially and unofficially, without any legal or other limitations. The only laws in effect were those dictated by National Socialist leaders, such as the executive order of Generalgouverneur Hans Frank introduced two months after the outbreak of war. It is enough to state a few provisions of this order to understand the entire issue. The provisions read as follows:

> The whole public possession of works of art in the General gouvernement is to be confiscated unless it was confiscated

as a property of the former Polish State according to another law (section 1).

The public possession of works of art includes:
1. private property . . . ;
2. church property with the exception of liturgical objects that are necessary for ordinary service (section 2).

All persons are subject to imprisonment:
1. who intend to hide, sell or export works of art from the Generalgouvernement;
2. who refuse to give or give false or incomplete information that is to be given according to this order (section 5).[3]

In such a situation, even the intense work on the documentation of losses carried out in secret by the Polish underground movement could bring only limited results. Data collected during 1939–43 were sent to the Polish government in London, where they were soon published.[4] In fact, that was the only result of all this work, because the government-in-exile was forced to stop its activities at the end of the war. The same fate fell to the efforts of the Commission for Protection and Restitution of Cultural Material, set up in 1944 by the Conference of Allied Ministers of Education to gather information on losses in the occupied countries. The commission was required to give all the documentary material collected by underground anti-Nazi movements to the archives of the British Council early in 1945, before that material could be put to practical use.[5]

The original documentation collected by the Polish underground movement also followed the same path, although the destination of the material was different. After the war, almost all files were taken over by the state police of the new regime and, as materials of an enemy organization, were deposited in the archives of the Communist Party. I was the first person who was allowed access to that material, at the end of the 1970s. The Bureau for Restitution and Reparations of the Ministry of Culture and Art, which was officially in charge of restitution matters after 1945, began the documentation work again, but due to the political changes of the late 1940s, its task could not be completed.[6] The bureau was closed down and the problem of restitution declared closed. The situation seemed to be hopeless. The issue of the removal of works of art to the former USSR could not even be mentioned, as this was politically unacceptable. Later, Polish museums had to appear grateful for "gifts" received from Moscow and Leningrad in 1956 after Khrushchev took power.[7]

For the same political reasons, Poland could not claim any property from the former German Democratic Republic (GDR). Neither could property be claimed from West Germany, because of the poor relations that existed between Poland and that country for many years.

The situation described explains precisely the reasons for the feelings of the museologists in Cracow noted by Thomas Hoving. Another reason was the general lack of progress achieved in Poland in the field of restitution of cultural property. The example often given was the fate of the claims that Poland had submitted to the Paris peace conference after World War I. Although the United States delegation and some others supported the idea of restitution in kind and reparations, the conference did not accept the Polish viewpoint in the end.[8] What could Polish museologists expect in the context of World War II, if such a conference had not even been planned in the many years since the war had ended?

Also very distressing for them was the attitude of official Polish authorities toward the still unsolved problem of the effects of World War II in the field of culture. The Ministry of Culture had no interest whatsoever in this issue. No one officially collected data on losses during the entire postwar period. That must be recognized as serious neglect, especially when we learn that such work has been continuously carried out in Germany, despite the negative political climate.[9] As a good example of the way that the Ministry of Culture has dealt with the problem, I refer to the talk I had with the ministry in 1979 when looking for some information on war losses. A senior officer I met answered my question: "My boy, you are talking about treasures removed by Nazis, but you are also thinking about treasures looted by Russians, and in that instance you are a liability not only for us but especially for yourself."

The political events of 1989 and 1990 have changed the situation totally; because of my publications, I was asked by the ministry to reopen and organize the repatriation and reparations bureau that had closed about forty years earlier. We had to start once again the work that our colleagues began in 1939–50. All old catalogues of lost works of art had to be verified and new information collected. As the political climate was completely different, we had no limitations, and work was to a certain extent easier. Computers contributed significantly to our progress.

At the same time, we started difficult negotiations on the new treaties with Russia, Ukraine, Belarus, and other countries. After extensive discussion, we were able to obtain a most important provision in the Polish-Russian Treaty of 1992. It reads:

> In accord with the international standards and agreements . . . the Sides will regard with favor the mutual efforts to reveal and return the cultural and historical goods, including archival material which had been seized and unlawfully removed or that by some other unlawful manner had come to be found in the territories of the other Side.[10]

The new political era helped also to accelerate some practical cases of restitution. Poland received back the collection of important Renaissance bronze tomb plaques removed by the Nazis from Poznań cathedral to Nuremberg in 1940 and finally found in a depot of the State Hermitage Museum in Leningrad in 1989. As the result of Polish-German talks in 1992, museums in Poznań and Warsaw have recovered over thirty pieces of ancient gold jewelry and over seven hundred coins.

By the end of 1994, about forty thousand lost works of art and collections were registered, and sixteen court restitution proceedings had been initiated in various countries. The cultural losses suffered by Poland as a result of World War II are no longer merely a historical issue but, I hope for the last time, have become a "hot" political and legal topic.

UNDER DURESS:

THE SALE OF

THE FRANZ KOENIGS

COLLECTION

Christine F. Koenigs

The art collection that Franz Koenigs had put together devotedly over many years amounted by 1935 to forty-six paintings, including twenty by Rubens, and nearly three thousand old master drawings. That year, Koenigs offered his collection on loan to the Boymans Museum in Rotterdam. The museum's director, Dr. D. Hannema, wrote triumphantly to the mayor and city council of Rotterdam on April 2, 1935, announcing an important long-term loan to the Boymans Museum in honor of the official opening of the museum's new building, and referring to this loan as "the famous 'Koenigs Collection,' a collection of old master paintings and a special collection of drawings, in possession of F. Koenigs." Stating that the collection was insured for 3.5 million guilders, as evidence of its great importance, Hannema went on: "I am very much delighted to be in personal contact with the great collector who is the source of this loan; the undersigned would greatly appreciate it if your Council would send F. Koenigs a letter of appreciation to show your satisfaction."[1] In Hannema's letter, as more often in correspondence of the succeeding years, the drawings were recognized as comprising a collection in their own right within the larger collection, with a special status. When the Koenigs collection is referred to today, as in publications and discussions relating to the "spoils of war" controversy, it is usually the drawings that are meant.

The close relationship of the Koenigs family to the collection, and the personal character of the loan to the museum, is attested, for example, by a letter from Koenigs' wife, Anna Koenigs, Countess von Kalckreuth, to Hannema on April 28, 1935: "Dr. Lütjens [the administrator of the Koenigs collection and the representative of Paul Cassirer in Amsterdam] must have told you that I would like to see you here in order to arrange a few things with you. My husband did on the whole arrange everything with you, but many questions remain, such as the date of transport of our treasures to Rotterdam, the question of framing the drawings. . . . Though it will be difficult to part with them, I am glad they will be in your hands, because you will surely really love them. If you would come to tea one afternoon with Lütjens also present, we will then soon have discussed all important matters."[2] On May 15, 1935, a transportation insurance policy was issued in the name of F. Koenigs for 2.2 million guilders,[3] and on November 20, 1935, Hannema sent to Koenigs an official receipt and acceptance of the loan, "until further notice."[4]

Subsequently, Dr. Hannema sought to purchase the Koenigs collection for the Boymans Museum. On August 31, 1939, some four years later, Hannema wrote to Goudstikker, the Amsterdam art dealer: "I just wanted to update you on the negotiations for the acquisition of the Koenigs collection for the Boymans Museum. As you know, I consider this collection to be of the very greatest importance. I have already taken a number of steps toward finding a solution, but circumstances really are not very favorable. Many important friends of the museum are out of the country, and the international situation occupies people's thoughts more than anything else."[5] On September 4, 1939, Goudstikker replied that Koenigs had given him "the right to continue negotiations with you and the other gentlemen in Rotterdam [that is, the Boymans Museum Foundation, recently founded on June 7, 1939] concerning the purchase of his collection. He has, however, under the present circumstances, fixed no terms, so that he retains, of course, the freedom to make other arrangements for his collection. It must be taken into account, as well, that he cannot consider himself as bound to the named price in the event of an unforeseen devaluation of our currency."[6] Goudstikker ends the letter by saying that in his opinion it is now the right moment to conclude a sale, underscoring Hannema's evident reluctance.

As is apparent from this exchange, Koenigs was preparing for the sale of his collection and had instructed Goudstikker to negotiate with the Boymans Museum Foundation. Koenigs had used his collection as collateral in a long-standing credit arrangement with S. Kramarsky, a German Jew living in Amsterdam, who was a business associate and friend of long standing and the majority shareholder in the Lisser & Rosen- kranz Bank, Amsterdam. With Kramarsky preparing to emigrate to America, and the Lisser & Rosenkranz Bank's existence jeopardized by an increasing German hegemony and the very real possibility of invasion, Koenigs foresaw a need to repay his loan.

Through his German descent and his activities as a banker, Koenigs had important business interests in Germany, but wartime conditions in Germany made impossible the liquidation of substantial assets and their transfer out of Germany, even to what was formally still a neutral country. Moreover, Koenigs' own personal situation was delicate, to say the least. In 1923, he had moved himself and his family to the Netherlands, long before the rise to power of the National Socialists, which only made more obvious the political connotations of his taking on Dutch nationality in February 1939. Over the years, he had maintained extensive business and social contacts on the highest levels in Germany, but he was known to be strongly critical of National Socialism, and documentation exists for his secret engagement in work against the Nazi regime.

The deteriorating international situation had rapidly restricted Koenigs' room to maneuver, and Kramarsky and the Lisser & Rosenkranz Bank were being forced to take urgent action. On November 11, 1939, after the announcement of an immediate threat of German invasion, Kramarsky and his family left overnight for Lisbon on their way to America. In the meantime, no proposals had been forthcoming from Rot- terdam concerning acquisition of the collection. On March 13, 1940, Hannema wrote to Van der Vorm, a benefactor of the museum, informing him that the taxation report on the Koenigs collection was ready. Hannema continued: "Today Koenigs has telephoned me and announced that within fourteen days his collection will be transported to Lisbon. A longer delay is not possible, because the bank where his collection is given as a collateral is now in liquidation. Mr. Koenigs assured me, though, that he will undertake everything

possible to keep the collection here. As you know, in 1935 the collection was insured for 4.5 million guilders, which is about what Mr. Koenigs has spent on it over the years. It is now being offered for 2.2 million guilders. At first, the important nineteenth-century French drawings were not included, but now they are. Two drawings by Dürer and Grünewald, which are at the moment in America, also belong to it. My evaluation could be called low. I would apply another standard for an eventual sale of only a part of the collection. It would be a disaster if it [the collection] were to leave Rotterdam for good."[7] Without mention of the telephone conversation with Koenigs, Hannema sent this very same letter to another benefactor, D. G. van Beuningen, on March 21, 1940.[8]

Despite the intense interest in the collection evident in Hannema's letter to Van der Vorm and Van Beuningen, Koenigs received no response to his most recent offer.

On April 2, 1940, Koenigs wrote to Hannema: "Since I haven't heard anything more from you, I have been obliged to give over these drawings as payment to the private banking firm of Lisser & Rosenkranz, in liquidation, by which these drawings have become the full and free property of the above named. I kindly request that you take careful note of this, as I am under the necessity of ending your loan and of placing these drawings at the complete disposal of the private banking firm of Lisser & Rosenkranz, in liquidation as previously described, whose instructions you are kindly requested to follow."[9] From the point of view of Hannema and his associates, this must have been a very promising development, as now the transaction was in the hands of an especially vulnerable party. On that same day, the directors of the Lisser & Rosenkranz Bank wrote to the Boymans Museum: "We have the honor of informing you that we have taken in payment from Mr. F. Koenigs the collection of drawings that some time ago he gave to you on loan, and of which we have a detailed description. In relation to this transaction, by which the above-mentioned drawings have become our full and free property, we are planning to have our shipping agent pick up the drawings in the course of this week, and kindly request that you inform us as to which day is most convenient for you to have these items picked up."[10]

On April 8, 1940, Hannema wrote to Van Beuningen: "I have given the whole Koenigs affair more thought and would like you to take the following into account, as I have always pointed out: a number of paintings can easily be sold without damaging the entirety. If we keep the four pieces by Hierony- mus Bosch and, by Rubens, the big Bath of Diana, the landscape from the former Northbrook collection, the five small sketches (studies for decorations in the Torre de la Parada), The Union of England and Scotland, The Three Crosses, and perhaps still another painting, then the rest of the paintings, something like twenty, could be disposed of. If push comes to shove, I would advise letting even the Bath of Diana go. I cannot emphasize enough the importance of the drawings. This is the largest and most important collection of its kind existing in private possession. Seeing that the material is no longer available, to make a comparable new collection is out of the question. Staying with your offer of one million guilders, the paintings thus represent a margin."[11]

In the letters to Hannema on April 2 from Koenigs and the Lisser & Rosenkranz Bank, it is the collection of drawings that is mentioned as having been given over to settle Koenigs' debt to the bank. The waiting game proved successful as a result of the rapidly deteriorating situation, so that by the second week of April, Hannema and Van Beuningen were able to assume that a large portion of Koenigs' collection of paintings was to be included in the sale, and that the whole could be had for less than half the price that had been asked only a few weeks before.

On April 9, 1940, Dr. Hannema wrote to the Lisser & Rosenkranz Bank: "On Friday, April 5, we had a conference at the Boymans Museum with Mr. Koenigs, who was to let you know how things stood. The same afternoon, Mr. D. G. van Beuningen visited you and made an offer for the collection as it is now held at the Boymans Museum. Today Mr. Goudstikker, representing you [Goudstikker was now representing the Lisser & Rosenkranz Bank] had a talk with Mr. van Beuningen, on which occasion you were made a new offer, which will remain in force until ten o'clock tonight. It is my opinion that in the present circumstances this new offer can be said to be better than good, and I am convinced that you would not easily get a better offer elsewhere. Meanwhile, we have started to ready the entire collection for shipping." Then follows some information about the preparations: "The paintings, which were hidden in different locations because of the threat of war, are being assembled. You should be able to pick up the entire collection any time from Tuesday morning on. I expect at the same time to be discharged then of all responsibility. In ending, I must draw your attention to the fact that the Boymans Museum was promised as a gift a choice of one of the paintings, when the collection leaves Rotterdam. I hesitate between the Saint Christopher by Jeroen [Hieronymus] Bosch and the landscape The Wagon by P. P. Rubens."[12] The nearly indifferent, administrative tone taken by Hannema in the above letter, by the man who had written to Van der Vorm and Van Beuningen that "it would be a disaster if it [the collection] were to leave Rotterdam," and that "to make a comparable new collection is out of the question," was probably intended to tighten the screws further on Koenigs and his associates.

Still representing the bank, Goudstikker sent a telegram to Hannema at 6:42 P.M. on the same day as the above letter: "Everything turned out exactly as we had hoped, cordial congratulations—Goudstikker."[13] Hannema sent a telegram in reply to Goudstikker: "Accomplishment of the deal delights me thanks for great cooperation—Hannema."[14]

The Lisser & Rosenkranz Bank sent two letters to the museum also on April 9: "We have just received your letter of April 9. Although in a strictly business sense a reply is not required, we would nevertheless like to take advantage of this opportunity to congratulate you on the fact that this important collection has been kept for the Netherlands and the Boymans

Museum, and we are pleased to have been able to contribute to this. Moreover, because of the promise made to us by Mr. D. G. van Beuningen, namely, that the present name for the collection of drawings and paintings will be maintained, Mr. Koenigs' wish has also been fulfilled."[15] The second letter reads as follows:

To the director of the Boymans Museum in Rotterdam:

Following on our correspondence of yesterday, we have the honor of informing you that the frequently referred to collection of drawings, "The F. Koenigs Collection," has been placed by us at the disposition of D. G. van Beuningen, *a costi* [in this town]. We have, moreover, also placed at the disposition of Mr. D. G. van Beuningen paintings from the F. Koenigs collection which are named as follows:

Hieronymus Bosch —The Marriage at Cana
" " —two panels, Hell and The Flood
" " — Saint Christopher
Peter Paul Rubens —The Three Crosses
" " —Ariadne and Bacchus on the Shore of the Lake
" " —The Triumph of Bacchus
" " —The Death of Eurydice
" " —Narcissus
" " —Nereid Riding on a Triton
" " —The Union of England and Scotland
" " —The Wagon

While we kindly request you to take note of these, we would like to receive a list from you naming any paintings remaining there at present, and for this we thank you in advance."[16]

At the cost of one million guilders, Van Beuningen came into possession of the complete collection of drawings, as well as the above-mentioned twelve paintings.

On April 12, 1940, Hannema wrote to Koenigs: "I can't refrain from writing you a word, now that the biggest part of your collection has definitely become the property of Rotterdam. I can well imagine that you had mixed feelings about this transaction, having built over the years with so much knowledge and love this very important whole, which to relinquish is a major matter. However, I do assure you that in the future your name will always be attached to the collection, which will be kept with the greatest care. I do hope wholeheartedly that the tie between the Boymans Museum, the Koenigs collection, and the two of you will continue to exist."[17] Anna Koenigs–von Kalckreuth replied two days later: "My husband and I thank you for your kind letter. This life seems to me to consist of becoming attached to people and possessions, and having to part from them. But it is a comfort that these art pieces stay together in the Netherlands in the Boymans Museum, and last but not least in your care. Perhaps the collection will still impart a feeling for tradition to our children and grandchildren and keep their love for art awake. In these times, one possesses nothing with certainty, except that which is within ourselves and which the circumstances of these times cannot take from us."[18]

Koenigs wrote to Hannema on April 17, 1940:

I thank you very much for your friendly letter of the 12th of this month.

It also gladdens us that the collection is staying in Holland, and the Boymans Museum is of course our place of preference for it.

To give expression to these feelings, I have, through the agency of Mr. Lütjens, sent to the Boymans Museum two drawings by Carpaccio from the Oppenheimer collection. Perhaps they will go some way toward filling a gap that I have always felt existed in the sequence of the Venetian drawings.[19]

In this letter, Koenigs evidences the spirit of the collector, not knowing that his collection is now owned by Van Beuningen and is not in the possession of the Boymans Museum, underlining the continuance of his personal bond with the collection. Heartsick over his loss, Koenigs tried to find some comfort in the Boymans Museum director's promise that what had been built "over the years with so much knowledge and love this very important whole" would be kept intact and continue to bear his name.

On May 10, a few weeks after the sale, the German invasion of the Netherlands was a fact, and the occupier went immediately on a hunt for art. In June, July, and August 1940, Professor Hans Posse, director of the Staatliche Gemälde-galerie, Dresden, and of Sonderauftrag Linz, frequently visited Rotterdam. Through Lukas Peterich (the German son-in-law of Mr. van Beuningen, acting in his name), Van Beuningen had offered the Koenigs collection to Posse for sale for 5 million guilders. Posse visited Rotterdam a number of times in order to make a selection of drawings from the Koenigs collection and to discuss their purchase. On October 23, 1940, Dr. Hannema found it necessary to write a statement in German: "Memorandum: Because Mr. van Beuningen cannot be present during the lengthy negotiations, I am putting my view into writing, as agreed. I do also hope that Professor Posse, as my colleague, might show understanding for my way of seeing things, and would desire to put before his principal, the Honorable Führer, this exceptional situation."[20] Later, Dr. Hannema would be appointed a member of the Dutch Culture Council and Supervisor of Museums in the Nether-lands, within the administration of the Reichskommissar SS-Obergruppenführer Arthur Seyss-Inquart.

In his memorandum, Dr. Hannema argued for a significant increase in price for the drawings: "But only at the advice and wish of Mr. Peterich did I stop the price increase at 35 percent. Myself, I would have considered an increase of 50 percent or 60 percent as absolutely justified. Others, like Dr. H. Schneider, director of the State Office of Art-Historical and Iconographical Documentation, even defended a 100 percent increase in price. As far as the Private Counselor [Geheimrat] Friedländer's appraisal, I must say with emphasis that Private Counselor Friedländer underestimated the French drawings by at least 110,000 guilders, the German drawings certainly by about 30,000 guilders, and the drawings selected by Professor Posse by 25,000 guilders. I can say this with a clear conscience, because I have known the collection for

years, whereas Private Counselor Friedländer has just now, for the first time, been able to study the collection in detail."[21]

On December 5, 1940, Dr. Hannema wrote to Van Beuningen: "I have just heard from Peterich that a deal has been concluded for a part of the Koenigs collection. I sincerely wish you the best of luck in this. I am delighted, as well, that the Boymans Museum Foundation has in this way come into the possession of such a magnificent collection. The Printroom of the Boymans Museum has now grown to become by far the most important in the Netherlands, a rival to even the greatest collections in this field, namely, those of London and Paris. Also, the collection of Primitives of the Boymans has been enriched by the four paintings by Hieronymus Bosch and the five sketches by Rubens for the Torre de la Parada."[22]

From Dresden, on January 15, 1941, Posse wrote to Martin Bormann: "I have been informed by a reliable source that up to the end of 1940, paintings amounting to 8 million guilders have been exported from Holland to Germany. This amount does not include my latest purchase, namely, drawings from the Koenigs collection (1,400,000 guilders), and about 250,000 guilders for the most recent purchases, which, by the way, should arrive in Dresden tomorrow. My own purchases to date in Holland come to more than 1.5 million guilders, and those for the Reichsmarschall to approximately the same amount."[23]

In summary, the Lisser & Rosenkranz Bank had sold approximately 3,000 drawings and 12 paintings to Van Beuningen for 1 million guilders, with a guarantee that they would remain together as a collection under the name of the collector Franz Koenigs. Van Beuningen had then offered the Koenigs collection to Posse for 5 million guilders.[24] Posse selected 527 drawings, something less than a quarter of the collection, purchased them for 1.4 million guilders, and had them removed to Germany. The drawings were packed and sent to The Hague, after which Peterich, Van Beuningen's son-in-law, accompanied the drawings by train to Dresden. In that very same week, on May 6, 1941, Franz Koenigs was murdered, pushed under a train at the Cologne station. On May 26, 1941, Posse wrote to Hannema that he had received the collection:

The very Honorable Dr. Hannema:

After the arrival in Dresden of that part of the Koenigs collection of drawings which we acquired from its owner, Mr. van Beuningen, and our acceptance of it today in the presence of Mr. Peterich, I would not want to fail to express to you my warmest gratitude for your friendly cooperation, and your equally friendly furtherance of my commission. Since it was easy for me to put myself in your place, I was all the more thankful for your helpfulness when I was obliged to pick a few raisins out of your beautiful cake.

Feeling as a colleague, I have found my only consolation to be that the lion's share of that wonderful collection remains with your museum.

With appreciative greetings,

Your very devoted,
H. Posse[25]

RETURN OF CULTURAL

PROPERTY: HOSTAGES OF WAR

OR HARBINGERS OF PEACE?

HISTORICAL FACTS,

POLITICAL POSITIONS, AND

AN ASSESSMENT FROM

THE GERMAN POINT OF VIEW

Hagen Graf Lambsdorff

When German soldiers crossed the Bug River in 1941 in order to wage an ideological war and seize Lebensraum in the Soviet Union, the services behind the occupation army included not only the notorious task forces that killed people but also art historians in uniform who hunted down cultural property for Rosenberg, Göring, and Himmler. Göring was motivated by personal greed, Himmler by racism and his quest for testimonies to the Germanic heritage, while Rosenberg followed Hitler's instructions to transfer works of art, libraries, and valuable archives to Germany. Many people took part in this large-scale theft of art treasures: Gauleiters, party functionaries, and military authorities, as well as some German soldiers of their own accord. The war, which was waged with brutal severity and a scorched-earth strategy on both sides, destroyed churches, museums, and collections; some of the works of art stolen by Himmler, Rosenberg, or Göring were lost in transit or destroyed in rearguard actions. The rest reached their destinations in Germany and were put away in the cellars of museums, in mine shafts or other dungeons. There were more than a thousand such art depots in total.

Russians, Ukrainians, and others therefore rightly call attention today to their inestimable loss of cultural property. And there is not one on the German side who would contradict them. The German theft of art treasures in the USSR was a breach of international law. It was a barbaric attack on the cultural identity of the Slavic peoples, as indeed it was intended to be according to the inhumane ideology underlying the German war of conquest. It is a dictate of justice and decency, as well as of respect for the victims of the National Socialist plundering of art treasures, that this be said openly and publicly. Without this clear admission there would be no legitimate legal or moral justification for discussing the return of cultural property removed in time or as a consequence of the war.

However, those who restrict themselves to this assessment without adding with equal decisiveness that such thefts aimed at damaging the cultural identity of peoples must not be repeated nor justified do not go far enough and risk carrying over the spirit and actions of an evil past into a future that is no better. The return of cultural property is not a matter of compensation and reparations, trophies or spoils of war, or the difference between aggression in contravention of international law and legitimate defense. Rather, it concerns quite a different dimension: respect for an inalienable cultural identity which cannot be taken away by anyone even in war and defeat, not even by the victors. It is protected by international law, as it forms part of the dignity of individuals and peoples and enjoys great respect in all civilized nations.

After 1945, the greater part of the cultural property carried off from the Soviet Union to Germany fell into the hands of the Allies, who gathered this property at so-called Collecting Points and returned it to the Soviet Union. In their own occupied zone, the Soviets removed the stolen cultural property they found to the Soviet Union directly and not via the

Collecting Points. According to American records, more than two million objects had been returned to thirteen European countries by 1948. These included well over five hundred thousand works of art from the Collecting Points that were sent back to the Soviet Union in closed consignments, not including those items returned directly to the Baltic states. Some of these objects were returned to the various regions of the USSR in which they originated. The Soviet Union was very selective in this process, and by no means everything that the Germans had taken from Ukrainian and Belarusan museums was returned there. These former states of the USSR are now independent countries, which seek to secure the return of their cultural property brought back from Germany in 1945.

During the war, Stalin ordered his advancing army to requisition German works of art in the conquered areas as spoils of war. So-called trophy and booty commissions employing art historians and museum experts were charged with tracing German cultural property, seizing it, and ensuring its transport to the Soviet Union. Large quantities of German cultural property were thus removed to the Soviet Union from Pomerania or East Prussia, where they had been sheltered from Allied bomb attacks or, later, from the Soviet occupation zone, which offered unrestricted access to these objects. The booty commissions seized entire inventories of museums, libraries, and collections—among them, the world-famous Dresden collection of paintings and the treasures from the Grünes Gewölbe (Green Vault), and in Berlin prestigious objects from the Pergamon Museum and almost the entire collection of the Museum of East Asian Art. The lists of objects seized and removed to the Soviet Union, largely known today, give an idea of the scale of these operations. In Bonn, in June 1994, during the second meeting of the joint commission charged with conducting bilateral negotiations on the return of cultural property, the Russian side was presented with a provisional and by-no-means complete survey of German treasures taken to the Soviet Union during and after the war: two hundred thousand museum artifacts, two million books, and several kilometers of archives—cultural property of such quality and proportions that it can legitimately be described as an essential part of the German cultural heritage.

At the same meeting of the joint commission, the Russians submitted a list of about forty thousand items. There is little doubt on either side, however, that a large part of these undisputed losses fell victim to the war and are irretrievable. Such lists can thus more or less only serve as historical documentation. This applies, for example, to the Amber Room, which was taken by the German Wehrmacht from Pushkin to Königsberg (Kaliningrad). There, as is now known, it was destroyed in the terrible battle of Kaliningrad.* Yet, both sides are aware that, although there is very little Russian cultural property left in Germany after the repatriation operations from

the Collecting Points and the undisputed destruction of many cultural objects, nevertheless, the search for it is still going on. The German authorities are doing everything they can through search operations in museums and public collections, as well as calls in specialist publications also directed at private individuals, to trace any works of art that might still be in Germany and to return them to their rightful owners in Russia.

One must know these facts to realize that the charges voiced in the Russian press and by Russian authorities that Germany is demanding the return of cultural property from Russia but is not prepared to reciprocate are simply not true. They ignore the fact that Germany lost the war and that after the war the Soviet Union, as a victorious power, rightly received back the cultural property stolen by the National Socialists. If German cultural property were now to be returned, this would indeed constitute "reciprocity"—a symmetry of returns—albeit with a fifty-year delay. A final word on this: to those who respect the prohibition under international law of theft of works of art during wartime it is self-explanatory that reciprocity or symmetry implies the obligation of each state to restore, in accordance with a contractually agreed return clause, works of art seized or removed in time or as a consequence of war.

Out of respect for international law and in view of its history, Germany has always taken this obligation seriously. It will continue to do so, regardless of whether it is dealing with Russia or another country. In spring 1994, German Chancellor Helmut Kohl returned to President François Mitterrand of France twenty-eight important works of art that had been taken from France to Germany during the war in unknown circumstances. They included pictures by Delacroix, Monet, Renoir, Manet, Cézanne, Gauguin, and other famous artists. The paintings had been in East Germany (GDR) since the end of the war. Immediately after reunification, the Federal Republic of Germany entered into negotiations with France on restitution. It was established that the works of art did not come from state collections. It is therefore likely that at least some of them belonged to French Jews from whom the Nazi tyrants with perfidious logic first took their property and then their lives. The German government thus returned these works of art to France on trust with the request that everything possible be done to find the rightful owners. For us, this was more than a gesture of Franco-German friendship and of close cooperation between two civilized European nations. It was a mark of reconciliation and of the endeavors being made to give back the stolen works of art to those to whom they belong legally and morally.

In the 1950s, the Soviet Union decided to return to its brother nation the GDR some of the German cultural property it had requisitioned. During that period, for example, the cities of Dresden and Berlin received back a number of objects that had been taken from them in 1945. Almost the entire Gotha library, which is playing a special role in the German-Russian negotiations on the return of cultural property, was given back.

Only about six thousand books from Gotha, some of them very valuable, however, remained in Moscow and are the subject of bilateral negotiations. The Soviets declared at that time that this major operation closed the chapter on returns. The Cold War and the rift between East and West set their own standards and limits, which left no room for investigation or even talks between Bonn and Moscow on the subject. Furthermore, due to its particular understanding of international law, the communist Kremlin was neither able nor prepared to admit that a substantial amount of Germany's stolen cultural property was still in its territory and thus simply made this a state secret. And whatever bore the stamp of secrecy in the Soviet Union just did not exist according to the official interpretation. In this manner, world-famous works of art from all eras—paintings, sculptures, and drawings, libraries and collections—were made permanent hostages of war and banished to a vast cultural gulag.

Not until glasnost and the political upheaval at the end of the 1980s did this change. The rumors and suspicions gradually condensed into the regained certainty that the German cultural property missing since the end of the war was in the Soviet Union, most of it in Russia, and the authorities eventually ceased to deny it. For most Russian experts, museum directors, art historians, and heads of libraries and archives, who knew or at least suspected that there were works of art, books, and archives hidden in cellars and KGB bunkers, this was a great relief and eased the burden on their personal and professional consciences. Free of the entanglements of a totalitarian system, they no longer had to deny facts they knew were true to their foreign colleagues and on the international stage, thus jeopardizing their personal credibility and professional integrity. Many have stated this publicly; others, in view of their office and interests, expressed it indirectly but no less clearly. It goes without saying that these groups in Russia belonged to the forces that fought for democracy, the rule of law, and reforms, and that from the outset they advocated a just arrangement in keeping with international law and continue to do so.

It must be added, however, that in the current difficult restructuring phase there are also forces in Russia that are neither able nor willing to free themselves from the old totalitarian ways of thinking and acting. For them, international law and treaties are entities that can be used arbitrarily as long as this serves what they regard as Russian interests. These groups and persons did not admit the existence of the secret depots and the art gulag until they had no alternative. This unnecessary dishonesty was harmful to their credibility and reputation.

The return of cultural property removed in time or as a consequence of war is undoubtedly one of the difficult tasks facing German and Russian foreign-policy makers today. This is the legacy of a war that even after fifty years evokes more than mere memories of a distant past. It rekindles strong emotions in Russia, on which untold suffering and destruction was inflicted by German aggression. It is as important for the new German-Russian relations that we respect these sentiments and respond to them with sympathy and a desire for reconciliation, as it would be disastrous to jeopardize the foundations of this new partnership through nationalist sentiments or other domestic considerations.

Germany has a vital interest in drawing Russia closer, in a spirit of partnership, to a democratic and merging Europe as laid down in the Good-Neighborliness Treaty of 1990 (see Appendix 14). Care in dealing with the sentiments of those who have had to endure two world wars and a communist dictatorship in this century is just as much a tenet of German foreign policy as is consideration for the difficult political, economic, and social processes of reform that Russia is currently undergoing. Germany has, to a degree not matched by any other country, declared its readiness to provide material and moral support, and has acted accordingly. It will continue to pursue this policy—without preconditions but in the firm belief that partnership is not a one-way street: that both sides must do everything possible to ensure that the burden of their history, of which the return of cultural property forms an integral part, does not evolve into a new burden for their future relations. At the CSCE (Conference on Security and Cooperation in Europe) summit in Budapest in November 1990, President Boris Yeltsin asked in reference to the democratic reforms in Russia, "Why this distrust?"—and added, "After all, we are partners now and no longer adversaries." He was probably not thinking of the negotiations on returning cultural property, but he did touch on the basic problem: contractual fidelity, international law, and respect for cultural identity are not arbitrary but essential elements of partnership and trust among democratic states.

CAPTURED ARCHIVES AND RESTITUTION PROBLEMS ON THE EASTERN FRONT: BEYOND THE BARD GRADUATE CENTER SYMPOSIUM

Patricia Kennedy Grimsted

While the Second World War was at its height, an *Information Bulletin* was issued in November 1942 by the embassy of the USSR in Washington, D.C., condemning the Nazi cultural atrocities and looting that were taking place on the Eastern Front. Soviet authorities appropriately criticized "the Hitlerite clique [which] in criminal manner tramples upon the rules and laws of warfare universally accepted by all civilized nations," quoting Article 56 of the 1907 Hague Convention (see Appendix 3), to which Germany was a party, and which forbids the seizure, damaging, and destruction of property of educational and art institutions.[1] The fiftieth anniversary of the end of that war and the defeat of Nazi Germany has come and passed, but civilized nations are still agonizing over the cultural treasures ravaged and looted in the course of that war and its aftermath, many of which still remain displaced.

In her address to the concluding session of the Bard Graduate Center symposium (see above, pages 221–24), Ekaterina Genieva, the director of the Rudomino State Library for Foreign Literature in Moscow, suggested that, if art-restitution issues were going to leave the European continent still divided, perhaps the further restitution of library books, such as being planned by her library, could again "make us friends." Indicative of alternative Russian attitudes against restitution, a full-page diatribe on the Bard symposium—"The 'Cold War' behind Museum Blinds"—in the Russian Communist Party newspaper *Pravda* considered Genieva's "anti-Russian rhetoric" a disgrace to the Russian delegation.[2] A few weeks after the opening of the exhibition of Impressionist paintings, "Hidden Treasures Revealed," at the State Hermitage Museum in St. Petersburg in March 1995, an overwhelming vote in the Russian Parliament (Duma) on April 21 declared a moratorium on all restitution until a newly drafted Russian law could be passed.

The proof of the efficacy of restitution, however, was demonstrated a year later, when another group of international specialists was gathered in Amsterdam for a conference, "On the Return of Looted Collections," honoring the fiftieth anniversary of the restitution of Dutch and other European collections from the United States Zone of Occupation in Germany.[3] Genieva was invited to present the concluding address to that conference as well, and there she heard a movingly appreciative report on the disposition of the six hundred books seized by the Nazis from the Netherlands during the war that her library returned to the University of Amsterdam in 1992.

When the drawings from the Koenigs collection from the Netherlands went on display in October 1995 in Moscow, the Russian minister of culture, Evgenii Sidorov, introduced the exhibit as symbolizing "a liberation of the last prisoners of war."[4] Six months later, in March 1996, a book by Vladimir Teteriatnikov, the same author who wrote the *Pravda* article condemning the Bard symposium, appeared in Moscow and Tver', justifying the Russian seizure of the Koenigs collection, and also presenting the text of the proposed Russian law to nationalize all of the cultural treasures transferred to Russia at the end of the war.[5] After the Russian Duma passed a first reading of that law a week after Victory Day 1996, *Pravda* published another full-page diatribe against restitution by Teteriatnikov, lamenting "treasures stolen from the Russian people" as a result of "returns or promises by the 'liberals.' "[6] After the presidential elections in July, the Duma passed the law almost unanimously, but the upper house refused approval. The conflict over restitution remains intense, and in the meantime, all possible restitution of the cultural "spoils of war" is suspended.

Archives were only mentioned in passing at the Bard symposium, but already in May 1994 an angry Russian Parliament halted the archival restitution process to France, despite official diplomatic agreements for the completion of archival restitution by the end of 1994. The newly revealed paintings and the "Trojan gold" long hidden in Russia, like the two Gutenberg Bibles held hostage in Moscow libraries, may claim more public attention, but the world must deal with the displaced archives as well. Never before World War II have archives been subject to such rationally calculated destruction, or to such massive looting for political, ideological, and operational purposes as was wrought by the Nazi invader throughout the European continent. And then at the end of the war, as if in retribution, Soviet authorities were involved in archival plunder that rivaled that of their vanquished Nazi foe. Although there was considerable progress in archival restitution during the Soviet regime, it was only in 1990 and 1991 that the extent of captured archives in Moscow became known. Since the collapse of the USSR, no other European country aside from France has been able to retrieve any part of its archives that are still held in Moscow.

The international legal basis and precedents for the restitution of displaced unique official records of state and private agencies are even stronger than is the case for art, and indeed, according to international law and archival precedents, archives should be considered in a separate category in terms of restitution issues. Already in 1976, reinforcing the Hague Conventions of 1907 and 1954, UNESCO adopted the position that "military and colonial occupation do not confer any special right to retain archives acquired by virtue of that occupation."[7] In October 1994 in Thessalonica, the International Council of the Round Table on Archives (CITRA) reaffirmed "accepted archival principles that archives are inalienable and imprescriptible and should not be regarded as 'trophies' or objects of exchange."[8] A position paper of the International Council on Archives (ICA) in April 1995 calls upon the international community to take further steps to remedy the persisting problems of displaced archives,[9] as millions of displaced files of many nations remain hostage in Russia, alongside their more illustrious artistic company. What is often forgotten is that many of those displaced archives retain the clues to the displacement of art and other cultural treasures.

Serious historical analysis of archival displacements on the Eastern Front has been impossible until recently.[10] The truth of what was lost, and what was destroyed and plundered—and by whom—has been hidden amid the half-truths that cultural atrocities in the former USSR were wrought by the "fascist invaders" alone. Now that many—although regrettably still not all—of the relevant archives are open, a more balanced study of the fate of Soviet-area archives, along with libraries and other cultural treasures, during and immediately after the war is at last possible. Preliminary findings have shown the extent to which many of the exaggerated Soviet claims about the massive losses and transfers of archival materials from Soviet lands now need to be reinterpreted.[11]

WARTIME SOVIET ARCHIVAL DESTRUCTION

One important component in the "revisionist" interpretation of wartime archival losses is the extensive Soviet intentional destruction of archives that could not be evacuated to the east during the summer of 1941. The extent to which Soviet authorities were ordered to destroy archives to prevent their falling into enemy hands has now been documented in shocking detail. To cite only a few examples, seven times as many records of the central state economic planning agency (Gosplan) were destroyed as were evacuated to the east for protection; only 4,980 files from the Supreme Council (Verkhovnyi Sovet) were saved, while 748,633 burned, and from the Main Administration of Labor Camps and Colonies (GULAG), 95,714 files were evacuated, while 1,172,388 were destroyed.[12]

Ironically, almost all the archival materials that the Nazis found, "protected," and evacuated during their retreat from the Eastern Front survived the war and were retrieved afterward, although such a conclusion runs counter to the party line and widespread conceptions. For example, as late as May 1993, the former director of the Special Archive in Moscow (now TsKhIDK) argued that because the Nazis looted the Kyiv (Kiev) Archive of Early Acts, the Russians should not return Soviet-seized German archives now in Moscow.[13] In fact, that portion of the Kyiv Archive that the Nazis did not succeed in evacuating (approximately half) was blown up when the Red Army liberated the city in early November 1943. Most of the Nazi-evacuated parts of that archive survived—half of it close to home in Kam'ianets'-Podil's'kyi. Part was recovered by Ukrainian archivists after the war in Czechoslovakia, and the most valuable part was restituted by the United States Army from Western Bohemia. By contrast, the official Soviet attestation submitted to the Moscow commission investigating wartime damage and subsequently to the Nuremberg war-crimes trials claimed the entire archive was looted and dynamited by the Nazis.[14]

SOVIET ARCHIVAL RETRIEVALS

Although little has been published about the extensive Soviet archival recovery operations after the war, recently opened files reveal new details about the highly successful missions sent to Romania, Czechoslovakia, Poland, Finland, and East Prussia, as well as Germany, to retrieve the archival treasures the Nazis had evacuated from the USSR. During 1945 alone, according to one top-secret report from the Main Archival Administration (Glavarkhiv), that agency retrieved eighty-nine freight-train wagonloads, and that did not include Soviet archives recovered by other Soviet agencies.[15]

Indeed, almost all the archival materials looted by the Nazis from the USSR have been accounted for. Furthermore, given Nazi archival policies and the now known evacuation destinations, we can ascertain that relatively few archives from occupied Soviet lands reached Germany itself or other areas that were liberated by the Western Allies.

WAR LOSSES AND WESTERN ARCHIVAL RESTITUTION

As a result of another major "blank spot" in the traditional Soviet presentation of the war and postwar developments, many Russian cultural leaders and politicians today are virtually unaware of the extent of Western cultural restitution to the USSR from various collection centers in occupied Germany. Facts about such restitution have not been published in the West either, and at the Bard symposium the participating directors of the postwar United States restitution centers had no recollection about shipments to the USSR. Complete archival records of the American transfers have long been open in the West, including detailed inventories of thirteen restitution shipments with over half a million items that were turned over to Soviet authorities between September 1945 and the fall of 1948. These included a wide range of cultural treasures, from the Neptune Fountain in Petrodvorets (Peterhof) to hundreds of early icons from Kyiv. One United States Army report noted that these shipments contained "a far greater number of items than the number of items officially claimed [by Soviet authorities]."[16]

That report confirmed that archives alone comprised the first United States Army restitution transfer of four railway freight cars to Soviet authorities (on September 20, 1945), namely, about one thousand packages of archival material taken by the Germans in 1943 from Novgorod, which were found in Berlin-Dahlem. A second shipment to the USSR a month later (on October 25, 1945), totaling twenty-five freight cars, comprised extensive archives and museum exhibits from Riga and Kyiv. These included over twenty-five hundred units from the Kyiv Archive of Early Acts, found in a Bohemian castle near Pilsen (Plzeň), Czechoslovakia. Three of the thirteen shipments comprised books and archival materials sent to the USSR from the Offenbach Archival Depository near Frankfurt, which was the centralized Collecting Point and restitution center for books and archives in the United States Zone of Occupation.

WESTERN NON-RESTITUTION

Although it is fair to say that almost all Soviet-area archives that reached the West were restituted after the war, there were, nevertheless, some major exceptions. Because of the

Nazi annihilation of Jewish communities in Eastern Europe, many Jewish collections were not returned to the USSR, including collections from the Jewish research institute YIVO (in Vilnius) that were turned over to the successor YIVO in New York City. Other valuable books and manuscripts of Jewish provenance were turned over to the Commission on Jewish Cultural Reconstruction and have ended up in Yad Vashem and the National and University Library in Jerusalem.

Because the Western Allies did not recognize the Soviet annexation of the Baltic republics, they also refused to return looted Baltic materials to Soviet authorities. The large holdings from the Tallinn City Archive discovered in the Grasleben salt mine (British Zone of Occupation) were held back by British authorities, as they tried unsuccessfully to negotiate the restitution of the Hanseatic records from Bremen, Hamburg, and Lübeck that they knew Soviet authorities had seized from the salt mines near Magdeburg.[17] The Königsberg (Kaliningrad) archive, and with it the medieval archive of the Order of Teutonic Knights, was also held back (now in Berlin-Dahlem), in this case due to the forced resettlement of the ethnic German population and the unresolved legal status of those parts of East Prussia that had been annexed to the USSR as Kaliningradskaia oblast' (Kaliningrad Oblast).[18]

A final category of materials not returned to the USSR involves documents of interest to American intelligence agencies, including the now famous files from the Communist Party Archive of Smolenskaia oblast' (Smolensk Oblast), over five hundred units of which are now still held by the National Archives in Washington, D.C. The much more voluminous part of the Smolensk archive, approximately four freight-wagon loads, was found by Soviet forces in Polish Silesia, in March 1945, and returned to Smolensk—although information about the Soviet retrieval was published only in 1991. In the case of the Smolensk files in Washington: by 1963, both the United States Army and the Department of State were prepared to return them to the Soviet Union. At that point, however, the Central Committee of the Communist Party of the Soviet Union (CPSU) decided against filing an official request for restitution, fearing further United States Cold War propaganda exploitation. Now it is the United States Congress that has unanimously voted to hold the "Smolensk Archive" hostage.[19]

ANGLO-AMERICAN-CAPTURED RECORDS AND RESTITUTION TO GERMANY

All of the Allies were anxious to capture records of the Nazi regime as justified by Allied Control Council Law No. 2, Providing for the Termination and Liquidation of Nazi Organizations (October 10, 1945), which ordered confiscation by military commands "of all archives [records], documents, and other property" of Nazi agencies and organizations.[20] Anglo-American authorities had been working closely together on captured Nazi records from the outset, and pressed for quadripartite Allied cooperation in the collection and analysis of Nazi records in connection with denazification efforts and war-crimes trials. Almost all of the Western-captured Nazi records were, however, subsequently returned to Germany in the 1950s. But Russian authorities still do not want to believe the extent of British and American restitution, and argue that the Allied Control Council laws justify their own continued retention of Nazi records.

SOVIET CULTURAL PLUNDER

On January 5, 1943, representatives of seventeen governments, including those of the USSR and the Western Allies, signed the Inter-Allied Declaration, or Declaration of London (see Appendix 9), opposing looting and plunder of cultural property. By the time the Red Army was on its triumphal march to Berlin in 1945, however, Stalin had long forgotten that declaration and the above-cited "rules and laws of warfare, universally accepted by all civilized nations," which Soviet authorities had themselves cited against the Nazis. When victory came, Stalin and other Soviet leaders were quite prepared to seize what spoils of war they could, not unlike their vanquished Nazi foes.

SOVIET-CAPTURED RECORDS

Archives constituted a small percentage of the overall Soviet cultural plunder after the war. But unlike art, most of the archival seizures were made chiefly for purposes of intelligence utilization and political control. Instructions for captured archives had already been prepared in February 1945, and, early in April 1945, NKVD Deputy Commissar for Internal Affairs Sergei Kruglov recommended to his chief, Lavrentii Beriia, and Beriia to Viacheslav Molotov, a special mission "to search thoroughly through all German archives and libraries to effect means of preservation and bring to the Soviet Union materials including printed editions, that have scientific-historical and operational significance for our country."[21]

It is still virtually impossible to estimate the quantity of archives involved. Various shipments were alternately measured in freight cars, crates, or tons. Many of them included printed books and art—and, in one case, seven freight cars of steel shelving—along with the records themselves. One top-secret year-end report for 1945 notes fifty-five wagonloads of German and Romanian materials and forty-four wagonloads of other foreign materials (predominantly French and Polish) brought to Moscow during the year, but the specific figures listed do not jibe with reports found elsewhere on individual shipments.[22] Besides, other archival seizures were made by military intelligence authorities, the trophy commissions, and other agencies.

As more and more documentation becomes available, general patterns emerge. Soviet-captured records can, for the purpose of analysis, be classified into three principal categories (although invariably there is considerable overlap): (1) records of the Nazi regime itself; (2) Russian émigré or other Russian/Soviet-related archives; and (3) displaced archives of other European nations, most of which had previously been seized

by Nazi authorities. The twin concepts of "scientific-historical" and "operational" value became the official euphemistic passwords for archival plunder in all three categories.

While Soviet authorities refused to cooperate with the Western Allies in regard to Nazi records, they actively collected as many as they could find, which, as noted above, was authorized by the Allied Control Commission. A large part of the Nazi/German component within Soviet-captured records came under the purview of the Main Archival Administration under Beriia's People's Commissariat for Internal Affairs (GAU pri NKVD), later known as Glavarkhiv. This component was specifically designated for "operational" analysis, which among other designated aims involved establishing Nazi collaborators and other "enemies of the Fatherland." A particularly important find was what Soviet authorities first identified as the "Archive of the Intelligence Division of the German General Staff, in Berlin-Wannsee," which also included vast quantities of French and Belgian military records earlier captured by the German Army Archive Heeresarchiv)—"approximately thirty wagons of documents." Also in Berlin they found the remains of the "Archive of the Ministry of the Navy"—approximately ten wagons of documents.[23]

Among the many other Nazi records, Soviet authorities found (in the Potsdam vicinity), a collection of over two thousand microcopies of high-level documents from the Reich Chancellery, which in April 1946 merited a special report to Stalin. Equally important to Beriia, they found some two hundred thousand files of an SS intelligence branch, including "many who were German foreign ('fifth-column') agents abroad."[24] In a Prague railway depot, they found thirty sealed wagons of high-level scientific and technological files from what Soviet scouts identified as "the Central Military-Technical Archive of the Wehrmacht." These latter captured records immediately went back to Moscow to unidentified technical-scientific agencies for immediate analysis.[25]

The Russian émigré and other Soviet-related components of the postwar archival seizures consisted in two prime categories. *First*, twentieth-century Russian émigré materials relating to the Civil War and foreign intervention, the White political emigration, and records of émigré communities abroad during the interwar period were retrieved everywhere they were found—from Prague to Sofia, from Cracow to Manchuria. Most of this category was deposited initially in the former Central State Archive of the October Revolution (TsGAOR SSSR), where a special NKVD analysis team was at work, although later, parts of the haul were transferred to many other archives. A *second* high-level priority was the Russian/Soviet-related materials pertaining to the international labor and revolutionary movement that were considered of prime "historico-scientific" value. Most of this latter category of records were eventually deposited in the former Central Party Archive (now RTsKhIDNI).

The well-known Bolshevik intellectual Vladimir Bonch-Bruevich, who survived the 1930s as director of the State Literary Museum in Moscow, wrote a now famous letter to

Stalin in February 1945, identifying major collections of Russian-related materials "held within the aggressor countries and their satellites":

> I recommend that such archives should be seized from those countries completely and entirely—Russian manuscripts, documents, correspondence, portraits, engravings, paintings, valuable rare books from libraries, substantial specialty objects among others, and even all Slavonic manuscript books. Most important from Germany—all Russian materials, all Slavic materials, with nothing left behind.[26]

In contrast to his NKVD contemporaries, Bonch-Bruevich added the important caveat that such confiscation had as its ultimate aim "thorough study, and—even more important— quality scholarly publications." His recommendations were not completely followed, however, because Beriia and his archival scouts were most interested in such documentation because it could serve as a tool for "operational" security aims, not because it represented "lost elements" of Russian culture as the basis "for scholarly editions."

This was most pointedly true for the Russian Foreign Historical Archive in Prague (RZIA), which, as Bonch-Bruevich had recommended, was officially presented as a "gift" of the Czech government to the Academy of Sciences of the USSR. The significance of this acquisition is apparent in the recently revealed two-page "Special File" (*Osobaia papka*), sent to Stalin from the NKVD Secretariat announcing the arrival in December 1945 of nine sealed freight cars.[27] Immediately after their arrival in Moscow, however, the president of the Academy of Sciences, "recognizing the intrinsic value of the materials," formally signed the archive over to Glavarkhiv under Beriia's NKVD.[28] Security chief Kruglov assured Andrei Zhdanov in May 1946 that the Prague archive would be expeditiously analyzed for "data on anti-Soviet activities of the White emigration to be used in operational work of security organs."[29] The massive card files remaining today in the State Archive of the Russian Federation (GA RF) attest to that activity. Subsequently, the RZIA and other émigré collections have been dispersed in close to thirty archives in the former USSR.

Another major cache from many European countries that reached Moscow in the fall of 1945 was the relatively complete remains of the infamous Seventh Division archive of the Reich Security Services Headquarters (RSHA), which by the end of the war was centered in and around the Silesian castle of Count von Althann in the village of Wölfelsdorf (now Polish Wilkanów). Along with RSHA records of capture and exploitation, the archive included many collections from European socialist sources, such as those from the International Institute for Social History in Amsterdam and its Paris office, and the archival records of the Second International that had been seized by the Nazis, predominantly from Belgium. Many of the massive RSHA Jewish and Masonic holdings, found in a former beer factory in nearby Habelschwerdt (now Polish Bystrzyca Kłodzka), were of less operational interest to the Soviet regime than they had been to the Nazis. The chancery and personal papers of Léon Blum and those of various European royalty, which were also part of the RSHA loot, were all but forgotten for half a century, along with other materials of lesser "operational" interest, such as early parchment charters from Greece and over three hundred Torah scrolls.[30] There were also many additional holdings of Russian émigré origin found in Silesia—even some files from the administrative records of the Turgenev Library, along with the library itself, which the Nazis had looted from Paris in 1940.

Plunder pure and simple served as a rationale for other major archival seizures. A Glavarkhiv team "examined documentary materials in the mines of Saxony, totaling over three hundred wagons from the period of the eleventh to the twentieth centuries," from which they chose "only seven wagons of the most topical fonds [record groups] presenting interest for Soviet historical sciences and activities of operational organs that should be brought to the USSR."[31] By November, the Soviet Trophy Commission had selected nearly nine thousand crates of literary and museum collections. In terms of archival materials, these included many manuscripts and early printed books from various German collections, ranging from collections of Oriental manuscripts, drawings and engravings, negatives of art and architecture, and ethnographic materials, including folklore recordings from Berlin, to the Ferdinand Lassalle papers and a collection of charters and manuscript books from the Magdeburg City Archive. As Georgii Aleksandrov explained to Georgii Malenkov in December 1945, "[B]ringing them to the USSR might to some extent serve as compensation for the losses wrought by the German occupiers on scholarly and cultural institutions in the Soviet Union."[32] That same attitude is being expressed today by those in the Duma who refuse to permit further restitution.

Among the other displaced foreign archives, and of greatest importance for Beriia and his security organs, was the major Nazi archival cache of some 6.5 kilometers of French intelligence and counterintelligence records—from the Sûreté Nationale and the Deuxième Bureau—found in May 1945 in a village manor house a few miles northwest of Česká Lípa in Czechoslovakia (part of the Sudetenland under the Reich). Twenty-eight freight cars and one first-class wagon were dispatched from Česká Lípa under Beriia's personal order, and on August 8, 1945, the tight-security shipment arrived in Moscow.[33]

THE SPECIAL ARCHIVE

As soon as the prize French intelligence materials arrived in Moscow in August 1945, Glavarkhiv chief Nikitinskii, in a memorandum to Beriia, deemed them of such "great state interest" for the various security organs that he recommended "the formation of a special central state archive of foreign fonds, in which would be concentrated the above-mentioned materials from the French archives, as well as earlier received Romanian *Siguranţe*, former Polish military and political organs, and various German occupation agencies."[34]

Soviet leaders and archival specialists were not, however, of one opinion as regards such a separate "special" archive. For example, the historian-archivist Professor V. V. Maksakov, who then directed the Central State Historical Archive in Moscow (TsGIAM) and favored scholarly use as well, explained, "Fonds such as those brought from Czechoslovakia . . . —we only have a right to them until such time when the international matters are regulated." In any case, the archive "would probably exist for only three, four, or maybe at most five years."[35]

It was the words of NKVD Captain A. A. Iur'ev in August 1945, however, that best reflected what proved to be the ultimate government policy in regard to the Special Archive for foreign captured records:

> Use [of that archive], in my opinion, should have an exclusively specific, limited character, namely utilization only with the meaning of *operational aims* of the NKVD, VD, MO [Defense], and ID [Foreign Affairs]. No scholarly research whatsoever can be carried out on the basis of that archive, and to be sure, no access whatsoever can be permitted to that archive for representatives of any scholarly institutions. . . . There is no need for compiling full inventories (*opisi*), nor is there need for arranging the files [according to archival principles]. The only immediate need is to use the documents there for operational aims."[36]

The top-secret Central State Special Archive (TsGOA) was formally established in March 1946, with separate national divisions of French, German, and Polish materials. Initially, a Romanian division was also planned, but then most of the captured Romanian records were transferred to the Moldavian SSR in Kishinev.

From a cultural standpoint, the vast quantities of captured archives, and even those of purely "historical significance" that Soviet authorities—in justifying their seizure— considered of the "utmost value to the Academy of Sciences," remained tightly closed to researchers. Even more serious from an archival standpoint, many of the documents were pulled out of their original archival context and transferred to other repositories. In the case of many fragmentary files, the facts and whereabouts of their seizure were likewise concealed; usually, those receiving archives did not themselves know, and were never able to record, from whence they came. Equally tragic, many of these "trophy" materials became subject to theft and dispersal, either en route or due in part to their suspect and not fully registered status within the archives where they were placed. In the case of the Bremen City Archive alone, as a result of its migration, some 248 early charters and 1,387 maps are now missing.[37]

The existence of the Special Archive was first revealed to the public in February 1990 by a Moscow journalist's "Five Days in the 'Osobyi arkhiv'," but then only Nazi records were mentioned.[38] It was not until two months after the attempted August coup, in October 1991, that another Moscow journalist could publish revelations regarding the even more extensive holdings from other Western European countries.[39] A week later the former director confirmed publicly that over a million

files of French intelligence records, to say nothing of many other "lost" foreign archives, were indeed ensconced in the so-called Special Archive.[40]

SOVIET RESTITUTION

Even before the public learned about the Special Archive, Soviet authorities did return some of the looted records, but mostly to East Germany and other Eastern-bloc nations— over two million file units in the 1950s and 1960s, including some of the Hanseatic records—and then noted euphemistically that the files had been "rescued by the Soviet army."[41] Through additional restitution in the late 1970s, in the spirit of the international archival resolutions from the 1977 ICA Cagliari CITRA conference, the Soviet Union was "helping other countries reunify their national archival heritage."[42] Unfortunately, however, in the process many fonds were split up and individual files broken out of integral groups of records.

During the late 1980s, some forty additional tons were returned to East Germany. In October 1990, remaining treasures from the medieval Hanseatic city archives of Bremen, Hamburg, and Lübeck (other parts of these collections had been transferred earlier to East Germany) were finally restored to their proper home in direct exchange for the counterpart medieval treasures from the Tallinn City Archive that were returned to Estonia from the Bundesarchiv in Koblenz. Only in 1989 were microfilm copies of the long-suppressed "death books" from Auschwitz (now Polish Oświęcim), made available to the Red Cross.

POST-SOVIET RESTITUTION EFFORTS IN RUSSIA

Following the demise of the Soviet Union, Russian archival authorities were more receptive to open discussion of restitution. In June 1992, the Special Archive (TsGOA SSSR) was euphemistically renamed the Center for the Preservation of Historico-Documentary Collections (TsKhIDK), and gradually started opening its doors. An unauthorized guide appeared in Germany late in 1992, covering only about half of the 870 trophy fonds officially reported as then held in the archive.[43] But even that TsKhIDK figure itself is misleading as, for example, in the case of one fond that comprises a massive collection of Masonic files from all over Europe, which were never broken down into separate fonds on the basis of their provenance. And there has been scant attention to the many trophy files that were transferred to other archives, such as the socialist materials transferred to the former Central Party Archive (now RTsKhIDNI), and the trophy files from émigré Russian and Ukrainian sources that have ended up in many other repositories.

There was hope in 1992 when the Netherlands was the first to sign an archival restitution agreement, and Dutch archivists started an extensive program of archival assistance in Russia. Bilateral archival agreements were also under negotiation with Belgium and Liechtenstein. Restitution to Germany had earlier been assured under the mutual friendship pact of 1990 (see Appendix 14). Begrudgingly, the German government even came up with half a million deutsche marks (as the first of three promised installments) for microfilming equipment, since Russian archival authorities insisted that the captured records be filmed before their return, as provided for by an archival agreement in connection with the bilateral German cultural agreement in 1992 (see Appendix 15).

A high-level Franco-Russian diplomatic agreement was signed in November 1992 for the restitution of the estimated 6.5 kilometers of French records by the end of 1994. France agreed to pay a quoted 3.5 million francs for microfilming and an additional high charge for xerographic copies of the Russian-language archival inventories (opisi). As part of the additional barter arrangement, on Russian insistence, France also agreed to give Russia some original Russian-related archival materials—including some Russian naval logs and papers of the Russian diplomat Ignat'ev—held in France. Between January and May of 1994, at least two-thirds of the French archives held in TsKhIDK were actually returned to France before the Russian Parliament angrily put a stop to the process in May 1994.

RUSSIAN NON-RESTITUTION

Since the collapse of the Soviet Union, France is the only Western country to have received back any of its archives from Moscow. When archival restitution to France was stymied in the Russian Parliament on May 20, 1994, one deputy went so far as to suggest that it would be appropriate also to exact storage charges from France for the million files that had been preserved in Moscow for fifty years. The issue became much broader, as the Russian Parliament further cited the example of the United States, which now holds hostage the so-called Smolensk Archive, as further justification for its actions curtailing the archival restitution process to France.[44]

During the bitter debates, the Russian Duma cited the lack of international laws and the inadequacy of domestic legislation to justify their refusal to permit further restitution of archival records and other cultural treasures displaced during World War II. A highly placed academic legal specialist and representative in the Russian legislature cried out again, "We do not owe anything to anyone," arguing in a later press account a Soviet-style legal justification for not surrendering wartime trophies, despite already signed bilateral agreements.[45] The phrase was earlier used in an article by Pushkin State Museum of Fine Arts director Irina Antonova, who followed the same line of reasoning at the Bard symposium, that her museum had in fact saved and preserved the artistic master-pieces, as indicated by the title of the 1995 Moscow exhibition, "Twice Saved."[46] There are, nevertheless, other circles in Russia, including the Yeltsin government, that are arguing for better solutions, with even the pro-government Izvestiia carrying a September 1994 headline "Scandal—Not Russian

Property," for an article denouncing the parliamentary prohibition on French archival restitution.[47]

During 1995 and 1996, the Russian Parliament considered new legislation to nationalize and prohibit export of all captured art, books, and archives.[48] A draft Russian law—On the Right of Ownership of Cultural Treasures Transferred to the Territory of the Russian Federation as a Result of the Second World War—was adopted by an overwhelming majority of the Council of the Russian Federation and sent to the State Duma, just before the "Hidden Treasures" exhibition of Impressionist art opened at the State Hermitage Museum in March 1995.[49] According to the preamble, the proposed law aimed "to estab-lish a firm legal basis for considering those treasures as partial compensation for the loss to the Russian cultural heritage as a result of the colossal looting and destruction of cultural treasures in the course of the Second World War by the German occu-pation army and their allies." The second paragraph affirmed the international legal basis for the law with the citation of several postwar agreements and treaties, although there was mention neither of the Hague Conventions of 1907 and 1954, nor of the London Declaration of 1943, as mentioned above. Later paragraphs made limited provision for the restitution of cultural treasures claimed by those who fought against the Nazi regime, but foreign governments, in cases decided in their favor, would have been required to pay the full value of the objects claimed, as well as storage, appraisal, and trans-portation costs.[50]

Statements pointing out the inadequacies of the proposed law were submitted to the Duma in April by the Ministry of Culture and the State Archival Service of Russia (Rosarkhiv), among others, but the politicians were not ready to listen. A parliamentary regulation enacted on April 21, 1995, prohib-ited any further restitution by Russian agencies until a law on wartime booty could be passed. An alternative draft law was prepared at the request of an opposing Duma group which, recognizing Russia's adherence to the Hague Conventions, gave more possibility for dialogue on serious restitution issues.[51] But when the drafts came up for full hearings in May, soon after the Fiftieth Anniversary of Victory celebrations, politicians gave little consideration to points raised by government officials who spoke against the draft law. A first reading of the law on June 7, 1995, was inconclusive, and the restitu-tion issue was again left in abeyance. Indicative of support for nationalization and opposition to restitution was the newspaper interview in Pravda, entitled "Blood and Gold," with the same museum specialist who had earlier spoken out so strongly against the Bard symposium.[52]

In a press interview, Deputy Minister of Culture Mikhail Shvidkoi appropriately went on record with his fears of the international consequences for Russia if the law passed in that formulation.[53] As noted above, the Duma passed the law in July 1996; but after an avid debate, and strong opposing statements from the presidential administration and a deputy foreign minister, it was narrowly defeated in the upper house. Nevertheless, the April 1995 moratorium still stands.

PRUSZYŃSKI: POLAND

1. *Intérêt national,* the French term, or *Heimatschutz,* the German term. However these terms are to be interpreted, they are nonetheless legally unclear. There is no general understanding as to the attitude of modern societies to their history as documented in, among other things, the monuments and relics of the past.

2. See, e.g., the Lieber Code for land warfare of 1863, articles 34–36 (see Appendix 1); the Hague Convention of 1907, articles 25–28, especially article 28 (see Appendix 3); the Hague Convention of 1954, Regulations for the Execution of the Convention for the Protection of Cultural Property in the Event of Armed Conflict (see Appendix 10).

3. Each German Wehrmacht soldier had in his *Soldbuch* (paybook) the following regulation: "Monuments of historical value and objects used for religious, artistic, scientific, or welfare purposes should be held in special respect." See also S. Kania, "Stosunek faszyzmu hitlerowskiego do Kultury polskiej" ("The Nazis' Attitude toward Polish Culture"), in C. Pilichowski, *Zbrodnie i sprawcy (Crimes and Delinquents)* (Warsaw, 1980), 658.

4. "Schutzmassnahmen für kulturgeschichtliche Denkmäler in Polen" of 10 October 1939; "Erlass des Führers über die Gliederung und Verwaltung der Ostgebiete" of 8 October 1939; "Verordnung über die Beschlagnahme des Vermögens des früheren polnischen Staates innerhalb des Generalgouvernements" of 15 November 1939; "Verordnung des Generalgouvernements für die Beschlagnahme des gesamten öffentlichen Kunstbesitzes" of 16 December 1939; "Verordnung über die Beschlagnahme von privaten Vermögen" of 24 January 1940; "Verordnung über die kulturelle Betätigung im Generalgouvernement" of 8 March 1940. Also, respectively, resolutions and provisions of the War Council of the Ukrainian Front concerning the provisional local administration of regions of the Western Ukraine.

5. Secret protocol to the German-Soviet Treaty of Non-Aggression, 23 August 1939, Article 2. This treaty preceded the German-Soviet Treaty of Friendship, Cooperation, and Demarcation of September 28, 1939. See *Nazi-Soviet Relations 1939–1941,* Documents of the Archives of the German Foreign Office, Washington, D.C., 1948, p. 78. Such "regulations" concerning Poland have a historic tradition. An additional protocol to the Treaty of St. Petersburg of 26 January 1797 between the copartitioning parties, Russia, Prussia, and Austria, stated: "It is necessary to abolish everything that refers to the existence of the Kingdom of Poland, in view of its annihilation as a political unit.

Hence, the contracting parties agree never to use the name 'Kingdom of Poland,' since it is now canceled forever."

6. From Hitler's widely known speech to his high commanders in Obersalzberg, Bavaria, 23 August 1939.

7. From Hans Frank's speech to the Nazi Society of Friends of the Generalgouvernement. See *Krakauer Zeitung,* May 1942. Frank took the occasion to enrich his private collection as well, plundering private property according to the Nazi directive of 16 December 1939, regarding the confiscation of artworks in the Generalgouvernement.

8. See Decision-Appeal to the Provisional Administration of Stanisławów, Tarnopol, Łuck, and Lwów ("Fair dawn of new life is arisen over our lands of Western Ukraine. . . . the artificially created Polish state founded on anarchy and oppression of nations has fallen . . . and our brothers, mighty nations of the Soviet Union, gave us their mighty hand . . ."), *Krasnoe Znamia,* no. 11, 5 October 1939. See also TASS Communiqué ("Today, Comrade Khrushchev visited certain election committees in Stanislavov . . . discussing changes in the people's lives after liberation of Western Ukraine from the oppression of the Polish landowners"), *Pravda,* 23 October 1939. See also Operational Orders of the Commanders of the Belarusan (M. Kovalov) and Ukrainian (S. Timoshenko) fronts, *Izvestiia,* nos. 221 (6991), 222 (6992), 223 (6993), 224 (6994), 226 (6996), of 23, 24, 26, 27, and 29 September 1939.

9. The Group for the Safekeeping of Objects of Art and Science in Warsaw, consisting of: Kajetan Mühlmann, Special Commissioner for the Protection of Monuments and Art Objects in the Generalgouvernement; Einsatzkommando P. Paulsen; Dr. E. Trathing (Cracow and Katowice); I. Löffler (Gniezno); H. Appel (Toruń); Reichskommissar for the Strengthening of Germandom, B. Galke; Wolfram Sievers, SS unit commander and general secretary of the SS Ahnenerbe (Scientific and Research Association for Ancestral Heritage), and Hermann Harmjenz (State Museums, Berlin), professor and SS Hauptsturmführer—both of whom were collaborators of Paulsen's; Groups of Operation; ERR. See the report of Robert Scholz on the Nuremberg trial session of 1 October 1946. Members of the ERR and various special action squads (*Einsatzgruppen*) headed a large network of civilian and military units. Some documents in Polish archives show that Polish museums had been targeted for immediate looting: a list, posted to Sievers, dated 18 September 1939, contains fifty-five museums of archaeology.

10. The so-called *Grossaktion,* which involved the arrest of scholars and professors of the University of Cracow.

11. See C. [K.] Estreicher, ed., *Cultural Losses of Poland: Index of Polish Cultural Losses during the German Occupation 1939–43* (London, 1944); J. Gross, *Polish Society under German Occupation: The General-government, 1939–1944* (New York, 1979); Pilichowski, *Zbrodnie i sprawcy;* and A. Mezyński, *Kommando Paulsen, October–December 1939* (Warsaw, 1994). See also note 9, above.

12. This was Kajetan Mühlmann, responsible for the plunder of museums and other collections in the private interest of Adolf Hitler, Hermann Göring, and Hans Frank.

13. Especially the Branicki collection in Wilanów, the Czartoryski Museum in Cracow, the Krasinski collection in Warsaw, the Potocki collection in Jablonna, and the Tarnowski collection in Dzików and Sucha.

14. For example, the index "schädlicher und deutschfeindlicher Bücher." Among the artworks to be found and seized were two big paintings by the Polish nineteenth-century painter J. Matejko entitled *The Battle of Grunvald* and *The Grand Master of the Teutonic Order Swearing Allegiance to the King of Poland.*

15. "Sichergestellte Kunstwerke im Generalgouvernement." The majority of the objects was found immediately after World War II ended, owing to the cooperation of the Polish envoys K. Estreicher and J. Morawinski with United States Monuments, Fine Arts, and Archives officers.

16. The catalogue of the exhibition "Sichergestellte Kunstwerke im Generalgouvernement," Berlin, 1940, was prepared with the collaboration of Professors H. von Dehmel, D. Frey, A. Haberlandt, K. Dittmer, L. Ruprecht, and others, who, along with members of the ERR, had previously visited Poland in a program of scholarly exchange.

17. See S. Lorentz, *Warszawa oskarza (Warsaw Accuses),* catalogue of the 1945 exhibition in the National Museum, Warsaw; S. Lorentz, *Walka o dobra kultury, Warszawa 1939–45 (Struggling for Culture, Warsaw, 1939–45),* vols. 1–2 (Warsaw, 1970).

18. The contents of museums and other collections are known in part from E. Chwalewik, *Zbiory polskie archiwa biblioteki gabinety galerie muzea i inne zbiory pamiątek przeszłości w ojczyźnie i na obczyźnie (The Polish Collections, Archives, Libraries, Cabinets, Galleries, Museums and Other Groupings of Monuments of the Past, in Poland and Abroad),* vols. 1–2 (Warsaw, 1926–27); and R. Aftanazy, *Materiały do dziejów rezydencji (Materials for the History of Residences),* 12 vols. (Warsaw, 1986–93).

19. The collection of the Krasinski Foundation consisted of over 250,000 volumes in 1844. During World War II, the most important works from the National Library and Library of the University of Warsaw were brought to the Krasinski

Library and burned together with its contents. See B. Bieńkowska, *Straty bibliotek polskich w czasie II wojny światowej (The Spoils of Polish Libraries from World War II)*, abridged (Warsaw: Office of the Commissioner for the Polish Heritage, 1994).

20. For the most part, these objects were stolen and melted down by Prussians in the middle of the eighteenth century; some were lost during the Austrian rule in Cracow in the nineteenth century, and partly restituted from Russia according to the terms of the Treaty of Riga of 1921 (objects from the Royal Castle in Warsaw). The crowns and scepters of the Saxon kings of Poland from the collection of the Royal Castle in Warsaw have had an interesting fate: taken by the Soviet army, they were returned by the government of the USSR to Germans (the German Democratic Republic), in accordance with the terms of a special protocol. Finally, they returned to the National Museum in Warsaw.

21. See M. Morelowski, "Memorandum on Cultural Reparations," below, note 22.

22. M. Morelowski, "Memorandum on Cultural Reparations," prepared for the peace conference in Paris, 1919, manuscript in the Modern Archive, Warsaw, sheet 387/115.

23. Archive of the Ministry of Culture and Art, Warsaw.

24. See note 16, above.

LEISTRA:
A SHORT HISTORY OF ART LOSS AND ART RECOVERY IN THE NETHERLANDS

1. L. de Jong, *Het Koninkrijk der Nederlanden in de Tweede Wereldoorlog*, 14 vols. (The Hague and Leiden, 1969–91), X.B.I: 97, 277; X.B.II: 1440–45; XII.I: 287–93; XIV.II: 707. Emile van Konijnenburg, *Roof, restitutie, reparatie. Samengesteld in opdracht van het Ministerie van Economische Zaken*, The Hague ('s-Gravenhage), 1947 (dissertation), especially 206, 227. *Ministerie van Economische Zaken. Commissariaat Generaal voor de Nederlandse Economische Belangen in Duitsland. Verslag over het jaar 1948, waaraan toegevoegd opstel over "Restitutie in theorie en practijk"* (Amsterdam, 1949), 83.

2. De Jong, *Het Koninkrijk*, III: 394–95; F. J. Duparc, *Een eeuw strijd voor Nederlands cultureel erfgoed* (The Hague ['s-Gravenhage], 1975), 231; Pieter J. J. van Thiel, "Chronological History of the Rijksmuseum Painting Collection," in *All the Paintings of the Rijksmuseum in Amsterdam* (Amsterdam and Maarssen, 1976), 41. For the damage caused to buildings and monuments, see *Lost Treasures of Europe. 427 Photographs*, ed. Henry LaFarge (New York, 1946), 24–45; and *Voorloopig overzicht van de oorlogsschade toegebracht aan de Nederlandse monumenten van geschiedenis en kunst. Aangeboden door de Rijkscommissie voor de monumentenzorg*, 3 vols. (The Hague ['s-Gravenhage], 1945).

3. Günther Haase, *Kunstraub und Kunstschutz. Eine Dokumentation* (Hamburg: privately printed, 1991), 81; De Jong, *Het Koninkrijk*, VI.I: 335–37; VII.I: 45–48. Konijnenburg, *Roof, restitutie, reparatie*, 111–16.

4. Duparc, *Een eeuw strijd*, 230; Konijnenburg, *Roof, restitutie, reparatie*, 178; Gladys E. Hamlin, "European Art Collections and the War: Part II," *College Art Journal* 4, no. 4 (May 1945): 212.

5. De Jong, *Het Koninkrijk*, IV.I: 372, 386–87; Konijnenburg, *Roof, restitutie, reparatie*, 61–68, 76–81; *Ministerie van Economische Zaken. Commissariaat Generaal voor de Nederlandse Economische Belangen in Duitsland. Verslag over de jaren 1945 en 1946* (Amsterdam, 1947) (hereafter cited as *Verslag EZ over 1945–46*), 47; Royal Decree A 6, 7 June 1940, and Statute H 251, 18 July 1948.

6. De Jong, *Het Koninkrijk*, IV.I: 372; S. L. Faison, Jr., *Consolidated Interrogation Report No. 4. Linz: Hitler's Museum and Library*, RIOD (Rijksinstituut voor Oorlogsdocumentatie: State Institute for War Documentation, Amsterdam) Doc. 685B.g, 15 December 1945, 9, 28, 45; M. F. Hennus, "Frits Lugt, Kunstvorscher, kunstkeurder, kunstgaarder," *Maandblad voor beeldende kunsten* 26, nos. 4–5 (April-May 1950): 76–140, especially 131; *Reflets du siècle d'or. Tableaux Hollandais du dix-septième siècle. Collection Frits Lugt—Fondation Custodia* (Paris, 1983), VI; J. G. van Gelder, "In memoriam Frits Lugt," in *Dessins Flamands du dix-septième siècle. Collection Frits Lugt, Institut Néerlandais Paris* (London and Paris, etc., 1972), IX–XV, especially XII; Janet Flanner, *Men and Monuments* (London, 1957), 242.

7. Faison, *Consolidated Interrogation Report* 4, 28, 45; Flanner, *Men and Monuments*, 243.

8. Faison, *Consolidated Interrogation Report* 4, 9, 12, 36; De Jong, *Het Koninkrijk*, IV.I: 372. On Mannheimer, see M. D. Haga, "Mannheimer, de onbekende verzamelaar," *Bulletin van het Rijksmuseum* 22, nos. 2–3 (September 1974): 87–95.

9. Albert J. Elen, *Missing Old Master Drawings from the Franz Koenigs Collection, Claimed by the State of the Netherlands* (The Hague, 1989). The catalogue lists 526 drawings. One additional drawing, by J. Tintoretto, is listed in an addendum to the catalogue as no. 396a; this work was mistakenly not catalogued, because it had not been included in the inventory of sold drawings that was kept in the Boymans–van Beuningen Museum (and which was the basis for the 1989 catalogue), possibly because of its similarity to cat. no. 396.

10. H. W. van Os, "Otto Lanz en het verzamelen van vroege Italiaanse kunst in Nederland," *Bulletin van het Rijksmuseum* 26, no. 4 (1978): 147–74, especially 165–68.

11. De Jong, *Het Koninkrijk*, IV.I: 370–71.

12. Ibid., 374; Jolande Withuis, "Archief wacht op Russische zending. Laat vrachtwagens rijden en vliegtuigen vliegen," *NRC-Handelsblad*, 21 January 1992; Konijnenburg, *Roof, restitutie, reparatie*, 179.

13. De Jong, *Het Koninkrijk*, XII.II: 681; J.C.E. Belinfante, *Joods historisch Museum* (Haarlem, 1978), 13–14.

14. Konijnenburg, *Roof, restitutie, reparatie*, 179; *Verslag EZ over 1945–46*, 55.

15. Flanner, *Men and Monuments*, 295; Michael J. Kurtz, *Nazi Contraband: American Policy on the Return of European Cultural Treasures, 1945–1955* (New York and London, 1985), 179–81; *Verslag EZ over 1945–46*, 55–56; De Jong, *Het Koninkrijk*, XII.I: 292; Belinfante, *Joods historisch Museum*, 16; Van Os, "Otto Lanz," 168; *Reflets du siècle d'or*, VI; Hennus, "Frits Lugt," 131; Haga, "Mannheimer," 87–95, especially 92.

16. C. Hugh Smyth, *Repatriation of Art from the Collecting Point in Munich after World War II: Background and Beginnings, with Reference Especially to the Netherlands* (Maarssen/The Hague, 1988), 68; "News Reports / Restitution of Looted Art," *College Art Journal* 6, no. 3 (Spring 1947): 237; *Verslag EZ over 1945–46*, 56.

17. *Verslag EZ over 1945–46*, 55. The original art-recovery files are kept at the Ministry of Finance in The Hague. Other useful material is at the Rijksarchief (State Archives), also in The Hague, and at the Rijksinstituut voor Oorlogsdocumentatie (State Institute for War Documentation) in Amsterdam.

18. *Five Centuries of European Drawings: The Former Collection of Franz Koenigs*, exhib. cat. (Moscow and Milan, 1995).

19. *Counterparts: Old Master Drawings from the Koenigs Collection in the Museum Boymans–van Beuningen in Rotterdam. A Selection of Drawings Closely Related to the Recovered Drawings Exhibited in the Pushkin Museum, Moscow*, exhib. cat. (Moscow, 1995). Both exhibitions closed on 21 January 1996.

20. This short presentation can only cover some aspects of the history and present state of Dutch art-recovery work. As regards the recovery of archives, mention should be made here of the announcement in January 1992 by the Archival Committee of the State Archive of the Russian Federation stating that the Special Archive in Moscow held more than thirty archival collections from the Netherlands containing several thousands of dossiers. Among these are archives of the Freemasons, of the International Institute for Social History, of Jewish communities and institutions, and of the

International Archive of the Women's Movement, which after the war had recovered only four of the forty crates taken by the Germans. The Archival Committee stated that the Russian authorities were willing to return the material. See Marc Jansen, "Oorlogsbuit 'herontdekt.' Rusland geeft Nederlandse archieven terug," *NRC-Handelsblad,* 14 January 1992. Until now, the restitution process has been held up by political circumstances; however, one other restitution did take place—in June 1992, six hundred books were returned to the Netherlands by the Rudomino State Library for Foreign Literature in Moscow.

LUST:
THE SPOILS OF WAR REMOVED FROM BELGIUM DURING WORLD WAR II

1. E. Verhoeyen, *België bezet 1940–1944* (Brussels, 1993), is the first systematic synthesis of the history of occupied Belgium during the Second World War. It has an extensive bibliography.
2. "Anliegender Tätigkeitsbericht der Militärverwaltung, 18 July 1940," Navorsings- en Studiecentrum voor de Geschiedenis van de Tweede Wereldoorlog, Brussels (hereafter cited as NCWOII).
3. R. Bollmus, *Das Amt Rosenberg und seine Gegner* (Stuttgart, 1970), 145–52.
4. Stabschef G. Utikal, Netherlands State Institute for War, to Reichsleiter A. Rosenberg, 18 January 1941: "Es ist weiter abgesprochen und schriftlich bestätigt worden, dass die Arbeitsgruppe Belgien das Recht hat, die Wohnungen und Diensträume ehemaliger Politiker in Belgien aufzusuchen und eine Auswertung der vorhandenen Bibliotheken und Akten vorzunehmen. Das Gleiche gilt für sämtliche belgischen Professoren, die nicht zurückgekehrt sind bezw. durch den Militärbefehlshaber abgesetzt worden sind," Ministry of Economic Affairs, Brussels. Part of these political and military archives were discovered by Dr. W. Steenhaut and M. Vermote (Archive and Museum of the Socialist Labour Movement, Ghent) in the Osoby-archives in Moscow.
5. "Urfassung der ersten Auswertungsarbeiten des Einsatzstabes. Bericht über die Akten des Duc de Guise und Comte de Paris, gefunden in Mansion d'Anjou, Brussel, November 1940," Bundesarchiv Koblenz (Federal Archive of Germany, Koblenz), NS 30, no. 71.
6. "Urfassung der ersten Auswertungsarbeiten des Einsatzstabes. Bericht über die im Hause des Prof. Gunzberg in Antwerpen gefundenen Freimaurerakte, Februar 1941," Bundesarchiv Koblenz NS 30, no. 71.
7. A. Despy-Meyer, A. Dierkens, F. Scheelings, 25.11.1941. *De Université Libre de Bruxelles sluit haar deuren* (Brussels, 1991).
8. "Erfassung der eingehenden und vorhandenen Bestände," Aktenvermerk, Bundesarchiv Koblenz NS 30, no. 22.
9. "Bibliothèque de la Fédération Internationale de l'Habitation et de l'Urbanisme," Dossier XI, Ministry of Economic Affairs, Brussels. (After the war, documentation was discovered in Gailsdorf, Germany, and was sent back to Brussels on 28 June 1947.)
10. "Bericht über die Arbeit an der Auswertung des Archivs des Jesuitenkollegs Enghien," Bundesarchiv Koblenz NS 30, no. 74, 2.
11. W. Schivelbusch, *Die Bibliothek von Löwen. Eine Episode der Zeit der Weltkriege* (Munich, 1988).
12. J. Lust and R. Marijnissen, "De wedervaardigheden van het Lam Gods en de Nazi-Kulturpolitik," in *Academia Analecta, Mededelingen van de Koninklijke Academie van Wetenschappen, Letteren en Schone Kunsten van België* (1992), 21–43.
13. J. Lust, "De recuperatie van Belgische kunst na de oorlog (1946–1962)," *'30/'50: Berichten van het Navorsings- en Studiecentrum voor de Geschiedenis van de Tweede Wereldoorlog,* no. 25 (1994), 42–46.
14. R. Van Doorslaer, ed., *Les juifs de Belgique de l'immigration au génocide, 1925–1945* (Brussels, 1994).
15. M. Steinberg, *L'étoile et le fusil,* 4 vols., *La question juive* (Brussels, 1983), *Les cent jours de la déportation* (Brussels, 1984), *La traque des Juifs,* 2 vols. (Brussels, 1986).
16. I. Shirman, "Een aspect van de Endlösung. De ekonomische plundering van de joden in België," in *Bijdragen tot de Geschiedenis van de Tweede Wereldoorlog* (Brussels, 1974), 163–82.
17. "Devisenschutzkommando, Ermittlungssache Andriesse," NCWOII.
18. Dossier E. Lyndhurst, Ministry of Economic Affairs, Brussels.
19. Dossiers E. Renders, Ministry of Economic Affairs, Brussels.
20. Dossiers Office de Récupération, Ministry of Economic Affairs, Brussels.

HAMON:
SPOLIATION AND RECOVERY OF CULTURAL PROPERTY IN FRANCE, 1940–94

1. Rose Valland, *Le Front de l'Art* (Paris, 1961).
2. A catalogue of works from the Schloss collection that had not been returned as of December 31, 1993—which is based on the inventory of August 1943 and known as List 1943—is ready for publication and should soon appear in print.
3. Bureau Central des Restitutions, *Répertoire des biens spoliés en France durant la guerre 1939–1945* (Berlin, 1947), 2: XII.
4. This figure includes 1,661 identifiable antique rugs. In addition, 1,776 unidentifiable Oriental rugs and 57 North African rugs were declared stolen. They were recorded in the file of the Bureau Central des Restitutions but were not mentioned in the catalogue because of difficulty in identifying them.
5. This figure includes bedroom and living- and dining-room sets, 475- and 350-piece porcelain sets, 100- and 150-piece crystal sets and toiletry sets, collections of incense burners and of gold- and silver-plated tables—each set and collection counted as one item.
6. The figure given is much lower than the actual number because the documents representing the archive resources and autograph collections could not be appraised since detailed information was lacking. The same is true for newspaper and periodical collections. Moreover, in a report of December 1949, Rose Valland mentioned sorting *two million returned books;* this means that many more than two million were taken since it is known that quantities are held in libraries in Eastern Europe.
7. Only the quantities given for certain collections were considered. The numbers are therefore also underestimated.
8. The signatory governments of the Declaration of London and the French National Committee reserved the right to invalidate all transfers of ownership or transactions involving rights or interests whatsoever located in the occupied territories under the direct or indirect control of enemy countries. This warning applied to transfers or transactions in the form of outright plundering or ransacking as well as to transactions that seemed legal, even if they appeared to have been made with the victim's consent.
9. This department deals with everything involving French citizens abroad and in particular, as in this instance, with protecting their property and private interests.

MALDIS:
THE TRAGIC FATE OF BELARUSAN MUSEUM AND LIBRARY COLLECTIONS DURING THE SECOND WORLD WAR

1. *Golas Radzimy,* 14 May 1981.
2. *Kultura: Infarmatsyina-analitychny biuleten Agentstva RID,* no. 1 (1995), 5.
3. *Izvestiia,* 7 September 1940.
4. *Litaratura i mastatstva,* 26 March 1993.
5. *Gazeta Wyborcza,* 24–27 December 1992.
6. *Sovetskaia Belorussiia,* 28 September 1990; *Vestnik Mogileva,* no. 39, 1991.

MANN:
JEWISH CEREMONIAL ART AND PRIVATE PROPERTY

1. I would like to acknowledge the generous help of Grace Cohen Grossman, Curator of Judaica at the Skirball Museum, Los Angeles, who graciously made available to me her research materials on the Jewish Cultural Reconstruction.
2. Hillel Kieval, "The Lands Between: The Jews of Bohemia, Moravia and Slovakia to 1918," in *Where Cultures Meet. The Story of the Jews of Czechoslovakia*, ed. Natalia Berger, exhib. cat., Nahum Goldmann Museum of the Jewish Diaspora, Beit Hatefutsoth, 1990, 23, 27; for a more detailed historical survey, see *The Jews of Czechoslovakia*, ed. Avigdor Dagan et al., 3 vols. (Philadelphia, 1968, 1971, 1984).
3. Vlastimila Hamackova, "Débuts du mouvement assimilateur tchéco-juif," *Judaica Bohemia* XIV, no. 1 (1978): 15–23.
4. Linda A. Altshuler and Anna R. Cohen, "The Precious Legacy," in *The Precious Legacy: Judaic Treasures from the Czechoslovak State Collections*, ed. David Altshuler (New York and Washington, D.C., 1983), 19–23.
5. This information is recorded in the original, handwritten catalogue still in the museum today. On wartime cataloguing and exhibitions, see Vladimir Sadek, "From the Documents Related to the War Time Central Jewish Museum in Prague," *Judaica Bohemiae* XVI, no. 1 (1980): 5–6. Sadek states that the Nazis wished the collection catalogued to establish its financial worth. See also Hana Volavková, ed., *A Story of the Jewish Museum in Prague* (Prague, 1968).
6. Sadek, "From the Documents Related to the War Time," 6. Altshuler and Cohen, "Precious Legacy," 24–38.
7. For an account of Jewish museum exhibitions under the Nazis, see "The Secret Presentation of the Museum Collections in the Second World War," in *A Story of the Jewish Museum in Prague*, 125–41.
8. *The Precious Legacy*, fig. 37.
9. Gershon C. Bacon, "Danzig Jewry: A Short History," in J. Gutmann and V. B. Mann, *Danzig 1939: Treasures of a Destroyed Community*, exhib. cat., The Jewish Museum, New York, 1980, 24–35; and Samuel Echt, *Die Geschichte der Juden in Danzig* (Leer in Ostfriesland, 1972).
10. On the period of Nazi rule in Danzig, see Erwin Lichtenstein, *Die Juden der Freien Stadt Danzig unter der Herrschaft des Nationalsozialismus* (Tübingen, 1973).
11. The Jewish Museum, New York, was likewise founded in 1904, as part of the Library of the Jewish Theological Seminary of America.
12. For an account of the interwar period, see Christoph M. Kimmich, *The Free City—Danzig and German Foreign Policy 1919–34* (New Haven, Conn., 1968).
13. See Gutmann and Mann, *Danzig 1939*, 20, for a reproduction of the packing list.
14. For the architectural history of the synagogue, see Otto Bocher, "Die Alte Synagoge zu Worms," *Der Wormsgau* XVIII (1960).
15. The list that follows is based on Bocher, "Die Alte Synagoge zu Worms," 88–95; it was reprinted in Ernst Roth, ed., *Festschrift zur Wiedereinweihung der Alten Synagoge zu Worms* (Frankfurt am Main, 1961), 88–95.
16. The Jewish Museum, New York: JM 29–51, and 31–51.
17. "Jewish Cultural Reconstruction," *Encyclopaedia Judaica*, X, col. 49; Lynn H. Nicholas, *The Rape of Europa: The Fate of Europe's Treasures in the Third Reich and the Second World War* (New York, 1994), 433–34.
18. See, most recently, Nicholas, *Rape of Europa*, 120–26, 157–72; and, for art collections confiscated by Nazis, country headings.
19. George Mihan, *Looted Treasure: Germany's Raid on Art* (London, 1944).
20. *Liste mit einer Kurzbeschreibung des im Gewahrsam des Bundesdenkmalamtes, öffentlicher Sammlungen und anderer Dienststellen befindlichen Kunst- und Kulturgutes, dessen Herausgabe von ehemaligen Eigentümern oder deren Rechtsnachfolgern von Todes wegen in der Zeit bis 30. September 1986 beansprucht werden kann.* Brochure published by the Bundesministerium für Finanzen, Vienna, November 1985.
21. For a recent evaluation of the settlement of Jewish claims to artworks in Austria, see Sharon Waxman, "Austria: Ending the Legacy of Shame," *ARTnews* 94, no. 7 (September 1995): 122–25.

SAILER:
AUSTRIA

1. *Jahrbuch des Kunsthistorischen Museums* (Vienna) 76 (1980): 139–71.
2. Ibid.
3. Declaration of 25 November 1992.
4. Hans Tietze, *Die Sammlungen des Schlosses Grafenegg* (Vienna: Verlag Anton Schroll, 1908).
5. U.S. Army Fact Sheet: Art Restitution, APO 777, National Archives, Washington D.C.

KAYE:
LAWS IN FORCE AT THE DAWN OF WORLD WAR II

The author expresses his appreciation to Lucille A. Roussin, a recent graduate of Benjamin N. Cardozo School of Law, for her assistance in the preparation of this chapter.

1. Convention with Respect to the Laws and Customs of War on Land, July 29, 1899, 32 Stat. 1803 (1903), T.S. No. 403; Convention Respecting the Laws and Customs of War on Land, Oct. 18, 1907, 36 Stat. 2277 (1911), T.S. No. 539 [hereinafter Hague Convention].
2. See generally 1 OPPENHEIM'S INTERNATIONAL LAW 4 (Sir Robert Jennings & Sir Arthur Watts, eds., 1992).
3. *Id.* at 41.
4. *Id.* at 341, 353–54.
5. *See, e.g.*, Lyndel V. Prott, *The Protocol to the Convention for the Protection of Cultural Property in the Event of Armed Conflict (The Hague Convention) 1954*, 5 INT'L ART TRADE & L. (forthcoming 1996) (from the proceedings of the 5th Symposium on the Legal Aspects of International Trade in Art: Licit Trade in Works of Art, Vienna, Sept. 28–30, 1994).
6. See generally Lawrence M. Kaye, *Cultural Property Theft During War—Application of the Statute of Limitations*, 5 INT'L ART TRADE & L. (forthcoming 1996) (from the proceedings of the 5th Symposium on the Legal Aspects of International Trade in Art: Licit Trade in Works of Art, Vienna, Sept. 28–30, 1994).
7. EMHERIC DE VATTEL, THE LAW OF NATIONS 367 (Joseph Chitty, ed., 1844).
8. HENRY WHEATON, ELEMENTS OF INTERNATIONAL LAW 395 (3d ed. 1846).
9. Alan Marchisotto, *The Protection of Art in Transnational Law*, 7 VAND. J. TRANSNAT'L L. 689, 697 (1974).
10. *Id.* at 693.
11. Letter from the Duke of Wellington to Lord Castlereagh, Sept. 23, 1815, *cited in* Marchisotto, *supra* note 9, at 693.
12. George B. Davis, *Doctor Francis Lieber's Instructions for the Government of Armies in the Field*, 1 AM. J. INT'L L. 13 (1907).
13. The Lieber Code, Washington, D.C., Apr. 24, 1863, art. 34, *reprinted in* 1 *The Law of War: A Documentary History* 165 (Leon Friedman ed., 1972) [hereinafter *Law of War*]. See generally Sharon A. Williams, *The International and National Protection of Movable Cultural Property: A Comparative Study* (1978), 16.
14. The Lieber Code, art. 35, *reprinted in Law of War, supra* note 13, at 165.
15. The Lieber Code, art. 36, *reprinted in Law of War, supra* note 13, at 165.
16. Davis, *supra* note 12, at 22.
17. Project of an International Declaration Concerning the Laws and Customs of War, *adopted by* the Conference of Brus-

sels, Aug. 27, 1874, art. 8, *reprinted in* 1
AM. J. INT'L L. 96 (Supp. 1907).

18. James Brown Scott, *The Hague Peace
Conferences: A Series of Lectures Delivered
Before the Johns Hopkins University in the
Year 1908*, vol. 1 (1909), 526.

19. Hague Convention, *supra* note 1, art. 56.

20. Hague Convention, *supra* note 1, arts. 28,
46, 47, 53, 55.

21. Stanislaw E. Nahlik, *International Law
and the Protection of Cultural Property in
Armed Conflicts*, 27 HASTINGS L. J. 1069,
1074 (1976).

22. *Id.* at 1075; Hague Convention, *supra*
note 1, Preamble.

23. Hague Convention, *supra* note 1, art. 3.

24. *Id.* art. 56. It should be noted that this
provision of the Convention formed one
basis for the Nuremberg trials after World
War II. See Telford Taylor, *The Anatomy of
the Nuremberg Trials* (1992), 54, 85, 305,
et passim.

25. Charles de Visscher, *La protection des
patrimoines artistiques et historiques
nationaux: Nécessité d'une réglementation
internationale*, 43–44 MOUSEION 7, 8–9
(1938).

26. *Id.* at 11–12.

27. Williams, *supra* note 13, at 154 n.215.

28. The arrival in Europe during the first
decades of the twentieth century of newly
wealthy Americans in search of art objects
of all description and at any cost played
no small part in this development. *See*
Stanislaw E. Nahlik, *La protection internationale des biens culturels en cas de conflit armé*, 1 RECUEIL DES COURS DE
L'ACADÉMIE DE DROIT INTERNATIONAL· DE
LA HAYE 61, 82 (1967).

29. Treaty of Peace with Germany, June 28,
1919, art. 245, 2 Bevans 43 [hereinafter
Treaty of Versailles].

30. *Id.* art. 247.

31. *Id.* art. 247; Marchisotto, *supra* note 9, at
699.

32. Treaty of Versailles, *supra* note 29, art. 247.

33. Lyndel V. Prott and P. J. O'Keefe, *Law and
the Cultural Heritage*, vol. 3, *Movement*
(London and Edinburgh: Butterworths,
1989), 804.

34. Treaty of Peace Between the Allied and
Associated Powers and Hungary (Treaty
of Trianon), June 4, 1920, *reprinted in*
15 AM. INT'L L. 1, 63 (Supp. 1921). See
generally Prott and O'Keefe, *Law and the
Cultural Heritage*, vol. 3, 804.

35. Treaty of Peace Between the Allied and
Associated Powers and Austria, Sept. 10,
1919, §2, arts. 195, 196 [hereinafter
Treaty of St. Germain], *reprinted in* 112
BRITISH AND FOREIGN STATE PAPERS 317,
350. See generally Prott and O'Keefe,
Law and the Cultural Heritage, vol. 3,
804f.

36. Treaty of St. Germain, *supra* note 35,
§2, art. 195, at 350. *See also International
Arbitrations under the Treaty of St. Germain*,
1923–24 BRITISH Y. B. INT'L L. 124, 126.

37. *International Arbitrations under the Treaty
of St. Germain*, supra note 36, at 126.

38. *Id.* at 127, 129.

39. Treaty of Peace Between Poland, Russia
and the Ukraine, March 18, 1921, art. 11,
§ 1, 6 L.N.T.S. 123, 139 [hereinafter
Treaty of Riga].

40. J. Chrzaszczewska, *Un exemple de restitution. Le traité de Riga de 1921 et le patrimoine artistique de la Pologne*, 17–18
MOUSEION 205, 207 (1932).

41. Treaty of Riga, *supra* note 39, art. 11, § 7
at 141.

42. 14 LEAGUE OF NATIONS O.J. 1394 (1933).
The International Museums Office was
the official international association of
national museums between the two world
wars. It has been succeeded by the International Council of Museums, founded in
1946. See Prott and O'Keefe, *Law and
the Cultural Heritage*, vol. 3, 101.

43. 14 LEAGUE OF NATIONS O.J. at 1395
(1933).

44. *Id.* at 1394.

45. *Id.* at 1396.

46. *Id.*, art. 7 at 1395.

47. *Id.* at 1396.

48. Prott and O'Keefe, *Law and the Cultural
Heritage*, vol. 3, 709.

49. 17 LEAGUE OF NATIONS O.J. 1310 (1936).

50. Office International des Musées, *Art et
Archéologie*, no. 2 (1940): 60–70. A more
successful effort is reflected by a regional
treaty drafted in the 1930s. The Treaty on
the Protection of Artistic and Scientific
Institutions and Historic Monuments—
more commonly known as the Roerich
Pact—was drafted by the governing board
of the Pan American Union and adopted
by it in 1935 (see Appendix 8); it has
been ratified by Brazil, Chile, Colombia,
Cuba, Dominican Republic, El Salvador,
Guatemala, Mexico, and the United States.
Although the Roerich Pact provides that
historic monuments and cultural, educational, and scientific institutions should
be protected during times of peace as well
as in war, no enforcement mechanism is
provided for in the treaty, and its potential
effectiveness has been questioned. 167
L.N.T.S. 279 (1935). *See* Prott and
O'Keefe, *Law and the Cultural Heritage*,
vol. 3, 689.

51. *Kunstsammlungen zu Weimar v. Elicofon*,
536 F. Supp. 829 (E.D.N.Y. 1981), *aff'd*,
678 F.2d 1150 (2d Cir. 1982) [hereinafter
Elicofon].

52. Elicofon, 536 F. Supp. at 833.

53. *Id.* at 830–33.

54. *Id.* at 851–52.

55. *DeWeerth v. Baldinger*, 658 F. Supp. 688
(S.D.N.Y. 1987), *rev'd*, 836 F.2d 103 (2d
Cir. 1987); 804 F. Supp. 539 (S.D.N.Y.
1992), *rev'd*, 28 Fed.R.Serv.3d (Callaghan)
1231 (2d Cir. 1994), *amended opinion
filed after petition for rehearing*, 38 F.3d
1266 (2d Cir. 1994), *cert. denied*, 15 S.
Ct. 512 (1994).

56. As it has been argued, the premise was
also implicitly rejected in the Declaration
of London of 1943 and in the Protocol
to the Convention for the Protection of
Cultural Property in the Event of Armed
Conflict (1954 Hague Convention). *See*
Prott, *The Protocol to the Convention for
the Protection of Cultural Property in the
Event of Armed Conflict*, supra note 5.
The Declaration of London and 1954
Hague Convention, with its Protocol and
Resolutions, are reprinted as, respectively,
Appendix 9 and Appendix 10 in this book.

57. See Kaye, *supra* note 6.

PETROPOULOS:
GERMAN LAWS AND DIRECTIVES
BEARING ON THE APPROPRIATION
OF CULTURAL PROPERTY IN
THE THIRD REICH

1. See Nolde's appeal to Joseph Goebbels,
reproduced in William Bradley, *Emil
Nolde and German Expressionism* (Ann
Arbor: UMI, 1986). See also the claims
by the Osthaus family, who had donated
paintings to the Folkwang Museum in
Essen and who objected to the purges, in
Wilhelm Arntz, "Bildersturm in Deutsch-
land: das Schicksal der Bilder," in *Das
Schönste*, July 1962, 28–29.

2. Mario Andreas von Lüttichau, " 'Deutsche
Kunst' und 'entartete Kunst,' " in Peter-
Klaus Schuster, ed., *Nationalsozialismus
und "Entartete Kunst." Die "Kunststadt"
München 1937* (Munich: Prestel, 1987),
96. Annegret Janda, "The Fight for Mod-
ern Art," in Stephanie Barron, ed.,
*"Degenerate Art": The Fate of the Avant-
Garde in Nazi Germany* (New York: Harry
N. Abrams, 1991), 113.

3. Joseph Goebbels, *Die Tagebücher von
Joseph Goebbels: Sämtliche Fragmente*,
vol. 3 (Munich: K. G. Sauer, 1988),
202–3 (entry for 15 July 1937).

4. Hildegard Brenner, *Die Kunstpolitik des
Nationalsozialismus* (Reinbek: Rowohlt,
1963), 109.

5. See Bundesarchiv Koblenz (Federal
Archive of Germany, Koblenz; hereafter
cited as BAK), R43II/1646, Bl. 133, for
Göring's order of 28 July 1937.

6. For the negotiations between Goebbels,
Rust, Frick, and others concerning this
law, see BAK R2/4868. The law is reproduced in Joseph Wulf, *Die bildenden
Künste im Dritten Reich* (Frankfurt: Ull-
stein, 1963), 377.

7. Paul Hofmann, *The Viennese: Splendor,
Twilight, and Exile* (New York: Anchor
Press, 1988), 277–78.

8. For the "Verordnung über die Anmeldung
des Vermögens der Juden," see the *Reichs-
gesetzblatt* I (1938): 414.

9. Himmler quoted by Hans Lammers in a

Vermerk (note to file), 30 January 1939. BAK, R43II/1269a, Bl. 157–60.

10. Wulf, *Die bildenden Künste,* 337.

11. *Vermerk* by Hans Lammers, 7 November 1942. BAK, R43II/1269a, Bl. 53–54. The *Führervorbehalt* was extended to the entire Reich on 9 October 1940; to the newly occupied territories on 18 November 1940; to Bohemia and Moravia on 11 May 1941; and again to the newly occupied territories on 25 July 1941.

12. For the "Verordnung über die Einziehung Volks- und Staatsfeindlichen Vermögens" and the "Verordnung über den Einsatz des jüdischen Vermögens," see Diemut Majer, *Recht, Verwaltung und Justiz im Nationalsozialismus. Ausgewählte Schriften, Gesetze und Gerichtsentscheidungen* (Cologne: Bund-Verlag, 1984), 269.

13. Lucy Dawidowicz, *The War Against the Jews, 1933–1945* (New York: Holt, Rinehart, and Winston, 1975), 58.

14. Ibid., 115.

15. See the 16 July 1943 report on Mühlmann's activities, "Bericht über die Überprüfung der Gesamttätigkeit des Sonderbeauftragten für die Erfassung der Kunst- und Kulturschätze im Generalgouvernement," in BAK, R43II/1341a, Bl. 63.

16. For Frank's 15 November 1939 "Verordnung über die Beschlagnahme des Vermögens des früheren polnischen Staates innerhalb des Generalgouvernements," and his 16 December 1939 "Verordnung des Generalgouvernements für die Beschlagnahme des gesamten öffentlichen Kunstbesitzes," see BAK, R43II/1341a, Bl. 47. See above, Pruszyński, note 4.

17. Werner Präg and Wolfgang Jacobmeyer, *Das Diensttagebuch des deutschen Generalgouverneurs in Polen* (Stuttgart: Deutsche Verlags-Anstalt, 1975), 59.

18. For Himmler's order of 16 December 1939, see Michael Kater, "Das Ahnenerbe. Die Forschungs- und Lehrgemeinschaft in der SS" (Ph.D. diss. Ruprecht-Karl Universität, Heidelberg, 1966), 135. Previously, on 10 November 1939, Himmler had ordered his forces to cooperate with Mühlmann's commando. See Lynn Nicholas, *The Rape of Europa: The Fate of Europe's Treasures in the Third Reich and the Second World War* (New York: Alfred A. Knopf, 1994), 67.

19. Helmut Lehmann-Haupt, *Cultural Looting of the Ahnenerbe* (Washington, D.C.: Office of the Military Governor of the United States, 1 March 1948).

20. Robert Koehl, *RKFDV: German Resettlement and Population Policy* (Cambridge, Mass.: Harvard University Press, 1957).

21. The best overview of the laws and directives for France is found in the report of the Militärbefehlshaber (Military Commander) for France, reproduced in Wilhelm Treue, "Dokumentation: Zum Nationalsozialistischen Kunstraub in Frankreich. Der 'Bargatzky-Bericht,'" in *Vierteljahreshefte für Zeitgeschichte* 13, no. 3 (July 1965): 285–337.

22. Rudolf Schleier to the German embassy in Paris, 31 July 1940, Centre de Documentation Juive Contemporaire, Paris (hereafter cited as CDJC), LXXI–104.

23. Treue, "Der 'Bargatzky-Bericht,'" 295.

24. Jacob Kurz, *Kunstraub in Europa, 1938–1945* (Hamburg: Facta Oblita, 1989), 136–38.

25. For this project, see BAK, R55/1476; and BAK, R55/1201.

26. Hans Lammers to Joseph Goebbels, 13 August 1940, BAK, R55/1476, Bl. 18.

27. Albert Speer, *Inside the Third Reich* (New York: Macmillan, 1969), 243.

28. BAK, NS 8/264.

29. Hitler's order was articulated by the head of the armed forces (Oberkommando der Wehrmacht) Field Marshal Wilhelm Keitel to General Walther von Brauchitsch, the head of the military administration in France. See Jean Cassou, *Le pillage par les Allemands des oeuvres d'art et des bibliothèques appartenant à des Juifs en France* (Paris: CDJC, 1947), 84.

30. Ibid., 145.

31. For Göring's order of 5 November 1940, see BAK, NS8/259, Bl. 25–27.

32. Rosenberg requested permission to confiscate "ownerless Jewish property" on 18 December in a letter to Hitler. This was granted in a 31 December 1941 response sent via Hans Lammers. See Günther Haase, *Kunstraub und Kunstschutz. Eine Dokumentation* (Hamburg: privately printed, 1991), 81.

33. For Hitler's order to all offices of the Wehrmacht, the National Socialist Party, and the state, dated 1 March 1942, see Haase, *Kunstraub and Kunstschutz,* 303–5. The struggle between Rosenberg and Bormann is reflected in the documents in BAK, NS8/157.

34. A. J. van der Leeuw, "Die Bestimmung der vom deutschen Reich entzogenen und von der Dienststelle Mühlmann übernommenen Kunstgegenstände," Rijksinstituut voor de Oorlogsdocumentatie, Amsterdam, 1962.

35. For Verordnung 189/1940, see Kurz, *Kunstraub in Europa,* 256.

36. The ERR-Ost (Einsatzstab Reichsleiter Rosenberg–East) did not receive a formal commission from Hitler to secure artworks until 1 March 1942; but because much of the personnel in this group also had positions in Rosenberg's Reichsministerium für die besetzten Ostgebiete (Reich Ministry for the Occupied Eastern Territories), they had other means prior to that date to secure artworks. See Kurz, *Kunstraub in Europa,* 320. For the ERR in the East, see also Patricia Kennedy Grimsted, "The Fate of Ukrainian Cultural Treasures during World War II: Archives, Libraries, and Museums under the Third Reich," in *Jahrbücher für Geschichte Osteuropas* 39, no. 1 (1991): 53–80.

37. A fourth battalion was later sent to North Africa. International Military Tribunal (IMT), *Trial of the Major War Criminals,* vol. 10 (Nuremberg: International Military Tribunal, 1947), 441.

38. Baron von Künsberg to Generalmajor Herff, 4 January 1943, Berlin Document Center, Künsberg file.

39. Quoted in Desmond Seward, *Napoleon and Hitler: A Comparative Biography* (New York: Viking, 1988), 209.

40. IMT, *Trial,* vol. 7, 100.

41. Hitler's order is mentioned in a report of 15 April 1943 by Robert Scholz of the ERR. See IMT, *Trial,* vol. 8, 60. The importation of modern art into the Slovakian Protectorate is noted in Pierre Assouline, *An Artful Life: A Biography of D. H. Kahnweiler, 1884–1979* (New York: Fromm International, 1991), 295.

42. See Martin Broszat's chapter "Departmental Polyocracy and Führer Absolutism," in *The Hitler State: The Foundation and Development of the Internal Structure of the Third Reich* (London and New York: Longman, 1981), 294–327.

43. See Jonathan Petropoulos, *Art as Politics in the Third Reich* (Chapel Hill and London: The University of North Carolina Press, 1996).

44. Hans Safrian, *Die Eichmann Männer* (Vienna and Zurich: Europaverlag, 1994). See also Götz Aly and Susanne Heim, *Vordenker der Vernichtung. Auschwitz und die deutschen Pläne für eine neue europäische Ordnung* (Hamburg: Hoffmann und Campe, 1991).

45. J. S. Conway, *The Nazi Persecution of the Churches, 1933–1945* (Toronto: Ryerson Press, 1968), 393–97.

46. Günter Bischof, "Die Instrumentalisierung der Moskauer Erklärung nach dem 2. Weltkrieg," in *Zeitgeschichte* 20 (November–December 1993): 345–66.

47. Herbert Rosenkranz, *Verfolgung und Selbstbehauptung. Die Juden in Österreich, 1938–1945* (Vienna: Herold Druck, 1978).

48. Robert Koehl, *The Black Corps: The Structure and Power Struggles of the Nazi SS* (Madison: University of Wisconsin Press, 1983), 173.

KURTZ:
THE END OF THE WAR AND THE OCCUPATION OF GERMANY, 1944–52. LAWS AND CONVENTIONS ENACTED TO COUNTER GERMAN APPROPRIATIONS

1. Richard A. Johnson, Protection, Restitution, and Reparation of Objets d'Art, and other Cultural Objects, 17 November 1944, File "Restituhon Background Material," London Files, 1943–1945, Record Group 239, Records of the American Commission for the Protection and Sal-

vage of Artistic and Historic Monuments in War Areas, National Archives at College Park, College Park, Maryland.

2. Ibid.

3. Ibid.; U.S. Department of State, *Foreign Relations of the United States, Diplomatic Papers, 1942,* vol. 1, *General* (Washington, D.C.: U.S. Government Printing Office, 1960), 72–88.

4. Ibid.

5. Ibid.

6. Ibid.

7. Ibid.

8. Ibid.

9. Ibid.

10. Ibid.

11. U.S. Department of State, *Foreign Relations of the United States, Diplomatic Papers, 1943,* vol. 1, *General* (Washington, D.C.: U.S. Government Printing Office, 1963), 443–44.

12. U.S. Department of State, *Foreign Relations of the United States, Diplomatic Papers, 1942,* vol. 1, *General,* 83.

13. U.S. Department of State, *Foreign Relations of the United States, Diplomatic Papers, 1943,* vol. 1, *General,* 449–51.

14. Ibid., 451–59.

15. Ibid.

16. In the fall of 1942, leaders of the art world met to discuss possible strategies and plans of action. Participants included: William B. Dinsmoor, president of the Archaeological Institute of America; Francis Henry Taylor, director of New York's Metropolitan Museum of Art; Paul J. Sachs, associate director of the Fogg Museum of Art at Harvard University; and David Finley, director of the National Gallery of Art in Washington, D.C. See *Report of the American Commission for the Protection and Salvage of Artistic and Historic Monuments in War Areas* (Washington, D.C.: U.S. Government Printing Office, 1946), 1.

17. Ibid., 3.

18. Ibid., 1, 3.

19. William B. Dinsmoor, Memorandum No. 4, Restitution of Art Objects and Other Cultural Materials, 25 May 1944, File "Restitution Background Material," London Files, 1943–1945, Record Group 239.

20. Ibid. In addition to the Conference of Allied Ministers of Education and the Interallied Commission for the Study of the Armistice, other groups focusing on cultural restitution schemes included the London International Assembly, the International Committee of the Central Institute of Art and Design, and the Interallied Commission for the Protection and Restitution of Cultural Materials. See Richard A. Johnson, Explanatory Note on Restitution Scheme of the Conference of Allied Ministers of Education, 15 December 1944, File "134.4: Directive No. 2—Works of Art," Record Group 43, Records of the European Advisory Commission,

Part 1: Records of Philip E. Mosely, U.S. Political Adviser, National Archives at College Park, College Park, Maryland.

21. Ibid.

22. U.S. Department of State, *Foreign Relations of the United States, Diplomatic Papers, 1944,* vol. 1, *General* (Washington, D.C.: U.S. Government Printing Office, 1966), 252–61, 299–301, 385–87, 395–96, 404.

23. U.S. Department of State, *Foreign Relations of the United States, Diplomatic Papers, 1945, Conferences at Malta and Yalta* (Washington, D.C.: U.S. Government Printing Office, 1955), 121, 124.

24. U.S. Department of State, *Foreign Relations of the United States, Diplomatic Papers, 1945,* vol. 3, *European Advisory Commission: Austria, Germany* (Washington, D.C.: U.S. Government Printing Office, 1968), 1345–46.

25. Ibid., 1426–27; CONL/P(45)65, 4 December 1945, File "CONL/P(45)," Record Group 43, Records of the Allied Control Council, Germany, 1941–1950, National Archives at College Park, College Park, Maryland.

26. Ibid.

27. U.S. Department of State, *Foreign Relations of the United States, Diplomatic Papers, 1945,* vol. 2, *General: Political and Economic Matters* (Washington, D.C.: U.S. Government Printing Office, 1967), 955–57; U.S. Department of State, *Foreign Relations of the United States, Diplomatic Papers, 1945,* vol. 3, *European Advisory Commission: Austria, Germany,* 1463; Minutes of the Twenty-Sixth Meeting of the Coordinating Committee (CORC/M(45)26), 12 December 1945, File "CORC/M(45)," Record Group 43, Records of the Allied Control Council, Germany, 1941–1950.

28. U.S. Department of State, *Foreign Relations of the United States, Diplomatic Papers, 1945,* vol. 3, *European Advisory Commission: Austria, Germany,* 1427–29.

29. Minutes of the Seventeenth Meeting of the Allied Control Council (CONL/M(46)2), 21 January 1946, File "CONL/M(46)," Record Group 43, Records of the Allied Control Council, Germany, 1941–1950.

30. CONL/P(45)65, 4 December 1945, File "CONL/P(45)," Record Group 43, Records of the Allied Control Council, Germany, 1941–1950.

31. Minutes of the Seventeenth Meeting of the Allied Control Council, (CONL/M(46)2), 21 January 1946, File "CONL/M(46)," Record Group 43, Records of the Allied Control Council, Germany, 1941–1950.

32. Minutes of the Thirty-Second Meeting of the Coordinating Committee, 17 January 1946, File "CORC/M(46)," Record Group 43, Records of the Allied Control Council, Germany, 1941–1950.

33. U.S. Department of State, *Foreign Relations of the United States, Diplomatic Papers, 1946,* vol. 5, *The British Commonwealth; Western and Central Europe* (Washington, D.C.: U.S. Government Printing Office, 1969), 488–89.

34. Quadripartite Procedures for Restitution (CORC/P(46)143), 17 April 1946, File "CORC/P(46)76–150," Record Group 43, Records of the Allied Control Council, Germany, 1941–1950.

35. Ibid.

36. Soviet Removals of Cultural Materials, 13 May 1947, File "WDSCA 000.4, 13 June 1946–31 May 1947," Record Group 165, Records of the Civil Affairs Division, General Records, Security Classified General Correspondence, 1943–July 1945, National Archives at College Park, College Park, Maryland; War Chronicle of the Museums of Berlin, May 1946, File "Interzonal Exchange," Record Group 59, General Records of the Department of State, Records Maintained by the Fine Arts and Monuments Adviser ("Ardelia Hall Collection"), 1945–1960, National Archives at College Park, College Park, Maryland.

37. CORC/P(46)80 revise, 28 June 1946, File "CORC/P(46)76–150," Record Group 43, Records of the Allied Control Council, Germany, 1941–1950.

38. Minutes of the Sixty-Third Meeting of the Coordinating Committee (CORC/M(46)34, Appendix A), 9 July 1946, File "CORC/M(46)," Record Group 43, Records of the Allied Control Council, Germany 1941–1950.

39. Ibid.

40. Ibid.

41. Minutes of the Sixty-First Meeting of the Reparations, Deliveries, and Restitution Directorate (DRDR/M(47)7), 25 February 1947, Record Group 260, Records of the U.S. Occupation Headquarters, World War II, Records of the U.S. Elements of Interallied Organizations, Records of the U.S. Element, Allied Control Authority, DRDR General Records, 1945–1948, National Archives at College Park, College Park, Maryland.

42. Ibid.

43. Owen R. McJunkins to Maj. Gen. L. I. Zorin, October 1948, File "Correspondence, October 1948," Record Group 260, Records of the Reparations and Restitution Branch, Correspondence and Related Records of the Restitution Section, 1946–1949; Maj. Gen. L. I. Zorin to Col. John Allen, 26 May 1947, File "May 1947," Record Group 260, Records of the Reparations and Restitution Branch, Correspondence and Related Records of the Restitution Section, 1946–1949; Soviet Removals of Cultural Materials, 13 May 1947, File "WDSCA 000.4, 13 June 1946–31 May 1947," Record Group 165, Records of the Civil Affairs Division.

44. Control Council Proclamation No. 2, Abolition of the Nazi Party, 20 September 1945; Control Council Law No. 2, Providing for the Termination and Liquidation of Nazi Organizations, 10 October 1945; Control Council Law No. 10, Punishment of Individuals Guilty of War Crimes and Crimes Against Peace and Against Humanity, 20 December 1945; Control Council Law No. 58, Addendum to Law No. 2 of the Control Council, 20 August 1947; Control Council Directive No. 30, Elimination of German Military and Nazi Monuments and Museums, 13 May 1946; Control Council Directive No. 38, Arrest and Punishment of War Criminals, 12 October 1946; File "Enactments and Approval Papers of the Control Council and Coordinating Committee, 1945–1948," Record Group 260, Records of the U.S. Elements of Interallied Organizations, Records of the U.S. Element of the Allied Control Authority, Records of Unidentified Allied Control Authority Units.

45. Ibid.

46. Transfer of Works of Art or Cultural Materials of Value or Importance, 6 December 1946, File "387, Restitution Reports," Record Group 260, Records of the Property Division, Records of the Reparations and Restitution Branch, Headquarters Records Relating to Reparations, 1945–1959.

47. Final Report—Monuments, Fine Arts and Archives Section, 30 December 1948, File "Final Reports—Reparations and Restitution," Record Group 260, Records of Property Division, Records of the Reparations and Restitution Branch, Reports and Related Records Re: Restitution, 1945–1950.

48. Ibid.

49. War Department Cablegram to OMGUS, External Restitution from Germany, 28 August 1948, File "Correspondence, August 1948," Record Group 260, Records of the Reparations and Restitution Branch, Correspondence and Related Records of the Restitution Section, 1946–1949. While American policy changed in this regard, there is little documentation on how the policy was implemented, if at all. From a practical point of view, former U.S. officials Seymour J. Pomrenze (chief of the Offenbach Archival Depot in the American Zone) and Richard F. Howard (chief of the Monuments, Fine Arts, and Archives Section of OMGUS) could recall few, if any, examples to document implementation of this policy. Personal correspondence: Seymour J. Pomrenze to Michael J. Kurtz, 10 May 1981; Richard F. Howard to Michael J. Kurtz, April 1981.

PLAUT:
INVESTIGATION OF THE MAJOR NAZI ART-CONFISCATION AGENCIES

1. Theodore Rousseau, "The Göring Collection," National Archives (NA), Record Group (RG) 239/85, Office of Strategic Services (OSS)/Art Looting Investigation Unit (ALIU) Consolidated Interrogation Reports (CIR) 1945, 13 September 1945.

2. S. Lane Faison, Jr., "Linz: Hitler's Museum and Library," NA, RG 239/77, OSS/ALIU CIR 1945, 14 December 1945.

3. James S. Plaut, "Activity of the ERR in France," NA, RG 239/85, OSS/ALIU CIR 1945, 15 August 1945, Attachment 4.

4. Lynn H. Nicholas, *The Rape of Europa: The Fate of Europe's Treasures in the Third Reich and the Second World War* (New York: Alfred A. Knopf, 1994).

SMYTH:
THE ESTABLISHMENT OF THE MUNICH COLLECTING POINT

1. Craig H. Smyth, *Repatriation of Art from the Collecting Point in Munich after World War II: Background and Beginnings, with Reference Especially to the Netherlands* (Maarssen/The Hague: Gary Schwartz/SDU Publishers, 1988).

2. Lynn H. Nicholas, *The Rape of Europa: The Fate of Europe's Treasures in the Third Reich and the Second World War* (New York: Alfred A. Knopf, 1994), 357–61, 374–76, 396.

3. These diaries are on deposit in the National Gallery of Art, Washington, D.C. The entry for 5 June is included in Smyth, *Repatriation,* Appendix II, 84–85.

4. The budget that was prepared for 1945 by the paymaster is reproduced in Smyth, *Repatriation,* Appendix III, 102–4.

5. This letter is included in Smyth, *Repatriation,* Appendix I, 77–78.

FARMER:
CUSTODY AND CONTROVERSY AT THE WIESBADEN COLLECTING POINT

1. The 373d Engineers G. S. Regiment was activated in April 1943: to England, November 1943; to France, August 1944; to Germany, January 1945; and returned to the United States June 1945. The regiment was commanded by Colonel Frank F. Bell. For a full account of my experiences in the army and as Monuments Specialist Officer, please see my forthcoming publication *The Safekeepers: A Memoir of the Arts at the End of World War II.* Further documentation will be found with my papers, which will be deposited in the archives at the National Gallery of Art in Washington, D.C.

2. Monuments, Fine Arts, and Archives (MFA&A) branch of the Reparations, Deliveries and Restitution (RDR) division of the United States Group, Control Council (USGCC).

3. In civilian life, Lieutenant Commander Charles Kuhn was a professor at Harvard University, and Major Bancel LaFarge was an architect practicing in New York City.

4. The Wiesbaden Landesmuseum was built in 1915, and its architecture represented the most advanced German museum design of that time.

5. Schloss Weilburg, Schloss Biebrich, Schloss Wiesbaden, and the Schoenbusch Palace were the properties we preserved in addition to the Wiesbaden Staatsarchiv.

6. James Rorimer, *Survival* (New York, 1950), 154–57, recounts the story of the safekeeping of the Hungarian crown and royal regalia, which were returned to the Hungarian people by President Carter in 1978, following a period of storage in the United States.

7. Twenty-four officers signed the document, and five others wrote letters in support.

8. Genêt, "The Beautiful Spoils," *New Yorker* 21, no. 40 (17 November 1945): 71.

9. Charles L. Kuhn, "German Paintings in the National Gallery: A Protest," *College Art Journal* 5, no. 2 (January 1946): 78–79.

10. Thomas Carr Howe, *Salt Mines and Castles* (Indianapolis, 1946), 304–11 (Appendix). The text of the resolution, organized by Frederick Mortimer Clapp, director of the Frick Collection, New York City, and by Juliana Force, director of the Whitney Museum, New York City, is as follows: "Whereas in all civilized countries one of the most significant public reactions during the recent war was the horrified indignation caused by the surreptitious or brazen looting of works of art by German officials in countries they had conquered; and whereas that indignation and abhorrence on the part of free peoples was a powerful ingredient in the ardor and unanimity of their support of the war effort of democratically governed states in which the private opinions of citizens are the source and controlling directive of official action; and whereas two hundred important and valuable pictures belonging to the Kaiser Friedrich and other Berlin museums have been removed from Germany and sent to this country on the still unestablished ground of ensuring their safety; and whereas it is apparent that disinterested and intelligent people believe that this action cannot be justified on technical, political or moral grounds and that many, including the Germans themselves, may find it hard to distinguish

between the resultant situation and the 'protective custody' used by the Nazis as a camouflage for the sequestration of the artistic treasures of other countries; be it therefore resolved that we, the undersigned, respectfully request the President to order the immediate safe return to Germany of the aforesaid paintings, the cancellation of any plans that may have been made to exhibit them in this country and the countermanding without delay of further shipments of the kind that may have been contemplated." More than one hundred museum directors and academicians signed the resolution.

11. Lynn H. Nicholas, *The Rape of Europa* (New York, 1994), 401–5.

12. Our planning for the exhibition also included the preparation of a catalogue in both German and English, with a checklist and a few illustrations. The foreword set forth the brief history of the Central Collecting Point at Wiesbaden and recognized the contributions of our German specialists and advisers, chief of whom was Dr. Ernst Holzinger, director of the Städelsches Kunstinstitut, Frankfurt. Since, until that time, little had appeared that announced the vital purposes of MFA&A, we used the opportunity to state our objectives in the catalogue: "Restoration of civil agencies for administration of fine arts activities, and protection and preservation of the cultural heritage indigenous to Land Greater Hesse; custody, care and protection of displaced, German-owned works of art and cultural material now stored in repositories and central collecting points in Land Greater Hesse; location, identification, and restitution of works of art and other cultural material acquired in Allied Countries during German occupation; emergency measures to prevent further deterioration of war-damaged cultural monuments." Copies of this catalogue will be found with my papers, which will be deposited in the archives of the National Gallery of Art, Washington, D.C. Captain Edith Standen, my successor as director at the Collecting Point, recalls that the famous bust of Queen Nefertiti was on display at every exhibition in order to reassure the German people that the sculpture had not been returned to Egypt.

13. Lucy S. Dawidowicz, *From That Place and Time* (New York, 1989), 322. According to Edith Standen, additionally a major collection of Freemasons archives, seized during the German occupation of the Isle of Jersey, was returned by the Americans to the British from the Offenbach Collecting Point.

TAPER:
INVESTIGATING ART LOOTING FOR THE MFA&A

1. Bernard Taper and Otto Wittman, Jr., "Detailed Interrogation Report, 18 September 1946, Subject: Hans Wendland," War Department, Office of the Assistant Secretary of War, Strategic Services Unit; Art Looting Investigation Unit, Washington; and Office of Military Government for Germany (U.S.), Economics Division, Restitution Branch (Monuments, Fine Arts, and Archives Section). National Archives, Washington, D.C.

2. "Vernehmung von Hermann Goering am 30 August, 1946, 1800.Uhr." National Archives, Washington, D.C.

FAISON:
TRANSFER OF CUSTODY TO THE GERMANS

1. For an account of this visit, see pages 435–36 in Lynn H. Nicholas's marvelous book, *The Rape of Europa: The Fate of Europe's Treasures in the Third Reich and the Second World War* (New York: Alfred A. Knopf, 1994).

MAURER:
THE ROLE OF THE STATE DEPARTMENT REGARDING NATIONAL AND PRIVATE CLAIMS FOR THE RESTITUTION OF STOLEN CULTURAL PROPERTY

1. This is in reference to a panel of Monuments, Fine Arts, and Archives (MFA&A) officers whose presentation received a standing ovation at the New York symposium. These officers of the United States Army conducted investigations and served at Collecting Points in Germany, where they restituted great amounts of artworks and where they strongly opposed, in the Wiesbaden Manifesto (reproduced in Farmer, above, p.133), the use of 202 German works of art for reparations purposes.

2. The State Department has summarized its policy on several occasions as follows: "The governments which have been victimized have been disturbed at the outflow of these objects to foreign lands, and the appearance in the United States of objects has often given rise to outcries and urgent requests for return by other countries. The United States considers that on grounds of principle, good foreign relations, and concern for the preservation of the cultural heritage of mankind, it should render assistance in these situations" (U.S. Code Cong. & Adm. News 4100 [1982]).

3. We found through the Defense Department that the culprit, Joe Tom Meador, had in fact been court-martialed in an unrelated case of theft of cultural property.

4. See *Department of State Bulletin* 16, no. 399 (23 February 1947): 359–60 (Appendix B).

5. See Ardelia R. Hall, "The Recovery of Cultural Objects Dispersed during World War II," *Department of State Bulletin* 25, no. 635 (27 August 1951): 337–44; also 345.

6. Ardelia R. Hall, "U.S. Program for Return of Historic Objects to Countries of Origin, 1944–1954," *Department of State Bulletin* 31, no. 797 (4 October 1954): 493–98; and see notes 10–11 for additional bibliography.

7. Some cases have surfaced in which the person who originally acquired the looted object died, and his heirs may not have known the background or were indifferent to it, and were eager to realize the monetary value of the object involved.

8. Lynn H. Nicholas, *The Rape of Europa: The Fate of Europe's Treasures in the Third Reich and the Second World War* (New York: Alfred A. Knopf, 1994), 444.

LOWENTHAL:
INTRODUCTION TO "THE QUEDLINBURG CHURCH TREASURES"

1. See Anne Bromberg et al., *The Quedlinburg Treasury,* exhib. cat., Dallas Museum of Art, 1991: no. 9, figs. 1–2. See also Dietrich Kötzsche, ed., *Der Quedlinburger Schatz,* exhib. cat. (Berlin: Ars Nicolai, 1993).

2. Constance Lowenthal, "German Booty in Texas," *Wall Street Journal,* 3 August 1990; and "The Quedlinburg Embarrassment," *ARTnews* 91 (Summer 1992): 158.

3. *The Quedlinburg Treasury,* no. 1, figs. 1–6.

4. *The Quedlinburg Treasury,* no. 7.

5. *The Quedlinburg Treasury,* nos. 2–6.

6. *The Quedlinburg Treasury,* no. 2.

7. *The Quedlinburg Treasury,* nos. 4–5.

8. *The Quedlinburg Treasury,* no. 8.

9. *The Quedlinburg Treasury,* no. 10.

HONAN:
JOURNALIST ON THE CHASE

1. William H. Honan, "A Trove of Medieval Art Turns Up in Texas," *New York Times,* 14 June 1990, A1, D22. The author has told the complete story of his involvement with the Quedlinburg treasures in *Treasure Hunt: A New York Times Reporter Tracks the Quedlinburg Hoard* (Fromm International Publishing Corp., in press).

KLINE:
LEGAL ISSUES RELATING TO THE RECOVERY OF THE QUEDLINBURG TREASURES

1. In that case, the Church of Cyprus and the Republic of Cyprus brought a successful suit against Carmel, Indiana, art dealer Peg Goldberg. The mosaics, which are world-famous, had been stripped from the walls of a church in the Turkish-occupied area of Cyprus, and found their way to Indiana through a circuitous route that apparently included Munich and Geneva. The United States courts applied Indiana law to the question of ownership and returned the mosaics to Cyprus because—in Indiana as elsewhere in the United States—the statute of limitations had not run out, even though suit was brought many years after the theft, because Cyprus had been diligent in searching for its stolen property. *Autocephalous Greek-Orthodox Church v. Goldberg and Feldman Fine Arts, Inc.,* 717 F. Supp. 1374 (S.D. Ind. 1989), *aff'd.* 917 F.2d 278 (7th Cir. 1990) [hereinafter *Church of Cyprus*]; Michel Van Rijn, *Hot Art, Cold Cash* (London: Warner Books, 1994); Dan Hofstadter, *Goldberg's Angel* (New York: Farrar Straus Giroux, 1994).

2. William H. Honan, "Germans to Get Priceless Gospels Lost in '45," *New York Times,* 1 May 1990, A1, A9.

3. Siegfried Kogelfranz and Willi A. Korte, *Quedlinburg—Texas und zurück* (Munich: Droemer Knaur, 1994).

4. William H. Honan, "A Trove of Medieval Art Turns Up in Texas," *New York Times,* 14 June 1990, A1, D22.

5. *Stiftskirche-Domgemeinde of Quedlinburg v. Jack Meador,* Civil Action No. CA3-90-1440-D (N.D. Tex. June 18, 1990); William H. Honan, "Texas Bank Admits It Has Missing Art," *New York Times,* 19 June 1990, C18.

6. Lee Hancock and David Thorne Park, "E. German Church Files Suit for Return of Art Treasures," *Dallas Morning News,* 19 June 1990, 1A.

7. William H. Honan, "Judge Refuses to Order Silence about Stolen Art," *New York Times,* 21 June 1990, B3.

8. William H. Honan, "Church Lawyers Say Stolen Art Was Moved," *New York Times,* 24 June 1990, 19.

9. Lee Hancock, "Judge Extends Order Forbidding Removal of Art," *Dallas Morning News,* 28 June 1990, n.p.

10. William H. Honan, "Treasured Art Stolen in WWII to Be Returned to W. Germany," *Dallas Morning News,* 1 May 1990, 1A, 10A; William H. Honan, "Germans Send Lawyers to Texas," *New York Times,* 15 June 1990, The Living Arts section, C22.

11. William H. Honan, "Letters Show Thief Knew Value of the Quedlinburg Treasures," *New York Times,* 3 September 1994, A1.

12. Ralph Blumenthal, "A Stolen Old Master Painting Is Bought Back for Poland," *New York Times,* 17 November 1994, C15.

13. *Church of Cyprus, supra* note 1.

14. David D'Arcy, "The Long Way Home," *Art and Antiques* 17 (April 1994): 65–69; Mark Rose and Özgen Acar, "Turkey's War on the Illicit Antiquities Trade," *Archaeology* 48 (March/April 1995): 44; *Republic of Turkey v. Metropolitan Museum of Art,* 762 F. Supp. 44 (S.D.N.Y. 1990).

15. William H. Honan, "Greece Sues Gallery for Return of Mycenaean Jewelry," *New York Times,* 26 May 1993, C14.

16. David D'Arcy, "Two New York Lawyers Who Fight the Illicit Trade in Works of Art—and Win," *The Art Newspaper,* May 1994, 25; David D'Arcy, "The Long Way Home," 64.

17. *United States of America v. Yuly Saet,* No. 93 Civ. 8330 (PKL), 1995 U.S. Dist. LEXIS 23 (S.D.N.Y. Jan. 5, 1995).

18. JoAnn Lewis, "The Art That Came Out of the Woodwork," *Washington Post,* 14 February 1995, B1.

19. *Menzel v. List,* 49 Misc.2d 300, 267 N.Y.S.2d 804 (Sup. Ct. 1966).

20. *O'Keeffe v. Snyder,* 416 A.2d 862 (N.J. 1980); *Erisoty v. Rizik Co.,* No. Civ. AQ.93-6215, 1995 WL 91406 (E.D. Pa. Feb. 23, 1995).

21. *Church of Cyprus, supra* note 1.

22. *Solomon R. Guggenheim Found. v. Lubell,* 77 N.Y.2d 311, 567 N.Y.S.2d 623 (1991).

LOWENTHAL:
INTRODUCTION TO "RECENT CONFIRMATIONS OF RUSSIAN HOLDINGS"

1. Albert Kostenevich, *Hidden Treasures Revealed: Impressionist Masterpieces and Other Important French Paintings Preserved by The State Hermitage Museum, St. Petersburg* (New York: Harry N. Abrams, in association with the Ministry of Culture of the Russian Federation and the State Hermitage Museum, St. Petersburg, 1995).

AKINSHA AND KOZLOV:
THE DISCOVERY OF THE SECRET REPOSITORIES

1. Konstantin Akinsha and Grigorii Kozlov, "Spoils of War: The Soviet Union's Hidden Art Treasures," *ARTnews* 90, no. 4 (April 1991): 130–41.

2. Alexei Rastorgouev, "Trofei 2-i mirovoi voiny v Sovetskom Soiuze," *Russkaia Mysl'* (Paris), 18 January 1991.

3. Natalia Mishina, interview with Viktor Baldin, "Spasi i sokhrani," *Pravda,* 27 May 1990.

4. Konstantin Akinsha and Grigorii Kozlov, "The Soviet War Treasures: A Growing Controversy," *ARTnews* 90, no. 7 (September 1991): 112–19.

5. Konstantin Akinsha, "The Turmoil over Soviet War Treasures," *ARTnews* 90, no. 10 (December 1991): 110–15.

6. Konstantin Akinsha and Grigorii Kozlov, "Trophäen der Roten Armee: Die Kostbarkeiten des Berliner Museums für Vor- und Frühgeschichte," *Antike Welt* 25 Jahrgang Sonderausgabe (1994), 67–72.

7. Interview with Nikolai Gubenko, "Trudno plyt' v kislote," *Pravda,* 4 August 1993.

8. Maria Dement'eva, interview with Evgenii Sidorov, "Kul'turnye tsennosti dolzhny byt' vozvrashcheny chelovechestvu," *Segodnia,* 11 November 1993.

9. State Archive of the Russian Federation, Moscow, coll. 7021, inv. 121, file 17, p. 144.

10. The Bureau of Experts was established by Decree 12 of the Extraordinary State Commission, 8 September 1943. See Konstantin Akinscha [Akinsha], Grigori Koslow [Grigorii Kozlov], and Clemens Toussaint, *Operation Beutekunst: Die Verlagerung deutscher Kulturgüter in die Sowjetunion nach 1945* (Nuremberg: Germanisches Nationalmuseum, 1995), 12–21.

11. "Report on Museum Equivalents in German Museums the USSR Desires to Receive in Compensation for Damage Done to Soviet Museums," Archive of the Research Institute for the Study of Culture, Moscow, inv. 1, file 299.

12. "Report on Museum Equivalents," p. 77.

13. State Archive of the Russian Federation, coll. 7021, inv. 121, file 17, p. 29.

14. Ibid.

15. "Report on Museum Equivalents," inv. 1, file 243.

16. Russian State Archive of Literature and Art, Moscow, coll. 962, inv. 6, file 1345, p. 7.

17. Ibid., pp. 15–20.

18. Russian Center for the Preservation and Study of Documents of Modern History, Moscow, coll. 644, inv. 1, file 430, p. 177.

19. Ibid., coll. 17, inv. 125, file 308, p. 20.

20. Konstantin Akinsha and Grigorii Kozlov, with Sylvia Hochfield, *Beautiful Loot: The Soviet Plunder of Europe's Art Treasures* (New York: Random House, 1995), 183–86.

RASTORGOUEV:
DISPLACED ART IN PRIVATE HANDS

1. Werner Schmidt, Preface in C. Dittrich, *Vermisste Zeichnungen des Kupferstich-Kabinettes Dresden* (Dresden, 1987).

2. This drawing is number 773 in the cata-

logue of lost Dresden drawings: Dittrich, *Vermisste Zeichnungen*, 2, 78.

3. This drawing is number 82 in the catalogue of lost drawings from the Franz Koenigs Collection: Albert J. Elen, *Missing Old Master Drawings from the Franz Koenigs Collection, Claimed by the State of the Netherlands* (The Hague, 1989), 83.

4. These drawings are numbers 1556–2938 in the catalogue of lost Dresden drawings: Dittrich, *Vermisste Zeichnungen.*

FIEDLER:
LEGAL ISSUES BEARING ON THE RESTITUTION OF GERMAN CULTURAL PROPERTY IN RUSSIA

1. Treaty Between the Federal Republic of Germany and the Union of Soviet Socialist Republics on Good-Neighborliness, Partnership and Cooperation, Nov. 9, 1990, 30 I.L.M. 505 (1991) [hereinafter Treaty on Good-Neighborliness, Partnership and Cooperation]; Treaty on the Development of Comprehensive Cooperation in the Field of Trade, Industry, Science and Technology, Nov. 9, 1990, F.R.G.-U.S.S.R., BGBl.II, 799.

2. Bulletin des Presse- und Informationsamtes der Bundesregierung 1409ff. (1990).

3. Agreement Between the Government of the Federal Republic of Germany and the Government of the Russian Federation on Cultural Cooperation (German-Russian Cultural Agreement), July 8, 1993, BGBl.II, 1256 (1993).

4. Moscow Protocol, Mar. 24, 1994, para. 5.

5. Moscow Protocol, Mar. 24, 1994, para. 3.

6. 1 *Procès des grands criminels de guerre devant le Tribunal Militaire International* 61ff., 254ff. (1947) [hereinafter *Procès des grands criminels*].

7. Thomas C. Howe, *Salt Mines and Castles: The Discovery and Restitution of Looted European Art* (1946); M. J. Kurtz, *Nazi Contraband: American Policy on the Return of European Cultural Treasures, 1945–1955* (1985), 163ff.; S. Turner, "Das internationale Kulturgüterrecht und die Zerstreuung des deutschen Kulturbesitzes nach dem zweiten Weltkrieg," in *Internationaler Kulturgüterschutz und deutsche Frage,* ed. W. Fiedler (1991), 109ff., 154f.

8. Turner, *supra* note 7, at 127.

9. Bonn Protocol, June 30, 1994, para. 4.

10. In 1958 the Central Committee named "2,614,874 objects of art and culture located in the USSR."

11. *Id.* "The great importance of these treasures for the history of the national culture (*National-Kultur*) of Germany."

12. Klaus Goldmann, "Heinrich Schliemanns 'Sammlung trojanischer Altertümer,'" in *Schliemanns Gold und die Schätze Alt-*

europas aus dem Museum für Vor- und Frühgeschichte (1993), 13–17; K.-E. Murawski, *Die Verlagerung von Kulturgütern in Deutschland im Zweiten Weltkrieg und die damit zusammenhängenden aktuellen Fragen, in* 1 Königssteiner Kreis 2ff. (1981).

13. See, e.g., for Berlin, Irene Kühnel-Kunze, *Bergung—Evakuierung—Rückführung: Die Berliner Museen in den Jahren 1939–1959,* 2d ed. Jahrbuch Preussischer Kulturbesitz, Sonderband 2 (1984), 102–5.

14. *See* Murawski, *supra* note 12, at 2.

15. *Id.* at 4.

16. Vienna Convention on the Law of Treaties, Preamble, BGBl.II, 926 (1985), 25 I.L.M. 543 (1986).

17. Treaty on Good-Neighborliness, Partnership and Cooperation, Preamble, *supra* note 1, 30 I.L.M. at 505.

18. Turner, *supra* note 7, at 132f.

19. Convention Respecting the Laws and Customs of War on Land, Oct. 18, 1907, art. 56 [hereinafter Hague Convention]. *See* 1 *The Law of War: A Documentary History* 308ff. (Leon Friedman, ed., 1972) [hereinafter *Law of War*].

20. S. A. Williams, *The International and National Protection of Movable Cultural Property: A Comparative Study* (1972), 5ff., 8f.; D. M. Quynn, "The Art Confiscations of the Napoleonic Wars," *American Historical Review* 50, no. 3 (April 1945): 437ff.; P. Wescher, *Kunstraub unter Napoleon* (2d ed. 1978); S. von Schorlemer, *Internationaler Kulturgüterschutz* 261ff. (1992); M. P. Wyss, *Kultur als eine Dimension der Völkerrechtsordnung* 86ff. (1992); for the changed legal situation in the nineteenth centu*ry, see* F. de Martens, 3 TRAITÉ DE DROIT INTERNATIONAL, §§ 119, 120 (1987).

21. *Procès des grands criminels, supra* note 6, at 251.

22. *Id.*

23. Preamble to the Hague Convention. *See Law of War, supra* note 19, at 309.

24. *See* UNESCO [Charter], Preamble, BGBl.II, 473 (1971); 4 U.N.T.S. 275; *see* Wyss, *supra* note 20, at 187ff.

25. Turner, *supra* note 7, at 311.

26. In a characteristic manner, one of the German participants described the importance of the Russian activities during the Hague peace conferences: P. Zorn, "Die beiden Haager Friedenskonferenzen von 1899 und 1907," in *Handbuch des Völkerrechts,* vol. 5 (1915), 22ff., 30ff.; and P. Zorn, *Weltunionen, Haager Friedenskonferenzen und Völkerbund* (1925), 11.

HILLER:
THE GERMAN-RUSSIAN NEGOTIATIONS OVER THE CONTENTS OF THE RUSSIAN REPOSITORIES

1. To date (May 1996), no presidential decree has been issued. On 21 April 1995, the Russian State Duma decided on a moratorium that makes any restitutions of cultural property dependent on a pertinent Russian law coming into force. Since then, several proposed laws have been submitted by the Russian Federation Council and the Duma, but none of them has yet been passed. The proposed laws so far known to the German government all contradict international law and the bilateral treaties, because, among other things, they unilaterally declare transferred cultural treasures as Russian property and/or ask for compensation in return for restitution.

BOGUSLAVSKY:
LEGAL ASPECTS OF THE RUSSIAN POSITION IN REGARD TO THE RETURN OF CULTURAL PROPERTY

1. *Nurenbergskii protsess,* vol. VII, Moscow, 1961, 217.

2. Lynn H. Nicholas, *The Rape of Europa* (New York, 1994).

3. Inter-Allied Declaration Against Acts of Dispossession Committed in Territories Under Enemy Occupation or Control, 5 Jan. 1943, signed by Australia, Belgium, Canada, the Netherlands, Greece, India, China, Luxemburg, New Zealand, Norway, Poland, the United States of America, the United Kingdom of Great Britain and Northern Ireland, the Union of Soviet Socialist Republics, the Czechoslovak Republic, Yugoslavia, the Union of South Africa, and the French National Committee. *Vneshniaia politika Sovetskogo Soiuza v period Velikoi Otechestvennoi Voiny,* vol. 1, 337–38.

4. L. N. Galenskaia, *Muzy i pravo, Pravovye voprosy mezhdunarodnogo sotrudnichestva v oblasti kultury* (Leningrad, 1987), 215.

5. See V. V. Evgen'ev, *Mezhdunarodno-pravovoe regulirovanie reparatsii posle vtoroi mirovoi voiny* (Moscow, 1950).

6. All of these facts have been repeatedly cited in the German legal literature, e.g.: L. Engstler, *Die territoriale Bindung von Kulturgütern im Rahmen des Völkerrechts* (Cologne, 1964), 156; Rudolf, Internationaler Schutz von Kulturgütern, p. 859; I. S. Pereterskii and M. M. Boguslavsky, "Mirnye dogovory 1947 goda," in L. Oppenheim, *Mezhdunarodnoe pravo,* vol. II (Moscow, 1950), 479ff.

7. Galenskaia, *Muzy i pravo,* 221.

8. Control Council Law No. 2 of 10 October 1945: Providing for the Termination and

Liquidation of Nazi Organizations; and Control Council Law No. 58 of 20 August 1947: Addendum to Law No. 2 of the Control Council. Control Council Directive No. 30 of 13 May 1946: Elimination of German Military and Nazi Monuments and Museums. Control Council Directive No. 38 of 12 October 1946: Arrest and Punishment of War Criminals. Control Council Law No. 10 of 20 December 1945: Punishment of Individuals Guilty of War Crimes and Crimes Against Peace and Against Humanity.

9. For details, see M. M. Boguslavsky, *Mezhdunarodnaia okhrana kul'turnykh tsennostei* (Moscow, 1979), 111.

10. See W. Kowalski, *Restitucja dziel sztuki* (Katowice, 1993).

11. Quoted from the written text of the statement of the director of the State Archive of the Russian Federation, R. Pikhoia, at the Commission on Culture of the State Duma (Russian parliament) at the Federal Meeting of 6/9/94.

12. Am. J. Int'l L. 195, (Supp. 1936).

13. N. K. Roerich, "Listy dnevnika," in N. Roerich, *Zazhigaite serdtsa!* (Moscow: Dozor, 1975), 176.

SIMPSON:
SCHLIEMANN'S "TREASURES" FROM THE SECOND CITY OF TROY

1. For a brief summary of theories on the destruction of the city, see J. Leslie Fitton, *The Discovery of the Greek Bronze Age* (Cambridge, Mass.: Harvard University Press, 1996).

2. Thucydides 1.10.

3. Herodotus 7.43.2.

4. Plutarch, *Life of Alexander* 8.2.

5. Diodorus 17.17.1–2.

6. Lucan, *Civil War* 9.964–79.

7. On the search for the ancient city, see Michael Wood, *In Search of the Trojan War* (New York: New American Library, Plume, 1985).

8. Frank Calvert's trial trench of 1863 constitutes the first scientific archaeological excavation at the site, and Calvert is often credited with the identification of Hisarlık as the Homeric city of Troy. See Susan Heuck Allen, " 'Finding the Walls of Troy': Frank Calvert, Excavator," *American Journal of Archaeology* 99 (1995): 379–407 for a study of Calvert's publications and previously unpublished correspondence. See also Marcelle Robinson, "Pioneer, Scholar, and Victim: An Appreciation of Frank Calvert (1828–1908)," *Anatolian Studies* 44 (1994): 153–68. The site was identified earlier by Charles Maclaren, whose first publication on the subject appeared in *The Edinburgh Magazine* 85 (1820), brought to my attention by Donald Easton.

9. Heinrich Schliemann was born January 6, 1822, in Neubukow, Germany, and died in 1890 in Naples. For details of his life and work and for illustrations of many of his finds, see Katie Demakopoulou, ed., *Troy, Mycenae, Tiryns, Orchomenos. Heinrich Schliemann: The 100th Anniversary of His Death*, exhib. cat., 15 June–2 September, 1990, National Archaeological Museum, Athens (Athens: Ministry of Culture of Greece, Greek Committee ICOM, and Ministry of Culture of the German Democratic Republic, 1990). For a comprehensive bibliography, see Georgios S. Korres, *Bibliographia Herrikou Sleman* (Athens: He en Athenais Archaiologike Hetaireia, 1974). The most recent biography of Schliemann is David A. Traill's *Schliemann of Troy: Treasure and Deceit* (London: John Murray; New York: St. Martin's Press, 1995).

10. Allen, " 'Finding the Walls of Troy,' " 393–94.

11. Ibid., 394. In a letter to Schliemann, dated 3 February 1869, Calvert makes the following stipulation: "I am willing nevertheless to meet you halfway, if you agree to it, which is that half of the objects found are to be my property after deduction made of duplicates which may or may not be claimed by Turkish Govt. The division to be made as follows the objects to be separated into two portions of as equal value as possible and then to draw lots—afterwards exchanges can be made between us."

12. Schliemann's character has been the subject of much discussion, resulting in a number of recent "exposés," notably William M. Calder's "A New Picture of Heinrich Schliemann" and David A. Traill's "Schliemann's Acquisition of the Helios Metope and His Psychopathic Tendencies" in *Myth, Scandal and History: The Heinrich Schliemann Controversy* (Detroit: Wayne State University Press, 1986), edited by these two scholars. For a more measured approach, see, *inter alia,* Donald Easton, "Schliemann's Mendacity —A False Trail?" *Antiquity* 58 (1984): 197–204. It is now difficult to ascertain the degree of truthfulness in Schliemann's accounts of his finds.

13. Schliemann claimed to have been obsessed with Troy from a very young age, agreeing with his father that he should one day excavate the site, although the accuracy of this account has been questioned. Nonetheless, Schliemann was an ardent Hellenist and by 1856 had begun to learn Greek. He mastered the language (along with many others), reporting that he had read the *Iliad* and the *Odyssey* several times. H. Schliemann, *Ilios. The City and Country of the Trojans*, 3, 14 (for full citation, see note 14, below).

14. Schliemann excavated at the site in 1870–73, 1878–79, 1882 (with Wilhelm Dörpfeld), and 1890. His major publications of his excavations at Hisarlık follow, with English versions given where available: *Trojanische Alterthümer. Bericht über die Ausgrabungen in Troja* (Leipzig: F. A. Brockhaus, 1874); *Atlas trojanischer Alterthümer. Photographische Abbildungen zu dem Bericht über die Ausgrabungen in Troja* (Leipzig: F. A. Brockhaus, 1874); *Troy and Its Remains. A Narrative of Researches and Discoveries Made on the Site of Ilium, and in the Trojan Plain*, ed. P. Smith, trans. L. D. Schmitz (London: John Murray, 1875); *Ilios. The City and Country of the Trojans: The Results of Researches and Discoveries on the Site of Troy and throughout the Troad in the Years 1871, 72, 73, 78, 79, including an Autobiography of the Author* (London: John Murray, 1880); *Troja: Results of the Latest Researches and Discoveries on the Site of Homer's Troy, and the Heroic Tumuli and other Sites Made in the Year 1882* (London: John Murray; New York: Harper & Bros., 1884); *Bericht über die Ausgrabungen in Troja im Jahre 1890* (Leipzig: F. A. Brockhaus, 1891).

15. Excavated by Schliemann in 1874 and 1876 (Grave Circle A); see H. Schliemann, *Mycenae. A Narrative of Researches and Discoveries at Mycenae and Tiryns* (London: John Murray, 1878; in a new edition, New York: Charles Scribner's Sons, 1880) and *Catalogue des trésors de Mycènes au Musée d'Athènes avec un plan de l'acropole de Mycènes* (Leipzig: F. A. Brockhaus, 1882).

16. Excavated by Schliemann in 1876 and 1884–85 (with W. Dörpfeld); see H. Schliemann, *Tiryns. The Prehistoric Palace of the Kings of Tiryns. The Results of the Latest Excavations* (New York: Charles Scribner's Sons, 1885) and *Mycenae. A Narrative of Researches and Discoveries at Mycenae and Tiryns* (see note 15, above).

17. Excavated by Schliemann in 1880–81 and 1886; see H. Schliemann, *Orchomenos. Bericht über meine Ausgrabungen im Böotischen Orchomenos* (Leipzig: F. A. Brockhaus, 1881) and "Exploration of the Boeotian Orchomenus," *Journal of Hellenic Studies* 2 (1881): 122–63. Schliemann also investigated a site on Ithaca in 1868, which he mistook for the ruins of the palace of Odysseus (H. Schliemann, *Ithaque, le Péloponnèse et Troie. Recherches archéologiques* [Paris: Reinwald, 1869]).

18. W. Dörpfeld, *Troja und Ilion. Ergebnisse der Ausgrabungen in den vorhistorischen und historischen Schichten von Ilion, 1870–1894* (Athens: Beck and Barth, 1902).

19. Carl W. Blegen et al., *Troy: Excavations Conducted by the University of Cincinnati 1932–1938*, 4 vols. (Princeton: Princeton University Press, 1950–58); C. W. Blegen, *Troy and the Trojans* (London: Thames and Hudson, 1963).

20. See the series *Studia Troica* (Mainz:

Philipp von Zabern), beginning with volume 1 (1991), and M. Korfmann, below, pp. 207–11.

21. See note 1, above.

22. The objects are recorded in photographs published in Schliemann's *Atlas trojanischer Alterthümer*: plate 204 is said to show the "Treasure of Priam," although there is now some uncertainty as to whether all of the objects pictured were found together. See D. Easton, "Priam's Gold: The Full Story," *Anatolian Studies* 44 (1994): 226–27 and note 81. The famous plate 204 of the *Atlas* was reproduced in an engraving for publication in *Troy and Its Remains*, plate II, and *Ilios*, fig. 14, which is illustrated here as figure 83. See also Hubert Schmidt, *Heinrich Schliemann's Sammlung trojanischer Altertümer* (Berlin: Georg Reimer, 1902), which catalogues the collection as it existed in Berlin.

23. Schliemann, *Ilios*, 41.

24. David Traill, "Schliemann's 'Discovery' of 'Priam's Treasure,' " *Antiquity* 57 (1983): 184.

25. The objects were removed to Schliemann's house in Athens in 1873 and subsequently sent to London, where they were displayed (along with additional objects from Troy) in the South Kensington Museum between 1877 and 1880. The pieces were then sent to Berlin, arriving in 1881, where they remained until the end of World War II. See D. Easton, "Priam's Gold: The Full Story," and Easton, below, pp. 197–99.

26. For a full account of the remarkable discovery that the Trojan treasures had been kept in secret storage in the Pushkin State Museum of Fine Arts in Moscow, see Konstantin Akinsha and Grigorii Kozlov, with Sylvia Hochfeld, *Beautiful Loot: The Soviet Plunder of Europe's Art Treasures* (New York: Random House, 1995), 3–11; and see Akinsha and Kozlov, above, pp. 162–65.

EASTON:
THE EXCAVATION OF THE TROJAN TREASURES, AND THEIR HISTORY UP TO THE DEATH OF SCHLIEMANN IN 1890

1. The treasures are listed in W. Dörpfeld, *Troja und Ilion*, 2 vols. (Athens, 1902), 325–43; and H. Schmidt, *Heinrich Schliemann's Sammlung trojanischer Altertümer* (Berlin, 1902), 225–47. All except Treasure L, found in Schliemann's final year, are also described in his publications: *Trojanische Alterthümer* (Leipzig, 1874); *Atlas trojanischer Alterthümer* (Leipzig, 1874); *Troy and Its Remains*, ed. P. Smith, trans. L. D. Schmitz (London, 1875); *Ilios: The City and Country of the Trojans* (London, 1880); and *Troja: Results of the Latest Researches and Discoveries on the Site of Homer's Troy . . . 1882* (London, 1884). Treasures found in 1870–73 and 1890 are also documented, to varying degrees, in his unpublished notebooks in the Gennadius Library of the American School of Classical Studies, Athens. For details of the Schliemann archive there, see D. F. Easton, "The Schliemann Papers," *Annual of the British School of Archaeology at Athens* 77 (1982): 93–110.

2. Schmidt himself subdivides H; for R and S, see D. F. Easton, "Schliemann's Mendacity—A False Trail?" *Antiquity* 58 (1984): 200–202.

3. *Treasure R2*: H. Schliemann, Unpublished Troy Excavation Notebook for 1872, Schliemann Archive, Gennadius Library, American School of Classical Studies, Athens, 478; Schliemann, *Trojanische Alterthümer*, 168; Schliemann, *Atlas*, plate 17, no. 521; Schliemann, *Ilios*, 272; Dörpfeld, *Troja*, 342, nos. 5 and 6; not listed in Schmidt, *Heinrich Schliemann's Sammlung*, 246f. See also Easton, "Schliemann's Mendacity," 200f.

4. M. Korfmann and B. Kromer, "Demircihüyük, Beşik-Tepe, Troia: Eine Zwischenbilanz zur Chronologie dreier Orte in Westanatolien," *Studia Troica* 3 (1993): 138. It seems likely to the present writer that structural timbers of Troy II were old components reused in Troy II, and that the new carbon-14 determinations for Troy II have produced excessively early dates. When the obvious distortions are removed, the new carbon-14 dates appear to be consistent with the chronology proposed in D. F. Easton, "Reconstructing Schliemann's Troy," in W. M. Calder III and J. Cobet, eds., *Heinrich Schliemann nach hundert Jahren* (Frankfurt am Main, 1990), 431–47. These are therefore the dates used here. But the whole question remains under review.

5. In the present writer's provisional terminology, Troy II.5. It is with this phase that the Early Bronze 3 period (EB3) begins; see D. F. Easton, "Schliemanns Ausgrabungen in Troia," in J. Cobet and B. Patzek, eds., *Archäologie und historische Erinnerung: nach 100 Jahren Heinrich Schliemann* (Essen, 1992), 60, fig. 5.

6. *Treasure G*: Schliemann, *Ilios*, 498; Dörpfeld, *Troja*, 334f.; Schmidt, *Heinrich Schliemann's Sammlung*, 240. In Schmidt's Berlin catalogue, *Ilios* no. 835 is wrongly placed in Treasure O. *Treasure N*: Schliemann, Unpublished Troy Excavation Notebook for 1872, 379, 403; Schliemann, *Trojanische Alterthümer*, 117; Schliemann, *Atlas*, plate 98, nos. 2070, 2075–2079; Schliemann, *Ilios*, 491–93; Dörpfeld, *Troja*, 340f.; Schmidt, *Heinrich Schliemann's Sammlung*, 245. The lists in Dörpfeld and Schmidt are confused and only partially relate to the genuine Treasure N—to which, in fact, also belong item nos. 6–12 in Dörpfeld, *Troja*, 332, attributed there to Treasure D. *Treasure R1*: Schliemann, Unpublished Troy Excavation Notebook for 1872, 349; Schliemann, *Trojanische Alterthümer*, 168; Schliemann, *Atlas*, plate 17, nos. 514, 516, 517, 520, 522; Schliemann, *Ilios*, 272; Dörpfeld, *Troja*, 324, nos. 1–4; Schmidt, *Heinrich Schliemann's Sammlung*, 246f., nos. 6141–6145. Treasure R1 was wrongly associated by Schliemann with the skeleton of Treasure R2: see Easton, "Schliemann's Mendacity," 200f. *Treasure Q*: Schliemann, *Troja*, 106; Dörpfeld, *Troja*, 341f.; Schmidt, *Heinrich Schliemann's Sammlung*, 246.

7. D. F. Easton, "Schliemann's Excavations at Troy, 1870–1873," 3 vols. (Ph.D. diss., University of London, 1989) (copies at Senate House Library, University of London; Troja Projekt, Tübingen; Troy; Department of Classics, University of Cincinnati), 519f., tables XXIII, XXIV; Easton, "Reconstructing Schliemann's Troy," 435; Easton, "Schliemanns Ausgrabungen," 58.

8. M. Korfmann, "Troia—Ausgrabungen 1990 und 1991," *Studia Troica* 2 (1992): 20. The findings seem to harmonize with the present writer's reconstruction. The second burned layer would mark the end of Troy II.6 (broadly corresponding to Blegen's Troy IIg); and the first, which destroyed Megaron IIA, would mark the end of Troy II.5.

9. In the present writer's terminology, Troy II.6. See Easton, "Schliemanns Ausgrabungen," 61, fig. 6. The phase dates to EB3b.

10. E.g., Schliemann, *Ilios*, 433–35.

11. *Treasure A*: Schliemann, *Trojanische Alterthümer*, 289–303; Schliemann, *Atlas*, plates 192–209; Schliemann, *Troy and Its Remains*, 323–40; Schliemann, *Ilios*, 453–85; Dörpfeld, *Troja*, 326–31; Schmidt, *Heinrich Schliemann's Sammlung*, 225–37. For a detailed discussion of the circumstances of the find, for a revised list of its original contents, and for an outline of its subsequent history, see D. F. Easton, "Priam's Treasure," *Anatolian Studies* 34 (1984): 141–69; and D. F. Easton, "Priam's Gold: The Full Story," *Anatolian Studies* 44 (1994): 221–44. These articles also discuss the improbable claim that the treasure was a hoax, for which view see D. A. Traill, *Excavating Schliemann*, Illinois Classical Studies Supplement 4, ed. W. M. Calder III (Atlanta, 1993), chapters 10–16.

12. As reconstructed by W. Kuckenburg in K. Demakopoulou, ed., *Troja, Mykene, Tiryns, Orchomenos: Heinrich Schliemann zum 100. Todestag* (Athens, 1990), 171f., no. 41.

13. *Treasure B*: H. Schliemann, Unpublished Troy Excavation Notebook for 1873, Schliemann Archive, Gennadius Library,

American School of Classical Studies, Athens, 268; H. Schliemann, "Ausgrabungen in Troja," *Allgemeine Zeitung* (Augsburg), Beilage zu Nr. 165, 14 June 1873: 2528; Schliemann, *Trojanische Alterthümer*, 296f.; Schliemann, *Atlas*, plates 171, nos. 3303 3306, and 176, no. 3401; Schliemann, *Troy and Its Remains*, 333f.; Schliemann, *Ilios*, 472f; Dörpfeld, *Troja*, 331; Schmidt, *Heinrich Schliemann's Sammlung*, 237; Easton, "Priam's Treasure," 165–67.

14. *Treasure J:* Schliemann, *Ilios*, 502f.; Dörpfeld, *Troja*, 336f.; Schmidt, *Heinrich Schliemann's Sammlung*, 240f.

15. *Treasure L:* Schliemann, Unpublished Troy Excavation Notebook for 1890, Schliemann Archive, Gennadius Library, American School of Classical Studies, Athens, 59–61; Dörpfeld, *Troja*, 338–40; Schmidt, *Heinrich Schliemann's Sammlung*, 242–44; Easton, "Schliemann's Mendacity," 199.

16. See D. F. Easton, "The Troy Treasures in Russia," *Antiquity* 69 (1995): 11–14.

17. Alfred Götze, "Die Kleingeräte aus Metall, Stein, Knochen, Thon und ähnlichen Stoffen: Die II.–V. Schicht," in Dörpfeld, *Troja*, 340.

18. *Treasure F:* Schliemann, *Ilios*, 494–98; Dörpfeld, *Troja*, 333f.; Schmidt, *Heinrich Schliemann's Sammlung*, 239f.

19. Schliemann, *Ilios*, 490, 493.

20. In other groups, where the white powder was not noticed, it also happens that jewelry could be kept in a jar (cf. Treasures A and C) and could be associated with a loose collection of bronzes (Treasure C) or even with ingots (Treasures A and C). Moreover, Treasure D and Treasure E appear to have been in fallen jars, while Treasure F, like Treasure A, was placed in safe storage and found as it had been left.

21. Korfmann, "Troia—Ausgrabungen," 20.

22. Easton, "Schliemann's Excavations," 462.

23. *Treasure C:* Schliemann, *Ilios*, 43, 485–88; Dörpfeld, *Troja*, 332; Schmidt, *Heinrich Schliemann's Sammlung*, 237.

24. *Treasure M:* Schliemann, *Ilios*, 429; Dörpfeld, *Troja*, 340; Schmidt, *Heinrich Schliemann's Sammlung*, 244f.

25. *Treasure D:* Schliemann, *Ilios*, 490f.; Dörpfeld, *Troja*, 332, nos. 1–5 (nos. 6–12 belong in reality to Treasure N); Schmidt, *Heinrich Schliemann's Sammlung*, 237f. *Treasure K:* Schliemann, *Troja*, 165–69; Dörpfeld, *Troja*, 337f.; Schmidt, *Heinrich Schliemann's Sammlung*, 241f.

26. *Treasure E:* Schliemann, *Ilios*, 493f.; Dörpfeld, *Troja*, 333; Schmidt, *Heinrich Schliemann's Sammlung*, 238.

27. *Treasure O:* Schliemann, *Ilios*, 488f.; Dörpfeld, *Troja*, 341; Schmidt, *Heinrich Schliemann's Sammlung*, 245, no. 6133 (no. 6134 does not belong to the original Treasure O).

28. Schliemann, *Ilios*, no. 834. The jars across the top of the pin have voluted wings not clearly visible in the illustration. In pottery, volutes in the form of wings or feet on jars and in the form of handles on bowls are typical of West Anatolian EB3b, being attested in Tarsus final EB3, Beycesultan VIII–VIA, and Poliochni Yellow. At Troy, they are especially characteristic of Troy III. As feet and handles, however, they do also occur in Late Troy II in both pottery and metalwork (Schliemann, *Ilios*, nos. 795, 797, 798, 979; C. W. Blegen et al., *Troy: Excavations Conducted by the University of Cincinnati, 1932–1938: The First and Second Settlements*, vol. I [Princeton, N.J., 1950], fig. 403, no. 37.1113); and there is clearly a relationship to the double- and quadruple-spiral motifs present in much of the Troy II jewelry. A Late Troy II date cannot therefore be excluded.

29. *Treasures S1 and S2:* Schliemann, Unpublished Troy Excavation Notebook for 1873, 136, 152–56; Schliemann, *Trojanische Alterthümer*, 232; Schliemann, *Troy and Its Remains*, 267f.; Schliemann, *Ilios*, 506–13; Dörpfeld, *Troja*, 342; Schmidt, *Heinrich Schliemann's Sammlung*, 247. For the subdivision of Treasure S and a definition of its contents, see Easton, "Schliemann's Mendacity," 202; and Easton, "Schliemann's Excavations," 412.

30. *Treasures Ha and Hb:* Schliemann, *Ilios*, 499–502; Dörpfeld, *Troja*, 335f.; Schmidt, *Heinrich Schliemann's Sammlung*, 240. *Treasure P:* Schliemann, Unpublished Troy Excavation Notebook for 1872, 484; Dörpfeld, *Troja*, 394f.; Schmidt, *Heinrich Schliemann's Sammlung*, 246; Easton, "Schliemann's Mendacity," 202. The lists in Dörpfeld and Schmidt are incomplete; see Easton, "Schliemann's Excavations," 342.

31. Schliemann, *Ilios*, 43.

32. M. Siebler, *Troia: Geschichte, Grabungen, Kontroversen* (Mainz, 1994), 48, figs. 58–60.

33. Schliemann, *Troy and Its Remains*, 52f.; E. Meyer, ed., *Heinrich Schliemann: Briefwechsel*, vol. I (Berlin, 1953), 178ff.; E. Meyer, ed., *Heinrich Schliemann: Kaufmann und Forscher* (Göttingen, 1969), 258.

34. Schliemann, *Troy and Its Remains*, 144, recording an arrangement similar to that made with Safvet Paşa, Minister of Public Instruction. It seems likely that the eastern border of the projected trench shown in Schliemann, *Atlas*, plate 116, from the beginning of the 1872 season reflects the western limit of Calvert's land. The line runs from approximately the intersection of F/G 2/3 in the north to that of E/F 8/9 in the south. On Calvert, see D. F. Easton, "Troy before Schliemann," *Studia Troica* 1 (1991): 119–25; M. Robinson, "Pioneer, Scholar and Victim: An Appreciation of Frank Calvert (1828–1908)," *Anatolian Studies* 44 (1994): 153–68; and S. H. Allen, " 'Finding the Walls of Troy': Frank Calvert, Excavator," *American Journal of Archaeology* 99 (1995): 379–407.

35. D. F. Easton, "Schliemann's Discovery of Priam's Treasure: Two Enigmas," *Antiquity* 55 (1981): 179–83; Easton, "Priam's Gold," 225f.; Traill, *Excavating Schliemann*, chapter 12.

36. For details, see Easton, "Priam's Gold," 226–30.

37. Schliemann, *Ilios*, 44; E. Meyer, ed., *Briefe von Heinrich Schliemann* (Berlin/Leipzig, 1936), 145f.; Meyer, *Briefwechsel*, vol. I, 282.

38. G. Saherwala, K. Goldmann, and G. Mahr, *Heinrich Schliemanns "Sammlung trojanischer Altertümer": Beiträge zur Chronik einer grossen Erwerbung der Berliner Museen*, Berliner Beiträge zur Vor- und Frühgeschichte, NF 7 (Berlin, 1993), 26–35, 223f. Thus, any claim to these treasures based on an entitlement to inherit what Schliemann owned at the time of his death must be irrelevant.

39. Schliemann, *Ilios*, 51; Meyer, *Heinrich Schliemann: Kaufmann und Forscher*, 305. An earlier permit had been issued in 1876, but had expired: Schliemann, *Ilios*, 44f.; E. Meyer, ed., *Heinrich Schliemann: Briefwechsel*, vol. II (Berlin, 1958), 41f., 47, 50; Meyer, *Heinrich Schliemann: Kaufmann und Forscher*, 281, 304.

40. Cf. Siebler, *Troia*, figs. 58–60.

41. Saherwala et al., *Heinrich Schliemanns "Sammlung*," 81, 225.

42. Detailed in the footnotes in Schmidt, *Heinrich Schliemann's Sammlung*, 237–47.

43. Saherwala et al., *Heinrich Schliemanns "Sammlung*," 36f.

44. See Victoria and Albert Museum, London, photo library, negative nos. 10,712–14, dated 31 January 1879; cf. Meyer, *Briefe*, 155.

45. Dora Konsola, "The Trojan Collection in the National Archaeological Museum," in Demakopoulou, *Troja, Mykene*, 79, 85, 149–52; Dörpfeld, *Troja*, 334.

46. Saherwala et al., *Heinrich Schliemanns "Sammlung*," 228. In 1881 Schliemann claimed still to have two-thirds of his collection in Athens (Meyer, *Briefwechsel*, vol. II, 430 n.125), and there were well over ten thousand items there at his death: Saherwala et al., *Heinrich Schliemanns "Sammlung*," 231f.

47. E.g., Saherwala et al., *Heinrich Schliemanns "Sammlung*," 227f., from 1882 and 1886.

48. One-third of the finds going to the excavator, one-third to the owner of the land, and one-third to the state. Thus, from the western half of the site the Turkish state could expect two-thirds of the finds, and from the eastern half one-third. Meyer, *Briefe*, 181; cf. Schliemann, *Troja*, 6. The law itself had been enacted in 1874, but had apparently been unevenly applied. For this information I am indebted to Miss Ilknur Türkoğlu.

49. The permit granted in 1878 had expired. Schliemann, *Troja*, 5; J. Herrmann and E. Maass, eds., *Die Korrespondenz zwischen Heinrich Schliemann und Rudolf Virchow, 1876–1890* (Berlin, 1990), 284.

50. Saherwala et al., *Heinrich Schliemanns "Sammlung,"* 36, 97–99, 103. Note that Schliemann also had secured agreement from Calvert to renounce any claim on certain objects, presumably items found on Calvert's property (ibid., 103); but this has no relevance to Treasures K and Q, which came from the western half of the site.

51. Ibid., 99.

52. Ibid.

53. Ibid., 105, 227.

54. Schliemann, Unpublished Troy Excavation Notebook for 1890, 1; Meyer, *Briefe*, 291, 293; Meyer, *Briefwechsel*, vol. II, 326f.; Herrmann and Maass, *Die Korrespondenz*, 521; Saherwala et al., *Heinrich Schliemanns "Sammlung,"* 140. It seems that in 1890 Schliemann required only the permission of Hamdy Bey, director of the Imperial Museum, to resume excavations. But possibly this was on the basis of an official *firman* (permit) already issued, perhaps that dated October 1887, which is illustrated in K. Goldmann, "Heinrich Schliemanns 'Sammlung Trojanischer Altertümer,'" in Staatliche Museen zu Berlin–Preussischer Kulturbesitz, *Schliemanns Gold und die Schätze Alteuropas aus dem Museum für Vor- und Frühgeschichte: Eine Dokumentation* (Mainz, 1993), 15.

55. But it is not presently known at what date Calvert ceased to own the eastern part of the mound.

56. E. Zengel, "Die Geschichte der Schliemann-Sammlung," *Das Altertum* 36 (1990): 161; cf. Saherwala et al., *Heinrich Schliemanns "Sammlung,"* 141 and n.2. Whether this applied equally to material from western and eastern halves of the site is as yet unclear. Schliemann certainly acted as though it did.

57. Herrmann and Maass, *Die Korrespondenz*, 548; Saherwala et al., *Heinrich Schliemanns "Sammlung,"* 142f., n.1.

58. Saherwala et al., *Heinrich Schliemanns "Sammlung,"* 142f; cf. Meyer, *Briefwechsel*, vol. II, 378ff.

59. Saherwala et al., *Heinrich Schliemanns "Sammlung,"* 232.

60. Schliemann, *Troy and Its Remains*, 53.

61. It is not referred to in the Athenian court records. See Easton, "Priam's Gold," 227–30.

62. According to Schliemann himself, his 1874 declaration of the contents of his collection, made for the Greek administration, showed four to five times the true number of objects in order to allow room for maneuver; and Treasure L may have been imported to Greece under the guise of deriving from Egypt. Saherwala et al.,
Heinrich Schliemanns "Sammlung," 107f., 142f.

63. Meyer, *Briefwechsel*, vol. II, 381; Saherwala et al., *Heinrich Schliemanns "Sammlung,"* 107f., 119, 142, 191f. n.1.

64. Saherwala et al., *Heinrich Schliemanns "Sammlung,"* 108.

65. Ibid., 99, 105, 227.

GOLDMANN: THE TROJAN TREASURES IN BERLIN

1. Konstantin Akinsha and Grigorii Kozlov, "Spoils of War: The Soviet Union's Hidden Art Treasures," *ARTnews* 90 (April 1991): 130–41.

2. Geraldine Saherwala, Klaus Goldmann, and Gustav Mahr, *Heinrich Schliemanns "Sammlung trojanischer Altertümer": Beiträge zur Chronik einer grossen Erwerbung der Berliner Museen*, Berliner Beiträge zur Vor- und Frühgeschichte, NF 7 (Berlin, 1993).

3. "At the reception given in Berlin on the evening of 25 August 1939, for the participants of the Sixth International Congress for Archaeology, we heard of the forthcoming hostilities with Poland. It was the Prussian Minister of Finance, [Johannes] Popitz, who told Carl Weickert, Director of the Department of Classical Antiquities, Berlin State Museums, that he should secure all irreplaceable holdings of the museums, as there would be no peaceful solution of the tense political situation. (Popitz was executed on 2 February 1945, because he had shared in the preparations for the planned assassination of Hitler on 20 July 1944.)" See Irene Kühnel-Kunze, *Bergung—Evakuierung—Rückführung. Die Berliner Museen in den Jahren 1939–1959*, Jahrbuch Preussischer Kulturbesitz, Sonderband 2 (Berlin, 1984), 18.

4. Full documentation of the contents of these three crates was published in 1993: see the chapters by Klaus Goldmann and Wilfried Menghin, in Staatliche Museen zu Berlin–Preussischer Kulturbesitz, *Schliemanns Gold und die Schätze Alteuropas aus dem Museum für Vor- und Frühgeschichte: Eine Dokumentation* (Mainz, 1993).

URICE: CLAIMS TO OWNERSHIP OF THE TROJAN TREASURES

1. Perhaps the best-known multilateral treaty is the UNESCO Convention on the Means of Prohibiting and Preventing the Illicit Import, Export and Transfer of Ownership of Cultural Property, Nov. 14,
1970, 823 U.N.T.S. 231 (1972). Much recent discussion has focused on the UNIDROIT Convention on Stolen or Illegally Exported Cultural Objects (see Appendix 17). For an example of a bilateral treaty, see Treaty of Cooperation Providing for the Recovery and Return of Stolen Archaeological, Historical, and Cultural Properties, July 17, 1970, U.S.-Mex., 22 U.S.T. 494, 791 U.N.T.S. 313. Perhaps the most comprehensive source for citations to and discussions of treaty materials is Lyndel V. Prott and P. J. O'Keefe, *Law and the Cultural Heritage*, vol. 3, *Movement* (London and Edinburgh: Butterworths, 1989).

2. For example, the so-called Kanakaria mosaics case, *Autocephalous Greek-Orthodox Church v. Goldberg and Feldman Fine Arts, Inc.*, 717 F. Supp. 1374 (S.D. Ind. 1989), aff'd, 917 F.2d 278 (7th Cir. 1990), cert. denied, 112 S. Ct. 918 (1992) (involving Byzantine mosaics taken from a church on Cyprus and ordered returned by a United States district court judge); *Peru v. Johnson*, 720 F. Supp. 810 (C.D. Cal. 1989), aff'd sub nom. *Peru v. Wendt*, 933 F.2d 1013 (9th Cir. 1991) (unpublished opinion) (in which Peru unsuccessfully sought the return of certain antiquities; and the recent litigation between Turkey and the Metropolitan Museum of Art in New York, resulting in a 1993 settlement under which the so-called Lydian Hoard was returned to Turkey).

3. *Menzel v. List*, 267 N.Y.S.2d 804 (Sup. Ct. 1966), modified as to damages, 279 N.Y.S.2d 608 (1st Dep't 1967), rev'd as to modifications, 246 N.E.2d 742 (N.Y. 1969) (involving an action to recover a Marc Chagall painting left in the plaintiff's Brussels apartment when the plaintiff and her husband fled the Nazis in March 1941; the painting was seized by the Einsatzstab Reichsleiter Rosenberg that month); *Kunstsammlungen zu Weimar v. Elicofon*, 536 F. Supp. 829 (E.D.N.Y. 1981), aff'd, 678 F.2d 1150 (2d Cir. 1982) (involving two portraits painted by Albrecht Dürer taken from Germany at the end of World War II and discovered in private hands in New York); *DeWeerth v. Baldinger*, 658 F. Supp. 688 (S.D.N.Y. 1987), rev'd, 836 F.2d 103 (2d Cir. 1987) (involving a painting by Claude Monet that disappeared from Germany at the end of World War II, discovered to be in a private New York collection).

4. I am most grateful to those who supplied me with materials for this presentation: Prof. Dr. Engin Özgen, General Director of Monuments and Museums of the Republic of Turkey; Stefano Weinberger of the German Federal Foreign Office; and Valery Koulichov, Director, Department of Restitution, at the Ministry of Culture of the Russian Federation. I hope that they will find this digest of their

5. Of course, one might consider that Greece also has some claim to the treasures, for Schliemann housed them for a period in his home in Athens before taking them to Germany. The attenuated nature of any such claim, however, precludes its treatment here.

6. Germany and Russia have ratified the convention; Turkey has acceded to it.

7. Marie Malaro, *Museum Governance* (Washington, D.C.: Smithsonian Institution Press, 1994), 17.

KORFMANN:
THE VALUE OF THE FINDS TO THE SCIENTIFIC COMMUNITY

1. Especially in Heinrich Schliemann, *Bericht über die Ausgrabungen in Troja in den Jahren 1871 bis 1873*, foreword by Manfred Korfmann (Munich and Zurich, 1990); Heinrich Schliemann, *Ilios, Stadt und Land der Trojaner. Forschungen und Entdeckungen in der Troas und besonders auf der Baustelle von Troja* (Leipzig, 1881); Alfred Götze, "Die Kleingeräte aus Metall, Stein, Knochen, Thon und ähnlichen Stoffen: Die II–V. Schicht," in Wilhelm Dörpfeld, *Troja und Ilion. Ergebnisse der Ausgrabungen in den vorhistorischen und historischen Schichten von Ilion 1870–1894* (Athens, 1902), 325–93; and Hubert Schmidt, *Heinrich Schliemann's Sammlung trojanischer Altertümer* (Berlin, 1902).

2. See Manfred Korfmann, "Die Schatzfunde in Moskau—ein erster Eindruck," *Antike Welt* 4 (1994): special report, within cover of journal.

3. Manfred Korfmann and Bernd Kromer, "Demircihüyük, Beşik-Tepe, Troia: Eine Zwischenbilanz zur Chronologie dreier Orte in Westanatolien," *Studia Troica* 3 (1993): 162–69.

4. Michael Siebler, *Troia: Geschichte, Grabungen, Kontroversen* (Mainz, 1994), 74 and fig. 103a-b.

5. Schmidt, *Heinrich Schliemann's Sammlung,* no. 6116.

6. Ernst Pernicka, "Gewinnung und Verbreitung der Metalle in prähistorischer Zeit," *Jahrbuch des Römisch-Germanischen Zentralmuseums* 37/38 (1990–91): 61 and n.23, in contrast with Schmidt, *Heinrich Schliemann's Sammlung,* 244.

7. Jane C. Waldbaum, "The First Archaeological Appearance of Iron and the Transition to the Iron Age," in Theodore A. Wertime and James H. Muhly, *The Coming of the Age of Iron* (New Haven and London, 1980), 71–73.

8. Ibid., 71.

9. Schmidt, *Heinrich Schliemann's Sammlung,* no. 6119; published with photograph in Richard Greeff, *Die Erfindung der Augengläser: Kulturgeschichtliche Darstellungen nach urkundlichen Quellen* (Berlin, 1921), plate VI.

10. Schmidt, *Heinrich Schliemann's Sammlung,* nos. 6065–6106, 6112–6114.

11. On ancient lenses, see George Sines and Yannis A. Sakellarakis, "Lenses in Antiquity," *American Journal of Archaeology* 91 (1987): 191–96.

12. Schmidt, *Heinrich Schliemann's Sammlung,* nos. 6009–6013. Many similar pieces from Troia are in the Istanbul Archaeological Museum; cf. Ufuk Esin, *Troya. Heinrich Schliemann Kazı Raporları ve Mektuplarından seçme Parçaları* (Istanbul, 1991), 38, and Siebler, *Troia,* fig. 58 (11 pieces).

13. Schmidt, *Heinrich Schliemann's Sammlung,* no. 5822.

14. Ibid., no. 5817.

15. Kurt Bittel, "Beitrag zur Kenntnis anatolischer Metallgefässe der zweiten Hälfte des dritten Jahrtausends v. Chr.," *Jahrbuch des Deutschen Archäologischen Instituts* 74 (1959): 13.

16. Schmidt, *Heinrich Schliemann's Sammlung,* nos. 6055–6058.

17. Korfmann, "Die Schatzfunde in Moskau," 31–34.

18. N. I. Veselovskii, "Kubanskaia oblast," *Otchet Arkheologicheskoi Komissii,* St. Petersburg, 1897, 2ff.

19. Remzi O. Arik, *Les fouilles d'Alaca Höyük, entreprises par la Société d'Histoire Turque. Rapport préliminaire sur les travaux en 1935* (Ankara, 1937); Hamit Z. Koşay, *Ausgrabungen von Alaca Höyük. Ein Vorbericht über die im Auftrage der Türkischen Geschichtskommission im Sommer 1936 durchgeführten Forschungen und Entdeckungen* (Ankara, 1944); Hamit Z. Koşay, *Les fouilles d'Alaca Höyük, entreprises par la Société d'Histoire Turque. Rapport préliminaire sur les travaux en 1937–39* (Ankara, 1951); Hamit Z. Koşay and Mahmut Akok, *Ausgrabungen von Alaca Höyük. Vorbericht über die Forschungen und Entdeckungen von 1940–48* (Ankara, 1966); Hamit Z. Koşay and Mahmut Akok, *Alaca Höyük Excavations. Preliminary Report on Research and Discoveries 1963–1967* (Ankara, 1973).

20. Tahsin Özgüç and Mahmut Akok, *Horoztepe—an Early Bronze Age Settlement and Cemetery* (Ankara, 1958); Burhan Tezcan, "New Finds from Horoztepe," *Anatolia* 5 (1960): 29–46.

21. Tahsin Özgüç and Raci Temizer, "The Eskiyapar Treasure," in Machteld J. Mellink, Edith Porada, and Tahsin Özgüç, eds., *Aspects of Art and Iconography: Anatolia and Its Neighbors. Studies in Honor of Nimet Özgüç* (Ankara, 1993), 613–28.

22. L. Bernabo Brea, *Città preistorica nell'Isola di Lemnos* (Rome, 1964).

23. C. L. Woolley, *Ur Excavations II: The Royal Cemetery* (London, 1934).

24. Manfred Korfmann, "Seefahrtbeziehungen zwischen Schwarzem Meer und der Ägäis im 3. und 2. Jahrtausend v.u.Z.," Sixth International Colloquium on Aegean Prehistory, Athens (forthcoming).

25. Schmidt, *Heinrich Schliemann's Sammlung,* no. 6058: "Der Stein ist blau, *wie* Lapislazuli, mit bräunlichen Adern und Flecken."

26. Korfmann, "Seefahrtbeziehungen" (forthcoming).

27. Schmidt, *Heinrich Schliemann's Sammlung,* nos. 6117–6118.

28. Ibid., nos. 6108–6111.

29. Schliemann, *Ilios,* 510 and figs. 689–693: "Armbänder"; Schmidt, *Heinrich Schliemann's Sammlung,* nos. 5940–5942: "Armringe (?)"; one might possibly also think that they are "Halsringe."

30. Özgüç and Temizer, "The Eskiyapar Treasure," plate 110, nos. 1a–1b.

31. Cf. Manfred Korfmann, "Troia—Ausgrabungen 1990 und 1991," *Studia Troica* 2 (1992): 24–27.

32. Ibid., 24.

33. Schliemann, *Bericht über die Ausgrabungen,* plates 192–209, especially plate 204.

TOLSTIKOV:
SOME ASPECTS OF THE PREPARATION OF THE CATALOGUE FOR THE EXHIBITION "THE TREASURE OF TROY: HEINRICH SCHLIEMANN'S EXCAVATIONS" AT THE PUSHKIN STATE MUSEUM OF FINE ARTS, MOSCOW

1. Heinrich Schliemann, *Atlas trojanischer Alterthümer* (Leipzig, 1874); Hubert Schmidt, *Heinrich Schliemann's Sammlung trojanischer Altertümer* (Berlin, 1902).

ESTEROW:
INTRODUCTION TO "CURRENT ISSUES AND COOPERATIVE EFFORTS"

1. Meir Ronnen, "Sinai: A Shared Heritage," *ARTnews* 93, no. 8 (October 1994): 147.

PROTT:
PRINCIPLES FOR THE RESOLUTION OF DISPUTES CONCERNING CULTURAL HERITAGE DISPLACED DURING THE SECOND WORLD WAR

Author's note: This paper expresses the personal views of the author, which are not necessarily those of UNESCO.

1. See Mann, above, p. 85.

2. A. R. Hall, *The Recovery of Cultural*

Objects Dispersed During World War II, 25 DEP'T ST. BULL. 337, 339 (1951).

3. The key decisions were taken in the cases of *Rosenberg v. Fischer* JdT 1946 I 25, Note, 149; *Bührle v. Fischer* (unreported decision) (Fed. Ct., Booty Chamber, July 5, 1951); and *Fischer v. Schweizerische Eidgenossenschaft* (unreported decision) (Fed. Ct., Booty Chamber, June 25, 1952). See the detailed discussions in E. Thilo, *La revendication de biens se trouvant en Suisse, dérobés en pays occupés pendant la guerre,* 1 JOURNAL DES TRIBUNAUX 25 (1946); *La restitution des rapines de guerre,* 1 JOURNAL DES TRIBUNAUX 418 (1948); and *La restitution des rapines de guerre,* 1 JOURNAL DES TRIBUNAUX 25 (1952).

4. International Council of Museums (ICOM), *Study on the Principles, Conditions and Means for the Restitution and Return of Cultural Property in View of Reconstituting Dispersed Heritages* (1977), 2.

5. For a list of parties to the UNESCO Convention for the Protection of Cultural Property in the Event of Armed Conflict (Hague Convention) and to the Protocol, May 14, 1954, see Appendix 10.

6. For a list of parties to the UNESCO Convention on the Means of Prohibiting and Preventing the Illicit Import, Export and Transfer of Ownership of Cultural Property, Nov. 14, 1970, see Appendix 11.

7. Adopted on 24 June 1995, at a diplomatic conference held in Rome at the invitation of the Italian government.

8. Such as those suggested for the return of objects in general repatriation programs: see the nine principles proposed in Lyndel. V. Prott and P. J. O'Keefe, *Law and the Cultural Heritage,* vol. 3, *Movement* (London and Edinburgh: Butterworths, 1989), 863–94.

9. S. E. Nahlik, *La protection internationale des biens culturels en cas de conflit armé,* 1 RECUEIL DES COURS DE L'ACADÉMIE DE DROIT INTERNATIONAL DE LA HAYE 61, 100 (1967).

10. Such documents include the Guidelines for the Final Report of the Committee of Experts on the Establishment of an Intergovernmental Committee concerning the Restitution or Return of Cultural Property, Dakar, Mar. 20–23, 1978, UNESCO Doc. CC-78/CONF.609/6; Guidelines for the Use of the Standard Form Concerning Requests for Return or Restitution of the UNESCO Intergovernmental Committee for Promoting the Return of Cultural Property to its Countries of Origin or its Restitution in Case of Illicit Appropriation, UNESCO Doc. CC-86/WS/3.

11. ICOM, *supra* note 4.

KOWALSKI: WORLD WAR II CULTURAL LOSSES OF POLAND

1. This symbolic act was noted in the New York press. See Laura Leivick, "Return Art Stolen during Wars, Now," *Wall Street Journal,* 16 February 1995.

2. See Appendix 7. According to article 11, section 1, Russia was required to return all cultural objects she had taken from Polish territories since 1 January 1772. Treaty of Peace between Poland, Russia, and the Ukraine signed at Riga on 18 March 1921. G. F. Martens, *Nouveau recueil général de traités,* 3d ser., vol. 13 (Göttingen, 1924), 152.

3. Verordnung über die Beschlagnahme von Kunstgegenständen im Generalgouvernement. Exec. Ord. Journal G. G. No. 12. 1939. See also R. Lemkin, *Axis Rule in Occupied Europe* (Washington, D.C., 1944).

4. C. [K.] Estreicher, ed., *Cultural Losses of Poland. Index of Polish Cultural Losses during the German Occupation 1939–43* (London, 1944). See also Ministerswo Informacji Poland, *The Nazi Kultur in Poland* (London: H. M. Stationery Office, 1945).

5. See W. Kowalski, *Liquidation of the Effects of World War II in the Area of Culture* (Warsaw, 1994), 48.

6. W. Tomkiewicz, *Catalogue of Paintings Removed from Poland by the German Occupation Authorities during the Years 1939–1945,* vol. 1, *Foreign Paintings* (Warsaw, 1950); vol. 2, *Polish Paintings* (Warsaw, 1953).

7. At that time, Poland was given back 835 paintings, over 2,000 prints and drawings, and over 2,000 objets d'art.

8. P. Burnett, *Reparation at the Paris Peace Conference from the Standpoint of the American Delegation,* vol. 1 (New York, 1940), 885.

9. M. Bernhard and K. Martin, *Verlorene Werke der Malerei in Deutschland in der Zeit von 1939 bis 1945. Zerstörte und verschollene Gemälde aus Museen und Galerien* (Berlin, 1965).

10. Treaty between the Republic of Poland and the Russian Federation on Friendship and Good-Neighborly Cooperation, 22 May 1992.

KOENIGS: UNDER DURESS: THE SALE OF THE FRANZ KOENIGS COLLECTION

Author's note: The translation and editing were done by Jonathan Bragdon, Amsterdam.

1. Hannema to the mayor and city council of Rotterdam, 2 April 1935, Archives of the Boymans–van Beuningen Museum, Rotterdam.

2. Anna Koenigs–von Kalckreuth to Hannema, 28 April 1935, Archives of the Boymans–van Beuningen Museum.

3. Insurance Company De Waal & Zoon to the Boymans Museum in Rotterdam, 15 May 1935, Archives of the Boymans–van Beuningen Museum.

4. Hannema to Koenigs, acceptance of the loan, 20 November 1935, Archives of the Boymans–van Beuningen Museum.

5. Hannema to Goudstikker, 31 August 1939, Archives of the Boymans–van Beuningen Museum.

6. Goudstikker to Hannema, 4 September 1939, Archives of the Boymans–van Beuningen Museum.

7. Hannema to Van der Vorm, 13 March 1940, Archives of the Boymans–van Beuningen Museum.

8. Hannema to D. G. van Beuningen, 21 March 1940, Archives of the Boymans–van Beuningen Museum.

9. Koenigs to the director of the Boymans Museum, 2 April 1940, Archives of the Boymans–van Beuningen Museum.

10. Lisser & Rosenkranz Bank to the director of the Boymans Museum, 2 April 1940, Archives of the Boymans–van Beuningen Museum.

11. Hannema to Van Beuningen, 8 April 1940, Archives of the Boymans–van Beuningen Museum.

12. Hannema to the directors of the Lisser & Rosenkranz Bank, 9 April 1940, Archives of the Boymans–van Beuningen Museum.

13. Goudstikker to Hannema, telegram, 9 April 1940, Archives of the Boymans–van Beuningen Museum.

14. Hannema to Goudstikker, telegram, 9 April 1940, Archives of the Boymans–van Beuningen Museum.

15. Lisser & Rosenkranz Bank to Hannema, 9 April 1940, Archives of the Boymans–van Beuningen Museum.

16. Lisser & Rosenkranz Bank to Hannema, 9 April 1940, Archives of the Boymans–van Beuningen Museum.

17. Hannema to Koenigs, 12 April 1940, Archives of the Boymans–van Beuningen Museum.

18. Anna Koenigs–von Kalckreuth to Hannema, 14 April 1940, Archives of the Boymans–van Beuningen Museum.

19. Koenigs to Hannema, 17 April 1940, Archives of the Boymans–van Beuningen Museum.

20. Memorandum by Hannema, 23 October 1940, Archives of the Boymans–van Beuningen Museum.

21. Ibid.

22. Hannema to Van Beuningen, 5 December 1940, Archives of the Boymans–van Beuningen Museum.

23. Posse to Bormann, 15 January 1941, U.S. National Archives, Office of Strategic Services (OSS)/Art Looting Investigation Unit (ALIU), Consolidated Interrogation Reports (CIR), Attachment 38.

24. Documents from the Central State Archive Moscow. Sonderarchiv 1524 (2) 202. Transferred Collected Material from the Pushkin Museum.

25. Posse to Hannema, 26 May 1941, Archives of the Boymans–van Beuningen Museum.

GRIMSTED: CAPTURED ARCHIVES AND RESTITUTION PROBLEMS ON THE EASTERN FRONT

Author's note: An earlier version of this essay appeared as *IISH Research Paper* no. 18, International Institute for Social History (Amsterdam), in October 1995 (revised February 1996), and is reprinted with minor revisions in *Janus: Revue archivistique/Archival Review,* no. 2 (1996): 42–77. A revised article is forthcoming in *Contemporary European History.*

In citations from Soviet-area archives, numbers are given sequentially for *fond* (record group)/*opis'* (inventory within *fond*)/and *delo* (or file) numbers.

1. Embassy of the USSR, Information Bulletin No. 138 (19 November 1942), 6.

2. Vladimir Teteriatnikov, "'Kholodnaia voina' za muzeinymi shtorami—Kak rossiiskie iskusstvovedy sdaiut v plen shedevry, okazavashiesia v SSSR posle pobedy nad Germaniei v 1945 godu," *Pravda,* 29 March 1995, 4.

3. Publication of the conference proceedings is planned under the auspices of the International Institute for Social History and the university library in Amsterdam.

4. Evgenii Sidorov, in the foreword to the elaborate catalogue *Five Centuries of European Drawings: The Former Collection of Franz Koenigs,* exhib. cat., 2 October 1995–21 January 1996 (Moscow and Milan: Leonardo Arte, 1995). A Russian edition was also available. On the Koenigs collection, see editor's note, above, p. 161.

5. Vladimir Teteriatnikov, *Problema kul'turnykh tsennostei peremeshchennykh v rezul'tate vtoroi mirovoi voiny: (dokazatel' stvo rossiiskikh prav na "Kollektsiiu Kenigsa")* (Moscow/Tver', 1996); published as a special issue of *Obozrevatel'/ Observer: Informatsionno-analiticheskii zhurnal* as a joint publication of *Obozrevatel'* and *Tverskaia starina*).

6. Vladimir Teteriatnikov, "Ograbiat li vnov' russkii narod? Tragicheskaia sud'ba kul'turnykh tsennostei, peremeshchennykh v resul'tate vtoroi mirovoi voiny," *Pravda,* no. 73, 22 May 1996.

7. "Report of the [UNESCO] Director-General on the Study on the Possibility of Transferring Documents from Archives Constituted within the Territory of Other Countries or Relating to their History, within the Framework of Bilateral Agreements," Nairobi, 1976 (UNESCO Doc. 19C/94, § 3.1.1).

8. Resolution 1 of the Thirtieth International Conference of the Round Table on Archives (CITRA), Conseil International des Archives/International Council on Archives, *Bulletin,* no. 43 (December 1994): 14–15.

9. "The View of the Archival Community on the Settling of Disputed Claims: Position Paper adopted by the Executive Committee of the International Council on Archives at its meeting in Guangzhou, 10–13 April 1995." A typescript of this document was furnished to the author by the ICA Secretary General.

10. The most thorough study to date of the fate of archives during the war, prepared in the 1960s, could never be published: V. V. Tsaplin, "Arkhivy, voina i okkupatsiia (1941–1945 gody)," Moscow, 1968; Tsaplin kindly made his typescript (with hand corrections, signed and dated 20 January 1969) available to the present author.

11. See the initial revelations in P. K. Grimsted, "The Fate of Ukrainian Cultural Treasures during World War II: Archives, Libraries, and Museums under the Third Reich," *Jahrbücher für Geschichte Osteuropas* 39, no. 1 (1991): 53–80. The Ukrainian booklet version, with the collaboration of Hennadii Boriak, includes many original documents: *Dolia skarbiv Ukrains'koi kul'tury pid chas druhoi svitovoi viiny: Vynyshchennia arkhiviv, bibliotek, muzeiv* (Kiev: Arkheohrafichna komisiia AN URSR, 1991; 2d ed., L'viv, 1992). Some of the material presented here is summarized from these publications.

12. Quoted from an extensive chart prepared by Glavarkhiv NKVD SSSR, 1 April 1942, GA RF, 5325/10/836, fols. 45–46. O. N. Kopylova analyzed figures for the evacuation and destruction of central archives in Moscow and Leningrad in a significant "revisionist" article, "K probleme sokhrannosti GAF SSSR v gody Velikoi Otechestvennoi voiny," *Sovetskie arkhivy,* 1990, no. 5: 37–44.

13. V. N. Bondarev, as quoted by Maria Dement'eva, "Osobaia sud'ba osobogo arkhiva," *Obshchaia gazeta,* no. 13, 4 May 1993, 8.

14. These details are documented in Grimsted, "The Fate of Ukrainian Cultural Treasures," 58–59. The official Soviet report was first published in *Pravda,* no. 52, 1 March 1944. A copy was submitted as one of the Soviet depositions at the Nuremberg trials in 1945. See GA RF, 7445/2/94, fols. 194–97. I have recently found the top-secret Soviet reports of the retrieval of a large part of the archive in Czechoslovakia.

15. "Spravka o rezul'tatakh raboty GAU NKVD SSSR po vozvrashcheniiu v Sov. Soiuz dokumental'nykh materialov GAF SSSR . . . ," 15 December 1945, GA RF, 5325/10/2148, fols. 1–4. For example, not included in the Glavarkhiv list, three freight-car loads taken by the Künsberg Commando (Sonderkommando Künsberg) from the Odessa archives were found in a salt mine in Saxony: Chechkov to Glavarkhiv chief Nikitinskii, GA RF, 5325/2/1620, fols. 158–159. Four trainloads of the Communist Party (CPSU) archives from Smolensk were retrieved in Silesia (see below).

16. See the official army list and explanatory text published as an appendix to Grimsted, *Dolia skarbiv Ukrains'koi kul'tury,* 117–19.

17. The fate and holdings of the Tallinn archive were well documented in the West: See P. K. Grimsted, *Archives and Manuscript Repositories in the USSR: Estonia, Latvia, Lithuania, and Belorussia* (Princeton, 1981), 743–46, 748–52. The Tallinn City Archive was returned to Estonia in 1990.

18. See ibid., 748–52.

19. These details and the current refusal of the United States to return the Smolensk files in Washington are documented in P. K. Grimsted, *The Odyssey of the Smolensk Archive: Plundered Communist Records for the Service of Anti-Communism,* Carl Beck Occasional Papers in Russian and East European Studies, no. 1201 (Pittsburgh: University of Pittsburgh, Center for Russian and East European Studies, 1995).

20. Law No. 2, as published in *Official Gazette of the Control Council for Germany,* no. 1 (2d ed., corrected), Berlin, 29 October 1945.

21. Kruglov to Beriia, 5 April 1945, GA RF, 5325/10/2025, fol. 4; a copy was addressed from Beriia to Molotov on 6 April 1945, fol. 5.

22. "Spravka . . . o vyvoze v SSSR arkhivov inostrannogo proiskhozhdeniia," 15 December 1945, GA RF, 5325/10/2148, fols. 1–4, and the accompanying top-secret memorandum by Golubtsov, "Svedeniia o dokumental'nykh materialakh inostrannogo proiskhozhdeniia vyvezennykh v Sovetskii Soiuz v 1945 godu," fol. 5, with indication of the archives in Moscow to which they were directed.

23. Zapevalin to Nikitinskii, 20 July 1945, GA RF, 5325/2/1353, fol. 207.

24. Nikitinskii to Beriia, GA RF, 5325/2/1353, fol. 210 (a handwritten endorsement is dated 12 October 1945).

25. L. Gaidukov to G. M. Malenkov, 20 August 1945, RTsKhIDNI, 71/125/308, fol. 28.

26. Bonch-Bruevich to Stalin, 24 February 1945, RTsKhIDNI, 71/125/308, fol. 3.

27. GA RF, 9401/2/134, fols. 1–2. The official protocol of transfer (Prague, 13 December 1945) and inventory of the 396 crates

from RZIA are found in GA RF, 5325/10/2024, fols. 3–4v.

28. Details about its arrival and transfer to TsGAOR SSSR appear in a report dated 3 January 1946, in GA RF, 5325/10/2023, fol. 40. Nikitinskii's receipt on behalf of TsGAOR SSSR (2 January 1946) is found in GA RF 5326/2/1705A.

29. Kruglov to Zhdanov, 15 May 1946, GA RF, 5325/10/2023, fol. 46.

30. Many of the foreign holdings from Wölfelsdorf are listed in the initial top-secret reconnaissance and shipping reports found in GA RF, 5325/10/2027.

31. Golubtsov to I. A. Serov, "Dokladnaia zapiska o rezul'tatakh obsledovaniia dokumental'nykh materialov germanskikh arkhivov, evakuirovannykh i ukrytykh v shakhtakh Saksonii" (Berlin, 24 October 1945), GA RF, 5325/2/1353, fol. 216. A list of fonds chosen is attached.

32. Aleksandrov to Malenkov, RTsKhIDNI, 17/125/308, fols. 49–51 (the quote is from fol. 51).

33. This shipment is documented in GA RF, 5325/10/2029.

34. Nikitinskii to Beriia, "Dokladnaia zapiska," 21 August 1945, GA RF, 5325/10/2029, fols. 20–23.

35. "Protokol soveshchaniia pri zam. nachal'nika Glavnogo arkhivnogo upravleniia NKVD SSSR—Izuchenie voprosa o sozdanii Osobogo Tsentral'nogo gosudarstvennogo arkhiva," 21 August 1945, GA RF, 5325/2/3623, fols. 2–3, fol. 8.

36. Ibid.

37. These figures are based on lists (data as of 11 February 1993) furnished to me by the deputy director of the Bremen Stadtsarchiv.

38. See Ella Maksimova, "Piat' dnei v Osobom arkhive," *Izvestiia*, nos. 49–53, 17–21 February 1990 (which started with an interview with the then director A. S. Prokopenko).

39. See the interview with P. K. Grimsted by Evgenii Kuz'min, "Vyvezti . . . unichtozhit'. . . spriatat' . . . , Sud'by trofeinykh arkhivov," *Literaturnaia gazeta* 39 (2 October 1991): 13; publication of that interview was delayed for almost a year.

40. Ella Maksimova, interview with the former director of the Special Archive, A. S. Prokopenko, "Arkhivy frantsuzskoi razvedki skryvali na Leningradskom shosse," *Izvestiia*, no. 240, 3 November 1991.

41. An unpublished 1969 Glavarkhiv report made available to the present author lists over two million files by country of origin: "Spravka o dokumental'nykh materialakh, peredannykh pravitel'stvam inostrannykh gosudarstv," typescript with handwritten corrections, signed by V. V. Tsaplin, 13 February 1969. These figures do not take into account manuscript treasures restituted by libraries under other controlling agencies, such as the German and Polish materials restituted in 1957 by the

Manuscript Division of the Russian State Library (former Lenin Library) and the library of Moscow State University.

42. S. L. Tikhvinskii, "Pomoshch' Sovetskogo Soiuza drugim gosudarstvam v vossozdanii natsional'nogo arkhivnogo dostoianiia," *Sovetskie arkhivy*, no. 2 (1979): 11–16. Again, most went back to GDR and other East-bloc countries.

43. Götz Aly and Susanne Heim, *Das Zentrale Staatsarchiv in Moskau ("Sonderarchiv"): Rekonstruktion und Bestandsverzeichnis verschollen geglaubten Schriftguts aus der NS-Zeit* (Düsseldorf: Hans-Böckler-Stiftung, 1993). A full list of French holdings has yet to appear.

44. See the official transcript of the Federal'noe Sobranie, parlament Rossiiskoi Federatsii, *Biulleten'*, no. 34, *Zasedaniia Gosudarstvennoi Dumy, 20 maia 1994 goda* (Moscow, 1994), 4, 26–33. A transcript of the June hearings is not available. Regarding the current refusal of the United States to return the Smolensk Archive, and for an analysis of the Russian parliamentary discussion, see Grimsted, *Odyssey of the Smolensk Archive*, 80–88.

45. Evgenii Stroev, "Pora poniat'—My nikomu nichego ne dolzhny," *Rossiiskaia gazeta*, 4 August 1994.

46. See the earlier article by Irina Antonova, "My nikomu nichego ne dolzhny: Eshche raz o vozvrate kul'turnykh tsennostei," *Nezavisimaia gazeta*, 5 May 1994.

47. "Skandal, ne dostoinyi Rossii," headlines separate articles by Iurii Kovalenko (Paris) and Ella Maksimova (Moscow), *Izvestiia*, no. 172, 8 September 1994, 5. The articles mention details of some of the Russian-related archival material presented to Russia in connection with the restitution process.

48. Already in March 1994, a new Russian archival decree defined the so-called Archival Fond of the Russian Federation to include "archival fonds and archival records (or documents) of juridical and physical entities (persons), which have been received through legal means into state proprietorship, including those from abroad" (Article 7). This conceptualization of Russian pretensions to archival materials of foreign provenance now held in Russia could further complicate restitution, given current Russian legal arguments, which would consider a Soviet "decree" or government order as a *de facto* legal instrument.

49. Albert Kostenevich, *Hidden Treasures Revealed: Impressionist Masterpieces and Other Important French Paintings Preserved by The State Hermitage Museum, St. Petersburg* (New York: Harry N. Abrams in association with the Ministry of Culture of the Russian Federation and the State Hermitage Museum, St. Petersburg, 1995).

50. Rossiiskaia Federatsiia, Federal'nyi zakon, proekt: "O prave sobstvennosti na kul'-

turnye tsennosti, peremeshchennye na territoriiu Rossiiskoi Federatsii v resul'tate vtoroi mirovoi voiny," Prilozhenie k postanovleniiu Soveta Federatsii Federal'nogo Sobraniia RF ot 23 marta 1995 goda, no 405-I-SF.

51. Federal'nyi zakon, proekt, "O zashchite kul'turnogo dostoianiia Rossii v vooruzhennykh konfliktakh." The alternative draft was prepared by the Institute of Analysis and Management of Conflicts and Stability (Institut analiza i upravleniia konfliktami i stabil'nost'iu).

52. Vladimir Vishniakov, "Krov' i zoloto," interview with Vladimir Teteriatnikov, *Pravda*, 16 May 1995, 1, 4. See also Vladimir Teteriatnikov, "Zakon obuzdaet chinovnikov," *Pravda*, 13 June 1995, 2. For the earlier interview with Teteriatnikov, see note 2, above.

53. Shvidkoi was quoted in a two-part commentary on the present debate in *Moskovskii komsomolets*, 7 June 1995, 2: Marina Ovsova and Anna Kovaleva, "Vse ob'iavliaiu moim: Duma v dvukh chastiakh," part 1, "U deputatov zabolela golovka."

54. Resolution 1, Thirtieth CITRA Conference, ICA *Bulletin*, 14–15.

APPENDICES

TREATIES, CONVENTIONS, AND

OTHER OFFICIAL DOCUMENTS:

COMPLETE DOCUMENTS

AND SELECTED SECTIONS

RELATING TO THE PROTECTION

AND RETURN OF

CULTURAL PROPERTY

Appendix I

INSTRUCTIONS FOR THE GOVERNMENT OF ARMIES OF THE UNITED STATES IN THE FIELD*
Also known as the "Lieber Code"
(Section 2)

Prepared by Francis Lieber, promulgated as General Orders No. 100 by President Lincoln, April 24, 1863

Section 2. Public and Private Property of the Enemy—Protection of Persons, and Especially of Women: of Religion, the Arts and Sciences—Punishment of Crimes against the Inhabitants of Hostile Countries

Article 31
A victorious army appropriates all public money, seizes all public movable property until further direction by its government, and sequesters for its own benefit or of that of its government all the revenues of real property belonging to the hostile government or nation. The title to such real property remains in abeyance during military occupation, and until the conquest is made complete.

Article 32
A victorious army, by the martial power inherent in the same, may suspend, change, or abolish, as far as the martial power extends, the relations which arise from the services due, according to the existing laws of the invaded country, from one citizen, subject, or native of the same to another.

   The commander of the army must leave it to the ultimate treaty of peace to settle the permanency of this change.

Article 33
It is no longer considered lawful—on the contrary, it is held to be a serious breach of the law of war—to force the subjects of the enemy into the service of the victorious government, except the latter should proclaim, after a fair and complete conquest of the hostile country or district, that it is resolved to keep the country, district, or place permanently as its own and make it a portion of its own country.

Article 34
As a general rule, the property belonging to churches, to hospitals, or other establishments of an exclusively charitable character, to establishments of education, or foundations for the promotion of knowledge, whether public schools, universities, academies of learning or observatories, museums of the fine arts, or of a scientific character—such property is not to be considered public property in the sense of paragraph 31; but it may be taxed or used when the public service may require it.

Article 35
Classical works of art, libraries, scientific collections, or precious instruments, such as astronomical telescopes, as well as hospitals, must be secured against all avoidable injury, even when they are contained in fortified places whilst besieged or bombarded.

Article 36
If such works of art, libraries, collections, or instruments belonging to a hostile nation or government can be removed without injury, the ruler of the conquering state or nation may order them to be seized and removed for the benefit of the said nation. The ultimate ownership is to be settled by the ensuing treaty of peace.

   In no case shall they be sold or given away, if captured by the armies of the United States, nor shall they ever be privately appropriated, or wantonly destroyed or injured.

Article 37

The United States acknowledge and protect, in hostile countries occupied by them, religion and morality; strictly private property; the persons of the inhabitants, especially those of women; and the sacredness of domestic relations. Offenses to the contrary shall be rigorously punished.

This rule does not interfere with the right of the victorious invader to tax the people or their property, to levy forced loans, to billet soldiers, or to appropriate property, especially houses, lands, boats or ships, and churches, for temporary and military uses.

Article 38

Private property, unless forfeited by crimes or by offenses of the owner, can be seized only by way of military necessity, for the support or other benefit of the army or of the United States.

If the owner has not fled, the commander officer will cause receipts to be given, which may serve the spoliated owner to obtain indemnity.

Article 39

The salaries of civil officers of the hostile government who remain in the invaded territory, and continue the work of their office, and can continue it according to the circumstances arising out of the war—such as judges, administrative or police officers, officers of city or communal governments—are paid from the public revenue of the invaded territory, until the military government has reason wholly or partially to discontinue it. Salaries or incomes connected with purely honorary titles are always stopped.

Article 40

There exists no law or body of authoritative rules of action between hostile armies, except that branch of the law of nature and nations which is called the law and usages of war on land.

Article 41

All municipal law of the ground on which the armies stand, or of the countries to which they belong, is silent and of no effect between armies in the field.

Article 42

Slavery, complicating and confounding the ideas of property (that is, of a *thing*), and of personality (that is, of *humanity*), exists according to municipal or local law only. The law of nature and nations has never acknowledged it. The digest of the Roman law enacts the early dictum of the pagan jurist, that "so far as the law of nature is concerned, all men are equal." Fugitives escaping from a country in which they were slaves, villains, or serfs, into another country, have, for centuries past, been held free and acknowledged free by judicial decisions of European countries, even though the municipal law of the country in which the slave had taken refuge acknowledged slavery within its own dominions.

Article 43

Therefore, in a war between the United States and a belligerent which admits of slavery, if a person held in bondage by that belligerent be captured by or come as a fugitive under the protection of the military forces of the United States, such person is immediately entitled to the rights and privileges of a freeman. To return such person into slavery would amount to enslaving a free person, and neither the United States nor any officer under their authority can enslave any human being. Moreover, a person so made free by the law of war is under the shield of the law of nations, and the former owner or State can have, by the law of postliminy, no belligerent lien or claim of service.

Article 44

All wanton violence committed against persons in the invaded country, all destruction of property not commanded by the authorized officer, all robbery, all pillage or sacking, even after taking a place by main force, all rape, wounding, maiming, or killing of such inhabitants, are prohibited under the penalty of death, or such other severe punishment as may seem adequate for the gravity of the offense.

A soldier, officer or private, in the act of committing such violence, and disobeying a superior ordering him to abstain from it, may be lawfully killed on the spot by such superior.

Article 45

All captures and booty belong, according to the modern law of war, primarily to the government of the captor.

Prize money, whether on sea or land, can now only be claimed under local law.

Article 46

Neither officers nor soldiers are allowed to make use of their position or power in the hostile country for private gain, not even for commercial transactions otherwise legitimate. Offenses to the contrary committed by commissioned officers will be punished with cashiering or such other punishment as the nature of the offense may require; if by soldiers, they shall be punished according to the nature of the offense.

Article 47

Crimes punishable by all penal codes, such as arson, murder, maiming, assaults, highway robbery, theft, burglary, fraud, forgery, and rape, if committed by an American soldier in a hostile country against its inhabitants, are not only punishable as at home, but in all cases in which death is not inflicted, the severer punishment shall be preferred.

---

* Instructions for the Government of Armies of the United States in the Field, prepared by Francis Lieber, promulgated as General Orders No. 100 by President Lincoln, Apr. 24, 1863, *reprinted in* Leon Friedman, ed. 1 *The Law of War: A Documentary History* 158 (1972).

Appendix 2

PROJECT OF AN INTERNATIONAL DECLARATION CONCERNING THE LAWS AND CUSTOMS OF WAR*
Also known as the "Declaration of the Conference of Brussels"

Adopted by the Conference of Brussels, August 27, 1874; not ratified

Article 1
A territory is considered as occupied when it is actually placed under the authority of the hostile army.

The occupation only extends to those territories where this authority is established, and can be exercised.

Article 2
The authority of the legal power being suspended, and having actually passed into the hands of the occupier, he shall take every step in his power to re-establish and secure, as far as possible, public safety and social order.

Article 3
With this object he will maintain the laws which were in force in the country in time of peace, and he will only modify, suspend, or replace them by others if necessity obliges him to do so.

Article 4
The functionaries and officials of every class who, at the instance of the occupier, consent to continue to perform their duties, shall be under his protection. They shall not be dismissed or be liable to summary punishment (*punis disciplinairement*) unless they fail in fulfilling the obligations they have undertaken, and shall be handed over to justice, only if they violate those obligations by unfaithfulness.

Article 5
The army of occupation shall only levy such taxes, dues, duties, and tolls as are already established for the benefit of the State, or their equivalent, if it be impossible to collect them, and this shall be done as far as possible in the form of and according to existing practice. It shall devote them to defraying the expenses of the administration of the country to the same extent as was obligatory on the legal Government.

Article 6
The army occupying a territory shall take possession only of the specie, the funds, and bills, etc. (*valeurs exigibles*), which are the property of the State in its own right, the depots of arms, means of transport, magazines and supplies, and, in general, all the personal property of the State which may be of service in carrying on the war.

Railway plant, land telegraphs, steam and other vessels, not included in cases regulated by maritime law, as well as depots of arms, and generally every kind of munitions of war, although belonging to companies or to private individuals, are to be considered equally as means of aid in carrying on a war, which cannot be left at the disposal of the enemy. Railway plant, land telegraphs, as well as the steam and other vessels above-mentioned shall be restored, and indemnities be regulated on the conclusion of peace.

Article 7
The occupying State shall only consider itself in the light of an administrator and usufructuary of the public buildings, real property, forests, and agricultural works belonging to the hostile State, and situated in the occupied territory. It is bound to protect these properties (*fonds de ces propriétés*) and to administer them according to the laws of usufruct.

Article 8
The property of parishes (*communes*), or establishments devoted to religion, charity, education, arts and sciences, although belonging to the State, shall be treated as private property.

Every seizure, destruction of, or wilful damage to, such establishments, historical monuments, or works of art or of science, should be prosecuted by the competent authorities.

Article 9
The laws, rights, and duties of war are applicable not only to the army, but likewise to militia and corps of volunteers complying with the following conditions:
1. That they have at their head a person responsible for his subordinates;
2. That they wear some settled distinctive badge recognizable at a distance;
3. That they carry arms openly; and
4. That, in their operations, they conform to the laws and customs of war.
In those countries where the militia forms the whole or part of the army, they shall be included under the denomination of "army."

Article 10
The population of a non-occupied territory, who, on the approach of the enemy, of their own accord take up arms to resist the invading troops, without having had time to organize themselves in conformity with Article 9, shall be considered as belligerents, if they respect the laws and customs of war.

Article 11
The armed forces of the belligerents may be composed of combatants and non-combatants. In the event of being captured by the enemy, both one and the other shall enjoy the rights of prisoners of war.

Article 12
The laws of war do not allow to belligerents an unlimited power as to the choice of means of injuring the enemy.

Article 13
According to this principle are strictly forbidden:
(a) The use of poison or poisoned weapons.
(b) Murder by treachery of individuals belonging to the hostile nation or army.
(c) Murder of an antagonist who, having laid down his arms, or having no longer the means of defending himself, has surrendered at discretion.
(d) The declaration that no quarter will be given.
(e) The use of arms, projectiles, or substances (*matières*) which may cause unnecessary suffering, as well as the use of the projectiles prohibited by the Declaration of St. Petersburg in 1868.
(f) Abuse of the flag of truce, the national flag, or the military insignia or uniform of the enemy, as well as the distinctive badges of the Geneva Convention.
(g) All destruction or seizure of the property of the enemy which is not imperatively required by the necessity of war.

Article 14
Stratagems (*ruses de guerre*), and the employment of means necessary to procure intelligence respecting the enemy or the country (*terrain*) (subject to the provisions of Article 36), are considered as lawful means.

Article 15
Fortified places are alone liable to be seized. Towns, agglomerations of houses or villages, which are open and undefended, cannot be attacked or bombarded.

Article 16
But if a town or fortress, agglomeration of houses, or villages be defended, the commander of the attacking forces should, before commencing a bombardment, and except in the case of surprise, do all in his power to warn the authorities.

Article 17
In the like case all necessary steps should be taken to spare, as far as possible, buildings devoted to religion, arts, sciences, and charity, hospitals and places where sick and wounded are collected, on condition that they are not used at the same time for military purposes.

It is the duty of the besieged to indicate these buildings by special visible signs to be notified beforehand by the besieged.

Article 18
A town taken by storm shall not be given up to the victorious troops to plunder.

Article 19
No one shall be considered as a spy but those who, acting secretly or under false pretences, collect, or try to collect, information in districts occupied by the enemy with the intention of communicating it to the opposing force.

Article 20
A spy if taken in the act shall be tried and treated according to the laws in force in the army which captures him.

Article 21
If a spy who rejoins the army to which he belongs is subsequently captured by the enemy, he is to be treated as a prisoner of war, and incurs no responsibility for his previous acts.

Article 22
Military men (*les militaires*) who have penetrated within the zone of operations of the enemy's army, with the intention of collecting information, are not considered as spies if it has been possible to recognize their military character.

In like manner military men (and also non-military persons carrying out their mission openly) charged with the transmission of despatches either to their own army or to that of the enemy, shall not be considered as spies if captured by the enemy.

To this class belong, also, if captured, individuals sent in balloons to carry despatches, and generally to keep up communications between the different parts of an army, or of a territory.

Article 23
Prisoners of war are lawful and disarmed enemies. They are in the power of the enemy's Government, but not of the individuals or of the corps who made them prisoners.

They should be treated with humanity.

Every act of insubordination authorizes the necessary measures of severity to be taken with regard to them.

All their personal effects except their arms are considered to be their own property.

Article 24
Prisoners of war are liable to internment in a town, fortress, camp, or in any locality whatever, under an obligation not to go beyond certain fixed limits; but they may not be placed in confinement (*enfermés*) unless absolutely necessary as a measure of security.

Article 25
Prisoners of war may be employed on certain public works which have no immediate connection with the operations on the theater of war, provided the employment be not excessive, nor humiliating to their military rank, if they belong to the army, or to their official or social position, if they do not belong to it.

They may also, subject to such regulations as may be drawn up by the military authorities, undertake private work.

The pay they receive will go towards ameliorating their position or will be placed to their credit at the time of their release. In this case the cost of their maintenance may be deducted from their pay.

Article 26
Prisoners of war cannot be compelled in any way to take any part whatever in carrying on the operations of the war.

Article 27
The Government in whose power are the prisoners of war undertakes to provide for their maintenance.

The conditions of such maintenance may be settled by a mutual understanding between the belligerents.

In default of such an understanding, and as a general principle, prisoners of war shall be treated, as regards food and clothing, on the same footing as the troops of the Government who made them prisoners.

Article 28
Prisoners of war are subject to the laws and regulations in force in the army in whose power they are.

Arms may be used, after summoning, against a prisoner attempting to escape. If retaken, he is subject to summary punishment (*peines disciplinaires*) or to a stricter surveillance.

If, after having escaped, he is again made prisoner, he is not liable to any punishment for his previous escape.

Article 29
Every prisoner is bound to declare, if interrogated on the point, his true name and rank, and in the case of his infringing this rule he will incur a restriction of the advantages granted to the prisoners of the class to which he belongs.

Article 30
The exchange of prisoners of war is regulated by mutual agreement between belligerents.

Article 31
Prisoners of war may be released on parole if the laws of their country allow it, and in such a case they are bound on their personal honour to fulfil scrupulously, as regards their own Government, as well as that which made them prisoners, the engagements they have undertaken.

In the same case their own Government should neither demand nor accept from them any service contrary to their parole.

Article 32
A prisoner of war cannot be forced to accept release on parole, nor is the enemy's Government obliged to comply with the request of a prisoner claiming to be released on parole.

Article 33
Every prisoner of war liberated on parole, and retaken carrying arms against the Government to which he had pledged his honour, may be deprived of the rights accorded to prisoners of war, and may be brought before the tribunals.

Article 34
Persons in the vicinity of armies, but who do not directly form part of them, such as correspondents, newspaper reporters, "vivandiers," contractors, etc., may also be made prisoners of war.

These persons should, however, be furnished with a permit issued by a competent authority, as well as with a certificate of identity.

Article 35
The duties of belligerents, with regard to the treatment of sick and wounded, are regulated by the Convention of Geneva of the 22d August, 1864, subject to the modifications which may be introduced into that convention.

Article 36
The population of an occupied territory cannot be compelled to take part in military operations against their own country.

Article 37
The population of occupied territories cannot be compelled to swear allegiance to the enemy's power.

Article 38
The honour and rights of the family, the life, and property of individuals, as well as their religious convictions and the exercise of their religion, should be respected.

Private property cannot be confiscated.

Article 39
Pillage is expressly forbidden.

Article 40
As private property should be respected, the enemy will demand from parishes (*communes*) or the inhabitants, only such payments and services as are connected with the necessities of war generally acknowledged in proportion to the resources of the country, and which do not imply, with regard to the inhabitants, the obligation of taking part in the operations of war against their own country.

Article 41
The enemy, in levying contributions, whether as equivalents for taxes (*vide* Art. 5), or for payments which should be made in kind, or as fines, will proceed, as far as possible, according to the rules of the distribution and assessment of the taxes in force in the occupied territory.

The civil authorities of the legal Government will afford their assistance, if they have remained in office.

Contributions can be imposed only on the order and on the responsibility of the General-in-Chief, or of the superior civil authority established by the enemy in the occupied territory.

For every contribution a receipt shall be given to the person furnishing it.

Article 42
Requisitions shall be made only by the authority of the Commandant of the locality occupied.

For every requisition an indemnity shall be granted or a receipt given.

Article 43
An individual authorized by one of the belligerents to confer with the other, on presenting himself with a white flag, accompanied by a trumpeter (bugler or drummer), or also by a flag-bearer, shall be recognized as the bearer of a flag of truce. He, as well as the trumpeter (bugler or drummer), and the flag-bearer, who accompany him, shall have the right of inviolability.

Article 44
The commander to whom a bearer of a flag of truce is despatched is not obliged to receive him under all circumstances and conditions.

It is lawful for him to take all measures necessary for preventing the bearer of the flag of truce taking advantage of his stay within the radius of the enemy's position to the prejudice of the latter; and if the bearer of the flag of truce is found guilty of such a breach of confidence, he has the right to detain him temporarily.

He may equally declare beforehand that he will not receive bearers of flags of truce during a certain period. Envoys presenting themselves after such a notification from the side to which it has been given forfeit their right of inviolability.

Article 45
The bearer of a flag of truce forfeits his right of inviolability if it be proved in a positive and irrefutable manner that he has taken advantage of his privileged position to incite to, or commit, an act of treachery.

Article 46
The conditions of capitulations shall be discussed by the Contracting Parties.

These conditions should not be contrary to military honour.

When once settled by a Convention, they should be scrupulously observed by both sides.

Article 47
An armistice suspends warlike operations by a mutual agreement between the belligerents. Should the duration thereof not be fixed, the belligerents may resume operations at any moment; provided, however, that proper warning be given to the enemy, in accordance with the conditions of the armistice.

Article 48
An armistice may be general or local. The former suspends all warlike operations between the belligerents; the latter only those between certain portions of the belligerent armies, and within a fixed radius.

Article 49
An armistice should be notified officially and without delay to the competent authorities and to the troops. Hostilities are suspended immediately after the notification.

Article 50
It rests with the Contracting Parties to define in the clauses of the armistice the relations which shall exist between the populations.

Article 51
The violation of the armistice by either of the parties gives to the other the right of terminating it (*le dénoncer*).

Article 52
The violation of the clauses of an armistice by private individuals, on their own personal initiative, only affords the right of demanding the punishment of the guilty persons, and, if there is occasion for it, an indemnity for losses sustained.

Article 53
The neutral State receiving in its territory troops belonging to the belligerent armies will intern them, so far as it may be possible away from the theater of war.

They may be kept in camps, or even confined in fortresses or in places appropriated to this purpose.

It will decide whether the officers may be released on giving their parole not to quit the neutral territory without authority.

Article 54
In default of a special agreement, the neutral State which receives the belligerent troops will furnish the interned with provisions, clothing, and such aid as humanity demands.

The expenses incurred by the internment will be made good at the conclusion of peace.

Article 55
The neutral State may authorize the transport across its territory of the wounded and sick belonging to the belligerent armies, provided that

the trains which convey them do not carry either the *personnel* or *material* of war.

In this case the neutral State is bound to take the measures necessary for the safety and control of the operation.

Article 56
The Convention of Geneva is applicable to the sick and wounded interned on neutral territory.

FINAL PROTOCOL

The Conference assembled at Brussels, on the invitation of the Government of His Majesty the Emperor of Russia, for the purpose of discussing a Project of International Rules on the Laws and Usages of War, has examined the Project submitted to it in a spirit in accordance with the elevated sentiment which had led to its being convoked, and which all the Governments represented had welcomed with sympathy.

This sentiment had already found expression in the Declaration exchanged between the Governments at St. Petersburg in 1868, with reference to the exclusion of explosive bullets.

It had been unanimously declared that the progress of civilization should have the effect of alleviating, as far as possible, the calamities of war; and that the only legitimate object which States should have in view during war is to weaken the enemy without inflicting upon him unnecessary suffering.

These principles met at that time with unanimous approval. At the present time the Conference, following the same path, participates in the conviction expressed by the Government of His Majesty the Emperor of Russia, that a further step may be taken by revising the laws and general usages of war, whether with the object of defining them with greater precision, or with the view of laying down, by a common agreement, certain limits which will restrain, as far as possible, the severities of war.

War being thus regulated would involve less suffering, would be less liable to those aggravations produced by uncertainty, unforeseen events, and the passions excited by the struggle; it would tend more surely to that which should be its final object, viz., the re-establishment of good relations, and a more solid and lasting peace between the belligerent States.

The Conference could respond to those ideas of humanity in no better way than by entering in the same spirit into the examination of the subject they were to discuss.

The modifications which have been introduced into the Project, the comments, the reservations, and separate opinions which the Delegates have thought proper to insert in the Protocols, in accordance with instructions, and the particular views of their respective Governments, or their own private opinions, constitute the *ensemble* of their work. It is of opinion that it may be submitted to the respective Governments which it represents, as a conscientious inquiry of a nature to serve as a basis for an ulterior exchange of ideas, and for the development of the provisions of the Convention of Geneva of 1864 and of the Declaration of St. Petersburg of 1868. It will be their task to ascertain what portion of this work may become the object of an agreement, and what portion requires still further examination.

The Conference, in concluding its work, is of opinion that its debates will have in every case thrown light on those important questions, the regulations of which, should it result in a general agreement, would be a real progress of humanity.

Done at Brussels, 27 August 1874.

[The Final Protocol was signed on 27 August 1874 by the representatives of the following States:]

Austria-Hungary	Netherlands
Belgium	Portugal
Denmark	Russia
France	Spain
Germany	Sweden and Norway
Great Britain	Switzerland
Greece	Turkey
Italy	

---

* Project of an International Declaration Concerning the Laws and Customs of War, adopted by the Conference of Brussels, Aug. 27, 1874, 4 Martens Nouveau Recueil (2d) 219.

Appendix 3

CONVENTION RESPECTING THE LAWS AND CUSTOMS OF WAR ON LAND*
Also known as the "Hague Convention of 1907" (Preamble; Convention; Annex, Section 2, Chapter 1: Articles 27–28, and Section 3: Articles 46–47, 53, 55–56)

Signed at The Hague, October 18, 1907; entry into force, January 26, 1910

(List of Contracting Parties)

Seeing that, while seeking means to preserve peace and prevent armed conflicts between nations, it is likewise necessary to bear in mind the case where the appeal to arms has been brought about by events which their care was unable to avert;

Animated by the desire to serve, even in this extreme case, the interests of humanity and the ever progressive needs of civilization;

Thinking it important, with this object, to revise the general laws and customs of war, either with a view to defining them with greater precision or to confining them within such limits as would mitigate their severity as far as possible;

Have deemed it necessary to complete and explain in certain particulars the work of the First Peace Conference, which, following on the Brussels Conference of 1874, and inspired by the ideas dictated by a wise and generous forethought, adopted provisions intended to define and govern the usages of war on land.

According to the views of the High Contracting Parties, these provisions, the wording of which has been inspired by the desire to diminish the evils of war, as far as military requirements permit, are intended to serve as a general rule of conduct for the belligerents in their mutual relations and in their relations with the inhabitants.

It has not, however, been found possible at present to concert regulations covering all the circumstances which arise in practice;

On the other hand, the High Contracting Parties clearly do not intend that unforeseen cases should, in the absence of a written undertaking, be left to the arbitrary judgment of military commanders.

Until a more complete code of the laws of war has been issued, the High Contracting Parties deem it expedient to declare that, in cases not included in the Regulations adopted by them, the inhabitants and the belligerents remain under the protection and the rule of the principles of the law of nations, as they result from the usages established among civilized peoples, from the laws of humanity, and the dictates of the public conscience.

They declare that it is in this sense especially that Articles 1 and 2 of the Regulations adopted must be understood.

The High Contracting Parties, wishing to conclude a fresh Convention to this effect, have appointed the following as their Plenipotentiaries:

(Here follow the names of Plenipotentiaries)

Who, after having deposited their full powers, found in good and due form, have agreed upon the following:

Article 1
The Contracting Powers shall issue instructions to their armed land forces which shall be in conformity with the Regulations respecting the Laws and Customs of War on Land, annexed to the present Convention.

Article 2
The provisions contained in the Regulations referred to in Article 1, as well as in the present Convention, do not apply except between Contracting Powers, and then only if all the belligerents are parties to the Convention.

Article 3
A belligerent party which violates the provisions of the said Regulations shall, if the case demands, be liable to pay compensation. It shall be responsible for all acts committed by persons forming part of its armed forces.

Article 4
The present Convention, duly ratified, shall as between the Contracting Powers, be substituted for the Convention of the 29th July, 1899, respecting the Laws and Customs of War on Land.

The Convention of 1899 remains in force as between the Powers which signed it, and which do not also ratify the present Convention.

Article 5
The present Convention shall be ratified as soon as possible.

The ratifications shall be deposited at The Hague.

The first deposit of ratifications shall be recorded in a *procès-verbal* signed by the Representatives of the Powers which take part therein and by the Netherland Minister for Foreign Affairs.

The subsequent deposits of ratifications shall be made by means of a written notification, addressed to the Netherland Government and accompanied by the instrument of ratification.

A duly certified copy of the *procès-verbal* relative to the first deposit of ratifications, of the notifications mentioned in the preceding paragraph, as well as of the instruments of ratification, shall be immediately sent by the Netherland Government, through the diplomatic channel, to the Powers invited to the Second Peace Conference, as well as to the other Powers which have adhered to the Convention. In the cases contemplated in the preceding paragraph the said Government shall at the same time inform them of the date on which it received the notification.

Article 6
Non-Signatory Powers may adhere to the present Convention.

The Power which desires to adhere notifies in writing its intention to the Netherland Government, forwarding to it the act of adhesion, which shall be deposited in the archives of the said Government.

This Government shall at once transmit to all the other Powers a duly certified copy of the notification as well as of the act of adhesion, mentioning the date on which it received the notification.

Article 7
The present Convention shall come into force, in the case of the Powers which were a party to the first deposit of ratifications, sixty days after the date of the *procès-verbal* of this deposit, and, in the case of the Powers which ratify subsequently or which adhere, sixty days after the notification of their ratification or of their adhesion has been received by the Netherland Government.

Article 8
In the event of one of the Contracting Powers wishing to denounce the present Convention, the denunciation shall be notified in writing to the Netherland Government, which shall at once communicate a duly certified copy of the notification to all the other Powers, informing them of the date on which it was received.

The denunciation shall only have effect in regard to the notifying Power, and one year after the notification has reached the Netherland Government.

Article 9
A register kept by the Netherland Ministry for Foreign Affairs shall give the date of the deposit of ratifications made in virtue of Article 5, paragraphs 3 and 4, as well as the date on which the notifications of

adhesion (Article 6, paragraph 2) or of denunciation (Article 8, paragraph 1) were received.

Each Contracting Power is entitled to have access to this register and to be supplied with duly certified extracts.

In faith whereof the Plenipotentiaries have appended their signatures to the present Convention.

Done at The Hague, the 18th October, 1907, in a single copy, which shall remain deposited in the archives of the Netherland Government, and duly certified copies of which shall be sent, through the diplomatic channel, to the Powers which have been invited to the Second Peace Conference.

[The following states signed the convention October 18, 1907:]

Argentina	Luxembourg
Austria-Hungary (Res.)[1]	Mexico
Belgium	Montenegro (Res.)
Bolivia	The Netherlands
Brazil	Norway
Bulgaria	Panama
Chile	Paraguay
Colombia	Persia
Republic of Cuba	Peru
Denmark	Portugal
Dominican Republic	Romania
Ecuador	Russia (Res.)
El Salvador	Serbia
France	Siam
Germany (Res.)	Sweden
Great Britain	Switzerland
Greece	Turkey (Res.)
Guatemala	United States of America
Haiti	Uruguay
Italy	Venezuela
Japan (Res.)	

ANNEX TO THE CONVENTION
REGULATIONS RESPECTING THE LAWS AND CUSTOMS OF WAR ON LAND

Section 2. Hostilities
Chapter 1. Means of Injuring the Enemy, Sieges, and Bombardments

Article 27
In sieges and bombardments all necessary steps must be taken to spare, as far as possible, buildings dedicated to religion, art, science, or charitable purposes, historic monuments, hospitals, and places where the sick and wounded are collected, provided they are not being used at the time for military purposes.

It is the duty of the besieged to indicate the presence of such buildings or places by distinctive and visible signs, which shall be notified to the enemy beforehand.

Article 28
The pillage of a town or place, even when taken by assault, is prohibited.

Section 3. Military Authority over the Territory of the Hostile State

Article 46
Family honour and rights, the lives of persons, and private property, as well as religious convictions and practice, must be respected.

Private property cannot be confiscated.

Article 47
Pillage is formally forbidden.

Article 53
An army of occupation can only take possession of cash, funds, and realizable securities which are strictly the property of the State, depôts of arms, means of transport, stores and supplies, and, generally, all movable property belonging to the State which may be used for military operations.

All appliances, whether on land, at sea, or in the air, adapted for the transmission of news, or for the transport of persons or things, exclusive of cases governed by naval law, depôts of arms, and, generally, all kinds of ammunition of war, may be seized, even if they belong to private individuals, but must be restored and compensation fixed when peace is made.

Article 55
The occupying State shall be regarded only as administrator and usufructuary of public buildings, real estate, forests, and agricultural estates belonging to the hostile State, and situated in the occupied country. It must safeguard the capital of these properties, and administer them in accordance with the rules of usufruct.

Article 56
The property of municipalities, that of institutions dedicated to religion, charity and education, the arts and sciences, even when State property, shall be treated as private property.

All seizure of, destruction or wilful damage done to institutions of this character, historic monuments, works of art and science, is forbidden, and should be made the subject of legal proceedings.

---

*   Convention Respecting the Laws and Customs of War on Land, Oct. 18, 1907, 36 Stat. 2277; 1 Bevans 631.
1. "Res." refers to states that signed under reservations.

Appendix 4

TREATY OF PEACE WITH GERMANY*
Also known as the "Treaty of Versailles"
(Preamble; Part 8, Section 1: Articles 231–38, and Section 2: Articles 245–47)

Signed at Versailles, June 28, 1919; entry into force, January 10, 1920

The United States of America, the British Empire, France, Italy and Japan,

These Powers being described in the present Treaty as the Principal Allied and Associated Powers,

Belgium, Bolivia, Brazil, China, Cuba, Ecuador, Greece, Guatemala, Haiti, the Hedjaz, Honduras, Liberia, Nicaragua, Panama, Peru, Poland, Portugal, Roumania, the Serb-Croat-Slovene State, Siam, Czecho-Slovakia and Uruguay,

These Powers constituting with the Principal Powers mentioned above the Allied and Associated Powers, of the one part;

And Germany, of the other part;

Bearing in mind that on the request of the Imperial German Government an Armistice was granted on November 11, 1918, to Germany by the Principal Allied and Associated Powers in order that a Treaty of Peace might be concluded with her, and

The Allied and Associated Powers being equally desirous that the war in which they were successively involved directly or indirectly and which originated in the declaration of war by Austria-Hungary on July 28, 1914, against Serbia, the declaration of war by Germany against Russia on August 1, 1914, and against France on August 3, 1914, and in the invasion of Belgium, should be replaced by a firm, just and durable Peace,

For this purpose the High Contracting Parties represented as follows:

(Here follow the names of Plenipotentiaries)

Who having communicated their full powers found in good and due form have agreed as follows:

From the coming into force of the present Treaty the state of war will terminate. From that moment and subject to the provisions of this Treaty official relations with Germany, and with any of the German States, will be resumed by the Allied and Associated Powers.

PART 8. REPARATION

Section 1. General Provisions

Article 231
The Allied and Associated Governments affirm and Germany accepts the responsibility of Germany and her allies for causing all the loss and damage to which the Allied and Associated Governments and their nationals have been subjected as a consequence of the war imposed upon them by the aggression of Germany and her allies.

Article 232
The Allied and Associated Governments recognize that the resources of Germany are not adequate, after taking into account permanent diminutions of such resources which will result from other provisions of the present Treaty, to make complete reparation for all such loss and damage.

The Allied and Associated Governments, however, require, and Germany undertakes, that she will make compensation for all damage done to the civilian population of the Allied and Associated Powers and to their property during the period of the belligerency of each as an Allied or Associated Power against Germany by such aggression by land, by sea and from the air, and in general all damage as defined in Annex 1 hereto.

In accordance with Germany's pledges, already given, as to complete restoration for Belgium, Germany undertakes, in addition to the compensation for damage elsewhere in this Part provided for, as a consequence of the violation of the Treaty of 1839, to make reimbursement of all sums which Belgium has borrowed from the Allied and Associated Governments up to November 11, 1918, together with interest at the rate of five per cent. (5%) per annum on such sums. This amount shall be determined by the Reparation Commission, and the German Government undertakes thereupon forthwith to make a special issue of bearer bonds to an equivalent amount payable in marks gold, on May 1, 1926, or, at the option of the German Government, on the 1st of May in any year up to 1926. Subject to the foregoing, the form of such bonds shall be determined by the Reparation Commission. Such bonds shall be handed over to the Reparation Commission, which has authority to take and acknowledge receipt thereof on behalf of Belgium.

Article 233
The amount of the above damage for which compensation is to be made by Germany shall be determined by an Inter-Allied Commission, to be called the Reparation Commission and constituted in the form and with the powers set forth hereunder and in Annexes 2 to 7 inclusive hereto.

This Commission shall consider the claims and give to the German Government a just opportunity to be heard.

The findings of the Commission as to the amount of damage defined as above shall be concluded and notified to the German Government on or before May 1, 1921, as representing the extent of that Government's obligations.

The Commission shall concurrently draw up a schedule of payments prescribing the time and manner for securing and discharging the entire obligation within a period of thirty years from May 1, 1921. If, however, within the period mentioned, Germany fails to discharge her obligations, any balance remaining unpaid may, within the discretion of the Commission, be postponed for settlement in subsequent years, or may be handled otherwise in such manner as the Allied and Associated Governments, acting in accordance with the procedure laid down in this Part of the present Treaty, shall determine.

Article 234
The Reparation Commission shall after May 1, 1921, from time to time, consider the resources and capacity of Germany, and, after giving her representatives a just opportunity to be heard, shall have discretion to extend the date, and to modify the form of payments, such as are to be provided for in accordance with Article 233; but not to cancel any part, except with the specific authority of the several Governments represented upon the Commission.

Article 235
In order to enable the Allied and Associated Powers to proceed at once to the restoration of their industrial and economic life, pending the full determination of their claims, Germany shall pay in such instalments and in such manner (whether in gold, commodities, ships, securities or otherwise) as the Reparation Commission may fix, during 1919, 1920 and the first four months of 1921, the equivalent of 20,000,000,000 gold marks. Out of this sum the expenses of the armies of occupation subsequent to the Armistice of November 11, 1918, shall first be met, and such supplies of food and raw materials as may be judged by the Governments of the Principal Allied and Associated Powers to be essential to enable Germany to meet her obligations for reparation may also, with the approval of the said Governments, be paid for out of the above sum. The balance shall be reckoned towards liquidation of the amounts due for reparation. Germany shall further deposit bonds as prescribed in paragraph 12 (c) of Annex 2 hereto.

Article 236
Germany further agrees to the direct application of her economic resources to reparation as specified in Annexes 3, 4, 5, and 6, relating respectively to merchant shipping, to physical restoration, to coal and derivatives of coal, and to dyestuffs and other chemical products; provided always that the value of the property transferred and any services rendered by her under these Annexes, assessed in the manner therein prescribed, shall be credited to her towards liquidation of her obligations under the above Articles.

Article 237
The successive instalments, including the above sum, paid over by Germany in satisfaction of the above claims will be divided by the Allied and Associated Governments in proportions which have been determined upon by them in advance on a basis of general equity and of the rights of each.

For the purposes of this division the value of property transferred and services rendered under Article 243, and under Annexes 3, 4, 5, 6, and 7, shall be reckoned in the same manner as cash payments effected in that year.

Article 238
In addition to the payments mentioned above Germany shall effect, in accordance with the procedure laid down by the Reparation Commission, restitution in cash of cash taken away, seized or sequestrated, and also restitution of animals, objects of every nature and securities taken away, seized or sequestrated, in the cases in which it proves possible to identify them in territory belonging to Germany or her allies.

Until this procedure is laid down, restitution will continue in accordance with the provisions of the Armistice of November 11, 1918, and its renewals and the Protocols thereto.

Section 2. Special Provisions

Article 245
Within six months after the coming into force of the present Treaty the German Government must restore to the French Government the trophies, archives, historical souvenirs or works of art carried away from France by the German authorities in the course of the war of 1870–1871 and during this last war, in accordance with a list which will be communicated to it by the French Government; particularly the French flags taken in the course of the war of 1870–1871 and all the political papers taken by the German authorities on October 10, 1870, at the chateau of Cerçay, near Brunoy (Seine-et-Oise) belonging at the time to Mr. Rouher, formerly Minister of State.

Article 246
Within six months from the coming into force of the present Treaty, Germany will restore to His Majesty the King of the Hedjaz the original Koran of the Caliph Othman, which was removed from Medina by the Turkish authorities and is stated to have been presented to the ex-Emperor William II.

Within the same period Germany will hand over to His Britannic Majesty's Government the skull of the Sultan Mkwawa which was removed from the Protectorate of German East Africa and taken to Germany.

The delivery of the articles above referred to will be effected in such place and in such conditions as may be laid down by the Governments to which they are to be restored.

Article 247
Germany undertakes to furnish to the University of Louvain, within three months after a request made by it and transmitted through the intervention of the Reparation Commission, manuscripts, incunabula, printed books, maps and objects of collection corresponding in number and value to those destroyed in the burning by Germany of the Library of Louvain. All details regarding such replacement will be determined by the Reparation Commission.

Germany undertakes to deliver to Belgium, through the Reparation Commission, within six months of the coming into force of the present Treaty, in order to enable Belgium to reconstitute two great artistic works:
1. The leaves of the triptych of the Mystic Lamb painted by the Van Eyck brothers, formerly in the Church of St. Bavon at Ghent, now in the Berlin Museum;
2. The leaves of the triptych of the Last Supper, painted by Dierick Bouts, formerly in the Church of St. Peter at Louvain, two of which are now in the Berlin Museum and two in the Old Pinakothek at Munich.

[The following states signed the treaty June 28, 1919:]

Australia (R)[1]	Honduras
Belgium (R)	Italy (R)
Bolivia	Japan (R)
Brazil	Liberia
British India (R)	New Zealand (R)
Canada (R)	Nicaragua
Czechoslovakia (R)	Panama
Ecuador	Poland (R)
France (R)	Portugal
Germany (R)	Romania
Greece	South Africa (R)
Guatemala	Uruguay
Haiti	United States of America
Hedjaz	Yugoslavia (R)

* Treaty of Peace with Germany, June 28, 1919, T.S. 658; 2 Bevans 43.
1. "R" refers to states that subsequently ratified the treaty.

Appendix 5

TREATY OF PEACE BETWEEN THE ALLIED AND ASSOCIATED POWERS AND AUSTRIA*
Also known as the "Treaty of St. Germain"
(Preamble; Part 8, Section 1: Article 184, and Section 2: Articles 191–93, 195–96)

Signed at St. Germain-en-Laye, September 10, 1919; entry into force, November 8, 1921

The United States of America, the British Empire, France, Italy and Japan,

These Powers being described in the present Treaty as the Principal Allied and Associated Powers;

Belgium, China, Cuba, Greece, Nicaragua, Panama, Poland, Portugal, Roumania, the Serb-Croat-Slovene State, Siam, Czecho-Slovakia,

These Powers constituting, with the Principal Powers mentioned above, the Allied and Associated Powers, of the one part;

And Austria, of the other part;

Whereas on the request of the former Imperial and Royal Austro-Hungarian Government an Armistice was granted to Austria-Hungary on November 3, 1918, by the Principal Allied and Associated Powers in order that a Treaty of Peace might be concluded, and

Whereas the Allied and Associated Powers are equally desirous that the war in which certain among them were successively involved, directly or indirectly, against Austria-Hungary, and which originated in the declaration of war against Serbia on July 28, 1914, by the former Imperial and Royal Austro-Hungarian Government, and in the hostilities conducted by Germany in alliance with Austria-Hungary, should be replaced by a firm, just and durable Peace, and

Whereas the former Austro-Hungarian Monarchy has now ceased to exist, and has been replaced in Austria by a republican government, and

Whereas the Principal Allied and Associated Powers have already recognized that the Czecho-Slovak State, in which are incorporated certain portions of the said Monarchy, is a free, independent and allied State, and

Whereas the said Powers have also recognized the union of certain portions of the said Monarchy with the territory of the Kingdom of Serbia as a free, independent and allied State, under the name of the Serb-Croat-Slovene State, and

Whereas it is necessary, while restoring peace, to regulate the situation which has arisen from the dissolution of the said Monarchy and the formation of the said States, and to establish the government of these countries on a firm foundation of justice and equity;

For this purpose the High Contracting Parties represented as follows:

(Here follow the names of Plenipotentiaries)

Who, having communicated their full powers, found in good and due form, have agreed as follows:

From the coming into force of the present Treaty the state of war will terminate.

Austria is recognized under the name of the "Republic of Austria."

From that moment, and subject to the provisions of the present Treaty, official relations will exist between the Allied and Associated Powers and the Republic of Austria.

PART 8. REPARATION

Section 1. General Provisions

Article 184
In addition to the payments mentioned above, Austria shall effect, in accordance with the procedure laid down by the Reparation Commission, restitution in cash of cash taken away, seized or sequestrated, and also restitution of animals, objects of every nature and securities taken away, seized or sequestrated in the cases in which it proves possible to identify them on territory belonging to, or during the execution of the present Treaty in the possession of, Austria or her allies.

Section 2. Special Provisions

Article 191
In carrying out the provisions of Article 184 Austria undertakes to surrender to each of the Allied and Associated Powers respectively all records, documents, objects of antiquity and of art, and all scientific and bibliographical material taken away from the invaded territories, whether they belong to the State or to provincial, communal, charitable or ecclesiastical administrations or other public or private institutions.

Article 192
Austria shall in the same manner restore objects of the same nature as those referred to in the preceding Article which may have been taken away since June 1, 1914, from the ceded territories, with the exception of objects bought from private owners.

The Reparation Commission will apply to these objects the provisions of Article 208, of Part 9 (Financial Clauses) of the present Treaty, if these are appropriate.

Article 193
Austria will give up to each of the Allied and Associated Governments respectively all the records, documents and historical material possessed by public institutions which may have a direct bearing on the history of the ceded territories and which have been removed during the last ten years. This last-mentioned period, as far as concerns Italy, shall be extended to the date of the proclamation of the Kingdom (1861).

The new States arising out of the former Austro-Hungarian Monarchy and the States which receive part of the territory of that Monarchy undertake on their part to hand over to Austria the records, documents and material dating from a period not exceeding twenty years which have a direct bearing on the history or administration of the territory of Austria and which may be found in the territories transferred.

Article 195
Within a period of twelve months after the coming into force of the present Treaty a Committee of three jurists appointed by the Reparation Commission shall examine the conditions under which the objects or manuscripts in possession of Austria, enumerated in Annex 1 hereto, were carried off by the House of Hapsburg and by the other Houses which have reigned in Italy. If it is found that the said objects or manuscripts were carried off in violation of the rights of the Italian provinces the Reparation Commission, on the report of the Committee referred to, shall order their restitution. Italy and Austria agree to accept the decisions of the Commission.

Belgium, Poland and Czecho-Slovakia may also submit claims for restitution, to be examined by the same Committee of three jurists, relating to the objects and documents enumerated in Annexes 2, 3, and 4 hereto. Belgium, Poland, Czecho-Slovakia and Austria undertake to accept the decisions taken by the Reparation Commission as the result of the report of the said Committee.

Article 196

With regard to all objects of artistic, archaeological, scientific or historic character forming part of collections which formerly belonged to the Government or the Crown of the Austro-Hungarian Monarchy and are not otherwise provided for in this present Treaty, Austria undertakes:

(a) To negotiate, when required, with the States concerned for an amicable arrangement whereby any portion thereof or any objects belonging thereto which ought to form part of the intellectual patrimony of the ceded districts may be returned to their districts of origin on terms of reciprocity, and

(b) For twenty years, unless a special arrangement is previously arrived at, not to alienate or disperse any of the said collections or to dispose of any of the above objects but at all times to ensure their safety and good condition and to make them available, together with inventories, catalogues and administrative documents relating to the said collections, at all reasonable times to students who are nationals of any of the Allied and Associated Powers.

---

* Treaty of Peace Between the Allied and Associated Powers and Austria, Sept. 10, 1919, T.S. 659; 112 B.F.S.P. 317.

Appendix 6

TREATY OF PEACE BETWEEN THE ALLIED POWERS AND HUNGARY*

Also known as the "Treaty of Trianon"

(Preamble; Part 8, Section 1: Article 168, and Section 2: Articles 175–78)

Signed at Trianon, June 4, 1920; entry into force, December 17, 1921

The United States of America, the British Empire, France, Italy and Japan,

These Powers being described in the present Treaty as the Principal Allied and Associated Powers,

Belgium, China, Cuba, Greece, Nicaragua, Panama, Poland, Portugal, Roumania, the Serb-Croat-Slovene State, Siam, and Czecho-Slovakia,

These Powers constituting with the Principal Powers mentioned above the Allied and Associated Powers, of the one part;

And Hungary, of the other part;

Whereas on the request of the former Imperial and Royal Austro-Hungarian Government an Armistice was granted to Austria-Hungary on November 3, 1918, by the Principal Allied and Associated Powers, and completed as regards Hungary by the Military Convention of November 13, 1918, in order that a Treaty of Peace might be concluded, and

Whereas the Allied and Associated Powers are equally desirous that the war in which certain among them were successively involved, directly or indirectly, against Austria-Hungary, and which originated in the declaration of war by the former Imperial and Royal Austro-Hungarian Government on July 28, 1914, against Serbia, and in the hostilities conducted by Germany in alliance with Austria-Hungary, should be replaced by a firm, just, and durable Peace, and

Whereas the former Austro-Hungarian Monarchy has now ceased to exist, and has been replaced in Hungary by a national Hungarian Government:

For this purpose the High Contracting Parties have appointed as their Plenipotentiaries:

(Here follow the names of Plenipotentiaries)

Who, having communicated their full powers found in good and due form, have agreed as follows:

From the coming into force of the present Treaty the state of war will terminate.

From that moment and subject to the provisions of the present Treaty official relations will exist between the Allied and Associated Powers and Hungary.

PART 8. REPARATION

Section 1. General Provisions

Article 168

In addition to the payments mentioned above, Hungary shall effect, in accordance with the procedure laid down by the Reparation Commission, restitution in cash of cash taken away, seized or sequestrated, and also restitution of animals, objects of every nature and securities taken away, seized or sequestrated in the cases in which it proves possible to identify them on territory belonging to, or during the execution of the present Treaty in the possession of, Hungary or her allies.

Section 2. Special Provisions

Article 175

In carrying out the provisions of Article 168, Hungary undertakes to surrender to each of the Allied and Associated Powers respectively all records, documents, objects of antiquity and of art, and all scientific and bibliographical material taken away from the invaded territories, whether they belong to the State or to provincial, communal, charitable or ecclesiastical administrations or other public or private institutions.

Article 176

Hungary shall in the same manner restore objects of the same nature as those referred to in Article 175 which may have been taken away since June 1, 1914, from the ceded territories, with the exception of objects bought from private owners.

The Reparation Commission will apply to these objects the provisions of Article 191, Part 9 (Financial Clauses), of the present Treaty, if these are appropriate.

Article 177

Hungary will give up to each of the Allied and Associated Governments respectively all the records, documents and historical material possessed by public institutions which may have a direct bearing on the history of the ceded territories and which have been removed since January 1, 1868. This last-mentioned period, as far as concerns Italy, shall be extended to the date of the proclamation of the Kingdom (1861).

With regard to all objects or documents of an artistic, archaeological, scientific or historic character forming part of collections which formerly belonged to the Government or the Crown of the Austro-Hungarian Monarchy and are not otherwise provided for in the present Treaty, Hungary undertakes:

(a) To negotiate, when required, with the States concerned for an amicable arrangement whereby any portion thereof or any objects or documents belonging thereto which ought to form part of the intellectual patrimony of the said States may be returned to their country of origin on terms of reciprocity, and

(b) For twenty years, unless a special arrangement is previously arrived at, not to alienate or disperse any of the said collections or to dispose of any of the above objects, but at all times to ensure their safety and good condition and to make them available, together with inventories, catalogues and administrative documents relating to the said collections, at all reasonable times to students who are nationals of any of the Allied and Associated Powers.

Reciprocally, Hungary will be entitled to apply to the said States, particularly to Austria, in order to negotiate, in the conditions mentioned above, the necessary arrangements for the return to Hungary of the collections, documents and objects referred to above, to which the guarantees referred to in paragraph (b) will apply.

Article 178

The new States arising out of the former Austro-Hungarian Monarchy and the States which receive part of the territory of that Monarchy undertake to give up to the Hungarian Government the records, documents and material dating from a period not exceeding twenty years which have a direct bearing on the history or administration of the territory of Hungary and which may be found in the territories transferred.

---

* Treaty of Peace Between the Allied Powers and Hungary, June 4, 1920, T.S. 660; 113 B.F.S.P. 486.

Appendix 7

TREATY OF PEACE BETWEEN POLAND, RUSSIA, AND THE UKRAINE*
Also known as the "Treaty of Riga"
(Preamble; Article 11)

Signed at Riga, March 18, 1921; entered into force upon signature

Poland, of the one hand, and Russia and the Ukraine, of the other, being desirous of putting an end to the war and of concluding a final, lasting and honorable peace based on a mutual understanding and in accordance with the peace preliminaries signed at Riga on October 12, 1920, have decided to enter into negotiations and have appointed for this purpose as plenipotentiaries:

(Here follow the names of Plenipotentiaries)

Article 11

1. Russia and the Ukraine shall restore to Poland the following objects which were removed from the territory of the Polish Republic to Russia and the Ukraine subsequent to January 1, 1772.
   (a) all war trophies (e.g., flags, colours, military insignia of all kinds, cannons, weapons, regimental and other insignia), together with the trophies taken from the Polish nation after 1792, during the struggle for independence which was maintained by Poland against Czarist Russia. Nevertheless, trophies of the Polish-Russo-Ukrainian war of 1918–1921 shall not be restored.
   (b) libraries, archaeological collections and archives, collections of works of art, collections of any nature and objects of historical, national, artistic, archaeological, scientific and general educational value.
   The collections of objects included under letters (a) and (b) of this paragraph shall be restored irrespective of the conditions under which, and the pretexts upon which they were carried off and irrespective of the authorities responsible for such removal and without regard to the person whether physical or legal to whom they belonged prior to, or subsequent to their removal.
2. The obligation to make restitution shall not apply to:
   (a) objects carried off from the territories situated on the east of the frontiers of Poland, as determined by the present Treaty, in so far as it shall be proved that such objects are a product of White-Ruthenian or Ukrainian civilisation, and that they were subsequently removed to Poland otherwise than as the result of a voluntary transaction or of succession;
   (b) objects which passed from the possession of their legal owner into Russian or Ukrainian territory as the result of a voluntary transaction or of succession, or were removed to the territories of Russia and the Ukraine by their legal owner.
3. If there exists in Poland any collections or objects falling within the class specified in letters (a) and (b) of § 1 of this Article, which have been removed from Russia or the Ukraine during the same period, such collections and objects shall be restored to Russia and the Ukraine under the conditions laid down in § 1 and § 2 of this Article.
4. Russia and the Ukraine shall restore to Poland objects carried off from the territory of the Polish Republic subsequent to January 1, 1772, which relate to the territory of the Polish Republic, such as archives, registers, extracts from archives, deeds, documents, maps, plans, sketches, together with plates and discs, seals, etc., of all State institutions and self-governing, private and ecclesiastical institutions.

Nevertheless, such of the above-mentioned objects as although not exclusively connected with the territory of the present Polish Republic, cannot be divided up, shall be restored in their entirety to Poland.

5. Russia and the Ukraine shall hand over the archives, registers, extracts from archives, deeds, documents, maps, plans and sketches belonging to legislative institutions and central, provincial and local organisations of all ministries, services, administrations, autonomous bodies and private and public institutions, which date from the period between January 1, 1772, and November 9, 1918—the period during which Russia administered the territory of the Polish Republic—in so far as such objects relate to the territory of the present Polish Republic and are actually within the territories of Russia and the Ukraine.

If objects referred to in the same paragraph which are of special interest to territories remaining part of Russia or the Ukraine exist in Poland, the latter country undertakes to restore such objects to Russia and the Ukraine, under the same conditions.

6. The provisions of § 5 of this Article shall not apply to:
   (a) archives, registers, etc., relating to operations subsequent to 1876 which were carried on by the former Czarist authorities against the revolutionary movements in Poland, until such time as a special convention shall be concluded between the two Parties as to the restitution of such objects to Poland;
   (b) objects of a secret military nature relating to the period subsequent to 1870.

7. The two Contracting Parties fully recognise that the value of systematic, scientifically prepared and complete collections, such as form a fundamental part of collections of world-wide scientific importance, ought in no way to be impaired and accordingly agree to the following provisions: should the handing over of a certain object, which is to be restored to Poland, under § 1 (b) of this article, prove likely to impair the completeness of such a collection, such object shall, save where it is closely bound up with the history and culture of Poland, remain on the spot, subject to the approval of both Parties represented on the Mixed Commission referred to in § 15 of the present article; it shall in that case be exchanged for an object of the same artistic or scientific value.

8. The two Contracting Parties declare themselves ready to conclude special Conventions concerning the restitution, purchase, or exchange of objects included in the categories defined in § 1 (b) of this Article, if these objects shall have been transferred from the territory of one Party to that of the other as the result of a voluntary transaction, or of succession, in so far as such objects are the product of the scientific, artistic, etc., activities of the Party concerned.

9. Russia and the Ukraine agree to make restitution to Poland of such of the following objects as belong to the State or to National institutions, autonomous bodies, private or public institutions, and in general to all legal and physical persons, and were taken with or without consent into Russia and the Ukraine from the territory of the Polish Republic after August 1st, 1914, that is to say, in the period from the outbreak of the great war until October 1, 1915:
   (a) archives, acts, documents, registers, account books and mercantile books, journals and correspondence, geodesic and land surveying instruments, photographic plates and negatives, seals, maps, plans and drawings with corresponding sketches and scales, with the exception of objects referring to military matters of a secret nature which belong to military institutions;
   (b) libraries, collections of books, collections of archives and objets d'art and their inventories, catalogues and bibliographical material, works of art, antiquities, all collections and objects of historical, national, artistic or scientific interest, bells and objects belonging to any religious denomination;
   (c) scientific and scholastic laboratories, collections of all kinds, scholastic and scientific accessories, instruments and apparatus and all auxiliary and experimental material.

It shall be permissible to make restitution of the individual objects referred to under the heading (c) of this paragraph or to replace them by an equivalent object to be decided upon by agreement between the two Parties represented on the mixed Committee provided for in § 15 of this article. Objects, however, which date from a period prior to 1870 or which have been offered by the Poles may only be replaced by a suitable equivalent after agreement between the two Parties represented on the aforementioned mixed Committee.

10. The two Contracting Parties undertake reciprocally to make restitution in a similar manner of collections and objects specified in § 9 of this article, taken with or without consent from the territory of the other Party after October 1, 1915.

11. Restitution shall be made of objects specified in §§ 9 and 10 of this article which are not the property of the State or State institutions upon the request of the Governments, made in accordance with the declarations of the owners, in order that such objects may be restored to the owners.

12. Restitution shall be made of the objects specified in §§ 9 and 10 of this article in so far as they are or may be actually in the possession of State institutions or private institutions belonging to the State which makes restitution. The obligation to prove that the object has been lost or destroyed shall rest with the State making restitution.

If the objects enumerated in §§ 9 and 10 of this article are in the possession of third persons, legal or physical, these persons shall be obliged to deliver them up with a view to their restitution. Upon the request of the owner, such of the objects enumerated in §§ 9 and 10 of this article, as may be already in his possession, shall also be restored.

13. The State making restitution shall pay the expenses incurred in connection with the return and the restitution of the objects within the limits of its own territory as far as the frontier.

The return and the restitution of objects shall be made notwithstanding prohibitions or restrictions on export, and such objects shall not be liable to any duty or any tax.

14. Each of the Contracting Parties agrees to return to the other Party property of an educational or artistic value given or bequeathed before November 7, 1917 (New Style) to their own State or to the private, scientific and artistic institutions within that State by individuals or public bodies of the other Party in so far as such gifts or bequests have been made in conformity with the laws of the said State.

The two Contracting Parties reserve the right of concluding special Conventions with regard to the aforementioned gifts and bequests made after November 7, 1917.

15. For the purpose of putting into force the provisions of this article, a special mixed paritary Commission shall be established within a period of six months at the latest of the ratifications of this Treaty, and shall sit at Moscow; this Commission shall be composed of three representatives of each Party and such experts as may be required.

In the exercise of its duties the Commission shall conform to the instructions contained in Annex No. 3 of this Treaty.

---

* Treaty of Peace Between Poland, Russia, and the Ukraine, Mar. 18, 1921, 6 L.N.T.S. 123.

Appendix 8

TREATY ON THE PROTECTION OF ARTISTIC AND SCIENTIFIC INSTITUTIONS AND HISTORIC MONUMENTS*
Also known as the "Roerich Pact"

Signed at Washington, D.C., April 15, 1935; entry into force, August 26, 1935

The High Contracting Parties, animated by the purpose of giving conventional form to the postulates of the Resolution approved on December 16, 1933, by all the States represented at the Seventh International Conference of American States, held at Montevideo, which recommended to "the Governments of America which have not yet done so that they sign the 'Roerich Pact,' initiated by the Roerich Museum in the United States, and which has as its object, the universal adoption of a flag, already designed and generally known, in order thereby to preserve in any time of danger all nationally and privately owned immovable monuments which form the cultural treasure of peoples," have resolved to conclude a treaty with that end in view, and to the effect that the treasures of culture be respected and protected in time of war and in peace, have agreed upon the following articles:

Article 1
The historic monuments, museums, scientific, artistic, educational and cultural institutions shall be considered as neutral and as such respected and protected by belligerents.

The same respect and protection shall be due to the personnel of the institutions mentioned above.

The same respect and protection shall be accorded to the historic monuments, museums, scientific, artistic, educational and cultural institutions in time of peace as well as in war.

Article 2
The neutrality of, and protection and respect due to, the monuments and institutions mentioned in the preceding article, shall be recognized in the entire expanse of territories subject to the sovereignty of each of the signatory and acceding States, without any discrimination as to the State allegiance of said monuments and institutions. The respective Governments agree to adopt the measures of internal legislation necessary to insure said protection and respect.

Article 3
In order to identify the monuments and institutions mentioned in Article 1, use may be made of a distinctive flag (red circle with a triple red sphere in the circle on a white background) in accordance with the model attached to this treaty.

Article 4
The signatory Governments and those which accede to this treaty, shall send to the Pan American Union, at the time of signature or accession, or at any time thereafter, a list of the monuments and institutions for which they desire the protection agreed to in this treaty.

The Pan American Union, when notifying the Governments of signatures or accessions, shall also send the list of monuments and institutions mentioned in this article, and shall inform the other Governments of any changes in said list.

Article 5
The monuments and institutions mentioned in Article 1 shall cease to enjoy the privileges recognized in the present treaty in case they are made use of for military purposes.

Article 6
The States which do not sign the present treaty on the date it is opened for signature, may sign or adhere to it at any time.

Article 7
The instruments of accession, as well as those of ratification and denunciation of the present treaty, shall be deposited with the Pan American Union, which shall communicate notice of the act of deposit to the other signatory or acceding States.

Article 8
The present treaty may be denounced at any time by any of the signatory or acceding States, and the denunciation shall go into effect three months after notice of it has been given to the other signatory or acceding States.

In witness whereof, the undersigned Plenipotentiaries, after having deposited their full powers found to be in due and proper form, sign this treaty on behalf of their respective governments, and affix thereto their seals, on the dates appearing opposite their signatures.

[The following states signed the treaty on April 15, 1935:]

Argentine Republic	Haiti
Bolivia	Honduras
Brazil	Mexico
Chile	Nicaragua
Colombia	Panama
Costa Rica	Paraguay
Cuba	Peru
Dominican Republic	United States of America
Ecuador	Uruguay
El Salvador	Venezuela
Guatemala	

And whereas the said Treaty has been duly ratified by the United States of America, whose instrument of ratification was deposited with the Pan American Union on July 13, 1935;

And whereas the said Treaty has been duly ratified also by the Republic of Cuba, whose instrument of ratification was deposited with the Pan American Union on August 26, 1935;

Now, therefore, be it known that I, Franklin D. Roosevelt, President of the United States of America, have caused the said Treaty to be made public to the end that the same and every article and clause thereof may be observed and fulfilled with good faith by the United States of America and the citizens thereof.

In testimony whereof, I have caused the Seal of the United States of America to be hereunto affixed.

Done at the city of Washington this twenty-fifth day of October in the year of our Lord one thousand nine hundred and thirty-five, and of the Independence of the United States of America the one hundred and sixtieth.

Franklin D. Roosevelt

By the President:
Cordell Hull
Secretary of State

---

* Treaty on the Protection of Artistic and Scientific Institutions and Historic Monuments, Apr. 15, 1935, 49 Stat. 3267; 167 L.N.T.S. 279.

Appendix 9

INTER-ALLIED DECLARATION AGAINST ACTS OF DISPOSSESSION COMMITTED IN TERRITORIES UNDER ENEMY OCCUPATION OR CONTROL*
Also known as the "Declaration of London"

January 5, 1943

The Governments of the Union of South Africa; the United States of America; Australia; Belgium; Canada; China; the Czechoslovak Republic; the United Kingdom of Great Britain and Northern Ireland; Greece; India; Luxemburg; the Netherlands; New Zealand; Norway; Poland; the Union of Soviet Socialist Republics; Yugoslavia; and the French National Committee:

Hereby issue a formal warning to all concerned, and in particular to persons in neutral countries, that they intend to do their utmost to defeat the methods of dispossession practised by the Governments with which they are at war against the countries and peoples who have been so wantonly assaulted and despoiled.

Accordingly, the Governments making this Declaration and the French National Committee reserve all their rights to declare invalid any transfers of, or dealings with, property, rights and interests of any description whatsoever which are, or have been, situated in the territories which have come under the occupation or control, direct or indirect, of the Governments with which they are at war, or which belong, or have belonged, to persons (including juridical persons) resident in such territories. This warning applies whether such transfers or dealings have taken the form of open looting or plunder, or of transactions apparently legal in form, even when they purport to be voluntarily effected.

The Governments making this Declaration and the French National Committee solemnly record their solidarity in this matter.

---

* Inter-Allied Declaration Against Acts of Dispossession Committed in Territories Under Enemy Occupation or Control, 8 DEP'T ST. BULL. 21 (1943).

Appendix 10

UNESCO CONVENTION AND PROTOCOL FOR THE PROTECTION OF CULTURAL PROPERTY IN THE EVENT OF ARMED CONFLICT*
Also known as the "Hague Convention and Protocol of 1954"

Done at The Hague, May 14, 1954; entry into force, August 7, 1956

The High Contracting Parties,

Recognizing that cultural property has suffered grave damage during recent armed conflicts and that, by reason of the developments in the technique of warfare, it is in increasing danger of destruction;

Being convinced that damage to cultural property belonging to any people whatsoever means damage to the cultural heritage of all mankind, since each people makes its contribution to the culture of the world;

Considering that the preservation of the cultural heritage is of great importance for all peoples of the world and that it is important that this heritage should receive international protection;

Guided by the principles concerning the protection of cultural property during armed conflict, as established in the Conventions of The Hague of 1899 and of 1907 and in the Washington Pact of 15 April, 1935;

Being of the opinion that such protection cannot be effective unless both national and international measures have been taken to organize it in time of peace;

Being determined to take all possible steps to protect cultural property;

Have agreed upon the following provisions:

Chapter I. General provisions regarding protection

Article 1. Definition of cultural property
For the purposes of the present Convention, the term "cultural property" shall cover, irrespective of origin or ownership:
(a) movable or immovable property of great importance to the cultural heritage of every people, such as monuments of architecture, art or history, whether religious or secular; archaeological sites; groups of buildings which, as a whole, are of historical or artistic interest; works of art; manuscripts, books and other objects of artistic, historical or archaeological interest; as well as scientific collections and important collections of books or archives or of reproductions of the property defined above;
(b) buildings whose main and effective purpose is to preserve or exhibit the movable cultural property defined in sub-paragraph (a) such as museums, large libraries and depositories of archives, and refuges intended to shelter, in the event of armed conflict, the movable cultural property defined in sub-paragraph (a);
(c) centres containing a large amount of cultural property as defined in sub-paragraphs (a) and (b), to be known as "centres containing monuments."

Article 2. Protection of cultural property
For the purposes of the present Convention, the protection of cultural property shall comprise the safeguarding of and respect for such property.

Article 3. Safeguarding of cultural property
The High Contracting Parties undertake to prepare in time of peace for the safeguarding of cultural property situated within their own territory against the foreseeable effects of an armed conflict, by taking such measures as they consider appropriate.

Article 4. Respect for cultural property

1. The High Contracting Parties undertake to respect cultural property situated within their own territory as well as within the territory of other High Contracting Parties by refraining from any use of the property and its immediate surroundings or of the appliances in use for its protection for purposes which are likely to expose it to destruction or damage in the event of armed conflict; and by refraining from any act of hostility directed against such property.

2. The obligations mentioned in paragraph 1 of the present Article may be waived only in cases where military necessity imperatively requires such a waiver.

3. The High Contracting Parties further undertake to prohibit, prevent and, if necessary, put a stop to any form of theft, pillage or misappropriation of, and any acts of vandalism directed against, cultural property. They shall refrain from requisitioning movable cultural property situated in the territory of another High Contracting Party.

4. They shall refrain from any act directed by way of reprisals against cultural property.

5. No High Contracting Party may evade the obligations incumbent upon it under the present Article, in respect of another High Contracting Party, by reason of the fact that the latter has not applied the measures of safeguard referred to in Article 3.

Article 5. Occupation

1. Any High Contracting Party in occupation of the whole or part of the territory of another High Contracting Party shall as far as possible support the competent national authorities of the occupied country in safeguarding and preserving its cultural property.

2. Should it prove necessary to take measures to preserve cultural property situated in occupied territory and damaged by military operations, and should the competent national authorities be unable to take such measures, the Occupying Power shall, as far as possible, and in close co-operation with such authorities, take the most necessary measures of preservation.

3. Any High Contracting Party whose government is considered their legitimate government by members of a resistance movement, shall, if possible, draw their attention to the obligation to comply with those provisions of the Convention dealing with respect for cultural property.

Article 6. Distinctive marking of cultural property

In accordance with the provisions of Article 16, cultural property may bear a distinctive emblem so as to facilitate its recognition.

Article 7. Military measures

1. The High Contracting Parties undertake to introduce in time of peace into their military regulations or instructions such provisions as may ensure observance of the present Convention, and to foster in the members of their armed forces a spirit of respect for the culture and cultural property of all peoples.

2. The High Contracting Parties undertake to plan or establish in peace-time, within their armed forces, services or specialist personnel whose purpose will be to secure respect for cultural property and to co-operate with the civilian authorities responsible for safeguarding it.

Chapter 2. Special protection

Article 8. Granting of special protection

1. There may be placed under special protection a limited number of refuges intended to shelter movable cultural property in the event of armed conflict of centres containing monuments and other immovable cultural property of very great importance, provided that they:

(a) are situated at an adequate distance from any large industrial centre or from any important military objective constituting a vulnerable point, such as, for example, an aerodrome, broadcasting station, establishment engaged upon work of national defence, a port or railway station of relative importance or a main line of communication;

(b) are not used for military purposes.

2. A refuge for movable cultural property may also be placed under special protection, whatever its location, if it is so constructed that, in all probability, it will not be damaged by bombs.

3. A centre containing monuments shall be deemed to be used for military purposes whenever it is used for the movement of military personnel or material, even in transit. The same shall apply whenever activities directly connected with military operations, the stationing of military personnel, or the production of war material are carried on within the centre.

4. The guarding of cultural property mentioned in paragraph 1 above by armed custodians specially empowered to do so, or the presence, in the vicinity of such cultural property, of police forces normally responsible for the maintenance of public order shall not be deemed to be used for military purposes.

5. If any cultural property mentioned in paragraph 1 of the present Article is situated near an important military objective as defined in the said paragraph, it may nevertheless be placed under special protection if the High Contracting Party asking for that protection undertakes, in the event of armed conflict, to make no use of the objective and particularly, in the case of a port, railway station or aerodrome, to divert all traffic therefrom. In that event, such diversion shall be prepared in time of peace.

6. Special protection is granted to cultural property by its entry in the "International Register of Cultural Property under Special Protection." This entry shall only be made, in accordance with the provisions of the present Convention and under the conditions provided for in the Regulations for the execution of the Convention.

Article 9. Immunity of cultural property under special protection

The High Contracting Parties undertake to ensure the immunity of cultural property under special protection by refraining, from the time of entry in the International Register, from any act of hostility directed against such property and, except for the cases provided for in paragraph 5 of Article 8, from any use of such property or its surroundings for military purposes.

Article 10. Identification and control

During an armed conflict, cultural property under special protection shall be marked with the distinctive emblem described in Article 16, and shall be open to international control as provided for in the Regulations for the execution of the Convention.

Article 11. Withdrawal of immunity

1. If one of the High Contracting Parties commits, in respect of any item of cultural property under special protection, a violation of the obligations under Article 9, the opposing Party shall, so long as this violation persists, be released from the obligation to ensure the immunity of the property concerned. Nevertheless, whenever possible, the latter Party shall first request the cessation of such violation within a reasonable time.

2. Apart from the case provided for in paragraph 1 of the present Article, immunity shall be withdrawn from cultural property under special protection only in exceptional cases of unavoidable military necessity, and only for such time as that necessity continues. Such necessity can be established only by the officer commanding a force the equivalent of a division in size or larger. Whenever circumstances permit, the opposing Party shall be notified, a reasonable time in advance, of the decision to withdraw immunity.

3. The Party withdrawing immunity shall, as soon as possible, so inform the Commissioner-General for cultural property provided for in the Regulations for the execution of the Convention, in writing, stating the reasons.

Chapter 3. Transport of cultural property

Article 12. Transport under special protection
1. Transport exclusively engaged in the transfer of cultural property, whether within a territory or to another territory, may, at the request of the High Contracting Party concerned, take place under special protection in accordance with the conditions specified in the Regulations for the execution of the Convention.
2. Transport under special protection shall take place under the international supervision provided for in the aforesaid Regulations and shall display the distinctive emblem described in Article 16.
3. The High Contracting Parties shall refrain from any act of hostility directed against transport under special protection.

Article 13. Transport in urgent cases
1. If a High Contracting Party considers that the safety of certain cultural property requires its transfer and that the matter is of such urgency that the procedure laid down in Article 12 cannot be followed, especially at the beginning of an armed conflict, the transport may display the distinctive emblem described in Article 16, provided that an application for immunity referred to in Article 12 has not already been made and refused. As far as possible, notification of transfer should be made to the opposing Parties. Nevertheless, transport conveying cultural property to the territory of another country may not display the distinctive emblem unless immunity has been expressly granted to it.
2. The High Contracting Parties shall take, so far as possible, the necessary precautions to avoid acts of hostility directed against the transport described in paragraph 1 of the present Article and displaying the distinctive emblem.

Article 14. Immunity from seizure, capture and prize
1. Immunity from seizure, placing in prize, or capture shall be granted to:
   (a) cultural property enjoying the protection provided for in Article 12 or that provided for in Article 13;
   (b) the means of transport exclusively engaged in the transfer of such cultural property.
2. Nothing in the present Article shall limit the right of visit and search.

Chapter 4. Personnel

Article 15. Personnel
As far as is consistent with the interests of security, personnel engaged in the protection of cultural property shall, in the interests of such property, be respected and, if they fall into the hands of the opposing Party, shall be allowed to continue to carry out their duties whenever the cultural property for which they are responsible has also fallen into the hands of the opposing Party.

Chapter 5. The distinctive emblem

Article 16. Emblem of the convention
1. The distinctive emblem of the Convention shall take the form of a shield, pointed below, per saltire blue and white (a shield consisting of a royal-blue square, one of the angles of which forms the point of the shield, and of a royal-blue triangle above the square, the space on either side being taken up by a white triangle).

2. The emblem shall be used alone, or repeated three times in a triangular formation (one shield below), under the conditions provided for in Article 17.

Article 17. Use of the emblem
1. The distinctive emblem repeated three times may be used only as a means of identification of:
   (a) immovable cultural property under special protection;
   (b) the transport of cultural property under the conditions provided for in Articles 12 and 13;
   (c) improvised refuges, under the conditions provided for in the Regulations for the execution of the Convention.
2. The distinctive emblem may be used alone only as a means of identification of:
   (a) cultural property not under special protection;
   (b) the persons responsible for the duties of control in accordance with the Regulations for the execution of the Convention;
   (c) the personnel engaged in the protection of cultural property;
   (d) the identity cards mentioned in the Regulations for the execution of the Convention.
3. During an armed conflict, the use of the distinctive emblem in any other cases than those mentioned in the preceding paragraphs of the present Article, and the use for any purpose whatever of a sign resembling the distinctive emblem, shall be forbidden.
4. The distinctive emblem may not be placed on any immovable cultural property unless at the same time there is displayed an authorization duly dated and signed by the competent authority of the High Contracting Party.

Chapter 6. Scope of application of the Convention

Article 18. Application of the Convention
1. Apart from the provisions which shall take effect in time of peace, the present Convention shall apply in the event of declared war or of any other armed conflict which may arise between two or more of the High Contracting Parties, even if the state of war is not recognized by one or more of them.
2. The Convention shall also apply to all cases of partial or total occupation of the territory of a High Contracting Party, even if the said occupation meets with no armed resistance.
3. If one of the Powers in conflict is not a Party to the present Convention, the Powers which are Parties thereto shall never-theless remain bound by it in their mutual relations. They shall furthermore be bound by the Convention, in relation to the said Power, if the latter has declared that it accepts the provisions thereof and so long as it applies them.

Article 19. Conflicts not of an international character
1. In the event of an armed conflict not of an international character occurring within the territory of one of the High Contracting Parties, each party to the conflict shall be bound to apply, as a minimum, the provisions of the present Convention which relate to respect for cultural property.
2. The parties to the conflict shall endeavour to bring into force, by means of special agreements, all or part of the other provisions of the present Convention.
3. The United Nations Educational, Scientific and Cultural Organization may offer its services to the parties to the conflict.
4. The application of the preceding provisions shall not affect the legal status of the parties to the conflict.

Chapter 7. Execution of the Convention

Article 20. Regulations for the execution of the Convention
The procedure by which the present Convention is to be applied is defined in the Regulations for its execution, which constitute an integral part thereof.

Article 21. Protecting powers

The present Convention and the Regulations for its execution shall be applied with the co-operation of the Protecting Powers responsible for safeguarding the interests of the Parties to the conflict.

Article 22. Conciliation procedure

1. The Protecting Powers shall lend their good offices in all cases where they may deem it useful in the interests of cultural property, particularly if there is disagreement between the Parties to the conflict as to the application or interpretation of the provisions of the present Convention or the Regulations for its execution.

2. For this purpose, each of the Protecting Powers may, either at the invitation of one Party, of the Director-General of the United Nations Educational, Scientific and Cultural Organization, or on its own initiative, propose to the Parties to the conflict a meeting of their representatives, and in particular of the authorities responsible for the protection of cultural property, if considered appropriate on suitably chosen neutral territory. The Parties to the conflict shall be bound to give effect to the proposals for meeting made to them. The Protecting Powers shall propose for approval by the Parties to the conflict a person belonging to a neutral Power or a person presented by the Director-General of the United Nations Educational, Scientific and Cultural Organization, which person shall be invited to take part in such a meeting in the capacity of Chairman.

Article 23. Assistance of UNESCO

1. The High Contracting Parties may call upon the United Nations Educational, Scientific and Cultural Organization for technical assistance in organizing the protection of their cultural property, or in connexion with any other problem arising out of the application of the present Convention or the Regulations for its execution. The Organization shall accord such assistance within the limits fixed by its programme and by its resources.

2. The Organization is authorized to make, on its own initiative, proposals on this matter to the High Contracting Parties.

Article 24. Special agreements

1. The High Contracting Parties may conclude special agreements for all matters concerning which they deem it suitable to make separate provision.

2. No special agreement may be concluded which would diminish the protection afforded by the present Convention to cultural property and to the personnel engaged in its protection.

Article 25. Dissemination of the Convention

The High Contracting Parties undertake, in time of peace as in time of armed conflict, to disseminate the text of the present Convention and the Regulations for its execution as widely as possible in their respective countries. They undertake, in particular, to include the study thereof in their programmes of military and, if possible, civilian training, so that its principles are made known to the whole population, especially the armed forces and personnel engaged in the protection of cultural property.

Article 26. Translations reports

1. The High Contracting Parties shall communicate to one another, through the Director-General of the United Nations Educational, Scientific and Cultural Organization, the official translations of the present Convention and of the Regulations for its execution.

2. Furthermore, at least once every four years, they shall forward to the Director-General a report giving whatever information they think suitable concerning any measures being taken, prepared or contemplated by their respective administrations in fulfilment of the present Convention and of the Regulations for its execution.

Article 27. Meetings

1. The Director-General of the United Nations Educational, Scientific and Cultural Organization may, with the approval of the Executive Board, convene meetings of representatives of the High Contracting Parties. He must convene such a meeting if at least one-fifth of the High Contracting Parties so request.

2. Without prejudice to any other functions which have been conferred on it by the present Convention or the Regulations for its execution, the purpose of the meeting will be to study problems concerning the application of the Convention and of the Regulations for its execution, and to formulate recommendations in respect thereof.

3. The meeting may further undertake a revision of the Convention or the Regulations for its execution if the majority of the High Contracting Parties are represented, and in accordance with the provisions of Article 39.

Article 28. Sanctions

The High Contracting Parties undertake to take, within the framework of their ordinary criminal jurisdiction, all necessary steps to prosecute and impose penal or disciplinary sanctions upon those persons, of whatever nationality, who commit or order to be committed a breach of the present Convention.

Final provisions

Article 29. Languages

1. The present Convention is drawn up in English, French, Russian and Spanish, the four texts being equally authoritative.

2. The United Nations Educational, Scientific and Cultural Organization shall arrange for translations of the Convention into the other official languages of its General Conference.

Article 30. Signature

The present Convention shall bear the date of 14 May, 1954 and, until the date of 31 December, 1954, shall remain open for signature by all States invited to the Conference which met at The Hague from 21 April, 1954 to 14 May, 1954.

Article 31. Ratification

1. The present Convention shall be subject to ratification by signatory States in accordance with their respective constitutional procedures.

2. The instruments of ratification shall be deposited with the Director-General of the United Nations Educational, Scientific and Cultural Organization.

Article 32. Accession

From the date of its entry into force, the present Convention shall be open for accession by all States mentioned in Article 30 which have not signed it, as well as any other State invited to accede by the Executive Board of the United Nations Educational, Scientific and Cultural Organization. Accession shall be effected by the deposit of an instrument of accession with the Director-General of the United Nations Educational, Scientific and Cultural Organization.

Article 33. Entry into force

1. The present Convention shall enter into force three months after five instruments of ratification have been deposited.

2. Thereafter, it shall enter into force, for each High Contracting Party, three months after the deposit of its instrument of ratification or accession.

3. The situations referred to in Articles 18 and 19 shall give immediate effect to ratifications or accessions deposited by the Parties to the conflict either before or after the beginning of hostilities or occupation. In such cases the Director-General of the United Nations Educational, Scientific and Cultural Organization shall

transmit the communications referred to in Article 38 by the speediest method.

Article 34. Effective application
1. Each State Party to the Convention on the date of its entry into force shall take all necessary measures to ensure its effective application within a period of six months after such entry into force.
2. This period shall be six months from the date of deposit of the instruments of ratification or accession for any State which deposits its instrument of ratification or accession after the date of the entry into force of the Convention.

Article 35. Territorial extension of the Convention
Any High Contracting Party may, at the time of ratification or accession, or at any time thereafter, declare by notification addressed to the Director-General of the United Nations Educational, Scientific and Cultural Organization, that the present Convention shall extend to all or any of the territories for whose international relations it is responsible. The said notification shall take effect three months after the date of its receipt.

Article 36. Relation to previous conventions
1. In the relations between Powers which are bound by the Conventions of The Hague concerning the Laws and Customs of War on Land (IV) and concerning Naval Bombardment in Time of War (IX), whether those of 29 July, 1899 or those of 18 October, 1907, and which are Parties to the present Convention, this last Convention shall be supplementary to the aforementioned Convention (IX) and to the Regulations annexed to the aforementioned Convention (IV) and shall substitute for the emblem described in Article 5 of the aforementioned Convention (IX) the emblem described in Article 16 of the present Convention, in cases in which the present Convention and the Regulations for its execution provide for the use of this distinctive emblem.
2. In the relations between Powers which are bound by the Washington Pact of 15 April, 1935 for the Protection of Artistic and Scientific Institutions and of Historic Monuments (Roerich Pact) and which are Parties to the present Convention, the latter Convention shall be supplementary to the Roerich Pact and shall substitute for the distinguishing flag described in Article 3 of the Pact the emblem defined in Article 16 of the present Convention, in cases in which the present Convention and the Regulations for its execution provide for the use of this distinctive emblem.

Article 37. Denunciation
1. Each High Contracting Party may denounce the present Convention, on its own behalf, or on behalf of any territory for whose international relations it is responsible.
2. The denunciation shall be notified by an instrument in writing, deposited with the Director-General of the United Nations Educational, Scientific and Cultural Organization.
3. The denunciation shall take effect one year after the receipt of the instrument of denunciation. However, if, on the expiry of this period, the denouncing Party is involved in an armed conflict, the denunciation shall not take effect until the end of hostilities, or until the operations of repatriating cultural property are completed, whichever is the later.

Article 38. Notifications
The Director-General of the United Nations Educational, Scientific and Cultural Organization shall inform the States referred to in Articles 30 and 32, as well as the United Nations, of the deposit of all the instruments of ratification, accession or acceptance provided for in Articles 31, 32 and 39 and of the notifications and denunciations provided for respectively in Articles 35, 37 and 39.

Article 39. Revision of the Convention and of the Regulations for its execution
1. Any High Contracting Party may propose amendments to the present Convention or the Regulations for its execution. The text of any proposed amendment shall be communicated to the Director-General of the United Nations Educational, Scientific and Cultural Organization who shall transmit it to each High Contracting Party with the request that such Party reply within four months stating whether it:
    (a) desires that a Conference be convened to consider the proposed amendment;
    (b) favours the acceptance of the proposed amendment without a Conference; or
    (c) favours the rejection of the proposed amendment without a Conference.
2. The Director-General shall transmit the replies, received under paragraph 1 of the present Article, to all High Contracting Parties.
3. If all the High Contracting Parties which have, within the prescribed time-limit, stated their views to the Director-General of the United Nations Educational, Scientific and Cultural Organization, pursuant to paragraph 1(b) of this Article, inform him that they favour acceptance of the amendment without a Conference, notification of their decision shall be made by the Director-General in accordance with Article 38. The amendment shall become effective for all the High Contracting Parties on the expiry of ninety days from the date of such notification.
4. The Director-General shall convene a Conference of the High Contracting Parties to consider the proposed amendment if requested to do so by more than one-third of the High Contracting Parties.
5. Amendments to the Convention or to the Regulations for its execution, dealt with under the provisions of the preceding paragraph, shall enter into force only after they have been unanimously adopted by the High Contracting Parties represented at the Conference and accepted by each of the High Contracting Parties.
6. Acceptance by the High Contracting Parties of amendments to the Convention or to the Regulations for its execution, which have been adopted by the Conference mentioned in paragraphs 4 and 5, shall be effected by the deposit of a formal instrument with the Director-General of the United Nations Educational, Scientific and Cultural Organization.
7. After the entry into force of amendments to the present Convention or to the Regulations for its execution, only the text of the Convention or of the Regulations for its execution thus amended shall remain open for ratification or accession.

Article 40. Registration
In accordance with Article 102 of the Charter of the United Nations, the present Convention shall be registered with the Secretariat of the United Nations at the request of the Director-General of the United Nations Educational, Scientific and Cultural Organization.

In faith whereof the undersigned, duly authorized, have signed the present Convention.

Done at The Hague, this fourteenth day of May, 1954, in a single copy which shall be deposited in the archives of the United Nations Educational, Scientific and Cultural Organization, and certified true copies of which shall be delivered to all the States referred to in Articles 30 and 32 as well as to the United Nations.

REGULATIONS FOR THE EXECUTION OF THE CONVENTION FOR THE PROTECTION OF CULTURAL PROPERTY IN THE EVENT OF ARMED CONFLICT

Chapter 1. Control

Article 1. International list of persons
On the entry into force of the Convention, the Director-General of the United Nations Educational, Scientific and Cultural Organization shall compile an international list consisting of all persons nominated by the High Contracting Parties as qualified to carry out the functions of Commissioner-General for Cultural Property. On the initiative of the Director-General of the United Nations Educational, Scientific and Cultural Organization, this list shall be periodically revised on the basis of requests formulated by the High Contracting Parties.

Article 2. Organization of control
As soon as any High Contracting Party is engaged in an armed conflict to which Article 18 of the Convention applies:
(a) It shall appoint a representative for cultural property situated in its territory; if it is in occupation of another territory, it shall appoint a special representative for cultural property situated in that territory;
(b) The Protecting Power acting for each of the Parties in conflict with such High Contracting Party shall appoint delegates accredited to the latter in conformity with Article 3 below;
(c) A Commissioner-General for Cultural Property shall be appointed to such High Contracting Party in accordance with Article 4.

Article 3. Appointment of delegates of Protecting Powers
The Protecting Power shall appoint its delegates from among the members of its diplomatic or consular staff or, with the approval of the Party to which they will be accredited, from among other persons.

Article 4. Appointment of Commissioner-General
1. The Commissioner-General for Cultural Property shall be chosen from the international list of persons by joint agreement between the Party to which he will be accredited and the Protecting Powers acting on behalf of the opposing Parties.
2. Should the Parties fail to reach agreement within three weeks from the beginning of their discussions on this point, they shall request the President of the International Court of Justice to appoint the Commissioner-General, who shall not take up his duties until the Party to which he is accredited has approved his appointment.

Article 5. Functions of delegates
The delegates of the Protecting Powers shall take note of violations of the Convention, investigate, with the approval of the Party to which they are accredited, the circumstances in which they have occurred, make representations locally to secure their cessation and, if necessary, notify the Commissioner-General of such violations. They shall keep him informed of their activities.

Article 6. Functions of the Commissioner-General
1. The Commissioner-General for Cultural Property shall deal with all matters referred to him in connexion with the application of the Convention, in conjunction with the representative of the Party to which he is accredited and with the delegates concerned.
2. He shall have powers of decision and appointment in the cases specified in the present Regulations.
3. With the agreement of the Party to which he is accredited, he shall have the right to order an investigation or to conduct it himself.
4. He shall make any representations to the Parties to the conflict or to their Protecting Powers which he deems useful for the application of the Convention.
5. He shall draw up such reports as may be necessary on the appli-cation of the Convention and communicate them to the Parties concerned and to their Protecting Powers. He shall send copies to the Director-General of the United Nations Educational, Scientific and Cultural Organization, who may make use only of their technical contents.
6. If there is no Protecting Power, the Commissioner-General shall exercise the functions of the Protecting Power as laid down in Articles 21 and 22 of the Convention.

Article 7. Inspectors and experts
1. Whenever the Commissioner-General for Cultural Property considers it necessary, either at the request of the delegates concerned or after consultation with them, he shall propose, for the approval of the Party to which he is accredited, an inspector of cultural property to be charged with a specific mission. An inspector shall be responsible only to the Commissioner-General.
2. The Commissioner-General, delegates and inspectors may have recourse to the services of experts, who will also be proposed for the approval of the Party mentioned in the preceding paragraph.

Article 8. Discharge of the mission of control
The Commissioners-General for Cultural Property, delegates of the Protecting Powers, inspectors and experts shall in no case exceed their mandates. In particular, they shall take account of the security needs of the High Contracting Party to which they are accredited and shall in all circumstances act in accordance with the requirements of the military situation as communicated to them by that High Contracting Party.

Article 9. Substitutes for Protecting Powers
If a Party to the conflict does not benefit or ceases to benefit from the activities of a Protecting Power, a neutral State may be asked to undertake those functions of a Protecting Power which concern the appointment of a Commissioner-General for Cultural Property in accordance with the procedure laid down in Article 4 above. The Commissioner-General thus appointed shall, if need be, entrust to inspectors the functions of delegates of Protecting Powers as specified in the present Regulations.

Article 10. Expenses
The remuneration and expenses of the Commissioner-General for Cultural Property, inspectors and experts shall be met by the Party to which they are accredited. Remuneration and expenses of delegates of the Protecting Powers shall be subject to agreement between those Powers and the States whose interests they are safeguarding.

Chapter 2. Special protection

Article 11. Improvised refuges
1. If, during an armed conflict, any High Contracting Party is induced by unforeseen circumstances to set up an improvised refuge and desires that it should be placed under special protection, it shall communicate this fact forthwith to the Commissioner-General accredited to that Party.
2. If the Commissioner-General considers that such a measure is justified by the circumstances and by the importance of the cultural property sheltered in this improvised refuge, he may authorize the High Contracting Party to display on such refuge the distinctive emblem defined in Article 16 of the Convention. He shall commun-icate his decision without delay to the delegates of the Protecting Powers who are concerned, each of whom may, within a time-limit of 30 days, order the immediate withdrawal of the emblem.
3. As soon as such delegates have signified their agreement or if the time-limit of 30 days has passed without any of the delegates concerned having made an objection, and if, in the view of the Commissioner-General, the refuge fulfils the conditions laid down in Article 8 of the Convention, the Commissioner-General

shall request the Director-General of the United Nations Educational, Scientific and Cultural Organization to enter the refuge in the Register of Cultural Property under Special Protection.

Article 12. International Register of Cultural Property under Special Protection
1. An "International Register of Cultural Property under Special Protection" shall be prepared.
2. The Director-General of the United Nations Educational, Scientific and Cultural Organization shall maintain this Register. He shall furnish copies to the Secretary-General of the United Nations and to the High Contracting Parties.
3. The Register shall be divided into sections, each in the name of a High Contracting Party. Each section shall be subdivided into three paragraphs, headed: Refuges, Centres containing Monuments, Other Immovable Cultural Property. The Director-General shall determine what details each section shall contain.

Article 13. Requests for registration
1. Any High Contracting Party may submit to the Director-General of the United Nations Educational, Scientific and Cultural Organization an application for the entry in the Register of certain refuges, centres containing monuments or other immovable cultural property situated within its territory. Such application shall contain a description of the location of such property and shall certify that the property complies with the provisions of Article 8 of the Convention.
2. In the event of occupation, the Occupying Power shall be competent to make such application.
3. The Director-General of the United Nations Educational, Scientific and Cultural Organization shall, without delay, send copies of applications for registration to each of the High Contracting Parties.

Article 14. Objections
1. Any High Contracting Party may, by letter addressed to the Director-General of the United Nations Educational, Scientific and Cultural Organization, lodge an objection to the registration of cultural property. This letter must be received by him within four months of the day on which he sent a copy of the application for registration.
2. Such objection shall state the reasons giving rise to it, the only valid grounds being that:
   (a) the property is not cultural property;
   (b) the property does not comply with the conditions mentioned in Article 8 of the Convention.
3. The Director-General shall send a copy of the letter of objection to the High Contracting Parties without delay. He shall, if necessary, seek the advice of the International Committee on Monuments, Artistic and Historical Sites and Archaeological Excavations and also, if he thinks fit, of any other competent organization or person.
4. The Director-General, or the High Contracting Party requesting registration, may make whatever representations they deem necessary to the High Contracting Parties which lodged the objection, with a view to causing the objection to be withdrawn.
5. If a High Contracting Party which has made an application for registration in time of peace becomes involved in an armed conflict before the entry has been made, the cultural property concerned shall at once be provisionally entered in the Register, by the Director-General, pending the confirmation, withdrawal or cancellation of any objection that may be, or may have been, made.
6. If, within a period of six months from the date of receipt of the letter of objection, the Director-General has not received from the High Contracting Party lodging the objection a communication stating that it has been withdrawn, the High Contracting Party

applying for registration may request arbitration in accordance with the procedure in the following paragraph.
7. The request for arbitration shall not be made more than one year after the date of receipt by the Director-General of the letter of objection. Each of the two Parties to the dispute shall appoint an arbitrator. When more than one objection has been lodged against an application for registration, the High Contracting Parties which have lodged the objections shall, by common consent, appoint a single arbitrator. These two arbitrators shall select a chief arbitrator from the international list mentioned in Article 1 of the present Regulations. If such arbitrators cannot agree upon their choice, they shall ask the President of the International Court of Justice to appoint a chief arbitrator who need not necessarily be chosen from the international list. The arbitral tribunal thus constituted shall fix its own procedure. There shall be no appeal from its decisions.
8. Each of the High Contracting Parties may declare, whenever a dispute to which it is a Party arises, that it does not wish to apply the arbitration procedure provided for in the preceding paragraph. In such cases, the objection to an application for registration shall be submitted by the Director-General to the High Contracting Parties. The objection will be confirmed only if the High Contracting Parties so decide by a two-third majority of the High Contracting Parties voting. The vote shall be taken by correspondence, unless the Director-General of the United Nations Educational, Scientific and Cultural Organization deems it essential to convene a meeting under the powers conferred upon him by Article 27 of the Convention. If the Director-General decides to proceed with the vote by correspondence, he shall invite the High Contracting Parties to transmit their votes by sealed letter within six months from the day on which they were invited to do so.

Article 15. Registration
1. The Director-General of the United Nations Educational, Scientific and Cultural Organization shall cause to be entered in the Register, under a serial number, each item of property for which application for registration is made, provided that he has not received an objection within the time-limit prescribed in paragraph 1 of Article 14.
2. If an objection has been lodged, and without prejudice to the provision of paragraph 5 of Article 14, the Director-General shall enter property in the Register only if the objection has been withdrawn or has failed to be confirmed following the procedures laid down in either paragraph 7 or paragraph 8 of Article 14.
3. Whenever paragraph 3 of Article 11 applies, the Director-General shall enter property in the Register if so requested by the Commissioner-General for Cultural Property.
4. The Director-General shall send without delay to the Secretary-General of the United Nations, to the High Contracting Parties, and, at the request of the Party applying for registration, to all other States referred to in Articles 30 and 32 of the Convention, a certified copy of each entry in the Register. Entries shall become effective thirty days after despatch of such copies.

Article 16. Cancellation
1. The Director-General of the United Nations Educational, Scientific and Cultural Organization shall cause the registration of any property to be cancelled:
   (a) at the request of the High Contracting Party within whose territory the cultural property is situated;
   (b) if the High Contracting Party which requested registration has denounced the Convention, and when that denunciation has taken effect;
   (c) in the special case provided for in Article 14, paragraph 5, when an objection has been confirmed following the procedures mentioned either in paragraph 7 or in paragraph 8 or Article 14.

2. The Director-General shall send without delay, to the Secretary-General of the United Nations and to all States which received a copy of the entry in the Register, a certified copy of its cancellation. Cancellation shall take effect thirty days after the despatch of such copies.

Chapter 3. Transport of cultural property

Article 17. Procedure to obtain immunity
1. The request mentioned in paragraph 1 of Article 12 of the Convention shall be addressed to the Commissioner-General for Cultural Property. It shall mention the reasons on which it is based and specify the approximate number and the importance of the objects to be transferred, their present location, the location now envisaged, the means of transport to be used, the route to be followed, the date proposed for the transfer, and any other relevant information.
2. If the Commissioner-General, after taking such opinions as he deems fit, considers that such transfer is justified, he shall consult those delegates of the Protecting Powers who are concerned, on the measures proposed for carrying it out. Following such consultation, he shall notify the Parties to the conflict concerned of the transfer, including in such notification all useful information.
3. The Commissioner-General shall appoint one or more inspectors, who shall satisfy themselves that only the property stated in the request is to be transferred and that the transport is to be by the approved methods and bears the distinctive emblem. The inspector or inspectors shall accompany the property to its destination.

Article 18. Transport abroad
Where the transfer under special protection is to the territory of another country, it shall be governed not only by Article 12 of the Convention and by Article 17 of the present Regulations, but by the following further provisions:
(a) while the cultural property remains on the territory of another State, that State shall be its depositary and shall extend to it as great a measure of care as that which it bestows upon its own cultural property of comparable importance;
(b) the depositary State shall return the property only on the cessation of the conflict; such return shall be effected within six months from the date on which it was requested;
(c) during the various transfer operations, and while it remains on the territory of another State, the cultural property shall be exempt from confiscation and may not be disposed of either by the depositor or by the depositary. Nevertheless, when the safety of the property requires it, the depositary may, with the assent of the depositor, have the property transported to the territory of a third country, under the conditions laid down in the present article;
(d) the request for special protection shall indicate that the State to whose territory the property is to be transferred accepts the provisions of the present Article.

Article 19. Occupied territory
Whenever a High Contracting Party occupying territory of another High Contracting Party transfers cultural property to a refuge situated elsewhere in that territory, without being able to follow the procedure provided for in Article 17 of the Regulations, the transfer in question shall not be regarded as misappropriation within the meaning of Article 4 of the Convention, provided that the Commissioner-General for Cultural Property certifies in writing, after having consulted the usual custodians, that such transfer was rendered necessary by circumstances.

Chapter 4. The distinctive emblem

Article 20. Affixing of the emblem
1. The placing of the distinctive emblem and its degree of visibility shall be left to the discretion of the competent authorities of each High Contracting Party. It may be displayed on flags or armlets; it may be painted on an object or represented in any other appropriate form.
2. However, without prejudice to any possible fuller markings, the emblem shall, in the event of armed conflict and in the cases mentioned in Articles 12 and 13 of the Convention, be placed on the vehicles of transport so as to be clearly visible in daylight from the air as well as from the ground. The emblem shall be visible from the ground:
   (a) at regular intervals sufficient to indicate clearly the perimeter of a centre containing monuments under special protection;
   (b) at the entrance to other immovable cultural property under special protection.

Article 21. Identification of persons
1. The persons mentioned in Article 17, paragraph 2(b) and (c) of the Convention may wear an armlet bearing the distinctive emblem, issued and stamped by the competent authorities.
2. Such persons shall carry a special identity card bearing the distinctive emblem. This card shall mention at least the surname and first names, the date of birth, the title or rank, and the function of the holder. The card shall bear the photograph of the holder as well as his signature or his fingerprints, or both. It shall bear the embossed stamp of the competent authorities.
3. Each High Contracting Party shall make out its own type of identity card, guided by the model annexed, by way of example, to the present Regulations. The High Contracting Parties shall transmit to each other a specimen of the model they are using. Identity cards shall be made out, if possible, at least in duplicate, one copy being kept by the issuing Power.
4. The said persons may not, without legitimate reason, be deprived of their identity card or of the right to wear the armlet.

PROTOCOL

The High Contracting Parties are agreed as follows:

I

1. Each High Contracting Party undertakes to prevent the exportation, from a territory occupied by it during an armed conflict, of cultural property as defined in Article 1 of the Convention for the Protection of Cultural Property in the Event of Armed Conflict, signed at The Hague on 14 May, 1954.
2. Each High Contracting Party undertakes to take into its custody cultural property imported into its territory either directly or indirectly from any occupied territory. This shall either be effected automatically upon the importation of the property or, failing this, at the request of the authorities of that territory.
3. Each High Contracting Party undertakes to return, at the close of hostilities, to the competent authorities of the territory previously occupied, cultural property which is in its territory, if such property has been exported in contravention of the principle laid down in the first paragraph. Such property shall never be retained as war reparations.
4. The High Contracting Party whose obligation it was to prevent the exportation of cultural property from the territory occupied by it, shall pay an indemnity to the holders in good faith of any cultural property which has to be returned in accordance with the preceding paragraph.

II

5. Cultural property coming from the territory of a High Contracting Party and deposited by it in the territory of another High Contracting Party for the purpose of protecting such property against the dangers of an armed conflict, shall be returned by the latter, at the end of hostilities, to the competent authorities of the territory from which it came.

III

6. The present Protocol shall bear the date of 14 May, 1954 and, until the date of 31 December, 1954, shall remain open for signature by all States invited to the Conference which met at The Hague from 21 April, 1954 to 14 May, 1954.

7. (a) The present Protocol shall be subject to ratification by signatory States in accordance with their respective constitutional procedures.

   (b) The instruments of ratification shall be deposited with the Director-General of the United Nations Educational, Scientific and Cultural Organization.

8. From the date of its entry into force, the present Protocol shall be open for accession by all States mentioned in paragraph 6 which have not signed it as well as any other State invited to accede by the Executive Board of the United Nations Educational, Scientific and Cultural Organization. Accession shall be effected by the deposit of an instrument of accession with the Director-General of the United Nations Educational, Scientific and Cultural Organization.

9. The States referred to in paragraphs 6 and 8 may declare, at the time of signature, ratification or accession, that they will not be bound by the provisions of Section I or by those of Section II of the present Protocol.

10. (a) The present Protocol shall enter into force three months after five instruments of ratification have been deposited.

    (b) Thereafter, it shall enter into force, for each High Contracting Party, three months after the deposit of its instrument of ratification or accession.

    (c) The situations referred to in Articles 18 and 19 of the Convention for the Protection of Cultural Property in the Event of Armed Conflict, signed at The Hague on 14 May, 1954, shall give immediate effect to ratifications and accessions deposited by the Parties to the conflict either before or after the beginning of hostilities or occupation. In such cases, the Director-General of the United Nations Educational, Scientific and Cultural Organization shall transmit the communications referred to in paragraph 14 by the speediest method.

11. (a) Each State Party to the Protocol on the date of its entry into force shall take all necessary measures to ensure its effective application within a period of six months after such entry into force.

    (b) This period shall be six months from the date of deposit of the instruments of ratification or accession for any State which deposits its instrument of ratification or accession after the date of the entry into force of the Protocol.

12. Any High Contracting Party may, at the time of ratification or accession, or at any time thereafter, declare by notification addressed to the Director-General of the United Nations Educational, Scientific and Cultural Organization, that the present Protocol shall extend to all or any of the territories for whose international relations it is responsible. The said notification shall take effect three months after the date of its receipt.

13. (a) Each High Contracting Party may denounce the present Protocol, on its own behalf, or on behalf of any territory for whose international relations it is responsible.

    (b) The denunciation shall be notified by an instrument in writing, deposited with the Director-General of the United Nations Educational, Scientific and Cultural Organization.

    (c) The denunciation shall take effect one year after receipt of the instrument of denunciation. However, if, on the expiry of this period, the denouncing Party is involved in an armed conflict, the denunciation shall not take effect until the end of hostilities, or until the operations of repatriating cultural property are completed, whichever is the later.

14. The Director-General of the United Nations Educational, Scientific and Cultural Organization shall inform the States referred to in paragraphs 6 and 8, as well as the United Nations, of the deposit of all the instruments of ratification, accession or acceptance provided for in paragraphs 7, 8 and 15 and the notifications and denunciations provided for respectively in paragraphs 12 and 13.

15. (a) The present Protocol may be revised if revision is requested by more than one-third of the High Contracting Parties.

    (b) The Director-General of the United Nations Educational, Scientific and Cultural Organization shall convene a Conference for this purpose.

    (c) Amendments to the present Protocol shall enter into force only after they have been unanimously adopted by the High Contracting Parties represented at the Conference and accepted by each of the High Contracting Parties.

    (d) Acceptance by the High Contracting Parties of amendments to the present Protocol, which have been adopted by the Conference mentioned in sub-paragraphs (b) and (c), shall be effected by the deposit of a formal instrument with the Director-General of the United Nations Educational, Scientific and Cultural Organization.

    (e) After the entry into force of amendments to the present Protocol, only the text of the said Protocol thus amended shall remain open for ratification or accession.

In accordance with Article 102 of the Charter of the United Nations, the present Protocol shall be registered with the Secretariat of the United Nations at the request of the Director-General of the United Nations Educational, Scientific and Cultural Organization.

In faith whereof the undersigned, duly authorized, have signed the present Protocol.

Done at The Hague, this fourteenth day of May, 1954, in English, French, Russian and Spanish, the four texts being equally authoritative, in a single copy which shall be deposited in the archives of the United Nations Educational, Scientific and Cultural Organization, and certified true copies of which shall be delivered to all the States referred to in paragraphs 6 and 8 as well as to the United Nations.

RESOLUTIONS

Resolution 1

The Conference expresses the hope that the competent organs of the United Nations should decide, in the event of military action being taken in implementation of the Charter, to ensure application of the provisions of the Convention by the armed forces taking part in such action.

Resolution 2

The Conference expresses the hope that each of the High Contracting Parties, on acceding to the Convention, should set up, within the framework of its constitutional and administrative system, a national advisory committee consisting of a small number of distinguished persons: for example, senior officials of archaeological services, museums, etc., a representative of the military general staff, a representative of the Ministry of Foreign Affairs, a specialist in international law and two or three other members whose official duties or specialized knowledge are related to the fields covered by the Convention.

The Committee should be under the authority of the minister of State or senior official responsible for the national service chiefly concerned with the care of cultural property. Its chief functions would be:

(a) to advise the government concerning the measures required for the implementation of the Convention in its legislative, technical or military aspects, both in time of peace and during an armed conflict;

(b) to approach its government in the event of an armed conflict or when such a conflict appears imminent, with a view to ensuring that cultural property situated within its own territory or within that of other countries is known to, and respected and protected by the armed forces of the country, in accordance with the provisions of the Convention;

(c) to arrange, in agreement with its government, for liaison and co-operation with other similar national committees and with any competent international authority.

Resolution 3

The Conference expresses the hope that the Director-General of the United Nations Educational, Scientific and Cultural Organization should convene, as soon as possible after the entry into force of the Convention for the Protection of Cultural Property in the Event of Armed Conflict, a meeting of the High Contracting Parties.

LIST OF THE 88 STATES PARTIES (75 STATES PARTIES TO THE PROTOCOL) AS AT 15 JUNE 1996

States	Convention		Protocol	
	Date of ratification (R) accession (A) succession (S)	Date of entry into force	Date of ratification (R) accession (A) succession (S)	Date of entry into force
Albania	20.12.1960 (A)	20.03.1961	20.12.1960 (A)	20.03.1961
Argentina	22.03.1989 (A)	22.06.1989		
Armenia (Republic of)[1]	05.09.1993 (S)	Note 1	05.09.1993 (S)	Note 1
Australia	19.09.1984 (R)	19.12.1984		
Austria	25.03.1964 (R)	25.06.1964	25.03.1964 (R)	25.06.1964
Azerbaijan (Republic of)	20.09.1993 (A)	20.12.1993	20.09.1993 (A)	20.12.1993
Belarus	07.05.1957 (R)	07.08.1957	07.05.1957 (R)	07.08.1957
Belgium	16.09.1960 (R)	16.12.1960	16.09.1960 (R)	16.12.1960
Bosnia-Herzegovina (Republic of)[2]	12.07.1993 (S)	Note 2	12.07.1993 (S)	Note 2
Brazil	12.09.1958 (R)	12.12.1958	12.09.1958 (R)	12.12.1958
Bulgaria	07.08.1956 (A)	07.11.1956	09.10.1958 (A)	09.01.1959
Burkina Faso	18.12.1969 (A)	18.03.1970	04.02.1987 (A)	04.05.1987
Cambodia	04.04.1962 (A)	04.07.1962	04.04.1962 (A)	04.07.1962
Cameroon	12.10.1961 (A)	12.01.1962	12.10.1961 (A)	12.01.1962
Côte d'Ivoire	24.01.1980 (A)	24.04.1980		
Croatia (Republic of)[2]	06.07.1992 (S)	Note 2	06.07.1992 (S)	Note 2
Cuba	26.11.1957 (R)	26.02.1958	26.11.1957 (R)	26.02.1958
Cyprus	09.09.1964 (A)	09.12.1964	09.09.1964 (A)	09.12.1964
Czech Republic[3]	26.03.1993 (S)	Note 3	26.03.1993 (S)	Note 3
Dominican Republic	05.01.1960 (A)	05.04.1960		
Ecuador	02.10.1956 (A)	02.01.1957	08.02.1961 (A)	08.05.1961
Egypt[4]	17.08.1955 (R)	07.08.1956	17.08.1955 (R)	07.08.1956
Estonia	04.04.1995 (A)	07.07.1995		
Finland	16.09.1994 (A)	16.12.1994	16.09.1994 (A)	16.12.1994
France	07.06.1957 (R)	07.09.1957	07.06.1957 (R)	07.09.1957
Gabon	04.12.1961 (A)	04.03.1962	04.12.1961 (A)	04.03.1962
Georgia (Republic of)[1]	04.11.1992 (S)	Note 1	04.11.1992 (S)	Note 1
Germany (Federal Republic of)[5]	11.08.1967 (R)	11.11.1967	11.08.1967 (R)	11.11.1967
Ghana	25.07.1960 (A)	25.10.1960	25.07.1960 (A)	25.10.1960
Greece	09.02.1981 (R)	09.05.1981	09.02.1981 (R)	09.05.1981
Guatemala	02.10.1985 (A)	02.01.1986	19.05.1994 (A)	19.08.1994
Guinea	20.09.1960 (A)	20.12.1960	11.12.1961 (A)	11.03.1962
Holy See	24.02.1958 (A)	24.05.1958	24.02.1958 (A)	24.05.1958
Hungary	17.05.1956 (R)	17.08.1956	16.08.1956 (A)	16.11.1956
India	16.06.1958 (R)	16.09.1958	16.06.1958 (R)	16.09.1958
Indonesia	10.01.1967 (R)	10.04.1967	26.07.1967 (A)	26.10.1967
Iran (Islamic Republic of)	22.06.1959 (R)	22.09.1959	22.06.1959 (R)	22.09.1959
Iraq	21.12.1967 (R)	21.03.1968	21.12.1967 (R)	21.03.1968
Israel	03.10.1957 (R)	03.01.1958	01.04.1958 (A)	01.07.1958
Italy	09.05.1958 (R)	09.08.1958	09.05.1958 (R)	09.08.1958
Jordan	02.10.1957 (R)	02.01.1958	02.10.1957 (R)	02.01.1958
Kuwait	06.06.1969 (A)	06.09.1969	11.02.1970 (A)	11.05.1970
Kyrghyz Republic	03.07.1995 (A)	03.10.1995		
Lebanon	01.06.1960 (R)	01.09.1960	01.06.1960 (R)	01.09.1960
Libyan Arab Jamahiriya	19.11.1957 (R)	19.02.1958	19.11.1957 (R)	19.02.1958
Liechtenstein	28.04.1960 (A)	28.07.1960	28.04.1960 (A)	28.07.1960
Luxembourg	29.09.1961 (R)	29.12.1961	29.09.1961 (R)	29.12.1961
Madagascar	03.11.1961 (A)	03.02.1962	03.11.1961 (A)	03.02.1962
Malaysia	12.12.1960 (A)	12.03.1961	12.12.1960 (A)	12.03.1961
Mali	18.05.1961 (A)	18.08.1961	18.05.1961 (A)	18.08.1961
Mexico	07.05.1956 (R)	07.08.1956	07.05.1956 (R)	07.08.1956
Monaco	10.12.1957 (R)	10.03.1958	10.12.1957 (R)	10.03.1958
Mongolia	04.11.1964 (A)	04.02.1965		
Morocco	30.08.1968 (A)	30.11.1968	30.08.1968 (A)	30.11.1968
Myanmar[4]	10.02.1956 (R)	07.08.1956	10.02.1956 (R)	07.08.1956
Netherlands	14.10.1958 (R)	14.01.1959	14.10.1958 (R)	14.01.1959
Nicaragua	25.11.1959 (R)	25.02.1960	25.11.1959 (R)	25.02.1960
Niger	06.12.1976 (A)	06.03.1977	06.12.1976 (A)	06.03.1977
Nigeria	05.06.1961 (A)	05.09.1961	05.06.1961 (A)	05.09.1961
Norway	19.09.1961 (R)	19.12.1961	19.09.1961 (R)	19.12.1961
Oman	26.10.1977 (A)	26.01.1978		
Pakistan	27.03.1959 (A)	27.06.1959	27.03.1959 (A)	27.06.1959
Panama	17.07.1962 (A)	17.10.1962		
Peru	21.07.1989 (A)	21.10.1989	21.07.1989 (A)	21.10.1989
Poland	06.08.1956 (A)	06.11.1956	06.08.1956 (R)	06.11.1956
Qatar	31.07.1973 (A)	31.10.1973		
Romania	21.03.1958 (R)	21.06.1958	21.03.1958 (A)	21.06.1958
Russian Federation[6]	04.01.1957 (R)	04.04.1957	04.01.1957 (R)	04.04.1957
San Marino[4]	09.02.1956 (R)	07.08.1956	09.02.1956 (R)	07.08.1956
Saudi Arabia	20.01.1971 (A)	20.04.1971		
Senegal	17.06.1987 (A)	17.09.1987	17.06.1987 (A)	17.09.1987
Slovak Republic[3]	31.03.1993 (S)	Note 3	31.03.1993 (S)	Note 3
Slovenia (Republic of)[2]	05.11.1992 (S)	Note 2	05.11.1992 (S)	Note 2
Spain	07.07.1960 (R)	07.10.1960		
Sudan	23.07.1970 (A)	23.10.1970		
Sweden	22.01.1985 (A)	22.04.1985	22.01.1985 (A)	22.04.1985
Switzerland	15.05.1962 (A)	15.08.1962	15.05.1962 (A)	15.08.1962
Syrian Arab Republic	06.03.1958 (A)	06.06.1958	06.03.1958 (R)	06.06.1958
Tajikistan (Republic of)[1]	28.08.1992 (S)	Note 1	28.08.1992 (S)	Note 1
Thailand	02.05.1958 (A)	02.08.1958	02.05.1958 (A)	02.08.1958
Tunisia	28.01.1981 (A)	28.04.1981	28.01.1981 (A)	28.04.1981
Turkey	15.12.1965 (A)	15.03.1966	15.12.1965 (A)	15.03.1966
Ukraine	06.02.1957 (A)	06.05.1957	06.02.1957 (R)	06.05.1957
United Republic of Tanzania	23.09.1971 (A)	23.12.1971		
Uzbekistan	21.02.1996 (A)	21.05.1996	21.02.1996	21.05.1996
Yemen (Republic of)[7]	06.02.1970 (A)	06.05.1970	06.02.1970 (A)	06.05.1970
Yugoslavia (Federal Republic of)[4]	13.02.1956 (R)	07.08.1956	13.02.1956 (R)	07.08.1956
Zaire	18.04.1961 (A)	18.07.1961	18.04.1961 (A)	18.07.1961

---

* UNESCO Convention and Protocol for the Protection of Cultural Property in the Event of Armed Conflict, *done* May 14, 1954, 249 U.N.T.S. 215.

1. This State lodged a notification of succession at the mentioned date, by

which it stated that it was bound by the Convention and its Protocol which the USSR ratified on 4 January 1957.

2. This State lodged a notification of succession at the mentioned date, by which it stated that it was bound by the Convention and its Protocol which Yugoslavia ratified on 13 February 1956.

3. This State lodged a notification of succession at the mentioned date, by which it stated that it was bound by the Convention and its Protocol which Czechoslovakia ratified on 6 December 1957.

4. In conformity with the procedure set forth in the Convention and the Protocol, both agreements entered into force, for the first States, three months after the deposit of instrument of ratification by the fifth State, Mexico.

5. The German Democratic Republic deposited an instrument of accession to the Convention and its Protocol on 16 January 1974. Through the accession of the German Democratic Republic to the Basic Law of the Federal Republic of Germany, with effect from 3 October 1990, the two German States have united to form one sovereign State.

6. The instrument of ratification was deposited by the USSR, on 4 January 1957. The Director-General has been informed that the Russian Federation would continue the participation of the USSR in UNESCO conventions.

7. The People's Democratic Republic of Yemen deposited its instrument of accession on 6 February 1970. After the unification of the People's Democratic Republic of Yemen and the Yemen Arab Republic into a single sovereign State called "the Republic of Yemen," the Ministers of Foreign Affairs of the Yemen Arab Republic and the People's Democratic Republic of Yemen informed the Secretary-General of the United Nations on 19 May 1990 that all treaties and agreements concluded between either the Yemen Arab Republic or the People's Democratic Republic of Yemen and other States and international organizations in accordance with international law which are in force on 22 May 1990 would remain in effect.

Appendix II

UNESCO CONVENTION ON THE MEANS OF PROHIBITING AND PREVENTING THE ILLICIT IMPORT, EXPORT AND TRANSFER OF OWNERSHIP OF CULTURAL PROPERTY*

Opened for signature November 14, 1970; entry into force, April 24, 1972

The General Conference of the United Nations Educational, Scientific and Cultural Organization, meeting in Paris from 12 October to 14 November 1970, at its sixteenth session,

Recalling the importance of the provisions contained in the Declaration of the Principles of International Cultural Co-operation, adopted by the General Conference at its fourteenth session,

Considering that the interchange of cultural property among nations for scientific, cultural and educational purposes increases the knowledge of the civilization of Man, enriches the cultural life of all peoples and inspires mutual respect and appreciation among nations,

Considering that cultural property constitutes one of the basic elements of civilization and national culture, and that its true value can be appreciated only in relation to the fullest possible information regarding its origin, history and traditional setting,

Considering that it is incumbent upon every State to protect the cultural property existing within its territory against the dangers of theft, clandestine excavation, and illicit export,

Considering that, to avert these dangers, it is essential for every State to become increasingly alive to the moral obligations to respect its own cultural heritage and that of all nations,

Considering that, as cultural institutions, museums, libraries and archives should ensure that their collections are built up in accordance with universally recognized moral principles,

Considering that the illicit import, export and transfer of ownership of cultural property is an obstacle to that understanding between nations which it is part of UNESCO's mission to promote by recommending to interested States, international conventions to this end,

Considering that the protection of cultural heritage can be effective only if organized both nationally and internationally among States working in close co-operation,

Considering that the UNESCO General Conference adopted a Recommendation to this effect in 1964,

Having before it further proposals on the means of prohibiting and preventing the illicit import, export and transfer of ownership of cultural property, a question which is on the agenda for the session as item 19,

Having decided, at its fifteenth session, that this question should be made the subject of an international convention,

Adopts this Convention on the fourteenth day of November 1970.

Article 1

For the purposes of this Convention, the term "cultural property" means property which, on religious or secular grounds, is specifically designated by each State as being of importance for archaeology, prehistory, history, literature, art or science and which belongs to the following categories:

(a) Rare collections and specimens of fauna, flora, minerals and anatomy, and objects of palaeontological interest;

(b) property relating to history, including the history of science and technology and military and social history, to the life of national leaders, thinkers, scientists and artists and to events of national importance;

(c) products of archaeological excavations (including regular and clandestine) or of archaeological discoveries;

(d) elements of artistic or historical monuments or archaeological sites which have been dismembered;

(e) antiquities more than one hundred years old, such as inscriptions, coins and engraved seals;
(f) objects of ethnological interest;
(g) property of artistic interest, such as:
  (i) pictures, paintings and drawings produced entirely by hand on any support and in any material (excluding industrial designs and manufactured articles decorated by hand);
  (ii) original works of statuary art and sculpture in any material;
  (iii) original engravings, prints and lithographs;
  (iv) original artistic assemblages and montages in any material;
(h) rare manuscripts and incunabula, old books, documents and publications of special interest (historical, artistic, scientific, literary, etc.) singly or in collections;
(i) postage, revenue and similar stamps, singly or in collections;
(j) archives, including sound, photographic and cinematographic archives;
(k) articles of furniture more than one hundred years old and old musical instruments.

Article 2
1. The States Parties to this Convention recognize that the illicit import, export and transfer of ownership of cultural property is one of the main causes of the impoverishment of the cultural heritage of the countries of origin of such property and that international co-operation constitutes one of the most efficient means of protecting each country's cultural property against all the dangers resulting therefrom.
2. To this end, the States Parties undertake to oppose such practices with the means at their disposal, and particularly by removing their causes, putting a stop to current practices, and by helping to make the necessary reparations.

Article 3
The import, export or transfer of ownership of cultural property effected contrary to the provisions adopted under this Convention by the States Parties thereto, shall be illicit.

Article 4
The States Parties to this Convention recognize that for the purpose of the Convention property which belongs to the following categories forms part of the cultural heritage of each State:
(a) Cultural property created by the individual or collective genius of nationals of the State concerned, and cultural property of importance to the State concerned created within the territory of that State by foreign nationals or stateless persons resident within such territory;
(b) cultural property found within the national territory;
(c) cultural property acquired by archaeological, ethnological or natural science missions, with the consent of the competent authorities of the country of origin of such property;
(d) cultural property which has been the subject of a freely agreed exchange;
(e) cultural property received as a gift or purchased legally with the consent of the competent authorities of the country of origin of such property.

Article 5
To ensure the protection of their cultural property against illicit import, export and transfer of ownership, the States Parties to this Convention undertake, as appropriate for each country, to set up within their territories one or more national services, where such services do not already exist, for the protection of the cultural heritage, with a qualified staff sufficient in number for the effective carrying out of the following functions:
(a) contributing to the formation of draft laws and regulations designed to secure the protection of the cultural heritage and particularly prevention of the illicit import, export and transfer of ownership of important cultural property;

(b) establishing and keeping up to date, on the basis of a national inventory of protected property, a list of important public and private cultural property whose export would constitute an appreciable impoverishment of the national cultural heritage;
(c) promoting the development or the establishment of scientific and technical institutions (museums, libraries, archives, laboratories, workshops . . .) required to ensure the preservation and presentation of cultural property;
(d) organizing the supervision of archaeological excavations, ensuring the preservation "in situ" of certain cultural property, and protecting certain areas reserved for future archaeological research;
(e) establishing, for the benefit of those concerned (curators, collectors, antique dealers, etc.) rules in conformity with the ethical principles set forth in this Convention; and taking steps to ensure the observance of those rules;
(f) taking educational measures to stimulate and develop respect for the cultural heritage of all States, and spreading knowledge of the provisions of this Convention;
(g) seeing that appropriate publicity is given to the disappearance of any items of cultural property.

Article 6
The States Parties to this Convention undertake:
(a) To introduce an appropriate certificate in which the exporting State would specify that the export of the cultural property in question is authorized. The certificate should accompany all items of cultural property exported in accordance with the regulations;
(b) to prohibit the exportation of cultural property from their territory unless accompanied by the above-mentioned export certificate;
(c) to publicize this prohibition by appropriate means, particularly among persons likely to export or import cultural property.

Article 7
The States Parties to this Convention undertake:
(a) To take the necessary measures, consistent with national legislation, to prevent museums and similar institutions within their territories from acquiring cultural property originating in another State Party which has been illegally exported after entry into force of this Convention, in the States concerned. Whenever possible, to inform a State of origin Party to this Convention of an offer of such cultural property illegally removed from that State after the entry into force of this Convention in both States;
(b) (i) to prohibit the import of cultural property stolen from a museum or a religious or secular public monument or similar institution in another State Party to this Convention after the entry into force of this Convention for the States concerned, provided that such property is documented as appertaining to the inventory of that institution;
  (ii) at the request of the State Party of origin, to take appropriate steps to recover and return any such cultural property imported after the entry into force of this Convention in both States concerned, provided, however, that the requesting State shall pay just compensation to an innocent purchaser or to a person who has valid title to that property. Requests for recovery and return shall be made through diplomatic offices. The requesting Party shall furnish, at its expense, the documentation and other evidence necessary to establish its claim for recovery and return. The Parties shall impose no customs duties or other charges upon cultural property returned pursuant to this Article. All expenses incident to the return and delivery of the cultural property shall be borne by the requesting Party.

Article 8
The States Parties to this Convention undertake to impose penalties or administrative sanctions on any person responsible for infringing the prohibitions referred to under Articles 6(b) and 7(b) above.

Article 9
Any State Party to this Convention whose cultural patrimony is in jeopardy from pillage of archaeological or ethnological materials may call upon other States Parties who are affected. The States Parties to this Convention undertake, in these circumstances, to participate in a concerted international effort to determine and to carry out the necessary concrete measures, including the control of exports and imports and international commerce in the specific materials concerned. Pending agreement each State concerned shall take provisional measures to the extent feasible to prevent irremediable injury to the cultural heritage of the requesting State.

Article 10
The States Parties to this Convention undertake:
(a) To restrict by education, information and vigilance, movement of cultural property illegally removed from any State Party to this Convention and, as appropriate for each country, oblige antique dealers, subject to penal or administrative sanctions, to maintain a register recording the origin of each item of cultural property, names and addresses of the supplier, description and price of each item sold and to inform the purchaser of the cultural property of the export prohibition to which such property may be subject;
(b) to endeavour by educational means to create and develop in the public mind a realization of the value of cultural property and the threat to the cultural heritage created by theft, clandestine excavations and illicit exports.

Article 11
The export and transfer of ownership of cultural property under compulsion arising directly or indirectly from the occupation of a country by a foreign power shall be regarded as illicit.

Article 12
The States Parties to this Convention shall respect the cultural heritage within the territories for the international relations of which they are responsible, and shall take all appropriate measures to prohibit and prevent the illicit import, export and transfer of ownership of cultural property in such territories.

Article 13
The States Parties to this Convention also undertake, consistent with the laws of each State:
(a) To prevent by all appropriate means transfers of ownership of cultural property likely to promote the illicit import or export of such property;
(b) to ensure that their competent services co-operate in facilitating the earliest possible restitution of illicitly exported cultural property to its rightful owner;
(c) to admit actions for recovery of lost or stolen items of cultural property brought by or on behalf of the rightful owners;
(d) to recognize the indefeasible right of each State Party to this Convention to classify and declare certain cultural property as inalienable which should therefore *ipso facto* not be exported, and to facilitate recovery of such property by the State concerned in cases where it has been exported.

Article 14
In order to prevent illicit export and to meet the obligations arising from the implementation of this Convention, each State Party to the Convention should, as far as it is able, provide the national services responsible for the protection of its cultural heritage with an adequate budget and, if necessary, should set up a fund for this purpose.

Article 15
Nothing in this Convention shall prevent States Parties thereto from concluding special agreements among themselves or from continuing to implement agreements already concluded regarding the restitution of cultural property removed, whatever the reason, from its territory of origin, before the entry into force of this Convention for the States concerned.

Article 16
The States Parties to this Convention shall in their periodic reports submitted to the General Conference of the United Nations Educational, Scientific and Cultural Organization on dates and in a manner to be determined by it, give information on the legislative and administrative provisions which they have adopted and other action which they have taken for the application of this Convention, together with details of the experience acquired in this field.

Article 17
1. The States Parties to this Convention may call on the technical assistance of the United Nations Educational, Scientific and Cultural Organization, particularly as regards:
   (a) Information and education;
   (b) consultation and expert advice;
   (c) co-ordination and good offices.
2. The United Nations Educational, Scientific and Cultural Organization may, on its own initiative conduct research and publish studies on matters relevant to the illicit movement of cultural property.
3. To this end, the United Nations Educational, Scientific and Cultural Organization may also call on the co-operation of any competent non-governmental organization.
4. The United Nations Educational, Scientific and Cultural Organization may, on its own initiative, make proposals to States Parties to this Convention for its implementation.
5. At the request of at least two States Parties to this Convention which are engaged in a dispute over its implementation, UNESCO may extend its good offices to reach a settlement between them.

Article 18
This Convention is drawn up in English, French, Russian and Spanish, the four texts being equally authoritative.

Article 19
1. This Convention shall be subject to ratification or acceptance by States members of the United Nations Educational, Scientific and Cultural Organization in accordance with their respective constitutional procedures.
2. The instruments of ratification or acceptance shall be deposited with the Director-General of the United Nations Educational, Scientific and Cultural Organization.

Article 20
1. This Convention shall be open to accession by all States not members of the United Nations Educational, Scientific and Cultural Organization which are invited to accede to it by the Executive Board of the Organization.
2. Accession shall be effected by the deposit of an instrument of accession with the Director-General of the United Nations Educational, Scientific and Cultural Organization.

Article 21
This Convention shall enter into force three months after the date of the deposit of the third instrument of ratification, acceptance or accession, but only with respect to those States which have deposited their respective instruments on or before that date. It shall enter into force with respect to any other State three months after the deposit of its instrument of ratification, acceptance or accession.

Article 22
The States Parties to this Convention recognize that the Convention is applicable not only to their metropolitan territories but also to all territories for the international relations of which they are responsible; they undertake to consult, if necessary, the governments or other competent authorities of these territories on or before ratification, acceptance or accession with a view to securing the application of the Convention to those territories, and to notify the Director-General of the United Nations Educational, Scientific and Cultural Organization of the territories to which it is applied, the notification to take effect three months after the date of its receipt.

Article 23
1. Each State Party to this Convention may denounce the Convention on its own behalf or on behalf of any territory for whose inter-national relations it is responsible.
2. The denunciation shall be notified by an instrument in writing, deposited with the Director-General of the United Nations Educational, Scientific and Cultural Organization.
3. The denunciation shall take effect twelve months after the receipt of the instrument of denunciation.

Article 24
The Director-General of the United Nations Educational, Scientific and Cultural Organization shall inform the States members of the Organization, the States not members of the Organization which are referred to in Article 20, as well as the United Nations, of the deposit of all the instruments of ratification, acceptance and acces-sion provided for in Articles 19 and 20, and of the notifications and denunciations provided for in Articles 22 and 23 respectively.

Article 25
1. This Convention may be revised by the General Conference of the United Nations Educational, Scientific and Cultural Organization. Any such revision shall, however, bind only the States which shall become Parties to the revising convention.
2. If the General Conference should adopt a new convention revising this Convention in whole or in part, then, unless the new convention otherwise provides, this Convention shall cease to be open to ratification, acceptance or accession, as from the date on which the new revising convention enters into force.

Article 26
In conformity with Article 102 of the Charter of the United Nations, this Convention shall be registered with the Secretariat of the United Nations at the request of the Director-General of the United Nations Educational, Scientific and Cultural Organization.

Done in Paris this seventeenth day of November 1970, in two authentic copies bearing the signature of the President of the sixteenth session of the General Conference and of the Director-General of the United Nations Educational, Scientific and Cultural Organization, which shall be deposited in the archives of the United Nations Educational, Scientific and Cultural Organization, and certified true copies of which shall be delivered to all the States referred to in Articles 19 and 20 as well as to the United Nations.

The foregoing is the authentic text of the Convention duly adopted by the General Conference of the United Nations Educa-tional, Scientific and Cultural Organization during its sixteenth session, which was held in Paris and declared closed the fourteenth day of November 1970.

In faith whereof we have appended our signatures this seventeenth day of November 1970.

The President of the General Conference   The Director-General

LIST OF THE 85 STATES PARTIES TO THE CONVENTION AS AT 15 JUNE 1996

States	Date of deposit ratification (R) acceptance (Ac) accession (A) succession (S)	Date of entry into force
Algeria	24.06.1974 (R)	24.09.1974
Angola	07.11.1991 (R)	07.02.1992
Argentina	11.01.1973 (R)	11.04.1973
Armenia (Republic of)[1]	05.09.1993 (S)	Note 1
Australia	30.10.1989 (Ac)	30.01.1990
Bangladesh	09.12.1987 (R)	09.03.1988
Belarus	28.04.1988 (R)	28.07.1988
Belize	26.01.1990 (R)	26.04.1990
Bolivia	04.10.1976 (R)	04.01.1977
Bosnia-Herzegovina (Republic of)[2]	12.07.1993 (S)	Note 2
Brazil	16.02.1973 (R)	16.05.1973
Bulgaria[5]	15.09.1971 (R)	24.04.1972
Burkina Faso	07.04.1987 (R)	07.07.1987
Cambodia	26.09.1972 (R)	26.12.1972
Cameroon	24.05.1972 (R)	24.08.1972
Canada	28.03.1978 (Ac)	28.06.1978
Central African Republic	01.02.1972 (R)	01.05.1972
China (People's Republic of)	28.11.1989 (Ac)	28.02.1990
Colombia	24.05.1988 (Ac)	24.08.1988
Costa Rica	06.03.1996 (R)	06.06.1996
Côte d'Ivoire	30.10.1990 (R)	30.01.1991
Croatia (Republic of)[2]	06.07.1992 (S)	Note 2
Cuba	30.01.1980 (R)	30.04.1980
Cyprus	19.10.1979 (R)	19.01.1980
Czech Republic[3]	26.03.1993 (S)	Note 3
Democratic People's Republic of Korea	13.05.1983 (R)	13.08.1983
Dominican Republic	07.03.1973 (R)	07.06.1973
Ecuador[5]	24.03.1971 (Ac)	24.04.1972
Egypt	05.04.1973 (Ac)	05.07.1973
El Salvador	20.02.1978 (R)	20.05.1978
Estonia	27.10.1995 (R)	27.01.1996
Georgia (Republic of)[1]	04.11.1992 (S)	Note 1
Greece	05.06.1981 (R)	05.09.1981
Grenada	10.09.1992 (Ac)	10.12.1992
Guatemala	14.01.1985 (R)	14.04.1985
Guinea	18.03.1979 (R)	18.06.1979
Honduras	19.03.1979 (R)	19.06.1979
Hungary	23.10.1978 (R)	23.01.1979
India	24.01.1977 (R)	24.04.1977
Iran (Islamic Republic of)	27.01.1975 (Ac)	27.04.1975
Iraq	12.02.1973 (Ac)	12.05.1973
Italy	02.10.1978 (R)	02.01.1979
Jordan	15.03.1974 (R)	15.06.1974
Kuwait	22.06.1972 (Ac)	22.09.1972
Kyrghyz Republic	03.07.1995 (A)	03.10.1995
Lebanon	25.08.1992 (R)	25.11.1992
Libyan Arab Jamahiriya	09.01.1973 (R)	09.04.1973
Madagascar	21.06.1989 (R)	21.09.1989
Mali	06.04.1987 (R)	06.07.1987
Mauritania	27.04.1977 (R)	27.07.1977
Mauritius	27.02.1978 (Ac)	27.05.1978
Mexico	04.10.1972 (Ac)	04.01.1973
Mongolia	23.05.1991 (Ac)	23.08.1991
Nepal	23.06.1976 (R)	23.09.1976
Nicaragua	19.04.1977 (R)	19.07.1977
Niger	16.10.1972 (R)	16.01.1973
Nigeria	24.01.1972 (R)	24.04.1972
Oman	02.06.1978 (Ac)	02.09.1978
Pakistan	30.04.1981 (R)	30.07.1981
Panama	13.08.1973 (R)	13.11.1973
Peru	24.10.1979 (Ac)	24.01.1980
Poland	31.01.1974 (R)	30.04.1974
Portugal	09.12.1985 (R)	09.03.1986
Qatar	20.04.1977 (Ac)	20.07.1977
Republic of Korea	14.02.1983 (Ac)	14.05.1983

Romania	06.12.1993 (R)	06.03.1994
Russian Federation[4]	28.04.1988 (R)	28.07.1988
Saudi Arabia	08.09.1976 (Ac)	08.12.1976
Senegal	09.12.1984 (R)	09.03.1985
Slovak Republic[3]	31.03.1993 (S)	Note 3
Slovenia (Republic of)[2]	05.11.1992 (S)	Note 2
Spain	10.01.1986 (R)	10.04.1986
Sri Lanka	07.04.1981 (Ac)	07.07.1981
Syrian Arab Republic	21.02.1975 (Ac)	21.05.1975
Tajikistan (Republic of)[1]	28.08.1992 (S)	Note 1
Tunisia	10.03.1975 (R)	10.06.1975
Turkey	21.04.1981 (R)	21.07.1981
Ukraine	28.04.1988 (R)	28.07.1988
United Republic of Tanzania	02.08.1977 (R)	02.11.1977
United States of America	02.09.1983 (Ac)	02.12.1983
Uruguay	09.08.1977 (R)	09.11.1977
Uzbekistan	15.03.1996 (R)	15.06.1996
Yugoslavia (Federal Republic of)	03.10.1972 (R)	03.01.1973
Zaire	23.09.1974 (R)	23.12.1974
Zambia	21.06.1985 (R)	21.09.1985

---

* UNESCO Convention on the Means of Prohibiting and Preventing the Illicit Import, Export and Transfer of Ownership of Cultural Property, *opened for signature* Nov. 14, 1970, 823 U.N.T.S. 231; 9 I.L.M. 289.

1. This State lodged a notification of succession at the mentioned date, by which it stated that it was bound by the Convention that the USSR ratified on 28 April 1988.

2. This State lodged a notification of succession at the mentioned date, by which it stated that it was bound by the Convention which Yugoslavia ratified on 3 October 1972.

3. This State lodged a notification of succession at the mentioned date, by which it stated that it was bound by the Convention which Czechoslovakia accepted on 14 February 1977.

4. The instrument of ratification was deposited by the USSR on 28 April 1988. The Director-General has been informed that the Russian Federation would continue the participation of the USSR in UNESCO conventions.

5. In conformity with the procedure set forth in the Convention, this agreement entered into force, for the first States, three months after the deposit of ratification by the third State, Nigeria.

Appendix 12

A PLEA FOR THE RETURN OF AN IRREPLACEABLE CULTURAL HERITAGE TO THOSE WHO CREATED IT*
Amadou-Mahtar M'Bow, former Director-General of UNESCO

June 7, 1978

One of the most noble incarnations of a people's genius is its cultural heritage, built up over the centuries by the work of its architects, sculptors, painters, engravers, goldsmiths and all the creators of forms, who have contrived to give tangible expression to the many-sided beauty and uniqueness of that genius.

The vicissitudes of history have nevertheless robbed many peoples of a priceless portion of this inheritance in which their enduring identity finds its embodiment.

Architectural features, statues and friezes, monoliths, mosaics, pottery, enamels, masks and objects of jade, ivory and chased gold—in fact everything which has been taken away, from monuments to handicrafts—were more than decorations or ornamentation. They bore witness to a history, the history of a culture of a nation whose spirit they perpetuated and renewed.

The peoples who were victims of this plunder, sometimes for hundreds of years, have not only been despoiled of irreplaceable masterpieces but also robbed of a memory which would doubtless have helped them to greater self-knowledge and would certainly have enabled others to understand them better.

Today, unbridled speculation, fanned by the prices prevailing in the art market, incites traffickers and plunderers to exploit local ignorance and take advantage of any connivance they find. In Africa, Latin America, Asia, Oceania and even in Europe, modern pirates with substantial resources, using modern techniques to satisfy their greed, spoil and rob archaeological sites almost before the scholars have excavated them.

The men and women of these countries have the right to recover these cultural assets which are part of their being.

They know, of course, that art is for the world and are aware of the fact that this art, which tells the story of their past and shows what they really are, does not speak to them alone. They are happy that men and women elsewhere can study and admire the work of their ancestors. They also realize that certain works of art have for too long played too intimate a part in the history of the country to which they were taken for the symbols linking them with that country to be denied, and for the roots they have put down to be severed.

These men and women who have been deprived of their cultural heritage therefore ask for the return of at least the art treasures which best represent their culture, which they feel are the most vital and whose absence causes them the greatest anguish.

This is a legitimate claim; and UNESCO, whose Constitution makes it responsible for the preservation and protection of the universal heritage of works of art and monuments of historic or scientific interest, is actively encouraging all that needs to be done to meet it.

The return of cultural assets to their countries of origin nevertheless continues to pose particular problems which cannot be solved simply by negotiated agreements and spontaneous acts. It therefore seemed necessary to approach these problems for their own sake, examining both the principle underlying them and all their various aspects.

This is why, on behalf of the United Nations Educational, Scientific and Cultural Organization which has empowered me to launch this appeal,

I solemnly call upon the governments of the Organization's Member States to conclude bilateral agreements for the return of cultural property to the countries from which it has been taken; to promote long-term loans, deposits, sales and donations between institutions concerned in order to encourage a fairer international exchange of cultural property, and, if they have not already done so, to ratify and rigorously enforce the Convention giving them effective means to prevent illicit trading in artistic and archaeological objects.

I call on all those working for the information media—journalists of press and radio, producers and authors of television programmes and films—to arouse world-wide a mighty and intense movement of public opinion so that respect for works of art leads, wherever necessary, to their return to their homeland.

I call on cultural organizations and specialized associations in all continents to help formulate and promote a stricter code of ethics with regard to the acquisition and conservation of cultural property, and to contribute to the gradual revision of codes of professional practice in this connection, on the lines of the initiative taken by the International Council of Museums.

I call on universities, libraries, public and private art galleries and museums that possess the most important collections, to share generously the objects in their keeping with the countries which created them and which sometimes no longer possess a single example.

I also call on institutions possessing several similar objects or records to part with at least one and return it to its country of origin, so that the young will not grow up without ever having the chance to see, at close quarters, a work of art or a well-made item of handicraft fashioned by their ancestors.

I call on the authors of art books and on art critics to proclaim how much a work of art gains in beauty and truth, both for the uninitiated and for the scholar, when viewed in the natural and social setting in which it took shape.

I call on those responsible for preserving and restoring works of art to facilitate, by their advice and actions, the return of such works to the countries where they were created and to seek with imagination and perseverance for new ways of preserving and displaying them once they have been returned to their homeland.

I call on historians and educators to help others to understand the affliction a nation can suffer at the spoliation of the works it has created. The power of the fait accompli is a survival of barbaric times and a source of resentment and discord which prejudices the establishment of lasting peace and harmony between nations.

Finally, I appeal with special intensity and hope to artists themselves and to writers, poets and singers, asking them to testify that nations also need to be alive on an imaginative level.

Two thousand years ago, the Greek historian Polybius urged us to refrain from turning other nations' misfortunes into embellishments for our own countries. Today when all peoples are acknowledged to be equal in dignity, I am convinced that international solidarity can, on the contrary, contribute practically to the general happiness of mankind.

---

* Amadou-Mahtar M'Bow, former Director-General, UNESCO, *A Plea for the Return of an Irreplaceable Cultural Heritage to Those Who Created It*, June 7, 1978, *reprinted in* 31 MUSEUM 58 (1979).

Appendix 13

STATUTES OF THE INTERGOVERNMENTAL COMMITTEE FOR PROMOTING THE RETURN OF CULTURAL PROPERTY TO ITS COUNTRIES OF ORIGIN OR ITS RESTITUTION IN CASE OF ILLICIT APPROPRIATION*

Adopted by Resolution 4/7.6/5 of the twentieth session of the General Conference of UNESCO, October 24–November 28, 1978.

In accordance with UNESCO practice, instruments adopted by the General Conference are not signed by the Member States

Article 1[1]
An Intergovernmental Committee of an advisory nature whose services will be available to Member States and Associate Members of UNESCO involved, hereafter called the Committee, whose functions are defined in Article 4 below, is hereby established within the United Nations Educational, Scientific and Cultural Organization, hereafter called UNESCO.

Article 2
1. The Committee shall be composed of 20 Member States of UNESCO elected by the General Conference at its ordinary sessions, taking into account the need to ensure equitable geographical distribution and appropriate rotation, as well as the representative character of those States in respect of the contribution they are able to make to the restitution or return of cultural property to its countries of origin.
2. The term of office of members of the Committee shall extend from the end of the ordinary session of the General Conference during which they are elected until the end of its second subsequent ordinary session.
3. Notwithstanding the provisions of paragraph 2 above, the term of office of half of the members designated at the time of the first election shall cease at the end of the first ordinary session of the General Conference following that at which they were elected. The names of these members shall be chosen by lot by the President of the General Conference after the first election.
4. Members of the Committee shall be immediately eligible for re-election.
5. States members of the Committee shall choose their representatives with due attention to the terms of reference of the Committee as defined by these statutes.

Article 3
1. For the purposes of these statutes, "cultural property" shall be taken to denote historical and ethnographic objects and documents including manuscripts, works of the plastic and decorative arts, palaeontological and archaeological objects and zoological, botanical and mineralogical specimens.
2. A request for the restitution or return by a Member State or Associate Member of UNESCO may be made concerning any cultural property which has a fundamental significance from the point of view of the spiritual values and cultural heritage of the people of a Member State or Associate Member of UNESCO and which has been lost as a result of colonial or foreign occupation or as a result of illicit appropriation.
3. Cultural property restituted or returned shall be accompanied by the relevant scientific documentation.

Article 4

The Committee shall be responsible for:

1. seeking ways and means of facilitating bilateral negotiations for the restitution or return of cultural property to its countries of origin when they are undertaken according to the conditions defined in Article 9;
2. promoting multilateral and bilateral co-operation with a view to the restitution and return of cultural property to its countries of origin;
3. encouraging the necessary research and studies for the establishment of coherent programmes for the constitution of representative collections in countries whose cultural heritage has been dispersed;
4. fostering a public information campaign on the real nature, scale and scope of the problem of the restitution or return of cultural property to its countries of origin;
5. guiding the planning and implementation of UNESCO's programme of activities with regard to the restitution or return of cultural property to its countries of origin;
6. encouraging the establishment or reinforcement of museums or other institutions for the conservation of cultural property and the training of the necessary scientific and technical personnel;
7. promoting exchanges of cultural property in accordance with the Recommendation on the International Exchange of Cultural Property;
8. reporting on its activities to the General Conference of UNESCO at each of its ordinary sessions.

Article 5

1. The Committee shall meet in regular plenary session at least once and not more than twice every two years. Extraordinary sessions may be convened as specified in the Committee's Rules of Procedure.
2. Each member of the Committee shall have one vote, but may send to the Committee's sessions as many experts or advisers as it deems necessary.
3. The Committee shall adopt its own Rules of Procedure.

Article 6

1. The Committee may set up *ad hoc* subcommittees for the study of specific problems related to its activities, as described in paragraph 1 of Article 4. Membership of such subcommittees may also be open to Member States of UNESCO which are not represented in the Committee.
2. The Committee defines the mandate of any such *ad hoc* subcommittee.

Article 7

1. At the beginning of its first session, the Committee shall elect a Chairman, four Vice-Chairmen and a Rapporteur; these shall form the Committee's Bureau.
2. The Bureau shall discharge such duties as the Committee may lay upon it.
3. Meetings of the Bureau may be convened in between sessions of the Committee at the request of the Committee itself, of the Chairman of the Committee or of the Director-General of UNESCO.
4. The Committee shall elect a new Bureau whenever its own membership is changed by the General Conference in accordance with Article 2 above.
5. The members of the Bureau who are representatives of Member States of UNESCO shall remain in office until a new Bureau has been elected.[2]

Article 8

1. Any Member State which is not a member of the Committee or any Associate Member of UNESCO that is concerned by an offer or a request for the restitution or return of cultural property shall be invited to participate, without the right to vote, in the meetings of the Committee or of its *ad hoc* subcommittees dealing with that offer or request. The States which are members of the Committee that are concerned by an offer or request for the restitution or return of cultural property shall not have the right to vote when such offer or request is being examined by the Committee or its *ad hoc* subcommittees.
2. Member States and Associate Members of UNESCO which are not members of the Committee may attend meetings of the Committee and of its *ad hoc* subcommittees as observers.
3. Representatives of the United Nations and other organizations of the United Nations system may take part, without the right to vote, in all meetings of the Committee and of its *ad hoc* subcommittees.
4. The Committee shall determine the conditions under which international governmental and non-governmental organizations, other than those covered by paragraph 3 above, shall be invited to attend its meetings or those of its *ad hoc* subcommittees as observers.

Article 9

1. Offers and requests formulated in accordance with these statutes, concerning the restitution or return of cultural property, shall be communicated by Member States or Associate Members of UNESCO to the Director-General, who shall transmit them to the Committee, accompanied, in so far as is possible, by appropriate supporting documents.
2. The Committee shall examine such offers and such requests and the relevant documentation in accordance with Article 4, paragraph 1, of these statutes.

Article 10

1. The Secretariat of the Committee shall be provided by the Director-General of UNESCO, who shall place at the Committee's disposal the staff and other means required for its operation.
2. The Secretariat shall provide the necessary services for the sessions of the Committee and meetings of its Bureau and *ad hoc* subcommittees.
3. The Secretariat shall fix the date of the Committee's sessions in accordance with the Bureau's instructions, and shall take all steps required to convene such sessions.
4. The Committee and the Director-General of UNESCO shall make the greatest possible use of the services of any competent international non-governmental organization in order to prepare the Committee's documentation and to ensure that its recommendations are implemented.

Article 11

Each Member State and Associate Member of UNESCO shall bear the expense of participation of its representatives in sessions of the Committee and of subsidiary organs, its Bureau and its *ad hoc* subcommittees.

---

* Statutes of the Intergovernmental Committee for Promoting the Return of Cultural Property to its Countries of Origin or its Restitution in Case of Illicit Appropriation, G.A. Res. 4/7.6/5, UNESCO, 20th Sess., 1 Resolutions 92 (1979), *reprinted in* U.N. GAOR, 34th Sess., Annex 8, Agenda Item 20, U.N. Doc. A/34/529 (1979).

1. The General Conference of UNESCO adopted, at its twenty-eighth session (Paris, October–November 1995), Resolution 28 C/22 increasing the membership of the Intergovernmental Committee from twenty to twenty-two Member States.

2. Resolution of the Twenty-third Session of the General Conference of UNESCO, adopted on 4 November 1985.

Appendix 14

TREATY BETWEEN THE FEDERAL REPUBLIC OF GERMANY AND THE UNION OF SOVIET SOCIALIST REPUBLICS ON GOOD-NEIGHBORLINESS, PARTNERSHIP AND COOPERATION*

Done at Bonn, November 9, 1990

The Federal Republic of Germany and the Union of Soviet Socialist Republics,

Conscious of their responsibility for the preservation of peace in Europe and in the world,

Desiring to set the final seal on the past and, through understanding and reconciliation, render a major contribution towards ending the division of Europe,

Convinced of the need to build a new, united Europe on the basis of common values and to create a just and lasting peaceful order in Europe including stable security structures,

Convinced that great importance attaches to human rights and fundamental freedoms as part of the heritage of the whole of Europe and that respect for them is a major prerequisite for progress in developing that peaceful order,

Reaffirming their commitment to the aims and principles enshrined in the United Nations Charter and to the provisions of the Final Act of Helsinki of 1 August 1975 and of subsequent documents adopted by the Conference on Security and Cooperation in Europe,

Resolved to continue the good traditions of their centuries-long history, to make good-neighborliness, partnership and cooperation the basis of their relations, and to meet the historic challenges that present themselves on the threshold of the third millennium,

Having regard to the foundations established in recent years through the development of cooperation between the Union of Soviet Socialist Republics and the Federal Republic of Germany as well as the German Democratic Republic,

Moved by the desire to further develop and intensify the fruitful and mutually beneficial cooperation between the two States in all fields and to give their mutual relationship a new quality in the interests of their peoples and of peace in Europe,

Taking account of the signing of the Treaty of 12 September 1990 on the Final Settlement with respect to Germany regulating the external aspects of German unity,

Have agreed as follows:

Article 1

The Federal Republic of Germany and the Union of Soviet Socialist Republics will, in developing their relations, be guided by the following principles:

They will respect each other's sovereign equality, territorial integrity and political independence.

They will make the dignity and rights of the individual, concern for the survival of mankind, and preservation of the natural environment the focal point of their policy.

They reaffirm the right of all nations and States to determine their own fate freely and without interference from outside and to proceed with their political, economic, social and cultural development as they see fit.

They uphold the principle that any war, whether nuclear or conventional, must be effectively prevented and peace preserved and developed.

They guarantee the precedence of the universal rules of international law in their domestic and international relations and confirm their resolve to honour their contractual obligations.

They pledge themselves to make use of the creative potential of the individual and modern society with a view to safeguarding peace and enhancing the prosperity of all nations.

Article 2

The Federal Republic of Germany and the Union of Soviet Socialist Republics undertake to respect without qualification the territorial integrity of all States in Europe within their present frontiers.

They declare that they have no territorial claims whatsoever against any State and will not raise any in the future.

They regard and will continue to regard as inviolable the frontiers of all States in Europe as they exist on the day of signature of the present Treaty.

Article 3

The Federal Republic of Germany and the Union of Soviet Socialist Republics reaffirm that they will refrain from any threat or use of force which is directed against the territorial integrity or political independence of the other side or is in any other way incompatible with the aims and principles of the United Nations Charter or with the CSCE Final Act.

They will settle their disputes exclusively by peaceful means and never resort to any of their weapons except for the purpose of individual or collective self-defence. They will never and under no circumstances be the first to employ armed forces against one another or against third States. They call upon all other States to join in this non-aggression commitment.

Should either side become the object of an attack the other side will not afford any military support or other assistance to the aggressor and resort to all measures to settle the conflict in conformity with the principles and procedures of the United Nations and other institutions of collective security.

Article 4

The Federal Republic of Germany and the Union of Soviet Socialist Republics will seek to ensure that armed forces and armaments are substantially reduced by means of binding, effectively verifiable agreements in order to achieve, in conjunction with unilateral measures, a stable balance at a lower level, especially in Europe, which will suffice for defence but not for attack.

The same applies to the multilateral and bilateral enhancement of confidence-building and stabilizing measures.

Article 5

Both sides will support to the best of their ability the process of security and cooperation in Europe on the basis of the Final Act of Helsinki adopted on 1 August 1975 and, with the cooperation of all participating States, develop and intensify that cooperation further still, notably by creating permanent institutions and bodies. The aim of these efforts is the consolidation of peace, stability and security and the coalescence of Europe to form a single area of law, democracy and cooperation in the fields of economy, culture and information.

Article 6

The Federal Republic of Germany and the Union of Soviet Socialist Republics have agreed to hold regular consultations with a view to further developing and intensifying their bilateral relations and coordinating their positions on international issues.

Consultations at the highest political level shall be held as necessary but at least once a year.

The Foreign Ministers will meet at least twice a year.

The Defence Ministers will meet at regular intervals.

Other ministers will meet as necessary to discuss matters of mutual interest.

The existing mixed commissions will consider ways and means of intensifying their work. New mixed commissions will be appointed as necessary by mutual agreement.

Article 7
Should a situation arise which in the opinion of either side constitutes a threat to or violation of peace or may lead to dangerous international complications, both sides will immediately make contact with a view to coordinating their positions and agreeing on measures to improve or resolve the situation.

Article 8
The Federal Republic of Germany and the Union of Soviet Socialist Republics have agreed to substantially expand and intensify their bilateral cooperation, especially in the economic, industrial and scientific-technological fields and in the field of environmental protection, with a view to developing their mutual relations on a stable and long-term basis and deepening the trust between the two States and peoples. They will to this end conclude a comprehensive agreement on the development of cooperation in the economic, industrial and scientific-technological fields and, where necessary, separate arrangements on specific matters.

Both sides attach great importance to cooperation in the training of specialists and executive personnel from industry for the development of bilateral relations and are prepared to considerably expand and intensify that cooperation.

Article 9
The Federal Republic of Germany and the Union of Soviet Socialist Republics will further develop and intensify their economic cooperation for their mutual benefit. They will create, as far as their domestic legislation and their obligations under international treaties allow, the most favourable general conditions for entrepreneurial and other economic activity by citizens, enterprises and governmental as well as non-governmental institutions of the other side.

This applies in particular to the treatment of capital investment and investors.

Both sides will encourage the initiatives necessary for economic cooperation by those directly concerned, especially with the aim of fully exploiting the possibilities afforded by the existing treaties and programmes.

Article 10
Both sides will, on the basis of the Agreement of 22 July 1986 concerning Economic and Technological Cooperation, further develop exchanges in this field and implement joint projects. They propose to draw on the achievements of modern science and technology for the sake of the people, their health, and their prosperity. They will promote and support parallel initiatives by researchers and research establishments in this sphere.

Article 11
Convinced that the preservation of the natural sources of life is indispensable for prosperous economic and social development, both sides reaffirm their determination to continue and intensify their cooperation in the field of environmental protection on the basis of the Agreement of 25 October 1988.

They propose to solve major problems of environmental protection together, to study harmful effects on the environment, and to develop measures for their prevention. They will participate in the development of coordinated strategies and concepts for a transborder environmental policy within the international, and especially the European, framework.

Article 12
Both sides will seek to extend transport communications (air, rail, sea, inland waterway and road links) between the Federal Republic of Germany and the Union of Soviet Socialist Republics through the use of state-of-the-art technology.

Article 13
Both sides will strive to simplify to a considerable extent, on the basis of reciprocity, the procedure for the issue of visas to citizens of both countries wishing to travel, primarily for business, economic and cultural reasons and for purposes of scientific and technological cooperation.

Article 14
Both sides support comprehensive contacts among people from both countries and the development of cooperation among parties, trade unions, foundations, schools, universities, sports organizations, churches and social institutions, women's associations, environmental protection and other social organizations and associations.

Special attention will be given to the deepening of contacts between the parliaments of the two States.

They welcome cooperation based on partnership between municipalities and regions and between Federal States and Republics of the Union.

An important role falls to the German-Soviet Discussion Forum and cooperation among the media.

Both sides will facilitate the participation of all young people and their organizations in exchanges and other contacts and joint projects.

Article 15
The Federal Republic of Germany and the Union of Soviet Socialist Republics, conscious of the mutual enrichment of the cultures of their peoples over the centuries and of their unmistakable contribution to Europe's common cultural heritage, as well as of the importance of cultural exchange for international understanding, will considerably extend their cultural cooperation.

Both sides will give substance to and fully exploit the agreement on the establishment and work of cultural centres.

Both sides reaffirm their willingness to give all interested persons comprehensive access to the languages and cultures of the other side and will encourage public and private initiatives.

Both sides strongly advocate the creation of wider possibilities for learning the language of the other country in schools, universities and other educational institutions and will for this purpose assist the other side in the training of teachers and make available teaching aids, including the use of television, radio, audio-visual and computer technology. They will support initiatives for the establishment of bilingual schools.

Soviet citizens of German nationality as well as citizens from the Union of Soviet Socialist Republics who have their permanent abode in the Federal Republic of Germany and wish to preserve their language, culture or traditions will be enabled to develop their national, linguistic and cultural identity. Accordingly, both sides will make possible and facilitate promotional measures for the benefit of such persons or their organizations within the framework of their respective laws.

Article 16
The Federal Republic of Germany and the Union of Soviet Socialist Republics will advocate the preservation of cultural treasures of the other side in their territory.

They agree that lost or unlawfully transferred art treasures which are located in their territory will be returned to their owners or their successors.

Article 17
Both sides stress the special importance of humanitarian cooperation in their bilateral relations. They will intensify this cooperation with the assistance of the charitable organizations of both sides.

Article 18
The Government of the Federal Republic of Germany declares that the monuments to Soviet victims of the war and totalitarian rule

erected on German soil will be respected and be under the protection of German law.

The same applies to Soviet war graves; they will be preserved and tended.

The Government of the Union of Soviet Socialist Republics will guarantee access to the graves of Germans on Soviet territory, their preservation and upkeep.

The responsible organizations of both sides will intensify their cooperation on these matters.

Article 19

The Federal Republic of Germany and the Union of Soviet Socialist Republics will intensify their mutual assistance in civil and family matters on the basis of the Hague Convention relating to Civil Procedure to which they are signatories. Both sides will further develop their mutual assistance in criminal matters, taking into account their legal systems and proceeding in harmony with international law.

The responsible authorities in the Federal Republic of Germany and the Union of Soviet Socialist Republics will cooperate in combating organized crime, terrorism, drug trafficking, illicit interference with civil aviation and maritime shipping, the manufacture or dissemination of counterfeit money, and smuggling, including the illicit transborder movement of works of art. The procedure and conditions for mutual cooperation will be the subject of a separate arrangement.

Article 20

The two Governments will intensify their cooperation within the scope of international organizations, taking into account their mutual interests and each side's cooperation with other countries. They will assist one another in developing cooperation with international, especially European, organizations and institutions of which either side is a member, should the other side express an interest in such cooperation.

Article 21

The present Treaty will not affect the rights and obligations arising from existing bilateral and multilateral agreements which the two sides have concluded with other States. The present Treaty is directed against no one; both sides regard their cooperation as an integral part and dynamic element of the further development of the CSCE process.

Article 22

The present Treaty is subject to ratification; the instruments of ratification will be exchanged as soon as possible in Moscow.

The present Treaty will enter into force on the date of exchange of the instruments of ratification.

The present Treaty will remain in force for twenty years. Thereafter it will be tacitly extended for successive periods of five years unless either Contracting Party denounces the Treaty in writing subject to one year's notice prior to its expiry.

Done at Bonn on November the 9th, 1990 in duplicate in the German and Russian languages, both texts being equally authentic.

For the Federal Republic of Germany
Dr. Helmut Kohl

For the Union of Soviet Socialist Republics
Mikhail S. Gorbachev

---

* Treaty on Good-Neighborliness, Partnership and Cooperation, Nov. 9, 1990, F.R.G.-U.S.S.R., 30 I.L.M. 505.

Appendix 15

AGREEMENT BETWEEN THE GOVERNMENT OF THE FEDERAL REPUBLIC OF GERMANY AND THE GOVERNMENT OF THE RUSSIAN FEDERATION ON CULTURAL COOPERATION*
(Articles 1–2, 13–18)

Signed at Moscow, December 16, 1992; entry into force, May 18, 1993

The Government of the Federal Republic of Germany and the Government of the Russian Federation,

In their effort to strengthen the relations between the two countries and to deepen mutual understanding,

Guided by the principles and aims of the Conference on Security and Cooperation in Europe,

In the conviction that the cultural relations are in accordance with the basic interests of the peoples of both countries in all areas, including education and science; that they strengthen the further development of good neighborliness, partnership, and cooperation; and that they thereby promote the awareness of a European cultural community and the creation of a common and open cultural area in Europe,

Mindful of the historical contribution of the peoples of both countries to the common European cultural heritage, and in the awareness that care and preservation of cultural goods are binding obligations,

Wishing to cultivate the cultural relations, including education and science, between the peoples of both countries have agreed as follows:

Article 1

The Contracting Parties will strive to expand and improve mutual knowledge of the culture of their countries, and to contribute to the strengthening of the awareness of a European cultural community. They will encourage and support state, societal and other initiatives, in order to develop a comprehensive cultural cooperation and partnership on all levels.

Article 2

1. The Contracting Parties will endeavor to grant all interested persons free access to the culture of the other country, including art, literature and history. They will carry out the appropriate measures and assist each other, within their powers, especially in respect of
   • guest performances of artists and ensembles, the presentation of concerts, theater performances, and other artistic presentations;
   • the implementation of exhibitions as well as the organization of speeches and lectures;
   • the organization of mutual visits of representatives from the various fields of cultural life, especially art and literature, with a view to developing cooperation, sharing experiences, and participating in seminars and similar events;
   • the furthering of contacts as well as the exchange of experts and materials in the fields of publishing, libraries, archives, and museums;
   • the translation of literary, scientific and technical works.

Article 13

The Contracting Parties, in accordance with the aims of this Agreement, will facilitate and encourage friendly cooperation at regional and local levels between the states, regions, districts and communities of the Federal Republic of Germany and the republics belonging to the Russian Federation, as well as the administrative regions, administrative provinces, autonomous regional bodies, cities and administrative districts of the Russian Federation.

Article 14

1. The Contracting Parties will promote the foundation of cultural institutions of the other party to the contract within the territory of their countries, and facilitate their work in accordance with their domestic legislation and under conditions to be agreed between them.
2. Cultural institutions within the meaning of paragraph 1 are cultural institutes, cultural centers, institutions and subsidiaries of science organizations, research institutions, universities, general and vocational schools, institutions for teacher training and continuing education, adult education, vocational training and continuing education, libraries and reading rooms, which are entirely or predominantly publicly funded. Cultural, scientific or educational professionals who are sent on official individual missions will have the same status as home-based specialists working for these institutions.
3. The status of the cultural institutions and their home-based specialists referred to in paragraphs 1 and 2, as well as that of the other professionals dispatched on official individual missions by the parties to the contract within the framework of cultural cooperation, will be determined in the Annex to this Agreement, which is an integral part of the Agreement. The Annex will enter into force concurrently with the Agreement.

Article 15

The Contracting Parties agree that lost or unlawfully transferred cultural property which is located in their sovereign territory will be returned to its owners or their successors.

Article 16

The representatives of the Contracting Parties will meet as necessary or at the request of either Contracting Party as a Mixed Commission alternately in the Federal Republic of Germany and in the Russian Federation in order to analyze the results of the cooperation under this Agreement and in order to elaborate recommendations as to the future emphasis of cultural cooperation. Further details will be worked out through the diplomatic channels.

Article 17

1. This Agreement will enter into force as soon as the Contracting Parties have notified each other that the domestic conditions for the Agreement's entry into force have been fulfilled. The day of receipt of the last notification will be regarded as the day of entry into force of the Agreement.
2. Upon the entry into force of this Agreement, the Agreement of May 19, 1973 between the Government of the Federal Republic of Germany and the Government of the Union of Soviet Socialist Republics on Cultural Cooperation in the relationship between the Federal Republic of Germany and the Russian Federation as the state succeeding the Union of Soviet Socialist Republics will cease to have effect.

Article 18

This Agreement shall be concluded for the duration of five years beginning on the day of its entry into force. It will be extended tacitly for successive periods of five years unless it is terminated in writing by either Contracting Party at least six months prior to its expiry.

Done at Moscow on December 16, 1992. In duplicate in German and Russian languages, both being equally authentic.

For the Federal Republic of Germany
Dr. Helmut Kohl

For the Russian Federation
Viktor S. Chernomyrdin

* Approved translation by the government of the Federal Republic of Germany, based on a translation by Katrin A. Velder.

Appendix 16

PROTOCOL OF THE JOINT MEETING OF THE RUSSIAN AND GERMAN GROUPS OF EXPERTS ON "PRIAM'S TREASURE"*

Signed at Moscow, October 26, 1994

1. On October 24 and 25, 1994, German and Russian groups of experts jointly examined "Priam's Treasure," which has been kept in the State Pushkin Museum of Fine Arts since 1945. This took place in accordance with point 14 of the protocol of the joint meeting of the Russian-German Commission for the Mutual Restitution of Cultural Treasures of March 23/24, 1994.
2. The German group of experts headed by the Director of the Museum für Vor- und Frühgeschichte, Staatliche Museen Berlin, Preussischer Kulturbesitz, Professor Wilfried Menghin; as well as Chief Curator Dr. Klaus Goldmann; Chief Restorer Hermann Born; and Dr. Burkhardt Goeres as interpreter; was able to establish that all the items from Schliemann's collection of Trojan antiquities mentioned in the "Category Irreplaceable" evacuation lists of 1939 are extant at the Pushkin Museum.
3. The 260 gold, silver, bronze and stone objects were scientifically examined together with the Russian group of experts headed by Dr. Irina A. Antonova, Director of the State Pushkin Museum; as well as Dr. Vladimir P. Tolstikov, Director of the Department of Old World Art and Archaeology; Professor Liudmila I. Akimova, Director of the Section for Art and Archaeology of the Ancient World; Professor Mikhail J. Treister, Chief Curator of the Section for Art and Archaeology of the Ancient World; and Dr. Olga V. Tugusheva, Scientific Assistant of the Section for Art and Archaeology of the Ancient World. The condition of the objects and the presentation of the collection were found to be outstanding. The German side therefore expresses its gratitude to the museum staff.
4. The first experience of the joint work of the German and Russian groups of experts showed that there were no problems or reservations whatsoever on either side, but that an entirely scientific and friendly agreement prevailed. The continuation of the joint work of the groups of experts provides for the implementation of the necessary discussions in the appropriate channels.

Signed at Moscow on October 26, 1994 in duplicate in the Russian and German languages. Both copies are equally valid.

(signed)
I. A. Antonova
(signed)
V. P. Tolstikov

(signed)
W. Menghin
(signed)
K. Goldmann

* Approved translation by the government of the Federal Republic of Germany, based on a translation by Katrin A. Velder.

Appendix 17

THE UNIDROIT CONVENTION ON STOLEN OR ILLEGALLY EXPORTED CULTURAL OBJECTS*

Opened for signature June 24, 1995

The States Parties to this convention,

Assembled in Rome at the invitation of the Government of the Italian Republic from 7 to 24 June 1995 for a Diplomatic Conference for the adoption of the draft UNIDROIT Convention on the International Return of Stolen or Illegally Exported Cultural Objects,

Convinced of the fundamental importance of the protection of cultural heritage and of cultural exchanges for promoting understanding between peoples, and the dissemination of culture for the well-being of humanity and the progress of civilisation,

Deeply concerned by the illicit trade in cultural objects and the irreparable damage frequently caused by it, both to these objects themselves and to the cultural heritage of national, tribal, indigenous or other communities, and also to the heritage of all peoples, and in particular by the pillage of archaeological sites and the resulting loss of irreplaceable archaeological, historical and scientific information,

Determined to contribute effectively to the fight against illicit trade in cultural objects by taking the important step of establishing common, minimal legal rules for the restitution and return of cultural objects between Contracting States, with the objective of improving the preservation and protection of the cultural heritage in the interest of all,

Emphasising that this Convention is intended to facilitate the restitution and return of cultural objects, and that the provision of any remedies, such as compensation, needed to effect restitution and return in some States, does not imply that such remedies should be adopted in other States,

Affirming that the adoption of the provisions of this Convention for the future in no way confers any approval or legitimacy upon illegal transactions of whatever kind which may have taken place before the entry into force of the Convention,

Conscious that this Convention will not by itself provide a solution to the problems raised by illicit trade, but that it initiates a process that will enhance international cultural co-operation and maintain a proper role for legal trading and inter-State agreements for cultural exchanges,

Acknowledging that implementation of this Convention should be accompanied by other effective measures for protecting cultural objects, such as the development and use of registers, the physical protection of archaeological sites and technical co-operation,

Recognising the work of various bodies to protect cultural property, particularly the 1970 UNESCO Convention on illicit traffic and the development of codes of conduct in the private sector,

Have agreed as follows:

Chapter 1. Scope of application and definition

Article 1
This Convention applies to claims of an international character for:
(a) the restitution of stolen cultural objects;
(b) the return of cultural objects removed from the territory of a Contracting State contrary to its law regulating the export of cultural objects for the purpose of protecting its cultural heritage (hereinafter "illegally exported cultural objects").

Article 2
For the purposes of this Convention, cultural objects are those which, on religious or secular grounds, are of importance for archaeology, prehistory, history, literature, art or science and belong to one of the categories listed in the Annex to this Convention.

Chapter 2. Restitution of stolen cultural objects

Article 3
1. The possessor of a cultural object which has been stolen shall return it.
2. For the purposes of this Convention, a cultural object which has been unlawfully excavated or lawfully excavated but unlawfully retained shall be considered stolen, when consistent with the law of the State where the excavation took place.
3. Any claim for restitution shall be brought within a period of three years from the time when the claimant knew the location of the cultural object and the identity of its possessor, and in any case within a period of fifty years from the time of the theft.
4. However, a claim for restitution of a cultural object forming an integral part of an identified monument or archaeological site, or belonging to a public collection, shall not be subject to time limitations other than a period of three years from the time when the claimant knew the location of the cultural object and the identity of its possessor.
5. Notwithstanding the provisions of the preceding paragraph, any Contracting State may declare that a claim is subject to a time limitation of 75 years or such longer period as is provided in its law. A claim made in another Contracting State for restitution of a cultural object displaced from a monument, archaeological site or public collection in a Contracting State making such a declaration shall also be subject to that time limitation.
6. A declaration referred to in the preceding paragraph shall be made at the time of signature, ratification, acceptance, approval or accession.
7. For the purposes of this Convention, a "public collection" consists of a group of inventoried or otherwise identified cultural objects owned by:
   (a) a Contracting State;
   (b) a regional or local authority of a Contracting State;
   (c) a religious institution in a Contracting State; or
   (d) an institution that is established for an essentially cultural, educational or scientific purpose in a Contracting State and is recognised in that State as serving the public interest.
8. In addition, a claim for restitution of a sacred or communally important cultural object belonging to and used by a tribal or indigenous community in a Contracting State as part of that community's traditional or ritual use, shall be subject to the time limitation applicable to public collections.

Article 4
1. The possessor of a stolen cultural object required to return it shall be entitled, at the time of its restitution, to payment of fair and reasonable compensation provided that the possessor neither knew nor ought reasonably to have known that the object was stolen and can prove that it exercised due diligence when acquiring the object.
2. Without prejudice to the right of the possessor to compensation referred to in the preceding paragraph, reasonable efforts shall be made to have the person who transferred the cultural object to the possessor, or any prior transferor, pay the compensation where to do so would be consistent with the law of the State in which the claim is brought.
3. Payment of compensation to the possessor by the claimant, when this is required, shall be without prejudice to the right of the claimant to recover it from any other person.
4. In determining whether the possessor exercised due diligence, regard shall be had to all the circumstances of the acquisition, including the character of the parties, the price paid, whether the possessor consulted any reasonably accessible register of stolen cultural objects, and any other relevant information and documentation which it could reasonably have obtained, and whether the possessor consulted accessible agencies or took any other step that a reasonable person would have taken in the circumstances.

5. The possessor shall not be in a more favourable position than the person from whom it acquired the cultural object by inheritance or otherwise gratuitously.

Chapter 3. Return of illegally exported cultural objects

Article 5
1. A Contracting State may request the court or other competent authority of another Contracting State to order the return of a cultural object illegally exported from the territory of the requesting State.
2. A cultural object which has been temporarily exported from the territory of the requesting State, for purposes such as exhibition, research or restoration, under a permit issued according to its law regulating its export for the purpose of protecting its cultural heritage and not returned in accordance with the terms of that permit shall be deemed to have been illegally exported.
3. The court or other competent authority of the State addressed shall order the return of an illegally exported cultural object if the requesting State establishes that the removal of the object from its territory significantly impairs one or more of the following interests:
   (a) the physical preservation of the object or of its context;
   (b) the integrity of a complex object;
   (c) the preservation of information of, for example, a scientific or historical character;
   (d) the traditional or ritual use of the object by a tribal or indigenous community,
   or establishes that the object is of significant cultural importance for the requesting State.
4. Any request made under paragraph 1 of this article shall contain or be accompanied by such information of a factual or legal nature as may assist the court or other competent authority of the State addressed in determining whether the requirements of paragraphs 1 to 3 have been met.
5. Any request for return shall be brought within a period of three years from the time when the requesting State knew the location of the cultural object and the identity of its possessor, and in any case within a period of fifty years from the date of the export or from the date on which the object should have been returned under a permit referred to in paragraph 2 of this article.

Article 6
1. The possessor of a cultural object who acquired the object after it was illegally exported shall be entitled, at the time of its return, to payment by the requesting State of fair and reasonable compensation, provided that the possessor neither knew nor ought reasonably to have known at the time of acquisition that the object had been illegally exported.
2. In determining whether the possessor knew or ought reasonably to have known that the cultural object had been illegally exported, regard shall be had to the circumstances of the acquisition, including the absence of an export certificate required under the law of the requesting State.
3. Instead of compensation, and in agreement with the requesting State, the possessor required to return the cultural object to that State, may decide:
   (a) to return ownership of the object; or
   (b) to transfer ownership against payment or gratuitously to a person of its choice residing in the requesting State who provides the necessary guarantees.
4. The cost of returning the cultural object in accordance with this article shall be borne by the requesting State, without prejudice to the right of that State to recover costs from any other person.
5. The possessor shall not be in a more favourable position than the person from whom it acquired the cultural object by inheritance or otherwise gratuitously.

Article 7
1. The provisions of this Chapter shall not apply where:
   (a) the export of a cultural object is no longer illegal at the time at which the return is requested; or
   (b) the object was exported during the lifetime of the person who created it or within a period of fifty years following the death of that person.
2. Notwithstanding the provisions of sub-paragraph (b) of the preceding paragraph, the provisions of this Chapter shall apply where a cultural object was made by a member or members of a tribal or indigenous community for traditional or ritual use by that community and the object will be returned to that community.

Chapter 4. General provisions

Article 8
1. A claim under Chapter 2 and a request under Chapter 3 may be brought before the courts or other competent authorities of the Contracting State where the cultural object is located, in addition to the courts or other competent authorities otherwise having jurisdiction under the rules in force in Contracting States.
2. The parties may agree to submit the dispute to any court or other competent authority or to arbitration.
3. Resort may be had to the provisional, including protective, measures available under the law of the Contracting State where the object is located even when the claim for restitution or request for return of the object is brought before: the courts or other competent authorities of another Contracting State.

Article 9
1. Nothing in this Convention shall prevent a Contracting State from applying any rules more favourable to the restitution or the return of stolen or illegally exported cultural objects than provided for by this Convention.
2. This article shall not be interpreted as creating an obligation to recognise or enforce a decision of a court or other competent authority of another Contracting State that departs from the provisions of this Convention.

Article 10
1. The provisions of Chapter 2 shall apply only in respect of a cultural object that is stolen after this Convention enters into force in respect of the State where the claim is brought, provided that:
   (a) the object was stolen from the territory of a Contracting State after the entry into force of this Convention for that State; or
   (b) the object is located in a Contracting State after the entry into force of the Convention for that State.
2. The provisions of Chapter 3 shall apply only in respect of a cultural object that is illegally exported after this Convention enters into force for the requesting State as well as the State where the request is brought.
3. This Convention does not in any way legitimise any illegal transaction of whatever nature which has taken place before the entry into force of this Convention or which is excluded under paragraphs (1) or (2) of this article, nor limit any right of a State or other person to make a claim under remedies available outside the framework of this Convention for the restitution or return of a cultural object stolen or illegally exported before the entry into force of this Convention.

Chapter 5. Final provisions

Article 11
1. This Convention is open for signature at the concluding meeting of the Diplomatic Conference for the adoption of the draft UNIDROIT Convention on the International Return of Stolen or Illegally Exported Cultural Objects and will remain open for signature by all States at Rome until 30 June 1996.

2. This Convention is subject to ratification, acceptance or approval by States which have signed it.

3. This Convention is open for accession by all States which are not signatory States as from the date it is open for signature.

4. Ratification, acceptance, approval or accession is subject to the deposit of a formal instrument to that effect with the depositary.

Article 12

1. This Convention shall enter into force on the first day of the sixth month following the date of deposit of the fifth instrument of ratification, acceptance, approval or accession.

2. For each State that ratifies, accepts, approves or accedes to this Convention after the deposit of the fifth instrument of ratification, acceptance, approval or accession, this Convention shall enter into force in respect of that State on the first day of the sixth month following the date of deposit of its instrument of ratification, acceptance, approval or accession.

Article 13

1. This Convention does not affect any international instrument by which any Contracting State is legally bound and which contains provisions on matters governed by this Convention, unless a contrary declaration is made by the States bound by such instrument.

2. Any Contracting State may enter into agreements with one or more Contracting States, with a view to improving the application of this Convention in their mutual relations. The States which have concluded such an agreement shall transmit a copy to the depositary.

3. In their relations with each other, Contracting States which are Members of organisations of economic integration or regional bodies may declare that they will apply the internal rules of these organisations or bodies and will not therefore apply as between these States the provisions of this Convention the scope of application of which coincides with that of those rules.

Article 14

1. If a Contracting State has two or more territorial units, whether or not possessing different systems of law applicable in relation to the matters dealt with in this Convention, it may, at the time of signature or of the deposit of its instrument of ratification, acceptance, approval or accession, declare that this Convention is to extend to all its territorial units or only to one or more of them, and may substitute for its declaration another declaration at any time.

2. These declarations are to be notified to the depositary and are to state expressly the territorial units to which the Convention extends.

3. If, by virtue of a declaration under this article, this Convention extends to one or more but not all of the territorial units of a Contracting State, the reference to:
   (a) the territory of a Contracting State in Article 1 shall be construed as referring to the territory of a territorial unit of that State;
   (b) a court or other competent authority of the Contracting State or of the State addressed shall be construed as referring to the court or other competent authority of a territorial unit of that State;
   (c) the Contracting State where the cultural object is located in Article 8 (1) shall be construed as referring to the territorial unit of that State where the object is located;
   (d) the law of the Contracting State where the object is located in Article 8 (3) shall be construed as referring to the law of the territorial unit of that State where the object is located; and
   (e) a Contracting State in Article 9 shall be construed as referring to a territorial unit of that State.

4. If a Contracting State makes no declaration under paragraph 1 of this article, this Convention is to extend to all territorial units of that State.

Article 15

1. Declarations made under this Convention at the time of signature are subject to confirmation upon ratification, acceptance or approval.

2. Declarations and confirmations of declarations are to be in writing and to be formally notified to the depositary.

3. A declaration shall take effect simultaneously with the entry into force of this Convention in respect of the State concerned. However, a declaration of which the depositary receives formal notification after such entry into force shall take effect on the first day of the sixth month following the date of its deposit with the depositary.

4. Any State which makes a declaration under this Convention may withdraw it at any time by a formal notification in writing addressed to the depositary. Such withdrawal shall take effect on the first day of the sixth month following the date of the deposit of the notification.

Article 16

1. Each Contracting State shall at the time of signature, ratification, acceptance, approval or accession, declare that claims for the restitution, or requests for the return, of cultural objects brought by a State under Article 8 may be submitted to it under one or more of the following procedures:
   (a) directly to the courts or other competent authorities of the declaring State;
   (b) through an authority or authorities designated by that State to receive such claims or requests and to forward them to the courts or other competent authorities of that State;
   (c) through diplomatic or consular channels.

2. Each Contracting State may also designate the courts or other authorities competent to order the restitution or return of cultural objects under the provisions of Chapters 2 and 3.

3. Declarations made under paragraphs 1 and 2 of this article may be modified at any time by a new declaration.

4. The provisions of paragraphs 1 to 3 of this article do not affect bilateral or multilateral agreements on judicial assistance in respect of civil and commercial matters that may exist between Contracting States.

Article 17

Each Contracting State shall, no later than six months following the date of deposit of its instrument of ratification, acceptance, approval or accession, provide the depositary with written information in one of the official languages of the Convention concerning the legislation regulating the export of its cultural objects. This information shall be updated from time to time as appropriate.

Article 18

No reservations are permitted except those expressly authorised in this Convention.

Article 19

1. This Convention may be denounced by any State Party, at any time after the date on which it enters into force for that State, by the deposit of an instrument to that effect with the depositary.

2. A denunciation shall take effect on the first day of the sixth month following the deposit of the instrument of denunciation with the depositary. Where a longer period for the denunciation to take effect is specified in the instrument of denunciation it shall take effect upon the expiration of such longer period after its deposit with the depositary.

3. Notwithstanding such a denunciation, this Convention shall nevertheless apply to a claim for restitution or a request for return of a cultural object submitted prior to the date on which the denunciation takes effect.

Article 20

The President of the International Institute for the Unification of Private Law (UNIDROIT) may at regular intervals, or at any time at the request of five Contracting States, convene a special committee in order to review the practical operation of this Convention.

Article 21

1. This Convention shall be deposited with the Government of the Italian Republic.
2. The Government of the Italian Republic shall:
   (a) inform all States which have signed or acceded to this Convention and the President of the International Institute for the Unification of Private Law (UNIDROIT) of:
      (i) each new signature or deposit of an instrument of ratification, acceptance, approval or accession, together with the date thereof;
      (ii) each declaration made in accordance with this Convention;
      (iii) the withdrawal of any declaration;
      (iv) the date of entry into force of this Convention;
      (v) the agreements referred to in Article 13;
      (vi) the deposit of an instrument of denunciation of this Convention together with the date of its deposit and the date on which it takes effect;
   (b) transmit certified true copies of this Convention to all signatory States, to all States acceding to the Convention and to the President of the International Institute for the Unification of Private Law (UNIDROIT);
   (c) perform such other functions customary for depositaries.

In witness whereof the undersigned plenipotentiaries, being duly authorised, have signed this Convention.

Done at Rome, this twenty-fourth day of June, one thousand nine hundred and ninety-five, in a single original, in the English and French languages, both texts being equally authentic.

ANNEX

(a) Rare collections and specimens of fauna, flora, minerals and anatomy, and objects of palaeontological interest;

(b) property relating to history, including the history of science and technology and military and social history, to the life of national leaders, thinkers, scientists and artists and to events of national importance;

(c) products of archaeological excavations (including regular and clandestine) or of archaeological discoveries;

(d) elements of artistic or historical monuments or archaeological sites which have been dismembered;

(e) antiquities more than one hundred years old, such as inscriptions, coins and engraved seals;

(f) objects of ethnological interest;

(g) property of artistic interest, such as:
   (i) pictures, paintings and drawings produced entirely by hand on any support and in any material (excluding industrial designs and manufactured articles decorated by hand);
   (ii) original works of statuary art and sculpture in any material;
   (iii) original engravings, prints and lithographs;
   (iv) original artistic assemblages and montages in any material;

(h) rare manuscripts and incunabula, old books, documents and publications of special interest (historical, artistic, scientific, literary, etc.), singly or in collections;

(i) postage, revenue and similar stamps, singly or in collections;

(j) archives, including sound, photographic and cinematographic archives;

(k) articles of furniture more than one hundred years old and old musical instruments.

[As of June 29, 1996, the following states had signed the convention:]

States	Date of Signature
Bolivia	29.06.1966
Burkina Faso	24.06.1995
Cambodia	24.06.1995
Côte d'Ivoire	24.06.1995
Croatia	24.06.1995
Finland	01.12.1995
France (*ad referendum*)	24.06.1995
Georgia	27.06.1995
Guinea	24.06.1995
Hungary	24.06.1995
Italy	24.06.1995
Lithuania	24.06.1995
Netherlands	28.06.1996
Pakistan	27.06.1996
Paraguay	13.06.1996
Peru	28.06.1996
Portugal	23.04.1996
Romania	27.06.1996
Russian Federation	29.06.1996
Senegal	29.06.1996
Switzerland	26.06.1996
Zambia	24.06.1995

* The UNIDROIT Convention on Stolen or Illegally Exported Cultural Objects, *opened for signature* June 24, 1995, 34 I.L.M. 1322.

ACC: Allied Control Council. Governing body set up to administer occupied Germany at the end of World War II; composed of the commanders in chief of the American, British, French, and Soviet Zones of Occupation.

Ahnenerbe: Ancestral Heritage Foundation. An organization administered by the SS as part of its campaign to promote ideological indoctrination; the Ahnenerbe was established to research German history and archaeology.

ALIU: Art Looting Investigation Unit, U.S. Office of Strategic Services (OSS).

Anschluss: annexation of Austria by Germany, proclaimed March 13, 1938.

Arbeitsamt: Labor Exchange. State employment exchange affiliated with the German Labor Ministry.

Big Four: the United States of America, Great Britain, France, and the USSR.

Big Three: the United States of America, Great Britain, and the USSR.

BSSR: Belorussian Soviet Socialist Republic.

Bundesamt für aussere Restitutionen: Federal Office for External Restitution.

CCP: Central Collecting Point.

C.I.A.: Central Intelligence Agency (U. S.).

CITRA: Conférence Internationale de la Table Ronde des Archives/International Council of the Round Table on Archives.

Commonwealth of Independent States: union of former Soviet states, established after the dissolution of the USSR, in 1991.

convention: agreement between states for regulation of matters affecting them all.

CORC: Coordinating Committee of the Allied Control Council.

CP: Collecting Point.

CPSU: Communist Party of the Soviet Union.

CSCE: Conference on Security and Cooperation in Europe (November 21, 1990).

defense of laches: legal defense whereby a defendant can defeat the claim of a plaintiff seeking to obtain non-monetary relief in a lawsuit, e.g., to recover stolen property from a good-faith purchaser. The defense of "laches" is established by showing, among other things, that the plaintiff unreasonably delayed bringing the lawsuit, and that this delay prejudiced the defendant. This defense may be asserted even if the lawsuit was commenced within the time limits prescribed by the applicable statute of limitations.

Devisenschutzkommando: Foreign Currency Control Commando (Reich).

Dienststelle Mühlmann: Mühlmann Agency. Nazi looting agency under the direction of Kajetan Mühlmann, created in 1939 to confiscate artworks in conquered Poland, and later active in Belgium and the Netherlands.

discovery rule: a rule generally providing that the period of time during which a plaintiff must commence a lawsuit, pursuant to the statute of limitations, does not begin to run until the plaintiff knew (i.e., discovered), or with reasonable diligence should have known, the facts underlying its claim. In cases brought to recover stolen property, those facts include the whereabouts of the property.

DRDR: Reparations, Deliveries and Restitution Directorate.

due diligence: the measure of prudence that would be expected from or exercised by a reasonable person under the particular circumstances.

EAC: European Advisory Commission.

EBA: Early Bronze Age.

Einsatzkommando: special German security unit, often with explicit ideological character. These units were used by the Nazis for such tasks as looting and ethnic cleansing.

ERR: Einsatzstab Reichsleiter Rosenberg (Special Task Force of the Reich Leader [Alfred] Rosenberg). Nazi looting agency headed by party philosopher Alfred Rosenberg, which seized archives and artworks in both the occupied western and the eastern territories from 1940 to 1945.

flak tower: tower on which anti-artillery guns are mounted.

FRG: Federal Republic of Germany.

Führererlass: decree by the Führer.

Führervorbehalt: prerogative of the Führer.

GAF: Gosudarstvennyi arkhivnyi fond (State Archival Record Group, USSR).

GA RF: Gosudarstvennyi arkhiv Rossiiskoi Federatsii (State Archive of the Russian Federation), Moscow; formerly TsGAOR SSSR.

GAU: Glavnoe arkhivnoe upravlenie (Main Archival Administration, USSR); alternatively, Glavarkhiv.

Gau: Nazi administrative district.

Gauleiter: district leader of the Nazi Party.

Gauleitung: office of a Nazi administrative district.

GDR: German Democratic Republic (the former East Germany).

Generalgouvernement: General Government. Area created by the Nazi partition of Poland, administered under German control.

Gestapo: Geheime Staatspolizei (State Secret Police). Instituted by Göring in 1933 and operating under the control of Himmler by 1936, the Gestapo was instrumental in the Nazis' pursuit of repression and terror.

Glavarkhiv: Glavnoe arkhivnoe upravlenie pri Sovete Ministrov SSSR (Main Archival Administration under the Council of Ministers of the USSR), 1960–91; alternatively, GAU.

Gosplan: central state economic planning agency of the USSR.

GULAG: Glavnoe upravlenie lagerei (Main Administration of Labor Camps and Colonies, USSR).

Haupttreuhandstelle Ost: Main Trustee Agency East.

HICOG: United States High Commissioner in Germany.

Hohe Schule: research and teaching institution established to facilitate the policies of the National Socialist Party (NSDAP)

ICA: International Council on Archives.

Institut zur Erforschung der Judenfrage: Institute for Research on the Jewish Question.

International Court of Justice: principal judicial body of the United Nations since 1945, when it replaced the Permanent Court of International Justice.

JCR: Jewish Cultural Reconstruction.

KGB: Komitet Gosudarstvennoi Bezopasnosti (Committee for State Security, USSR).

Kunstschutz: Art Protection Agency of the German army.

Lebensraum: German word meaning "living space," used by the Nazis to promote German expansionist policies.

Maginot Line: an advanced defensive system constructed between World War I and World War II along the eastern border of France. Considered unbreachable by the French military command, the line created a false sense of security, contributing to the fall of France in June 1940.

M-Aktion: Möbel-Aktion. Furniture project, whereby Germans confiscated objects in the occupied West and distributed them in the Reich.

mala fide: Latin term meaning "with or in bad faith."

MFA&A: Monuments, Fine Arts, and Archives section of the Office of Military Government, United States (OMGUS).

Militärverwaltung: German Military Administration.

Nationalsozialismus: National Socialism, Nazism.

National Stolen Property Act: United States law declaring it a crime to transport across state or natural borders objects worth $5,000 or more that are known to be stolen.

Nazi: member of the Nationalsozialistische Deutsche Arbeiterpartei (NSDAP).

NKVD: Narodnyi komissariat vnutrennikh del (People's Commissariat for Internal Affairs, USSR).

OBEA: Office Belge de l'Economie et de l'Agriculture (Office of the Economy and Agriculture, Belgium).

OLCB: Office of the Land Commissioner of Bavaria.

OMGUS: Office of Military Government, United States. The United States military government in occupied Germany.

ORE: Office de Récupération Economique (Office of Economic Recovery, Belgium).

OSS: Office of Strategic Services. Created in 1942, the OSS operated as the principal U.S. intelligence organization during World War II.

Pacta sunt servanda: Latin term meaning "agreements of the parties must be observed."

Permanent Court of International Justice: principal judicial body of the League of Nations from 1920 until 1945, when its functions were transferred to the International Court of Justice. Also known as the World Court.

protocol: document that supplements a treaty, either recording compliance of a party with the conditions of the treaty, or extending the scope and interpretation of the treaty.

RDR: Reparations, Deliveries and Restitution (division overseen by CORC).

Regierungsbezirk: German word for a locally governed district.

Reichskommissar: Reich Commissioner.

Reichsministerium für die besetzten Ostgebiete: Reich Ministry for the Occupied Eastern Territories.

reparation: payment to redress injury or damage.

restitution: return of property wrongfully taken, or compensation for the wrongful taking of or damage to property.

restitution-in-kind: restituion by substituting other, usually similar, property for property wrongfully taken or damaged.

Roberts Commission: American Commission for the Protection and Salvage of Artistic and Historic Monuments in War Areas, established in 1943; known as the Roberts Commission after its chairman, Justice Owen J. Roberts.

Rosarkhiv: Gosudarstvennaia arkhivnaia sluzhba Rossii (State Archival Service of Russia), after 1991.

RSFSR: Rossiiskaia Sovetskaia Federativnaia Sotsialisticheskaia Respublika (Russian Soviet Federated Socialist Republic).

RSHA: Reichssicherheitshauptamt (Reich Security Services Headquarters).

RTsKhIDNI: Rossiiskii tsentr khraneniia i izucheniia dokumentov noveishei istorii (Russian Center for the Preservation and Study of Documents of Modern History), Moscow; formerly, Central Party Archive: TsPa.

RZIA: Russkii zagranichnyi istoricheskii arkhiv (Russian Foreign Historical Archive), Prague.

SA: Sturmabteilung (Storm Detachment). A paramilitary organization founded by Hitler in 1920, which proved crucial to the Nazis' rise to power.

SD: Sicherheitsdienst. Security Service of the SS, concerned not only with intelligence and surveillance, but also with operations of the mobile killing squads on the Eastern Front.

SHAEF: Supreme Headquarters, Allied Expeditionary Forces.

SIPO-SD: Sicherheitspolizei-Sicherheits-dienst (security police-security service, Reich).

SMAG: Sovetskaia voennaia administratsiia v Germanii (Soviet Military Administration in Germany); Soviet acronym: SVAG.

Sonderauftrag Linz: Special Project Linz. Created by Hitler to collect artworks for his proposed Führermuseum in Linz, Austria.

Sonderkommando: special German security unit (see also Einsatzkommando).

Sonderkommando Künsberg: Special Commando Künsberg. This Nazi special unit was active in the confiscation of cultural goods, first in France and then on the Eastern Front (see also Einsatz-kommando).

sovereign immunity: doctrine, generally accepted by all nations, according to which a sovereign or nation is immune from being sued anywhere, at least with respect to acts considered to be governmental rather than commercial or private in nature.

SS: Schutzstaffeln (Protection Squads). Organization within the Nazi Party controlled by Heinrich Himmler, with wide-ranging responsibilities, including internal security, intelligence, and the persecution of enemies of the Reich.

SS Ahnenerbe: See Ahnenerbe.

Staatsarchiv: State Archive.

statute of limitations: law that provides specific time limitations for commencing lawsuits. Usually, the time period runs from the date the claim arises and varies depending on the particular kind of claim being asserted. Regardless of its merits, a claim is subject to dismissal if the de-fendant can establish that it was asserted after the prescribed time period had elapsed.

SVAG: See SMAG.

Treuhandgesellschaft: trustee corporation. Legal entity often used by the Nazis to liquidate confiscated property.

TsGAOR SSSR: Tsentral'nyi gosudarstvennyi arkhiv Oktiabr'skoi revoliutsii i vysshikh organov SSSR (Central State Archive of the October Revolution and High Organs of Government and State Administration of the USSR), Moscow; now part of GA RF.

Ts GIAM: Tsentral'nyi gosudarstvennyi istoricheskii arkhiv v Moskve (Central State Historical Archive, Moscow); now part of GA RF.

TsGOA SSSR: Tsentral'nyi gosudarstvennyi osobyi arkhiv SSSR (Central State Special Archive of the USSR), Moscow; now, TsKhIDK.

TsKhIDK: Tsentr khraneniia istoriko-dokumental'nykh kollektsii (Center for the Preservation of Historico-Documentary Collections), Moscow.

UNESCO: United Nations Educational, Scientific and Cultural Organization, established in 1945 for the purpose of advancing the objectives of international peace and the common welfare of humankind.

UNIDROIT: International Institute for the Unification of Private Law, created in 1926 as an independent body to facilitate the harmonization of national laws.

USGCC: United States Group Control Council.

USSR: Union of Soviet Socialist Republics.

VKPb: All-Union Russian Party of Bolsheviks.

Vugesta: Vermögensumzugsgut der Gestapo (Property Transfer Agency of the Gestapo).

Wehrmacht: armed forces of the Third Reich.

YIVO: research institute and academic center founded in 1925 for the preservation of the East European Jewish heritage.

SELECTED

BIBLIOGRAPHY

Adams, E. E. "Looted Art Treasures Go Back to France." *The Quartermaster Review,* September–October, 1946.

Akinsha, Konstantin, and Grigorii Kozlov. "Spoils of War: The Soviet Union's Hidden Art Treasures." *ARTnews,* April 1991.

_____. "Moscow: The Secret Depositories Slowly Open." *ARTnews,* April 1992.

_____. "Moscow: Yeltsin: Repatriation is a Long Way Off." *ARTnews,* Summer 1992.

_____. "Moscow. War Loot: Drawings for Deutsche Marks?" *ARTnews,* September 1992.

_____. "Moscow: Let the Museums Decide." *ARTnews,* December 1992.

_____. "To Return or Not to Return." *ARTnews,* October 1994.

Akinsha, Konstantin, and Grigorii Kozlov, with Sylvia Hochfield. *Beautiful Loot: The Soviet Plunder of Europe's Art Treasures.* New York: Random House, 1995.

Akinscha [Akinsha], Konstantin, Grigori Koslow [Grigorii Kozlov], and Clemens Toussaint. *Operation Beutekunst: Die Verlagerung deutscher Kulturgüter in die Sowjetunion nach 1945.* Nuremberg: Germanisches Nationalmuseum, 1995.

Alford, Kenneth D. *The Spoils of World War II: The American Military's Role in Stealing Europe's Treasures.* New York: Birch Lane Press Book, 1994.

Aly, Götz, and Susanne Heim. *Das Zentrale Staatsarchiv in Moskau ("Sonderarchiv"): Rekonstruktion und Bestandsverzeichnis verschollen geglaubten Schriftguts aus der NS-Zeit.* Düsseldorf: Hans-Böckler-Stiftung, 1993.

American Commission for the Protection and Salvage of Artistic and Historic Monuments in War Areas. *Report of the American Commission for the Protection and Salvage of Artistic and Historic Monuments in War Areas.* Washington, D.C.: U.S. Government Printing Office, 1946.

Antonova, Irina. "We Don't Owe Anybody Anything." *The Art Newspaper,* July–September 1994.

Barron, Stephanie, ed. *"Degenerate Art": The Fate of the Avant-Garde in Nazi Germany.* Catalogue of the exhibition held at the Los Angeles County Museum of Art, 17 February–12 May 1991, and at the Art Institute of Chicago, 22 June–8 September 1991. New York and Los Angeles: Harry N. Abrams, Inc., Publishers, and the Los Angeles County Museum of Art, 1991.

Bator, Paul M. *The International Trade in Art.* Chicago: University of Chicago Press, 1983.

Beck, Ernest. "Budapest: Hungary Asks Russia for Missing Art Treasures." *ARTnews,* April 1992.

Bernhard, Marianne, and Kurt Martin. *Verlorene Werke der Malerei, 1939–1945.* Munich: F. A. Ackermann, 1965.

Bloedow, Edmund. "The Authenticity and Integrity of 'Priam's Treasure.'" *Boreas* 14/15 (1991/1992).

Boguslavsky, Mark M. *Mezhdunarodnaia okhrana kul'turnykh tsennostei.* Moscow, 1979.

_____. *Private International Law: The Soviet Approach.* Dordrecht: Nijhoff, 1988.

_____. "Contemporary Legal Problems of Return of Cultural Property to its Country of Origin in Russia and the Confederation of Independent States." *International Journal of Cultural Property* 3, no. 2 (1994).

Brauner, Lothar, Bernhard Maaz, and Ruth Strohschein, eds. *Nationalgalerie.* Vol. 3, *Dokumentation der Verluste.* Berlin: Staatliche Museen zu Berlin–Preussischer Kulturbesitz, 1996.

Brenner, Hildegard. *Die Kunstpolitik des Nationalsozialismus.* Reinbek bei Hamburg: Rowohlt, 1963.

Bureau Central des Restitutions. *Répertoire des biens spoliés en France durant la guerre 1939–1945.* Berlin, 1947.

Burkhard, Arthur. *The Cracow Altar of Veit Stoss.* Munich: Bruckmann, 1972.

Burnham, Bonnie. *Art Theft, Its Scope, Its Impact, Its Control.* New York: International Foundation for Art Research, 1978.

Cassou, J. *Le pillage par les Allemands des oeuvres d'art et des bibliothèques appartenant à des Juifs en France.* Paris: Editions du Centre [Centre de documentation juivre contemporaine], 1947.

Chamberlin, Russell. *Loot! The Heritage of Plunder.* London: Thames and Hudson, 1983.

Clark, Ian Christie, and Lewis E. Levy. *National Legislation to Encourage International Cooperation: The Challenge to Our Cultural Heritage.* Paris: UNESCO, 1986.

Clemen, Paul, ed. *Protection of Art during War: Reports.* Leipzig: Seeman, 1919.

Commune di Firenze [Italy]. *L'opera ritrovata: Omaggio a Rodolfo Siviero.* Florence: Cantini, 1984.

Conte, Luigi. "Restitution: Italy. Some Are Found—but Many Are Still Lost: Can You Help?" *The Art Newspaper,* October 1995.

Corémans, P. *La protection scientifique des oeuvres d'art en temps de guerre.* Brussels, 1946.

Counterparts: Old Master Drawings from the Koenigs Collection in the Museum Boymans–van Beuningen in Rotterdam. A Selection of Drawings Closely Related to the Recovered Drawings Exhibited in the Pushkin Museum, Moscow. Catalogue of the exhibition organized by the Netherlands Ministries of Foreign Affairs and Education, Culture and Science, Moscow, 30 November 1995–21 January 1996. Moscow: Rudomino State Library for Foreign Literature, 1995.

D'Arcy, David. "The Long Way Home." *Art and Antiques,* April 1994.

Decker, Andrew. "A Legacy of Shame." *ARTnews,* December 1984.

_____. "Austria's Bid for Justice." *ARTnews,* December 1996.

Demakopoulou, Katie, ed. *Troy, Mycenae, Tiryns, Orchomenos. Heinrich Schliemann:*

The 100th Anniversary of His Death. Catalogue of the exhibition held at the National Archaeological Museum, Athens, 15 June–2 September 1990 and at the Altes Museum, Berlin, 4 October–15 January 1991. Athens: Ministry of Culture of Greece, Greek Committee ICOM, and Ministry of Culture of the German Democratic Republic, 1990.

Dittrich, Christian. *Vermisste Zeichnungen des Kupferstich-Kabinettes Dresden.* Dresden: Staatliche Kunstsammlungen, 1987.

Dokumentation der durch Auslagerung im 2. Weltkrieg vermissten Kunstwerke der Kunsthalle Bremen. Bremen: Der Kunstverein in Bremen and Kunsthalle Bremen, 1991.

Domagala, Rosemarie. *Die Rüstkammer der Wartburg.* Kassel: Wartburg-Stiftung, 1990.

Dornberg, John. "The Mounting Embarrassment of Germany's Nazi Treasures." *ARTnews,* September 1988.

Duboff, Leonard D., and Mary Ann Crawford Duboff. *The Protection of Artistic National Patrimony against Pillaging and Theft in Law and the Visual Arts.* Law and the Visual Arts Conference, Portland, Oregon, 1974, sponsored by the Northwestern School of Law, Lewis and Clark College and others, 1974.

Duboff, Leonard D., ed. *Art Law: Domestic and International* (collection of papers). New Jersey: Fred B. Rothman, 1975.

Duparc, F. J. *Een eeuw strijd voor Nederland's cultureel erfgoed.* The Hague ('s-Gravenhage): Staatsuitgeverij, 1975.

Easton, Donald F. "Priam's Treasure." *Anatolian Studies* 34 (1984).

_____. "Schliemann's Mendacity: A False Trail?" *Antiquity* 58 (1984).

_____. "Was Schliemann a Liar?" In *Heinrich Schliemann: Grundlagen und Ergebnisse moderner Archäologie 100 Jahre nach Schliemanns Tod,* edited by J. Herrmann. Wienheim: Akademie-Verlag, 1992.

_____. "Priam's Gold: The Full Story." *Anatolian Studies* 44 (1994).

_____. "The Troy Treasures in Russia." *Antiquity* 69 (1995).

Eichwede, Wolfgang. "Wann wird aus Beutekunst wieder Kunst?" *Die Zeit,* 10 December 1993.

Eichwede, Wolfgang, and Marlene P. Hiller, eds. *Goten, Ikonen und Schmetterlinge—sowjetische Kulturgüter als deutsche Beute im Zweiten Weltkrieg.* Forthcoming.

Elen, Albert J. *Missing Old Master Drawings from the Franz Koenigs Collection, Claimed by the State of the Netherlands.* The Hague: Netherlands Office for Fine Arts, 1989.

Elsner, Tobias von. *Alles verbrannt? Die verlorene Gemäldegalerie des Kaiser Friedrich Museums in Magdeburg. Sammlungsverluste durch Kriegseinwirkungen und Folgeschäden.* Magdeburger Museumshefte 5. Magdeburg, 1995.

Esterow, Milton. *The Art Stealers.* New York: Macmillan, 1966.

_____. "A Little Justice in Austria." *ARTnews,* September 1995.

Estreicher, Charles [Karol], ed. *Cultural Losses of Poland: Index of Polish Cultural Losses during the German Occupation 1939–43.* London, 1944.

Faison, S. Lane, Jr. "Linz: Hitler's Museum and Library," National Archives, Record Group 239/77, Office of Strategic Services/Art Looting Investigation Unit Consolidated Interrogation Reports 1945, 14 December 1945.

Farmer, Walter I. *The Safekeepers: A Memoir of the Arts at the End of World War II.* Forthcoming.

Fasola, Cesare. *The Florentine Galleries and the War.* Florence: Monsalvato, 1945.

Fedoruk, Alexander K. *Sources of Cultural Relations.* 1974.

Feliciano, Hector. *Le musée disparu. Enquête sur le pillage des oeuvres d'art en France par les nazis.* Paris: Austral, 1995.

Fiedler, Wilfried. "Zur Entwicklung des Völkergewohnheitsrechts im Bereich des Internationalen Kulturgüterschutzes." In *Staat und Völkerrechtsordnung.* Berlin, 1989.

_____. "Neue völkerrechtliche Ansätze des Kulturgüterschutzes." In *Internationaler Kulturgüterschutz, Wiener Symposium, 1990.* Vienna: Gerte Reichelt, 1992.

_____. "Why Has the War Loot Question Still Not Been Resolved?" *The Art Newspaper,* January 1995.

_____. "Safeguarding of Cultural Property during Occupation—Modifications of the Hague Convention of 1907 by World War II." In *Fifth Colloquium on the Legal Aspects of International Trade in Art: Licit Trade in Works of Art* (Vienna, 28–30 September 1994). Paris: International Chamber of Commerce, forthcoming.

Fiedler, Wilfried, ed. *Internationaler Kulturgüterschutz und deutsche Frage.* Berlin, 1991.

Five Centuries of European Drawings: The Former Collection of Franz Koenigs. Catalogue of the exhibition held at the Pushkin State Museum of Fine Arts, Moscow, 10 October 1995–1 January 1996. Moscow: Ministry of Culture of the Russian Federation and Pushkin State Museum of Fine Arts, in association with Leonardo Arte, Milan, 1995.

Flanner, Janet. *Men and Monuments.* New York: Harper, 1957.

Friemuth, Cay. *Die geraubte Kunst. Der dramatische Wettlauf um die Rettung der Kulturschätze nach dem Zweiten Weltkrieg.* Braunschweig: Westermann, 1989.

Fry, Varian. *Surrender on Demand.* New York: Random House, 1945.

Ganslmayr, H., et al. "Study on the Principles, Conditions and Means for the Restitution or Return of Cultural Property in View of Reconstituting Dispersed Heritages." *Museum* 31, no. 1 (1979).

Gimaldinova, Z. "Ukraine's Libraries within the Great Patriotic War." In *Library Science and Bibliography.* 1985.

Glenny, Michael. "The Amber Room." *Art and Antiques,* March 1989.

Goldmann, Klaus. "Unternehmen 'Sonnenuntergang'—Operation 'Sunrise,' Berliner Museen zwischen 1937 und 1987." In *MuseumsJournal* (Berlin), no. 1, August 1987.

_____. "Berliner Kulturschätze—unterwegs." In *Die Reise nach Berlin* (herausgegeben von der Berliner Festspiele GmbH im Auftrag des Senats von Berlin zur 750–Jahr-Feier Berlins 1987). Berlin, 1987.

_____. ". . . das Schliemann-Gold vor Augen: Protokoll einer Dienstreise nach Moskau." *Antike Welt* 25, no. 4 (1994).

_____. "Protokoll einer Dienstreise." *MUT. Forum für Kultur, Politik und Geschichte,* December 1994.

Goldmann, Klaus, and Wolfgang Schneider. *Das Gold des Priamos: Geschichte einer Odyssee.* Leipzig: Gustav Kiepenheuer Verlag, 1995.

Goldmann, Klaus, and Günter Wermusch. *Vernichtet, Verschollen, Vermarktet: Kunstschätze im Visier von Politik und Geschäft.* Asendorf: MUT-Verlag, 1992.

Goldmann, Klaus, and Christine Reich, eds. *Museum für Vor- und Frühgeschichte.* Vol. 4, *Dokumentation der Verluste.* Berlin: Staatliche Museen zu Berlin–Preussischer Kulturbesitz, 1996.

Granin, Daniel, Ilya Gurevich, Galina Khodasevich, and Valeria Belanina. *Risen from the Ashes: Petrodvorets, Pushkin, Pavlosk.* Translated by Graham Whittaker. Leningrad: Aurora, 1992.

Greenfield, Jeannette. *The Return of Cultural Treasures.* 2d ed. Cambridge: Cambridge University Press, 1996.

Grimaldi, David A. *Amber: Window to the Past,* especially "The Amber Room," pp. 186–91. New York: Harry N. Abrams, Inc., Publishers, in association with the American Museum of Natural History, 1996.

Grimsted, Patricia Kennedy. "The Fate of Ukrainian Cultural Treasures during World War II: Archives, Libraries, and Museums under the Third Reich." *Jahrbücher für Geschichte Osteuropas* 39, no. 1 (1991).

_____. "New Revelations on Archival Evacuation and Destruction of Ukrainian Archives at the Beginning of World War II." In *Arkhivy Ukrainy,* 1994.

_____. *Displaced Archives on the Eastern Front: Restitution Problems from World War II and Its Aftermath.* International Institute for Social History, Research Paper no. 18. Amsterdam, 1995.

_____. *The Odyssey of the Smolensk Archive: Plundered Communist Records for the Service of Anti-Communism.* Carl Beck Occasional Papers in Russian and East European Studies, no. 1201. Pittsburgh: University of Pittsburgh, Center for Russian and East European Studies, 1995.

Haase, Günther. *Kunstraub und Kunstschutz. Eine Dokumentation.* Hamburg: privately printed, 1991.

Hall, Ardelia R. "The Recovery of Cultural Objects Dispersed during World War II."

Department of State Bulletin 25, no. 635 (27 August 1951).

Hammond, Mason. "Remembrance of Things Past." In *Proceedings of the Massachusetts Historical Society* 92. Boston, 1980.

Hamon, Marie. "The Working Group on Cultural Property." In *Cultural Treasures Moved Because of the War: A Cultural Legacy of the Second World War. Documentation and Research on Losses. Documentation of the International Meeting in Bremen,* edited by Jost Hansen and Doris Lemmermeier. Bremen: Koordinierungsstelle der Länder für die Rückführung von Kulturgütern, 1995.

_____. *La récupération des biens culturels, 1944–1994.* Forthcoming.

Hancock, Walker. "Experiences of a Monuments Officer in Germany." *College Art Journal,* May 1946.

Hartt, Frederick. *Florentine Art under Fire.* Princeton, N.J.: Princeton University Press, 1949.

Henry-Künzel, Ginger, and Andrew Decker, with Ekaterina Dyogot. "Bremen: Never Look a Gift Horse in the Mouth." *ARTnews,* April 1994.

Hentzen, Alfred. *Die Berliner National-Galerie im Bildersturm.* Berlin: Grote, 1971.

Heydenreuter, Reinhard. *Kunstraub. Die Geschichte des Quedlinburger Stiftsschatzes.* Esslingen, 1993.

Hiller, Marlene P. "Bücher als Beute—das Schicksal sowjetischer und deutscher Bibliotheken als Folge des Zweiten Weltkriegs." *Nordost-Archiv, n.s.,* 4, no. 1 (1995).

Hinz, Berthold. *Art in the Third Reich.* New York: Pantheon, 1979.

Hochfield, Sylvia. "Under a Russian Sofa: 101 Looted Treasures." *ARTnews,* April 1993.

_____. "The Russians Renege." *ARTnews,* Summer 1994.

Hoffman, Barbara. "The Spoils of War." *Archaeology,* November–December 1993.

Honan, William H. "Germans to Get Priceless Gospels Lost in '45." *New York Times,* 1 May 1990.

_____. "A Trove of Medieval Art Turns Up in Texas." *New York Times,* 14 June 1990.

_____. "Second Missing Manuscript Turns Up in German Hands." *New York Times,* 16 June 1990.

_____. "Letters Show Thief Knew Value of the Quedlinburg Treasures." *New York Times,* 3 September 1994.

_____. *Treasure Hunt: A New York Times Reporter Tracks the Quedlinburg Hoard.* Fromm International Publishing Corp., in press.

Howe, Thomas Carr. *Salt Mines and Castles: The Discovery and Restitution of Looted European Art.* Indianapolis and New York: Bobbs/Merrill, 1946.

Ilatovskaya, Tatiana. *Master Drawings Rediscovered: Treasures from Prewar German Collections.* Catalogue of the exhibition held at the State Hermitage Museum, St. Petersburg, 3 December 1996–31 March 1997. New York: Ministry of Culture of the Russian Federation and State Hermitage Museum, in association with Harry N. Abrams, Inc., Publishers, 1996.

International Council of Museums. *Code of Professional Ethics.* Paris: International Council of Museums, 1987.

Jackman, J. C., and C. M. Borden. *The Muses Flee Hitler.* Washington, D.C.: Smithsonian, 1983.

Jong, L. de. *Het Koninkrijk der Nederlanden in de Tweede Wereldoorlog.* 14 vols. The Hague and Leiden: Martinus Nijhoff, 1969–91.

Kater, M. *Das Ahnenerbe der SS.* Stuttgart: Deutsche Verlags-Anstalt, 1974.

Kirstein, Lincoln. "In Quest of the Golden Lamb." *Town and Country,* September 1945.

Klugmann, Claudia. "Kriegsverluste der Gemälde- und Plastiksammlung des Museums der bildenden Künste." In *Museum der bildenden Künste, Leipzig, Jahresheft 1994.* Leipzig: Museum der bildenden Künste, 1995.

Knott, Hermann J. *Der Anspruch auf Herausgabe gestohlenen und illegal exportierten Kulturguts.* Baden-Baden: Nomos, 1990.

Knyschewskij, Pawel Nikolaewitsch. *Moskaus Beute. Wie Vermögen, Kulturgüter und Intelligenz nach 1945 aus Deutschland geraubt wurden.* Munich: Landsberg, 1995.

Kogelfranz, Siegfried, and Willi A. Korte. *Quedlinburg—Texas und zurück. Schwarzhandel mit geraubter Kunst.* Munich: Droemer Knaur, 1994.

Korfmann, Manfred. "Troia—Ausgrabungen 1990 und 1991." *Studia Troica* 2 (1992).

_____. "Die Schatzfunde in Moskau—ein erster Eindruck." *Antike Welt* 25, no. 4 (1994).

Korfman, M., and B. Kromer. "Demircihüyük, Beşik-Tepe, Troia: Eine Zwischenbilanz zur Chronologie dreier Orte in Westanatolien." *Studia Troica* 3 (1993).

Kostenevich, Albert. *Hidden Treasures Revealed: Impressionist Masterpieces and Other Important French Paintings Preserved by the State Hermitage Museum, St. Petersburg.* Catalogue of the exhibition held at the State Hermitage Museum, St. Petersburg, opened 30 March 1995. New York: Ministry of Culture of the Russian Federation and State Hermitage Museum, in association with Harry N. Abrams, Inc., Publishers, 1995.

Kotrelev, N. V. *Katalog nemeckojazychnych izdanij XVI veka v fondach VGBIL.* Moscow, 1992.

Kötzsche, Dietrich, ed. *Der Quedlinburger Schatz.* Catalogue of the exhibition held at the Kunstgewerbemuseum Staatliche Museen zu Berlin–Preussischer Kulturbesitz, 31 October 1992–5 March 1993. Berlin: Ars Nicolai, 1993.

Kowalski, Wojciech. "Restytucja dwóch obrazów Dürera do zbiorów Weimaru" (The Restitution of Two Paintings by Dürer to the Weimar Collections). *Muzealnictwo* 28–29 (1985).

_____. "Udzial Karola Estreichera w alianckich przygotowaniach do restytucji dzieł sztuki zagrabionych w czasie II wojny światowej" (Contribution of Karol Estreicher to Allied Preparations for the Restitution of Works of Art Looted during the Second World War). *Muzealnictwo* 30 (1986).

_____. "Dzialalność restytucyjna Karola Estreichera po zakończeniu II wojny światowej" (Restitutional Activities of Karol Estreicher after the End of World War II). *Muzealnictwo* 31 (1988).

_____. *Restytucja dzieł sztuki. Studium z dziedziny prawa międzynarodowego (Restitution of Works of Art. A Study on Restitution of Looted Cultural Property Pursuant to Public International Law).* Katowice, 1993.

_____. *Liquidation of the Effects of World War II in the Area of Culture.* Warsaw: Institute of Culture, 1994.

Kubin, Ernst. *Sonderauftrag Linz.* Vienna, 1989.

Kuhn, Charles L. "German Paintings in the National Gallery: A Protest." *College Art Journal* 5, no. 2 (January 1946).

Kühnel-Kunze, Irene. *Bergung—Evakuierung—Rückführung. Die Berliner Museen in den Jahren 1939–1959.* Jahrbuch Preussischer Kulturbesitz, Sonderband 2. Berlin: Gebr. Mann, 1984.

Kümmel, Otto. *Geraubte Kulturgüter 2. Bericht auf Erlass des Herrn Reichsministers und Chefs der Reichskanzlei . . . und des Herrn Reichsministers für Volksaufklärung und Propaganda . . . betr. Kunstwerke und geschichtlich bedeutsame Gegenstände, die seit 1500 ohne unseren Willen oder auf Grund zweifelhafter Rechtsgeschäfte in ausländischen Besitz gelangt sind.* Berlin, 1941.

Kurtz, Michael. *Nazi Contraband: American Policy on the Return of European Cultural Treasures, 1945–1955.* New York: Garland, 1985.

Kurz, Jakob. *Kunstraub in Europa, 1938– 1945.* Hamburg: Facta Oblita, 1989.

LaFarge, Henry, ed. *Lost Treasures of Europe. 427 Photographs.* New York: Pantheon, 1946.

Lambacher, Lothar, ed. *Skulpturensammlung.* Vol. 2, *Dokumentation der Verluste.* Berlin: Staatliche Museen zu Berlin–Preussischer Kulturbesitz, 1996.

Lehmann, Klaus-Dieter, and Ingo Kolasa, eds. *Restitution von Bibliotheksgut: Runder Tisch deutscher und russischer Bibliothekare in Moskau am 11. und 12. Dezember 1992, Zeitschrift für Bibliothekswesen und Bibliographie,* Sonderheft 56. Frankfurt am Main: Vittorio Klostermann, 1993.

Lehmann-Haupt, Hellmut. *Art under a Dictatorship.* New York: Oxford, 1954.

Leiser, Erwin. "Hitlers Kunstraub für Linz." *Du* 11 (1987).

Liska, Pavel. *Nationalsozialistische Kunstpolitik.* Berlin: Neue Gesellschaft für bildende Kunst, 1974.

Lorentz, Stanislaw. *Museums and Collections in Poland, 1945–1955.* Warsaw: Polonia, 1956.

Lowenthal, Constance. "Pending Legislation about the Ownership of Stolen Art." In *Proceedings of the Fourth International Conference on Cultural Economics*. Akron: University of Akron, 1987.

———. "Quedlinburg Treasures Turn Up in Texas." *IFAR [International Foundation for Art Research] Reports*, July 1990.

Lust, Jacques. "La récupération des oeuvres d'art belges après la guerre (1946–1962)." *'30–'50: Bulletin de nouvelles du Centre de Recherches et d'Études Historiques de la Seconde Guerre mondiale*, no. 25 (Autumn 1994).

Maldis, Adam. *I azh'ivaiuts' spadch'in'i staronki: v'ibranae (Pages of History Speak)*. Minsk: Mastatskaia Litaratura, 1994.

Mazauric, Lucie. *Le Louvre en voyage, 1939–1945*. Paris: Plon, 1978.

McBryde, Isabel, ed. *Who Owns the Past?* London: Oxford University Press, 1985.

Merkert, Jörn, and Irina Antonova, eds. *Berlin—Moscow/ Moscow—Berlin*. Catalogue of the exhibition organized by the Berlinische Galerie in the Martin-Gropius-Bau, Berlin, 3 September 1995–7 January 1996, and the Pushkin State Museum of Fine Arts, Moscow, 1 March–1 July 1996. Munich and New York: Prestel-Verlag; Moscow: Galart, 1995.

Merryman, John Henry. "International Art Law: From Cultural Nationalism to a Common Cultural Heritage." *Journal of International Law and Politics* (New York University) 15, no. 4 (Summer 1983).

Merryman, John Henry, and Albert E. Elsen. *Law, Ethics, and the Visual Arts*. 2d ed., 2 vols. Philadelphia: University of Pennsylvania Press, 1983.

Messenger, Phyllis Mauch, ed. *The Ethics of Collecting Cultural Property: Whose Culture? Whose Property?* Albuquerque: University of New Mexico Press, 1989.

Meyer, Karl E. *The Plundered Past*. New York: Atheneum, 1973.

———. "The Hunt for Priam's Treasure." *Archaeology*, November–December, 1993.

Michaelis, Rainer, ed. *Gemäldegalerie*. Vol. 1, *Dokumentation der Verluste*. Berlin: Staatliche Museen zu Berlin–Preussischer Kulturbesitz, 1995.

Mihan, George. *Looted Treasure: Germany's Raid on Art*. London: Alliance, 1944.

Ministero degli Affari Esteri and Ministero per i Beni Culturali e Ambientali [Italy]. *Treasures Untraced: An Inventory of the Italian Art Treasures Lost during the Second World War*. Rome: Istituto Poligrafico e Zecca dello Stato, Rome, 1995.

Molajoli, Bruno. *Musei ed opere d'arte di Napoli attraverso la guerra*. Naples: Soprintendenza Alle Gallerie, 1948.

Moorehead, Caroline. *The Lost Treasures of Troy*. London: Weidenfeld and Nicolson, 1994.

Musée de l'Orangerie, Paris. *Les chefs-d'oeuvre des collections françaises retrouvés en Allemagne par la Commission de Récupération Artistique et les Services Alliés*. Catalogue of the exhibition held at the Orangerie des Tuileries, June–August 1946. Paris: Ministère de l'Education Nationale, 1946.

Museum der bildenden Künste, Leipzig, Jahresheft 1995. Leipzig: Herwig Guratzsch, 1996.

Nafziger, James A. R. "The New International Legal Framework for the Return, Restitution or Forfeiture of Cultural Property." *Journal of International Law and Politics* (New York University) 15, no. 4 (Summer 1983).

Nahlik, Stanislaw E. "International Law and the Protection of Cultural Property in Armed Conflicts." *Hastings Law Journal* 27 (May 1976).

The National Museums and Galleries: The War Years and After. London: His Majesty's Stationery Office, 1948.

Nicholas, Lynn H. *The Rape of Europa: The Fate of Europe's Treasures in the Third Reich and the Second World War*. New York: Alfred A. Knopf, 1994.

Norris, Christopher. "The Disaster at Flakturm Friedrichshain." *Burlington Magazine* 94, no. 597 (December 1952).

Office Belge de l'Économie et de l'Agriculture [Belgium]. *Missing Art Works of Belgium*. Part 1: *Public Domain*. Part 2: *Belgian State*. Brussels, 1994–95.

Office de Récupération Economique [Belgium]. *Répertoire d'oeuvres d'art dont la Belgique a été spoliée durant la guerre 1939–1945*. Brussels, 1948.

Opper, Dieter, and Doris Lemmermeier. *Cultural Treasures Moved Because of the War—A Cultural Legacy of the Second World War. Documentation and Research on Losses*. Documentation of the International Meeting in Bremen, 30 November–2 December 1994. Bremen: Koordinierungsstelle der Länder für die Rückführung von Kulturgütern, 1995.

Palais des Beaux-Arts, Brussels. *Chefs-d'oeuvre récupérés en Allemagne*. Catalogue of the exhibition held at the Palais des Beaux-Arts, Brussels, November–December 1948. Brussels: Editions de la Connaissance, 1948.

Petropoulos, Jonathan George. "Not a Case of 'Art for Art's Sake': The Collecting Practices of the National Socialist Elite." *German Politics and Society* 32 (Summer 1994).

———. "Bannerträger und Tiroler Bergjäger: Die von den USA beschlagnahmte NS-Kunst." In Jan Tabor, ed., *Kunst und Diktatur*. Vienna: Künstlerhaus Wien, 1994.

———. "The History of the Second Rank: The Case of the Art Plunderer Kajetan Mühlmann." *Contemporary Austrian Studies* 4 (1995).

———. *Art as Politics in the Third Reich*. Chapel Hill and London: University of North Carolina Press, 1996.

Piotrovsky, Mikhail. "Asymmetrische Situation: Ein MUT-Interview mit dem Eremitage-Direktor Prof. Dr. Michail Piotrowski." *MUT. Forum für Kultur, Politik und Geschichte*, December 1994.

Plaut, James S. "Activity of the ERR in France." National Archives, Record Group 239/85, Office of Strategic Services/Art Looting Investigation Unit Consolidated Interrogation Reports 1945, 15 August 1945, Attachment 4.

———. "Hitler's Capital: Loot for the Master Race." *Atlantic Monthly*, September 1946.

Pretzell, Lothar. *Das Kunstgutlager Schloss Celle 1945–1958*. Celle: Schlossmuseum, 1958.

The Protection of Cultural Resources against the Hazards of War. Washington, D.C.: Committee on the Conservation of Cultural Resources, U.S. National Resources Planning Board, February 1942.

Prott, Lyndel V. *The Latent Power of Culture and the International Judge*. Abingdon: Professional Books, 1979.

Prott, Lyndel V., and P. J. O'Keefe. *National Legal Control of Illicit Traffic in Cultural Property*. Paris: UNESCO, 1983.

———. *Law and the Cultural Heritage*. 5 vols. Vol. 1: *Discovery and Excavation*. Abingdon: Professional Books, 1984. Vol. 3: *Movement*. London and Edinburgh: Butterworths & Co., 1989. Vols. 2, 4, 5 forthcoming.

———. " 'Cultural Heritage' or 'Cultural Property'?" *International Journal of Cultural Property* 1, no. 2 (1992).

Pruszyński, Jan P. *The Legal Protection of Historical Architecture in Poland*. Warsaw: Law Publishers, 1977.

———. *Protection of Monuments: History, Organization, Law*. Warsaw: The State Scientific Publ. (PWN), 1989.

———. *Legal Protection of Cultural Property in Germany. Texts and Commentaries*. Warsaw: The State Ateliers for Monuments Conservation, 1992.

The Quedlinburg Treasury. Catalogue of the exhibition held at the Dallas Museum of Art, 16 February–14 April 1991. Dallas Museum of Art, 1991.

Rastorgouev, Alexei. "Trofei 2-i mirovoi voiny v Sovetskom Soiuze" (Trophies of the Second World War in the Soviet Union), *Russkaia Mysl'* (*La Pensée Russe*) (Paris), no. 3862, 18 January 1991.

———. "Voennoplennoe Iskusstvo," (Artworks as Prisoners of War), *Literaturnaia gazeta* (Moscow), no. 25 (5351), 26 June 1991.

Rave, Paul Ortwin. *Kunstdiktatur im Dritten Reich*. Hamburg: Gebr. Mann, 1949.

Rorimer, James J., in collaboration with G. Rabin. *Survival: The Salvage and Protection of Art in War*. New York: Abelard, 1950.

Rose, Mark. "What Did Schliemann Find—and Where, When, and How Did He Find It?" *Archaeology*, November–December 1993.

Rousseau, Theodore. "The Göring Collection." National Archives, Record Group 239/85, Office of Strategic Services/Art Looting Investigation Unit Consolidated Interrogation Reports 1945, 13 September 1945.

Roxan, David, and Ken Wanstall. *The Jackdaw*

of Linz: The Story of Hitler's Art Thefts. London: Cassell, 1964.

Schliemann, Heinrich. Troy and its Remains. A Narrative of Researches and Discoveries Made on the Site of Ilium, and in the Trojan Plain. Edited by P. Smith. Translated by L. D. Schmitz. London: John Murray, 1875; New York, 1876.

_____. Ilios. The City and Country of the Trojans: The Results of Researches and Discoveries on the Site of Troy and throughout the Troad in the Years 1871, 72, 73, 78, 79, including an Autobiography of the Author. London: John Murray, 1880; New York, 1881.

_____. [Trojanische Alterthümer.] Bericht über die Ausgrabungen in Troja in den Jahren 1871 bis 1873. Foreword by Manfred Korfmann. Munich and Zurich: Artemis, 1990.

Siehr, Kurt. "Manuscript of the Quedlinburg Cathedral Back in Germany." International Journal of Cultural Property 1, no. 1 (1992).

_____. "The UNIDROIT Draft Convention on the International Protection of Cultural Property." International Journal of Cultural Property 1, no. 2 (1992).

Simon, Matila. The Battle of the Louvre: The Struggle to Save French Art in World War II. New York: Hawthorne, 1971.

Siviero, Rodolfo. L'arte e il nazismo: Esodo e ritorno delle opere d'arte italiane 1938–1963. Florence: Cantini Edizioni d'Arte, 1984.

Skilton, John. Défense de l'art européen. Paris: Editions Internationales, 1948.

Smith, Arthur L., Jr. Hitler's Gold: The Story of the Nazi War Loot. Oxford: Berg, 1989.

Smyth, Craig Hugh. Repatriation of Art from the Collecting Point in Munich after World War II: Background and Beginnings, with Reference Especially to the Netherlands. Maarssen/The Hague: Gary Schwartz/SDU Publishers, 1988.

Spoils of War International Newsletter. Bremen: Koordinierungsstelle der Länder für die Rückführung von Kulturgütern, beginning in 1995.

Staatliche Kunstsammlungen Dresden. Vermisste Kunstwerke des Historischen Museums Dresden. Dresden, 1990.

Staatliche Museen zu Berlin–Preussischer Kulturbesitz. Schliemanns Gold und die Schätze Alteuropas aus dem Museum für Vor- und Frühgeschichte: Eine Dokumentation. Mainz: Verlag Philipp von Zabern, 1993.

Stout, George. "Preservation of Paintings in Wartime." Technical Studies, January 1942.

Strahle, Rochelle. "The Retention and Retrieval of Art and Antiquities through International and National Means: The Tug of War over Cultural Property." Brooklyn Journal of International Law 1 (1979).

Sutter, Sem C. "The Fall of the Bibliographic Wall: Libraries and Archives in Unified Germany." College and Research Libraries, September 1994.

Tolstikov, Vladimir, and Mikhail Treister. The Gold of Troy: Searching for Homer's Fabled City. Translated by Christina Sever and Mila Bonnichsen. New York: Ministry of Culture of the Russian Federation and Pushkin State Museum of Fine Arts, in association with Harry N. Abrams, Inc., Publishers, 1996.

Traill, David A. Schliemann of Troy: Treasure and Deceit. New York: St. Martin's Press, 1995.

Traill, David A., and William M. Calder III, eds. Myth, Scandal and History: The Heinrich Schliemann Controversy and a First Edition of the Mycenaean Diary. Detroit: Wayne State University Press, 1986.

United Nations Educational, Scientific and Cultural Organization (UNESCO). Convention on the Means of Prohibiting and Preventing the Illicit Import, Export and Transfer of Ownership of Cultural Property, adopted by the UNESCO General Conference at its sixteenth session, Paris, 14 November 1970.

_____. Conventions and Recommendations of UNESCO Concerning the Protection of the Cultural Heritage. Paris, 1983.

U.S. Congress. Senate. Committee on Armed Services. Hearings on S2439: A Bill to Provide for the Temporary Retention in the US of Certain German Paintings, 4 March and 10 April 1948. Washington, D.C.: U.S. Government Printing Office.

Urice, Stephen K. "Repatriation of Cultural Property: Recent Cases and Controversies." In Legal Problems of Museum Administration. Philadelphia: American Law Institute–American Bar Association, 1991.

_____. "A Contract Law Primer for the Museum Administrator." In Legal Problems of Museum Administration. Philadelphia: American Law Institute–American Bar Association, 1994.

Valland, Rose. Le Front de l'Art. Paris: Plon, 1961.

Van Rijn, Michel. Hot Art, Cold Cash. London: Warner Books, 1994.

Varine, Hugues de. "The Rape and Plunder of Cultures: An Aspect of the Deterioration of the Terms of Cultural Trade between Nations." Museum 35, no. 3 (1983).

Varshavsky, S. Saved for Humanity. Leningrad: Aurora, 1985.

Varshavsky, S., and B. Rest. The Hermitage during the War of 1941–1945. Translated by Arthur Shkarovsky-Raffe. St. Petersburg: Slavia, 1995.

Venema, A. Kunsthandel in Nederland, 1940–1945. Amsterdam: Arbeiderspers, 1986.

Visscher, Charles de. "La protection des patrimoines artistiques et historiques nationaux: Nécessité d'une réglementation internationale." Mouseion 43–44 (1938).

_____. Essays on International Protection of Works of Art. U.S. Department of State Documents and State Papers 1, no. 15 (June 1949).

Vries, Willem H. de. The Confiscation of Music in the Occupied Countries of Western Europe by the Sonderstab Musik of the Einsatzstab Reichsleiter Rosenberg (1940–1945). Amsterdam: Amsterdam University Press, 1995.

Warsaw Accuses. Exhibition catalogue. Warsaw: Ministry of Culture and Art and Ministry of Reconstruction of the Country, 1945.

Waxman, Sharon. "Justice in Austria . . . Finally?" ARTnews, January 1995.

_____. "Austria: Ending the Legacy of Shame." ARTnews, September 1995.

Wermusch, Günter. Tatumstände (un)bekannt, Kunstraub unter den Augen der Alliierten. Braunschweig: Westermann, 1991.

Williams, Robert C. Russian Art and American Money 1900–1940. Cambridge, Mass.: Harvard University Press, 1980.

Williams, Sharon A. The International and National Protection of Movable Cultural Property. A Comparative Study. Dobbs Ferry, N.Y.: Oceana Publications, 1978.

Woolley, Sir Charles Leonard. A Record of the Work Done by the Military Authorities for the Protection of the Treasures of Art and History in War Areas. London: His Majesty's Stationery Office, 1947.

Works of Art in Italy: Losses and Survivals in the War. Vol. 1 (Part 1): South of Bologna. Vol. 2 (Part 2): North of Bologna. London: His Majesty's Stationery Office, 1945 and 1946.

Zaldumbide, Rodrigo Pallares. "Return and Restitution of Cultural Property: Cases for Restitution." Museum 34, no. 2 (1982).

CONTRIBUTORS

Konstantin Akinsha, Contributing Editor of *ARTnews,* graduated from Moscow State University and received a Ph.D. degree from the All-Union Research Institute of Art History. In 1991 he wrote, with Grigorii Kozlov, the article that revealed Soviet "special repositories" of art missing from German and European collections since World War II. Akinsha and Kozlov's books *Beautiful Loot: The Soviet Plunder of Europe's Art Treasures* and *Operation Beutekunst* were published in 1995; the authors have also collaborated on numerous articles on looted art for international periodicals. In 1993, after discovering a cache of 101 drawings and prints from the Bremen Kunsthalle, they delivered them to the German Embassy in Moscow. Both Akinsha and Kozlov have received a number of awards, including the George Polk Memorial Award for investigative journalism.

Irina Antonova, Director of the Pushkin State Museum of Fine Arts in Moscow, is a graduate of Moscow State University. She has written widely in the fields of Italian Renaissance and twentieth-century art. From 1981 to 1993, she served as Vice President of the International Council of Museums (ICOM). She has participated in major international art exhibitions, including the 1960 Venice Biennale, "Moscow-Paris," "From Poussin to Matisse," "Marc Chagall," and others. She is a board member of the Russian Foundation for Culture; a member of the Russian State Commission on the Restitution of Cultural Property; and a member of the Russian Academy of Education. She has been elected an honorary member of ICOM. The French Government has awarded her the Order (Commandeur) for Art and Literature.

Jana Bahurinská is Head of the Gallery Information Center of the Slovenská národná galéria in Slovakia, where she specializes in the computerization and standardization of fine-art collection documentation and coordinates the computerized collections documentation of works of fine art in Slovakia. She received her M.A. and Ph.D. degrees in library science and science information from the Comenius University Faculty of Philosophy. From 1979 to 1990, she was affiliated with the Institute of Information and Management in Culture in Bratislava. She is the author of several articles for *Múzeum, Pamiatky a múzeá,* and a review, *GALERIA.*

Mark M. Boguslavsky is a Leading Research Fellow at the Institute of State and Law of the Russian Academy of Sciences and holds a doctoral degree in the field of law. He is the author of the textbooks *International Preservation of Cultural Treasures* and *International Private Law,* as well as numerous other books and articles. He serves as an expert for the Ministry of Culture of the Russian Federation; formerly, he served as expert to the Committee on International Affairs and Foreign Trade of the Supreme Soviet of the Russian Federation and other comparable committees of the Supreme Soviet of the USSR. Dr. Boguslavsky is a member of the Russian State Commission on the Restitution of Cultural Property.

Donald Fyfe Easton is a free-lance Near Eastern archaeologist, specializing in the archaeology, history, and languages of preclassical Turkey. He received his M.A. degree in theology from Oxford University, an M.A. degree from Cambridge University, and M.A. and Ph.D. degrees in Western Asiatic archaeology from the University of London. His doctoral dissertation reexamined Heinrich Schliemann's unpublished Troy excavation notebooks (publication forthcoming). He was appointed Research Fellow at the University of Liverpool from 1979 to 1982 and at Clare Hall, Cambridge, from 1982 to 1988. He is a member of the Troy excavation team and a member of the international advisory committee for the Troy excavations, and he has lectured and examined at the Institute of Archaeology, University College, London. In 1990, he was awarded the Heinrich Schliemann Medal by the Berlin Academy of Sciences, at the centenary of Schliemann's death. He was one of six Western scholars invited to Moscow and St. Petersburg in November 1994 to view the Troy treasures, inaccessible since 1945, and was a consultant on the English edition of the Pushkin Museum's exhibition catalogue *The Treasure of Troy* (1996). His writings include articles on "Priam's Treasure" in *Antiquity* and *Anatolian Studies,* and others in *Studia Troica, Journal of Cuneiform Studies,* and elsewhere.

Wolfgang Eichwede is Professor of Contemporary History and Policy in Eastern Europe at the University of Bremen and, since 1982, Director of the Research Institute for Eastern Europe in Bremen. He received a Ph.D. degree in history from the University of Tübingen. His publications focus on the social history of the Soviet Union and international affairs. Topics on which he is presently working include social movements (including human-rights movements) and the recent transformation of Eastern Europe. Most recently, he has edited *Der Shirinowski-Effekt* (1994). The Research Institute for Eastern Europe in Bremen is currently conducting the research project "The Fate of the Treasures of Art Removed from the Soviet Union during World War II."

Milton Esterow is Editor and Publisher of *ARTnews,* which he bought from *Newsweek* in 1972. Under his direction, *ARTnews* has achieved the world's largest circulation for an art magazine and has won most of the major journalism awards presented to periodicals. In 1992, the magazine received its second George Polk Award—for a series of articles revealing that cultural treasures seized by the

Red Army in Nazi Germany were still hidden in the former Soviet Union. The series also won an award for excellence from the Overseas Press Club. *ARTnews* also publishes *ARTnewsletter* (a biweekly), *ARTnews for Students,* and books on art, and sponsors conferences on the art market. Mr. Esterow has lectured extensively both in the United States and abroad.

S. Lane Faison, Jr., Professor of Art History at Williams College from 1936 to 1976, and Director of the Williams College Museum of Art from 1948 to 1976, received an M.F.A. degree from Princeton University in 1932 and an Honorary Litt.D. degree from Williams College in 1971. The recipient of numerous awards, he has written extensively on art for both scholarly and popular audiences. In 1945, he was assigned to the Art Looting Investigation Unit, Office of Strategic Services. For his work with the ALIU-OSS, Faison received the French Legion of Honor (Chevalier) in 1947. In 1950–51, he served as Director of the Munich Central Collecting Point, supervising the return of works of art acquired by the Nazis. Professor Faison is a past president of the College Art Association of America.

Walter I. Farmer, an architecture and interior-design consultant, received both an A.B. degree in architecture and an A.B. degree in mathematics from Miami University, Oxford, Ohio, in 1935. After three years as U.S. Army Captain C.E., he was Director of the Wiesbaden Collecting Point for German-owned works of art for the Monuments, Fine Arts, and Archives section of the U.S. Military Government in Germany (1945–46). A co-founder and first President of the Contemporary Arts Museum, Houston, Texas, and cofounder and major patron of the Miami University Art Museum, he was awarded a Doctorate in Humane Letters from Miami University in 1973. On September 27, 1995, he received the Commander's Cross of the Federal Order of Merit from German Foreign Minister Klaus Kinkel for sponsoring the Wiesbaden Manifesto. This document, signed by MFA&A officers on November 7, 1945, protested the transfer of German-owned works of art to the United States. He has written *In America Since 1607* (1987) and *The Safekeepers,* a memoir of the arts at the end of World War II (forthcoming).

Alexander Fedoruk is Chairman of the National Commission on the Restitution of Cultural Treasures to Ukraine. He received M.A. degrees from L'viv State University and the St. Petersburg Institute of Fine Arts, Sculpture, and Architecture, and a Ph.D. degree from the Kyiv Institute of the History of Art, Folklore, and Ethnography. Prof. Dr. Fedoruk has received numerous awards and published many books and articles on the history of national and international culture,

including *Sources of Cultural Relations* (1974), *German Art* (1986), and *Vassyl Khmeluk* (1996). He has organized several exhibitions, including "Slav Art and Its Contribution to the World's Culture" and "The Unknown Europe."

Wilfried Fiedler is Professor of Constitutional, Administrative, and Public International Law, University of the Saarland, Saarbrücken. He studied law at the universities of Tübingen, Hamburg, and Freiburg im Breisgau and received a C.E.S. from the University of Grenoble (France) and J.D. and *Habilitation* degrees from the University of Freiburg im Breisgau. Until 1984, he was Director of the Institute for International Law, University of Kiel; in 1986, he founded the Research Institute for the Protection and Restitution of Cultural Property in Contemporary Public International Law. In 1991, he was Visiting Professor at the Tohoku University in Sendai, Japan; in 1992–93, he was Dean of the Faculty of Law and Economics at the University of the Saarland. Within the field of public international law, his current work focuses on issues of state succession. He has written and edited numerous publications, including *Internationaler Kulturgüterschutz und deutsche Frage* (1991) and, in 1994, a study of Hermann Heller, a German researcher in public law (d. 1933). In 1995, Professor Fiedler published the protocols of the negotiations between the Federal Republic of Germany and Russia concerning the restitution of German and Russian cultural property (*Kulturgüter als Kriegsbeute?* [Heidelberg, 1995]).

István Fodor is Titular Director General of the Hungarian National Museum in Budapest and Professor of Archaeology at the University of Szeged. He received an A.M. degree from Lomonosov University in Moscow and a Ph.D. degree from the Hungarian Academy of Sciences. His field of research is the archaeology and early history of the Hungarian and Finno-Ugric peoples and of Eurasian nomads. He is the author of six books and many articles. He has organized museum exhibitions in Europe and the United States and is a Fellow of the Harvard Seminar in Salzburg, Austria. He has received awards for his scientific and cultural activities, including a prize for his book, *In Search of a New Homeland: The Prehistory of the Hungarian People and the Conquest* (1982).

Ekaterina Genieva, Director General of the Rudomino State Library for Foreign Literature, received her Ph.D. degree in philology from Moscow State University. She is the author of many publications in the fields of English and Irish literature. Her public activities include membership in various foundations and societies; she is Vice President of the Russian Federation of Library Associations, Member of the Board of the Russian Bible Society, and Member of the Board of the All-

Russian Culture Foundation. Dr. Genieva is affiliated with numerous international organizations: she is an Observer to the Russian-German Library Commission on Restitution, Member of the International Advisory Board of the Regional Library Program/Open Society Institute, and an Executive Board Member of the International Federation of Library Associations and Institutions (IFLA).

Klaus Goldmann is a Curator at the Museum for Pre- and Early History, Berlin State Museums, Prussian Heritage Foundation. He chairs the board of "Museumsdorf Düppel," a reconstruction of an excavated medieval village. Dr. Goldmann received his Dr. rer. nat. from Albertus Magnus University, Cologne. Since 1971, he has been involved in tracing objects that disappeared from his museum at the end of World War II. In October 1994, he was a member of the Berlin Museum Commission invited to Moscow to view objects from the Schliemann gold collection taken from the Museum for Pre- and Early History after the war, now held in the Pushkin State Museum of Fine Arts, Moscow. In September 1995, he was decorated with the German Cross of Merit.

Jeanette Greenfield is an Australian writer and lawyer who divides her time between London and Australia. She received an LL.B. degree from the University of Melbourne, as well as LL.B. and Ph.D. degrees in international law from Cambridge University. In 1986, she was the recipient of a British Academy Research Award for a definitive work, *China's Practice in the Law of the Sea,* which was published by Oxford University Press. She is the author of books and articles on diverse international legal issues embracing art, anthropology, culture, and heritage, and she is a contributor to such publications as *Antiquity* and *Apollo.* Her book *The Return of Cultural Treasures* appeared in 1989 and was reviewed internationally; a second, revised, edition was published by Cambridge University Press in 1996.

Patricia Kennedy Grimsted is a Research Fellow of the Russian Research Center and Associate at the Ukrainian Research Institute, Harvard University. She received her Ph.D. degree in Russian history from the University of California at Berkeley and has taught Russian/Soviet history at several universities. She is the author of a number of historical monographs and a multivolume directory of archives in the former USSR. She is currently working with Russian and Ukrainian colleagues in developing a multilingual data base as a directory and bibliography for archives in Russia and Ukraine; a major volume (covering over 260 repositories in Moscow and St. Petersburg) is currently in press in Moscow and New York. Since the opening of Soviet archives in the late 1980s, Dr. Grimsted has been investigating the displacement of cultural treasures during and after World War II, and especially of archives on the Eastern Front, and she is preparing an extensive monograph on the subject. Her article on the fate of Ukrainian cultural treasures during and immediately after the war appeared in 1991 in *Jahrbücher für Geschichte Osteuropas* and as a booklet in Ukrainian with appended documents. Her research paper "Displaced Archives on the Eastern Front" appeared as an International Institute for Social History Research Paper (Amsterdam, 1995), and her study "The Odyssey of the Smolensk Archive" appeared in the University of Pittsburgh's Carl Beck Occasional Papers series (1995).

Marie Hamon is Conservateur en chef du Patrimoine of the French Ministry of Foreign Affairs. She is a graduate of the Ecole des Chartes. The author of the book *L'Hôtel du Ministre des Affaires étrangères,* she has specialized for several years in researching the works of art stolen during the last world war. She was recently co-curator of the exhibition "Oeuvres d'art restituées par l'Allemagne" at the Musée d'Orsay (October–December 1994). Her study *La Récupération des biens culturels, 1944–1994,* is currently in press.

Armin Hiller is Head of the Policy Division, Directorate-General for Cultural Affairs, Foreign Office of the Federal Republic of Germany. After completing his training as a lawyer, he began his career in the private sector. Dr. Hiller entered the Federal Foreign Office in 1972. He was assigned to the German embassies in Washington, D.C., and Maputo, Mozambique, and served as the German Ambassador in Brazzaville, the Congo; from 1989 to 1993, he was Deputy Chief of Mission at the German Embassy in Prague. He is a member of both the German-Russian and the German-Ukrainian joint commissions on the return of cultural property removed in time of, or as a consequence of, war, as well as a member of the German delegation in the bilateral talks with Poland on the return of cultural property.

Marlene P. Hiller, Editor of the historical journal *DAMALS* (Deutsche Verlagsanstalt, Stuttgart), received a Ph.D. degree in history from the University of Tübingen. She headed the exhibition project "Stuttgart in the Second World War" (1986–90) and co-organized a conference, "Towns in the Second World War: An International Comparison." She participated in the research project "The Fate of the Treasures of Art Removed from the Soviet Union during World War II," conducted by the Research Institute for Eastern Europe, Bremen. Her publications include "Sowjetische und deutsche Bibliotheksverluste im Zweiten Weltkrieg," Sonderheft 56, *Zeitschrift für Bibliothekswesen und Bibliographie* (1993), which has been published also in Russian translation (Moscow, 1994).

William H. Honan is National Higher Education Correspondent for the *New York Times.* In 1991, he was nominated for a Pulitzer Prize for discovering the identity of the American soldier who stole the Quedlinburg treasures from Germany at the end of World War II. During his twenty-five-year career at the *New York Times,* Mr. Honan has served as Travel Editor, Sunday Arts and Leisure Editor, Culture Editor, and Chief Cultural Correspondent. The author of several books, he is presently working on a book about the Quedlinburg case. Born in New York, he graduated from Oberlin College and earned a master's degree from the University of Virginia.

Pavel Jirásek, Adviser on Security of Cultural Property, Ministry of Culture, Prague, Czech Republic, received a degree in systems analysis and economics at the Czech Technical College in Prague. In 1990, he became a programmer at the State Institute for the Care of Monuments in Prague and built a protection program for selected castles. He has been working at the Ministry of Culture of the Czech Republic since 1991 as head coordinator for the program against crime for museums, galleries, castles, and churches in the Czech Republic. He is active in cooperating with the Cultural Heritage Committee of the Council of Europe and with the International Council of Museums (ICOM). He is a member of the Czech ICOM National Committee (1993) and a member of the Executive Board of the International Committee on Museum Security of ICOM (1995). His writings include articles on the protection of cultural objects and the economic situation of the museums in the Czech Republic (*ICOM News*) and articles on protection against theft in cultural institutions for various Czech newspapers.

Lawrence M. Kaye is a partner in the law firm of Herrick, Feinstein and a graduate of St. John's Law School, where he was Editor-in-Chief of the *Law Review.* He has been involved in many important cultural-property litigations, including the landmark case of *Kunstsammlungen zu Weimar v. Elicofon,* in which two Dürer masterpieces stolen at the end of World War II were recovered by the Weimar Museum. He represents the Republic of Turkey in cultural-repatriation matters and lectures and writes extensively on cultural-property issues.

Thomas R. Kline is a partner in the law firm of Andrews & Kurth L.L.P., resident in the firm's Washington, D.C., office. He received his A.B. degree from Columbia College in 1968 and his J.D. degree from Columbia Law School in 1975. Mr. Kline has represented numerous clients in the recovery of stolen art and cultural property found in the United States, beginning with the Greek-Orthodox Church of Cyprus and the Republic of

Cyprus, which he represented in the Kanakaria mosaics litigation, *Cyprus v. Goldberg.* He represented the Church of St. Servatius, Quedlinburg, in recovering treasures stolen during World War II by a U.S. Army officer.

Christine F. Koenigs is a filmmaker and painter. In 1978, her film *Rain* received a first prize at the Bilbao Film Festival. Her work was selected for presentation at the Sydney Biennale (1982), where she realized the short film *Level,* which received the Diploma of Merit at the Melbourne Film Festival. On a commission from the Dutch Ministry of Culture, she traveled to India to research the film industry there; her report was published under the title "Tigers from Celluloid" (1987). A second journey to India, to visit traditional scroll painters, resulted in a book, *Carola Carambola Visits India* (1990). Since 1988, while creating numerous film installations, she has also established herself as a portrait painter. Research into the life and collection of her grandfather Franz W. Koenigs, begun in 1994, soon became her full-time occupation.The results will be published in two volumes: the first, a biography of her grandfather; the second, a catalogue raisonné of his collection, for which she is drawing on contributions by major collectors and international experts in the field of old master paintings and drawings.

Manfred Korfmann is Professor of Pre- and Protohistoric Archaeology at the University of Tübingen. He received his Ph.D. and *Habilitation* degrees from the University of Frankfurt am Main. He has directed several major excavations of archaeological sites in Turkey, at Beşik-Tepe, at Demircihüyük, and, since 1988, at Troy. From 1972 to 1977, he was Referent (Lecturer) at the German Archaeological Institute in Istanbul. Professor Korfmann has written and edited several books and numerous scholarly articles, predominantly on the Neolithic period and the Bronze Age. He is the editor of the annual *Studia Troica.* In 1994, he received the Max Planck Research Award.

Willi Korte is a researcher, investigator, lawyer, and writer, specializing in the identification and restitution of works of art that were lost during World War II and immediately thereafter. He studied history, law, and political science at the Free University, Berlin, Ludwig-Maximilians University, Munich, and Georgetown University, Washington, D.C. He has a Ph.D. degree in history. Dr. Korte has assisted many governments, individuals, and institutions in Europe and North America in their efforts to recover and return missing cultural property. He is coauthor of *Quedlinburg–Texas und zurück: Schwarzhandel mit geraubter Kunst* (1994) and a founding member of Trans-Art International, L.C., a company dedicated to inhibiting the international trade in stolen art.

Valery Koulichov, former Director of the Department of Restitution, Ministry of Culture of the Russian Federation, and former Special Assistant to the Minister of Culture on restitutional matters, holds degrees in international law from Moscow State University and in international journalism from L'viv State University. From 1986 to 1992, he served as Senior Editor for Western Europe of the press agency Novosti. He was formerly Secretary of the Russian State Commission on the Restitution of Cultural Property, and served as Expert to the Russian-German, Russian-Dutch, and Russian-Hungarian Commissions on Restitution. Mr. Koulichov has written on restitutional problems for Russian and Western periodicals. He is presently Consultant to the Minister of Culture on restitutional matters.

Wojciech Kowalski is Professor and Head of the Department of Intellectual and Cultural Property Law at the University of Silesia. He received his M.A. degree in law from the Jagiellonian University in Cracow and his Ph.D. degree from the University of Silesia. From 1991 to 1994, he was Commissioner for Polish Cultural Heritage Abroad for the Government of Poland, responsible for negotiating the restitution of works of art lost by Poland during World War II. In 1992, he successfully negotiated the return of a collection of ancient gold jewelry and coins from Berlin. He was formerly a Polish representative and Vice Chairman of the Cultural Heritage Committee of the Council of Europe. He is the author of *Art Treasures and War: A Study on Restitution of Looted Cultural Property Pursuant to Public International Law* (Katowice, 1994; English edition forthcoming), *Liquidation of the Effects of World War II in the Area of Culture* (Warsaw, 1994), and a number of articles on intellectual and cultural-property laws. He is currently Assistant Editor for Central and East European issues at *Art, Antiquity and Law*.

Grigorii Kozlov is a Research Fellow of the Bremen Kunstverein. He received his M.A. degree from Moscow State University. He has served as an Inspector with the Department of Museums, USSR Ministry of Culture, and Curator of the Museum of Private Collections affiliated with the Pushkin State Museum of Fine Arts, Moscow. In 1991 he published, with Konstantin Akinsha, an article revealing Soviet "special repositories" of art missing from German and European collections since World War II. In 1993, he and Akinsha published proof that the Trojan treasure and the treasures of Cottbus, Eberswalde, Holm, and Driesen were at the Pushkin Museum. Kozlov and Akinsha's books *Beautiful Loot: The Soviet Plunder of Europe's Art Treasures* and *Operation Beutekunst* were published in 1995. The two authors have received a number of awards, including the Overseas Press Club Citation of Excellence.

Michael J. Kurtz is Assistant Archivist for the National Archives in Washington, D.C. He received an A.B. degree from the Catholic University of America and A.M. and Ph.D. degrees from Georgetown University, Washington, D.C. He is the author of *Nazi Contraband: American Policy on the Return of European Cultural Treasures, 1945–1955* (1985) and essays and articles on the American Civil War, nineteenth-century religious and social history, and archives management. He is President of the Lutheran Historical Society and Chair of the Management Roundtable of the Society of American Archivists.

Hagen Graf Lambsdorff has been Head of the Foreign Affairs Department of the Press and Information Office of the Government of the Federal Republic of Germany since May 1995. After reading law, political science, and journalism, he became Editor and later Departmental Head at various German print media. In 1974, he joined the Foreign Service and was posted to Brussels as Press Officer at the Permanent Mission of the Federal Republic of Germany to the European Community. From there, he went to the Press and Information Office as Head of Division in the Foreign Affairs Department. From 1982 to 1985, he headed the Cultural Affairs Department of the German Embassy in Moscow and was thereafter appointed Head of Division in the Cultural Relations Directorate-General of the Federal Foreign Office in Bonn. From 1988 to 1991, Graf Lambsdorff was Minister Plenipotentiary for Economic Affairs at the German Embassy in Washington, D.C., and from 1991 to 1993 he served as German Ambassador in Riga, Latvia. As Deputy Head of the Cultural Relations Directorate-General of the Federal Foreign Office in Bonn (1993–95) he co-chaired the German-Ukrainian commission on the return of cultural property removed during the war.

Josefine E. P. Leistra is Inspector for Cultural Heritage and Executive of the Art Recovery Project, Netherlands Office for Fine Arts (RBK). After completing studies in the history of art at Utrecht University, she did research at the Mauritshuis Museum at The Hague and carried out several free-lance projects for the RBK. She is the author of *George Henry Boughton: God Speed! Pelgrims op weg naar Canterbury* (1987) and *Bredius, Rembrandt en het Mauritshuis* (1991). She has contributed articles to Macmillan's *Dictionary of Art*, is editor of the catalogue of acquisitions of the RBK for 1984–89 (1990), and collaborated on *Counterparts: Old Master Drawings from the Koenigs Collection in the Museum Boymans–van Beuningen in Rotterdam. A Selection of Drawings Closely Related to the Recovered Drawings Exhibited in the Pushkin Museum, Moscow* (1995). She is a member of the editorial board of *Spoils of War International Newsletter*.

Constance Lowenthal is Executive Director, International Foundation for Art Research (IFAR), a nonprofit organization working against art theft and forgery. IFAR maintains comprehensive art theft records and runs an authentication service. Dr. Lowenthal received a B.A. degree from Brandeis University and a Ph.D. degree from the Institute of Fine Arts, New York University. Among her numerous publications are an occasional column in the *Wall Street Journal* titled "Art Crime Update"; *Michelangelo* (1980); and articles in *Museum News* and *Art and Auction*. She was formerly an Assistant Museum Educator at the Metropolitan Museum of Art, New York, and a member of the art history faculty at Sarah Lawrence College.

Jacques Lust is an Expert at the Belgian Ministry of Economic Affairs, a bureau responsible for the recovery of cultural goods lost during World War II in Belgium. He received an M.A. degree in art history from Ghent University, where his research focused on cultural life during World War II, a field in which he has published and lectured extensively. He is also councillor of VLAKAM, the Flemish organization of art historians, archaeologists, ethnologists, and musicologists.

Adam Maldis is Director of the F. Skaryna National Center for Humanitarian Studies and Education; President of the International Association of Belarusists; and Chairman of the National Commission of the Republic of Belarus on the Restitution of Lost Cultural Property. He earned his undergraduate and Ph.D. degrees from the Belarusan State University. He won the Belarusan State Prize for his participation in writing *The History of Belarusan Literature*. Professor Maldis is the author of eleven books, two of which are dedicated to researching Belarusan material and cultural values. His books and articles have been translated into Polish, Russian, Latvian, and Lithuanian.

Vivian B. Mann is Morris and Eva Feld Chair of Judaica at The Jewish Museum, New York. Dr. Mann is Director of the Master's Program in Art and Material Culture and Adjunct Professor at the Jewish Theological Seminary of America. She received her Ph.D. degree from the Institute of Fine Arts, New York University. She has written and edited numerous books and catalogues, most recently, with Richard I. Cohen, *From Court Jews to the Rothschilds: Art, Patronage and Power, 1600–1800* (1996), and *The Jewish Museum* (1993). Her many articles, scholarly papers, and lectures cover a broad range of topics in medieval art and Jewish art history. Recently, Dr. Mann was the recipient of an NEH Fellowship for Independent Scholars and has been a Fellow at the Institute for Advanced Studies, The Hebrew University, Jerusalem.

Ely Maurer is Assistant Legal Adviser for Educational, Cultural, and Public Affairs at the U.S. Department of State. He received an LL.B. degree from Columbia Law School. In the State Department, he served as Assistant Legal Adviser for European Affairs, for Far Eastern Affairs, and for Military Affairs. He was the chief department spokesman to testify before Congress on legislation relating to the protection of cultural property. He served as State Department Representative on the UNESCO Committee of Governmental Experts for the Promotion of the Return of Cultural Property and was a member of the U.S. Delegation to UNIDROIT conferences on a draft convention for protection of cultural property. He is the author of articles in professional journals.

Lynn H. Nicholas is an independent scholar. She holds a B.A. degree from Oxford University and has studied at Radcliffe College, the University of Madrid, and the Institut Supérieur d'Histoire de l'Art et d'Archéologie de Bruxelles. She has worked in various capacities at the National Gallery of Art in Washington, D.C., and is the author of *The Rape of Europa: The Fate of Europe's Treasures in the Third Reich and the Second World War* (1994). In 1995, *The Rape of Europa* received the National Book Critics Circle Award for nonfiction.

Nikolai Nikandrov is Deputy Director of the Department of Restitution, Ministry of Culture of the Russian Federation. He received a degree in history and literature from the Novosibirsk Pedagogical Institute. He served in the military until 1992. Mr. Nikandrov is a member of the expert group of the Russian State Commission on the Restitution of Cultural Property and of the Russian-German Commission on the Mutual Return of Cultural Treasures, and he heads the Russian expert group of the Russian-Polish Commission on the Mutual Return of Cultural Treasures. He is also director of an expert interagency research group involved in the search for Russian art lost during World War II.

Jonathan Petropoulos is Associate Professor of History at Loyola College in Baltimore, Maryland. In 1990, he received a Ph.D. degree from Harvard University, where he continued as a Lecturer from 1990 to 1993. From 1989 to 1991, he served as Assistant to the Curator at the Los Angeles County Museum of Art, helping to prepare the exhibition "'Degenerate Art': The Fate of the Avant-Garde in Nazi Germany." Subsequently, he was a Scientific Colleague at the Künstlerhaus Wien, and contributed two articles to the exhibition catalogue of "Kunst und Diktatur" (1994). He has received numerous fellowships and awards and has published widely on culture in twentieth-century Germany. His book, *Art as Politics in the Third Reich*, was published by the University of North Carolina Press in 1996.

James S. Plaut (1912–1996) received B.A. and M.A. degrees in fine arts from Harvard University and an Honorary Doctorate of Fine Arts from Wheaton College. From 1935 to 1939, he was Assistant Curator of Paintings, Museum of Fine Arts, Boston, and from 1939 to 1956 served as first Director of the Institute of Contemporary Art, Boston. During his wartime service, Mr. Plaut was Director of the Art Looting Investigation Unit, Office of Strategic Services, from 1944 to 1946. He served as Secretary General of the World Crafts Council from 1967 to 1976 and subsequently directed Aid to Artisans, an organization that furthers the interests of third-world artisans. The author of numerous books and articles relating to the arts, Mr. Plaut was decorated in Belgium, France, Norway, and the United States for his achievements in the arts and in the advancement of international cultural relations.

Lyndel V. Prott is Chief of the International Standards Section of the Cultural Heritage Division of UNESCO, which provides the Secretariat for the UNESCO Intergovernmental Committee for Promoting the Return of Cultural Property to its Countries of Origin or its Restitution in Case of Illicit Appropriation. From 1991 to 1996, she also held a Personal Chair in Cultural Heritage Law at the University of Sydney. She received the degrees of B.A. and LL.B. from the University of Sydney, *Licence spéciale en Droit international* from the Brussels Free University, and a J.D. degree from the University of Tübingen. She is the author or coauthor of over 150 publications, including the series *Law and the Cultural Heritage*.

Jan P. Pruszyński is Professor of Public Law and Senior Researcher, Institute of Law Studies of the Polish Academy of Sciences. He received an M.A. degree in international public law from the Law Faculty of the University of Warsaw and Ph.D. and *Habilitation* degrees from the Institute of State and Law. He is the author of numerous books and essays on law and its relation to culture and science, including: *The Legal Protection of Historical Architecture in Poland* (1977), *Protection of Monuments: History, Organization, Law* (1989), and *Legal Protection of Cultural Property in German Texts and Commentaries* (1992). He has received many awards and lectured widely. Professor Pruszyński is currently a member of the Council for the Protection of Monuments, Ministry of Culture and Arts of Poland, and an Expert with the Parliamentary Commission.

Alexei L. Rastorgouev is Associate Professor in the Department of Art History, Faculty of History, Moscow State University. He lectures and publishes widely on the "displaced" art of World War II, as well as on Early Christian and medieval art and modern Russian poetry. Dr. Rastorgouev serves as Moscow correspon-

dent and art critic for the émigré newspaper *La Pensée Russe* (Paris). He has been a member of the Russian State Commission on the Restitution of Cultural Property and is a member of the Berlin society Missing Art in Europe.

Gerhard Sailer is President of the Bundesdenkmalamt, the Austrian Federal Office for the Preservation of Historical Monuments. He studied at the University of Vienna and received the degree of Doctor of Law. Until 1982, he worked at the Finanzprokuratur, mostly in cases of cultural law.

Werner Schmidt is Director General of the Dresden State Art Collections and Professor of Art History at the Dresden Technical University. He became a certified art historian following studies at Leipzig and Berlin; later he received a Ph.D. h.c. at Dresden Educational University. He headed the Department of Prints and Drawings in Dresden from 1959 to 1990, where he was responsible for numerous exhibitions and catalogues. Among his publications, *Russian Prints of the Nineteenth and Twentieth Centuries* (1967) is of particular significance. Since 1993, he has co-chaired the Museums/Collections group of specialists of the German-Russian Commission on the Restitution of Cultural Property.

Mikhail Shvidkoi, Deputy Minister of Culture of the Russian Federation, is a member of the Russian State Commission on the Restitution of Cultural Property. He received his Ph.D. degree from the Russian Academy of Theater Art; he has since served as Professor at this institution, as well as at the Russian State University. Former Deputy General Editor of the journal *Theater,* from 1991 to 1993 he was General Director of the Kultura Publishing Complex, Ministry of Culture of the Russian Federation. He has received the Russian Badge of Honor and has been named Polish Esteemed Cultural Authority. Besides books on theater, he has published over three hundred articles in Russia and abroad, including many on restitutional problems.

Elizabeth Simpson, Chairman of "The Spoils of War" symposium organizing committee and Editor of the present volume of proceedings, is Associate Professor at The Bard Graduate Center for Studies in the Decorative Arts. She received B.A. and M.A. degrees from the University of Oregon and a Ph.D. degree in classical archaeology from the University of Pennsylvania. She is director of the project to study and conserve the ancient wooden furniture excavated at Gordion, Turkey, and a Research Associate at the University Museum, University of Pennsylvania. A former curator at the Metropolitan Museum of Art, she has also taught at Sarah Lawrence College and Duke University. Dr. Simpson is the recipient of many grants and the author of numerous publications on ancient furniture and the reconstruction of ancient works of art.

Craig Hugh Smyth, Professor Emeritus, Harvard University, received M.F.A. and Ph.D. degrees from Princeton University. He served as Ensign to Lieutenant in the U.S. Navy from 1942 to 1946, and with the Monuments, Fine Arts, and Archives section of the American Military Government in Germany as Officer-in-Charge, Central Art Collecting Point, Munich, 1945–46. Appointed in 1950 to the faculty at the Institute of Fine Arts, New York University, he served as Director of the Institute and Head of the Department of Fine Arts, New York University Graduate School, from 1951 to 1973. He was Professor of Fine Arts at Harvard University and Director of the Villa I Tatti from 1973 to 1985. An alternate U.S. member of the Comité International de l'Histoire de l'Art (1970–83) and U.S. member (1983–85), he has lectured and written widely and has received numerous honors, fellowships, and awards, including the French Legion of Honor.

Susan Weber Soros, Founder and Director of The Bard Graduate Center for Studies in the Decorative Arts, received an A.B. from Barnard College and an M.A. from the Cooper-Hewitt Museum/Parsons School of Design. She founded and publishes *Source: Notes in the History of Art,* and is Director of Philip Colleck of London, specialists in English antiques. She was Assistant Director of the exhibition "New York: The State of Art" at the New York State Museum, and Associate Producer of the documentary films *In Search of Rothko* and *The Big Picture.* From 1985 to 1992, she was Executive Director of the Open Society Fund.

Edith A. Standen is Curator Emeritus in the Department of European Sculpture and Decorative Arts at the Metropolitan Museum of Art, where she was in charge of the Textile Study Room from 1949 to 1970. She received her B.A. degree from Oxford University and is now Honorary Fellow of her college, Somerville. In 1943, she joined the Women's Army Corps and from 1945 to 1947 was a member of the Monuments, Fine Arts, and Archives section of the American Military Government in Germany. She is the author of *European Post-Medieval Tapestries and Related Hangings in The Metropolitan Museum of Art,* as well as many articles on tapestries and other textiles.

Bernard Taper served as Art Intelligence Officer for the Monuments, Fine Arts, and Archives section of the U.S. Military Government in Germany from 1946 to 1948. During that time, he also wrote a number of articles on Nazi and postwar Germany for the *New Yorker, The Nation, Harper's,* and other magazines. For five years after his return to the United States, he was a reporter for the *San Francisco Chronicle.* From 1956 to 1995, he was a staff writer for the *New Yorker.* Since 1970, he has also been Professor of Journalism at the University of California, Berkeley. He received his B.A. degree from that university and his M.A. degree from Stanford University, which he attended on a creative-writing fellowship. He is the author of *Balanchine: A Biography; Cellist in Exile: A Portrait of Pablo Casals; The Arts in Boston;* and *Gomillion versus Lightfoot: The Tuskegee Gerrymander Case;* and is the editor of *Mark Twain's San Francisco.*

Vladimir Tolstikov is Director of the Department of Ancient Art and Archaeology, the Pushkin State Museum of Fine Arts, Moscow. He trained and worked as a designer before attending Moscow State University, from which he received his Ph.D. degree in archaeology. Since 1977, he has directed the Pushkin Museum's Bosphorus Archaeological Expedition (Kerch, Crimea, Panticapaeum), and since January 1994 he has served as Keeper of the Schliemann Gold Collection. Mr. Tolstikov has published and lectured extensively on ancient Greek art and archaeology.

Stephen K. Urice is Director of the Rosenbach Museum and Library and Lecturer in Law and the Visual Arts at the University of Pennsylvania Law School. Previously, he served as Deputy Director and Counsel to the Frederick R. Weisman Art Foundation and as Lecturer at the UCLA Law School. He received his Ph.D. degree in fine arts from Harvard University and his J.D. degree from Harvard Law School. He is a regular contributor to *Museum News* and is U.S. Correspondent Secretary of the *International Journal of Cultural Property.* With Linda F. Pinkerton, Esq., he is currently preparing *Cases on Art Law* for publication.

INDEX

Vyazhishchsk monastery, tiles from, 69
Vysotskaia, N., 80

W

Wagner, Gottfried, collection (Dresden), 168–69
Wald, Ernest T. De, 91, 129
Warsaw
Krasinski Library, 51
National Museum, 51, 88
Numismatic Society, University of Warsaw, 103
Palace-on-Water (Lazienki Park), 51
Royal Castle, collections, 51
Wilanów Royal Palace, 51
Warsaw Pact, 160
Warsaw Uprising (1944), 51
Wartburg Castle, armory of, 98
Washington, D. C.
National Archives, Office of. *See* United States
National Gallery of Art, 44, 132, 134
United States Holocaust Memorial Museum, 16, 73
Watteau, Antoine, 77, 97
Figure of a Child Blowing Bubbles, 55, 57
Wauters, Antoine, 59
Wauters, M., 89
Waxman, Sharon, 91
Webb, Geoffrey, 126
Weesenstein, Schloss, 43, 96, 161, 167–69
Wehrmacht. *See* Germany, Nazi
Weimar Museum, 95, 104, 143
Weinmüller auction house (Munich), 54
Wellington, Duke of, 101
Wendland, Hans, 137
Wermusch, G., 200
Westphalia, Kingdom of, 150

Wettin, House of, 98
Wheaton, Henry, 101
Wieluń, Reliquary of, 51
Wierzbowski, Edward, 12
Wiesbaden
Landesmuseum, 131
Regierungsbezirk (Wiesbaden Administrative District), 131
Wiesbaden Collecting Point, 13, 43, 60, 123, 131–34, *132,* 139–40, 182
Wiesbaden Manifesto, 133
Wildenstein collection, 64
Wildenstein Gallery, 143
Wilhelmina, Queen (Netherlands), 53
Willrich, Wolfgang, 106
Wilson, Woodrow, 59
Wintershalle mine storage depot (Bernburg, Saxony-Anhalt), 119
Wittman, Otto, Jr., 125, 137
Wolff-Metternich, Franz Count von, 41
Wolseley, Sir Garnet, 36
Woolley, Sir Leonard, 126
World War I, 39–40, 49, 52–53, 58–59, 85, 100, 102–3, 105, 187, 228–29. *See also* Treaty of St. Germain, Treaty of Trianon, Treaty of Versailles
World War II, 12–13, 15, 34, 37–45, 47–48, 51, 53, 58, 64, 68, 72, 88, 98, 100, 160, 171, 186, 225–30, 232–36, 250–51, and passim; see, in general, 47–98 (Part 2: Losses)
Wörlitz, museum, 96
Worms, Jewish community of, 20, 86–87
Worms Burial Society, two beakers of, *21*
Wrocław, Silesian Museum of Applied Arts, 233
Wurschen, Schloss, 167
Wu Yixian, *Rainstorm,* 97, 97

X

Xerxes, 191

Y

Yad Vashem. *See* Jerusalem
Yakovlev, Mr., 145
Yalta
museum, 74
museum of regional history, 74
Yalta conference, 221
Yasnaya Polyana (estate of Leo Tolstoy), looting of, *71*
Yeltsin, Boris, 163, 179, 181, 243
YIVO (Vilnius), 246, 314

Z

Zagorsk. *See* Sergeyev Posad
Zakharov (Soviet minister of culture), 145
Zaporizhya, library, 73
Zarianko, S., 78
Zenkevich, Alexander, 79
Zentralinstitut für Kunstgeschichte, 129–30, 140
Zhdanov, Andrei, 248
Zhukov, Marshal, 118, 167, 222
Ziegler, Adolf, 106–7
Zones of Occupation
British, 145, 201, 202, 246
French, 136
Soviet, 118–19, 176, 185, 203, 222, 241–42
United States, 13, 83, 92, 115–16, 129, 135, 139, 201, 244, 246
See also Allied Control Council; Soviet Union, Trophy Commissions; United States, Army, restitution efforts of
Zurbarán, Francisco de, 95

CREDITS

The Bard Graduate Center for Studies in the Decorative Arts wishes to thank the authors of the chapters in this book for permission to publish their contributions, to which they retain copyright on an individual basis.

PHOTOGRAPH CREDITS

Akinsha and Kozlov Archive: figs. 76, 78; Archivi Alinari, Florence: fig. 1; Courtesy of Viktor Baldin: fig. 74; The Belarussian Institute of Arts and Sciences in the USA: colorplate 4; Bildarchiv der Österreichischen Nationalbibliothek: figs. 34, 35, 36; Bildarchiv Preussischer Kulturbesitz, Berlin: colorplates 9, 10, figs. 72, 73, 82; Boymans–van Beuningen Museum, Rotterdam: fig. 80; The John Nicholas Brown Center for the Study of American Civilization, Providence, R. I.: fig. 56; Bundesarchiv, Koblenz: figs. 46, 48, 49, 53; Donald F. Easton: figs. 85, 86, 87, 88, 89; S. Lane Faison, Jr.: fig. 70; Walter I. Farmer: fig. 67; S. Gerloff, *Praehistorische Zeitschrift* 68 (1993): figs. 97, 98; Klaus Goldmann Archive: colorplate 16, figs. 9, 91, 92, 93; R. Greeff, *Die Erfindung der Augengläser* (Berlin, 1921): fig. 95; William H. Honan: fig. 71; Courtesy of the Hungarian National Gallery and Dr. László Mravik: figs. 37, 38, 39, 40, 41; Illustrated London News Picture Library: fig. 2; Institut Royal du Patrimoine Artistique, Brussels: figs. 21, 22; The International Institute for Conservation of Historic and Artistic Works, London: fig. 66; ITAR-TASS/Sovfoto: fig. 29; The Jewish Museum, New York: colorplates 5 (D254, D184a,b, D31), 6 (JM 30-51, JM 31-51, gifts of Michael Oppenheim), fig. 33; The Jewish Museum, Prague: figs. 31, 32; Courtesy of Dr. Pavel Knishevsky: fig. 77; M. Korfmann and B. Kromer, *Studia Troica* 3 (1993): fig. 94; Kultura Publishing House/Global American Television, Inc.: colorplates 11, 12; Kunstbibliothek SMPK, Berlin: colorplate 15; Kunsthalle Bremen: colorplate 8; Kupferstich-Kabinett Dresden: fig. 43; The Ministry of Economic Affairs, Belgium: figs. 19, 20; John Murray (Publishers) Ltd.: fig. 83; National Archives, Washington, D. C.: figs. 4, 5, 6, 7, 10; Netherlands State Institute for War Documentation, Amsterdam: fig. 47; Office of the Plenipotentiary of the Government of Poland for the Polish Cultural Heritage Abroad: colorplate 1, figs. 13, 14, 15, 16; Photo-Novosti/Sovfoto: figs. 25, 30; The Pushkin State Museum of Fine Arts, Moscow: colorplates 19, 20, 21; Courtesy of Alexei Rastorgouev, photograph by Elizabeth Simpson: fig. 81; Rijksdienst Beeldende Kunst, The Hague: colorplates 2, 3, figs. 17, 18, 69; Courtesy of the Rorimer Family: fig. 3; Rudomino State Library for Foreign Literature, Moscow: colorplates 22, 23, 24, 25; Senatsverwaltung für Bau- und Wohnungswesen, Berlin: fig. 90; Craig Hugh Smyth: figs. 8, 11, 12, 57, 58, 59, 60, 61, 62, 63, 64, 65; Sovfoto: jacket illus., figs. 23, 24, 26, 27, 28, 52; Staatliche Kunstsammlungen Dresden: figs. 45, 79; Staatliche Museen zu Berlin, Gemäldegalerie: fig. 42; Staatliche Museen zu Berlin, Museum für Ostasiatische Kunst: fig. 44; Staatliche Museen zu Berlin, Museum für Vor- und Frühgeschichte: colorplate 7; Edith Standen: fig. 55; Bernard Taper: fig. 68; Troia Excavations: colorplate 13 (Troia slide 21818), 14 (Troia slide 21351), 17 (Troia slide 15315), 18 (Troia slide 8803), fig. 96 (Troia slide 15319)